Abdelkébir Khatibi

Postcolonialism, Transnationalism and Culture in the Maghreb and Beyond

Contemporary French and Francophone Cultures, 72

Contemporary French and Francophone Cultures

This series aims to provide a forum for new research on modern and contemporary French and francophone cultures and writing. The books published in *Contemporary French and Francophone Cultures* reflect a wide variety of critical practices and theoretical approaches, in harmony with the intellectual, cultural and social developments which have taken place over the past few decades. All manifestations of contemporary French and francophone culture and expression are considered, including literature, cinema, popular culture, theory. The volumes in the series will participate in the wider debate on key aspects of contemporary culture.

Recent titles in the series:

59 Ari J. Blatt and Edward J. Welch, *France in Flux: Space, Territory, and Contemporary Culture*

60 Nicholas Harrison, *Our Civilizing Mission: The Lessons of Colonial Education*

61 Joshua Armstrong, *Maps and Territories: Global Positioning in the Contemporary French Novel*

62 Thomas Baldwin, *Roland Barthes: The Proust Variations*

63 Lucas Hollister, *Beyond Return: Genre and Cultural Politics in Contemporary French Fiction*

64 Naïma Hachad, *Revisionary Narratives: Moroccan Women's Auto/Biographical and Testimonial Acts*

65 Emma Wilson, *The Reclining Nude: Agnès Varda, Catherine Breillat, and Nan Goldin*

66 Margaret Atack, Alison S. Fell, Diana Holmes, Imogen Long, *Making Waves: French Feminisms and their Legacies 1975–2015*

67 Ruth Cruickshank, *Leftovers: Eating, Drinking and Re-thinking with Case Studies from Post-war French Fiction*

68 Etienne Achille, Charles Forsdick, Lydie Moudileno, *Postcolonial Realms of Memory: Sites and Symbols in Modern France*

69 Patrick Crowley and Shirley Jordan, *What Forms Can Do: The Work of Form in 20th and 21st-century French Literature and Thought*

70 Erin Twohig, *Contesting the Classroom: Reimagining Education in Moroccan and Algerian Literatures*

71 Keith Reader, *The Marais: The Story of a Quartier*

JANE HIDDLESTON
AND KHALID LYAMLAHY

Abdelkébir Khatibi

Postcolonialism, Transnationalism
and Culture in the Maghreb and Beyond

LIVERPOOL UNIVERSITY PRESS

First published 2020 by
Liverpool University Press
4 Cambridge Street
Liverpool
L69 7ZU

British Library Cataloguing-in-Publication data
A British Library CIP record is available

ISBN 978-1-78962-233-1 cased

Typeset by Carnegie Book Production, Lancaster
Printed and bound in Poland by BooksFactory.co.uk

Contents

Acknowledgements   vii

List of Photographs   ix

Introduction: Abdelkébir Khatibi, at Home and Abroad   1
    Jane Hiddleston and Khalid Lyamlahy

I Critical Thinking: From Decolonization to Transnationalism

1   The 'Souverainement Orphelin' of Abdelkébir Khatibi's
    Early Writings: Sociology in the *Souffles* Years   41
    Andy Stafford

2   Tireless Translation: Travels, Transcriptions, Tongues and
    the Eternal Plight of the '*Étranger professionnel*' in the
    Corpus of Abdelkébir Khatibi   65
    Alison Rice

3   Abdelkébir Khatibi's Mediterranean Idiom   89
    Edwige Tamalet Talbayev

4   Abdelkébir Khatibi and the Transparency of Language   111
    Assia Belhabib
    Translated from the French by Jane Hiddleston

5   Khatibi and Performativity, '*From where to speak?*':
    Living, Thinking and Writing with an
    'epistemological accent'   125
    Alfonso de Toro

II Cultural and Philosophical Dialogues

6   Khatibi and the Transcolonial Turn   149
     Olivia C. Harrison

7   Segalen and Khatibi: Bilingualism, Alterity and the Poetics
     of Diversity   173
     Charles Forsdick

8   Khatibi and Derrida: A 'Franco-Maghrebian' Dialogue   197
     Dominique Combe
     Translated from the French by Jane Hiddleston

9   Maghrebian Shadow: Abdelkébir Khatibi and Japanese Culture   219
     Nao Sawada

III Aesthetics and Art in the Islamic World and Beyond

10   Reading Signs and Symbols with Abdelkébir Khatibi:
     From the Body to the Text   237
     Rim Feriani, Jasmina Bolfek-Radovani and Debra Kelly

11   Abdelkébir Khatibi: The Other Side of the Mirror   261
     Lucy Stone McNeece

12   The Carpet as a Text, the Writer as a Weaver: Reading the
     Moroccan Carpet with Abdelkébir Khatibi   279
     Khalid Lyamlahy

13   The Artist's Journey, or, the Journey as Art: Aesthetics
     and Ethics in *Pèlerinage d'un artiste amoureux* and Beyond   305
     Jane Hiddleston

IV Translations

14   Excerpts from Abdelkébir Khatibi, *La Blessure
     du nom propre* (Paris: Editions Denoël, 1974)   329
     Translated from the French by Matt Reeck

15   Excerpts from Abdelkébir Khatibi and Jacques Hassoun,
     Le Même Livre (Paris: Editions de l'Eclat, 1985)   347
     Translated from the French by Olivia C. Harrison

Notes on Contributors   361

Bibliography   367

Index   387

Acknowledgements

The idea behind this volume originated in 2016 in Oxford and took some time to materialize into a coherent project. Long and numerous discussions about North African literature and culture have informed our thinking at various stages. During these discussions, we became increasingly aware that Abdelkébir Khatibi's original, wide-ranging and erudite contributions deserve to be not only duly acknowledged and further analysed but also shared with wider audiences. Therefore, our aim was to bring together a diverse group of international scholars to engage with Khatibi's works from different and complementary perspectives. We would like to thank all the contributors for producing thoughtful and well-presented papers in time and for their patience and understanding throughout the editing and revision process. It has been both an immense pleasure and a rewarding experience to work with all of them. We are also grateful to the reviewers for their insightful and very useful comments which helped us to improve the overall quality of the volume. We would like to express our deepest gratitude to Mme Lalla Mina El Alaoui Khatibi who supported this project and granted us permission to reproduce the photographs included in the volume.

The co-editors are extremely thankful to Liverpool University Press for welcoming this project at an early stage and, more specifically, to Chloe Johnson, the Commissioning Editor for Modern Languages and Postcolonial Studies, for her availability and responsiveness. We hope this volume will serve as a valuable resource and a starting point for further debates on Khatibi's works and legacies.

Photographs

Unless otherwise stated, all the following photographs are the property of Mrs Lalla Mina El Alaoui Khatibi and reproduced with her kind permission.

1 (August 1954) In the streets of Casablanca (Khatibi is second from the right).

2 (1957–8) Propaedeutic Year at the Lycée Lyautey in Casablanca (Khatibi is in the third row, fourth from the left).

3 (July 1959) Sant Miquel de Fluvià, in the Catalonia region, Spain.

4 (1959 or 1960) With a Mauritarian friend in Boulevard Saint-Michel, Paris.

5 (1966) In India with Zakir Husain, the then Vice-President of the country.

6 (1972) During the 'First Congress on Mediterranean Studies of Arabo-Berber Influence', hosted by the Royal University (currently University of Malta) in Msida, Malta (Khatibi is in the first row, first from the left).

7 (In the 1970s) With his mother.

8 (October 1980) With Moroccan sociologist and writer Fatema Mernissi during a visit to the Merinid Madrasa in Salé, Morocco.

9 (1987) In Paris with Algerian artist Rachid Koraïchi, Palestinian writer and diplomat Elias Sanbar and Palestinian poet Mahmoud Darwish during the preparation of the collective project *A Nation in Exile* (Amman: Darat al Funun, 1997), republished as *Une Nation en exil: hymnes gravés suivi de La Qasida de Beyrouth* (Algiers: Barzakh/Arles: Actes Sud, 2009). Photograph is published with the kind permission of Rachid Koraïchi. © Rachid Koraïchi.

10 (In the 1990s) With the Egyptian psychiatrist and writer Jacques Hassoun and his wife.

11 (In the 1990s) With Syrian poet Adonis.

12 (In the 1990s) Working at his desk.

13 (August 1990) In Herbeys (France) at Mrs Claudette Oriol-Boyer's home during the summer school, 'Lire, écrire, réécrire' (Chichilianne, University of Grenoble 3/CNRS).

14 (July 1992) With Jacques Derrida in Cerisy-la-Salle during the colloquium, 'Le Passage des frontières: Autour du travail de Jacques Derrida'.

15 (July 1992) With French writer Hélène Cixous (right) and French scholar Anne Emmanuelle Berger (left) in Cerisy-la-Salle during the colloquium, 'Le Passage des frontières: Autour du travail de Jacques Derrida'.

16 (1992) In London with Lebanese writer Elias Khoury.

17 (September 1994) In Jerusalem in front of the Dome of the Rock. Photograph by Mohammed Habib Samrakandi and published with his kind permission. © Mohammed Habib Samrakandi.

18 (September 1994) With Palestinian leader Yasser Arafat and Moroccan playwright Tayeb Saddiki. Photograph by Mohammed Habib Samrakandi and published with his kind permission. © Mohammed Habib Samrakandi.

19 (November 1995) In Cotonou with Nicéphore Soglo, the then President of Benin, before the Sixth Summit of the Francophonie.

20 (April 1996) In New York during a jazz concert.

21 (July 2000) In Rabat at the Faculty of Law, University Mohammed V.

22 (January 2002) In Rabat with Spanish writer Juan Goytisolo during the colloquium, 'Jean Genet: Féerie et dissidence'.

23 (March 2003) In Tokyo.

24 (November 2003) In Paris with Assia Djebar during the colloquium, 'Assia Djebar: Nomade entre les murs', organized by Mireille Calle-Gruber in the period 27–29 November 2003 at La Maison des Ecrivains. Photograph is property of Mireille Calle-Gruber and published with her kind permission. © Mireille Calle-Gruber – ARCS (Association 'Archive Claude Simon et ses Contemporains').

25 (2005) With Moroccan writer and psychiatrist Rita El Khayat.

26 (2006) In El Harhoura near Rabat with Moroccan journalist and writer Abdelkrim Ghallab (left) and Iraqi and Morocco-based writer Ali Al-Kasimi (right).

27 (March 2007) During his second visit to Tokyo.

Introduction

Abdelkébir Khatibi, at Home and Abroad

Jane Hiddleston and Khalid Lyamlahy

In the opening lines of his late autobiographical work, *Le Scribe et son ombre*, Khatibi makes what can be considered to be a wholehearted declaration of love and commitment to his homeland:

> Je vis et travaille au Maroc. Ce pays est de force vive. Je lui dois ma naissance, mon nom, mon identité initiale. Comment pourrais-je ne pas l'aimer avec bienveillance! Une bienveillance critique et vigilante. Une patrie n'est pas seulement le lieu de la venue au monde, mais un choix personnel qui fortifie le sentiment d'appartenance.[1]

> [I live and work in Morocco. This country is my lifeblood. I owe it my birth, my name and my initial identity. How could I not love it with benevolence? A critical and watchful benevolence. A native land is not only the place of one's coming into the world, but a personal choice that strengthens the feeling of belonging.]

Khatibi's moving words reveal one of the most distinctive and enduring features of his career as a Moroccan writer and intellectual: his native land with its history, culture, society and politics has always been at the centre of his prolific work. Morocco not only provides the backdrop to some of his fictional and autobiographical writings but also forms the central focus of his literary, sociological, semiological and philosophical investigations. Nevertheless, for all his commitment to Moroccan culture, history and politics, Khatibi's thought is also

---

1   Abdelkébir Khatibi, *Le Scribe et son ombre* (Paris: La Différence, 2008), p. 9.

throughout his career assertively outward-looking. Although he lived in Morocco for most of his life, his outlook remains unremittingly intercultural and transnational. When focusing on local cultures, Islamic history and art, for example, Khatibi is at pains to stress their plural, dialogic and open-ended form, and part of his passion for Moroccan culture stems precisely from its engagement and blurring with other cultures, languages and idioms. Conversely, his travels and interactions with other cultures at the same time inform and fuel his vision of his native 'Maghreb pluriel' ['plural Maghreb']. This introductory essay sets out to uncover the significance of Khatibi's work, first 'at home' and later 'abroad', to offer a backdrop to the essays collected here presenting original and revealing insights into the thought of this crucial but under-represented thinker.

The origins of Khatibi's relationship with Morocco and Moroccan culture can be found in his upbringing and early education. Khatibi was born on 11 February 1938 in El Jadida, a coastal city near Casablanca. The hometown also of his elder fellow writer Driss Chraïbi, the city was once called Mazagan, and can be recognized by its massive sixteenth-century Portuguese fortress facing the Atlantic Ocean. The history of El Jadida is reflected in the significant shift from its nickname 'El-Mahdouma' in the eighteenth century, which means 'The Ruined' in reference to the Portuguese vestiges, to its current name, which means 'the New' in Arabic: a metaphor for reconstruction and regeneration. Khatibi grew up in the medina, a labyrinthine and inspiring space that enhanced – as he explains in one of his interviews – his conception of the movement of the body in tandem with its surroundings. The game of movement and seduction with the maze-like old town can be construed as one of the triggers for his ongoing predilection for errantry. Having shaped his imagination as a child, this passion for movement and discovery informs at the same time his later readings of Moroccan art, culture and geography.

In addition to these childhood moments of errantry, however, two further preoccupations can be traced back to Khatibi's early years, namely language and death. Both of these resonate in his first name, 'Abdelkébir', a reference, according to Islamic scripture, to one of God's names (literally, 'Slave of God'), and to the day of his birth, which coincided with Eid el Kebir, the Feast commemorating Abraham's near-sacrifice of his son. Thus, Khatibi's first name bears the dual trace of loss and submission: 'je fus sacrifié en venant au monde, et ma tête fut, en quelque sorte, offerte à Dieu. L'ai-je jamais retrouvée, au-delà de tout destin métaphysique?' ['I was sacrificed upon my birth and my head was, in a way, offered to God. Did I ever find it beyond all metaphysical fate?'].[2] Khatibi's open question reveals an ongoing search for meaning, which would continue to fuel his deep interest in language and semiology. His later writings, moreover, can be considered as so many responses to this original 'blessure' ['wound'], further inscribed in his surname, a borrowed civil name chosen by his family only in the 1950s. The wound is at the same time inscribed more literally in the writer's body, not only through the memorable experience of circumcision but also through an early infection of his eyes and a minor myopia that would persist throughout his lifetime. Retrospectively, Khatibi's trajectory as a writer can be read, in his words, as 'la projection d'un enfant au-delà de ses signes' ['the projection of a child beyond all signs'],[3] a journey initiated and inflected by the wounds and tragedies of his early years.

The youngest of four, at an early age Khatibi lost his sister and one of his brothers, and at the age of seven, his father, initially a theologian who later became a trader of wheat and wood. At the age of four, Khatibi himself nearly perished in the Atlantic Ocean, when he was caught off guard by a huge wave at the beach in the coastal city of Essaouira, where he used to spend time with his aunt. As he suggests in the opening pages of *La Mémoire tatouée*, this early encounter with death led the writer to seek solace in language, as if he might learn how to resist loss and separation through the creation of linguistic connections: 'mer, mère, mémoire, lapsus échappés à cette frileuse nostalgie' ['ocean, mother, memory – lapses fleeing from this chill nostalgia'].[4] Khatibi's close relationship with his mother and his early engagement with the feminine also played a key role in developing his sensitivity and reinforcing his attention to intimate conversation, as well as to narratives and rituals. Also crucial are his first but difficult contact with calligraphy at the Qur'anic school, and his early experience of multilingualism when he joined the French school in

2 Abdelkébir Khatibi, 'Présentation', in *La Mémoire tatouée: autobiographie d'un colonisé* (Paris: Union générale d'éditions, Collection 10/18, 1979), pp. 9–13 (p. 10). Unless otherwise stated, all translations are ours.

3 Abdelkébir Khatibi, *La Mémoire tatouée: autobiographie d'un décolonisé* (Paris: Denoël, 1971), reprinted in *Œuvres de Abdelkébir Khatibi I: Romans et récits* (Paris: La Différence, 2008), pp. 9–113 (p. 17); *Tattooed Memory*, trans. Peter Thompson (Paris: L'Harmattan, 2016), p. 138; p. 18.

4 Khatibi, *La Mémoire tatouée*, p. 20; *Tattooed Memory*, p. 23.

1945: 'je devins triglotte, lisant le français sans le parler, jouant avec quelques bribes de l'arabe écrit, et parlant le dialecte comme quotidien. Où, dans ce chassé-croisé, la cohérence et la continuité?' ['I became trilingual, reading French without speaking it, fooling around with scraps of written Arabic, and speaking my everyday dialect. Where, in all this babble, was there any coherence and continuity?'].[5] This linguistic diversity and separation not only triggered Khatibi's yearning for exchange and dialogue beyond borders but also prefigured his continuous effort to turn his multilayered relationship with idioms into a powerful source of inspiration and creativity.

If translation and mobility are in this way inscribed in Khatibi's formative years, his first experience of writing took place in Marrakesh, where he attended a secondary boarding school between 1950 and 1957. This new move constituted yet another episode of rupture: 'séparation d'un adolescent, arraché d'un double exil, deux villes et deux mères [...] L'enfance allait mourir' ['An adolescent's separation, ripped from his double exile, two towns and two mothers [...] Childhood was about to die'].[6] Nevertheless, Khatibi's strolls in the Red City would prove instructive as a precocious experience of errantry and encounter. Similarly, classes of geography and Greek mythology allowed him to give free rein to his imagination, driven by these 'mots étranges, qui m'ouvraient le cœur de quelque pays lointain' ['strangest words, which opened the heart of some far country to me'].[7] Reading Gibran Khalil Gibran and a range of French authors, including Racine, Corneille, and Stendhal, Khatibi came closer to writing himself, first through imitation and parody. Mostly inspired by his early romances, his first poems in Arabic then in French were published in the literary supplement of *Maroc-Presse*, a daily newspaper in Casablanca. These would serve as a training lab for his subsequent poetry, especially his later collections around the concept of 'aimance', a term he deploys to refer to a particular, contingent and non-proprietary form of loving and friendship.

Khatibi was only 18 when Morocco gained its independence in 1956. At this time, writing provided him with a unique lens through which to explore and extend the period of his self-construction while reflecting on the postcolonial future of the country. During the last years of the French Protectorate, he took part in anticolonial protests in Marrakesh,

5   Ibid., p. 40; p. 50.
6   Ibid., p. 45; pp. 59–60.
7   Ibid., p. 54; p. 70.

although he describes his participation as 'relative et inorganisée' ['relative and unorganized'],[8] and seemed more interested in how myths and popular beliefs support resistance, and how the creation of freedom also draws on fantasies and idealized forms of representation. In the fervour of the country's newly won independence, his experience as an apprentice playwright with his older brother in the streets of Marrakesh launched his passion for theatre, which he later developed by writing his own plays, *La Mort des artistes* and *Le Prophète voilé*. Theatre became a space of performance and creativity, another way – alongside philosophy – to reflect on the ongoing historical changes in the country and beyond.

In 1957, Khatibi's intellectual formation took another turn as he moved to Casablanca, where he spent a pre-university year 'Propédeutique Lettres' at the French Lycée Lyautey. While he notes in *La Mémoire tatouée* that the experience of the industrial city confused him – he perceives it as an intricate and rather indecipherable web of signs – it still allowed Khatibi to develop his readings and reinforce his mastery of French language and literature. His success in the context of the 'French Mission' remained, however, conditioned by a form of cultural appropriation: 'on m'acceptait parce que j'étais semblable, annihilant d'avance toute mon enfance, toute ma culture. [...] J'apprenais aux autres à écrire leur propre langue' ['They accepted me because I was similar, annihilating in advance my whole childhood, my whole culture [...] I was teaching others how to write their own language'].[9] Rather than merely accepting or allowing himself to feel burdened by this paradoxical situation, Khatibi would later use his proficiency in French specifically to promote Moroccan art and literature, particularly in France. Furthermore, his impressive knowledge of French intellectual, literary and philosophical sources also served and fuelled his broader project of exploring North African popular culture in dialogue and contrast with that of France.

Already evident in *La Mémoire tatouée*, a book that redefines the act of remembering by weaving an impressive web of popular signs and social representations, Khatibi's interest in Moroccan culture and society was to develop and take on more concrete forms upon his return to Morocco in 1964. His training as a sociologist at the Sorbonne and his interaction in the period from 1958 to 1964 with eminent

8 Ibid., p. 63; p. 82.
9 Ibid., p. 71; p. 95.

French scholars such as Raymond Aron, Georges Gurvitch, André Leroi-Gourhan and Henri Lefebvre provided him with a transdisciplinary toolkit in sociology, ethnology and philosophy, also enriched by his first travels in Europe. After his appointment as a professor at the University Mohammed V in Rabat, Khatibi concentrated his efforts on the decolonization and reconstruction of sociology as a scientific discipline in Morocco, a task he would carry out from his position as the director of the Institut de Sociologie in the period 1966–70. In *Bilan de la sociologie au Maroc*, an early historical and bibliographical synthesis of the discipline after the French Protectorate, Khatibi insists that 'une décolonisation de la sociologie suppose une non-dépendance scientifique de la Métropole et une politique scientifique critique basée sur l'analyse comparative des pays sous-analysés ou plutôt mal analysés' ['a decolonization of sociology requires a scientific independence from the Metropole and a critically scientific politics based on the comparative analysis of under-analysed or rather poorly analysed countries'].[10] Alongside leading Moroccan sociologist Paul Pascon, Khatibi also trained the new generation of Moroccan scholars while conducting and supervising a series of studies on a wide range of themes including the rural economy, social development and class struggle in postcolonial Morocco. A number of these studies were regularly published in the *Bulletin économique et social du Maroc* (*Bulletin ESM*), a quarterly journal coordinated by Khatibi himself. In 1970, the Moroccan government decided to close the Institute on the pretext that it was serving as a space of political protest and social unrest. Although deeply affected by this decision, Khatibi continued to stress the necessity of redefining 'le statut d'une sociologie critique et au service de l'opinion publique' ['the status of a sociology that should both be critical and work in the service of public opinion'] by calling for the reconstruction of the history of the country and the reappropriation of Moroccan space, temporality and knowledge.[11] Khatibi's substantial effort not only laid the foundations of sociology as a scientific discipline in postcolonial Morocco but also reflected what he praised in Pascon's scholarship as 'une sociologie en mouvement' ['a

10   Abdelkébir Khatibi (ed.), *Bilan de la sociologie au Maroc* (Rabat: Publications de l'Association pour la Recherche en Sciences Humaines, 1967), p. 28.
11   Abdelkébir Khatibi, 'Avant-propos', in *Etudes sociologiques sur le Maroc* (Rabat: Publications de la Société d'Etudes économiques, sociales et statistiques, 1971).

sociology in motion'],[12] namely an area of research attuned to the local dynamics of social, economic and cultural transformations.

As Khatibi puts it in *Le Scribe et son ombre*, one of the main aims of his intensive activity in the field of sociology and beyond was to 'réhabiliter, ou plutôt restituer à la culture populaire, quand elle n'a pas disparu, sa dignité théorique' ['rehabilitate or rather return to popular culture its theoretical dignity, when it still exists'].[13] Working against both the dismissal of popular culture by local intellectual elites and its reduction to mere folklore by French orientalists, Khatibi's effort took the form of an intersemiotic and transdisciplinary study in *La Blessure du nom propre*, a groundbreaking volume that explores artistic forms as diverse as tattoos, proverbs, narratives and calligraphy. Popular culture is approached by Khatibi as a dynamic and interconnected system of signs, which he skilfully links to notions of identity, knowledge, pleasure and intertextuality. Khatibi's reading and translation of popular culture would often hinge on a thoughtful dialogue between texts and images, as his contributions move from contemplative readings of artistic objects to analytical commentaries on semiotic systems. This movement, already present in *La Blessure*, becomes more prominent in the two volumes written in collaboration with Moroccan doctor, photographer and writer Mohamed Sijelmassi, and dedicated to Arab-Muslim calligraphy,[14] as well as the collective volume on Moroccan civilization co-edited by them both.[15] With contributions from more than 40 specialists and scholars, the latter is considered one of the best encyclopaedic publications on Morocco, covering a wide range of topics, from history, mythology and religion to linguistic and cultural heritage, traditional and contemporary art, as well as modes of life and creation in rural and urban areas. In his introduction to the volume, Khatibi provides a brief overview of Moroccan civilization, showing how it has been not only shaped by the country's Amazigh (or Berber) roots and strategic location at the crossroads of the Atlantic, the Mediterranean and the Saharan but also enriched by the fruitful encounter

12   Abdelkébir Khatibi, 'Préface', in Paul Pascon, *Etudes rurales: idées et enquêtes sur la campagne marocaine* (Rabat: Société Marocaine des Editeurs Réunis, 1980), pp. i–viii (p. viii).
13   Abdelkébir Khatibi, *Le Scribe et son ombre* (Paris: La Différence, 2008), p. 49.
14   Abdelkébir Khatibi and Mohamed Sijelmassi, *L'Art calligraphique arabe* (Paris: Editions du Chêne, 1976), republished as *L'Art calligraphique de l'Islam* (Paris: Gallimard, 1994).
15   Abdelkébir Khatibi and Mohamed Sijelmassi (eds), *Civilisation marocaine: arts et cultures* (Arles: Actes Sud, 1999).

of Islamic influence and Western culture. As Khatibi would argue in a
number of subsequent publications, Moroccan culture has benefited from
the fusion of the sacred and the secular to create '*un art syncrétique,*
extrêmement composite, un bric-à-brac magique' ['a *syncretic,* extremely
composite *art,* a magical bric-a-brac'].[16] While reading Morocco as a site
of a violent yet productive confrontation between identity and difference,
the native and the foreign, Khatibi still insists that the perfection of any
piece of Moroccan art bares the talent of 'l'artiste anonyme qu'est l'artisan
dont la dignité esthétique est à respecter' ['the artisan as an anonymous
artist whose aesthetic dignity should be respected'].[17] This aesthetic and
theoretical dignity is what Khatibi relentlessly seeks to enlighten, promote
and transmit to the reader. For him, art is an invitation to reflect on acts
of creation and reception within a given historical and sociocultural
context. Calligraphy, for instance, can be conceived of as 'une écriture
et une lecture au second degré' ['a reading and a writing in the second
degree'] in the sense that it combines techniques of writing, outlining and
drawing while offering a multilayered composition of geometric figures,
signatures, miniatures and arabesques.[18]

In this respect, one of Khatibi's most valuable contributions to
the understanding of Moroccan art is the pivotal idea that artistic
disciplines and creations are not separate but interrelated entities, each
of which can be fruitfully used to read the other. With this theory,
Khatibi puts Moroccan plurality into practice through the very act of
reading. The circulation of meaning produced in this way is at the core
of *Du signe à l'image: le tapis marocain,* a book he wrote in collaboration with Moroccan anthropologist and museologist Ali Amahan.
As Khalid Lyamlahy develops in the present volume, Khatibi's reading
of the Moroccan carpet as an intersemiotic surface is an invitation not
only to explore the skilful handcrafted weaving of colours, symbols and
forms but also to unravel the polysemous nature of the carpet as a spatial
and social object that draws on religious practice, promotes feminine
agency and mirrors the art of narration.

If Khatibi's prolific *œuvre* can be read, just like the Moroccan carpet
and in his own words as 'une calligraphie des formes' ['a calligraphy

16   Khatibi, 'Paradigmes de civilisation', ibid., pp. 10–15 (p. 13).
17   Ibid., p. 12.
18   Khatibi and Sijelmassi, *L'Art calligraphique de l'Islam,* p. 6; *The Splendor of Islamic Calligraphy,* trans. James Hughes (London: Thames & Hudson, 1996), p. 6.

of shapes'],[19] this is essentially thanks to his impressive ability to identify, analyse and bring together various levels of interpretation. As he shrewdly elaborates in *Le Corps oriental*, an original study of the body in Islam, the physical is the meeting point of laws and prohibitions, sacred rituals and desacralized practices, lexical elements and symbolic images, political representations and erotic references, whose combined imprints constitute the multivalent nature of social identity. Khatibi's treatment of his object of study is never reducible to a one-dimensional discipline nor to a limited space of reflection. As with the corpus of Moroccan popular proverbs or ancestral tattoos, interpretation is always driven by variation, a word that proves fundamental in Khatibi's discourse, as if his exploration of the bottomless territories of artistic creation were but a continuation of his childhood strolls in the narrow streets of the medina.

As is made clear by his contributions to several art books,[20] Khatibi's interest in artistic and cultural production was not restricted to Morocco but expanded to include the Maghreb, and more broadly the Islamic and Arab worlds. This broader interest is first visible in his early contribution as a co-editor, alongside leading figures Albert Memmi, Jean Déjeux, Jacqueline Arnaud and Arlette Roth, to two of the pioneering anthologies and bibliographies of North African Francophone literature.[21] Khatibi's interest in the Maghreb in particular is confirmed in his thesis *Le Roman maghrébin*, an early sociological study of the North African novel in the

---

19   Abdelkébir Khatibi and Ali Amahan, *Du signe à l'image: le tapis marocain* (Casablanca: LAK International, 1994), p. 90; *From Sign to Image: The Moroccan Carpet* (Casablanca: LAK International, 1997), p. 90.

20   See, for instance, Abdelkébir Khatibi, E. A. El Maleh, Toni Maraini and Mohammed Melehi, *La Peinture de Ahmed Cherkaoui* (Casablanca: Shoof, 1976); Abdelkébir Khatibi, 'Un chasseur d'empreintes', in Daoud Aoulad-Syad, *Marocains* (Paris: Contrejour/Agadir: Belvisi, 1989); Abdelkébir Khatibi and Moulim El Aroussi, *Peintres de Doukkala* (Casablanca: Association des Doukkala, 1994); Abdelkébir Khatibi, 'L'Envol des racines', in *Ahmed Cherkaoui: la passion du signe* (Paris: IMA, 1996); Abdelkébir Khatibi, 'Témoigner en images', in *Regards des photographes arabes contemporains* (Paris: IMA, 2005).

21   See *Anthologie des écrivains maghrébins d'expression française* (Paris: Présence Africaine, 1964) and *Bibliographie de la littérature nord-africaine d'expression française* (Paris: Editions Mouton, 1965). Khatibi also co-edited an anthology of Moroccan literature: see Mohammed Benjelloun Touimi, Abdelkébir Khatibi and Mohammed Kably (eds), *Ecrivains marocains: du Protectorat à 1965* (Paris: Sindbad, 1974).

period between 1945 and independence, completed during his time at the Sorbonne. In his introduction, Khatibi explains that, beyond aesthetic and thematic approaches to the novel, a central concern of the book is 'la construction nationale' ['the national construction'] and the question of *'ce qu'est le roman pour nous, Maghrébins, maintenant en 1968, c'est-à-dire en période de décolonisation'* [*'what the novel is for us as Maghrebians in 1968, that is during the period of decolonization'*].[22] This emphasis on Maghrebian collective identity as it is treated in the novel – the Western literary genre par excellence – is clearly reflected in the structure of his book, which combines broad exploration of dominant themes such as acculturation, engagement and revolution with more focused studies of key figures, including Kateb, Chraïbi, Mammeri and Djebar. Also revealing is the fact that the closing section of *Le Roman maghrébin* reproduces excerpts and articles by Moroccan, Algerian and Tunisian writers. One of these is Abdellatif Laâbi's significant prologue to the first issue of *Souffles*, a leading avant-garde journal of culture and politics, founded in 1966 by a group of Moroccan poets and artists. Khatibi not only contributed to the journal but also transmitted the first poems by Tahar Ben Jelloun to Abdellatif Laâbi and recommended their publication.

In 2016, an Anglophone anthology of articles from *Souffles* made available, for the first time in English, some of Khatibi's early contributions to one of the most influential platforms for experimental writing and postcolonial thought in the Maghreb and beyond.[23] After three poems published in the second issue, Khatibi wrote an article in the following one entitled 'Roman maghrébin et culture nationale' ['The Maghrebian Novel and National Culture'], in which he praised Francophone Maghrebian writers for incorporating the novel in North African culture. He admitted, however, that these authors remain exposed to the dilemma of either describing the reality of their societies in a journalistic style or producing a disincarnated literature more or less distanced from their environment. In the post-independence age of nation-building, Khatibi described national culture in the region

---

22   Abdelkébir Khatibi, *Le Roman maghrébin* (Paris: Maspero, 1968), p. 17. Emphasis is the author's.

23   See Olivia C. Harrison and Teresa Villa-Ignacio, *Souffles-Anfas: A Critical Anthology from the Moroccan Journal of Culture and Politics* (Stanford, CA: Stanford University Press, 2016). The journal is available in digitized form at the Bibliothèque Nationale du Royaume du Maroc: http://bnm.bnrm.ma:86/ListeVol. aspx?IDC=3 (accessed 10 Mar. 2018).

as 'encore principalement traditionaliste ou imitative' ['still mostly traditional and imitative'] and therefore called writers to 'faire éclater cette tradition, la démystifier et trouver de nouvelles formules aptes à exprimer notre réalité et à incarner nos désirs les plus profonds' ['to debunk this tradition, to demystify it and to find new ways to appropriately express our reality and embody our deepest desires'].[24] This goal was achieved by Driss Chraïbi, whom Khatibi praises in a brief note in the same issue for having dismantled Moroccan conservative social structures in his first novel *Le Passé simple*. Interestingly, however, Khatibi criticizes Chraïbi's exile in France as 'irréaliste' ['unrealistic'], arguing that, 'malgré tout, c'est à l'intérieur du pays qu'il convient de travailler et de lutter' ['in spite of everything, it is necessary to work and struggle from inside the country'].[25] For Khatibi, the North African intellectual should remain in permanent contact with the reality of his society: too much distance would not only entail a lack of knowledge but also lead to misunderstandings on both sides. The Maghreb also needs from its intellectuals a strong yearning for renewal and regeneration. Writing should be driven, as Khatibi notes in his foreword to another issue of *Souffles* dedicated to North African literature, by 'le désir têtu de basculer le réalisme misérabiliste et le lyrisme des pauvres caractérisant la littérature inhibée de notre passé' ['the stubborn desire to overturn the miserable realism and lyricism of the poor that characterizes the inhibited literature of our past'].[26] Khatibi's enthusiasm for the new generation of North African authors stems from his conviction that the revival of literature in the region needs a twofold effort of 'rupture' and 'réappropriation du corps et de la mémoire' ['the reappropriation of the body and of memory'],[27] which he identifies in the early poetry of Abdellatif Laâbi and Mostafa Nissabouri, and praises as an efficient way to rebuild North African postcolonial identity.

Although Khatibi signed the 'Appeal to Maghrebian writers' published in the 'Special Issue for the Palestinian Revolution', he would clearly

24 Abdelkébir Khatibi, 'Roman maghrébin et culture nationale', *Souffles* 3 (1966), pp. 10–11 (p. 11); Abdelkébir Khatibi, 'The Maghrebi Novel and National Culture', trans. Claudia Esposito, in Harrison and Villa-Ignacio, *Souffles-Anfas: A Critical Anthology*, pp. 56–8 (p. 58).

25 Abdelkébir Khatibi, 'Justice pour Driss Chraïbi', *Souffles* 3 (1966), p. 48.

26 Abdelkébir Khatibi, 'Avant-propos', *Souffles* 10–11 (1968), pp. 4–5 (p. 4).

27 Abdelkébir Khatibi, 'Abdellatif Laâbi, *Race* and E. M. Nissabouri, *Plus haute mémoire*', *Souffles* 13–14 (1969), p. 35.

distance himself from the overtly political turn of *Souffles* after 1969 to develop his own thinking on Maghrebian and Arab issues from a more intellectual and scholarly perspective. In this respect, one of his most acclaimed contributions is his reimagining of the space of the Maghreb in *Maghreb pluriel*, a collection of essays published in 1983. In the first of these, which is a revised version of an article first published in a special issue of *Les Temps Modernes* in 1977, Khatibi redefines the Maghreb as a site of plurality, founded on the simultaneous critique of both Western and local heritage ('double critique') and the insurrectionary rejection of the theocratic, static and dogmatic foundations of North African subjectivity ('pensée autre' or 'other-thought'). While providing an overview of the three major movements that sought to reform and revive the Maghreb ('traditionalism', 'Salafism' and 'rationalism'), Khatibi criticizes the first two for having failed to question their theocratic foundations and to engage in a productive dialogue with the West. His most cited observations, however, are those directed at the work of Moroccan historian Abdallah Laroui, whom he criticizes for reading history as a continuous and rational concept while dismissing the movement of dissymmetry, disorder and disjunction in the historical construction of the subject. Laroui's denunciation of the dispossession of the Arab subject by both colonial scholarship and the nostalgic impulse of traditionalism leaves Khatibi unsatisfied. His ultimate goal is to extend freedom of thought by questioning the metaphysical, philosophical and psychoanalytical foundations of identity,[28] and by opening the Maghrebian self to a strategic and shifting dialogue with difference. Khatibi's championing of what he subsequently called 'la différence intraitable' ['intractable difference'] is an original and reinvigorating attempt to rethink the Maghreb, 'tel qu'il *est*, site topographique entre l'Orient, l'Occident et l'Afrique, et tel qu'il puisse se mondialiser pour son propre compte' ['as it *is*, topographical site between the East, the West, and Africa, and as such that it can become global for its own account'].[29] An immediate and practical application of this new thought can be found in Khatibi's subsequent and groundbreaking studies of bilingualism, sexuality and

28   Khatibi himself underwent psychoanalysis between September 1982 and July 1983 and gathered his reflections on the discipline and its practice in a fragmented diary and a series of studies published in *Par-dessus l'épaule* (Paris: Aubier, 1988), pp. 47–71 and 73–135.
29   Abdelkébir Khatibi, *Maghreb pluriel* (Paris: Denoël, 1983), pp. 38–9; *Plural Maghreb*, trans. P. Burcu Yalim (London: Bloomsbury, 2019), pp. 22–3.

art, all driven by his desire to open up unexplored or silenced lines of research in Maghreb studies. Regardless of its level of attainment, his contribution had the merit of regenerating the theoretical toolkit of the North African scholar while fostering a critical, constructive and updated thinking on contemporary issues. In his preface to *Penser le Maghreb*, published in 1993 as a sequel to *Maghreb pluriel*, Khatibi reaffirms that 'penser le Maghreb, c'est fixer notre attention sur le rapport de la pensée à la contemporanéité, à l'histoire que nous faisons et à celle que nous ne faisons pas' ['to think of the Maghreb is to direct our attention to the relationship between thought and contemporaneity, and with the history we are making as well as that we are not making'].[30] Following the foundation of the Arab Maghreb Union in 1989, Khatibi displayed his vision on the future of the region and pursued his reflections on Arab identity and culture, as well as on the relationship between the sacred and the political in North African societies and beyond.

Khatibi's intellectual production, however, never prevented him from intervening in political debates. In the 1960s, he briefly joined the Moroccan Communist Party and was for some time active within the powerful Moroccan National Students' Union (UNEM). Although his political activism remained relatively discreet, he wrote a number of articles discussing local, regional and international issues. In 1979, for instance, he published a column in *Le Monde* about the Saharan conflict between Morocco and Algeria. In line with his vision of a plural Maghreb, he called for an economic and political compromise between the two neighbours and wondered: 'pourquoi le Sahara ne serait-il pas le lien d'une volonté commune? Le Maghreb à partir du Sud?' ['why the Sahara could not be the link for a common will? For the Maghreb from the South?'].[31] Plurality as a paradigm for Maghrebian reality constitutes, as is aptly observed by Charles Forsdick, a position that 'is not merely aesthetic, but also influences Khatibi's political stance, consciously suspicious of homogenizing calls for pan-Arab solidarity'.[32] In so doing, Khatibi's thinking sought to connect aesthetics and politics while expanding and redefining the role of the North African intellectual.

30 Abdelkébir Khatibi, *Penser le Maghreb* (Rabat: Société Marocaine des Editeurs Réunis, 1993), p. 5.
31 Abdelkébir Khatibi, 'Pour un compromis saharien', *Le Monde*, 2–3 Sept. 1979, reprinted in *Penser le Maghreb*, pp. 117–19 (p. 119).
32 Charles Forsdick, *Victor Segalen and the Aesthetics of Diversity: Journeys between Cultures* (Oxford: Oxford University Press, 2000), p. 99.

In this respect, his forays into the realm of politics took various forms, from the scathing critique of both Zionism and the position of the French left towards the Palestinian question in his pamphlet *Vomito blanco*, published in 1973,[33] to the analytical study of the ideology and activity of Moroccan political parties in his brief essay *L'Alternance et les partis politiques*, written following the appointment in 1998 of the 'alternance' government led by the socialist and long-time opponents of the Union Socialiste des Forces Populaires (USFP).[34] In a foreword to the latter, Khatibi sees in the official photograph of the new Moroccan government, 'l'image de ma génération politique et intellectuelle, son long combat pour une société plus juste […] mes propres doutes, mes espérances, mes craintes du futur' ['the image of my intellectual and political generation, its long fight for a fairer society […] my own doubts, my hopes, and my fears for the future'].[35] If the book stems from what several observers have considered as a significant turn in Moroccan politics after the so-called 'Years of Lead', Khatibi's confessed fears and doubts retrospectively take on a special resonance. More than 20 years after the 'alternance' experiment, and despite the relative progress achieved on a legislative level in the aftermath of the 'Arab Spring', the Moroccan political scene is still facing challenges, including what Khatibi identified as the ongoing weakening of political parties and young people's lack of involvement in politics.

Throughout his career, Khatibi developed a substantial number of intellectual, literary and artistic friendships, including in the Maghreb. These relationships have almost all in common a sense of instructive dialogue and productive exchange. In 2003, for instance, Khatibi took part in a two-day colloquium in Paris organized by Mireille Calle-Gruber around Assia Djebar's work and contributed with a close analytical reading of *L'Amour, la fantasia*.[36] A volume of tributes entitled *Le Jour d'après* and published one year after Khatibi's death allows

33   Abdelkébir Khatibi, *Vomito blanco* (Paris: Union générale d'éditions, 1974) was republished alongside a series of articles in *Paradoxes du sionisme* (Rabat: Al Kalam, 1990).

34   'Union Socialiste des Forces Populaires' [Socialist Union of Popular Forces] was founded in 1974 following a split from the Union Nationale des Forces Populaires [National Union of Popular Forces], which was itself established in 1959 by leftist members who broke away from the Istiqlal Party [Independence Party].

35   Abdelkébir Khatibi, *L'Alternance et les partis politiques* (Casablanca: Eddif, 1998), p. 11.

36   Abdelkébir Khatibi, 'La Vestale et la guérillère: à propos de *L'Amour, la*

us to comprehend the significance of his impact on his Maghrebian colleagues. Tahar Ben Jelloun, for instance, admits having learned from his elder comrade how to read and interpret popular culture.[37] In 1970, he lauds *La Mémoire tatouée* as the first novel, alongside Beckett's and Artaud's works, that provided him with 'le sentiment de complicité et de récréation' ['the feeling of complicity and recreation'] and helped him to experience the joys of writing.[38] For Algerian artist Aïssa Ikken, Khatibi was a helpful and inspirational companion who enriched his understanding of language in relation to artistic production. Similarly, Algerian writer Nabile Farès praises him as 'l'ami précieux'[39] ['the precious friend'], while his fellow Beïda Chikhi highlights Khatibi's impressive ability to 'reprendre la main et la passer' ['take and hand over'] in reference to his commitment to sharing and disseminating knowledge.[40] In the same vein, Tunisian writer Abdelwahab Meddeb evokes his intense relationship with Khatibi in the period between the 1970s and 1990s and describes their first encounter in Paris in 1975 as an embodiment of 'la pensée qui se déploie'[41] ['thinking that spreads out'] and an early sign of their productive and far-reaching dialogue. Meddeb sees in Khatibi not only a friend but also a creative mentor who paved the way for the regeneration of Maghrebian identity and the reinvention of literary forms and mental frameworks in North Africa and beyond. Meddeb's and Khatibi's intersecting interests, from Arabic mysticism to Francophone experimental fiction, through the

fantasia', in Mireille Calle-Gruber (ed.), *Assia Djebar, nomade entre les murs: pour une poétique transfrontalière* (Paris: Maisonneuve & Larose, 2005), pp. 107–13.

37   Tahar Ben Jelloun, 'Abdel', in Assia Belhabib (ed.), *Le Jour d'après: dédicaces à Abdelkébir Khatibi* (Casablanca: Afrique Orient, 2010), pp. 35–8 (p. 36).

38   Tahar Ben Jelloun, 'Lettre à l'auteur', *Pro-Culture* 12 – Numéro spécial: 'Khatibi' (Rabat: Imprimerie culturelle et universitaire Mohammed V, 1978), p. 42. On Ben Jelloun's later break with Khatibi, see Tahar Ben Jelloun, *Eloge de l'amitié* (Paris: Arléa, 1994) and Abdelkébir Khatibi, 'Amitié truquée (Lettre ouverte à Tahar Ben Jelloun en réponse à son livre *La soudure fraternelle*)', *République Internationale des Lettres* 5 (8 July 1994), pp. 56–7.

39   Nabile Farès, 'Dans le temps, au-delà du temps à l'ami précieux, Abdelkébir Khatibi', in *Le Jour d'après: dédicaces à Abdelkébir Khatibi*, pp. 85–6.

40   Beïda Chikhi, 'Ce qui s'appelle "reprendre la main"', in *Le Jour d'après: dédicaces à Abdelkébir Khatibi*, pp. 51–6, p. 56.

41   Abdelwahab Meddeb, 'Adieu l'ami', ibid., pp. 161–7, p. 162. See also Abdelwahab Meddeb, 'Sonnet pour Abdelkébir Khatibi', in Ahmed Kohen Lamrhili (ed.), *Abdelkébir Khatibi* (Rabat: Okad, 1990), p. 43.

investigation of linguistic duality, the critique of dogmatism and the dialogue with foreign cultures, are particularly revealing. Khatibi's complementary and long-lasting North African friendships served to deepen his creative insight and often triggered a return to more personal writing, as suggested by his late autobiographical work *Le Scribe et son ombre*, written following the request of 'un ami bienveillant' ['a kindly friend'].[42] In a tribute to Khatibi, Moroccan scholar Abdelfettah Kilito interprets this process of stimulated writing as a continuation of an old tradition that dates back to ancient Latin and Arab writers.[43] This suggests that Khatibi's friendships were not only rooted in the Maghreb and open to the world but also driven by the ongoing dialogue between the individual and the collective, the present and the past.

Whether in political analysis or in cultural studies, a consistent element of Khatibi's activity has been his enthusiastic dialogue with, and transmission of knowledge to, young people and early-career scholars and writers. It is particularly revealing, for instance, that *L'Alternance et les partis politiques* ends with a brief 'Lettre à un jeune militant' ['Letter to a Young Activist'] in which Khatibi provides Moroccan youth with a didactic redefinition of political activity as *'loi du partage'* ['the law of sharing'], grounded in ethical, social and ideological values.[44] Also revealing is the fact that Khatibi wrote several prefaces and afterwords to a number of fictional, poetic and theoretical texts published by both Moroccan well-known figures and emerging talents, including a volume by Fatima Mernissi, an autobiography by musician Abdellatif El Bayati, a long prose poem by writer Siham Issami, a novel by journalist and literary critic Abdallah Bensmain, an essay on Muslim community by political leader and diplomat Kacem Zhiri and a catalogue by painter Mohammed Cherkaoui.[45] Furthermore, Khatibi enthusiastically encouraged several writers such as Moroccan poet Maria Zaki whose

---

42   Khatibi, *Le Scribe et son ombre*, p. 13.
43   Abdelfattah Kilito, '"Fuguer, toujours fuguer"', in *Le Jour d'après: dédicaces à Abdelkébir Khatibi*, pp. 109–14 (p. 113).
44   Khatibi, *L'Alternance et les partis politiques*, pp. 103–6 (p. 106).
45   Abdelkébir Khatibi, 'Exergue', in Fatima Mernissi, *Le Maroc raconté par ses femmes* (Rabat: Société Marocaine des Editeurs Réunis, 1986), pp. 7–10; 'Préface', in Abdellatif El Bayati, *La Symphonie des nuits diaprées: récit autobiographique* (Rabat: Marsam, 2001), pp. 9–10; 'Préface', in Kacem Zhiri, *Panorama Islamique* (Casablanca: Najah el Jadida, 1999), p. 7; 'Préface', in Mohammed Cherkaoui, *Exposition des tableaux des merveilles cosmiques* (Rabat: Imprimerie Al Maarif Al Jadida, 2006), pp. 5–6; 'Préface', in Siham Issami, *Les Amants de l'ailleurs*

early poetry appeared in the special issue of *Poésie 94* he initiated in 1994 around the concept of 'aimance'.[46] Starting from 2005, Khatibi pursued this role while serving as a Chairman of the Moroccan Centre of PEN International, established the same year. As part of his activities within the association, Khatibi organized a series of literary and academic events starting with the first colloquium in 2005 on 'L'intellectuel, la société et le pouvoir' ['The Intellectual, Society and Power']. In his contribution to the proceedings, Khatibi argues that the intellectual is most likely to be efficient in civil society through 'sa vocation d'initiateur, de formateur et de directeur d'opinion publique' ['his vocation as an initiator, instructor and director of public opinion'],[47] three roles he himself played throughout his career.

In Morocco as abroad, Khatibi's works have been the subject of several academic events and conferences, most of which involved both Moroccan and international scholars. In 1985, the first event organized by the newly created 'Centre National d'Art Contemporain' in Grenoble was dedicated to Morocco and included a colloquium on the notion of difference in Khatibi's works. The proceedings were published under the title of *Imaginaires de l'autre: Khatibi et la mémoire littéraire*, with contributions from academics that included leading Moroccan scholars Abdelfattah Kilito, Abdesslam Benabdelali and Abdallah Bounfour.[48] In March 2008, the Université Chouaïb Doukkali at El Jadida organized a two-day conference dedicated to Khatibi followed by a publication entitled *Hommage à Abdelkébir Khatibi*.[49] More recently, in March 2019, a four-day international colloquium was organized in El Jadida,

(Neuilly-sur-Seine: Al Manar, 2005), pp. 7–8; 'Postface', in Abdallah Bensmain, *Le Retour du muezzin* (Paris: Publisud, 2011), pp. 195–8.

46   See *Poésie 94*, n° 53 (June 1994): 'L'Aimance', ed. Abdelkébir Khatibi (Paris: Seghers/Maison de la Poésie). The issue features poems by Adonis, Maria Zaki, Abdelmajid Benjelloun and others.

47   Abdelkébir Khatibi, 'L'Intellectuel et le mondialisme', in Centre Marocain de Pen International (collective), *L'Intellectuel, la société, le pouvoir* (El Jadida: Editions Okad, 2007), pp. 9–20 (p. 11).

48   Christine Buci-Glucksmann, Antoine Raybaud, Abdelhaï Diouri, Marc Gontard, Abdesslam Benabdelali, Abdelfattah Kilito, Abdallah Bounfour, Jacques Hassoun and Réda Bensmaïa, *Imaginaires de l'autre: Khatibi et la mémoire littéraire* (Paris: L'Harmattan, 1987).

49   Abdelouahad Mabrour (ed.), *Hommage à Abdelkébir Khatibi: Actes du Colloque international du 26 et 27 mars 2008* (El Jadida: Publications de la Faculté des Lettres et des Sciences Humaines d'El Jadida, 2009).

Rabat and Kenitra to commemorate the tenth anniversary of Khatibi's death, followed shortly by a three-day conference held at the Académie du Royaume du Maroc with an opening keynote by Syrian poet Adonis.[50] Three of the earliest studies of Khatibi's works in Morocco, published in the mid-1990s, are Hassan Wahbi's *Les Mots du monde: Khatibi et le récit* and Rachida Saïgh Bousta's *Lecture des récits de Abdelkébir Khatibi*.[51] More recent monographs include Assia Belhabib's *La Langue de l'hôte: lecture de Abdelkébir Khatibi* and Hassan Wahbi's *Abdelkébir Khatibi: l'esprit de la lettre*.[52] A number of journals have dedicated special issues to Khatibi and his works, including *Pro-Culture* in Morocco in 1978 and two issues of the journal *Celaan Revue* (formerly *Revue Celfan/Celfan Review*), in 1990 and 2011, with contributions by Moroccan and international scholars.[53] In a foreword to the 1990 issue, Eric Sellin considers that the 'humanist' Khatibi stands 'at the center of the circle'[54] constituted by Maghrebian intellectuals and writers. As the figure of Khatibi was held in high esteem by his peers, tributes were regularly paid to his works. Among the first of these was a collective volume published in 1990 on the initiative of the director of the monthly Moroccan journal 'Al-Asas'.[55] After Khatibi's death in 2009, more publications continued to pay tribute to his memory while reflecting on his intellectual legacy, including in 2010 the aforementioned collective

50 'Abdelkébir Khatibi: Cheminements et empreintes', El Jadida, Rabat, Kenitra, 12–15 Mar. 2019. See https://kha2019.sciencesconf.org and 'Abdelkébir Khatibi: Quels héritages?', Rabat: 20–22 Mar. 2019.

51 Hassan Wahbi, *Les Mots du monde: Khatibi et le récit* (Agadir: Publications de la Faculté des Lettres et Sciences Humaines, 1995); Rachida Saïgh Bousta, *Lecture des récits de Abdelkébir Khatibi: ecriture, memoire et imaginaire* (Casablanca: Afrique Orient, 1996).

52 Assia Belhabib, *La Langue de l'hôte: lecture de Abdelkébir Khatibi* (El Jadida: Okad, 2009); Hassan Wahbi, *Abdelkébir Khatibi: l'Esprit de la lettre* (Rabat: Marsam, 2014).

53 *Pro-Culture* 12, Numéro spécial: 'Khatibi' (Rabat: Imprimerie culturelle et universitaire Mohammed V, 1978); *Revue Celfan/Celfan Review* 8.1–2 (Nov. 1988–Feb. 1989) (Philadelphia: Temple University, 1990); *Celaan* 9.2–3, Fall 2011, 'Hommage à Abdelkébir Khatibi (1938–2009)' (New York: Skidmore College, 2011); *Celaan* 16.2–3, Spring & Summer 2020, 'Khatibi in English' (New York: Skidmore College, 2020).

54 Eric Sellin, 'Editorial: Abdelkébir Khatibi, Humanist', *Revue Celfan/Celfan Review* 8.1–2 (Nov. 1988–Feb. 1989), p. 1.

55 Ahmed El Kohen Lamrhili (ed.), *Abdelkébir Khatibi* (Rabat: Okad, 1990).

volume *Le Jour d'après*, edited by Assia Belhabib.[56] In 2012, a series of interviews that had taken place four years earlier between Abdelkébir Khatibi and American thinker Samuel Weber were finally published by University Mohammed V in Rabat.[57] Two years later appeared a bilingual collective volume in tribute to Khatibi and coordinated by his nephew, poet and translator Mourad El Khatibi.[58] In 2019, Moroccan philosopher Abdesslam Benabdelali published a short monograph about Khatibi in a series supported by the Institut du Monde Arabe in Paris, and more recently, another collective volume was edited by Abdelghani Fennane and published by Editions Toubkal.[59]

The recognition of Khatibi's unique contribution to the intellectual and cultural scene in Morocco and the Arab world sparked considerable interest in the translation of his works into Arabic. One of the earliest is Moroccan Arabophone novelist and literary critic Mohammed Berrada's translation of *Le Roman maghrébin* in 1971, later republished alongside the translation of *La Mille et Deuxième Nuit* and an interview with Khatibi.[60] Berrada, also known for his translation of Barthes into Arabic, would later translate Khatibi's volume written with Sijelmassi, *L'Art calligraphique arabe*.[61] The 1980s and 1990s witnessed an acceleration in the translation of Khatibi's works: *Le Lutteur de classe à la manière taoïste*, *La Blessure du nom propre* and a collective volume featuring articles from *Maghreb pluriel* alongside *Vomito blanco* in 1980, *La Mémoire tatouée* in 1984, *Le Prophète voilé* and *Un été à Stockholm* in 1992 and *Triptyque de*

56 Assia Belhabib (ed.), *Le Jour d'après: dédicaces à Abdelkébir Khatibi* (Casablanca: Afrique Orient, 2010).

57 Abdelkébir Khatibi and Samuel Weber, *Le Chemin vers l'autre: entretiens (27–31 Octobre 2008)* (Rabat: Faculté des Lettres et des Sciences Humaines de Rabat, 2012).

58 Mourad El Khatibi (ed.), *Né demain: hommage à Abdelkébir Khatibi (11 février 1938–16 mars 2009)* (Tangier: Slaiki Akhawayne, 2014).

59 Abdesslam Benabdelali, *Abdelkebir Khatibi: l'étranger professionnel* (Casablanca: Centre Culturel du Livre, 2019); Abdelghani Fennane (ed.), *Celui qui vient de l'avenir: Abdelkébir Khatibi* (Casablanca, Editions Toubkal, 2020).

60 Mohammed Berrada (trans.), *Al-Riwaya Al-Magharibia* (Rabat: Publications du Centre Universitaire de la Recherche Scientifique, 1971); Mohammed Berrada, *Fi Al-Kittaba wa Ttajriba* (Beirut: Dar Al-Aouda, 1980/Rabat: Okad, 1989).

61 Mohammed Berrada (trans.), *Diwan Al-Khatte Al-Arabi* (Beirut: Dar Al-Aouda, 1981).

Rabat in 1998.[62] More recently, a volume in Arabic appeared entitled 'Towards a Different Thought', including a translation of Khatibi's article 'Le Maghreb comme horizon de pensée', first published in *Les Temps Modernes* in 1977, followed by a translation of *Vomito blanco*.[63] The Arabic translation of Khatibi's and Hassoun's collective book *Le Même Livre* is expected to be published in Rabat in 2020. Furthermore, a substantial number of articles and excerpts from Khatibi's works were translated in various Arabophone literary journals and cultural magazines and newspapers, including 'Mawakif' in Lebanon, 'Al-Yawm Assabi' in Paris, as well as 'Al-Alam', 'Al-Ittihad Al-Ichtiraki' and the 'Annales marocaines de sociologie' in Morocco.[64]

Interestingly, the translation of Khatibi's works was carried out as much by Moroccan novelists (Mohammed Berrada), poets (Mohammed Bennis), philosophers (Abdesslam Benabdelali) and scholars (Farid Zahi), as by international academics (Boutros Hallaq, professor of Modern Arabic Literature at Paris 3, and Kadhim Jihad Hassan, professor at INALCO). Moreover, the translations were published in both Morocco and other centres of the book industry in the Middle East, including Lebanon and Qatar. This diversity is not surprising given the broad spectrum of Khatibi's interests and the curiosity it has generated across disciplines. The blurb of one of the most recent translations celebrates him as 'one of the rare Arab encyclopaedists and independent thinkers after the pioneering generation of Al-Nahda'.[65] This anachronistic reference to the Arab renaissance is particularly significant as it not

---

62   Kadhim Jihad (trans.), *Al-Mounadil Al-Tabaki Ala Al-Tarika Al-Taouia* (Casablanca: Toubkal, 1980); Mohammed Bennis (trans.), *Al-Issmo Al-Arabiyo Al-Jarih* (Beirut: Dar Al-Aouda, 1980); Adonis, Abdesslam Benabdelali and Zoubida Bourhil (trans.), *Annakd Al-Mouzdawaj* (Beirut: Dar Al-Aouda, 1980/ Rabat: Okad, 1990); Boutros Hallaq (trans.), *Addakira Al-Mawchouma* (Rabat: Institut Arabe pour la Recherche et la Publication and Société Marocaine des Editeurs Réunis, 1984); Mohammed Kaghat (trans.), *Annabiy Al-Moukanaa* (Kuwait City: Ministère de la Communication, 1993); Farid Zahi (trans.), *Sayf fi Stockholm* (Casablanca: Toubkal, 1992); Farid Zahi (trans.), *Thoulathiat Al-Ribat* (Casablanca: Arrabita, 1998).

63   Abdesslam Benabdelali (trans.), *Nahwa Fikr Moughayir* (Doha: Ministry of Culture, Arts, and Heritage, 2013).

64   For more bibliographical references, see *L'Œuvre de ... Abdelkébir Khatibi* (Rabat: Marsam, 1997) and Saïd Nejjar, *Bibliographie de l'œuvre de Abdelkébir Khatibi* (Rabat: Institut Universitaire de la Recherche Scientifique, 2001).

65   Benabdelali (trans.), *Nahwa Fikr Moughayir*, blurb.

only acknowledges Khatibi's impact on Arab cultural and intellectual history but it also suggests that he responded to a pressing need in the Arab world to renew knowledge and scholarship while providing a lens through which to look at both the Eastern and Western worlds.

Khatibi has still, however, not quite received the recognition he deserves, including in Morocco. Although he intervened on a number of public television and radio programmes,[66] and gave conferences and talks in a series of schools and universities, his name has suffered from a relative lack of acknowledgement from the general public. If this issue has certainly more to do with the influence of intellectuals in Morocco, generally limited to academic and professional circles, than with the figure of Khatibi himself, the author of *La Mémoire tatouée* has still been criticized for his difficult prose style and highly intellectualized use of the French language. This widespread reputation has produced a general misunderstanding that has probably kept some potential readers away from his texts. Another issue has been the tremendous difficulty of finding some of his books, not only in Moroccan bookstores but also through online platforms. The only way to get hold of many of his works is to wander between booksellers and spend hours in second-hand bookshops, an activity he himself particularly enjoyed. Also significant is the absence of translations into Amazigh languages, although this is mostly due to the slow development of government support for Tamazight in Morocco, following its recognition as an official language alongside Arabic in the constitutional reform of July 2011.

Despite these difficulties, Khatibi remains an acclaimed author and a leading intellectual in both Morocco and the Arab world. He was decorated as 'Chevalier de l'ordre du Trône' in 1996 and awarded a number of prizes including the 'Grand Prix Atlas' in 1997, the 'Grand Prix du Maroc' in 1998 and the 'Prix de l'Afrique méditerranéenne/Maghreb' in 2003. Furthermore, his name has been given to an exhibition space in El Jadida, a communal school in the region of the same city, and more temporarily to a room at the International Book and Publishing Fair 'SIEL' in Casablanca in 2010, the year following his death. Khatibi's presence is still vibrant in Morocco, calling for more initiatives to perpetuate his intellectual legacy.

---

66 For references, see *L'Œuvre de … Abdelkébir Khatibi*.

Khatibi's commitment and influence in Morocco should be recognized, however, alongside his strikingly international outlook and significance. His autobiographical works demonstrate how, although he resided in Morocco for most of his life and his trips abroad were for the most part relatively short-term, international culture nevertheless plays a central role in his evolution as a thinker. As both *La Mémoire tatouée* and *Le Scribe et son ombre* attest, he spent six years studying sociology and philosophy at the Sorbonne in Paris, where he also completed his thesis on *Le Roman maghrébin*, and the experience had a transformational impact on his thinking. Reflecting on these years in *La Mémoire tatouée*, for example, he evokes his fascination with France and indeed Western culture, and yet performs in his writing and in his relationships with European women a playful game of both seduction and distancing with French culture. In the concluding fragments to the work, the writer addresses the West directly, yet uses a mixed vocabulary of praise as well as of rejection; he still desires the West as he would a woman, yet beseeches, 'ravale, Occident, tes vipères, tes pierres dressées' ['swallow your vipers, Occident, your stones erected'].[67] In confronting in Paris the West that was nevertheless present throughout his upbringing in Morocco, Khatibi's narrator reaches an understanding of his own subject position as a space both of tension and of meeting, where 'l'Occident est une partie de moi, que je ne peux nier que dans la mesure où je lutte contre tous les occidents et orients qui m'oppriment ou me désenchantent' ['the Occident is a part of me, and I can only deny it to the extent that I struggle against all the occidents and orients that either oppress or disillusion me'].[68] At the same time, however, he also imagines the French capital as a space of diversity and openness. Indeed, 'dans Paris, il y a autant de villes que de suggestions (Dieu merci!), autant de villes que de groupes d'étrangers, autant de quartiers que d'autres quartiers' ['in Paris there are as many cities as suggestions (thank God!), as many cities as groups of foreigners, as many neighborhoods as there are other neighborhoods'].[69] This place of encounter provokes the philosopher to confront his own hybridization, to address his own subjectivity as indeterminate and necessarily evolving as a result of his background and education and his continuing development. His relationship with France, moreover, was crystallized when he was decorated as 'Chevalier de

---

67   Khatibi, *La Mémoire tatouée*, p. 103; *Tattooed Memory*, p. 141.
68   Ibid., p. 68; p. 90.
69   Ibid., p. 77; p. 103.

l'ordre français des Arts et des Lettres' in 1997, and received the equally prestigious 'Grand Prix de l'Académie Française' in 1994 and the 'Grand Prix de Poésie de la Société des Gens de Lettres' in 2008.

Alongside his stay in Paris and the accompanying reflection on both French and Western cultures, Khatibi also figures himself in these autobiographical works as a wanderer. Paris itself is admired to the extent that it offers a space for errantry and encounter, and the later sections of *La Mémoire tatouée* also refer to visits to Berlin, Cordoba, Delhi, London, Havana and Stockholm. The experience of travel is represented as a trigger for self-questioning, initiating a call for encounter, for self-transformation through contacts with different cultures and peoples. Even more, the journey inaugurates new forms of representation, it brings about encounters with other sign systems, which again in turn engender a form of transcendence of the self, the liberation of subjectivity from the constraints of cultural determinism:

> Voyages ou danse? Mon errance chez tous ces peuples, dont je reprendrai un jour les interférences, face à face, interminable fascination dont je dénonce les signes, et quelle fable racontera mon mouvement? Furtif échange, une fantaisie, une équation de visions qui me font flotter, à la croisée des différences, vers ma propre divination.

> [Travels or dancing? My roaming among all these peoples – and one day I'll recapture its interferences again, face to face – an interminable fascination whose signs I renounce, and what fable could retell my movements? Furtive exchange, a whim, an equation of visions that make me drift – where differences meet – toward my own divining.][70]

Khatibi's stay in Stockholm is of course also explored at more length in *Un été à Stockholm*, published in 1990, a work where travel and the experience of living in Sweden generate a philosophical reflection that knits together many crucial aspects of Khatibi's thinking on errantry and encounter. The city of Stockholm, associated with political neutrality, is also the setting for new friendships and love affairs liberated by the transience and openness of 'aimance', as well as the backdrop for the work of a simultaneous interpreter whose activity inspires a conception of writing itself as translation, as an attentive process of listening as well as recreation. While on some level Khatibi remains anchored in and deeply committed to Morocco, then, and while he never chose to live abroad for the long term, his thinking is itself an embrace of travel and of

---

70 Ibid., p. 102; p. 139.

the contacts and transformations it may bring. His writing throughout strives at the same time to record the trace of that cultural movement, as if his language itself, though ostensibly French, always captures echoes of Arabic and other languages, and stretches both allusion and syntax in order to seek new resonances.

If Khatibi is perhaps best known for his reimagining of the space of the Maghreb in *Maghreb pluriel*, he has also often been cited for his theorizations of language, translation and bilingualism. The collective volume *Du bilinguisme*, published in 1985, is itself an international enterprise, based on a conference held in Rabat in 1981, with a set of diverse participants from a range of different cultural and linguistic backgrounds. Contributors to the volume include François Cheng, Jacques Hassoun and Tzvetan Todorov, as well as several Moroccan writers such as Abdallah Bounfour and Abdelfattah Kilito, and Khatibi's own article, 'Incipits', reprinting the illuminating reading of Abdelwahab Meddeb's *Talismano* from *Maghreb pluriel*. The work is a paradigm-changing study of the limits of monolingualism, of the ways in which languages can come together, overlap, subvert and also conflict with one another, and aptly anticipates more recent studies of multilingualism and 'translanguaging' well in advance. While Todorov writes movingly of the sense of incompatibility between the French and Bulgarian languages, Hassoun, for example, deconstructs more comprehensively the notion of the 'mother tongue', and while Jalil Bennani explores the significance of bilingualism in psychoanalysis, Eliane Formentelli examines how poetic language in particular can challenge overly reassuring notions of a language of origins. Khatibi's own reading of *Talismano* is a stunning demonstration, moreover, of the hidden presence of Arabic in Meddeb's French, as if traces of Arabic do leave their mark on the French, but for the most part these traces are imperceptible, testifying to the meeting between languages but also their untranslatability. This combination of linguistic merging and blending with untranslatability provides at the same time the theoretical backdrop to the poetic narrative *Amour bilingue*, first published close to *Maghreb pluriel* in 1983. Khatibi's complex vision of cultural encounter is perhaps played out here in its most intensified form, where a richly allusive style associates language with breath, body, movement and gesture, and with a desire that both calls to and welcomes the other while at the same time embracing a confrontation with the difference, indeed the potential unintelligibility and intractability, of that other language.

   This recurrent preoccupation with errantry and bilingualism makes Khatibi as philosopher and writer an 'étranger professionnel' ['professional stranger'], committed not only to conceptualizing travel and cultural encounter but also to allowing it to shape all aspects of his writing and thought. The necessary consequence of the embrace of 'pensée autre' and the 'bi-langue', the 'étranger professionnel' perceives the pursuit of and encounter with other cultures and languages as the guiding principle of his life and work, as an approach to intellectual activity that will be present throughout his career and his lived experiences. The central character of *Un été à Stockholm*, Gérard Namir, for example, is described as a 'voyageur professionnel qui veut traverser les frontières avec une souplesse d'esprit' ['a professional traveller who crosses borders with a flexible mind'], as if the role necessitates both a commitment to travel and an intellectual and spiritual openness that would be present at all times.[71] In *Figures de l'étranger dans la littérature française*, Jean Genet is held up as an apt example of the professional stranger, always seeking new encounters and experiences and keeping his thought alive through that restlessness.[72] And, most importantly, Khatibi himself is an 'étranger professionnel', as he asserts in the essay 'Nationalisme et internationalisme littéraires' ['Literary Nationalism and Internationalism'], in *Figures de l'étranger*,[73] and later in an essay entitled 'Un étranger professionnel', published in *Etudes françaises* in 1997. Here, as in *Figures*, a series of writers and thinkers are taken to have performed this gesturing towards the other, and towards the other within the self, as he mentions Rimbaud, Mallarmé, Michaux, Kourouma and Beckett. Yet Khatibi evokes his own experience of writing in French as accomplishing a comparable uniqueness through its interweaving with other languages, and asserts that it is this curiously singular duality that characterizes the 'étranger professionnel' par excellence:

71   Abdelkébir Khatibi, *Un été à Stockholm* (Paris: Flammarion, 1990), reprinted in *Œuvres de Abdelkébir Khatibi I: Romans et récits*, pp. 285–379 (p. 287).
72   On Genet, see also Abdelkébir Khatibi and Marie Redonnet (eds), *Féerie et dissidence: colloque Jean Genet* (Rabat: Okad, 2003) – the proceedings of a two-day colloquium organized by Khatibi in Rabat, 16–17 Jan. 2002.
73   See also 'Literary Nationalism and Internationalism', in Kenneth W. Harrow, Jonathan Ngaté and Clarisse Zimra (eds), *Crisscrossing Boundaries in African Literatures*, Annual Selected Papers of the ALA 12/1986 (Washington, DC: Three Continents Press/African Literature Association, 1991), pp. 3–10.

une expérience, mon expérience de la langue d'écriture tissée à une double, multiple langue m'a appris au moins ceci: toute œuvre réside, habite dans son unicité solitaire. À cette unicité si singulière, je donne depuis quelques années le nom d'étranger professionnel.[74]

[an experience, my experience of a written language interwoven with a double, a multiple language, has taught me at least this: that every work resides in its solitary uniqueness. To this singular uniqueness I have given for a few years the name a professional stranger.]

As Alison Rice also elaborates in the present volume, the vision and experience of the professional stranger will always be inscribed in the very fabric of Khatibi's writing.

In addition to both the conceptualization and the experiencing of professional strangeness, Khatibi's transnational outlook is amply demonstrated by his multiple and diverse engagements with other writers and thinkers throughout his work. If *La Mémoire tatouée* traces his cultural evolution, from his upbringing in Morocco through his studies in Paris, *Le Scribe et son ombre* tracks a sort of intellectual trajectory. The narrative stresses his disciplinary eclecticism, as is testified by his publications in sociology, philosophy, literature and art, and also alludes to the multiplicity of highly varied intellectual companions who have accompanied him as his thought has evolved. The list is long but also striking in its disregard for historical or cultural categorization: the texts he cites are 'ceux de Héraclite et de Lao Tseu, Platon, Al Maari et Ibn Khaldûn, Marc Aurèle et Montaigne, Leopardi, Marx, Kierkegaard, Nietzsche, Freud, sans oublier Bachelard, Leroi-Gourhan, Valéry, Borges, Blanchot, Foucault, Barthes, Derrida' ['those of Heraclitus and Lao Tzu, Plato, Al Ma'arri and Ibn Khaldun, Marcus Aurelius and Montaigne, Leopardi, Marx, Kierkegaard, Nietzsche, Freud, not forgetting Bachelard, Leroi-Gourhan, Valéry, Borges, Blanchot, Foucault, Barthes, Derrida'].[75] And while this philosophical diversity evidently informs his conceptual work throughout his career and testifies to his intellectual suppleness, voracious and wide-ranging literary reading shapes his poetics and his passion for mining the secrets and potentialities of language. In the series of interviews with Hassan Wahbi entitled *La Beauté de l'absent*, for example, he cites the Arabic writer Gibran Khalil Gibran alongside

---

74 Abdelkébir Khatibi, 'Un étranger professionnel', *Etudes françaises* 33.1 (1997), pp. 123–6 (p. 126).
75 Khatibi, *Le Scribe et son ombre*, p. 24.

Baudelaire, Maeterlinck, Verhaeren, Rimbaud, Mallarmé and Valéry as initiators of his interest in poetry, together with Stendhal and Dostoevsky as introductions to the novel. Yet he also writes, he insists, under the influence of the Chinese philosopher Lao Tzu, for example, and of an even broader range of international figures, including Tanizaki, Borges, Cervantès, Goethe and Rilke.[76] And it is through reading literature, he argues, that we are able to discover new worlds, worlds as unfamiliar and as distinct as that of the 'Esquimau' (whose love of seals is revealed to him through an immersion in their poetry). Khatibi's close engagements with literature in works such as *Figures de l'étranger*, as well as *Ombres japonaises*, published in 1988, at the same time themselves privilege writers and works who transgress borders and expand meaning, as Tanizaki's *Eloge de l'ombre*, for example, is in the latter work examined for its use of shadows to figure a subtle suggestiveness. It is perhaps unsurprising that figures as diverse as Martinican writer Patrick Chamoiseau, Senegalese scholar Papa Samba Diop and Japanese artist Minol Kolin-Kobayashi all recognize Khatibi's legacy and pay tribute to his contributions in various forms and across areas and disciplines.[77]

Khatibi's disregard for cultural frontiers in his intellectual life is the result, moreover, of a commitment to denouncing oppressive and atavistic thinking of all kinds. The 'double critique' of *Maghreb pluriel* vilifies both colonialism and theocracy, and in this way targets authoritarianism and cultural determinism on both sides of the Mediterranean. Olivia Harrison, in the present volume as well as in her book-length study, *Transcolonial Maghreb: Imagining Palestine in the Era of Decolonisation*, published in 2015, dubs this critique of both European and Arab metaphysics a form of 'transcolonial' thinking, responding to parallel forms of oppression operating in different but inter-related contexts. And Khatibi's engagement with different cultures significantly includes a reflection on the Palestinian question, most controversially in *Vomito blanco*, published in 1974, where he voices a severe critique of Zionist ideology as well as of Arab ethno-nationalism. Once again, the philosophical backdrop to this most acerbic work is Khatibi's

---

76 Hassan Wahbi, *La Beauté de l'absent: entretiens avec Abdelkébir Khatibi* (Paris: L'Harmattan, 2010), p. 48.

77 See Patrick Chamoiseau, 'Pour Abdelkébir Khatibi', in *Ecarts d'identité* 114 (2009), p. 4; Papa Samba Diop, 'Abdelkébir Khatibi: une plume qui accroche', in *Le Jour d'après: dédicaces à Abdelkébir Khatibi*, pp. 67–77; Minol Kolin-Kobayashi, 'Vers la plage d'El Harhoura', ibid., pp. 115–20.

'pensée autre', working against ethnic and religious as well as cultural determinism, and responding to other cultures in a spirit of openness and generosity.[78] The critique of Zionism, moreover, is followed in Khatibi's philosophical evolution by the crucial dialogue with Jewish culture accomplished in the exchange with Jacques Hassoun, in *Le Même Livre*, first published in 1985, some extracts of which are for the first time translated in the present volume. The volume's title alludes to the parallels between the Torah and the Qur'an, relating these to the cross-fertilization of practices and rituals between the two religions, and this complicity is emphasized in fierce resistance to the disastrous division between Islam and Judaism in the twentieth century. Khatibi's and Hassoun's own correspondence at the same time dramatizes the spirit of dialogue, celebrating a spontaneous and personal style, and open to unpredictability. It accomplishes in its very form a vital 'exercice d'altérité, qui tombe sous la loi de la langue et de l'écriture' ['exercise in alterity, which falls under the law of language and writing'], one which is also an 'exercice de reconnaissance parmi d'autres' ['an exercise in recognition among others'].[79]

Exchange, moreover, has always been fundamental in Khatibi's writing, as his works are often readings of or responses to other thinkers. *Maghreb pluriel*, for example, famously associates decolonization with Derridean deconstruction, though it also consists of readings of the Moroccan historian Abdallah Laroui, as well as the French Orientalist Jacques Berque and the Tunisian writer Abdelwahab Meddeb, as mentioned above. The text opens, moreover, with a reference to Frantz Fanon, to whose call the 'pensée autre' responds directly, as Khatibi insists, 'quelque temps avant sa mort, Franz Fanon avait lancé cet appel: "allons, camarades, le jeu européen est définitivement terminé, il faut trouver autre chose"' ['shortly before his death, Frantz Fanon made the following call: "Come, then, comrades, the European game has finally ended; we must find something different"'].[80] It is perhaps the dialogue with Derrida, however, outlined here by Dominique Combe, that

78   On the question of Palestine, see also Khatibi's article, 'Comment fonder poétiquement une nation en exil?', in Mahmoud Darwich and Rachid Koraïchi, *Une nation en exil: hymnes gravés* suivi de *La Qasida de Beyrouth* (Algiers: Barzakh/Arles: Actes Sud, 2009), pp. 15–21.

79   Abdelkébir Khatibi and Jacques Hassoun, *Le Même Livre* (Paris: Editions de l'éclat, 1985), pp. 9–10.

80   Khatibi, *Maghreb pluriel*, p. 11; *Plural Maghreb*, p. 1.

has generated the most attention in Europe and the USA, and which helped Khatibi to gain some of the recognition outside Morocco that he deserves. Indeed, it is with a brief 'Exergue' by Derrida that the three volumes of *Œuvres* published by La Différence in 2008 opens, so as to crystallize, perhaps, the ways in which he pursues his commitment to Derridean thinking throughout his career. He participated, for example, in the 1992 Colloque de Cerisy, 'Le Passage des frontières: autour du travail de Jacques Derrida', the proceedings of which were subsequently published in 1994, and produced an article responding to Derrida's reflection on language subsequently published in *Le Monolinguisme de l'autre* and imagining the creative and liberating potential of the invention of impure and hybridized idiomatic forms.[81] After Derrida famously cited Khatibi's *Amour bilingue* in the epigraph to *Le Monolinguisme*, published in 1996, Khatibi further responded with *La Langue de l'autre*, reprinting the Cerisy article and continuing with a 'Lettre ouverte à Jacques Derrida', and addressing his friend in the intimate 'tu' form. The text develops the reflection on language and alienation in the Maghreb, supplementing Derrida's discussion of Algeria with a consideration of language usage in Morocco, while referring also to thinkers beyond the Maghreb, including Kafka, Cixous and Claude Ollier.[82] Some of this material then appears again in *Jacques Derrida, en effet*, published in 2007, where Khatibi also develops his own conception of 'aimance', explored, for example, in *Un été à Stockholm*, conceptualized by Derrida in *Politiques de l'amitié*, expanded in Khatibi's *Le Livre de l'aimance* in 1995 and translated into poetry in *Aimance* in 2003. The term aptly captures, moreover, the intermittent but recurring conversation between Khatibi and Derrida and the reflective, responsive form of intellectual friendship that their interaction performs.

Prior to the exchange with Derrida, however, Khatibi had already entered into a dialogue with Roland Barthes, whose essay celebrating what he learned from Khatibi is now printed as the 'Exergue' to volume

---

81 Abdelkébir Khatibi, 'Le point de non-retour', *Le Passage des frontières: autour du travail de Jacques Derrida* (Paris: Galilée, 1994), pp. 445–9.

82 Abdelkébir Khatibi, *La Langue de l'autre* (New York and Tunis: Les Mains secrètes, 1999). On Cixous, see also Abdelkébir Khatibi, 'Témoigner à distance', in Mireille Calle-Gruber and Marie Odile Germain (eds), *Genèses, généalogies, genres: autour de l'œuvre d'Hélène Cixous* (Paris: Galilée and Bibliothèque Nationale de France, 2006), pp. 153–61.

III of the selected *Œuvres* printed by Editions de la Différence in 2008. There may be a degree of Orientalism in Barthes's eulogy to the Moroccan thinker, and the consecration of Khatibi's work by the French academy that the essay performs is no doubt on some level tinged with a form of exoticist reappropriation. Yet Barthes welcomes the subtlety of Khatibi's vision of linguistic hybridization while nevertheless stressing the distinctiveness of the context with which he works:

> Ce qu'il nous faut apprendre, ce n'est pas à réciter un modèle (la langue nous en sépare absolument), mais à inventer pour nous une langue 'hétérologique', un 'ramassis' de différences, dont le brassage ébranlera un peu la compacité terrible (parce qu'historiquement très ancienne) de l'*ego* occidental.[83]

> [What we have to learn, is not to recite a model (language separates us from it completely), but to invent for ourselves a 'heterological' language, a 'mass' of differences, whose mixing will slightly weaken the terrible density of the Western *ego*.]

According to Barthes, then, Khatibi's 'heterological' language serves to critique the assumed stability and hegemony of the Western ego. In *Le Scribe et son ombre*, moreover, Khatibi recalls Barthes's membership of the jury for his thesis and stresses his discretion at the same time as his bold rejection of rigid systems of thought. The two thinkers met several times, and indeed had planned future collaborations, cut short by Barthes's untimely death in 1980.

Khatibi's interactions with Derrida and Barthes are the starting points, moreover, for further parallels and engagements with other major European and postcolonial thinkers, the richness of which is only now starting to be addressed. Nasrin Qader's study of *Narratives of Catastrophe* reads Khatibi's 'pensée autre' as a significant intervention into philosophy and theology themselves, and argues that 'Khatibi wants to take thought, in its traditional sense of reason, to the limit and therefore point to the fracture within thought that, by fragmenting it, opens thought up'.[84] Qader's reading of Khatibi is also heavily inflected with the thought of Jean-Luc Nancy, with whom she perceives Khatibi can be understood to enter into dialogue, and who also imagines a

---

83 Roland Barthes, 'Exergue', in *Œuvres de Abdelkébir Khatibi III: Essais* (Paris: La Différence, 2008), pp. 7–8.
84 Nasrin Qader, *Narratives of Catastrophe: Boris Diop, Ben Jelloun, Khatibi* (New York: Fordham University Press, 2009), p. 126.

conception of thought beyond the dictates of reason, a thought that pushes itself to the limit. More recently, Matt Reeck has developed this parallel between Khatibi and Nancy in his analysis of the 'poetics of the orphan' in *Le Lutteur de classe à la manière taoïste* as a starting point for an ethics of encounter, built out of a positively constructed rootedness. The last part of Reeck's article juxtaposes Khatibi's ethics with Nancy's conception of 'mondialisation' ['globalization'], sketched in *La Création du monde, ou la mondialisation*, where myths of founding origins are replaced with an embrace of the 'groundlessness of the world'.[85] This connection with Nancy's global thinking should also be construed as the result of Khatibi's friendship with Edouard Glissant, for whom the flattening and universalizing implications of 'mondialisation' can be countered by the more open-ended and dialogic network of 'mondialité' ['globality'].[86] These readings uncover far-reaching philosophical significance in Khatibi's thought, taking him outside the context of the Maghreb and establishing his work as a major intervention into contemporary philosophies contemplating the state of the world in the context of globalization. Khatibi's thought can in this way be conceived as continually relevant in its relentless critique of authoritarianism and of dangerously deterministic categories of identity, culture and thought.

Khatibi's significance, more specifically, for postcolonial thought in the Anglophone world has also been noted by critics, though still needs to be more fully recognized. It is perhaps intriguing that, in one of the interviews with Hassan Wahbi in *La Beauté de l'absent*, Khatibi insists that he has not read postcolonial theory and has little to say about it, though he goes on to explain that this is because, in writing *La Mémoire tatouée*, he felt, 'ce récit prend en charge la question de passage (personnel, certes) de la colonisation à la décolonisation' ['this narrative takes on the question of the (certainly personal) passage from colonization to decolonization'].[87] The rejection of postcolonial theory appears, then, to be based on the misapprehension that postcolonial thought has not properly mourned the passing of the period of colonial rule. Yet Khatibi's work in fact offers a vital contribution to postcolonial

85 Matt Reeck, 'The Poetics of the Orphan in Khatibi's Early Work', *Journal of French and Francophone Philosophy* 35.1 (2017), pp. 132–49 (p. 146).
86 See, for example, Edouard Glissant, *Traité du tout-monde* (Paris: Gallimard, 1997).
87 Hassan Wahbi, *La Beauté de l'absent: entretiens avec Abdelkébir Khatibi*, p. 74.

studies on a number of levels. Alfonso de Toro's contribution to the present volume suggests that his conception of the movement of identity through different cultures resonates with Homi Bhabha's use of the notion of 'unhomeliness' in the postcolonial context. And there is no doubt that Bhabha's much cited conceptions of hybridity and the third space as they are theorized in *The Location of Culture*, published in 1994, are strongly reminiscent of Khatibi's 'pensée autre', with its rejection of identitarian and deterministic thinking and its openness to the significatory possibilities of the 'bi-langue'. Françoise Lionnet, moreover, has written a revealing article reading Khatibi alongside Edward Said, where she notes the parallel development of their careers, and the fruitful association between Said's 'contrapuntal' mode of analysis and Khatibi's 'double critique'. Even more, however, Lionnet also notes that Said paid insufficient attention to Khatibi, and that the latter goes further in his imagination of 'as yet unthought exteriority beyond the "archeology of silence" that represses *other* languages, genders, and peoples in their unheard difference'.[88] While Said still looks for 'common ground or translatability', Khatibi's thinking allows a more far-reaching contemplation of modes of being not reducible to existing identity categories and frameworks.

It is in this sense that Khatibi can also be associated not only with postcolonial thought but also, as Andy Stafford suggests in the present volume, with the 'decolonial'. His thought not only condemns the authoritarianism of colonial ideology; the 'pensée autre' calls also for a mode of thinking that completely transcends the structures that allow for that kind of hierarchy. In this sense, it can indeed be construed as 'decolonial' in the sense that Walter Mignolo gives to the term as 'a relentless effort to understand, in order to overcome, the logic of coloniality underneath the rhetoric of modernity'.[89] In his study *Local Histories, Global Designs*, published in 2012, moreover, Mignolo argues that Khatibi exemplifies what he calls 'border thinking' in his alertness to the movement and transfer of languages and signs. This 'border thinking' is precisely not only a deconstruction of colonial categories

---

88 Françoise Lionnet, 'Counterpoint and Double Critique in Edward Said and Abdelkébir Khatibi: A Transcolonial Comparison', in Dominic Thomas and Ali Behdad (eds), *A Companion to Comparative Literature* (Chichester: Wiley Blackwell, 2011), pp. 387–407 (p. 404).
89 Walter Mignolo, *The Darker Side of Western Modernity: Global Futures, Decolonial Options* (Durham, NC: Duke University Press, 2011), p. 10.

but a deeper rejection of the 'subalternization of knowledges and the coloniality of power'.[90] It requires an alternative language as well as an anticolonial critique, and proposes a thinking more radically divorced from colonial modernity and from global capitalism than those versions of critique that remain conditioned by these structures. The lack of attention that Khatibi's thought has won in the West is at the same time symptomatic of the limited scope of neo-imperialist thought, which has failed to take on board critical approaches originating in the Arab and Islamic world, for example. As Qader, Reeck and Lionnet too suggested, Khatibi's 'pensée autre' overturns the very systems of imperialism and modernity, rather than merely terms within those systems.

Khatibi's work, then, has been slow to receive the critical attention it deserves, though is steadily generating more interest, which this volume seeks to fuel and inspire in turn. In addition to the studies published in Morocco mentioned earlier, Marc Gontard discusses his work in *Le Moi étrange* and *La Violence du texte*, each of which offers helpful surveys of Moroccan literature and are both published by L'Harmattan in France.[91] Leading critics in English include Réda Bensmaïa, whose chapters on Khatibi in *Experimental Nations* offer sophisticated readings of his challenging novels, as well as Debra Kelly, with her study of his autobiography in *Autobiography and Independence*, and Alison Rice, whose *Time Signatures* offers a subtle appreciation of his language with its musical cadences and rhythms.[92] Many of the

---

90 Walter Mignolo, *Local Histories, Global Designs: Coloniality, Subaltern Knowledges, and Border Thinking* (Princeton, NJ: Princeton University Press, 2012), p. 338.

91 Marc Gontard, *Le Moi étrange: littérature marocaine de langue française* (Paris: L'Harmattan,1981); *La Violence du texte: étude sur la littérature marocaine* (Paris: L'Harmattan, 1993). See also Abdallah Memmes, *Abdekébir Khatibi: l'écriture de la dualité* (Paris: L'Harmattan, 1994) and more recently Fatima Ahnouch, *Abdelkébir Khatibi: la langue, la mémoire et le corps* (Paris: L'Harmattan, 2004); Nabil El Jabbar, *L'Œuvre romanesque d'Abdelkébir Khatibi: enjeux poétiques et identitaires* (Paris: L'Harmattan, 2014); Lahoucine El Merabet, *Abdelkébir Khatibi: la sensibilité pensante à l'œuvre dans* Le Livre du sang (Paris: L'Harmattan, 2018); Olga Hél-Bongo, *Roman francophone et essai: Mudimbe, Chamoiseau, Khatibi* (Paris: Honoré Champion, 2019).

92 See Réda Bensmaïa, *Experimental Nations: Or, the Invention of the Maghreb*, trans. Alyson Waters (Princeton, NJ: Princeton University Press, 2003); Debra Kelly, *Autobiography and Independence: Selfhood and Creativity in North African Writing in French* (Liverpool: Liverpool University Press, 2005); Alison

contributors to the present volume have also published lucid readings of his works in a range of volumes and journals. It should be noted, perhaps, that Khatibi's work has not been received without criticism, and Winifred Woodhull notably objects to Khatibi's potential occlusion of particular manifestations of otherness, such as femininity, Arabness, Jewishness, blackness, which ultimately in his thought 'circulate indifferently in a space of "immemorial bewitchment" divorced from the particular intersecting histories of those groups'.[93] Woodhull is evidently uncomfortable with the lack of historical grounding in the philosophy of the 'pensée autre', and appreciates Khatibi's work most when it is most clearly bound up with a vision of social change. Yet, while it may be true that Khatibi does not provide us with the foundations for a politics based on a particular, asserted identity, its conceptual implications clearly call for freedom and for anti-authoritarian thinking, and in many instances clearly responds to particular historical situations of oppression. The present volume will seek to uncover these significant implications at once for political questions such as those raised by colonialism and neo-imperialism, and for the particular unfolding of transnationalism in the recent period, as well as for both European and Arabic philosophy and aesthetics.

The reticence with which Khatibi has been met in the international arena is finally, inevitably, the result of the absence of available translations, beyond those in Arabic referred to earlier, of even his best-known works. The present volume seeks to intervene as this situation appears to be coming to an end. *Amour bilingue* is one of the few works to have been available in English for some time, as Richard Howard's translation *Love in Two Languages* came out with the University of Minnesota Press in 1990. It is much more recently, however, in 2016, that L'Harmattan published *Tattooed Memory*, translated by Peter Thompson, and Bloomsbury released the long-awaited translation of *Maghreb pluriel* (*Plural Maghreb*) in November 2018 by P. Burcu Yalim, who previously translated an essay from the journal *Cahiers intersignes*.[94] The first section of Khatibi's

Rice, *Time Signatures: Contextualizing Contemporary Francophone Writing from the Maghreb* (Oxford: Lexington Books, 2006).

93 Winifred Woodhull, *Transfigurations of the Maghreb: Feminism, Decolonisation, and Literatures* (Minneapolis: University of Minnesota Press, 1993), p. xxiii.

94 Abdelkébir Khatibi, 'Frontiers: Between Psychoanalysis and Islam', trans.

article 'Double critique' was published in English translation in 1985,[95] Cecile Lindsay translated the chapter on Claude Ollier from *Figures de l'étranger* for *The Review of Contemporary Fiction* in 1988,[96] Catherine Dana translated an excerpt from *Paradoxes du sionisme* for Yale French Studies in 1993,[97] Catherine Porter translated three essays from *La Langue de l'autre* as 'The Language of the Other: Testimonial Exercises' for *PMLA* in 2010,[98] and Matt Reeck published his translation of *Le Lutteur de classe à la manière taoïste* with Wesleyan University Press in 2017. Khatibi's beautiful study of Islamic calligraphy was translated by James Hughes and published by Thames & Hudson in 1976, and Ali Amahan's translation *From Sign to Image: The Moroccan Carpet* was published by LAK International Morocco in 1998. And Khatibi's moving correspondence around 'aimance' with Rita El Khayat after the death of her child was published in an English translation by Safoi Babana-Hampton, Valérie K. Orlando and Mary Vogl as *Open Correspondence: An Epistolary Dialogue* in 2010. It is astonishing, however, how long it has taken for such works to appear in English, and how much of Khatibi's work remains unavailable. Both Olivia Harrison's and Matt Reeck's translations of some sections respectively from *Le Même Livre* and *La Blessure du nom propre* included in the present volume hope to begin the process of filling this gap. In this respect, recent academic events such as the two-day workshop organized by Yasser Elhariry and Matt Reeck at Dartmouth College in November 2019 will certainly draw more attention to the translation, reception and rethinking of Khatibi's works abroad and across disciplines.[99]

P. Burcu Yalim, *Third Text* 23.6 (2009), pp. 689–96. Translated from 'Frontières', in 'Entre psychanalyse et Islam', *Cahiers Intersignes* 1 (1990), pp. 13–22.

95 See 'Double Criticism: The Decolonization of Arab Sociology', in Halim Barakat (ed.), *Contemporary North Africa: Issues of Development and Integration* (Washington, DC: Center for Contemporary Arab Studies, 1985), pp. 9–19.

96 Abdelkébir Khatibi, 'Traces of a Trauma: On *Marrakch medine*', *Review of Contemporary Fiction* 8.2 (1988), pp. 107–13.

97 Abdelkébir Khatibi, 'A Colonial Labyrinth', trans. Catherine Dana, *Yale French Studies* 83.2 (1993), pp. 5–11.

98 Abdelkébir Khatibi, 'The Language of the Other: Testimonial Exercises', trans. Catherine Porter, *PMLA* 125.4 (2010), pp. 1002–19. Translated from *La Langue de l'autre*.

99 'Abdelkébir Khatibi: Literature and Theory', Workshop and keynote speech by Brian Edwards of Tulane University on the thought of Abdelkébir Khatibi,

This volume is divided into three parts, with essays discussing 'Critical Thinking: From Decolonization to Transnationalism', 'Cultural and Philosophical Dialogues' and 'Aesthetics and Art in the Islamic World and Beyond'. Andy Stafford's essay opens the discussion with a turn to Khatibi's early years and a focus on his contribution to the human sciences in Morocco. Stafford's essay outlines Khatibi's critique of colonial sociology, as well as his reflections on the ways in which sociology might contribute to the modernization of Moroccan life, while also locating the seeds of his poetic thought in these early works. Alison Rice's essay reads Khatibi's transnationalism not so much through a particular space or history but through his understandings of the work of the 'étranger professionnel' and the translator. Concepts of travel and linguistic transfer inform Khatibi's own trajectory as it is traced in *Le Scribe et son ombre*, argues Rice, as well as his linguistically highly creative narratives *Un été à Stockholm* and *Amour bilingue*. Edwige Tamalet Talbayev goes on to link Khatibi's transnationalism with a mode of thinking specifically emanating from the Mediterranean. Khatibi's commitments to Morocco and the Maghreb for Talbayev should be read as part of his embrace of a Mediterranean space sedimented with layers of cultural interaction and superimposition through history. Assia Belhabib's creative and provocative discussion reads Khatibi against the background of contemporary global culture and technology and argues polemically for the retention of Khatibi's notions of opacity and intractability against facile and reductive demands for transparency. Finally, Alfonso de Toro's essay reads Khatibi using a more philosophical approach and concentrates in particular on language and performativity in order to argue that the thinker's works allow a conception of hybridity that is nevertheless clearly located in space and time, through an attention to 'accent'.

Khatibi's work is also, as we have suggested, committed to cultural and philosophical dialogues, and four authors address this commitment in their contributions to the second section of the volume. Olivia Harrison focuses more specifically on Khatibi's treatment of the question of Palestine. Finding parallels between the 'double critique' and Khatibi's outrage at the mistreatment of Palestinians in *Vomito blanco*, Harrison conceives Khatibi as a prime example of a 'transcolonial' thinker and associates his opening out of both Jewish and Arab cultures with his long-standing resistance to identitarian and

Dartmouth College, New Hampshire, 7–8 November 2019. See https://news. dartmouth.edu/events/event?event=58726 (accessed 2 Nov. 2019).

authoritarian thinking. Charles Forsdick goes on to discuss the dialogue between Khatibi and Segalen around decolonization, acculturation and deconstruction. Forsdick argues that understanding Segalen as an interlocutor with Khatibi at once illuminates the Moroccan thinker's reflection on translation, transnationalism and the aesthetics of diversity, and encourages a fresh reading of the French writer in a postcolonial context. Dominique Combe's essay tracks in detail Khatibi's relationship with the Franco-Algerian philosopher Jacques Derrida and shows how Khatibi's conception of diglossia can be seen to enter into dialogue and also potentially turn out to be more subversive than Derrida's 'monolinguisme'. Finally, Nao Sawada investigates Khatibi's dialogue with Japanese culture and literature from the perspective of his work on Japanese poet Junichiro Tanizaki. By focusing on the motifs of exoticism, the body and language, Eros and Thanatos, Sawada demonstrates that Khatibi offers a new insight into Japanese culture and, more specifically, into the work of Tanizaki, which he rightly reads as an ultra-modern writer.

In the final section, four contributors set out to show how Khatibi's aesthetic analyses of various art forms in turn tie in with his broader thinking on plurality and transnationalism. Rim Feriani, Jasmina Bolfek-Radovani and Debra Kelly analyse what Khatibi calls the 'intersé-miotique', the migration of signs, in dialogue also with a Sufi heritage. For Feriani, Bolfek-Radovani and Kelly, this elastic and dialogic conception of the movement of signs is also performed by calligraphy and by tattoo art, so as to sketch a more integrated conception of the relationship between body and text. Lucy McNeece then explores Khatibi's use of Asian sources and hermetic sciences and shows how these contribute to his reconfiguring of the very figure of the author in his writing. These are then associated with his blurring of the relationship between self and other, with diglossia, and with his engagement in plural sign systems, all dramatized in turn through Khatibi's own allusive and elusive style. Next, Khalid Lyamlahy offers a detailed reading of *Du signe à l'image: le tapis marocain* in order to link this work with Khatibi's anticolonial thinking and to demonstrate the philosopher's commitment to popular culture. The carpet too, Lyamlahy argues, is a meeting of signs reflecting at the same time the criss-crossing of cultures within society and the human imagination. Finally, Jane Hiddleston reads one of Khatibi's late novels, the substantial but scarcely discussed *Pèlerinage d'un artiste amoureux*, as a window onto his thinking as a whole. The novel builds on Khatibi's aesthetic vision in that it explicitly links art with the motif of the journey, and also juxtaposes reflections on sign systems, religion and colonialism in an expansive and illuminating portrait of Moroccan history since before the Protectorate. Matt Reeck's translations from *La Blessure du nom propre* serve to uncover the intricacies of Khatibi's thinking on semiotics and aesthetics. Olivia Harrison's translations from *Le Même Livre* close the volume with a salutary affirmation of dialogue and shared history between Jews and Arabs to form an aptly synthetic and concrete view of Khatibi's highly ethical and liberatory thinking.

If, as we have already argued, Khatibi's work has suffered from a lack of due recognition, the present volume opens the way for further analysis and debate. Far from providing a comprehensive overview of this dynamic and eclectic thinker's work, we introduce the reader to some of his most resonant and enduring ideas in the hope that critics will continue to mine his rich and extensive work for new resonances. We hope to provide a sense of the originality of his writing, as well as to stress the ethical and political significance of his thought in the critique of multiple forms of oppression, as crucial as ever still now in the twenty-first century. Alison Rice describes him here as a 'tireless' traveller, and without claiming to capture all aspects of his extraordinarily wide-ranging thought we hope to convey the restless and energetic form of his reflections on a range of questions. An enormously dynamic and challenging thinker, Khatibi opens up ideas for discussion, tests the structures we use to create meaning and probes at the seams of philosophical systems. The current book is conceived to continue these probings and to invite readers to return to his writing to consider further his potential impact on contemporary critical and cultural thought.

PART ONE

Critical Thinking:
From Decolonization to
Transnationalism

The 'Souverainement Orphelin' of Abdelkébir Khatibi's Early Writings

Sociology in the *Souffles* Years

Andy Stafford

Sociology as Decolonization

[T]out écrire et tout imaginer, voilà le motif de ma génération, voilà tout.

[Write it all and imagine everything, that was the code of my generation, that was the whole picture.]

Abdelkébir Khatibi[1]

There is always the danger when looking at the early career of a writer that the researcher arrogantly suggests that the early writings foresee, 'explain', even trump the later writings. Fortunately, the researchers working on the later career can fight back against this arrogance, mainly by teleologizing the early writings into the later writings; however, in so doing, the latter method risks an arrogance of its own, which is – almost if it were in a backwards direction through time – to look from

---

1   Abdelkébir Khatibi, *La Mémoire tatouée: autobiographie d'un décolonisé* (Paris: Denoël, 1971), reprinted in *Œuvres de Abdelkébir Khatibi I: Romans et récits* (Paris: La Différence, 2008), pp. 9–113 (p. 24); translated as *Tattooed Memory* by Peter Thompson (Paris: L'Harmattan, 2016), p. 29. Henceforth the French and then the English version will be referenced in the page numbers; all other translations of Khatibi's early work are mine.

above at the writer's trajectory and, abusively, to read the later in the earlier writings. This chapter – the first in this volume on Abdelkébir Khatibi – will seek to do neither of these; or rather, to avoid either of these extremes, by, on the one hand, not explicitly relating early to later Khatibi, and, on the other, keeping a period of his life as historical moment that is sovereign to the totality of that moment. In other words, this account of Khatibi's writings *before La Mémoire tatouée* in 1971 places those writings – especially the sociological research – in their historical and political milieu, involving the Moroccan specificities in journal culture, in intellectual and literary history, and Marxism. In this sense, we will respect, and apply carefully, Khatibi's notion of the 'sovereignly orphan', developed and explored in his first collection of poetry in 1976, *Le Lutteur de classe à la manière taoïste*.[2]

Indeed, applying the double notion of 'sovereignly orphan' to his earlier career seems particularly apt; except that, if we consider the 1966–71 period as sovereign in Khatibi's career, the orphaning may well be in the future direction, in the sense that there is a clear move away from his younger Marxist approach. We could suggest orphan in another sense: the three-volume series of Khatibi's *Œuvres* contains neither the sociological writings nor his first monograph, *Le Roman maghrébin*, published in France in 1968.[3] By considering some of these 'lost' pieces, we will consequently take seriously the break that *La Mémoire tatouée* represents.

In a later interview, Khatibi underlined the break this novel represented: 'j'avais envie de travailler à partir de mon … disons … désir' ['I wanted to work starting from my … shall we say … desire'].[4] By considering Khatibi, first and foremost, as an essayist – and certainly the most Barthesian of

---

2   First published in 1976 in Paris by Sindbad, this poetry collection is reprinted in *Œuvres de Abdelkébir Khatibi II: Poésie de l'aimance* (Paris: La Différence, 2008), pp. 9–35 (p. 12); it has been recently translated by Matt Reeck as *Class Warrior – Taoist Style* (Middletown, CT: Wesleyan University Press, 2017). On the 'orphan' in *La Mémoire tatouée*, see Matt Reeck, 'The Poetics of the Orphan in Abdelkébir Khatibi's Early Work', *Journal of French and Francophone Philosophy* 25.1 (2017), pp. 132–49.

3   For a complete bibliography of Khatibi's work, including his early sociology, see Abdelkébir Khatibi, *L'Œuvre de … Abdelkébir Khatibi* (Rabat: Marsam, 1997), pp. 168–70. In *La Mémoire tatouée* (p. 58; p. 76), Khatibi describes pieces that he wrote in the press in the 1950s, but this is juvenilia that we will not have time to consider here.

4   See the interview in *L'Œuvre de … Abdelkébir Khatibi*, p. 21.

Moroccan writers – this chapter will place his sociological writing in the intellectual and literary currents of late 1960s and early 1970s theory. By looking not so much at *Souffles* – for which Khatibi was a fellow traveller who only occasionally intervened in the journal and was never a member of the 'comité d'action' ['action committee'] – we will present Khatibi working – undoubtedly in parallel with *Souffles* and its aims of decolonizing Moroccan culture – as a pioneering sociologist and essayist.

The aspect of Khatibi's career that this investigation wants to stress then is his enormous contribution to the human and social sciences in Morocco and across the globe. For nearly four decades (1966–2004) he was the *rédacteur en chef* of the seminal *Bulletin ESM*, founded in 1934.[5] It is Khatibi's obituary in 2009, in the *Bulletin ESM*, that spells out this commitment, dedication and persistence, describing how, leading the *Bulletin ESM* through thick and thin for 38 years, Khatibi had to steer the journal following the (accidental) death of Paul Pascon.[6] Indeed, Khatibi's sociology has been immensely influential within Morocco. For example, Mohamed Berdouzi, having been imprisoned in the early 1970s alongside Abdellatif Laâbi and Abraham Serfaty, uses elements of Khatibi's early sociology in his 1981 DES thesis – a critique of the work of the colonial sociologist of Morocco Robert Montagne.[7]

The first published piece by Khatibi on sociological matters is an article in the second number of the liberal magazine *Lamalif*, published in Rabat in 1966, in which Khatibi critically assessed family planning and birth control in a 'patriarchal' society, asserting the issue's social and political ramifications, and finally proposing the IUD contraception coil for women – or 'scoubidou' – as a progressive and woman-friendly method.[8] The dates are important, since, in George Steinmetz's recent history of colonial and postcolonial sociology, Khatibi is listed as one

---

5 Alongside *Souffles* and *Lamalif*, the *Bulletin ESM* is available in digitized form at the Bibliothèque Nationale du Royaume du Maroc: http://bnm.bnrm. ma:86/ListeVol.aspx?IDC=45 (accessed 24 Apr. 2018).

6 Ahmed Zouggari, 'Abdelkébir Khatibi, une carrière dédiée aux Sciences humaines et sociales', *Bulletin ESM* (July 2009), pp. 7–9. See Khatibi's joint 'Avant-propos' in *Bulletin ESM* 156 (1986) following Pascon's death and Khatibi's homage to Pascon, 'Mémoire d'une quête' and his 'Conclusion', in *Bulletin ESM* 159-160-161, pp. 9–12, p. 293.

7 Mohamed Berdouzi, *Structures du Maroc précolonial* (Casablanca: Editions La Croisée des Chemins, 2012).

8 Abdelkébir Khatibi, 'Le Maroc à l'heure du scoubidou', *Lamalif* 2 (15 Apr. 1966), pp. 19–23.

of a group of 'indigenous' sociologists, alongside Anouar Abdelmalek, Albert Memmi and Abdelmalek Sayad, who began their careers before decolonization.[9] Steinmetz's suggestion is surely incorrect though. Born in 1938, Khatibi was 18 when Morocco was decolonized in 1956! This error, however, suggests the first and crucial point concerning Khatibi's sociology of decolonization. Too young to be decolonized as an adult, Khatibi left for France soon after Moroccan independence; and it was in France, the former colonizer, that he then launched the *intellectual* process of decolonization.

Beginning his sociological studies at the Sorbonne between 1958 and 1964, and completing his doctorate in 1965, Khatibi belongs to a slightly younger, later generation than Steinmetz suggests. It was only in 1966, recently returned from Paris, that Khatibi was appointed co-director, with Paul Pascon, of the 'Institut de Sociologie' in Rabat (and was also founder of the university teachers trade union, the 'Syndicat de l'enseignement supérieur'). He began his stewardship of the *Bulletin ESM* the same year, and, given the account by the journal's 'directeur', Nacer el Fassi, the number 100 of the *Bulletin ESM* in 1966 marked the relaunch of the journal after a three-year break.[10] One can only assume that Khatibi's return to Morocco and recruitment to the *Bulletin ESM* was a crucial development for the journal.[11] Indeed, as *rédacteur en chef* of the *Bulletin ESM* Khatibi soon introduced new sociological themes, such as urbanism in Morocco.[12] As well as surveying the existing colonial sociological material in 1967 – to which we will return in a moment – Khatibi was also one of the first to take up notions of acculturation in his sociological work.[13] He also made important links

9 George Steinmetz, 'Sociology and Colonialism in the British and French Empires, 1945–1965', *Journal of Modern History* 89 (2017), pp. 601–48 (p. 605 n. 17).

10 Nacer el Fassi, 'Avant-propos', *Bulletin ESM* 100 (1966), p. 5. As well as performing her secretarial work for *Souffles*, Jocelyne Laâbi – 'Mme J. Laâbi' – is credited as the 'secrétaire' for the *Bulletin ESM* for two years, from July to December 1967 (nos. 106–7) until summer 1969 (no. 114).

11 Furthermore, given Khatibi's piece on family planning in *Lamalif* in 1966, it is possible that it was he who led the (unsigned) 'enquête' on family planning published in the *Bulletin ESM* 104–5 (Jan.–June 1967).

12 Abdelkébir Khatibi, 'Avant-propos', *Bulletin ESM* 118–19 (1970), p. 3.

13 Abdelkébir Khatibi (ed.), *Bilan de la sociologie au Maroc* (Rabat: Publications de l'Association pour la Recherche en Sciences Humaines, 1967); 2nd edn (Rabat: Imprimerie de l'Agdal, 1968), which is a select and annotated bibliography of 67

between this journal and *Souffles* on the central topic of 'development'; and in his 'Avant-Propos' for the 1968 number on development, Khatibi underlined the widening of sociology's purview onto a 'sociologie du monde arabe' ['sociology of the Arab world'], and, aware of the dangers of generalness and exteriority, he expressed an 'incertitude' as to the usefulness of the notion of 'modernisation' ['modernization'] – 'économiste' ['economistic'] as it risked sounding – in understanding the differentials of and in Moroccan culture.[14]

Khatibi started his sociological career in Morocco in the mid-sixties then, at a moment when the discipline was not only young and short of postcolonial and Moroccan-based concepts, but also up against a Western tradition that was now being methodologically, politically and culturally challenged by the new postcolonial nations. It meant that newly qualified sociologists from these countries were having to negotiate what the French specialist on Tunisia and its sociology, Jean Duvignaud, called the 'double ambiguïté' ['double ambiguity'] for newly liberated 'third-world' countries: that of having to import European sociological concepts that favoured the fastest development in postcolonial countries, as well as having to defer to them by renouncing aspects of the newly independent culture that the 'intellectuel des jeunes nations' ['intellectual in new nations'] would have, previously, defended against colonialism.[15] This was precisely the main object of Khatibi's brief history of colonial sociology in Morocco, a critique of its ideological functions in the Moroccan history journal *Hespéris-Tamuda* in 1966.[16]

works. On acculturation, see A. Khatibi, 'Deux propositions sur le changement social et l'acculturation', *Annales marocaines de sociologie* 1 (1968), a theme that is criticized in Tahar Ben Jelloun's assessment in *Souffles* of his doctoral thesis and first book *Le Roman maghrébin*. See Tahar Ben Jelloun, 'Bibliographie critique maghrébine: Abdelkabir Khatibi, *Le Roman maghrébin*', *Souffles* 13–14 (1969), pp. 32–4 (p. 33).

14   Abdelkébir Khatibi, 'Avant-propos', *Bulletin ESM* 109 (Apr.–June 1968), p. 1. See A. Serfaty, 'Progrès technique et développement', ibid., pp. 3–17, which is echoed in Serfaty's two pieces in *Souffles*: 'Cultures et progrès scientifique', *Souffles* 13–14 (1969), pp. 7–15 and 'La Francophonie contre le développement', *Souffles* 18 (Mar.–Apr. 1970), pp. 26–34.

15   Jean Duvignaud, 'La Sociologie et le tiers monde', in *Introduction à la sociologie* (Paris: Gallimard, 1966), pp. 133–48 (p. 137).

16   Abdelkébir Khatibi, 'Histoire et sociologie au Maroc, note sur le problème de l'idéologie', *Hespéris-Tamuda* 7 (1966), pp. 101–5.

Aware of the danger of condemning all colonial sociology, Khatibi nevertheless pointed to its ideological function during the 44 years of a 'système d'oppression qui a échoué' ['system of oppression that failed'].[17] Seeing colonial sociology during the French Protectorate as a means of 'pacification', Khatibi underlined its ideological importance for colonialism on both sides of the divide:

> [I]l convient de se demander dans quelle mesure l'histoire et la sociologie ont participé à la politique de déculturation et de mystification scientifique, afin que les historiens nationaux ne soient plus prisonniers d'une certaine image de notre passé, restitué par les savants à tendance colonialiste ou raciste, et afin que notre culture ne soit plus brouillée par des techniques d'analyse dépassées.[18]

> [It is right to ask questions about the extent to which history and sociology have been involved in the policy of deculturation and scientific mystification; so that historians of the nation are no longer prisoners of a particular image of our past, one which has been drawn up by experts who are colonialist or racist, and so that our culture is not blurred by techniques of analysis that are out of date.]

Khatibi's analysis was devastating for the 'mission civilisatrice' ['civilizing mission'] mentality of colonial sociology. Bringing together General Lyautey's ideas, F. Le Chatelier's political science and G. Hardy's organizational skills, colonial sociology under the Protectorate had, he said, been carefully designed to help France colonize Morocco. One of the agents of this colonial sociology, E. Michaux-Bellaire, had placed the *Makhzen* – the Moroccan pre-colonial aristocratic establishment – at the centre of his analysis, partly with which to relegate the importance of Islam by looking at a pre-Islamic Morocco (and hence also the emphasis on Berber culture in Michaux-Bellaire's work). It was Montagne, however – former soldier in the French pacification of the Rif in 1925 – that Khatibi considered as the key agent of colonial sociology of Morocco. It was he who used sociology to justify French colonial control, first by failing to understand Moroccan nationalism – Khatibi was surprised that Montagne called the first coup of Moroccan independence in 1953, which deposed Mohammed V, a 'revolution'. Indeed, quoting from Montagne's 1954 study *La Révolution au Maroc*, Khatibi rejected the simplistic view of social forces in the

17   Ibid., p. 101.
18   Ibid., p. 101, p. 103.

Moroccan independence movement, in which Montagne, erroneously, presented the combat as one of 'absolutisme sultanien et d'un nationalisme xénophobe et totalitaire avec une féodalité berbère ou tribale qui guide une paysannerie traditionnelle' ['sultanate absolutism and of a xenophobic and totalitarian nationalism with a Berber or tribal feudalism which guides a traditional peasantry'].[19]

In his 1967 review, Jacques Cagne strongly recommended Khatibi's edited collection *Bilan de la sociologie au Maroc*.[20] Not only was Khatibi the best person to look at the history of sociology in Morocco, Cagne announced that Khatibi, having completed his *Le Roman maghrébin* thesis, was now preparing a 'thèse' on social stratification, a major study of pre-colonial definitions of class in Morocco (to which we will return). Furthermore, Cagne commended Khatibi's *Bilan* for its coverage of the crucial 50 years of sociology in Morocco, as well as the 'méthode du global et esprit synthétique' ['global method within a spirit of synthesis'] that Khatibi shared with Paul Pascon, 'qui doivent beaucoup à Marx et à Gurvitch' ['which owe much to Marx and to Gurvitch'].[21]

Nevertheless, according to one historian, Khatibi very quickly saw his hopes for sociology to help modernize, in a progressive way, the lives of Moroccan people blocked at every turn.[22] Indeed, the Institut de Rabat, which had been set up in 1960 with UNESCO help (and soon renamed the 'Institut de Sociologie'), was closed down in 1971, because,

19   Ibid., p. 105 n. 7.
20   Jacques Cagne, '"Bilan de la sociologie au Maroc" de Abdelkabir Khatibi', *Bulletin ESM* 106–7 (July–Dec. 1967), pp. 174–9.
21   Khatibi, cited ibid., p. 176. Impressed by the way Khatibi's history shows Moroccan sociology moving from 'apologétique' to 'critique', Cagne recommended Khatibi's 'autonomie scientifique', Cagne's only reservation being the limited definition of sociology in Khatibi's bibliography, whose 67 entries overlooked anthropological interventions in the field, including work carried out before 1912: ibid., pp. 177–8.
22   Khatibi called for a 'réforme du code pénal et du statut de la femme' ['reform of the penal code and of the status of women'], aware that Moroccan women were marrying at a very young age and were victims of the 'système de la répudiation' ['system of repudiation'] and accused of helping 'mauvais esprits' ['evil spirits']; but unable to overcome this backwardness, Khatibi 'se tourne vers la "micro-sociologie", vers la sociologie de la littérature puis, enfin, vers la littérature' ['turns towards "micro-sociology", towards sociology of literature, and finally towards literature']. See Olga Hél-Bongo, 'Polymorphisme et dissimulation du narratif dans *La Mémoire tatouée* d'Abdelkébir Khatibi', *Études littéraires* 43.1 (2012), pp. 45–61 (p. 49).

in Khatibi's words, the job of 'le sociologue doit [...] continuellement critiquer dans le sens profond du terme pour n'être jamais récupéré', but '[p]eu d'Etats acceptent facilement une grande dose critique' ['the sociologist must [...] continually perform a critique, in the deepest sense of the word, so as never to be recuperated; then again, there are very few States that are happy to accept a big dose of critique']:

> La sociologie est insérée, qu'elle le veuille ou non dans la lutte sociale. Elle peut également vouloir s'insérer dans un projet historique, une politique de transformation [...] La sociologie se situe dans une pratique politique réelle, bien qu'indirecte.[23]
>
> [Whether we like it or not, sociology is implicated in social struggle. And it is up to it to decide if it wants to be part of a historical project, a politics of transformation [...] Sociology is involved in a real political practice, albeit indirect.]

So, Marxian sociologist, trained in Paris, decolonizing Moroccan sociology and aware of the interventionist, albeit 'indirect', responsibility of sociology, Khatibi was in a singular position in late 1960s Morocco. But before we look at this early sociological work, we must first consider his work on sociology of literature, as well as his own literature. Indeed, in the 1973 interview cited above, Khatibi was acutely aware of the contradictions between being sociologist and writer.[24] The subtext of this chapter, by considering the fate of his pioneering work on Moroccan political economy and radical sociology, is to suggest that his sociological *engagement* became diverted, in the early to mid-1970s, through the post-structuralism of this period. Across the 1970s period, dubbed the *années de plomb* in a euphemism that covered (up) the enormity of state crimes in Morocco, we will see – and this is a bold and rather rash suggestion, worthy of consideration nonetheless – that culturalism came to dominate the radical intellectual horizons associated with Marxism.

---

23   See the interview with Abdelkébir Khatibi, 'Il faut s'essayer à une double critique permanente', *Lamalif* 57 (1973), pp. 32–4 (p. 33).
24   Ibid., p. 33.

Sociologist-*littérateur*?

[P]rofession – regard dédoublé sur les autres[.]

[Profession – this divided gaze toward others.]

Abdelkébir Khatibi[25]

Steinmetz may indeed be right to include Khatibi in the list – alongside Georges Balandier, Pierre Naville, Charles Le Cœur, Albert Memmi – of what he calls 'colonial sociologist-*littérateurs*', who 'combined social scientific and poetic discourse' whilst operating 'at the sensitive, vital border zone between coloniser and colonised in a period of turbulent cultural change'.[26] A 'sociologist in literature', Khatibi was also teaching literature at University Mohammed V, and saw himself as budding poet, publishing three poems in the third number of *Souffles*, just as he began his sociological career in Morocco.[27]

During his doctoral research in Paris between 1961 and 1964, following his undergraduate study in sociology with Georges Gurvitch and Raymond Aron, Khatibi had been supervised by the Jewish Tunisian writer and sociologist Albert Memmi.[28] Indeed, Khatibi's first editorial collaboration had been in 1964, on the project led by Memmi at the VIth section of the École Pratique des Hautes Études (EPHE) in Paris, called the 'Groupe de recherches sur la culture maghrébine'. With Jacqueline Arnaud, Jean Déjeux and Arlette Roth, Khatibi helped Memmi to produce an *Anthologie des écrivains maghrébins d'expression francaise* (one of a series of three volumes on North African writing in French published in Paris by Présence Africaine), and for which Khatibi supplied the choices and notices for the Moroccan writing in French.[29] Thus, as a

25 Khatibi, *La Mémoire tatouée*, p. 10; *Tattooed Memory*, p. 15.
26 Steinmetz, 'Sociology and Colonialism', p. 647 n. 197.
27 Sam Cherribi and Matthew Pesce, 'Khatibi: A Sociologist in Literature', in Kirsten Ruth Bratt *et al.* (eds), *Vitality and Dynamism: Interstitial Dialogues of Languages, Politics and Religion in Morocco's Literary Tradition* (Leiden: Leiden University Press, 2014), pp. 177–84.
28 Ibid., p. 179.
29 Khatibi prefaces extracts by Chraïbi (pp. 63–4), Mohammed Aziz Lahbabi (pp. 203–4) and Ahmed Sefrioui (p. 255) – and other Moroccan writers signalled by Khatibi are Abdelkader Bel Hachmy, Ahmed Belhachmi, Taieb Djemeri, Abdelkader Oulhaci and Kamel Zebdi. As a critic who will – alongside *Souffles*

model of the sociologist-*littérateur*, Khatibi had Memmi directly before him; and alongside Memmi, Jean Duvignaud, novelist, playwright, specialist on sociology and ethnography of Tunisia, and former popular-theatre colleague of Roland Barthes's.[30] Khatibi was also influenced in Paris by the work of Lucien Goldmann, the Romanian-born colleague of Barthes's at the EPHE and specialist on Hungarian Marxist and literary theorist Georg Lukács.

Soon after his return to Morocco, Khatibi put his sociological eye to work in his early poetry in *Souffles* in 1966.[31] 'La rue' ['The Street'], 'Devenir' ['Becoming'] and 'Emeute' ['Riot'] are three short poems that present elliptical voices of the Moroccan streets, emerging, almost certainly, from the 1965 riots in Casablanca in which students and unemployed Moroccan youth vented their anger about their stymied prospects. As well as their elliptical, notational style – not dissimilar to the Barthes of *Incidents* in Moroccan street scenes in 1969 and what Khatibi would later call 'l'instant qui déchire' ['that instant that tears itself open'] – these poems betray a deep, if brief, solidarity with the poor and disenfranchised youth of the street.[32]

Indeed, one of the tentative arguments of this chapter is that, with his complex moves towards decolonizing the self in the 1966–71 period, there was a marked poeticization of Khatibi's essayism. This is especially true in *La Mémoire tatouée* – a good example of what Driss Chraïbi

– reject Sefrioui's folkloric novel *La boîte à merveilles*, Khatibi is entirely consistent in his 1964 judgement: 'Qu'on ne se méprenne pas au pittoresque: il est pénétré de mélancolie' ['Let us not misunderstand the picturesque: it is shot through with melancholy']. He also collaborates with the same people on Memmi's *Bibliographie de la littérature nord-africaine d'expression française* (Paris: Editions Mouton, 1964). See also Khatibi's co-editing of another anthology, *Ecrivains marocains: du Protectorat à 1965*, with Mohammed Benjelloun Touimi and Mohammed Kably (Paris: Sindbad, 1974).

30   Memmi was his 'directeur de thèse de troisième cycle' on 'Le Roman maghrébin d'expression arabe et française depuis 1945', and, one might suggest, tentatively, that following Memmi's own colonized 'Portraits', not to mention his autobiographical novels of the 1950s, *La Statue de sel* and *Agar*, *La Mémoire tatouée* represents the Arab and Moroccan response to Memmi's own Jewish-Tunisian (and slightly older) generational specificities.

31   Abdelkébir Khatibi, 'Poèmes', *Souffles* 2 (1966), p. 16. For the English translation, see 'Poems', trans. Lucy R. McNair, in Olivia Harrison and Teresa Villa-Ignacio (eds), *Souffes-Anfas: A Critical Anthology from the Moroccan Journal of Culture and Politics* (Stanford, CA: Stanford University Press, 2016), pp. 37–8.

32   Khatibi, *La Mémoire tatouée*, p. 93; *Tattooed Memory*, p. 125.

called 'la mixture de l'essai et du roman' ['mixture of essay and novel'] – and Khatibi famously ended his 'autobiographie' theorizing the intergeneric and post-generic challenges of new Moroccan writing as 'l'œuvre à venir' ['the manuscript to come'].[33] This interest in genre – a new genre, such as the 'roman-itinéraire' devised in Laâbi's 1969 *L'Œil et la nuit* – dovetailed with Khatibi's experience as colonized, to the extent that his sociology of the novel in *Le Roman maghrébin* had made him sceptical of a modern Moroccan version of this most European and colonial of literary forms.[34]

Here, Khatibi seemed to be adapting Lukács's 1957 theory of the 'Ideology of Modernism', which takes the novel as an example of where modernism risks killing literature – modernism, argued Lukács, 'meant not the enrichment but the negation of art'.[35] Khatibi keenly adapted this to the postcolonial situation of the novel in Morocco, famously predicting in *Le Roman maghrébin* its demise – or rather its outmodedness.[36] This seemingly pessimistic critique of modernism became a moment of liberation for Khatibi, however, influencing his intergeneric essayism in *La Mémoire tatouée*. There is another sense in which Khatibi absorbed Lukácsian theory.

---

33 Khatibi, *La Mémoire tatouée*, p. 113; *Tattooed Memory*, p. 157. Driss Chraïbi, cited by Tahar Ben Aoun: www.limag.refer.org/new/index.php?inc= dspliv&liv=00024453 (accessed 3 May 2018). Khatibi's 'romanesque' essayism is continued in 1971 in two collections of 'bagatelles' published in *Les Lettres Nouvelles*. See Abdelkébir Khatibi, 'Vingt bagatelles sur la dépossession' and 'Bagatelles', in *Les Lettres Nouvelles* (Mar. and Nov. 1971), pp. 125–8 and pp. 29–37 respectively. The 'bagatelle' then becomes an important element of the 'discours parémiologique' ['paremiological discourse'] in Khatibi's 1974 essay *La Blessure du nom propre* (Paris: Denoël, 1974), pp. 23–58.

34 Khatibi's suspicion of the novel as a Western, francophone form is counterposed to Arabic culture's favouring of other, non-narrative forms, such as poetry, essay and short story; see *Le Roman maghrébin* (Paris: Maspero, 1968), p. 112.

35 Georg Lukács, 'The Ideology of Modernism' [1957], reprinted in T. Eagleton and D. Milne (eds), *Marxist Literary Theory* (Oxford: Blackwell, 1996), pp. 141–62 (p. 162).

36 In the 'Avant-propos' to the Maghrebian literature section of *Souffles* 3 (1966), Khatibi wrote: 'Je suis peut-être pour la mort provisoire de la littérature et pour l'engagement de l'intellectuel dans la lutte politique' ['Perhaps I am for the temporary death of literature and for the intellectual's commitment to the political struggle'] (p. 11): trans. Claudia Esposito, in Olivia C. Harrison and Teresa Villa-Ignacio, *Souffles-Anfas: A Critical Anthology from the Moroccan Journal of Culture and Politics* (Stanford, CA: Stanford University Press, 2016), pp. 56–8 (p. 58).

The early Lukács had famously underlined the necessarily tight relation between the essay form and its time, and this was particularly applicable to Khatibi.[37] Indeed, the mixture of literature and political sociology in Khatibi's *œuvre* is plain, especially in his 1974 essay on Palestine and on Marx's Judaism, *Vomito blanco*, which mixes historical materialism, anti-colonial politics and Henri Michaux's avant-garde poetry in an extraordinarily powerful – and persuasive – polemic against Zionism. So, the essay – at least for a budding sociologist-*littérateur* – was where political sociology met the literary. Khatibi's 1966 injunction, 'l'écriture est une praxis' ['writing is a praxis'] – as much Barthesian as Althusserian, as much Maoist as culturalist – represented the search for a new form of writing.[38] Sometimes violent – 'L'histoire est notre désir, noué [...] à la violence du temps' ['History is our desire, tied to the violence of time'] – Khatibi's writing became classically essayistic.[39] Essayism – the provisional and peremptory, fundamentally literary, engagement with one's political moment – is marked by a writing of prose that could easily be poetry. *La Mémoire tatouée* was not just a response to Memmi's literary sociology of self but also underscored the need for a new form, a new mode, of subjectivity in postcolonial Morocco.

Khatibi's 'memoirs', written at the ripe old age (!) of 33, are heavily situated, as the subtitle suggests: *autobiographie d'un colonisé*. The descriptions of poverty – by which we really mean a destitution, a bitter 'pénurie de la rue' ['street poverty'], if not hunger (and even famine in Morocco during the Second World War) – explain the near-uprising in Casablanca and other cities in 1965 that had taken the postcolonial regime by surprise. Pre-dating Mohammed Choukri's oral *plaidoyer* against destitution in *Le Pain nu* (1973), *La Mémoire tatouée* details the colonized subject's upbringing in impoverished El Jadida – 'Je me rappelle la rue, plus que mon père, plus que ma mère, plus que tout le monde' ['I recall the street, more than I do my father, more than my mother, more than anything there is'] – and tallies with Khatibi's 'incidental' poetry in *Souffles* that had echoed the 1965 riots.[40] His acute

37   Georg Lukács, 'On the Nature and Form of the Essay: Letter to Leo Popper' [1911], in *Soul and Form*, trans. Anna Bostock (New York: Columbia University Press, 2010), pp. 16–34.
38   Abdelkébir Khatibi, 'Avant-propos', *Souffles* 3 (1966), p. 11; Harrison and Villa-Ignacio, *Souffles-Anfas: A Critical Anthology*, p. 58.
39   Khatibi, *La Mémoire tatouée*, p. 111; *Tattooed Memory*, p. 152.
40   Ibid., p. 20; p. 22.

awareness of 'la rue' in his memoirs – what he calls 'une sociologie à la voix rauque' ['a gravel-voiced sociology'] – is balanced by a lively poetry in his prose, examples being regular if interspersed. However, the other, or complementary, side to this decolonial sociology *de littérateur* is the ironic, detached analysis and presentation of self.[41]

One critic has deemed Khatibi's interiorizing of the Orphic myth, in both *La Mémoire tatouée* and his next 'novel' in 1979, *Le Livre du sang*, a means to 'assurer [...] la réconciliation du moi divisé' ['achieve [...] a reconciliation of the divided self'].[42] Indeed, in a literary sociology of self, Khatibi brilliantly plays this out in *La Mémoire tatouée* through the notion and practice of *dédoublement* (split personality). No doubt indebted to new ethnographic techniques such as Edgar Morin's 'loop', Khatibi uses this sociological technique not, however, on an anthropological, ethnographic 'other' but on a decolonized (decolonizing) self. The eye of *La Mémoire tatouée* is a sociologized and thereby deconstructed form of analysis of self in which Khatibi appears to himself as if in a study. This is because the decolonial process – at least in Khatibi's case, as we have suggested – is accomplished (only) in 1971. It also means that the sociological 'bric à brac' that he has constructed during his time in Paris – such as the 'palier' ['level'] borrowed from Gurvitch – led in this period of Khatibi's intellectual decolonization to what he called in *La Mémoire tatouée* the 'militant divisé' ['split militant'] stuck in the 'entre-deux' of the 'intellectuel colonisé-décolonisé' ['colonized-decolonized intellectual'].[43] Whether this explains his distancing from *Souffles* during the 1969–71 period in which Laâbi and Serfaty move towards militant Marxism is a moot point; it is nevertheless clear, as we shall see, that Khatibi explored his contradictory Marxian praxis in this period. To complete this survey of Khatibi's early – and orphaned – writings, we will now consider whether, and if so how much, this sociology-*littérateur* appeared in, even interfered with, his 'academic' sociological scholarship.

41   Ibid., p. 87; p. 119. It is interesting to note that in this period Khatibi is unsure of the appropriate (Europeanized) spelling of his first name; in three different numbers of the *Bulletin ESM* he signs his name, first, 'Abdelkabir' (101–2 (Apr.–Sept. 1966), p. 172), then 'Abdelkebir' (118–19 (1970)) and finally 'Abdelkébir' (126 (1975), p. 1).

42   Jacques Madelain, *L'Errance et l'itinéraire: lecture du roman maghrébin de langue française* (Paris: Sindbad, 1983), p. 103.

43   Khatibi, *La Mémoire tatouée*, p. 79, p. 110; *Tattooed Memory*, p. 106, p. 150.

Sociology by a 'split militant'?

Il n'y a pas de sociétés sous-développées, mais des sociétés sous-analysées.

[There are no under-developed societies, only under-analysed societies.]

Jacques Berque[44]

There is another sense in which Khatibi's early sociological work is orphaned. The same year as *La Mémoire tatouée*, Khatibi published in the *Bulletin ESM* the first of two announced studies on social class in Morocco. The second study does not appear ever to have been published, but the first, his 1971 article 'Hiérarchies pré-coloniales – les théories', attempted to define Moroccan class society in the pre-colonial period. This lengthy and theoretically advanced article built on a series of sociological pieces that he had been writing since 1966.

We saw above how Khatibi had exposed the ideological function of colonial sociology in his 1966 piece in *Hespéris-Tamuda*. Then, in the *Chroniques* section of the journal in 1966, and his very first piece in the *Bulletin ESM*, Khatibi considered the difficulties of sounding the opinions of Moroccan students.[45] In a sensitive and thoughtful overview of the difficulties in sociological fieldwork, especially the questionnaire in a postcolonial population such as Morocco's that is (understandably) suspicious of Western-devised social intervention, Khatibi was pessimistic about the value of sociological inquiry. If the researcher is perceived as an 'agent' of the state, or if there is no defined outcome or solution for the persons undergoing the research, then, he argued, the results are heavily compromised.

Khatibi's 'vox pop' research in 1966, with 500 Moroccan students, used a 'loop' at the end, asking the respondents to say what they thought of the *enquête*, including their critiques and suggestions. Sensitive to the 'autoritarisme' ['authoritarianism'] of the questionnaire – with its closed, leading questions and its individualized approach – Khatibi noted how

---

44 Cited in Cagne, '"Bilan de la sociologie au Maroc" de Abdelkabir Khatibi', p. 176.

45 Abdelkébir Khatibi, 'Perception et fonction de l'enquête de l'opinion', *Bulletin ESM* 101–2 (Apr.–Sept. 1966), pp. 169–72.

the students preferred a group discussion or debate. Indeed, perceived
by students as the professor's or tutor's viewpoint, the questionnaire
appeared blind to their issues (such as love life, interaction between the
sexes). As Khatibi put it, their 'embarras' ['embarrassment'] was due not
to the interest being taken in them and in the expression of their views
but to the limited nature of the questions. Citing both negative views
['this "enquête" made me miss my sports class'] and wild optimism,
Khatibi was cynical about the whole exercise:

> L'illusion la plus importante est de croire que l'enquête d'opinion est
> un moyen de développement du pays [...] puisque cette information
> scientifique doit permettre aux responsables de connaître les besoins
> des étudiants donc d'améliorer leur situation. [...] [L]'étudiant ne peut
> comprendre qu'on entreprenne une étude uniquement dans le but de
> préparer un diplôme ou de faire de la recherche fondamentale.[46]

> [The most important illusion is to believe that the survey of opinions is
> a way to develop the country [...] since this scientific information must
> surely be used by the people in charge to find out the needs of the students
> and therefore how to improve their situation. [...] The student cannot
> believe that the study is undertaken purely to pass a qualification or as
> part of state-funded research.]

The 'enquête d'opinion, 'la fonction du questionnaire', concluded
Khatibi, 'est beaucoup plus une fonction d'*éducation* et de *décision* que
d'information et de catharsis' ['The survey of opinions, the function of
the questionnaire, has much more to do with *education* and *decision-
making* than with information or catharsis'].[47] Either, he wrote,
the questions were too weak and neutral, or they were perceived as
ideological. Questions about religiosity were considered insulting, and
the researcher often eyed with suspicion as an 'agent de renseignements'
['government spy'], a perception which forced certain questions off the
questionnaire. Given that the *enquête* was taking place in the wake of
the huge anti-government riots of 1965, this led Khatibi to an important,
subjectivist conclusion:

> [L]'enquête d'opinion ne doit pas être technique extérieure, mais doit
> essayer de poser des questions que le groupe ou la société se pose et dans
> les termes scientifiques équivalents aux termes qu'ils emploient.[48]

46 Ibid., p. 170
47 Ibid., p. 172.
48 Ibid.

[The survey of opinions does not have to be a technique coming from the outside; but it must try to ask questions that the group or society are asking, using scientific terminology equivalent to the terms that they use.]

Thus, in institutionally suspicious mode, Khatibi began his academic career in Moroccan sociology with a highly politicized, and anti-authoritarian, understanding of the *post*colonial state's use of sociology.[49]

It was in his next piece in the *Bulletin ESM*, 'Stratification sociale et développement', that Khatibi made his first foray into notions of 'social class'.[50] In his report on the conference with the same title, held in Hammamet in Tunisia in November 1965 – which brought together over 30 organizations from across North Africa and Europe to look at the 'Mediterranean question' – Khatibi regretted that, so far, sociology had failed to get beyond a naïve and simplistic view of social class. The conference, according to Khatibi, concentrated not on this key sociological and political question of social class but first on images of social stratification, secondly on the under-class (or 'sous-prolétariat') evident in Spain and Greece, and finally on the role of 'cadres' ['middle management'] as examples of the 'classe moyenne' ['middle class']. Despite the involvement of southern European dimensions alongside North-African realities, Khatibi finished his report with a level of dissatisfaction by suggesting that a comparative approach was far from being established as the 'appareil conceptuel' ['conceptual apparatus'] was yet to be set out; and he cited favourably the work by (former Surrealist and Trotskyist psychologist) Pierre Naville, who suggested ways of getting beyond a 'réalisme naïf' ['naïve realism'].[51] It is a topic to which he would return four years later, in 1971.

In the same year as *La Mémoire tatouée*, Khatibi published his most advanced work on historical and political sociology. 'Hiérarchies pré-coloniales – les théories' is the result of his research on Moroccan social classes that Jacques Cagne had announced in his review (mentioned

49   See the 1969 interview with Khatibi in *Lamalif* on the revolt by global youth, which considers the reasons and future of progressive social change from the younger Moroccan generation, 'La jeunesse est un espoir conditionné', *Lamalif* 31 (July–Aug. 1969), pp. 46–50.

50   Abdelkébir Khatibi, 'Stratification sociale et développement', *Bulletin ESM* 106–7 (July–Dec. 1967), pp. 171–3.

51   Pierre Naville, 'Classes sociales et classes logiques: note sur le réalisme des classes', *Année sociologique*, 1960, pp. 3–77, reprinted in *Classes sociales et classes logiques* (Paris: Presses universitaires de France, 1961).

above) of Khatibi's *Bilan de la sociologie au Maroc*.[52] A dense and
lengthy article, citing Barthes and Julia Kristeva on the one hand, and
Marx, Ibn Khaldun and Durkheim on the other, it displays Khatibi's
theoretical dexterity, and not to say his essayistic aplomb.

Khatibi had already looked at feudal and aristocratic society in his
doctoral research on literary form in the European novel. In 'Hiérarchies
pré-coloniales – les théories', he now turned his sights on the same feudal
period in Morocco. Announced as the first part of a wider study, the article
situates itself, implicitly, in a post-structuralism *d'époque*, in which,
Khatibi argued, a 'déconstruction du savoir élaboré' ['deconstruction
of received wisdom'] on Morocco's social classes necessarily involved
an 'analyse critique' [a 'critical analysis'] of concepts in both Arab
and Western epistemologies.[53] Setting out the central question of early
Moroccan social history – was Morocco, with Marx, an Asiatic mode
of production, or, with Durkheim, a 'système segmentaire' ['segmentary
system']? – Khatibi began his analysis in an earlier period, with Ibn
Khaldun's *Prolégomènes* (otherwise known as *The Muqaddimah*).
Indeed, considering Ibn Khaldun's late fourteenth-century treatise as an
early *urtext* of Arabic and Muslim sociology, Khatibi debated the recent
work of Yves Lacoste on whether – or how much – Ibn Khaldun could
be considered a precursor to Marx.[54]

Khatibi set out the 'double view' that Ibn Khaldun's writing held
with respect to history, both inside and outside, in what Khatibi called
(following Barthes) 'un discours sur l'histoire' ['a discourse on history'],

52 'Hiérarchies pré-coloniales – les théories' appears in the *Bulletin ESM* 120–1
(1971), pp. 27–62 and is republished as 'Etat et classes sociales', in Abdelkébir
Khatibi (ed.), *Etudes sociologiques sur le Maroc* (Rabat: Société d'études
économiques, sociales et statistiques, 1971; 2nd edn, Bulletin économique et social
du Maroc, 1978), pp. 3–15 alongside articles by M. Belghiti, A. Lahlimi, G. Lazarev
and P. Pascon which had appeared originally in the *Bulletin ESM*, 1966–71.
53 Khatibi, 'Hiérarchies pré-coloniales – les théories', p. 27.
54 Yves Lacoste, *Ibn Khaldoun: naissance de l'histoire, passé du Tiers-Monde*
(Paris: Maspero, 1966). See H. Rachik and R. Bourqia, 'La Sociologie au Maroc:
grandes étapes et jalons thématiques', *SociologieS: théories et recherches*.
Online. 18 Oct. 2011: http://journals.openedition.org/sociologies/3719, paras 3–4,
who suggest that the Ibn Khaldun/Marx debate was becoming central in late
1960s Morocco. However, Henry Corbin, in *Histoire de la philosophie islamique*
(Paris: Gallimard, 1986), writing his piece on Ibn Khaldun (pp. 385–90) and the
connections with Marx (p. 389) mentions (inexplicably) neither Khatibi's 1971
piece nor Lacoste's work.

and citing (and spelling incorrectly) Kristeva's *Semiotica* [*sic*].[55] By breaking with linear study, argued Khatibi, Ibn Khaldun had developed a dialectical method, and, as a social thinker following Aristotle, had combined a dialectical understanding with a cyclical one.[56] Khatibi thus analysed the *Prolégomènes* as a theocratic meditation on change and cyclicality, in which the three pre-colonial classes in Morocco – nomads ('chameliers' ['camel drivers']), sedentary nomads and city dwellers – played out God's requirements; and the resultant *'açabiyya* – or 'solidarité socio-agnatique' ['social-agnatic solidarity', that is, based on the male lineage of the 'noblesse'] – became the motor of history in Ibn Khaldun's schema.[57]

Khatibi pointed to an important exception in Ibn Khaldun's account: the Idrisids dynasty that ruled Morocco from 788 to 944 had not used the *'açabiyya*, leading Khatibi to suggest, following Ibn Khaldun, that 'le savoir est un art [...] un discours qui exige une lecture plurielle' ['learning is an art ... a discourse which requires a plural reading'], because, in class terms, the Khaldunist approach showed how hierarchy in pre-colonial Morocco was both 'un fait naturel et une valeur religieuse' ['a natural fact and a religious value'].[58] Consequently, the supra-clanic nationhood that then developed in Morocco could be based on *'açabiyya* on the one hand (so long as it included the army), but this assertion needed to be counterbalanced by the determinant of money on the other. Though this argument in Ibn Khaldun's schema confirmed the Marxian 'division of labour' theory, it was not, suggested Khatibi, a determinist explanation in economic terms. Indeed, Khatibi now set out the differences between Marx and Ibn Khaldun, the former basing his analysis on a finality (communism) versus the latter's cyclical justification of religious hierarchy.[59]

---

55   Continuing the culturalist approach to class, Khatibi underlined how Vladimir Propp's *Morphologie du conte*, '[c]ette réflexion sur le conte populaire[,] ne nous éloigne pas de notre objet, car le conte est la formalisation de rapports sociaux dans l'ordre du discours' ['this reflection on the popular folk-tale does not take us away from our object of study, because the folk-tale is the formalisation of social relations within discourse']; and, in this vein, he offered a surprising explanation of aspects of Moroccan homosexuality and prostitution ('Hiérarchies pré-coloniales – les théories', p. 59).

56   Ibid., pp. 30–1.

57   Ibid., pp. 32–3.

58   Ibid., p. 35.

59   Ibid., p. 39.

Khatibi nevertheless recognized that Ibn Khaldun had been used by colonial historians to justify Morocco's (and the Arab world's) ripeness for colonization. He also questioned the relevance of the *'açabiyya* in today's Arab and Moroccan world, rejecting Ibn Khaldun's insistence on the tribe as the motor of history in favour of a (Marxian) theory of the rising Moroccan state.[60] Khatibi also criticized the recent work of Abdallah Laroui for its tendency to overstate in the other direction, whereby Laroui exaggerated (as we saw with Michaux-Bellaire above) the role of the Makhzen and its state-like control; and it was the theory of the Makhzenite state that Khatibi aimed to treat in the second part of his analysis.[61]

Against Lacoste's interpretation of Ibn Khaldun and having outlined Marx's late writings on Algeria, Khatibi now devised a persuasive if elliptical account of socio-historical forces in Morocco. It was the *conflict* between the Makhzen on the one side and the Berber tribes on the other that, alone, explained peasant revolts:

> [N]ous pensons qu'un clivage de classe se combine avec un clivage tribal, et qu'une véritable lutte de classe s'engage entre le Makhzen et l'aristocratie tribale. Il s'agit de déterminer dans chaque cas les groupes moteurs, issus des hiérarchies multiples, et qui guident les mouvements sociaux.[62]

> [We think that a class divide combines with a tribal divide, and that a veritable class struggle takes place between the Makhzen and the tribal aristocracy. The task then is to determine in each case the groups that drive this, and who are part of multiple hierarchies and lead social movements.]

---

60 Khatibi cited Barthes's 1967 article, 'Le discours de l'histoire', pointing to the void left by the historian's facts which is then filled by the 'closure' of the narrative. Barthes's essay in English is translated by Peter Wexler as 'Historical Discourse' in M. Lane (ed.), *Structuralism: A Reader* (London: Jonathan Cape, 1970), pp. 145–55.

61 'Hiérarchies pré-coloniales – les théories', pp. 41–2. See Abdallah Laroui, *L'histoire du Maghreb: un essai de synthèse* (Paris: Maspero, 1970). Khatibi summarized this simplistic understanding by citing a Berber proverb: 'Moi contre mes frères; mes frères et moi, contre mes cousins; mes cousins, mes frères et moi contre le monde' ['I against my brothers; my brothers and I against my cousins; my cousins, my brothers and I against the world']. 'Hiérarchies pré-coloniales – les théories', p. 54.

62 Ibid., pp. 46–7.

Adopting the analysis of René Gallissot and other Communist historians, Khatibi set out the four 'paliers' ['levels'] – using Gurvitch's term – in Morocco's pre-modern class system: 'paysannerie communautaire' ['peasant community']; rural aristocracy; merchant bourgeoisie; and an 'aristocratie de commandement' ['ruling aristocracy'].[63] This stratification led Khatibi to discount Marx's theory of an Asiatic mode of production in Morocco, preferring the equilibrium-based explanation in Marcel Mauss's theory of *Le Don* ['The Gift'], that was famously taken up (Khatibi reminded in a footnote) by Georges Bataille in the notion of the *part maudite* ['accursed share']:

> [L]'échange maintient l'équilibre entre la rareté et les excès dangereux de l'inégalité des structures sociales. Mais quand la rationalité économique du système tribal a été brisée ou affaiblie par la rationalité économique capitaliste, le système tribal a continué à fonctionner selon un mode dégradé, segmentaire, en une résistance larvée. C'est sur l'illusion d'un système ayant perdu sa violence militaire qu'il faut pointer l'analyse. Et s'il y a un processus de féodalisation, il n'est qu'un processus induit: la propriété privée prend le pas sur la manipulation de la rareté et de la violence, le surplus économique prend le pas sur le surplus social.[64]

> [Exchange maintains the balance between scarcity and the dangerous excesses caused by the inequality of social structures. But when the economic rationality of the tribal system was smashed or weakened by capitalist economic rationality, the tribal system continued to function in a degraded, segmentary way, as a latent form of resistance. We must then direct our analysis towards the illusionary nature of a system that has lost its military violence. And if there is a process of feudalization, this process is merely an induced one: private property overtakes social manipulation through scarcity and violence, economic surplus overtakes social surplus.]

63 René Gallissot (ed.), *Sur le féodalisme* (Paris: éditions sociales, 1971). Khatibi's colleague Mohamed Guessous's unpublished work from this period is also concerned with social stratification and 'chefferie'. See Rachik and Bourqia, 'La Sociologie au Maroc', para. 12.
64 Khatibi, 'Hiérarchies pré-coloniales – les théories', p. 49. Ibn Khaldun is sharply differentiated from Marx in Muhammad Dhaouadi, 'The Concept of Change in the Thought of Ibn Khaldun and Western Classical Sociologists', *Islam Arastirmalari Dergisi Sayi* 16 (2006), pp. 43–87 (p. 46). On stratification and sociology, see P. Berger and B. Berger, *Sociology: A Biographical Approach* (Harmondsworth: Penguin, 1976 [1972]), chaps 7 and 8, 'The Stratified Community' and 'The Stratified Society'.

Therefore, concluded Khatibi, neither 'le discours khaldûnien' ['Khaldunian discourse'] nor 'le discours marxiste' ['Marxist discourse'] could replace the value of a segmentary analysis.[65] Khatibi now acknowledged the ethnographic work of Roger Bastide, a major influence during his time in Paris, which took the debate, via Jeanne Favret, to a discussion of the work of Emile Durkheim, Ernest Gellner, David Hart and, finally, his colleague Paul Pascon on segmentarity:

> Le système segmentaire est donc une espèce de jeu d'échiquier, une structure dans laquelle les différents segments ont la double caracté-ristique d'être homogènes et semblables.[66]

> [The segmentary system is therefore a kind of chess board, a structure in which the different segments have the dual characteristic of being both homogeneous and alike.]

Using E. E. Evans-Pritchard's structural-functional models used on the Nuer (published first in 1937 by this British scholar of Mauss), Khatibi now made a link between a segmentary, Durkheimian approach and a Marxian one, citing Durkheim's notion of communism as the subsumption of the individual within the collective:

> Dans le système segmentaire, la cohésion est maintenue par une prédom-inance de la religion sur le pouvoir. Si donc cette organisation est égalitaire, l'instance économique se trouve dominée par ce jeu d'échiquier [...] Durkheim rejoint ainsi Marx quand ils fondent tous les deux la différen-ciation sociale sur l'individualisation de la propriété.[67]

---

65 Khatibi does not mention John Waterbury's contemporaneous study on political segmentation, *The Commander of the Faithful: The Moroccan Political Elite. A Study in Segmented Politics* (New York: Columbia University Press, 1970).

66 Khatibi, 'Hiérarchies pré-coloniales – les théories', p. 51. On the importance of Bastide's work for Khatibi, see Cherribi and Pesce, 'Khatibi: A Sociologist in Literature'. Khatibi is (presumably) referring to Jeanne Favret's 'Présentation' of Siegfried F. Nadel, *La Théorie de la structure sociale*, trans. J. Favret (Paris: éditions de Minuit, 1970). On Gellner and stratification theories, see A. Hammoudi, 'Segmentarity, Social Stratification, Political Power and Sainthood: Reflections on Gellner's Theses', *Hespéris-Tamuda* 15 (1974), reprinted in *Economy and Society* 9.3 (1980). See also D. Hart, 'Making Sense of Moroccan Tribal Sociology and History', *Journal of North African Studies* 6.2 (2001). R. Bourqia lists Khatibi's work on pre-colonial classes in Morocco in *La Stratification sociale: note de synthèse* (2006) – available at www.ires.ma/wp-content/uploads/2017/02/GT2-1.pdf (consulted 30 March 2018) – but does not take up Khatibi's Marxian dilemmas.

67 Khatibi, 'Hiérarchies pré-coloniales – les théories', p. 53.

[In the segmentary system, cohesion is maintained by the predominance of religion over power. If then this organization is egalitarian, economic authority finds itself dominated by this chess-board [...] Thus Durkheim joins with Marx when both of them base social differentiation on the individualization of property.]

Though Khatibi questioned the relevance of the theory of segmentarity in a global context, it nonetheless became the basis of his critique, first of Favret, then of Gellner, for their inability fully to comprehend the role of segmentarity in social-class construction:

Il arrive que la segmentarité l'emporte sur la hiérarchie ou l'inverse; l'essentiel c'est d'étudier les deux systèmes dans leur déploiement historique. [...] Le saut épistémologique n'est pas aisé, et comme Alice peut passer du reflet du miroir au miroir lui-même, la segmentarité saute d'une illusion à une autre illusion. La tribu en tant que genre n'est pas statique.[68]

[It turns out that segmentarity overcomes hierarchy or the opposite happens; the important thing is to study the two systems in their historical unfurling. [...] This epistemological leap is not easy, and just as Alice can move from the mirror's reflection into the mirror itself, segmentarity leaps from one illusion to another. The tribe as a category is not static.]

Indeed, Khatibi's conclusion betrayed his suspicion of Western anthropology:

Le segmentarisme serait-il simplement la systématisation (occidentale) de l'idéologie dominatrice des chefs de tribu? Curieux paradoxe qui transforme une théorie anthropologique en une légitimation (inconsciente) du rapport de domination! Théorie de violence symbolique qui repose pour nous le problème du discours: qui parle à travers la parole de l'anthropologue?[69]

[Might segmentarism be simply the (Western) systematization of the tribal chiefs' dominant ideology? It is a curious paradox that transforms an anthropological theory into an (unconscious) legitimation of the relation of domination! It is a theory of symbolic violence which restates for us the problem of discourse: who speaks through the words of the anthropologist?]

68   Ibid., p. 56.
69   Ibid., p. 57.

In good post-structuralist fashion, Khatibi now played out the 'chess-board' analysis of social phenomena, in which changes of dimension – here globality – deconstruct 'local' determinants:

> [L]e modèle segmentaire rend plus intelligible les processus de stratification tribale, mais il est inopérant quand il s'agit d'expliquer la position du système tribal dans l'histoire et la société globale. [...] [C]e système ne rend pas compte des mouvements de déséquilibre des hiérarchies entre patrilignages, qui sont autant de facteurs de féodalisation et de développement de classes, de commandement. Le passage des formes élémentaires de la stratification à une structuration en classes n'intéresse pas les segmentaristes. Ce qui restreint la portée de leurs analyses.[70]

> [The segmentary model makes the processes of tribal stratification more intelligible, but it does not work when it is a question of explaining the place of the tribal system within history and global society. [...] This system does not account for the destabilizing effects on hierarchies between patrilineages, which are equally factors of feudalization and development of classes, of power structures. The move from elementary forms of social stratification to a structuring of social classes does not interest segmentarists. And this restricts the scope of their analyses.]

Furthermore, he added, a fluctuating tribal society such as pre-colonial Morocco meant that the Makhzen caste could dominate.

Finishing by hesitating between the three approaches – Khaldunist, Marxian and Durkheimian – and abruptly drawing a table of the three different areas of operation of the three theories, Khatibi concluded: 'ces trois logiques se déploient dans des discours spécifiques, dont chacun renvoie à une imbrication particulière de codes' ['these three logics are used in specific discourses, each of which points to a specific overlapping of codes'].[71] Thus, Khaldunist circularity, Marxian dialectics and Durkheimian segmentarity are all combined – or left floating – in Khatibi's thought. All are necessary, and, like a game of paper–scissors–stone, each one can trump only one other but not both others.[72]

---

70   Ibid., pp. 59–60.

71   Ibid., pp. 60–1.

72   Indeed, in the 1973 interview in *Lamalif*, 'Il faut s'essayer à une double critique permanente', Khatibi now questioned the appropriateness of Khaldunian circularity, preferring Marx's dialectical view of history and change.

Conclusion: Triple Entry

It would not be unfair to point out that the segmentarity thesis, as the third element in Khatibi's analysis of class, tends to ignore that which divides classes as a hierarchy, the segment reflecting difference not rank. Introducing difference into social explanation, a move typical of post-structuralism, allows segmentarism to collapse determinants, by making them, equally, multideterminant, and thereby, it neutralizes them, in utopian fashion, by pluralizing them in a non-hierarchy that – admittedly in an admirable fashion – tries to defy exclusion; but this multi-determinism merely concedes ground to hierarchy by not describing it as capable of being overthrown. The 'triple entry', in political terms, therefore, is a fudge.

The 'triple entry' deployed by Khatibi now appears as essayism's concession to the literary *œuvre*. Indeed, *La Mémoire tatouée* exemplifies the Khatibi of multiple voices and popular experiences, combining literature with sociological segmentation, dialectics with circularity. Furthermore, Khatibi's favourable reference to Jacques Prévert's trademark 'pirouette' at the end of his poems, is, for the essayist, the equivalent of the final 'renversement' ['reversal'] that allows a triple entry into the object of study.[73] 'Triple entry' is thus a response to the sociology of forms and the formalism of determinants, a cultural materialism – and a form of culturalism – that is redolent (ironically for an anti-Occidentalist writer such as Khatibi) of 'Western Marxism'.[74]

It was Barthes, in his 1970 reading of Balzac, *S/Z*, who famously theorized the 'triple entry'.[75] It may be that the pre-eminent *littérateur*-sociologist of French post-structuralism finds its Moroccan counterpart in the sociologist-*littérateur*. A comparison of Khatibian and Barthesian essayism is, however, for another day.

---

73   Khatibi, *La Mémoire tatouée*, p. 58; *Tattooed Memory*, p. 76.

74   Khatibi continued the discussion on popular culture in 'Culture nationale et culture de classe au Maroc' (*Intégral*, 5–6 (Sept. 1973), p. 20) and in his work on calligraphy (*Intégral*, 3–4 (Jan. 1973), p. 46).

75   See R. Barthes, 'The Three Points of Entry', *S/Z* [1970], trans. Richard Miller (New York: Hill & Wang, 1974), pp. 214–16.

CHAPTER TWO

Tireless Translation

Travels, Transcriptions, Tongues and the Eternal Plight of the *'Étranger professionnel'* in the Corpus of Abdelkébir Khatibi

Alison Rice

> identité différence deux mots pour nommer le même nœud
> dénouer ces mots c'est tracer une spirale
> tracer en son corps une spirale élastique
> c'est se mouvoir dans l'exil
> s'exiler sauvagement à l'autre
> c'est s'ouvrir à la différence sans retour
>
> [identity difference two words to point to the same knot
> to untie these words is to trace out a spiral
> to trace an elastic spiral in the body
> is to enter into exile
> to consign oneself wildly to the other
> is to open oneself to difference without return]
>
> Abdelkébir Khatibi[1]

In his final publication, the autobiographical *Le Scribe et son ombre*, Abdelkébir Khatibi asserts that he likes to introduce himself both as a Moroccan and as an *étranger professionnel*.[2] This latter expression

---

1   See Abdelkébir Khatibi, *Le Lutteur de classe à la manière taoïste* (Paris: Sindbad, 1976), reprinted in *Œuvres de Abdelkébir Khatibi II: Poésie de l'aimance* (Paris: La Différence, 2008), pp. 9–35 (p. 30); *Class Warrior – Taoist Style*, trans. Matt Reeck (Middletown, CT: Wesleyan University Press, 1976), p. 38.

2   Abdelkébir Khatibi, *Le Scribe et son ombre* (Paris: La Différence, 2008), p. 15.

emerges in Khatibi's corpus from time to time, and it is inevitably connected to numerous travels; in his contemplative last text, the author addresses the multiple trips he has personally engaged in: 'J'ai beaucoup voyagé, plus ou moins séjourné dans de nombreux pays. Mais je n'ai jamais été poussé à l'exil, ni par force, ni par un désir d'errance et de transplantation' ['I travelled a great deal, residing more or less in numerous countries. But I have never been pushed into exile, either by force or by my desire to err and be transplanted'].[3] If he never chose to make another nation his primary place of residence it is because he experienced a strong ongoing affiliation with his native country; this work contains a delineation of his decision to remain in this location: 'Une patrie n'est pas seulement le lieu de la venue au monde, mais un choix personnel qui fortifie le sentiment d'appartenance' ['A fatherland is not only the place of your birth but a personal choice that strengthens a feeling of belonging'].[4] Even if he affirms in this text that he will be forever attached to his homeland, Khatibi was a multifaceted individual who remains hard to pin down. He assumed so many positions in his life and work that he has rendered nearly impossible any attempt to create a simplified approach to his identity:

> Ici ou là, on me dit sociologue, chercheur, professeur, poète, romancier, essayiste, sémiologue, critique d'art, philosophe, politologue même. Je suis accablé par cette non-identification des rôles. Mais, me suis-je dit, cette confusion des rôles et des tâches est, en elle-même, un obstacle qui serait favorable à la connaissance de soi et d'autrui.[5]

> [Depending on whether I am here or there, I am called a sociologist, a researcher, a professor, a poet, a novelist, an essayist, a semiologist, an art critic, a philosopher, even a political scientist. I am overwhelmed by the non-identification of these roles. But, I told myself, this confusion of roles and tasks is, in itself, an obstacle favourable to the knowledge of oneself and others.]

Rather than select a single definition from this list of possible designations, Khatibi sought a singular term that he could choose to describe as he wished, a neologistic expression that would allow him to situate himself beyond the expectations of any particular profession in order to underscore a lifestyle, a way of being, concentrated outside the confines of a country or its customs.

---

3   Ibid.
4   Ibid., p. 9.
5   Ibid., p. 14.

The most effective way to communicate the specificity of this choice of conduct is to create a dialogue in the written text, and Khatibi opts in his last work to revisit and expand upon a passage from an earlier publication, imagining a conversation that would allow him to elucidate his invented term:

> Si un curieux ou une curieuse venait à m'interroger sur la signification de cette expression lancée en l'air, lors d'un colloque franco-maghrébin à Paris, en 1986, je lui répondrais comme le personnage de mon dernier récit publié:
> — C'est un étranger professionnel, dit-il.
> — Curieux métier!
> — Ce n'est pas un métier. C'est une position mobile dans le monde. On est à même de traverser les frontières: entre les langues, entre les civilisations, entre les marchés. Un jour, on s'arrête pour méditer.
> — Vous en êtes là, amigo! dit-elle.
> — Si, si toujours là. Quand on me cherche, on me trouve sur le chemin – la main sur le cœur.[6]

> [If a curious man or woman came to ask me about the significance of this expression that I put out there during a Franco-Maghrebian conference in Paris in 1986, I would respond just like the character in my most recent publication:
> 'He's a professional stranger', he said.
> 'Curious profession!'
> 'It's not a profession. It's a mobile position in the world. It means being capable of crossing borders: between languages, civilizations, markets. One day, you stop to meditate.'
> 'That is what you're doing, amigo!'
> 'Yes, yes, still there. When they look for me, they will find me on the path, my hand on my heart.']

In this exchange, the *étranger professionnel* provides the assurance that he can always be found *en route*, advancing along a path that is not determined by employment but is instead a behaviour motivated by sincere sentiment, by a profound openness to the other – to all others. While it wasn't necessarily a natural response to the conditions of his coming into the world, Khatibi nonetheless indicates that his birth in a colonized country on the eve of the Second World War made him sensitive to the widespread human propensity to exercise domination and exhibit cruelty. After making this observation early in life, he

6 Ibid., p. 15.

opted to pursue higher education in Paris, where, as a foreigner among many foreigners, he assumed the stance of the *étranger professionnel*, both at the Sorbonne and beyond the university's walls: 'À Paris, j'appris à être anonyme, mobile, circulant dans le labyrinthe d'une ville elle-même fluide, féeriquement fluide, ouverte aux aventures et aux aléas de l'agitation cosmopolite' ['In Paris, I learned to be anonymous, mobile, circulating in the labyrinth of a city that was itself fluid, fairily fluid, open to adventures and to the hazards of cosmopolitan agitation'].[7] This acceptance of the advantages of what the author often terms a 'position' in the world points to the disposition that Khatibi has adopted on the many travels that came to characterize his life and work.

A strikingly similar verbal exchange to the one defining the *étranger professionnel* above reveals in *Pèlerinage d'un artiste amoureux* that a 'perpetual itinerant' has taken on a lifestyle marked by movement that allows for considerable contemplation of his surroundings:

— Que faites-vous dans la vie?
— Itinérant perpétuel.
— C'est un métier?
— Non, c'est une manière de vivre. J'ai des rentes. Écoutez, si vous m'envoyez demain dans un bateau à destination, disons, d'une ville éloignée dans un pays inconnu de moi. Un pays dont je ne connais, ni la langue, ni les mœurs, pas même la physionomie de son peuple. Eh bien, je commence par m'installer dans un hôtel, au centre de la vieille ville. Je dépose mes valises, je sors me promener. Ainsi commence un certain apprentissage du monde.[8]

['What do you do?'
'Perpetual itinerant.'
'Is that a profession?'
'No, it's a way of living. I have annuities. Listen, if you send me on a boat tomorrow heading to a far-off city in a country unknown to me, a country whose language, mores, and even whose people's physiognomy are unknown to me, I will begin by settling into a hotel in the centre of the old town. I will put down my suitcases and go out for a walk. That's how a certain apprenticeship of the world begins.']

---

7 Ibid., p. 19.

8 Abdelkébir Khatibi, *Pèlerinage d'un artiste amoureux* (Monaco: Editions du Rocher, 2003), reprinted in *Œuvres de Abdelkébir Khatibi I: Romans et récits* (Paris: La Différence, 2008), pp. 471–672 (p. 598).

This 'apprenticeship' in the world comes with a commitment to immersion in the complete unknown of a foreign country. While this passage does not contain the words *étranger professionnel*, the term is found elsewhere in the book, when the narrative voice contemplates the exceptional status of the figure of the artist, throughout time: 'L'artiste serait-il en tous temps un étranger professionnel?' ['Is the artist a professional stranger in all eras?'].[9] There can be little doubt that Khatibi's creative written work benefits from the fact that the author could make a claim like that of the principal protagonist of *Un été à Stockholm*: 'Une vie, toute une partie de ma vie à voyager!' ['A life, a huge part of my life spent travelling!'].[10] The central character of this text set in Sweden puts into practice the approach of the professional foreigner or stranger through his multiple travels: 'de ville en ville, l'itinéraire de ma vie arpente son territoire. J'y apprenais aussi à explorer le secret des frontières, des passages, des issues ou des impasses: secret initiatique du voyageur' ['from one city to another, the itinerary of my life strides across its territory. I also learned to explore the secret of borders, passageways, exits and impasses: the initiatory secret of the traveller'].[11] The secret of the traveller seems to be hidden in the pages of various works by Khatibi, requiring the careful reader to examine well-chosen passages in order to find the key to their resonances, and ultimately to understand their wisdom. Travel therefore takes on tremendous importance in Khatibi's *œuvre*. It is a source of inspiration that propels the writer towards textual innovation: 'Pour chaque moyen de transport, il faudrait inventer un genre littéraire' ['For each mode of transportation, we need to invent a literary genre'].[12] But travel also constitutes a quest for something fundamental, a search for the redeeming features of humanity.

If the contentious context of Khatibi's early life made him question what positive traits made up his fellow human beings, this query moved him in the direction of a 'vie transmigratoire' ['transmigratory life'], as he articulates it in *Féerie d'un mutant*.[13] What drives the *étranger*

9   Ibid., p. 517.

10   Abdelkébir Khatibi, *Un été à Stockholm* (Paris: Flammarion, 1990), reprinted in *Œuvres de Abdelkébir Khatibi I: Romans et récits*, pp. 285–379 (p. 287).

11   Ibid., p. 318.

12   Ibid., p. 339.

13   Abdelkébir Khatibi, *Féerie d'un mutant* (Monaco: Editions du Rocher, 2005), reprinted in *Œuvres de Abdelkébir Khatibi I: Romans et récits*, pp. 673–711 (p. 700).

professionnel in his seemingly ceaseless travel is a deep desire to unearth what similarities and differences are present in others: 'L'humain! Montrez-nous votre visage, faites-nous écouter le timbre de votre voix. Êtes-vous comme vous-même … comme nous … comme quoi?' ['The human! Show us your face, let us listen to the timbre of your voice. Are you like yourself … like us … like what?'].[14] A wager on the human is what an interlocutor assumes is at the forefront of the foreigner's mind, according to this exchange: '— Nous faisons un pari sur l'humain, rien que l'humain. C'est ce que vous cherchez à défendre, n'est-ce pas, étranger professionnel? — Je cherche la trace du désastre dans le langage, la pensée, le corps, le comportement …' ['We are wagering on the human, nothing but the human. This is what you seek to defend, isn't it, professional stranger?' 'I seek the trace of disaster in language, thought, body, behaviour …"].[15] This response reminds us that, in the case of Khatibi, these travels are born of an inaugural loss bound up in colonization: 'L'accès à mon humanité ne m'est pas accordé par héritage. Plutôt par désir d'extranéité. Dans le sillage d'une fluidité identitaire, marquée de points mobiles d'adaptation à soi et à autrui' ['It isn't through an inheritance that I gain access to my humanity, but through the desire for foreignness. In the wake of a fluid identity, marked by mobile points of adaptation to the self and to others'].[16] The exuberance of the elected lifestyle of the *étranger professionnel*, the whirlwind excitement of an itinerary that moves from country to country, is exalted in exclamatory passages that claim a new human heritage through travel: 'L'Orient – ah oui! – est ma patrie, alors que je me désoriente vers d'autres continents. Voyager? Le voyage est toujours devant moi: je suis comblé' ['The Orient? – ah yes! – is my home, therefore I disorient myself towards other continents. Travel? Travel is always ahead of me: I am overjoyed'].[17] The joy of displacement is in large part connected to the diversity of discoveries, to the variety of views – and viewpoints – that are available to the person who is meeting people and visiting places that are ever new. But, as this passage suggests, part of the situation that permits

14   Ibid., p. 694.
15   Ibid., p. 695.
16   Khatibi, *Le Scribe et son ombre*, p. 120.
17   Abdelkébir Khatibi, *Amour bilingue* (Montpellier: Fata Morgana, 1983), reprinted in *Œuvres de Abdelkébir Khatibi I: Romans et récits*, pp. 205–83 (p. 282); *Love in Two Languages*, trans. Richard Howard (Minneapolis: University of Minnesota Press, 1990), p. 116.

the first-person narrator to embark on dizzying, disorienting transcontinental trips is that he has a homeland, a country that he can claim as his and to which he is always able to return. This stable home base, and his ongoing attachment to it, provides him with a sense of 'belonging' that he is free to criticize, but for which he is grateful: 'Je vis et travaille au Maroc. Ce pays est de force vive. Je lui dois ma naissance, mon nom, mon identité initiale' ['I live and work in Morocco. This country is a lively force. I owe it my birth, my name, my initial identity'].[18] Given that his native region was not independent in his early years, Khatibi learned not to take anything for granted but instead moved towards creating a stance that stands out in stark contrast to nationalist and xenophobic sentiments: 'Étranger, il faut que je m'attache à tout ce qui l'est sur cette terre' ['a foreigner, I must attach myself to all that is foreign on this earth'].[19] The ever-moving, ever-adjusting position that Khatibi extolls has consequences on multiple levels, affecting the body and the relationships of the *étranger professionnel*, but the effects are perhaps most evident on his use of language. The pleasure the traveller experiences is intricately connected to the multiple idioms he comes up against as he moves from one place to another, the numerous tongues into which he throws himself with such intensity.

Languages of the Other

The bipartite title of Khatibi's final work features first a recurring term from his *œuvre*: *Le Scribe et son ombre* refers not only to the author himself but also to the multiple alter egos that grace the pages of his creative work. It is interesting that he so often springs for the word 'scribe' when it recalls the profession of those who studied sacred scriptures, and carries the connotation of copying. The act of faithfully reproducing words that accompanies this calling is communicated in the figure who emerges in Khatibi's writings. In an era when emphasis is often placed on originality, this term tells of another possible relationship to the text: one dictated by careful representation and that is inspired by external forces as much as by internal insights. In the various written passages that employ the word, it becomes clear that Khatibi's conception of the scribe is in tune with the rhythms of life, and is especially encouraged by travel.

18 Khatibi, *Le Scribe et son ombre*, p. 9.
19 Ibid., p. 11.

The writing of the scribe accompanies movement on a grand scale, and Khatibi shows that travel can be taken down in meaningful manner.

The scribe is poised and prepared to render in written form what he experiences, observes, witnesses: 'Il écrivait avec sa vie' ['He wrote with his life'].[20] Serving as a scribe means transferring the traces of voice and emotion to written form, in order to leave a similar trace: 'Écrire! c'est laisser des empreintes de la voix et de l'émotion dans le dessin des mots' ['To write! Is to leave imprints of the voice and emotion in the design of words'].[21] This task requires an undeniably open attitude that enables the scribe to be moved by inspiration that can come from a variety of sources, external and internal, sometimes mystic and sometimes oneiric:

> Mais je crois que tout cela est encore abstrait, presque de seconde main. C'est le rêve qui *nous* rêve, n'est-ce pas, c'est lui qui nous écrit. Nous sommes en position de lecteurs. Mais la lecture entraîne le mouvement d'écrire, de telle manière que ce qui nous écrit, nous continuons à le transcrire, à le traduire. L'Inconscient comme une machine de traduction, oui, tout le monde le dit, mais j'ai tendance à diviser encore l'Inconscient, à en faire du pluriel … mais là je risque de m'embrouiller.[22]

> [But I believe that all that is still abstract, almost second hand. It's the dream that dreams *us*, right, it is the dream that writes us. We are in the position of readers. But reading pulls us into the movement of writing, in such a fashion that what writes us, we continue to transcribe it, to translate it. The Unconscious is like a translation machine, yes, everyone says it, but I have a tendency to divide the Unconscious even further, to make it a plural … but in this I risk confusing myself.]

In this co-authored text, Khatibi attests that often the dream *dreams* him, as states of altered awareness are prone to affect those who are open to their influence, and that it is therefore the dream that *writes* him as well. His reflections reveal that reading and writing become intermingled, and these are not the sole activities that become mixed up in this assessment of the ways the unconscious is similar to a machine that churns out words that have equivalents elsewhere. The evocation of technology in this passage points towards later texts in which Khatibi brings together body, mind and machine in thought-provoking passages

---

20   Khatibi, *Féerie d'un mutant*, p. 704.
21   Khatibi, *Un été à Stockholm*, p. 326.
22   Abdelkébir Khatibi and Jacques Hassoun, *Le Même Livre* (Paris: Editions de l'éclat, 1985), p. 133.

that explore the intersections of these aspects of existence and their implications for human development in an evolving world; while he accords importance to the machine and is actively interested in the ways humans are reacting to technological advances, he exhibits some hesitation with respect to the ways in which the body itself must adapt to these changes. One of the most significant parts of this passage is the revelation that what *writes* the writer, what provides the author with initial inspiration, continues to inhabit him long after the first spark, and the writing process comprises not only the *transcription* but also, perhaps simultaneously, the *translation* of that insight in the text. The juxtaposition of 'transcrire' and 'traduire' in this quotation reveals a great deal about the writer's understanding of these two actions as highly complementary and even, possibly, synonymous.

The scribe of Khatibi's corpus is immediately turned *both* towards the past *and* towards the future, furtively taking down what happens in between the two, furrowing an identity that in some cases depends on a memory that does not yet exist, that is present in the process of creation, that is caught up in the movement of becoming: 'Telle est mon identité de scribe, de narrateur et d'autobiographe, quête d'une mémoire en devenir' ['Such is my identity as a scribe, a narrator and an autobiographer, in search of a becoming of a memory'].[23] In order most aptly to render lived experience in written form, the scribe must debunk certain widespread presuppositions regarding language and translation, namely that the first can somehow be 'pure' and the second can somehow be 'faithful'. In *Maghreb pluriel*, Khatibi reflects on the French tongue that was imposed upon him in the Morocco of his childhood, emphasizing the multiple influences acting upon this language that, as a result, is neither steady nor immutable but instead is constantly in flux: 'La langue française n'est pas la langue française: elle est plus ou moins toutes les langues internes et externes qui la font et la défont' ['The French language is not the French language – it is more or less all the inside and outside languages that make it up and undo it'].[24] The formulation here is compelling, as it insists on the malleable nature of the language that is not only *marked by* but also, more strikingly, is *made up of* other

---

23 Abdelkébir Khatibi, *La Langue de l'autre* (New York: Editions Les Mains secrètes, 1999), p. 30.

24 Abdelkébir Khatibi, *Maghreb pluriel* (Paris: Denoël, 1983), p. 188; *Plural Maghreb: Writings on Postcolonialism*, trans. P. Burcu Yalim (London: Bloomsbury, 2019), p. 124.

tongues. Jacques Derrida, Khatibi's friend and fellow Maghrebian-born philosopher, underscores in provocative terms what such a resulting plurality in language implies for translation: 'Car il y a toujours plus d'une langue dans une langue, dans ce qu'on appelle une langue. Au moment où l'on traduit, on réduit le pluriel à un. Ce qui est toujours difficile à traduire […] c'est la multiplicité des langues dans une langue' ['For there is always more than one language in a language, in what we call a language. At the moment we translate it, we reduce the plural to one. That which is always difficult to translate […] is the multiplicity of languages in one language'].[25] It is this multiplicity in and around French that Khatibi teases out, translates and celebrates in his work.

Always attuned to plurality, Khatibi draws attention to the linguistic mixing that is part of the francophone world in a composite publication whose title, *La Langue de l'autre*, reveals that it is a response to Jacques Derrida's *Le monolinguisme de l'autre*. Khatibi reflects in this text on the fact that language does not exist in a vacuum, as he highlights the ways various tongues interact: 'le monde francophone est métissage, mixité avec des bilinguismes et des multilinguismes divers. C'est une loi de la langue, de s'entretenir avec une autre ou d'autres, de se brouiller avec, de se confondre avec' ['the Francophone world is crossing, mixing with different bilingualisms and multilingualisms. It is a law of language that they talk with each other, that they become blurred and confused'].[26] These diverse forms of multilingualism are often encouraged by travel, as Khatibi notes in the case of the French writer Claude Ollier who chose to go to Morocco in 1950, 'un exil volontaire' ['a voluntary exile'] that could only enhance the writer's work, in Khatibi's estimation: 'Faut-il s'exiler pour écrire? non, car l'exil nous précède, mais nous enrichissons cet exil par un surplus de vie que le désir d'écrire libère dans le déplacement' ['Is it necessary to go into exile in order to write? No, for exile precedes us, but we enrich this exile by a surplus of life that the desire to write liberates in displacement'].[27] Khatibi suggests that Ollier is an *étranger professionnel*, specifying that the writer changed countries and began to listen and observe. The

25 Jacques Derrida, 'Fidélité à plus d'un: Mériter d'hériter où la généalogie fait défaut', in *Idiomes, nationalités, déconstructions: rencontre de Rabat avec Jacques Derrida* (Paris: Intersigne/Casablanca: Editions Toubkal, 1998), pp. 221–65 (p. 252).
26 Khatibi, *La Langue de l'autre*, p. 66.
27 Ibid., p. 31.

Frenchman discovered Arabic and Berber and his relationship to his mother tongue was transformed in the process: he realized that this native language was not a 'natural' or a 'given' as he had previously supposed, but was instead an arbitrary construct that had been forced upon him. Ollier's observations carry particular weight for Khatibi, who was not on the side of the colonizer in this linguistic equation and was fully aware from the outset that French was not 'his own': 'La langue n'appartient à personne, elle appartient à personne et sur personne je ne sais rien. N'avais-je pas grandi, dans ma langue maternelle, comme un enfant adoptif? D'adoption en adoption, je croyais naître de ma langue même' ['Language belongs to no one, it belongs to no one and I know nothing about anyone. In my mother tongue, didn't I grow up as an adoptive child? From one adoption to another, I thought I was language's own child'].[28] Born not of a particular language but of language itself, Khatibi found himself free to adopt one tongue after another, becoming delirious at times with the linguistic aspects that exist outside the realm of reason: 'folie de la langue' ['madness of language'].[29]

Even if language in general is a liberating space when it has been freed from belonging, Khatibi contends that the French text of his creation is a freer place to inhabit as a writer because the tongue of composition remains a second language. Indeed, the author maintains during an interview that this is a means of expression that exists without the inhibitions that the mother tongue so often carries: 'j'ai plus de liberté que les écrivains d'origine française. La langue française n'est pas ma propriété, mon héritage direct. Elle m'a été imposée' ['I have more freedom than writers of French origin. The French language isn't my property, my direct inheritance. It was imposed upon me'].[30] Khatibi might have been intimidated by this language at first but he overcame such sentiments and soon entertained a very different relationship with French: 'Mais depuis longtemps, j'ai dépassé ce rapport de soumission, j'aime cette langue, je l'écris avec plaisir, parfois paradoxal' ['But for a long time now I have moved beyond this submissive relationship. I love this language. I write it with a sometimes paradoxical pleasure'].[31] The contradictory nature of his work in French is due in large part to a certain 'clean' or 'purified' form that he seeks when he writes in

---

28   Khatibi, *Amour bilingue*, p. 208; *Love in Two Languages*, pp. 4–5.
29   Ibid., p. 224; p. 27.
30   Khatibi, *La Langue de l'autre*, p. 80.
31   Ibid.

poetry or in 'artistic prose', all while demonstrating an attachment to a syntax that is more in line with his 'sensitivity' to languages and that pushes him to the limits of literary composition: 'C'est pourquoi j'aime les écrivains paradoxaux, qui vivent une expérience-limite du langage. Je suis un frontalier, un arpenteur, un "étranger professionnel"' ['that's why I love paradoxical writers who live an experience at the limits of language. I am surveying at the borders, "a professional stranger"'].[32] What is ultimately at work in texts that perch precariously at the edge of comprehensibility is creativity in language that is heavily influenced by multilingual abilities.

The implications of this approach to literary creation have not eluded literary critics like Françoise Lionnet who has found that texts like those penned by Khatibi make use of French as 'a means of translating into the colonizer's language a different sensibility, a different vision of the world, a means, therefore, of transforming the dominant conceptions circulated by the more standard idiom'.[33] While scholars are not unanimous in their praise for Khatibi's writing, they have nonetheless been influenced by his unique conceptions and idiosyncratic iterations, particularly when it comes to language. One of his salient contentions is that the mother tongue is present in the learned language. In his view, this first form of expression comes through in various ways in the printed publication in French; some of its influences may be hardly perceptible, but the mother tongue is nonetheless there. Khatibi articulates this reality with certainty in *Maghreb pluriel*: 'La langue dite maternelle est inaugurale corporellement, elle initie au dire du non-dit de la confusion avec le corps de la mère, et de ce fait, il initie à ce qui ne pourra s'effacer dans aucune autre langue apprise, même si ce parler inaugural tombe en ruine et en lambeaux' ['the so-called mother tongue is physically inaugural; it introduces to the saying of the non-said of the confusion with the mother's body, and thereby to what cannot be erased in any other learned language, even if this inaugural speech falls apart and crumbles'].[34] The ineffaceable connection between this inaugural way of speaking and the mother's body is what anchors this language in something much more solid than even the memory of it; it is not inconceivable that the writer should forget this mother tongue, but it is unfathomable that the

32 Ibid.
33 Françoise Lionnet, *Postcolonial Representations: Women, Literature, Identity* (Ithaca, NY: Cornell University Press, 1995), p. 13.
34 Khatibi, *Maghreb pluriel*, p. 191; *Plural Maghreb*, p. 127.

effects it has on his very being should ever fade away. As Khatibi argues, 'la langue "maternelle" est à l'œuvre dans la langue étrangère' ['the "mother" tongue is at work in the foreign language'].[35] But while the mother tongue is a strong influence on the text in the other language, it is not the only language that comes through; that is, while two languages are certainly perceptible in his French-language prose, Khatibi delights in the possibilities of proposing a plurality of expressions in the written work that reveal a familiarity with many tongues, thanks to travel and translation.

Translating in the Wings

Flight is what makes possible a great deal of the large-scale movement in which the *étranger professionnel* takes part, and *Un été à Stockholm* is a text that opens and closes with air travel. *Amour bilingue* is a complementary work that underscores the many places with which the frequent flyer is able to become acquainted, in passages such as the following:

> Il couchait partout, ne débandant pas de continent en continent: plaisirs à la chaîne et putains polyglottes de langue en langue. Il se drogua avec les Chinois: ah! ces Chinois qui se tiennent debout comme des idéogrammes: il faut une langue pareille pour les maintenir en vie! Et là-bas encore, il dansa avec les Balinais, entra presque nu, dans un théâtre d'ombres. Un jour, il s'encanailla dans les bordels de Bangkok et de Singapore: curieux, curieux idiomes! Plus tard, il traversa d'immenses forêts, parmi ces arbres dont il voyait les racines remonter au ciel. On l'accueillait partout, enfin étranger à tout, à lui-même et à ses hôtes.

> [He went from bed to bed, staying hard from one continent to the next: assembly-line ecstasies and multilingual whores from one language to the next. He took drugs with the Chinese, the Chinese who hold themselves upright like ideograms. They need a language like Chinese to keep them alive. There, too, he danced with Balinese, entering nearly naked into a theater of shadows. One day, he went slumming in the brothels of Bangkok and Singapore. Curious, curious idioms. Later, he traversed immense forests, where the roots of some of the trees climbed back toward the sky. He was received everywhere, a stranger to everything, both to himself and to his hosts.][36]

---

35 Ibid., p. 179; p. 117.
36 Khatibi, *Amour bilingue*, p. 235; *Love in Two Languages*, p. 45.

The sensual pleasure that the traveller experiences when changing continents is connected to the linguistic variation that accompanies such displacement. The body is thoroughly involved in this form of immersion, not only thanks to sexual stimulation but also because of the drugs that it partakes of and dances that it participates in. Language, however, is absolutely essential to these corporeal encounters, as sentence after sentence reveals; it is the different tongues that bring special vigour to travel. It is noteworthy as well that, nearly naked, the protagonist ventures into a theatre, a location where the body serves as a crucial element on stage. He may be hovering on the border of this space, a participant who is not at the centre of the play. In this setting, he is content to work as an outsider who can adapt to some of the codes of the society in which he is presently residing, but who will never be fully adept at navigating all the aspects of this performance. The foreigner comes into inspiring contact with many others, but remains on the outskirts, alone in ways that contribute to his work: 'cette jouissance de l'étranger qui doit continuellement travailler à la marge, c'est-à-dire pour son seul compte, solitairement' ['this *jouissance* of the foreigner who must constantly work on the margins, that is, only for himself, in solitude'].[37] The solitary scribe must continually search, striking a careful balance between acceptable forms and inventive fancy, and thereby never runs the risk of sinking into complacency and resting on habit. This practice of seeking out and cultivating the margins, of consistently working in the wings, is what allows the text truly to take off.

What the *étranger professionnel* who becomes intimate with more than two languages is compelled to engage in is a particular form of translation: 'écrire en quelque sorte à plusieurs mains, à plusieurs langues dans un texte qui ne soit qu'une perpétuelle traduction' ['to write in a way with many hands and many languages, in a text that is but a perpetual translation'].[38] The conception of the written work as a 'perpetual translation', as an ongoing exercise that involves movement among several tongues, unites Khatibi's concentration on plurality and his focus on translation in a powerful way. Indeed, this quotation could be seen to encompass the writer's *plight* in two senses of the term, taking into account the *difficulty* of the translator's task in Khatibi's *œuvre* and the *devotion* that that translator has shown to his work,

37   Khatibi, *Maghreb pluriel*, p. 179; *Plural Maghreb*, p. 117.
38   Ibid., p. 205; p. 134.

exhibiting throughout his writing a deep sense of what Derrida termed 'fidélité à plus d'un' ['faithfulness to more than one']. Constantly carrying out translation is what the *étranger professionnel* is wont to do, moving from the mother tongue to the learned language: 'De l'une à l'autre se déroulent une traduction permanente et un entretien en abyme, extrêmement difficile à mettre au jour' ['from one to the other takes place a constant translation and a conversation *en abyme*, extremely difficult to bring to light'].[39] This plight is characterized by its near impossibility, but that does not impede the writer from throwing himself into this work, and the resulting publication bears the prints of the struggle: 'tel est le texte bilingue, aux marges de l'intraduisible' ['such is the bilingual text, on the margins of the untranslatable'].[40] The text that flirts with the untranslatable, that balances on the brink of the *intraduisible*, of that which cannot be rendered in another tongue, may be quintessentially literary. It demonstrates the immense inventiveness to which Khatibi had recourse throughout his *œuvre* in order to speak of experiences outside the realm of the monolingual and uniform.

Khatibi chalks up to 'transdisciplinarité' the approach that became his as a researcher interested in the transformations his many travels and multiple tongues brought about in him, and in his writing: 'Méthode toujours filtrée par la question du langage à inventer, à travers l'épreuve de la vie' ['a method always filtered through the question of the language to be invented through the trial of life'].[41] This turn to invention resolves the dilemma posed by the imposition of the language of writing through colonization; this shift towards creation relieves some of the tension that comes with the burden of appropriation:

Dans la mesure où l'on se place dans la perspective de l'invention de la langue, l'appropriation tombe dans l'idéologie. Tout l'édifice monumental, qui constitue la forteresse du legs patrimonial qui enferme la langue dans ses institutions et ses enseignements, est chaque fois à mettre en crise dans toute pensée, toute œuvre, toute invention, qui en bouleverse les données. Alors l'invention de la langue prend toute sa force de transformation, de mise en forme de la dissidence. Dès lors, ta phrase: '*Je n'ai qu'une langue, ce n'est pas la mienne*', laisse place à toute liberté d'invention. N'importe qui participerait à cette invention. La langue est à donner, elle n'est pas

---

39   Ibid., p. 179; p. 117.
40   Ibid., p. 183; p. 120.
41   Khatibi, *Le Scribe et son ombre*, p. 22.

donnée, expérience-limite où chacun tente sa chance, joue son pari sur l'inconnu.[42]

[From the perspective of the invention of language, appropriation becomes ideology. The entire monumental edifice, which makes up the fortress of the patrimonial legacy that encloses the language in its institutions and its teachings, is continually put in crisis in every thought, product or invention that upsets its givens. The invention of language therefore takes on all its transformative strength as it assumes the shape of dissidence. Then the sentence 'I only have one language, it is not mine', opens up to total freedom of invention. Anybody can participate in this invention. Language is a gift, not a given, a limit-experience in which everyone can try their luck and place their bets on the unknown.]

Khatibi is in dialogue with Derrida here, citing one of his best-known phrases from a piece that was composed in part as a conversation with Khatibi on language and power. This response to his friend and fellow thinker places an emphasis on the ways in which destabilizing the link between a certain language and the laws of the land opens up to great possibility; eroding the edifices that tie tongues provides space for invention at the edges. In *Amour bilingue*, such potential is realized in breathless passages that brush against the boundaries of expression: 'il courait, parlant sans fin, se traduisant, traduisant tout, au seuil de l'indicible' ['he ran, talking incessantly, translating himself, translating everything, on the threshold of the unsayable'].[43] These words come from a larger passage that revels in the reveries afforded to those who allow themselves to move and speak at once, as they fully engage in translating as a way of life.

The love story that graces the pages of *Amour bilingue* with unconventional prose owes much to Khatibi's conception of simultaneity:

S'il m'arrivait de substituer un mot à un autre (je le savais pour mon compte), j'avais l'impression, non pas de commettre une faute ni d'enfreindre une loi, mais de prononcer deux paroles simultanées: l'une, qui parvenait à son écoute (sans cela, pouvait-elle me tenir tête?), et une autre, qui était là, et pourtant lointaine, vagabonde, retournée sur elle-même.

[If I happened to substitute one word for another (I knew it was on my own behalf) I didn't have the impression that I was making a mistake or

---

42 Khatibi, *La Langue de l'autre*, p. 33.
43 Khatibi, *Amour bilingue*, p. 236; *Love in Two Languages*, p. 47.

breaking a law but rather that I was speaking two words simultaneously: one which reached her hearing (failing that, could she have stood up to me?) and a second word, an other, which was there and yet was far away, a vagabond, turned in upon itself.][44]

The narrator bathes in multilingualism in various ways, including contemplating words that are alike in different tongues, and introducing phrases from languages such as Spanish and Swedish into the French-language text. All of this belongs to an understanding that difference is not to be shunned but is rather to be elevated for its constant inspiration: 'Différence qui m'exaltait. Ce que je visais aussi était de me maintenir en cet écart, le déportant dans une écoute où fût bannie toute opposition entre langue morte et langue vivante, où fût affirmé tout ce qui unit en séparant, sépare en se traduisant continuellement' ['Difference which exalted me. My objective was also to maintain myself in this gap, carrying it into a listening where all opposition between dead language and living language would be forbidden, where everything that unites through separation and everything that separates by continually translating itself would be affirmed'].[45] If translating in this manner is ever pressing and ever promising, then it can come as no surprise that a machine that might enhance the experience is brought into the mix: 'Un jour, devant une cabine de traduction simultanée, il lui avait dit: "Veux-tu que nous nous y enfermions pour nous traduire mutuellement?" Par la suite, il lui acheta une machine à traduire et qui lui eût servi – quelle idée! – lorsqu'elle découchait de continent en continent' ['One day, in front of a simultaneous interpretation booth, he said, "Shall we lock ourselves in there and translate each other"? Subsequently, he bought her a translation machine which would have been useful to her – what an idea! – when she stayed out all night from one continent to the next'].[46] The possibilities of connecting through the mutual comprehension that simultaneous translation proposes are fascinating, and their inspiration for the writer raises crucial questions about the relationship between the spoken word and the written text.

A striking paragraph in *Un été à Stockholm* permits the first-person narrative voice of the simultaneous translator to address his 'position de capteur' ['position of receiver'] who must maintain 'neutralité' ['neutrality'] in his line of work, in which he must devote himself to 'la transparence des

44 Ibid., p. 224; p. 28.
45 Ibid., p. 224; p. 28.
46 Ibid., pp. 237–8; pp. 48–9.

mots' ['the transparency of words']: 'Oui, oui, il m'arrive d'improviser. Improvisation sous contrôle, ma voix glissant entre les variations des exposés. Garder le ton, le rythme, l'invention vocale, telle est ma règle d'or' ['Yes, yes, I do happen to improvise. Controlled improvisation, with my voice slipping between the variations of the exposed notes. Keeping the tone and the rhythm of vocal invention, that's my golden rule'].[47] He underscores the self-control that is necessary at each step of the translation process, and provides insights into the various levels of attention required: 'Le timbre vocal de l'orateur? je l'articule à ma sensibilité. Je suis successivement moi-même, l'autre, et de nouveau moi-même, entre la vitesse et la parole, la vitesse et le silence' ['The vocal timbre of the orator? I articulate it according to my sensibility. I am successively myself, the other, and myself again, between speed and the spoken word, speed and silence'].[48] The translator must remain absolutely alert, entirely attentive to every syllable that is uttered, and explains that an important part of this readiness includes predicting what lies ahead in order properly to handle the words, sentences and turns of phrase as they come:

> Je suis là derrière la vitre pour capter, anticiper, comprendre tous les sens d'un mot, d'une phrase ou d'un calembour. Tous les sens: clairs ou pas, raisonnables et plus ou moins complexes ou fumeux; sens troués de pensées lumineuses, de bavardage, de sottise, de fausse rigueur insupportable, autant de positions instables dans l'équilibre entre les langues.[49]

> [I am there behind the glass to capture, anticipate, understand every meaning of a word, phrase or pun. All the meanings: clear or not, reasonable and more or less complex or smoky; meanings related to luminous thoughts, gossip, silliness, and unbearable false rigor. These are all unstable positions that come into the balance between languages.]

The delicate balance *between languages* that is evoked here is significant, for rather than highlighting a unilateral direction from a 'source' language to a 'target' language, the translator refers to his work with a different term, one that does not seek to move completely from one tongue to the other, one that actually valorizes this in-between state: 'interlangue'.[50]

47 Khatibi, *Un été à Stockholm*, p. 309.
48 Ibid.
49 Ibid.
50 Ibid., p. 310.

When Khatibi reflects on his writing process, he likens it to simultaneous translation: 'Ecrire le français, le traduire en l'écrivant, à l'intérieur de cette division active où se joue l'écriture. Je la sens comme une traduction en simultané, par une association rapide de signes et d'images' ['To write in French, to translate it while writing, in the active division where writing plays itself out. I feel it as if it were a simultaneous translation, through rapid association between signs and images'].[51] The speed of the writing begs this comparison, as do the ways in which silence comes through in the text; improvisation is another critical factor that has serious implications for the written work: 'C'est au gré des improvisations, du rythme sensitif et émotif que je m'applique à réduire les premières associations et leur anamorphose. Le tissage par la syntaxe' ['It is at the discretion of improvisations, from a sensitive and emotional rhythm that I apply myself to the reduction of the first associations and their anamorphosis. Weaving through syntax'].[52] According to Khatibi, there is less agency than inspiration in his literary compositions. Much as a simultaneous translator depends upon another to provide him with the words he must transform, so the writer allows the other tongue to make its mark on his text; rather than serving as a translator in a traditional sense, he becomes the one who transcribes: 'Par exemple, des mots ou expressions arabes. Parfois je traduis littéralement des fragments arabes, mais avec inquiétude. Plutôt laisser la langue maternelle arriver, transformée' ['For example, Arabic words or expressions. Sometimes I translate Arabic fragments literally, but with worry. I'd rather let the mother tongue arrive, transformed'].[53] In this version, Khatibi does not purport to be the omniscient author who imparts meaning that must be deciphered by readers; instead, he is received in his own text as a guest: 'Si je fais ainsi l'éloge de la syntaxe, c'est qu'elle élargit l'espace d'hospitalité où l'écrivain est reçu dans son propre texte comme un invité, à l'ombre du lecteur' ['If I praise syntax in this way, it is because it enlargens the hospitable space in which the writer is received in his own text like a guest, in the shadow of the reader'].[54] As other texts have shown, it is possible for the writer to play many roles, taking on a variety of different complementary tasks that lead to a more complex written work: 'Narrateur et traducteur, je m'incarne dans ces transfigurations: je

51 Khatibi, *La Langue de l'autre*, p. 38.
52 Ibid.
53 Ibid.
54 Ibid.

parle et j'écris, je parle et je traduis, je raconte et je suis le scribe de mon histoire' ['Narrator and translator, I take form in these transfigurations: I speak and I write, I speak and I translate, I recount and I am the scribe of my story'].[55] Assertions such as these lead literary critic and translator Matt Reeck to assess the changing, adaptable nature of identity that comes through in Khatibi's *œuvre*, especially but not only in texts that are autobiographical: 'writing is no longer a site merely to reproduce a previously existing and full self, but rather a site where the author exceeds previous limits to achieve a new iteration of the self'.[56] Khatibi does not display an eagerness to assign himself to any single definition, just as he does not wish in any of his texts to restrict himself to any single idiom, and he cultivates an in-between state with tact.

'Interlangue', the term the narrator of *Un été à Stockholm* elects to express how he prefers to work as a simultaneous translator in the passage above, is also found in *Eloge de la créolité*, the manifesto co-written by Jean Bernabé, Raphaël Confiant and Patrick Chamoiseau. According to these Antillean writers, this term can be employed to refer to the linguistic variation that characterizes their Caribbean island, a diversity that they celebrate in this creative text. But if 'interlangue' is useful, the co-authors nonetheless express their preference for the word 'interlecte', thanks to its potential: 'susceptible de conserver à notre créolité sa complexité fondamentale, son champ référentiel diffracté' ['capable of preserving for our creoleness its fundamental complexity, its diffracted referential space'].[57] What is interesting is that these theoreticians are drawn, like Khatibi, to a term that stresses an in-between location that does not necessarily privilege a native tongue or the colonizer's language, but that recognizes instead the value of lingering in another space. This might be the location of the 'entre-deux-langues' that Algerian writer Assia Djebar articulates so effectively: 'Entre-deux-langues, pour un écrivain ne pouvant être autrement qu'écrivain, c'est se placer dans l'aire nerveuse, énervée, désénervée, douloureuse et mystérieuse de toute langue: situation souvent fréquente pour les écrivains ex-colonisés, des

55   Khatibi, *Un été à Stockholm*, p. 368.
56   Matt Reeck, 'Translation and the Poetics of the Orphan: Abdelkébir Khatibi, Discourse and Difference', *International Journal of Francophone Studies* 20.1–2 (2017), pp. 123–33 (p. 128).
57   Jean Bernabé, Raphaël Confiant and Patrick Chamoiseau, *Eloge de la créolité* (Paris: Gallimard, 1989), p. 50; *In Praise of Creolness*, trans. M. B. Taleb-Khyar (Paris: Gallimard, 1993), p. 110.

terres de l'Empire français, anglais, espagnol, hollandais ou portugais d'hier' ['Between-two-languages, for a writer who could only be a writer, this is to place oneself in the nervous, enervated, unnerved, painful and mysterious zone of any language. This is a situation that is often frequent for formerly colonized writers, from the lands of the former French, English, Spanish, Dutch or Portuguese empires'].[58] The in-between that is a part of this formulation is what critics have underscored as a critical component of Khatibi's position on translation. David Fieni emphasizes the thinker's 'decolonial redeployment of the differences generated by the collision of French colonial language politics and Arabic and Islamic idioms in Morocco' by drawing attention to 'the interference or cancelling out that occurs during translation, understood as a condition of exile between languages'.[59] Khatibi's tireless translation – both the translation that characterizes his life's work and the translation that figures on the pages of that work – has led to a focus on the 'inter', on the in-between, that is especially powerful because it is not found in any centre but is instead found at the extreme, at the limits.

In his final work, the prefix 'inter' appears on its own in two different instances to mark the text: 'Je schématise la figure du voyage pour aller vite. Et vite vers l'*Inter*. L'inter qui divise le soi, l'autre, le proche, le voisin, l'étranger' ['I schematize the figure of the trip, in order to go quickly. And quickly toward the *Inter*. The *inter* that divides the self, the other, the loved one, the neighbour, the foreigner'];[60] 'L'*inter* est le point de gravité de toute rencontre virtuelle' ['The *inter* is the centre of gravity of every virtual encounter'].[61] In the first example, 'inter' intervenes to indicate the multiple roles that the self can adapt to take on, and the relationships that influence the self are rolled into these appellations; in the second sense, 'inter' is the meeting point where disparate beings can come together. The writer who is attentive to this term is carving out his own idiom thanks to his multilingual awareness. In a reflective moment, he ascertains that his work is indebted to another 'inter': 'Ma mémoire se rétrécit en mots, et quand je monologue comme n'importe qui, je le fais dans une troisième langue, une interlangue marquée par des trous

58   Assia Djebar, *Ces voix qui m'assiègent … en marge de ma francophonie* (Paris: Albin Michel, 1999), p. 30.
59   David Fieni, 'Introduction: Khatibi's "Place of Hostage"', *PMLA* 125.4 (2010), pp. 1002–19 (p. 1003).
60   Khatibi, *Le Scribe et son ombre*, p. 40.
61   Ibid., p. 62.

de mémoire, des associations imprévues, résurgence du refoulé en moi'
['My memory recedes in words, and when I create a monologue, like
anyone, I do it in a third language, an interlanguage marked by lapses
in memory, unforeseen associations, the emergence of that which is
repressed within me'].[62] The 'interlangue' that he makes use of when he
turns to the past is one that admits the faulty nature of memory. But it is
also one that makes space for faults in language, with the understanding
that it is often preferable to dwell in the in-between than to fully reside
in a single tongue, and the result is a text that allows for reading *entre
les lignes* on many levels that lead to a wealth of possible meanings.[63]

The individual familiar with more than one tongue draws from the
potential that is found in the interstices, the place where transformative
exchanges can take place, as Mireille Rosello expresses it: '*Bilingua* is
an unstable and elusive nonspace, the tension between two languages.
It is another name for a performative encounter'.[64] It is in this space
that progress can be made towards new forms of communication, and
the writer can create the idiosyncratic idiom of his text: 'L'écrivain est
une tête chercheuse de la trace, il a à inventer de nouveaux territoires'
['The writer is a head seeking traces to invent new territories'].[65] It
is the place where true differences can be entertained, in accord with
the transports Khatibi experienced through his many travels, and that
consistently pushed his identity in new directions, as he attested in
his final work: 'L'étranger en moi dominait mon identité intime, il
me montrait les chemins amoureux à parcourir, les stases et extases
à traverser' ['The foreigner in me took over my intimate identity. He
showed me the amorous paths to travel, the states of stasis and ecstasy
to pass through'].[66]

If Khatibi was convinced that all great literary works were translations,
even if their author was monolingual, then what tremendous potential
he perceived in textual creations that revealed familiarities that
encompassed more than the single tongue.

> Or, chaque œuvre est en elle-même une frontière, un passage et un obstacle
> entre les langues, un lieu de réincarnation, quitte, pour l'écrivain, qu'il

---

62   Ibid., p. 54.
63   Khatibi, *Un été à Stockholm*, p. 355.
64   Mireille Rosello, *France and the Maghreb: Performative Encounters*
(Gainesville: University Press of Florida, 2005), p. 78.
65   Khatibi, *La Langue de l'autre*, p. 31.
66   Khatibi, *Le Scribe et son ombre*, p. 101.

soit métropolitain ou extra-muros, à introduire – du français en français – des agencements idiomatiques, à y greffer des points de rupture, des noyaux de dissidence, de résistance, de telle sorte que cette langue que nous écrivons – si nous écrivons – soit disponible à une traduction infinie.[67]

[For each work is in itself a border, a passageway and an obstacle between languages, a place of reincarnation in which the writer, whether he be from within the walls of the city or outside them, can introduce— from French into French—idiomatic layouts, adding breaking points, kernels of dissidence, of resistance, in such a way that this language that we write—if we write—is opened to infinite translation.]

Khatibi's eternal plight as an *étranger professionnel* was to accept the challenge as well as the commitment to dwell in the interstices of multiple tongues, to inhabit the in-between spaces, to seek continual stimulation through exposure to additional modes of expression, and to never become satisfied. With an understanding of language and self that extended beyond questions of property or propriety, Khatibi engaged in tireless translation in texts that depict travel as synonymous with creation and innovation that benefit from transnational perspectives that render all things foreign, in deeply pleasurable ways that are ever new.

67   Abdelkébir Khatibi, *La Langue de l'autre*, p. 37.

CHAPTER THREE

Abdelkébir Khatibi's Mediterranean Idiom

Edwige Tamalet Talbayev

J'ai souvent demandé à la mer d'être moins barbare.
On lui doit, paraît-il, l'ordre de la mémoire

[I have often asked the sea to be less barbaric.
It is said that we owe to it the order of memory.]

Abdelkébir Khatibi[1]

Il faudrait réveiller la mémoire au tracé de ses
refoulements, de ses points aveugles, de ses passions
endormies.

[Memory should be awakened along the lines of its
repressions, its blind spots, its slumbering passions.]

Abdelkébir Khatibi[2]

Contexts

In the 1980s, Moroccan philosopher and writer Abdelkébir Khatibi's
reflections on the intrinsic plurality of the Maghrebian region – a legacy
that encompasses, yet extends far beyond, the European conquests of
the modern age of empire – have brought a groundbreaking corrective

---

1 Abdelkébir Khatibi, 'Bagatelles', in *Les Lettres Nouvelles* (Nov. 1971),
pp. 29–37 (p. 36).
2 Abdelkébir Khatibi, *Le Scribe et son ombre* (Paris: La Différence, 2008),
p. 44.

to binary conceptions of culture and identity born of the history of colonialism in North Africa. Engaging the monolith of teleological history (the Maghreb in the timeline of Islam or Western colonial modernity), Khatibi's theorizations reveal the region's sedimented temporality in all its incongruity and overlapping. Through its sustained focus on decolonization, Khatibi's approach unearths a local form of eclecticism, the watermark of his plural Maghreb, cutting across more dominant epistemological structures. 'Une pensée-autre, une pensée peut-être inouïe de la différence' ['an other-thought, a thought of difference, perhaps unheard of']:[3] such is the thrust of Khatibi's *pensée autre* through its effort to undermine the binary of European rationalism and Islamic theology, the two dominant epistemological paradigms credited with structuring postcolonial Maghrebian identity. Debunking conceptions of the Maghreb as a space beholden to a mystified sense of authenticity, Khatibi's reflections on other-thought reveal a fluctuating identity principle, a form of cultural and linguistic heterogeneity emerging in the interstices between disparate cultural traditions. Indexing true decolonization of thought to an intercultural inscription into the world, Khatibi's method erodes theories of identity tethered to religious or political absolutes. Against any form of nostalgia for atavistic, pre-colonial models of culture, other-thought thus lays claim to the promise of a truly decolonized future attuned to the Maghreb's intrinsic plurality. This approach fosters a *double critique* of long-established, hegemonic metaphysical categories, as well as a radical reshuffling of the most entrenched identitarian thinking in the context of postcolonialism:

> *Maghreb*, ici, désigne le nom de cet écart, de ce non-retour au modèle de sa religion et de sa théologie (si déguisées soient-elles sous des idéologies révolutionnaires) [...] d'autre part, le nom 'Arabe' désigne une guerre de nominations et d'idéologies qui mettent au jour la pluralité active du monde arabe [...] [une pluralité comprenant] ses marges spécifiques (berbères, coptes, kurdes ... et marge des marges: le féminin)

> [Here *Maghreb* designates the name of this gap, this nonreturn to the model of its religion and theology (no matter how well-disguised they may be under revolutionary ideologies) [...] On the other hand, the name 'Arab' designates a war of naming and ideologies, which bring to light

---

3   Abdelkébir Khatibi, 'Pensée-autre', in *Œuvres de Abdelkébir Khatibi III: Essais* (Paris: La Différence, 2008), pp. 9–27 (p. 9); *Plural Maghreb: Writings on Postcolonialism*, trans. P. Burcu Yalim (London: Bloomsbury, 2019), p. 1.

the active plurality of the Arab world [...] [a plurality comprising] its specific margins (Berber, Coptic, Kurdish ... and the margin of margins: the feminine).][4]

In Nasrin Qader's ascription, this approach 'does not oppose Islam and the West but questions the one and the other at the same time, in their distance and in their proximity'.[5]

It is this ongoing negotiation of the 'distance and proximity' between both terms that marks out the Maghreb's unique positionality. Situated on the margin of two metaphysical systems yet in dialectical tension to both, the Maghreb figures a rich in-between space that operates as a transitional '*marge en éveil*' ['*margin on alert*'][6] and enables the process of *double critique* to take hold. In 'Pensée-Autre', Khatibi ascribes the origin of his bi-directional reading to a trans-Mediterranean lineage running from the Syriac and the Greek in ancient times to Arabic and Islamic thought, a movement which he recasts as a 'traduction en arabe du monothéisme abrahamique' ['translation into Arabic of Abrahamic monotheism'].[7] Linking Islamic theology to Greek philosophy through Aristotle highlights the Maghreb's complex resonance, capitalizing on both its marginal position, which posits it at an angle to totalizing thought systems, and its centrality as a Mediterranean site lying at the confluence of multiple civilizations. Through its fruitful reorganization of dominant lineages and lines of demarcation between cultures, the Maghreb's *marginal centrality* is a product of its 'Media-terranean' character.[8] As a 'site topographique entre l'Orient, l'Occident et l'Afrique [qui peut] se mondialiser pour son propre compte' ['topographical site between the East, the West, and Africa, and such that it can become global for its own account'],[9] the Maghreb's mediating nature conveys fluidity and erosion, chipping away at the stability of land-rooted models

4   Ibid., pp. 10–11; pp. 2–3.

5   Nasrin Qader, *Narratives of Catastrophe: Boris Diop, Ben Jelloun, Khatibi* (New York: Fordham University Press, 2009), p. 123. See also Alfonso de Toro, 'Le "plurilinguisme de l'autre": performativité et transversalité de la langue', *Expressions maghrébines* 12.1 (2013), pp. 85–101 (p. 88).

6   Khatibi, 'Pensée-autre', p. 13; *Plural Maghreb*, p. 6.

7   Ibid., p. 16; p. 10.

8   Réda Bensmaïa, 'Media-Terranean, or Between Borders: Nabile Farès's *Un passager de l'Occident*', in Mauro Peressini and Ratiba Hadj-Moussa (eds), *The Mediterranean Reconsidered: Representations, Emergences, Recompositions* (Ottawa: University of Ottawa Press, 2005), pp. 109–23.

9   Khatibi, 'Pensée-autre', p. 26; *Plural Maghreb*, pp. 22–3.

of thought. This plural Maghreb thus resonates in its intermediacy, its nurturing relation to diversity. Limned anew along the contours of its Mediterranean interfaces, Khatibi's Maghreb coalesces as a vector of transnational connectivity, one whose unfolding momentum deploys across the rich, sedimented space of the sea.

In 'Diglossia', a text dedicated to the memory of Kateb Yacine, Khatibi further engages the multiple resonances of Maghrebian diversity in the context of the region's plurilingualism. As Khatibi shrewdly remarks, in a Maghrebian context, diglossia manifests as a long-standing historical condition extending back in time beyond the threshold of the colonial conquest. The interaction resulting from this enduring coexistence of languages, however, should not be construed as simple linguistic mixing or even a superimposition proceeding from the scrupulous layering of one language over another. The palimpsestic conjunction of the Maghreb's multiple idioms is revealed as a genuinely *transformative* process that alters the inner structure of each language through multiple imbrications in 'a vernacular foundation [...] transferred, deported into the language of the other'.[10] A vector of demultiplication and restructuring ('dividing myself, reincarnating myself – in the other's language'),[11] this interface between languages showcases their mutual dislocation. Harking back to Barthes's 'mouvement de déport' mobilized by Réda Bensmaïa,[12] this dynamism flags the unpredictable swerve of language's poetic and semantic deployment. Such is the foundation of *bi-langue*, Khatibi's notion of non-symbiotic bilingualism, which outlines a concept of hybridity that rests on the incommensurability between two linguistic (and cultural) systems. Rather than stake his concept on the overlap between two languages, Khatibi projects his *bi-langue* through a site of 'active [verbal] plurality', along the demarcation line 'between two exteriorities'.[13] *Bi-langue* then materializes along this double breach between languages and their respective referential domains. Eschewing the temptation of dialectical synthesis between the two, *bi-langue* maintains the nourishing tension that alone enables languages to

---

10   Khatibi, 'Diglossia', in Anne-Emmanuelle Berger (ed.), *Algeria in Others' Languages* (Ithaca, NY: Cornell University Press, 2002), pp. 157–60 (p. 158).

11   Ibid., p. 158.

12   Réda Bensmaïa, *Experimental Nations: Or, the Invention of the Maghreb*, trans. Alyson Waters (Princeton, NJ: Princeton University Press, 2003), p. 106.

13   Khatibi, 'Diglossia', p. 158.

'meet without merging, confront their respective graphic movements *without osmosis* and without a reconciling *synthesis*. If, then, we can speak of a '"translation," it is one that does not return to the *same*'.[14] In the vertiginous space of the interval (Khatibi evokes an 'entretien en abyme' ['conversation *en abyme*']15 between both languages), the lure of a return to origins proves untenable. *Bi-langue* thus transcends the complex cross-pollination uniting a writer's practice of the mother tongue and the foreign language, revealing the gaps and fissures running through their infinite dialogue and ongoing translation.

The subsequent essay 'Literary nationalism and internationalism' further lifts the veil on what Khatibi has quipped the 'lois de l'hospitalité dans le langage'16 ['the laws of hospitality in language']. Expanding his reflections on diglossia, Khatibi delves deeper into the 'untranslatable' buffer preserving the irreducible singularity of language, its otherness to itself and other languages, its resilience against any yearning for transparency; untranslatability is not only 'ce qui fait barrière d'une langue à une autre, à d'autres, mais c'est une force intérieure à toute écriture'17 ['what keeps one language from another or other languages but it is an inner force of all writing']. The domain of circulatory 'interlangues' ['interlanguages'], the untranslatable crystallizes along the line 'entre l'oral et l'écrit, entre le national et l'extra-national ou le transnational [...] le tout-autre veille sur la force poétique'18 ['between the oral and the written, between the national and the extra-national or the trans-national [...] the radically other watches over poetical force']. Declining language as *tout-autre* within itself, the act of writing is implicitly recast as a bilingual or inter-lingual process revealing a permeability between self and other: 'Dans chaque mot: d'autres mots; dans chaque langue: le séjour d'autres langues' ['in each word: other words; in each language: the sojourn of other languages'].19 This renewed attention to the permeability of the linguistic medium stems

14 Réda Bensmaïa, 'Multilingualism and National "Character": On Abdelkébir Khatibi's "Bilanguage"', in Anne-Emmanuelle Berger (ed.), *Algeria in Others' Languages* (Ithaca, NY: Cornell University Press, 2002), pp. 161–183 (p. 165).

15 Abdelkébir Khatibi, *Maghreb pluriel* (Paris: Denoël, 1983), p. 179; *Plural Maghreb*, p. 117.

16 Abdelkébir Khatibi, *Figures de l'étranger dans la littérature française* (Paris: Denoël, 1987), p. 203.

17 Ibid., p. 204.

18 Ibid., pp. 204–5.

19 Ibid., p. 205.

from the recognizance of the Maghreb's need to 'take charge of the active plurality of its utterances. [...] [so] that we may glimpse writing as it bursts forth, strong and free, as a historical event'.[20] Laying claim to this historicity boils down to securing new strategies through which to revitalize the writer's inscription into a fluid, trans-historical Maghreb. For though language exceeds its 'encadrement national' ['national framing'], it nevertheless performs a return via an intrinsic detour: 'Je viens d'Afrique et j'y reviens en recevant le tout-étranger'[21] ['I come from Africa and I go back to it as I receive the radically foreign']. Yet this ontological diversion portends no reterritorialization in the ferment of cultural authenticity. Refusing any form of metaphysical or scriptural co-optation, this return capitalizes on the differential space of the interval between idioms. It figures 'a metonymic displacement [that] opens the play of vertiginous shifts that, from one language to another, endlessly refer to a "spacing" that does not *legitimately* belong to either language'.[22]

In this irreducible space, a dissident form of identity coalesces through an '*exercice d'altérité cosmopolite*'[23] ['*exercise in cosmopolitan alterity*'] by which Khatibi designates an investment in otherness committed to 'parcourir des différences'[24] ['moving across differences']. This multi-directional connection to the world belies the rigid dichotomies of colonialism and privileges in their place a dialogue with *tout-autre* imaginaries – for instance, through the experience of alterity encapsulated in the use of the Spanish verb *vacilar* (to vacillate) culled from one of Khatibi's visits to Caracas:

> Chaque fois que je le prononçais au bon moment, j'avais l'impression qu'une joie se dégageait de son aura et irrésistiblement, j'aimais cette langue, ce peuple, ces voyages [...] chaque fois que je découvre l'autre en moi, l'autre séjournant dans mon esprit, dans mon corps.[25]

> [Every time that I pronounced it at the right time, I felt as if a joyfulness emanated from its aura and, irresistibly, I loved this language, this people, these journeys [...] every time that I discover the other in me, the other sojourning within my mind, within my body.]

20 Khatibi, 'Diglossia', p. 158.
21 Khatibi, *Figures de l'étranger*, p. 205.
22 Bensmaïa, 'Multilingualism', p. 169.
23 Khatibi, *Figures de l'étranger*, p. 211.
24 Ibid.
25 Ibid., pp. 211–12.

This dissident, dialogical idiom, inclusive of alterity, draws inspiration from the very semantics of Khatibi's Spanish detour – it stages a vacillation of identity, a fundamental instability that opens writing up to cross-cultural influences and linguistic polyphony. Yet this imaginative journey also expands into the realm of memory. It calls for a 'réappro-bation de cette mémoire, de cette pluralité'[26] ['reacceptance of this memory, this plurality'] that holds ground against the more pervasive forces of exclusion and delineates an *other-history*, a detour via other ordering narratives.

Drawing from the fluctuation of the Mediterranean as critical method, this chapter extends the purview of Khatibi's critique of any stable concept of origins to include other moments of trans-Mediterranean contact between the Maghreb and Europe – moments preceding the watershed of the European conquest and projecting the Maghreb towards its Western other along non-dichotomous lines. Khatibi has written that his core concept of *bi-langue* functions as a means to 'enter into the telling of forgetting and of anamnesia. [...] "I am an/other" i[s] an idiom that I owe it to myself to invent'.[27] Here, then, *bi-langue* concerns itself with probing the forgetting of another idiom, one incommensurable to the languages in which writing occurs – one ensconced in the multiple 'gaps and ruptures [...] this historical churning between peoples, between civilizations'.[28] This chapter argues that this 'forgotten idiom', born of interculturality, constitutes for the Maghreb an alternative form of memory stretching beyond the trauma of the colonial conquest to resurrect other forms of historical inscription into a long-reaching genealogy of Mediterranean existence. '[T]ak[ing] charge of the active plurality of [the Maghreb's] utterances', as Khatibi enjoins,[29] is but another avenue through which to move beyond *bi-langue*'s ethos of irremediable melancholia and loss, to engage in 'the telling of forgetting and of anamnesia'. For to embrace this loss, to give it expression, is to open the *bi-langue* to the *pluri-langue*, to disseminate it beyond the confines of the colonial relation and the cultures it forced together in the days of empire – to open it up to the anamnestic language of the sea to which ones owes 'l'ordre de la mémoire'[30] ['the order of memory']. The remainder of this essay will thus probe the form that this memorial idiom

---

26 Ibid., p. 210.
27 Khatibi, 'Diglossia', p. 158.
28 Ibid.
29 Ibid.
30 Khatibi, 'Bagatelles', p. 36.

is to take, beyond the comfort of Manichean visions of belonging and being, in the density of the Maghreb's *marge en éveil* – as the point of departure of a transcultural heuristic tethered to the contiguous space of the Mediterranean Sea, here conceived as a new form of 'spacing',[31] which portends the kind of ethical, relational project put forward in Khatibi's later writing.

'Our Common Song as Mediterraneans'

The product of multiple encounters and contacts across the sea, the Mediterranean surges as a slippery concept, deployed along two shorelines bearing the indelible imprimatur of multiple, rippling trauma: 'two worlds then', in Nabile Farès's memorable formula, 'deux; parfaitement vus, identifiés, dont l'un (le second) n'est pas le contraire, ni le miroir de l'autre, mais, l'exacte mesure de la séparation [...] sa frustration'[32] ['two; perfectly seen, identified, one of which (the second one) is not the opposite or the mirror-image of the other, but, the exact measure of its separation [...] its frustration']. Following from this lacunar deployment, the space of the Mediterranean weaves and unweaves identities across the boundless expanse of the sea, in the resounding echo of the water's fundamental indeterminacy, of its washing away of any principled notion of origin or ascription. Both forbidding demarcation and endless connectivity, the maritime space reverberates with the conceptual antinomy of the original *pontos* (Greek for sea and bridge), fluidly alternating between dispersion and concentration, contracting and expanding following the flow of historical events. The modularity of the maritime space proceeds from the sea's singular topography constellating from the Mediterranean's

> trois portes étroites [par lesquelles la mer s'ouvre] sur l'immense et multiple univers; mêlant à Gibraltar ses eaux à celles de l'Ouest atlantique; accueillant avec précaution par le canal de Suez le monde énigmatique et les dieux du Sud et de l'Est; tendant, entre les rives du Bosphore, ce qu'on appelle si joliment 'un bras de mer' vers les dieux, anciens et nouveaux, du Nord et du Nord-Est. Ainsi, par trois portes seulement, la Méditerranée parvient à regarder vers les quatre points cardinaux. Dans cette démarche improbable du trois qui sait être quatre, je veux voir un symbole du destin

31   Bensmaïa, 'Multilingualism', p. 169.
32   Nabile Farès, *Le Miroir de Cordoue* (Paris: L'Harmattan, 1994), p. 39.

singulier de la Méditerranée: où les mesures les plus précises sont faussées par l'intervention du miracle: où l'inspiration qui n'est, au demeurant, que la réponse à l'aspiration, vient faire, à chaque instant, voler en éclats le règne des règles.

[three gates, narrow ones [opening] onto the vast and multiple universe; mingling its waters at Gibraltar with those of the western Atlantic; cautiously greeting via the Suez Canal the enigmatic world and the gods of the South and the East; holding out, between the shores of the Bosphorus, what we so nicely call, in French, 'an arm of the sea', towards the gods, ancient and modern, of the North and the North-East. And so, via three gates only, the Mediterranean manages to look towards the four cardinal points. In this improbable process of three becoming four, I like to see a symbol of the Mediterranean's singular destiny; whereby the most precise measurements are bent through the intervention of the miraculous; whereby inspiration, which is, moreover, but the response to aspiration, comes along to shatter the reign of rules.][33]

In his provocative take on Mediterranean forms of thought, Salah Stétié uncovers the foundational vacillation undergirding the rebellious nature of Mediterranean thinking, a 'hésitation [...] cette réfutation permanente du pour par le contre, du contre par le pour' ['hesitation [...] the permanent refuting of the pros by the cons, the cons by the pros'].[34] Further reflecting on the hypothesis of a distinctive form of Mediterranean thought, Jewish Tunisian author Albert Memmi postulates a Mediterranean form of expression shared by all Mediterraneans: what he calls 'notre chanson commune de Méditerranéens' ['our common song as Mediterraneans'], adding that 'par-delà les accidents et les incidents de l'Histoire, qui nous a cruellement séparés, et fait souffrir les uns et les autres [...] ce sera cette chanson commune qui survivra le plus longtemps et nous donnera notre visage définitif et définitivement fraternel' ['beyond history's accidents and incidents, which have cruelly kept us apart and hurt all of us [...] it will be this common song that will survive the longest and that will give us our definitive face, a definitively fraternal one'].[35] Jacques Derrida's own musings on the forcible amnesia implied in any form

33 Salah Stétié, 'Questions sur un très vieux rivage'. Online. 8 Dec. 2011: http://salahstetie.net/?p=130; 'A Question upon a Very Old Shore'. Online. 10 Apr. 2014: http://salahstetie.net/?p=1007 (accessed 7 May 2018).

34 Stétié, 'Questions', unpag.; 'A Question', unpag.

35 Albert Memmi, *Anthologie des écrivains français du Maghreb* (Paris: Présence africaine, 1969), pp. 20–1.

of monolingualism highlight the plurality layering the dual Franco-Maghrebian identity model. Cautioning against the coercive violence of partisan historical discourse, Derrida writes: '[L]e statut [des juifs dans l'Algérie coloniale ...] on lui donne le titre de "franco-maghrébin" [...] Le silence de ce trait d'union ne pacifie ou n'apaise rien, aucun tourment, aucune torture. Il ne fera jamais taire leur mémoire' ['[The] status [of Jews in colonial Algeria ...] is given the title of "Franco-Maghrebian" [...] The silence of that hyphen does not pacify or appease anything, not a single torment, not a single torture. It will never silence their memory'].[36] One must then conceive of a Mediterranean form of expression which sets as its goal the perpetuation of repressed memory – its unearthing and dissemination against the weft of forced amnesias. For, as Jocelyne Dakhlia argues, in response to Derrida's conception of the monolingualism of the other, 'pour qu'un écrivain maghrébin puisse *jouir* de ce trouble de l'identité, il lui faut symétriquement oublier toutes les langues franques de son histoire'[37] ['for a Maghrebi writer to *benefit* from this identity trouble, he must symmetrically forget all the lingua francas of his history'].

Memmi's premise of a Mediterranean language common to all Mediterraneans on either side of the colonial divide, a language more readily embodied in an everlasting song of memory than in the divisive concatenation of events, rests on solid historical grounding. One such representation of a 'forgotten' Mediterranean idiom may be found in the pre-colonial lingua franca that reigned supreme over the Mediterranean and that Dakhlia's own eminent work has popularized. Made up of borrowings from various Romance languages (Italian, Spanish, Portuguese) as well as Arabic, Turkish and Amazigh languages, the lingua franca appeared in the sixteenth century as a testament to the rich cross-cultural effervescence of the Western region of the sea. The Mediterranean idiom rose to exceptional prominence, ranking third most commonly spoken language after Turkish and Arabic.[38]

---

36 Jacques Derrida, *Le Monolinguisme de l'autre, ou, La Prothèse d'origine* (Paris: Galilée, 1996), pp. 26–7; *The Monolingualism of the Other, or, The Prosthesis of Origin*, trans. Patrick Mensah (Stanford, CA: Stanford University Press, 1998), pp. 10–11.

37 Jocelyne Dakhlia, '"No man's langue": une rétraction coloniale', in Jocelyne Dakhlia (ed.), *Trames de langues: usages et métissages linguistiques dans l'histoire du Maghreb* (Paris: Maisonneuve et Larose, 2004), pp. 259–71 (p. 262).

38 Natividad Planas, 'L'Usage des langues en Méditerranée occidentale à l'époque moderne', in Jocelyne Dakhlia (ed.), *Trames de langues: usages et métissages*

Historically tied to the rise of the corsair cities of Algiers, Tunis and Tripoli, and to increasing mobility throughout the Ottoman Maghreb, the emergence of this hybrid form of speech served the purpose of facilitating communication between slaves of various origins, as well as between Christians, Jews and Muslims, whether they spoke Arabic in various forms, Turkish or Amazigh languages. A reflection of the manifold rivalries and tensions between competing empires, the lingua franca nevertheless reverberates with the polycentrism of the sea. Forming a liminal, shared *no man's langue* (Dakhlia), the lingua franca "par paradoxe, défini[t] la frontière même de l'altérité'[39] ['paradoxically define[s] the very threshold of alterity']. A continuum between two antagonistic regimes, the Mediterranean vernacular nevertheless stays clear of any consensus: it operates as a language of reciprocal exchange rather than a vector of syncretism. In point of fact, the strong dominance within the lingua franca of Romance languages over southern and eastern Mediterranean linguistic systems pre-empted any true linguistic creolization. Thus, the form of bilateralism that it promoted remained beholden to the very geopolitical rivalries animating Mediterranean relations. For that reason, the widespread use of the lingua franca, which came to an end in the middle of the nineteenth century, disproves any retrospective reading of the early modern Mediterranean in terms of a depoliticized, deterritorialized zone of felicitous hybridity. The lingua franca's very inability to foster any durable fusion between parties accentuates the enduring tensions that its very existence helped mitigate. It figures an idiom of openness and cooperation, yet one tributary to a historical context more inclined to brew discord than harmony. In this respect, its many similitudes with the later age of colonial conquests make it a particularly apt model not only to rethink (post)colonial relations between the Maghreb and Europe in our contemporary moment but also to take to task the enduring myths of fixed identities and of the impossibility of living together across cultures and faiths.

Khatibi himself drew inspiration from the lingua franca of yore when debating the issue of linguistic contact and hybridity. In a text reflecting on Derrida's position on monolingualism, Khatibi eases the philosopher's rigid conception of language in a colonial context. To

linguistiques dans l'histoire du Maghreb (Paris: Maisonneuve et Larose, 2004), pp. 241–57.

39 Jocelyne Dakhlia, *Lingua Franca: histoire d'une langue métisse en Méditerranée* (Arles: Actes Sud, 2008), p. 13.

the repressive dominance of French imposed by the colonial regime, Khatibi's inquiry adjoins the usual native corollaries: Arabic (both dialectal and 'la langue savante et liturgique' ['the learned and liturgical language'], which he likens to Hebrew)[40] and Tamazight. Yet, to this familiar enumeration, Khatibi adds older linguistic traditions preceding the French and Spanish conquests of the Maghreb: Turkish and Algeria's Judeo-Arabic. Somewhat apart from those models stands the 'lingua franqua', which, he tells us, is 'un idiome hybride' ['a hybrid idiom'], in tension with 'ce français dialectal d'Algérie'[41] ['this French Algerian dialect']. Drawing on linguist André Lanly's *Le Français d'Afrique du nord*, Khatibi establishes the latter as a mostly French-based pidgin that incorporated lexical units from local varieties of Arabic or Romance languages brought to the Maghreb by the Europeans, echoing through this composition well-known *pataouète*, the composite working-class dialect of colonial Algiers.[42] Khatibi distinguishes this vernacular from the 'lingua franqua' that historically preceded it – a language made up of 'mots italiens, espagnols et provençaux' ['Italian, Spanish and Provencal words'] and, according to Lanly, reserved exclusively for trade relations.[43] Khatibi does not provide much additional insight into either hybrid dialect other than to establish a transhistorical continuum between the two linguistic moments. Yet, as a methodological gesture, aligning the lingua franca of the early modern Mediterranean with its colonial successor performs several important critical moves.

First, it lays emphasis on the fundamental, historical hybridity of Maghrebian culture as the product of linguistic syncretism, both before and *during* the colonial period. By so doing, it positions the lingua franca to complicate dominant political assumptions regarding the dialectic of language and power in the colonial period. Here is an amalgamated form of expression that, though it does not do away with the existing tensions between colonizers and colonized, offers the alternative option of a language free from any exclusive identitarian

40   Abdelkébir Khatibi, 'Le Point de non-retour', in *Le Passage des frontières: autour du travail de Jacques Derrida*, Colloque de Cerisy (Paris: Galilée, 1994), pp. 445–9 (p. 448).
41   Ibid., p. 448.
42   See Roland Bacri, *Trésors des racines pataouètes* (Paris: Belin, 1983); Musette [Auguste Robinet], *Cagayous, ses meilleures histoires: introduction, notes et lexique par Gabriel Audisio* (Paris: Gallimard, 1931).
43   Khatibi, 'Le Point de non-retour', p. 448.

claims. Dakhlia proposes that Maghrebian forms of Arabic have long contained Romanic linguistic elements, whose incorporation pre-dated the European colonial conquests. Furthermore, as Dakhlia suggests and Khatibi himself emphasizes while citing Lanly in his consideration of lingua franca, 'cette langue [...] n'est revendiquée [par personne ...]. Les musulmans, à la parler, croiraient parler la langue des chrétiens, et les chrétiens, réciproquement, imagineraient parler la langue d'échange des musulmans'[44] ['this language [...] is not reclaimed [by anybody ...]. The Muslims, by speaking it, believe that they are speaking the language of the Christians, and the Christians, reciprocally, imagine that they are speaking the language through which the Muslims communicate']. This other-language is remarkable for its fundamental hospitality. It mediates a move towards the other through what one assumes in good faith to be a genuine form of his language, favouring conciliation over antagonism. Rehabilitating the enduring, historical dominance of the lingua franca thus subtly disengages the Maghreb from the straitjacket of binary colonial perspectives. It testifies to the existence of irrefutable transnational and plurilingual Maghrebian cultural forms that rest on the ferment of Mediterranean 'connectivity'[45] while amending any polarizing definition of the North African past under the aegis of Arab identity, Islam or its exclusive relation to France.

Second, Khatibi's perspective brings a nuanced corrective to Derrida's own musings on the acquisition of French as a prohibitive development. Against the idea of a cultural and linguistic ablation, Khatibi highlights the productive otherness to itself (*le tout-autre*) implied in the process of writing in a language carrying within itself the residue of another, repressed idiom. When posing his resonant question, 'quelle perte ou quel deuil du temps passé est-il laissé pour compte dans la Langue de l'autre?'[46] ['What loss or what mourning of the past is left aside in the other's Language?'], the philosopher intimates that this 'spacing' between languages directly engages the leftover traces of the traumatic, forced oblivion of alternative histories, pushing them back to the surface. Through the 'résistance inassimilable' ['unassimilable resistance'] it generates, this 'violence hospitalière' ['hospitable violence'] of the other's language functions as a revealing agent, delineating through its repression

44 Dakhlia, 'No man's langue', p. 265.
45 Peregrine Horden and Nicholas Purcell, *The Corrupting Sea: A Study of Mediterranean History* (Oxford: Wiley Blackwell, 2000).
46 Khatibi, 'Le Point de non-retour', p. 449.

the very contours of the realm of trauma.[47] Khatibi's 'partage' [sharing], instead, makes a tabula rasa of enduring resentment against the former colonial power, a sentiment which Khatibi sees as producing endless and eventually self-destructive mourning. Recognizing the potential of this passage through the other's language, then, advantageously deploys a regenerative memorial process that uncovers the entanglements and rich detours of the Maghreb's complex past with an eye towards the resolution of trauma.

Towards a Mediterranean Poetics of the 'Common Language'

Khatibi, like Memmi before him, poses the hypothesis of a 'common language', one that would remain distinct from the *bi-langue* and that the two lovers from *Love in Two Languages* would share: 'Peut-être aimait-il en elle deux femmes, celle qui vivait dans leur langue commune, et l'autre, cette autre qu'il habitait dans la bilangue' ['Perhaps he loved two women in her, the one who inhabited their common language and another as well, the one who inhabited the *bi-langue*'].[48] As he explains in *Maghreb pluriel,* Maghrebian literature is rooted in the realm of the untranslatable, which lies beyond binary inscriptions, for every language aspires to this condition of impenetrability, 'singulière, irréductible, rigoureusement autre' ['singular, irreducible and rigorously other'].[49] From this opacity surges the plurilingual layering of the Maghreb's literary idiom, which leads Khatibi to the groundbreaking pronouncement that 'cette literature maghrébine dite d'expressions française est un récit de traduction. Je ne dis pas qu'elle n'est que traduction, je précise qu'il s'agit d'un récit *qui parle en langues*' ['all this Maghrebi literature of French expression as they call it is a narrative of translation. I am not saying that it is only translation; I am pointing out that it is a narrative that *speaks in tongues*'].[50] Resonating with Dakhlia's discussion of the multiple lingua francas lurking beneath the surface

---

47   Ibid.
48   Abdelkébir Khatibi, *Amour bilingue* (Montpellier: Fata Morgana, 1983), reprinted in *Œuvres de Abdelkébir Khatibi I: Romans et récits* (Paris: La Différence, 2008), pp. 205–83 (p. 219); Abdelkébir Khatibi, *Love in Two Languages*, trans. Richard Howard (Minneapolis: University of Minnesota Press, 1990), p. 20.
49   Khatibi, *Maghreb pluriel*, p. 186; *Plural Maghreb*, p. 122.
50   Ibid., p. 186; pp. 122–3.

of monolingualism, these repressed 'tongues' animate any writing in French, populating its depth with the muffled echoes of past moments of plurilingualism. Against this inaudible linguistic ferment emerges the *indicible*, the unsayable, towards which the foreign woman endlessly entices the lover. Celine Piser conceives of the *indicible* as 'the meeting of two languages and two cultures that cannot be articulated'.[51] This ineffability doubles as a source of pain: 'cette souffrance de l'indicible. Chaque jour s'écrivait une blessure, chaque jour, de l'irréparable' ['this suffering of the unsayable. Every day a wound was written, every day, something irreparable'].[52] By contrast, the 'common language' shines on as an idiom of true sharing, one that a binary structure of thought tethered to colonial dichotomies finds itself unable to fathom, let alone express. The bilingualism induced by colonialism dons the shape of a rapt. By contrast, the 'common language' emphasizes shared ground under the guise of a 'trans-Mediterranean'[53] identity deployed transnationally on either shore of the Mediterranean Sea, on either side of the French/Maghrebian divide. Yet, for Piser, it rests on a hierarchically layered identity, since the 'common' language uniting the two lovers is in fact French, the colonial language: 'Que désirait-il? Qu'elle fût cet abîme entre lui et lui, dans leur langue commune? Lui demandait-il l'impossible?' ['What was it that he wanted? That she should be this abyss between him and himself, in their common language? Was he asking the impossible of her?'].[54] In the depth of the abyss, the utopian desire for a non-hierarchical, heterogeneous linguistic substrate vacillates, in Piser's eyes showing the limits of Khatibi's 'Mediterraneanism' as it unfolds in *Love in Two Languages*: its 'failure' and 'violence',[55] as it ultimately adds up to little more than a mere 'subversive echo of the colonial silence of Arabic'.[56] In many ways, Piser's binary reading construes Khatibi's definition of *bi-langue* in terms of 'the space between two exteriorities'[57] as a lacuna, a deficiency thematizing the inextricable dominance of French over Arabic. By contrast, I choose to see in this caesura a space of

---

51   Celine Piser, 'Silent Multilingualism: Language Politics in the Mediterranean', *Critical Multilingualism* 5.2 (2017), pp. 64–86 (p. 75).
52   Khatibi, *Amour Bilingue*, p. 238; *Love in Two Languages*, p. 49.
53   Piser, 'Silent Multilingualism', p. 72.
54   Khatibi, *Amour Bilingue*, p. 219; *Love in Two Languages*, p. 20.
55   Piser, 'Silent Multilingualism', p. 84.
56   Ibid., p. 78.
57   Khatibi, 'Diglossia', p. 158.

interlangue, a site displaying enduring modes of expression incommensurable to the individual languages involved in the colonial encounter and their play for dominance. It is a space of trauma and suffering, but also a space from which to displace the history of colonialism as the most meaningful framing of postcolonial Maghrebian identity. I thus read the yearning for a 'common language' steeped in the rich humus of Mediterranean diversity as an urging to excavate further-reaching genealogies of trauma that reveal a *longue durée* sense of Maghrebian identity – most notably through the anamnesis of another foundational moment of intercultural contact between the Maghreb and the West in a Mediterranean framework: al-Andalus.

For Khatibi, this rerouting of identity narratives along the axes of memory and loss is typified in the Maghrebian relation to the trope of Spain. In 'Au-delà du trauma', an allocution delivered at a literary gathering in the small Andalusian town of Ronda, Spain towers as the epitome of the Andalusian moment of *convivencia*, which united the three monotheistic religions in its embrace. The object of a novel amorous heuristics extending beyond the bilingual, binary relationship to the French lover in *Love in Two Languages* ('cette duplicité, ou plutôt cette multiplicité d'histoires, de cultures et de langues...secret qui ne se donne qu'à celui qui le déchiffre en l'aimant' ['this duplicity, or rather this multiplicity of histories, cultures and languages ... a secret that is only revealed to he who deciphers it through love']),[58] Spain materializes as the Maghreb's alter ego. It figures 'une expérience d'écriture [...] et de pensée'[59] ['a writing [...] and thinking experience'] for the Maghrebian writer separated from his Andalusian counterpart by the original trauma besmirching the Maghreb's self-consciousness well ahead of the European colonial conquests: the Andalusian *Reconquista* by the Catholic Kings. The text postulates a mode of writing able to delve into the aftermath of this originary traumatic rupture, not in the vain hope of restoring the famed 'lost paradise' of al-Andalus but rather in an effort to locate 'la force de l'inoublié entre Arabes et Espagnols'[60] ['the power of the unforgotten between the Arabs and the Spanish'] in its most indelible, if subtle, traces. Embarking on his commemorative journey in search of 'le chant de l'inoublié et de l'inoubliable' ['the song of the

---

58   Abdelkébir Khatibi, 'Au-delà du trauma', in *Par-dessus l'épaule* (Paris: Aubier, 1988), pp. 123–35 (p. 126).
59   Ibid., p. 124.
60   Ibid., p. 125.

unforgotten and the unforgettable'], Khatibi concludes that 'l'Espagne est un autre nom de la passion de ce souvenir' ['Spain is but another name for the passion for this rememoration'].[61] The trenchant awareness of Arab culture's traumatic truncation from its Spanish counterpart lies at the core of Khatibi's post-traumatic liturgy – an evocation of Spain both as a throbbing phantom limb, in an echo of Derrida's linguistic amputation, and as a contemporary space through which to enter a form of global modernity beyond the colonial relationship to France. As 'une expérience esthétique' ['aesthetic experience'],[62] the search for Spain sheds light on the irrefutable alterity at the heart of Arab culture from the days when Islamic civilization reigned over the Western Mediterranean: 'Cette Espagne historique a appris aux Arabes à se mesurer à l'autre, à le connaître et à le méconnaître dans le même geste d'appropriation et d'expropriation'[63] ['This historical Spain has taught the Arabs to pit themselves against the Other, to know him and misjudge him in the same gesture of appropriation and expropriation']. From this embedded history surges a new form of 'spacing'. In the context of the Maghreb's embedded history with Spain, this distantiation takes the form of an ontological estrangement, an *étrangeté* intrinsic to the sense of exile stemming from the expulsion from Spain: 'Nous revenons à un passé encore vivant, à une part exilée de nous-mêmes, à l'étrangeté de notre passé'[64] ['We return to a past that is still alive, to an exiled part of ourselves, to the strangeness of our past']. Identity – here the commensurability to one's deep self – crystallizes as an assimilation of this strangeness, as a 'réconcili[ation] avec ... *notre cœur étranger de ce pays*' ['reconciliation with [...] *our foreign heart in this country*'].[65] The space of Spain becomes coextensive with the constitutive absence which it comes to reflect. Only by restoring this missing alter ego can the writer rend baneful melancholia asunder (Khatibi alludes to 'l'être endeuillé' ['the mourning self']).

Building on the proposition developed in *Maghreb pluriel* that endless, blind resentment against alterity can only lead to an atrophied sense of identity, Khatibi encourages a radical reconceptualization of the Maghreb's relation to the West through a triangulation of desire

61 Ibid., pp. 125–6.
62 Ibid., p. 127.
63 Ibid.
64 Ibid.
65 Ibid., p. 128.

uniting Morocco, France and Spain in a cross-Mediterranean '*chaînon indestructible de filiation symbolique*'[66] ['*indestructible chain of symbolic filiation*']. This militant poetic gesture dissipates the intrinsic limitations of any outlook bearing the mark of trauma. In its place, it reactivates an ethos of encounter through

> une écriture de la géo-politique, qui romprait avec la vision folklorique et la complainte mélancolique, une écriture qui rendrait compte de sa profondeur mythologique, qui est à l'arrière-fond de notre être commun, comme si cette rencontre devait se réécrire sur les pages d'un palimpseste – ainsi qu'une lettre en souffrance'[67]

> [a geopolitical form of writing that would break with the folkloric vision and the melancholy complaint, a form of writing that would let its deep mythological foundation, which underpins our common being, shine through, as if this encounter was to be written anew on the pages of a palimpsest – like an overdue letter.]

By playfully resemanticizing the suffering of the *lettre en souffrance* though the phrase's idiomatic acception as an unclaimed or delayed missive, Khatibi de-emphasizes the debilitating grief obstructing any positive engagement with the other. As impossibility morphs into simple postponement, a 'récit intercontinental et interscripturaire' ['intercontinental and interscriptural narrative'] comes to life which delineates the Maghreb's newfound inscription into the world: 'L'Espagne est une question d'écriture … l'Espagne ne s'appartient pas, elle n'appartient à personne, elle est cet ailleurs où l'expérience de vivre, de mourir et de survivre au-delà du trauma, nous contraint à entrer dans la mondialisation du récit moderne'[68] ['Spain is a matter of writing … it isn't self-possessed, it isn't possessed by anybody, it is this other space where the experience of living, of dying, and of surviving beyond trauma compels us to enter the worlding of modern narrative'.] The triangulation of the Maghreb's relation to the West through this Spanish detour aligns Khatibi's conception with what Jane Hiddleston has quipped 'a universal conception of relationality and ethical exchange within and between all languages'.[69] A laboratory for intercultural contact, al-Andalus redraws

---

66   Ibid., p. 132.
67   Ibid.
68   Ibid., p. 134.
69   Jane Hiddleston, *Understanding Postcolonialism* (Oxford: Routledge, 2014 [2009]), p. 133.

identity as relational exteriority, as a form of *métissage* of which both Spain and the Maghreb have been the rightful heirs.

In a well-known missive to Egyptian writer Jacques Hassoun, Khatibi evokes the common destiny of Spain and the Arab world: 'Le romancier Goytisolo propose la notion de *"mudéjar"* pour désigner ce métissage culturel *actuel* entre l'hispanité et l'arabité'[70] ['The novelist Goytisolo proposes the notion of *"mudéjar"* to designate this *current* cultural hybridity between Spanish and Arab identities']. This ongoing mixing is conceived as the product of deep-time interaction lasting to this day and revealing the self as foundationally other, recognizing the stranger within: 'faire intervenir l'autre dans son écriture comme un élément intérieur de son corps propre'[71] ['to let the other interfere in one's own writing like an entity intrinsic to one's body']. This writing experience moves beyond objectifying exoticism. It stands closer in fact to the model of interculturality championed by Victor Segalen, who, to Khatibi, was the first to 'ouv[rir] la voie à une esthétique de l'étranger [...] dans sa différence irréductible'[72] ['clear the path for an aesthetics of the stranger [...] in his irreducible difference']. This interest in non-hierarchical interaction is reminiscent of the much-desired 'common language' of encounter fruitlessly pursued in *Love in Two Languages*. Through the mediation of Mediterranean cultural *mudéjar*, the Maghreb's historical destiny of plurality and mixing resurfaces, liberating the creative potential of its unfettered memory: 'Il faudrait réveiller la mémoire au tracé de ses refoulements, de ses points aveugles, de ses passions endormies'[73] ['Memory should be awakened along the lines of its repressions, its blind spots, its slumbering passions']. If Spain 'fait émerger la force de la mémoire' ['drives the force of memory to the surface'], this engagement takes the form of a 'return': 'Étrange impression de *revenir* en Espagne. En tant que Marocain, j'y reviens dans une intersection de deux chiasmes [...] traumatiques. L'un, celui de la défaite arabe [...]; et l'autre, le colonial'[74] ['The strange impression of *returning* to Spain. As a Moroccan, I return to it in the intersection between two [...] traumatic chiasmi. One is that of the Arab defeat [...] and the other, the

70 Abdelkébir Khatibi and Jacques Hassoun, *Le Même Livre* (Paris: Editions de l'éclat, 1985), p. 94 (my emphasis).

71 Ibid.

72 Ibid., p. 95.

73 Khatibi, *Le Scribe et son ombre*, p. 44.

74 Khatibi and Hassoun, *Le Même Livre*, p. 95.

colonial one']. From the transformation of 'the irremediable' colonial conquest into writing surges the ability to move beyond trauma: 'l'incisif d'une phrase qui doit accueillir la décomposition et l'humiliation pour témoigner au-delà du trauma'[75] ['the incisiveness of a sentence that must welcome the decomposition and the humiliation to testify beyond trauma']. In this appeased form of memory writing, the mediation of the Mediterranean lingers, restructuring the space of the *interlangue* as a space of encounter and mutual definition. 'All language, for Khatibi, contains traces of other languages, and, like Levinas's discourse, it is a site for encounter across differences, although its proper understanding does not allow the reduction of difference to the same', writes Jane Hiddleston.[76] This testimonial language beyond trauma could well be the 'common language' to all Mediterraneans that both Memmi and Khatibi called for in their musings. In his essay 'Paradigmes de civilisation', Khatibi explicitly links this *métissage* to the Mediterranean as civilization: 'nous sommes aujourd'hui au Maroc devant une civilisation dont on ne peut nier ni l'identité, ni la permanence, ni la singularité, ni le brassage. Elle est appelée à jouer son rôle dans la nouvelle Méditerranée'[77] ['today in Morocco we are witnessing a civilization whose identity, permanence, singularity, and mixing are undeniable. It is destined to play its full role in the new Mediterranean']. What Khatibi means by this 'new Mediterranean' formula is the 'ajustement des cultures riveraines et de leurs valeurs de civilisation à l'actuelle configuration géostratégique, régionale et mondiale'[78] ['adjustment of the neighbouring cultures and of their civilizing values to the current regional and worldwide geostrategic configuration']. This 'dispositif à faire de la civilisation' ['civilization-making apparatus'], following French poet Paul Valéry's metaphor for the Mediterranean, contains the germs of a more promising future for a Morocco going through 'ever greater Westernization' ('Le Maroc continue à s'occidentaliser') while attempting not to lose its roots.[79] Its participation in this expanding civilization is a function of its *brassage*, of its ability to invent for itself a 'langue "hétérologique", un "ramassis" de différences, dont le brassage ébranlera un peu la

75   Ibid.
76   Hiddleston, *Understanding Postcolonialism*, p. 133.
77   Abdelkébir Khatibi, 'Paradigmes de civilisation', in *L'Œuvre de … Abdelkébir Khatibi* (Rabat: Marsam, 1997), pp. 69–87 (p. 86).
78   Ibid., p. 86.
79   Ibid., pp. 86–7.

compacité terrible [...] de l'*égo* occidental'[80] ['"heterological" language, an "amalgam" of differences whose mixing will somewhat shake the terrible compactness [...] of the Western *ego*']. It has been this chapter's argument that Khatibi's restored Mediterranean idiom has been a precise incarnation of this 'heterological' language, whose reclaiming constitutes the first step towards implementing the civilizing mission ingrained in this 'new Mediterranean' – a crucial political project to dismantle ever-increasing global hierarchies and inequities.

80 Roland Barthes, 'Ce que je dois à Khatibi', in *L'Œuvre de ... Abdelkébir Khatibi* (Rabat: Marsam, 1997), pp. 121–3 (p. 123).

CHAPTER FOUR

Abdelkébir Khatibi and the Transparency of Language

Assia Belhabib
Translated from the French by *Jane Hiddleston*

Si je ne rêve pas une langue qui jaillisse et sourde de mon chant intérieur lui-même en alternance entre le réel et l'imaginaire, si cette question d'écriture n'est pas respectée, il n'y aura pas de moment exotique, pas de rencontre avec le pays exotique rêvé.

[If I do not dream of a language which rises up and emerges from my own inner song between the real and the imaginary, if this question of writing is not respected, there will be no exotic moment, no meeting with the exotic country I dream of.]

Abdelkébir Khatibi[1]

C'est d'avoir une langue qui est constitutif de notre humanité, non d'avoir telle langue.

[It is having a language that defines our humanity, not having a particular language.]

Tzvetan Todorov[2]

In the twenty-first century, transparency has become a requirement. Everything is expected to be transparent: the funding of electoral

---

1   Abdelkébir Khatibi, *Figures de l'étranger dans la littérature française* (Paris: Denoël, 1987), p. 37.
2   Tzvetan Todorov, *L'Homme dépaysé* (Paris: Editions du Seuil, 1996), p. 22.

campaigns, the success of the candidates, the management of businesses, individual financial status. But what justifies this demand for transparency? Modern society, which is going through many transformations, is determined by market value. In this situation where writing is threatened by extinction, what place is given to the writer? Having lived for a long time alongside the cinema, will the writer have to become a scriptwriter, a scribe of the image, in order to survive?

The way in which different parts of the social body touch, intersect, remain unaware of, or even repel each other, is something that undeniably interests the Moroccan poet, novelist, dramatist and essayist Abdelkébir Khatibi. Throughout his life, he repeatedly renewed his experience of reality. Crossing the borders between disciplines, his books, which have been translated into more than ten languages, express a search for a space and a language which tirelessly untie and knit together the link between the self, the other and the world. His death on 16 March 2009 marks the closure of a work which is now a part of world heritage and whose questioning does not cease to speak to its readers.

His essays *Maghreb pluriel*, *Du bilinguisme* and *Chemins de traverse*, as well as his dialogues with Jacques Derrida, Roland Barthes, Jacques Hassoun and Rita El Khayat, subtly dissect human relationships and the links between societies, which cannot be conceived independently from relationships with groups. Playing with words in a virtuoso performance, Khatibi reveals the importance of language in the formation of social barriers.

The Mercantilization of Art

The great venture bequeathed by the West is that of having subjected everything to the demands of the market. Even art is not spared. It proliferates in all different forms of expression. Yet while discourse about art is becoming more generalized, the concept of art is becoming insipid. Where has its ability to deny the real gone? What has its illusory force become? Art – as a symbolic contract distinct from culture, as an infinite production of signs, a recycling of past and present forms – has been deformed, and has lost its power to provoke judgement or pleasure. It is reduced to a stage of ultra-rapid circulation that leads to exchange at all costs. The lure of gain governs the art world and accentuates its mercantile aspect. Jean Baudrillard explains in *La Transparence du Mal*:

Derrière tout le mouvement convulsif de l'art contemporain, il y a une sorte d'inertie, quelque chose qui n'arrive plus à se dépasser et qui tourne sur lui-même dans une récurrence de plus en plus rapide [...]. Au fond, dans le désordre actuel de l'art, on pourrait lire une rupture du code secret de l'esthétique, comme dans certains désordres biologiques on peut lire une rupture du code génétique.

[Behind the whole convulsive movement of modern art lies a kind of inertia, something that can no longer transcend itself and has therefore turned in upon itself, merely repeating itself at a faster and faster rate [...]. Just as some biological disorders indicate a break in the genetic code, so the present disorder in art may be interpreted as a fundamental break in the secret code of aesthetics.][3]

Contemporary society has produced a generalized aestheticization in that it has liberated forms, colours and artistic concepts by means of a process of cultural internationalization. Entrenched in a utopian form, art migrates into the media, into information technology and more broadly into what we now call 'techno-science'. As a cosmopolitan staging which gives semiological organization over to the materialism of the market, art paradoxically 'democratizes' itself: the most marginal, the most banal, the most trivial and the most obscene reveals itself as a work of art. Everything is said, everything is shown, everything is formed by signs. It is less the added value of the object of exchange that functions in this system than the added aesthetic value of the sign. Whilst people willingly speak of the dematerialization of art in all its forms of expression (minimalist art, conceptual art, ephemeral art, anti-art), and today's is an aesthetics of transparency, in reality it is aesthetics that everywhere makes itself material in operational form. This is why art must make itself minimalist, must play out its own disappearance. This is what it has set out to bring about for more than a century, by doubling itself, by simulating its own negation, by progressively effacing itself to leave space for the image, in its triumph.

In his short book *Civilisation de l'intersigne*, Khatibi asks: 'sur quoi se développera cette culture mondiale? Sur la techno-science au service du divertissement, une sorte de culture de l'intersigne où l'image, le son, la lettre et le chiffre sont le prolongement magique de nos illusions'

3   Jean Baudrillard, *La Transparence du Mal: essai sur les phénomènes extrêmes* (Paris: Galilée, 1990), p. 23; Jean Baudrillard, *The Transparency of Evil: Essays on Extreme Phenomena*, trans. James Benedict (London and New York: Verso, 1993), p. 15.

['from what will this world culture develop? From techno-science in the service of entertainment, a sort of culture of the intersign where image, sound, words and figures are the magic extension of our illusions'].[4] In a culture of eclectic pleasures, of the creation of images without traces, contemporary production reveals everything and nothing. The plastic arts, painting, the audio-visual, advertisements, and computer-generated imagery are only the consequence of something that has disappeared, something that exists only by effacing itself.

Khatibi explains, 'nous sommes en devenir par la pensée dans la mesure où la modernité est invention du futur' ['we evolve through thought to the extent that modernity is an invention of the future'].[5] Two of his fictional works in particular illustrate the course of this galloping technology: *Un été à Stockholm* and *Féerie d'un mutant*. The first of these emphasizes the reign of the image as the new power of cinema, photography and the apparatus of simultaneous translation. He writes, 'j'étais assis près de la fenêtre, distrait par le va-et-vient des survenants et des partants. Lorsqu'ils étaient dans le premier état, ils disaient *Hej!* (Salut!) et: *Hej då!* (Au revoir!) dans le second, si bien que ces seuls deux mots avaient, pour mon oreille dépaysée, la résonance d'un premier chant' ['I was sitting next to the window, distracted by the coming and going of those arriving and leaving. Those arriving would say "Hej!" (Hi!) and those leaving would say "Hej da!" (Goodbye!) so that just these two words seemed for my unaccustomed ear to resonate like a first song'].[6] The second fictional work depicts Earth entirely given over to cloning and teleportation. During this period of globalization, Khatibi interrogates again our *being* in order to understand better the foundations of its evolution at a time when the laws of hospitality and sharing are also undergoing changes. Visionary, and profoundly optimistic, the author conceives this narrative as a hymn to the proximity of *being*: 'il [Med] sentit ensuite – au bout de ses doigts – une calligraphie sur peau de gazelle, diacritisée en points rouges. Saisi par le glissement du toucher sur la matière sensible du Livre qui s'ouvrit en forme d'éventail, il baissa

4 Abdelkébir Khatibi, 'Civilisation de l'intersigne', Conference presented at the Université de Rennes, 6 Apr. 1995 and at Berkeley, University of California, 14 Apr. 1995 (Rabat: Dossiers Ouverts, 1996), p. 7.

5 Ibid., p. 5.

6 Abdelkébir Khatibi, *Un été à Stockholm* (Paris: Flammarion, 1990), reprinted in *Œuvres de Abdelkébir Khatibi I: Romans et récits* (Paris: La Différence, 2008), pp. 285–379 (p. 299).

ses yeux et pointa son index sur cette devise: *Cultive l'art d'inventer la vie*. Devise qui s'effaça derrière une autre: *Adhère à ta nature créative*' ['he [Med] then felt at the end of his fingers a calligraphy as if on the skin of a gazelle, with diacritics marked in red. Compelled by the soft feel of the material of the Book which was open like a fan, he lowered his eyes and pointed his finger on this motto: *Cultivate art and invent life*. It was a motto that was hidden behind another: *Be faithful to your creative nature*'].[7]

A frenzy of communication has taken hold of the planet. Humanity finds itself propelled into an area where time and space are contracted and where every vague hope to escape is definitively compromised. Mobile phones, social networks, wireless connection and localization by satellite are technologies that create a mesh of all kinds of links from which it is more and more difficult to escape. When properly mastered, these means of communication can enrich both professional and private human relationships by maintaining links despite time differences and distances. We are permanently plunged today in a pool of Hertzian waves which transmit voices, sounds, photos and videos at the speed of light. The diffusion of information from any part of the world has become almost instantaneous.

Philosophers agree on the need for us to learn a new way to manage time and our relations with others. The future is projected into the image of our expectations and into our dream of time. The dream of art and culture is prolonged in an alert mode of thought that battles against the unknown. The construction of new objects and participation in the civilization of the world require a fictional knowledge and an imaginative power. The twenty-first century appears as a decisive stage in the history of humanity.

The Place of Literature in the Globalization of Culture

In the race for technological and financial performance, literature occupies a controversial place, and many voices demand what end it serves. It is for nothing, and this nothing is indispensable. Of course, it fuels authors, editors, critics and everyone in that small world that lives

---

7 Abdelkébir Khatibi, *Féerie d'un mutant* (Monaco: Editions du Rocher, 2005), reprinted in *Œuvres de Abdelkébir Khatibi I: Romans et récits*, pp. 673–711 (p. 704).

off the book market. But literature cannot be reduced to the economy of letters; it resides in the gap between history and form. Or at once in history and in form and in the absence of history. It is in the unsayable, in the play of language, in sensibility, in each author's imaginary. Literature is a form of creation, a pleasure, an opening onto the world. Is it not at the same time a transgression of borders? Even when it expresses a particularity and is tightly linked to a land or an epoch, is literature not above all universal? The universal truth of literature does not reside in its precision, nor in its clarity, nor in its beauty, but in all of these at the same time: it is in its emotion.

Of all genres, the novel is the one that lends itself the least to transparency. The novel is a space of free fiction adopted by its author. As a result, the novel displays the sensitive and necessarily subjective aspect of truth that the reader must decode through the palimpsest of his or her own personal references. With its profusion and scope (not necessarily the number of pages), the novel gains in density what it loses in clarity. When Khatibi published *Le Livre du sang* in 1979, he was already famous as a result of the interest he shows in fundamental questions of art and culture from a general point of view.[8] The essence of his thinking is clear; what is striking, by contrast, is the diversity of genres that he has drawn on since then. None of them seems to become a privileged form of expression. Autobiographical narrative, the essay, theatre, poetry or the novel translate a certain intellectual necessity – to the extent that a given genre is better suited to the demands of a particular question – rather than the supremacy of a given artistic genre. Theoretical reflection counts above all, and artistic expression is significant only insofar as it contributes to giving it a form. Man's creative power is, as Nietzsche reminds us, fully realized in his intelligence, his sensibility and instinct.

It is not necessary to tackle the fundamental question of the complex notion of the novel, which is ancillary to the main argument here. If the texts by Khatibi designated as 'novels' only partially fit in with the classic definition of the novel as a 'récit d'une histoire fictive' ['the narrative of a fictional story'], it is precisely because these three aspects do not enjoy a particular pertinence in his writing.[9] The narrative is often eclipsed in favour of theoretical commentary, the story has no real consistency – it

---

8   Abdelkébir Khatibi, *Le Livre du sang* (Paris: Gallimard, 1979), reprinted in *Œuvres de Abdelkébir Khatibi I: Romans et récits*, pp. 115–204.

9   Roland Bourneuf and Réal Ouellet, *L'Univers du roman* (Paris: Presses universitaires de France, 1981), p. 26.

is reduced to various scattered events and fiction appears above all as a parable to illustrate the work's reflection on a set of preoccupations. In *Amour bilingue*, for example, Khatibi weaves together a patchwork of discourses around the metaphor of the double. Linking together the cyclical structure of the plant world with scenes of the human world, the narrative unfolds through the metaphor of the 'bi-langue', which becomes the intimate song resonating through the epic. It offers an existential hypothesis: 'il pensait au soleil, et déjà son nom, celui de la lune s'inversent – du féminin au masculin – dans sa double langue. Inversion qui fait tourner les mots avec constellations, pour une étrange attraction de l'univers' ['he thought of the sun and even in doing so its name, that of the moon, inverted itself – from feminine to masculine – in his double language. Inversion which makes words wheel with the constellations, making for a strange attraction of the universe'].[10] Between narration and reflection, the text develops under the hold of the foreign language, 'plus [beau]' ['more beautiful'] and yet 'plus terrible pour un étranger' ['more terrible, for a foreigner'].[11] Language and self-knowledge are imagined as a result of a view of the world as a multitude of associated forces. Pleasure, seduction, but also rebellion. The alterity of language, alterity communicated through language is not only an immediate, irreducible presence but a true alterity, one that is represented and recognized as such by a form of writing whose trembling and deceptive nature (to use Barthes's terms) demonstrate that it refuses to announce that alterity fully or to fix it in a rigid language that would necessarily destroy it.

Khatibi's work shows that by transgressing entrenched dualities it becomes possible to keep hold of a new linguistic space. It is only in this way that language can open itself up in multiple ways. The 'bi-langue' should not be confused with bilingualism. It is rather a sort of third language, between French and Arabic, which results from their relationship with the abyss and their confrontation within the same being. 'La bi-langue? Ma chance, mon gouffre individuel, et ma belle énergie d'amnésie. Energie que je ne sens pas, c'est bien curieux, comme une déficience; mais elle serait ma troisième oreille' ['*Bi-langue*?

---

10   Abdelkébir Khatibi, *Amour bilingue* (Paris: Fata Morgana, 1983), reprinted in *Œuvres de Abdelkébir Khatibi I: Romans et récits*, pp. 205–83 (p. 208); *Love in Two Languages*, trans. Richard Howard (Minneapolis: University of Minnesota Press, 1990), p. 4.

11   Ibid., p. 207; p. 4.

My luck, my own individual abyss and my lovely amnesiac energy. An energy I don't experience as a deficiency, curiously enough. Rather, it's my third ear'], affirms the narrator on this notion held dear by the Moroccan author.[12]

The Language of Writers

The question remains of what novels, and in what languages, francophone writers should write after independence? Whatever the effects might be of 'la conscience malheureuse', this sort of challenge is no longer worrying. The francophone Maghrebian novelistic universe, for example, has entered a phase where its singularity is realized, what Khatibi calls its 'différence intraitable', which remains attentive to the constructions of the West without at that same time losing its own richness. The gesture of opening out that fights against modes of thought that are marginalized by trying to be superior to others consists in leaving behind any attempt at self-sufficiency to try to reach a 'pensée plurielle' ['plural thought']. Khatibi explains:

> Selon le modèle mondialiste, la vie est un laboratoire où l'identité de l'homme est une question et une réponse toujours différée, dans le mouvement des progrès cumulatifs. L'altermondialiste pense que le devenir problématique des pays – comme le nôtre – est lourd de conséquences.[13]

> [According to the globalizing model, life is a laboratory where man's identity is a constantly deferred question and answer, in the movement of cumulative progress. The proponents of alter-globalization think that the problematic future of countries like ours has serious consequences.]

The category of the universal is certainly in crisis. Globality throws into question the utopia of the universal, as market value prevails over the ideal of values.

Singularity can thwart globalization. To live in a climate of trust, it is necessary to accept to live out one's singularity, to accept its irreducible rituals. Perhaps this is a form of resistance to the hackneyed notion

---

12 Ibid., p. 208; p. 5.
13 Abdelkébir Khatibi, 'L'intellectuel et le mondialisme', in 'Positions et propositions', *Œuvres de Abdelkébir Khatibi III: Essais* (Paris: Editions de la Différence, 2008), pp. 319–23 (p. 322).

of universalism. In that case, the relationship with the other is not necessarily reciprocal. Research into language is a good example; it allows the multiplication of different approaches, the discovery of new relations, the short-circuiting of familiar old ideas and new spaces of reflection.

Khatibi approaches this ideal by working less on vocabulary than on syntax, as only syntax can encompass the meandering of thought and the aporias of perception. In this way the sentence either explodes (it contains so much information that it becomes difficult to order it), or, it is this information that crumbles into many sentences. The process of writing never reflects the traditional rules of language. The disintegration of language is never affirmed; it is accomplished within the linguistic system in insidious and multiple ways. If by chance the writer uses a local code, it is so that the constitutive elements of the language are interpenetrated with one another rather than juxtaposed. Khatibi explains, 'pour moi qui écris en français, ce processus d'autodestruction agit de la façon suivante: je prends une langue morte, dont les tenants peuvent comprendre les mots, mais sans entrer dans le système. En marge de cette altérité profonde, il y a bien sûr aussi complicité avec l'autre puisque je m'installe dans sa langue. Le langage, à un certain niveau, devient action' ['for myself, who write in French, this process of self-destruction functions in the following way: I take a dead language, whose words can be understood by those who know it, but without entering into the system. In the margins of this profound alterity, there is also a complicity with the other, as I set up a home in the language ["langue"]. The language ["langage"] on a certain level becomes an action.']¹⁴

A journey through language is like a dream of the other. The language of the other, which echoes the monolingualism of the other, lies on the borders of language, what Jacques Derrida calls '*au bord* du français' ['*on the shores* of the French language'].¹⁵ At this limit position, the space between two hands, between two languages, opens up. Khatibi positions himself in this quest for the trace, an 'étranger clandestin qui navigue dans

14   Akim Charoub, '*La Mémoire tatouée* de Abdelkébir Khatibi', *Jeune Afrique* 558 (1971), p. 50.

15   Jacques Derrida, *Le Monolinguisme de l'autre, ou, La Prothèse d'origine* (Paris: Galilée, 1996), p. 14; *The Monolingualism of the Other, or, The Prosthesis of Origin*, trans. Patrick Mensah (Stanford, CA: Stanford University Press, 1998), p. 2.

la nuit entre deux langues' ['a clandestine stranger who navigates between two languages at night'].[16] Night is the cult moment of silence. For Khatibi, learning the French language was realized in silence, a language that is written before being spoken. 'Ce pas furtif dans la nuit du langage est un début de séparation et d'isolement' ['this furtive step taken in the night of language is the start of a process of separation and isolation'].[17] 'Celui qui fait vœu et volonté de silence cherche le dépaysement de soi' ['he who seeks silence seeks the disorientation of himself'], he writes, no doubt during a night of solitary meditation.[18]

Is it possible to think of the form of the other as a destiny and not as a convenient psychological or social partner? Is it possible to believe in the existence of alterity other than as a sort of interactive superstructure? If, today, everything is conceived in terms of difference, alterity is not difference. It is a more autonomous notion that opens up broad modes of understanding. If a language is distributed in a system of differences, meaning is reduced to an effect of difference. Radical alterity is abolished and with it the dialectic between language and thought. The part of language that is irreducible to mediation, to articulation, to meaning, and that ensures that language cannot be confused with the subject, is removed. It is in this way that the book becomes, 'un exercice dans l'exploration de l'inconnu qui nous travaille' ['an exercise in the exploration of the unknown that troubles us'], affirms Khatibi.[19] The major feature that inhabits this dialectic is dialogue.

The Singularity and Universality of Language

Every individual belongs to the world of economic exchange as well as to his or her cultural group, and has both a private and spiritual and social and public life. It is no longer the case that one can either participate in the market or withdraw from it. Most people link in a volatile and

16   Abdelkébir Khatibi, *La Langue de l'autre* (New York: Editions Les Mains secrètes, 1999), p. 30.

17   Abdelkébir Khatibi, *Vœu de silence* (Neuilly-sur-Seine: Al Manar, 2000), reprinted in *Œuvres de Abdelkébir Khatibi II: Poésie de l'aimance* (Paris: La Différence, 2008), pp. 161–77 (p. 163).

18   Ibid., p. 176.

19   Abdelkébir Khatibi, 'La Passion du livre vivant', *Regards* 1 (1988), pp. 46–9 (p. 48).

versatile way their willingness to participate in industrialized production and consumption and a growing desire to preserve their intimate space, their identity and origin. Can the realm of objectification and trade communicate with that of personal and collective subjectivity in this situation? Certainly, their communication is necessary. A multicultural society is not constructed out of isolated and separate cultures; rather it is the link between them, every individual's recognition of a common language which allows them to understand one another at the same time as they can identify the differences between them, to be part of the social group at the same time as they assert their cultural specificity.

This leads to the central question, around which many of Khatibi's texts revolve: 'how do we unite what is separate, how do we enable individuals and groups of different cultures to live together?' It is a question of reconciling public activity with private experience. The combination of these only occurs within an individual's experience, and as a result beyond political and religious institutional solutions. This is borne out by Alain Touraine:

> C'est dans son histoire et son expérience de vie que chaque individu – ou chaque collectivité – combine instrumentalité et unité et cette combinaison est possible précisément parce que la rationalité n'est plus celle des fins mais seulement des moyens, car il n'est plus possible de combiner une vision rationaliste et une vision magique du monde, pas plus qu'il n'est possible d'être à la fois chrétien et musulman ou croyant et athée. En revanche, si la rationalité est dans l'ordre des moyens et l'identité dans l'ordre des fins, elles ne sont plus incompatibles.[20]

> [It is in his own history and experience that each individual – or each collectivity – combines instrumentality and unity, and this combination is possible precisely because rationality now seeks means not ends, because it is no longer possible to combine a rationalist vision and a magical vision of the world, no more than it is possible to be both Christian and Muslim or believer and atheist. Conversely, if rationality is bound up with means and identity with ends, these are no longer compatible.]

To believe this we just need to read Khatibi's *Pèlerinage d'un artiste amoureux*, where the protagonist meets characters of many religions and customs other than his own. There is no incomprehension and no

---

20 Alain Touraine, 'Faux et vrais problèmes', in Michel Wieviorka (ed.), *Une société fragmentée? Le multiculturalisme en débat* (Paris: Editions de la Découverte, 1997), p. 302.

rejection in his journey. On the contrary, benevolent curiosity and the call of the other contributes to an exchange of viewpoints as a sign of respect for humanity as a whole.

It is also more difficult to determine an identity which is constantly evolving. It takes into account every new encounter, records all our movements. It is 'fluid', Khatibi reminds us. He offers an excellent lesson in dialogue in his epistolary exchanges with Jacques Hassoun, and a few years later with Rita El Khayat, where the question of globalization enters into in their discussions of the universal and the particular. We have to face both our hopes and our fears, not so much in our economic use of one another as in our ethical obligations to one another as citizens of the world.

This is not a new idea, and as a hegemonic temptation, globalization is as old as the world. Today it takes the form of the West's crusade in pursuit of the universal. It fuels discussion, nourishes political and religious systems, blurs categories and develops in antithetical terms. Global morality provokes intolerance, and a collective frenzy, against plural values. A question remains, however, formulated clearly and concisely by Jean-Claude Guillebaud: 'existe-t-il un principe d'humanité, une valeur d'essence supérieure, capable de transcender les différences de race, de culture ou de sexe pour définir notre commune humanité? Cette valeur doit-elle l'emporter sur toutes les autres?' ['is there a human principle, an essentially superior value, capable of transcending racial, cultural or sexual differences, and of defining our common humanity? Should this value be set above all others?'].[21] This is a decisive question, relevant across all periods, and one which constantly divides people. Globalization, as it has been perverted by market society, is a threat both to universality and to difference. By altering the differences that unite us, it hinders the universality that allows us to transcend those differences. We have to learn to consider these two dimensions differently by adopting a renewed vision of our creative diversity and a greater confidence in ourselves that will lead us to perceive our resemblances. Universality or the concept of the universal that imbues Romance languages constitutes a chapter in the history of shared meaning that it is interesting to recall here. The linguistic gesture even when unconscious wears out this concept as if it was an obvious given. It has a heritage with its own

21   Jean-Claude Guillebaud, *La Refondation du monde* (Paris: Seuil, 1999), p. 185; *Re-Founding the World: A Western Testament*, trans. W. Donald Wilson (New York: Algora Publishing, 2001), p. 161.

effects and uses. But it is a legacy that has become naturalized so that the dialectic between the universal and the particular can be seen as one of the essential dichotomies of Western thought. In this way it becomes a normative distinction, like those between truth and falsity, between the beautiful and the ugly, between the useful and the useless. In all the uses of this opposition, what is at stake are forms of categorization and necessarily forms of judgement, whether evaluative or not. The domain of reference of the categories of the universal and the singular varies between law, philosophy, culture, and politics. But when we speak of a legacy that has become naturalized, it is above all to underline a mechanism that most often serves as a criterion for classification.

In 'L'Universalisme et l'invention du futur', Abdelkébir Khatibi concludes: 'comme beaucoup d'entre vous, je suis un étranger professionnel, c'est-à-dire une personne qui fait de la question des lieux de passage et de résistance entre civilisations une tâche de tous les jours, dans l'exercice de mon travail, dans mon pays et dans l'ailleurs. Pourquoi ne devrions-nous pas être, comme n'importe quel humain, les hôtes du futur?' ['like many of you, I am a professional stranger, that is, someone who thinks every day about the spaces of movement and resistance between civilizations, in my work, in my country and elsewhere. Why should we not be, like any human being, the hosts of the future?].[22]

The acquisition of a new cultural code without losing the old one is what makes all of us, in the polyphony of modern cosmopolitanism, into hybrids. It issues an invitation to make an inventory of the social world and its relations with other subjects in the same world in order to halt the fragmentation of human beings and objects. It is an invitation to journey around the planet not in order to explore it but to recreate it, not in order to conquer new lands but to feel under our step the harmony between soil and feet of which Albert Camus dreamt.

In a universe dominated by the blind forces of the financial markets, what in the last instance does a transparent language mean? Language is necessarily double-edged; the wish for transparency is a pious wish. Language often implies more than it says. Interpretation is a fault of language which fails because it is unable to express everything.

22 Abdelkébir Khatibi, *Chemins de traverse: essais de sociologie* (Rabat: Editions Okad, 2002), p. 291.

CHAPTER FIVE

Khatibi and Performativity, *'From where to speak?'*

Living, Thinking and Writing with an 'epistemological accent'

Alfonso de Toro

Je tiens à souligner que cette œuvre [...] est à la fois une immense invention poétique et une puissante réflexion théorique qui [...] s'attache à la problématique du bilinguisme ou du biculturalisme. Ce que Khatibi fait de la langue française, ce qu'il lui donne en y imprimant sa marque, est inséparable de ce qu'il analyse de cette situation, dans ses dimensions linguistiques, certes, mais aussi culturelles, religieuses, anthropologiques, politiques.

[I would like to point out that this œuvre [...] is both an immense poetic invention and a powerful theoretical reflection which [...] focuses on the problem of bilingualism or biculturalism. What Khatibi does with the French language, what he gives it by imprinting his mark on it, is inseparable from what he analyses of this situation, in its linguistic, of course, but also cultural, religious, anthropological, and political dimensions.]

Jacques Derrida[1]

---

1   Jacques Derrida, 'Exergue', in *Œuvres de Abdelkébir Khatibi I: Romans et récits* (Paris: La Différence, 2008), p. 7.

The philosopher, sociologist, novelist and poet Abdelkébir Khatibi is the author of a most impressive corpus of works, comprising novels, poetry, literary criticism, and essays on culture, language and literary theory. He is furthermore an intellectual of the first order, he represents one of the most exceptional and brilliant cultural personalities of the Maghreb and is a pioneer in many cultural and theoretical issues that, decades later, will become academically mainstream.[2]

Focusing on works such as *La Mémoire tatouée* (1971), *Amour bilingue* (1983), *Maghreb pluriel* (1983), *Figures de l'étranger dans la littérature française* (1987), *Imaginaires de l'autre: Khatibi et la mémoire littéraire* (1987), *Penser le Maghreb* (1993), *La Langue de l'autre* (1999), 'Cervantès et la modernité' (2005) and 'Goethe ou le poète masqué' (2006), which are located at the productive and innovative interface between the epistemai of 'Islam' and 'Christianity', of 'Orient' and 'Occident', I am going to describe his 'performative thinking and praxis' in relation to the actual theory and praxis of culture and 'identity', always dependent on language, on one's own chosen language and on an *'accent'* rooted in knowledge, epistemology and fiction that are inserted into the body and steered and driven by emotion.[3]

I consider the term 'accent' as Rosi Braidotti does, not in the sense of spoken language; rather we assign this term an epistemological status. I understand by 'epistemological accent' an intellectual, political, social, cultural and scientific attitude to inhabiting the world: living, thinking and writing at the intersection or interface of systems, for example, to belong to two or more cultures and to live with several identities. The 'epistemological accent' is equivalent to Derrida's term 'différance' or to Homi Bhabha's notion of the 'in-between' or 'third space': it means the experience of multiplicity. An 'epistemological accent' means to think and to write with my own scientific languages, languages that are crossed, superposed and intermeshed with each other. This thinking and writing at the same time in my own language, in my own scientific

2   Alfonso de Toro, *Epistémologies: Le Maghreb* (Paris: L'Harmattan, 2010 [2008]).

3   I owe my term of 'thinking with an accent' as a transcultural concept to Marta Segarra's inspiring and innovative lecture, 'Parler, écrire et penser avec un accent. La construction d'une identité diasporique, hybride et genrée chez Mélikah Abdelmoumen', held at the Conference of the French–Romances Association in September 2016 in Saarbrucken, a concept she takes from Rosi Braidotti's essay, 'Thinking with an Accent: Françoise Collin, *Les cahiers du Grif*, and French Feminism', *Signs* 39.3 (2014), pp. 597–626.

argot, patois or pidgin and in the language of the 'Other', that is at the interface, is what Deleuze calls the *'pensée mineure'*, and corresponds to Khatibi's *'pensée-autre'* and *'double critique'*. As we shall describe later in this chapter, Khatibi is one of the best examples of this figure of the 'epistemological accent' because he is always located in an 'in-between'; he leaves a permanent 'différance' that he calls *'la pensée-autre'* and *'la double critique'*.

We understand 'emotion' as an experience that is connected with the 'Blink', 'gaze' or 'glance', consequently with the 'body' and with 'desire', and it is expressed through cultural behaviour and through writing. 'Emotion' is an individual changing phenomenon and is not rooted in a 'national culture' but in several cultures, and not in the *'prothèse d'origine'*.[4]

The speaking subject builds with his body, desire, culture and *'accent'* in the space of the postcolonial interface, that of crossing cultures, the transcultural, nomadic and hybrid space that, as a consequence of a misunderstanding based on a logical mistake, is frequently defined or thought of as a *non or rootless space*. Rather, the terms 'trans', 'nomadism' and 'hybridity' are relational, and they demand fixed points of relation and only as such can we classify a phenomenon as 'trans', 'nomadic' or 'hybrid'. The fact that people, intellectuals, writers or artists live in places that do not correspond to their original regions of birth, that they speak different languages, share different identities and cultural and religious traditions, eliminates neither 'cultural difference' nor the 'location of culture', as Bhabha illustrates explicitly in the title of his book and in his theory of 'hybridity'.[5] 'Hybridity' and 'nomadism' are always located somewhere, but are also located in a specific individual, corresponding to the formula of 'from where to speak' as discussed by Edward Said and Fernando de Toro.[6] The latter has repeatedly insisted

---

4 See Jacques Derrida, *Le Monolinguisme de l'autre ou la prothèse d'origine* (Paris: Galilée, 1996), p. 29. Derrida means by *'prothèse d'origine'* the arbitrary reduction, interpretation and definition of an individual to his place of birth, as his exclusive and true origin. But experience in this field shows us that this reduction, especially in everyday life, is used as an instrument of exclusion and racism.

5 Homi Bhabha, *The Location of the Culture* (London and New York: Routledge, 1994).

6 Edward Said, *Orientalism* (New York: Vintage Books, 1994 [1978]) and Fernando de Toro, 'From Where to Speak', in Fernando de Toro (ed.), *Borders and Margins: Post-Colonialism and Post-Modernism* (Frankfurt am Main: Vervuert, 1995), pp. 131–48.

on and underlined this aspect: we speak always from somewhere and
that is *our place, our home, our 'accent'*. This pluricultural voice
with an *'accent'* and a body are new homes; as Fernando de Toro
expresses, an *'unhomely home'*.[7] The voice is always located in a
place, in a body, in the desire of someone, crossed by 'diversity' and
'hybridity'. All that builds the *new place*, the *nomadic pluricultural
place* and *individual*, makes this new home a place of enunciation
that is always performative, transversal and determined by *'différance'*.
When Fernando de Toro speaks of the displacement of literature and
culture,[8] he does not confuse what scholars usually mix up: 'it is not
that the subject producing the literature is displaced but rather the
stories, narrated, inhabit displacement'.[9] This is something completely
different; he is not eliminating the categories of 'home', 'identity' or the
particular 'place of enunciation' of *'my accent'*. We always have a home
and an 'identity'. The difference today is the particular way in which
we construct our home or new diaspora, and our new, 'multi-referential
and cultural identity'. What we have, as Fernando de Toro argues, is
a nomadic home, a nomadic language, which can also be understood
in the sense of Guillermo Gómez Peña's theory of the border. For him,
culture is a 'border' or 'borderland culture' and is equivalent to a new
notion of 'home' as an open cartography that builds proliferating lines.
Expressions such as 'home is always somewhere else. Home is both
"here" and "there" or somewhere in between. Sometimes it's nowhere'
formulate the oscillation of identities between and through different
cultures.[10] Here, a particular thinking is created, where 'home' gets the
same status as 'unhomely' (in the language of Homi Bhabha) and turns
into a source for building a 'third space'.[11]

---

7   Fernando de Toro, *New Intersections: Essays on Culture and Literature in the
Post-Modern and Post-Colonial Condition* (Madrid: Iberoamericana/Frankfurt
am Main: Vervuert, 2003), p. 87.

8   Ibid. pp. 87, 92.

9   Ibid.

10   Guillermo Gómez Peña, *The New World Border: Prophecies, Poems and
Loqueras for the End of the Century* (San Francisco: City Lights, 1996), p. 5.

11   Homi Bhabha, *The Location of Culture*, pp. 1–13 and 217; Alfonso de Toro,
'Globalization – New Hybridities – Transidentities – Transnations: Recognition
– Difference', in Frank Heidemann and Alfonso de Toro (eds), *New Hybridities*
(Hildesheim, Zurich and New York: Olms, 2006), pp. 19–37 (p. 30) and 'Introducción.
Más allá de la "postmodernidad", "postcolonialidad" y "globalización": hacia
una teoría de la hibridez', in Alfonso de Toro, *Cartografías y estrategias de la*

To conclude, to speak about 'nomadism', 'the nomadic', 'the hybrid' or 'displaced literature, culture or identity', and to speak about 'transculturalism' or 'transidentity' always means a fixed point from where we speak, think, write, feel and live. This fixed point is built as a 'hybrid-performative location', as speaking, thinking, writing, feeling and living crossed by many traditions and *'accents'*. That is exactly what Fernando de Toro is describing when he speaks about new 'sonorities and colours': he means the migrants that are coming to Canada from all over the world (e.g. Aborigines, Dutch, Germans, Italians, Portuguese, English Filipinos, Ukrainians, Chinese, Vietnamese, Indian, Latin-Americans, Lebanese, Maghrebian and so forth).[12] They are coming from different cultures, with different religions, with different languages and phonetic systems that inscribe themselves, in the case of Canada, in the English or French languages.

Khatibi's work can be placed in this line of cultural epistemology, and that is why the concept of 'cultural performance' and the idea of a 'performative pluri-language' are at the centre of Khatibi's thinking and writing; for him, these do not imply alienation, rootlessness or the impenetrability of history, amnesia or the undecipherable:

> Là réside son principe d'identité initial − dit ici schématiquement − par rapport auquel nous sommes inscrits, Français et francophones, avec *nos langues, nos idiomes, nos cultures*, bien avant la colonisation et l'Empire français.[13]

> [It is here that the principle of an initial identity resides − expressed here schematically − in relation to which we are inscribed as French or francophone, with *our languages, our idioms, our cultures*, well before colonization and the French empire.]

The concepts of 'performativity' and of a 'performative culture and language', as we understand them and as Khatibi developed them, means the reinvention of the self in an indeterminate process in which the past performs both itself and the present through literature, experience and emotion, 'Occident' and 'Orient'. He invents and re-invents himself in

---

'*postmodernidad*' y la '*postcolonialidad*' en Latinoamérica: '*hibridez*' y '*globalización*' (Frankfurt am Main: Vervuert, 2006), pp. 9–36.

12   Fernando de Toro, *New Intersections: Essays on Culture and Literature in the Post-Modern and Post-Colonial Condition*, p. 88.

13   Abdelkébir Khatibi, 'La Langue de l'autre', in *Œuvres de Abdelkébir Khatibi III: Essais* (Paris: La Différence, 2008), pp. 115–35 (p. 115) (my emphasis).

an endless process of '*translatio*',[14] or, in the language of Khatibi, of '*transposition*',[15] because he can only exist within a language, within a 'pluri-language':

> Or, chaque œuvre est en elle-même une frontière, un passage et un obstacle entre les langues, un lieu de réincarnation, quitte, pour l'écrivain, qu'il soit métropolitain ou extra-muros, à introduire – du français en français – des agencements idiomatiques, à y greffer des points de rupture, des noyaux de dissidence, de résistance, de telle sorte que cette langue que nous écrivons – si nous écrivons – soit disponible à une traduction infinie.[16]

> [For each work is in itself a border, a passageway and an obstacle between languages, a place of reincarnation, even if the writer, whether he is metropolitan or residing outside the metropole, can introduce from French into French idiomatic arrangements, he can graft breaks, knots of dissidence, of resistance, so that the language that we write, if we write, can be infinitely translated.]

Khatibi placed his thinking and writing at the 'peripheries', at the 'borders', but not ones understood in the traditional sense of marginalization, but of interfaces ('beyond binary borders'), and in the sense of 'post-coloniality' as an epistemological place of enunciation, as a laboratory of a subversive and innovative as well as a powerful production at the interfaces of cultures, thinking, traditions and writing. All this takes place in the context of hybrid processes – not only in the sense of Homi Bhabha's negotiation – but also in the sense of epistemological strategies.[17]

---

14 Alfonso de Toro, 'Jorge Luis Borges: Translatio e Historia', in Rafael Olea Franco (ed.), *In Memoriam Jorge Luis Borges*. Colóquio Internacional, Centro de Estudios Lingüísticos y Literarios, Cátedra Jaume Torres Bodet (Mexico City: Colegio de México, 2008), pp. 191–236.

15 Abdelkébir Khatibi, 'Goethe ou le poète masqué', in *Quatuor poétique: Rilke, Goethe Ekelof, Lundkvist* (Neuilly-sur-Seine: Al Manar, 2006), pp. 38, 44, 47, reprinted in *Œuvres de Abdelkébir Khatibi II: Poésie de l'aimance* (Paris: La Différence, 2008), pp. 179–91.

16 Khatibi, 'La Langue de l'autre', p. 116.

17 On the term 'post-coloniality', see Alfonso de Toro, 'Jorge Luis Borges. The Periphery at the Center/The Periphery as Center/The Center of the Periphery: Postcoloniality and Postmodernity', in Fernando de Toro and Alfonso de Toro (eds), *Borders and Margins: Post-Colonialism and Post-Modernism* (Frankfurt am Main: Vervuert, 1995), pp. 11–45; Alfonso de Toro, 'La postcolonialidad en Latinoamérica en la era de la globalización. ¿Cambio de paradigma en el

In this sense, Khatibi's work has to be considered from his first and hybrid text (novel? autobiography?), *La Mémoire tatouée,* as founding post-coloniality, and this all the more so as this theory was built on by Said's *Orientalism* and explicitly by the Australian group, Ashcroft, Griffiths and Tiffin, in *The Empire Writes Back: Theory and Practice in Post-Colonial Literatures* (1989). By 'post-coloniality' we understand a new form of pluralistic cultural and international dialogue between the periphery and the centre, between social, gender, religious and political minorities, between Occidental and Oriental epistemologies. The conception of 'post-coloniality', thought of in this way, surpasses the traditional binary oppositions of culture and of regions/areas. 'Post-coloniality', as part of 'post-modernity', is a form of a more transdisciplinary, transtextual and transcultural deconstructionist thinking that has the capacity to re-codify and decentre history, culture and language. It is a system of both subjective and radical particularity and diversity. 'Post-coloniality' is not exclusionary, rather it includes multidimensionality, the interaction of a diverse codified series of knowledge and experiences, which is ultimately capable of unmasking that which, in colonialism and neo-colonialism, have been established as power and tradition, as *the* history, as *the* irrefutable truth, as *the* culture, as *the* language, as something contradictory and irregular, as plural and multiple. This is what Khatibi performs in his work: 'post-coloniality' as '*cosmopolitanism*' in the sense of '*cosmo-humanism*'.

Living in Rabat, thinking in and travelling through the world, through literatures, cultures, sciences and systems, Khatibi, with his erudition and his privileged sensibility and intelligence, became an intellectual and travelling cosmopolitan and a great cosmo-humanist, in the sense that he takes as a 'bridge-builder' with cultural and ethical responsibility in dealing with Occidental as well as with Oriental culture, placing himself at the interfaces of thinking and of cultural worlds. His life was a 'worlding-life', his literature a 'worlding-literature' within the interface of deconstruction of the Occidental and Oriental logoi:

> Une déconstruction du logocentrisme et de l'ethnocentrisme, cette parole de l'autosuffisance par excellence que l'Occident, en se développant, a développée sur le monde. Et il nous reste beaucoup à méditer – de ce

pensamiento teórico-cultural latinoamericano?', in Alfonso de Toro and Fernando de Toro (eds), *El debate de la postcolonialidad en Latinoamérica: una postmodernidad periférica o Cambio de paradigma en el pensamiento latinoamericano* (Frankfurt am Main: Vervuert, 1999), pp. 31–77; and Gómez Peña, *The New World Border.*

côté – sur la solidarité structurelle qui lie l'impérialisme dans toutes ses instances (politique, militaire, culturelle) à l'expansion de ce qu'on appelle les sciences sociales. Tâche immense, il est vrai: entre le fait colonial et celui de la décolonisation, il y va du destin de la science et de la technique, en tant que forces, énergies de domination et de maîtrise sur la totalité du monde, et du sur-monde aussi bien. [...] Cela suppose aussi, exige, tout autant, une critique du savoir et des discours élaborés par les différentes sociétés du monde arabe sur elles-mêmes.

[A deconstruction of logocentrism and ethnocentrism, this speech of self-sufficiency par excellence that the West, in the course of its development, developed on the world. And we have much to reflect – here on this side – on the structural solidarity that links imperialism in all its aspects (political, military, cultural) to the expansion of the so-called social sciences. A huge task, it is true: between the fact of colonization and that of decolonization, what is at stake is the destiny of science and technology as forces, energies of domination and mastership over the totality of the world, and over the world as well. [...] This equally presupposes, or rather necessitates, a critique of the knowledge and discourses elaborated by different societies of the Arab world about themselves.][18]

His 'cosmopolitanism' and 'cosmo-humanism' are not just a fashion or a form of hedonist play. This is the result of the three previously described operations of 'translatio', the 'double critique' and the 'pensée autre', operations that open the possibility for Khatibi as an individual, as an intellectual, as a writer, as a philosopher and as a sociologist to place himself at the interface and think and hear both sides: the Occident and the Orient, what I have called in another context 'Occirient', following the line of thought of Khatibi and his term 'Tolédance':

Permutation permanente. [...] Passage multiple selon un chassé-croisé: ici, deux langues et une diglossie, scène de ses transcriptions. Il avait appris que toute langue est bilingue, oscillant entre le passage oral et un autre, qui s'affirme et se détruit dans l'incommunicable.

[Permanent permutation. [...] A passage involving many passes: here, two languages and a diglossia, stage for its transcriptions. He had learned that every language is bilingual, oscillating between the spoken portion and another, which both affirms and destroys itself in the incommunicable.][19]

18   Abdelkébir Khatibi, *Maghreb pluriel* (Paris: Denoël, 1983), pp. 48–9; *Plural Maghreb*, trans. P. Burcu Yalim (London: Bloomsbury, 2019), p. 26.
19   Abdelkébir Khatibi, *Amour bilingue* (Montpellier: Fata Morgana, 1983), reprinted in *Œuvres de Abdelkébir Khatibi I: Romans et récits*, pp. 205–83 (p. 219);

D'une part, il faut écouter le Maghreb résonner dans sa pluralité (linguistique, culturelle, politique), et d'autre part, seul le dehors repensé, décentré, subverti, détourné de ses déterminations dominantes, peut nous éloigner des identités et des différences informulées.

[On the one hand, one should listen to the Maghreb resonate in its (linguistic, cultural, political) plurality, and on the other, only the outside rethought, decentred, subverted, diverted from its dominant determinations, can allow us to go beyond unformulated identities and differences.][20]

In order to establish his own cultural location and to find his own voice, Khatibi performs a monumental act of '*translatio*' on the base of the axis of a '*double critique*' and of the '*pensée autre*', and he becomes an '*écrivain-voyageur infatigable*', a '*voyageur cosmopolite*', a '*voyageur ou migrant professionnel*' of diverse worlds.

By '*translatio*' we mean the idea that every enunciation and every movement constitutes a 'relinquishing' ['*Entäußerung*'], a 'distortion', or a 'warping' ['*Verwindung*' and not '*Überwindung*' or 'overcoming'] and a 'dissemination'. So culture exists in a permanently and evidently changing state.[21] All kinds of transformations, or 'refunctionalizations', represent 'transcultural changes' as a result of external relations. '*Translatio*' is just a part of what I call a '*translatio*-machine', understood as a complex interweaving of social, cultural, literary, medial, scientific, anthropological, ethnic, philosophical and historical processes. In practice, '*translatio*' reveals the modalities and the structure of the new object and underlines the fact that even a 1:1 assumption of a structure or element of content constitutes a cultural and semantic deterritorialization, simply by virtue of the conditions of temporal, spatial and cultural postponement. Therefore, repetition, adoption or transfer do not mean reproduction but implicit differences,[22] a productive disorder

---

Love in Two Languages, trans. Richard Howard (Minneapolis: University of Minnesota Press, 1990), p. 20.

20 Khatibi, *Maghreb pluriel*, p. 39; *Plural Maghreb*, p. 23.

21 See Alfonso de Toro, 'Jenseits von Postmoderne und Postkolonialität Materialien zu einem Modell der Hybridität und des Körpers als transrelationalem, transversalem und transmedialem Wissenschaftskonzept', in Christof Hamann and Cornelia Sieber (eds), *Räume der Hybridität. Postkoloniale Konzepte in Theorie und Literatur* (Hildesheim, Zurich and New York: Olms, 2003), pp. 15–52.

22 See Gilles Deleuze, *Différence et répétition* (Paris: Presses universitaires de France, 1968).

that makes the old-fashioned terms 'influence' or 'studies of sources' obsolete. 'Transformation' refers to concrete changes on the levels of structure, semantics and pragmatics, on the level of representation – and clearly on that of the constitution of significance.

As the result of the operation of '*translatio*', we have the '*double critique*'. By this term Khatibi means a reciprocal critical and deconstructive revision of the fundamental issues of Western and Occidental philosophy, of cultural, social and political systems, a critique that has its origins at the interfaces of Khatibi's intellectual locations. The '*double critique*' also deals with the deconstruction of the notion, idea and conception of what is an Arab-Muslim Identity as well what is a 'Christian-Occidental Identity'.

This cultural operation, as a form or strategy of '*translatio*', leads to another form or strategy, that of the '*pensée autre*' that represents a thinking beyond binary dichotomies as 'Orient vs. Occident' and at the same time overcomes, or better 'warps', the '*prothèse d'origine*' and makes possible a productive dialogue between them: on the one hand, the Maghreb as part of the Orient and of Western culture, and, on the other hand, Europe as part of Western Culture with an extensive influence. Both are thought in the frame of one episteme, that of Derridean '*différance*', where the 'one' and the 'other' are thought at the same time. This *va-et-vient*, this oscillation, presupposes evidently an act of permanent '*translatio*' of one system into the other (languages, cultural and religious practices, customs and traditions in everyday life) and leads to an interlacing of identities and cultural practices.

Multi-Polyphonic '*Accents*': 'Occirient'

In the following, I would like to describe Khatibi's '*accent*', meaning his multi-polyphonic '*accents*', his thinking, working and writing in the fissure of a double principle: that of the respect of idiomatic variety and of a plural universality placed on 'plusieurs langues [...] plusieurs élaborations techniques et scientifiques' ['several languages [...] several technical and scientific elaborations'] and 'plusieurs pôles de civilisation' ['several poles of civilization'].[23] According to him, this universalism implies 'une pensée qui prendrait l'univers des êtres et des choses pour un

---

23   Khatibi, *Maghreb pluriel*, p. 14; *Plural Maghreb*, p. 4.

palimpseste sans parchemin, jamais écrit – et par personne effacé – d'où qu'elle vienne' ['a thought that would understand the universe of beings and things as a palimpsest without a manuscript, never written down – and never effaced by anyone – wherever it comes from'].[24] Khatibi has, like Jorge Luis Borges, the capacity to decentre culture, a capacity of which Roland Barthes speaks in his 'Postface' in reference to Khatibi's *La Mémoire tatouée*, 'de quoi nous permettre de saisir "l'autre" à partir de notre "même"' ['what allows us to grasp the "other" on the basis of our sameness'].[25]

The passage from one cultural location to another can be a geographical displacement, or also a mental/intellectual movement and relocation of an individual or of a group, and the creation of one's own language and of one's own *'accent'*. 'Cosmo-humanism', particularly in Khatibi's work, generates the potential to find alternatives to nationalism, to monolithic and essentialist constructions of nation, culture and identity. One of these alternatives is to think of the world as an intellectual, psychological and emotionally open/nomadic cartography and to try to develop a sort of theory regarding it. We want to understand 'cosmopolitism' and 'cosmo-humanism' as a 'Beyond', as a process of transcendence of the local, as travel, as a perpetual passage of *'aves de paso'* ['bird of passage'] after Ortíz.[26] To think of cosmopolitism as 'cosmo-humanism' in the sense of an ethic of hospitality, as a 'beyond' of borders and ethnic essentialisms means more than considering it in terms of a change of place. They can, of course, be both, as Kant shows in his *Zum ewigen Frieden. Ein philosophischer Entwurf* [*Perpetual Peace: A Philosophical Sketch*].[27] The term 'cosmo-humanism', if it is to make any sense, must remain indeterminate. 'Cosmopolitanism' and 'cosmo-humanism' must be thought of as a permanent transition, as life at the interface, as *'une pensée*

24 Abdelkébir Khatibi, 'Repères', in *Pro-Culture* 12 – Numéro spécial: 'Khatibi' (Rabat: Imprimerie culturelle et universitaire Mohammed V, 1978), pp. 48–52 (p. 51).

25 Roland Barthes, 'Exergue', in Abdelkébir Khatibi, *Œuvres de Abdelkébir Khatibi III: Essais*, pp. 7–8 (p. 8).

26 Fernando Ortiz, *Contrapunteo cubano del tabaco y el azúcar* (Havana: Editorial de Ciencias Sociales, 1983 [1940]).

27 See Emmanuel Kant, *Perpetual Peace: A Philosophical Sketch* (Philadelphia: Slought Foundation *et al.*, 2010 [1795]). Text based on the 1891 William Hastie translation. Footnotes based on the 1903 Mary Campbell Smith translation. Online: https://slought.org/media/files/perpetual_peace.pdf (accessed 12 May 2017).

autre' or '*une double critique*' (Khatibi), as an individual modus in the context of universal norms. 'Cosmo-humanism' is the availability of hospitality, the willingness to receive someone, as Khatibi writes: 'annonciation qui reçoit l'autre, dans une hospitalité possible, et qui peut être un pari heureux, quel que soit le risque' ['an annunciation that receives the other in a possible hospitality, and which can be a fortunate wager, whatever the risk may be'].[28]

In this context, I would like to locate Khatibi's theory and praxis also in the context of a '*translatio* experience' in the sense of an enunciation act that creates a world with pluri-locations as a result of the epistemology of 'hybridity', and as a historical construction wherein the traces of individual and collective experiences are registered in the memory and in the body. This '*translatio* experience' always represents a phenomenon of *friction and tension*, of *transgression* and *subversion* of cultural, linguistic and intellectual worlds. Therein Khatibi brings the supposed and so-called Occidental and Oriental concepts to 'pullulate' and transport them beyond their habitual locations, as a result of a process of dissemination and contamination by the de- and reterritorialization of meaning, reception and perception of culture. Finally, for Khatibi, the '*translatio* experience' is an act of emancipation of encrusted and deadlocked ideas of what Occidental and Oriental culture is or is supposed to be:

> Ecrire le français, le *traduire en l'écrivant*, à l'intérieur de cette division active où se joue l'écriture. Je la sens comme une traduction en simultané, par une association rapide de signes et des images. Je les capte en évitant les néologismes, les scories, les télescopages des mots. Par exemple, des mots ou expressions arabes. Parfois je traduis littéralement des fragments arabes, mais avec inquiétude. Plutôt laisser la langue maternelle arriver, *transformée*. C'est au gré des improvisations, du *rythme sensitif et émotif* que je m'applique à réduire les premières associations et leur anamorphose.[29]

> [To write in French, to *translate it while writing it*, in that active division where writing plays out. I feel it as a simultaneous translation, by a rapid association between signs and images. I catch them, avoiding neologisms, dregs, condensations of words. For example, Arabic words. Sometimes I literally but anxiously translate Arabic fragments. It is better to allow the mother tongue to emerge transformed. It is as a result of improvisations,

28 Khatibi, 'Goethe ou le poète masqué', p. 186.
29 Khatibi, 'La Langue de l'autre', p. 116 (my emphasis).

of sensitive and emotive rhythm, that I try my hardest to reduce the first associations and their anamorphosis.]

This literary and writing praxis, this permanent *'translatio'*, which is always inherent in 'transculturality' and 'hybridity', becomes the laboratory and experimental home of Khatibi. Here he belongs, here he receives and creates himself a new concept of hospitality: *'hospitalité littéraire'*.[30] Here he builds his identity on the basis of the simultaneous acting of 'plural-multi-languages', of a transversal living, thinking and writing with an *'accent'*, which he describes with the term *'cicatrice'* ['scar'],[31] or with the terms *'errance'* ['wandering'], *'une permutation permanente'* ['a permanent permutation'], *'folie de la langue'* ['madness of language'],[32] as a result of the experience that all languages are *'bi-langue'*, and of an infinite series of significations, of an infinite textual production: *'un mot: déjà deux: déjà un récit'* ['one word: now two: it's already a story']:[33] 'Pour lui parler, il était traduit lui-même par un double mouvement: du parler maternel à l'étranger, et de l'étranger en étranger en se métamorphosant, dieu sait pour quelles extravagances' ['in order to speak to her, he himself was doubly translated: translated from his mother tongue to a foreign language, and from one foreign thing to another through an auto-metamorphosis, God only knows for what extravagances'].[34]

The *'hospitalité littéraire'*, the *'errance'*, the *'cicatrice'*, the 'epistemological *accent'*, the 'third space' of cultures and identities, the conjunctive and disjunctive *'différance'*, the oscillation between 'Orient' and 'Occident' is what we want to call 'Occirient' in line with Khatibi's concept of *'tolédance'*, which he develops in his essay 'Cervantès et la modernité',[35] referring to the episode of the captive in Cervantes's *Don Quixote*.[36] Here we can study Khatibi's hybrid thinking and cultural

---

30   Khatibi, 'Cervantès et la modernité', in *Œuvres de Abdelkébir Khatibi III: Essais*, pp. 233–41 (p. 240).

31   Khatibi, 'La Langue de l'autre', p. 116 (my emphasis).

32   Khatibi, *Amour bilingue*, pp. 26, 131; *Love in Two Languages*, pp. 20, 118 (my emphasis).

33   Ibid., pp. 11, 131; p. 5 (my emphasis).

34   Ibid., p. 27; p. 20.

35   Khatibi, 'Cervantès et la modernité', in *Œuvres de Abdelkébir Khatibi III: Essais*, pp. 233–41.

36   Miguel Cervantès Saavedra, *Don Quichotte de la Manche*, 2nd edn (Paris: Gallimard, 1973 [1605; 1615; 1961]), chaps 37–42 (pp. 742–804).

praxis, and what we call his *'epistemological accent'*,[37] when Zoraida
and the Captive undertake a series of translatological operations in
order to realize the substitutions and new distributions between the
'Muslim/Oriental' and the 'Christian/Occidental' worlds that are able to
overcome binary systems and to arouse a web of hybrid and transversal
relations in which the Captive and Zoraida discard foreignness in favour
of familiarity. They produce at the same time irritation and consensus
in the fracture of a new vision of 'hospitality' and 'belonging'; and here
is the aspect that Khatibi elaborates from Cervantes's 'Captive Episode'.
Khatibi – following Derrida[38] – knows that culture and language are
not the property of anyone and that Otherness has always determined
our lives:

> Commet décrire cet état, ce qui l'aura transformé? Quand j'écris, je le
> fais dans la Langue de l'autre. Cette langue n'est pas une propriété; c'est
> plutôt le lieu vide d'une identité que se réincarne. Rien n'est assuré, donné
> ou accordé par avance. [...] cette Langue de l'autre, cette monolangue
> tant défendue et illustrée par ses héritiers [...] par leur appartenance au
> terroir, à la société, à la culture, qui ont entretenu son enseignement et ses

37   In speaking about Cervantes, Khatibi also speaks about his own writing,
cultural location and position.

38   Derrida, *Le Monolinguisme de l'autre*, p. 45; *The Monolingualism of the
Other*, p. 23: 'Car contrairement à ce qu'on est le plus souvent tenté de croire,
le maître n'est rien. Et il n'a rien en propre. Parce que le maître ne possède pas
en propre, naturellement, ce qu'il appelle pourtant sa langue; parce que, quoi
qu'il veuille ou fasse, il ne peut entretenir avec elle des rapports de propriété ou
d'identité naturels nationaux, congénitaux, ontologiques; parce qu'il ne peut
accréditer et dire cette appropriation qu'au cours d'un procès non naturel de
constructions politico-phantasmatiques; parce que la langue n'est pas son bien
naturel, par cela même il peut historiquement, à travers le viol d'une usurpation
culturelle, c'est-à-dire toujours d'essence coloniale, feindre de se l'approprier pour
l'imposer comme "la sienne"'. ['For contrary to what one is often most tempted
to believe, the master is nothing. And he does not have exclusive possession of
anything. Because the master does not possess exclusively, and naturally, what
he calls his language, because, whatever he wants or does, he cannot maintain
any relations of property or identity that are natural, national, congenital, or
ontological, with it, because he can give substance to and articulate [dire] this
appropriation only in the course of an unnatural process of politicophantasmatic
constructions, because language is not his natural possession, he can, thanks to
that very fact, pretend historically, through the rape of a cultural usurpation,
which means always essentially colonial, to appropriate it in order to impose it as
"his own"'.]

belles-lettres, rien ne m'empêchait de la revendiquer à ma manière, disons comme un étranger professionnel.[39]

[How can we describe this state, what transformed it? When I write, I do it in the language of the other. That language is not a property: it is rather the empty space of an identity being reincarnated. Nothing is known, given, or bestowed in advance. [...] this language of the other, this monolingualism so defended and illustrated by its heirs [...] in the name of belonging to a territory, a society, a culture, who have maintained its teaching and its belles-lettres, nothing stops me from claiming it in my own way, let's say as a professional stranger.]

What Khatibi appreciates and admires in his 'post-colonial' and post-modern reading of Cervantes is the creation of a language of alterity, the language of the Other that encompasses all languages with an *'accent'* that he calls:

Si l'on définit 'la modernité' en tant qu'invention du futur [...] ce langage est hospitalier, empreint d'une grande humanité. C'est ce langage qui fait de l'amitié de Don Quichotte et Sancho Pança un passe-temps joyeux, vraisemblable et invraisemblable, si riche en trouvailles ironiques sur la condition de l'homme. Tant et si bien que l'amitié porte en elle-même un savoir vivre-ensemble, qui est une des bases de la civilisation conviviale.[40]

[If we define 'modernity' as an invention of the future [...] this language is hospitable, marked by a great humanity. It is this language that makes of Don Quixote and Sancho Pancha's friendship a joyful pastime, both realistic and unrealistic, so rich in revealing ironic discoveries about the human condition. So much so that the friendship carries within it a knowing how to live together, which is one of the bases of a convivial civilization.]

He also sees in this the *'modernité'* of Cervantes's cultural position and writings at the beginning of the Modern Age, a position that consists, as for Khatibi, in a *'langue hospitalière'* that is characterized by the *'humanité'* and *'amitié'* of the owners of the tavern, who welcome the two fugitives with open arms. This *'langue hospitalière'* is translated in concrete acts that make possible a *'vivre-ensemble'* constituted by 'hospitality' in the sense that the foreigners feel 'recognized', as if they 'belong' to the new culture.

39 Khatibi, 'La Langue de l'autre', p. 118–19.
40 Khatibi, 'Cervantès et la modernité', p. 234.

Khatibi considers the tolerant position of Cervantes until the point when he, Cervantes, has attributed the paternity of his *Don Quixote* to a Moresque historian in his long captivity in Algeria.[41] It enables Cervantes – and therefore Khatibi – to create a hybrid universe and a new kind of literature that he calls 'littérature qui porte en elle une vérité dangereuse' ['a literature that carries within it a dangerous truth'],[42] because it uses irony and humour as instruments of a revolution and emancipation, 'invent[ant] [le] futur et [la] diversité culturelle' ['inventing the future and cultural diversity'].[43] Here he sees a parallel with the creation of Franco-Maghrebian literature and culture as far as this new 'Arabic-Andalucian-Spanish' culture is characterized and marked by the '*plurilangue*' and by an oscillating duality that breaks the exultant polarities between 'Occident' and 'Orient', the 'Arab', 'Spanish' and 'French'. These new 'values', formulated by this literature and culture with an '*accent*', are always in danger and have to be protected, even nowadays:

> vu le comportement contradictoire des uns et des autres, attirés par l'instinct de destruction et de cruauté [...] Cervantès répond par le stoïcisme qui puisse sauver la tragi-comédie humaine, grâce à une stratégie de l'humilité qui convient au savoir vivre-ensemble. Pour un individu, l'humilité est de se mettre à distance des puissants, de respecter la dignité des démunis et des personnages vulnérables.[44]

> [Given the contradictory behaviour of different people, attracted by a destructive and cruel instinct [...] Cervantes responds with a stoicism that can save the human tragi-comedy by means of a strategy of humility appropriate to living together. For an individual, humility consists in distancing oneself from the powerful, in respecting the dignity of the disenfranchised and the vulnerable.]

It is precisely this '*littérature dangereuse*', with a '*vérité dangereuse*', that makes possible 'un art de vivre, qui exige de nous une imagination perpétuelle d'adaptation à une civilisation inventive et en devenir'[45] ['an art of living which demands from us that we constantly imagine adapting to an inventive and developing civilization'] and a construction

41 Ibid.
42 Ibid., pp. 234, 235.
43 Ibid., p. 237.
44 Ibid., p. 238.
45 Ibid.

of a '*savoir vivre-ensemble dans la civilité, la convivialité, la tolérance*'[46] ['a knowing how to live together based on civility, conviviality and tolerance'] which allow Khatibi to 'accéder à une réalité plus riche, plus varié, plus fertile, parce qu'il [l'art] traite la réalité comme une variation d'apparences' ['access a richer, more varied, more fertile reality, because it [art] treats reality as a variable appearance'].[47] In the context of this '*vérité dangereuse*' and this '*littérature dangereuse*', Khatibi gives imagination and playing with language the same central place given by Foucault when he speaks about *Don Quixote*:

> Don Quichotte est la première des œuvres modernes puisqu'on y voit la raison cruelle des identités et des différences se jouer à l'infini des signes et des similitudes; puisque le langage y rompt sa vieille parenté avec les choses, pour entrer dans cette souveraineté solitaire d'où il ne réapparaîtra, en son être abrupt, que devenu littérature; puisque la ressemblance entre là dans un âge qui est pour elle celui de la déraison et de l'imagination. La similitude et les signes une fois dénoués, deux expériences peuvent se constituer et deux personnages apparaître face à face. Le fou, entendu non pas comme malade, mais comme déviance constituée et entretenue, comme fonction culturelle indispensable, est devenu, dans l'expérience occidentale, l'homme des ressemblances sauvages. Ce personnage, tel qu'il est dessiné dans les romans ou le théâtre de l'époque baroque, et tel qu'il s'est institutionnalisé peu à peu jusqu'à la psychiatrie du XIXᵉ siècle, c'est celui qui s'est *aliéné* dans l'*analogie*. Il est le joueur déréglé du Même et de l'Autre. Il prend les choses pour ce qu'elles ne sont pas, et les gens les uns pour les autres; il ignore ses amis, reconnaît les étrangers; il croit démasquer, et il impose un masque. Il inverse toutes les valeurs et toutes les proportions, parce qu'il croit à chaque instant déchiffrer des signes: pour lui les oripeaux font un roi.

> [*Don Quixote* is the first modern work of literature, because in it we see the cruel reason of identities and differences make endless sport of signs and similitudes; because in it language breaks off its old kinship with things and enters into that lonely sovereignty from which it will reappear, in its separated state, only as literature; because it marks the point where resemblance enters an age which is, from the point of view of resemblance, one of madness and imagination. Once similitude and science are sundered from each other, two experiences can be established and two characters appear face to face. The madman, understood not as one who is sick but as an established and maintained deviant, as an

46 Ibid., p. 240.
47 Ibid., p. 238.

indispensable cultural function, has become, in Western experience, the man of primitive resemblances. This character, as he is depicted in the novels or plays of the Baroque age, and as he was generally institution-alized right up to the advent of nineteenth-century psychiatry, is the man who is *alienated* in *analogy*. He is the disordered player of the Same and the Other. He takes things for what they are not, and people for one another; he cuts his friends and recognizes complete estrangers; he thinks he is unmasking when in fact, he is putting on a mask. He inverts all values and all proportions, because he is constantly under the impression that he is deciphering signs; for him, the crown makes the king.][48]

Both Khatibi and Cervantes formulate through language and writing an absolutely new world that has a new capacity: 'l'art invente de la vie dans la mesure où il libère des forces inhibées et cachées dans le cœur et la conscience des hommes' ['art invents life to the extent that it liberates inhibited forces in the hearts and minds of men'].[49] Both Cervantes's and Khatibi's works build an *'accent'*-language of passages between 'French', 'Spanish' and 'Arabic', raising them to the Universal. And Khatibi underlines exactly this about Cervantes's writings: the power of the artist, of the language, of the imagination, of the visionary fool, of Zarathustras and of the subversive Harlequins, a writing that *'fait du roman un moyen de connaissance imaginaire, ouvert à toute découverte de l'esprit et de la vérité'* ['makes of the novel a form of imaginary knowledge, open to all discoveries of the mind and of truth'] and 'accueille l'étranger selon les lois de l'hospitalité littéraire. Cet étranger s'appelle Sidi Ahmed Begengeli' ['welcomes the stranger according to the laws of literary hospitality. This stranger is called Sidi Ahmed Begengeli'];[50] these foreigners are named Khatibi, Ben Jelloun, Memmi, Meddeb, Djebar, Sansal, Kilito, Laroui, Borges or Kafka, and many, many others.

The discovery of the manuscript of the *History of Don Quixote* at a market in Toledo is no less of an accident than the discovery of the modernity of Cervantes by Khatibi. What for Cervantes is Toledo, 'ville de convivialité intercommunautaire et interconfessionnelle' ['the city of conviviality between communities and faiths'],[51] ultimately of the

---

48   Michel Foucault, *Les Mots et les choses* (Paris: Gallimard, 1979 [1966]), pp. 62–3; *The Order of Things: An Archaeology of the Human Sciences* (London: Routledge, 2011), p. 54.
49   Khatibi, 'Cervantès et la modernité', p. 240.
50   Ibid.
51   Ibid.

'*tolédance*' and '*Occirient*', where he placed his *Don Quixote*, is, for Khatibi, the thinking at the interface, at the *hinge* between 'Occident' and 'Orient', his '*nomadic home*'. In the same way as Heidegger translates the Greeks and develops his own accent, Khatibi does this with both cultures, and thus from the beginning, with *La Mémoire tatouée*, steps beyond the theory of 'post-colonialism' towards 'post-coloniality':

> [...] la philosophie arabe [...] est grecque par essence [...].
> [...] le Dieu d'Aristote est entré dans l'islam avant l'arrivée de celui-ci. La théologie de l'islam et son épistémè globale étaient précédées par Aristote qui leur préexiste. Cette théologie de l'islam serait-elle d'abord une *traduction*? La traduction en arabe du monothéisme abrahamique par l'intermédiaire du syriaque et du grec?
> [...] l'islam qui est la métaphysique d'un dieu invisible a perdu le regard dans ce face-à-face avec les Grecs.
> [...] dédoublement de Dieu dans la philosophie arabe [...] les Arabes, en considérant la question de l'être selon leur *langue*, ont opéré une double traduction par l'intermédiaire du syriaque et du grec. Par cette double traduction, s'est renforcée une métaphysique du Texte.
> [Arabic philosophy [...] is Greek in essence [...].

> [...] The God of Aristotle entered Islam before the arrival of the latter. The theology of Islam and its global episteme were preceded by Aristotle who preexists them. Would this theology of Islam first be a *translation*? The translation into Arabic of Abrahamic monotheism via Syriac and Greek?
> [...] Islam, which is the metaphysics of an invisible god, lost its gaze in this face-to-face with the Greeks.
> [...] this splitting of God in Arabic philosophy. [...] the Arabs, in considering the question of being on the basis of their *language*, carried out a double translation via Syriac and Greek. Through this double translation, a metaphysics of the Text was reinforced.][52]

'Beyond' Postcolonialism and Postmodernism: *'Pensée autre'* – *'double critique'* – *'plurilinguisme'* – *'tatouage'*

Khatibi's hybrid condition and 'pluri-epistemological *accent*' are placed in his macro-theory or epistemology of the *'pensée-autre'* that reflects life at the interfaces of 'Orient' and 'Occident' in a simultaneous and

---

52 Khatibi, *Maghreb pluriel*, pp. 22–3; *Plural Maghreb*, pp. 9–10.

interwoven reciprocity between both. The 'double critique' is to be understood as an *operational category* of '*différance*', for the description of concrete pluri-cultural and pluri-lingual encounters that aim to deconstruct the conception of an essential being, of an essential 'Arabic-Muslim' and 'Christian identity', of an essentialism of 'Orient' and 'Occident'. It means to renounce the idea of a special, totalizing and fundamentalist construction of being that is exclusively Oriental or exclusively Occidental in favour of a performative and hybrid conception and praxis of being, and, as a consequence, of culture and identity.

This approach builds a 'beyond', opening a new cultural cartography, a '*pensée-dehors*'. Khatibi thinks — in translating both cultures related to each other — both himself and the other at the same time, as we have already stressed: 'pensée-autre' means to place oneself 'aux limites de ses possibilités. Car, nous voulons décentrer en nous le savoir occidental, nous décentrer par rapport à ce centre, à cette origine que se donne l'Occident' ['at the limits of its possiblities. For we seek to decenter in us Western knowledge, to decenter ourselves with respect to this center, this origin that the West gives itself'].[53]

Both the 'pensée-autre' and the 'double critique' represent an extraordinary act of 'translatio' where, Khatibi states, 'le chercheur arabe devient essentiellement le traducteur [...] d'un ensemble de pensées et de science' ['the Arab researcher essentially becomes the *translator* [...] of a set of thoughts and of sciences'].[54] He adds that:

> la traduction exige une pluralité de langues et de pensées qui s'y inscrivent. Et une pensée-autre, telle que nous l'envisageons, est une pensée en langues, une mondialisation traduisant des codes, des systèmes et des constellations de signes qui circulent dans le monde et au-dessus de lui (dans un sens non théologique).

> [Translation requires a plurality of languages and thoughts, inscribing themselves therein. And an other-thought, such as we envisage it, is a *thought in tongues*, a globalizing translation of the codes, systems, and constellations of signs that circulate in the world and above (in a nontheological sense).][55]

This is because cultural diversity, as the normal condition of civilization, imposes the imperative necessity of 'thinking in language' with an

53 Ibid., p. 54; p. 30.
54 Ibid., p. 59; pp. 34–5.
55 Ibid., pp. 59–60; p. 35.

'*accent*'[56] that is based on an 'obligation de dialogue avec la globalité de l'épistémè occidentale et universelle' ['obligation to engage in dialogue with the totality of the Western and universal apisteme'].[57] Such a concept of hybrid culture, that with an 'accent', is characterized by a performance ad libitum, in an endless chain of negotiations, recodifications and reinventions that correspond to Derrida's interpretation of the concept of '*tatouage*', as another term for 'hybridity' and '*accent*':

> L'absence d'un modèle d'identification stable pour un *ego* – dans toutes ses dimensions: linguistiques, culturelles, etc., – provoque des mouvements qui, se trouvant toujours *au bord* de l'effondrement, oscillent entre trois possibilités menaçantes.

> [The absence of a stable model of identification for an *ego* – in all its dimensions: linguistic, cultural and so on – gives rise to impulses that are always *on the brink* of collapse and oscillate, as a result, between three threatening possibilities.][58]

And, indeed, for Khatibi, the '*tatouage*' has the plural function of materializing and making visible the cultural '*différence*' ['difference'],[59] to liberate it from exoticism and stereotype in order to transform it into perceivable signs mediated by language and writing. The '*tatouage*' represents a phenomenon of the hybridization of diverse cultures, languages, '*accents*', passages, nomadism, de- and reterritorializations, a process of '*Entäußerung*', of '*Schizoglossia*' – as Khatibi formulates it – of a culture always 'on the move'.

Summary

Khatibi is the incarnation of 'hybridity' as well as of individual being, as an intellectual and as an indefatigable border crosser, as a 'border coyote', in the language of Gómez Peña,[60] placed on a sliding scale of

56 Ibid., p. 60; p. 35.
57 Ibid., p. 60; p. 35.
58 Jacques Derrida, *Le Monolinguisme de l'autre*, p. 116; *The Monolingualism of the Other*, p. 60.
59 Abdelkébir Khatibi, *La Mémoire tatouée: autobiographie d'un décolonisé* (Paris: Denoël, 1971), reprinted in *Œuvres de Abdelkébir Khatibi I: Romans et récits* (Paris: La Différence, 2008), pp. 9–113 (p. 111); *Tattooed Memory*, trans. Peter Thompson (Paris: L'Harmattan, 2016), p. 153.
60 Gómez Peña, *The New World Border*.

references and relations, in the '*accent*', in the '*cicatrice*' ['scar'], in the '*errance*' ['wandering'], in a '*permutation permanente*' ['permanent permutation'], in the '*folie de la langue*' ['the madness of language'] and in the '*Schizoglossia*' that build a '[t]opologie errante, schize, rêve androgyne, perte de l'identité – au seuil de la folie' ['wandering topology, separation, androgynous dream, loss of identity – at the threshold of madness'], a 'body-language', a 'corps imprononçable, ni arabe ni français, ni mort ni vivant, ni homme ni femme' ['an unpronounceable body, neither Arabic nor French, neither dead nor alive, neither man nor woman'].[61]

Khatibi finds in all kinds of literatures and cultures that practise diversity, so also in Cervantes, 'kindred spirits' opened to the world as principles of civilization, as a shared ethic and responsibility where the often discriminating question, resulting from the different 'sonorities and colours', *where do you come from?* is replaced by *who are you?* and by a '*langue hospitalière*', full of '*humanité*', '*amitié*' and '*vivre-ensemble*'. Cervantes is perhaps the first writer who thinks in terms of cultural 'hybridity' and Khatibi one of the most powerful voices in Oriental and Occidental culture and in the '*Occirient*', an exemplary case of tolerance, one who creates a real and substantial '*tolédance*'.

61   Khatibi, 'Repères', p. 49.

1. (August 1954) In the streets of Casablanca (Khatibi is second from the right).

2. (1957–8) Propaedeutic Year at the Lycée Lyautey in Casablanca
(Khatibi is in the third row, fourth from the left).

3. (July 1959)
Sant Miquel de Fluvià,
in the Catalonia region,
Spain.

4. (1959 or 1960)
With a Mauritarian friend
in Boulevard Saint-Michel,
Paris.

5. (1966) In India with Zakir Husain, the then Vice-President of the country.

6. (1972) During the 'First Congress on Mediterranean Studies of Arabo-Berber Influence', hosted by the Royal University (currently University of Malta) in Msida, Malta (Khatibi is in the first row, first from the left).

7. (In the 1970s) With his mother.

8. (October 1980) With Moroccan sociologist and writer Fatema Mernissi
during a visit to the Merinid Madrasa in Salé, Morocco.

9. (1987) In Paris with Algerian artist Rachid Koraïchi, Palestinian writer and diplomat Elias Sanbar and Palestinian poet Mahmoud Darwish during the preparation of the collective project *A Nation in Exile* (Amman: Darat al Funun, 1997), republished as *Une Nation en exil: hymnes gravés suivi de La Qasida de Beyrouth* (Algiers: Barzakh/Arles: Actes Sud, 2009). Photograph is published with the kind permission of Rachid Koraïchi. © Rachid Koraïchi.

10. (In the 1990s) With Egyptian psychiatrist and writer Jacques Hassoun and his wife.

11. (In the 1990s) With Syrian poet Adonis.

12. (In the 1990s) Working at his desk.

PART TWO

Cultural and
Philosophical Dialogues

CHAPTER SIX

Khatibi and the Transcolonial Turn

Olivia C. Harrison

Transcolonial Francophone Studies

Abdelkébir Khatibi has achieved canonical status in the field of postcolonial Francophone studies. Khatibi's work has, in fact, helped define the field, bringing questions of colonial acculturation, diglossia and bilingualism, travel and translation, and cultural, religious and racial plurality to bear on the study of literature of French expression. True to his self-styling as an 'étranger professionnel' ['professional stranger' or 'foreigner'], Khatibi is also one of the most well-travelled French-language thinkers.[1] His key concepts – 'double critique', 'pensée-autre' ['other-thinking'] and 'bi-langue' ['bifurcated tongue'] – have been deployed by key postcolonial theorists such as Walter Mignolo and Emily Apter, demonstrating the importance of his work beyond the Franco-Arabic context.[2] The renewed interest in translating Khatibi's

---

1 Abdelkébir Khatibi, *Figures de l'étranger dans la littérature française* (Paris: Denoël, 1987), p. 211. All translations are my own unless otherwise noted.

2 Walter Mignolo, *Local Histories/Global Designs: Coloniality, Subaltern Knowledges, and Border Thinking* (Princeton, NJ: Princeton University Press, 2012), chap. 1 (pp. 65–78). Emily Apter, *The Translation Zone: A New Comparative Literature* (Princeton, NJ: Princeton University Press, 2006), pp. 105–8. There is to date no authoritative translation of Khatibi's philosophical work. Critics have translated *pensée-autre* in a variety of ways: 'thought of otherness' [Réda Bensmaïa, *Experimental Nations: Or, the Invention of the Maghreb*, trans. Alyson Waters (Princeton, NJ: Princeton University Press, 2003), p. 141]; 'other thought' [Jane Hiddleston, *Understanding Postcolonialism* (London: Routledge, 2009), p. 127]; 'other-thought' [Abdelkébir Khatibi, 'Other-Thought', in *Plural Maghreb*, trans. P. Burcu Yalim (London: Bloomsbury, 2019), pp. 1–23]; 'thought-other' [Lucy Stone McNeece, 'Rescripting Modernity: Abdelkébir Khatibi and

œuvre into English attests to the generativity and continued relevance of his thought for the twenty-first century.[3]

Khatibi's canonization has coincided, to a large extent, with the institutionalization of postcolonial studies in the USA, UK, Australia and, much more recently and tentatively, France. It is by now a well-documented paradox that, despite the preponderance of anti- and postcolonial writing in French by the likes of Albert Memmi, Frantz Fanon, Edouard Glissant, Assia Djebar and Khatibi, French academia has been slow to embrace postcolonial theory, remaining until recently reticent to engage with a field perceived to be English language- and British Commonwealth-dominated, as well as overly politicized and governed by American-style identity politics.[4] Much has changed since the arrival of postcolonial theory in the metropole some 20 years ago, in no small part through the writings of Jacques Derrida, Hélène Cixous,

the Archeology of Signs', in Mildred Mortimer (ed.), *Maghrebian Mosaic: A Literature in Transition* (Boulder, CO: Lynne Rienner Publishers, 2011), pp. 81–98 (p. 94); Nasrin Qader, *Narratives of Catastrophe: Boris Diop, ben Jelloun, Khatibi* (New York: Fordham University Press, 2009), p. 123]; 'an other thinking' [Mignolo, *Local Histories/Global Designs*, p. 66], to name a few. I follow Mignolo's usage while preserving the hyphen; 'other-thinking' remains close to the original formulation while conveying the two senses present in the French: thinking otherwise and the other as horizon of thinking. For a succinct definition of 'pensée-autre', see Françoise Lionnet, 'Counterpoint and Double Critique in Edward Said and Abdelkébir Khatibi: A Transcolonial Comparison', in Ali Behdad and Dominic Thomas (eds.), *A Companion to Comparative Literature* (Oxford: Blackwell, 2011), pp. 387–407 (p. 401).

3   After the relatively quick translation of Khatibi's novel *Amour bilingue* [*Love in Two Languages*, trans. Richard Howard (Minneapolis: University of Minnesota Press, 1990)], the translation of Khatibi's work into English has been slow and piecemeal. Recent translations include: 'The Language of the Other: Testimonial Exercises', trans. Catherine Porter, *PMLA* 125.4 (2010), 1002–19; *Tattooed Memory*, trans. Peter Thompson (Paris: L'Harmattan, 2016); *Class Warrior – Taoist Style*, trans. Matt Reeck (Middletown, CT: Wesleyan University Press, 2017); and *Plural Maghreb*, trans. P. Burcu Yalim (London: Bloomsbury, 2019).

4   For a French perspective on the belated arrival of postcolonial studies in France, see Jean-Marc Moura, *Littératures francophones et théorie postcoloniale* (Paris: Presses universitaires de France, 1999) and Marie-Claude Smouts, 'Introduction: le postcolonial pour quoi faire?', in Marie-Claude Smouts (eds), *La Situation postcoloniale: les* postcolonial studies *dans le débat français* (Paris: Presses de la Fondation Nationale des Science Politiques, 2007), pp. 25–66 (pp. 55–66).

Glissant and the académicienne Djebar, which returned to France, so to speak, via their adoption in postcolonial studies departments in the USA and UK. The deprovincialization of French literature has expanded the corpus of French letters to include French-language writing from all corners of the earth, rivalling in its capaciousness the planetary reach of Commonwealth or Global English literature. Though the playing field is still far from level, the broad public interest generated by literary events such as the manifesto 'Pour une "littérature-monde" en français' attests to the profound nature of the shifts that have occurred in French academia over the past several decades. Without neglecting the pitfalls of the recent appeal for a 'world literature in French', it is hard to argue that the field of French letters is not considerably more hospitable today that it was a mere 15 years ago.[5]

An unexpected result of this belated adoption of postcolonial theory in the field of French and Francophone studies, I argue, is that it risks to recentre the colonial binary, a binary that was rightly the focus of French-language anticolonial theory – I am of course thinking of Memmi's *Portrait du colonisé* and Fanon's *Les Damnés de la terre* – and yet was already being undermined by its own theorists. Even Memmi, who admits to being caught in the colonial dialectic by virtue of his privileged position, as an assimilated Jew, in 'the pyramid of petty tyrants', calls in no uncertain terms for the destruction of the colonial dialectic and the complete decolonization of human relations. Building on Memmi's Hegelian understanding of decolonization, Fanon's magnum opus is an urgent appeal to leave Europe behind and 'find something different – something we might call the Third World project or, following Khatibi, an 'other-thinking' that eschews the double bind of assimilation and nativism.[6]

5   Muriel Barbery, Tahar Ben Jelloun, Alain Borer *et al.*, 'Manifeste pour une littérature-monde en français', *Le Monde des Livres*. Online. 15 Mar. 2007: www.lemonde.fr/livres/article/2007/03/15/des-ecrivains-plaident-pour-un-roman-en-francais-ouvert-sur-le-monde_883572_3260.html (accessed 14 Dec. 2017). For a thorough (and often critical) analysis of the manifesto, see Alec G. Hargreaves, Charles Forsdick and David Murphy (eds), *Transnational French Studies: Postcolonialism and Littérature-Monde* (Liverpool: Liverpool University Press, 2010). See also Jean-Marc Moura, 'Le Postcolonial dans les études littéraires en France', in Smouts, *La Situation postcoloniale*, pp. 98–119 (pp. 104–8).

6   Albert Memmi, *The Colonizer and the Colonized*, trans. Howard Greenfeld (New York: Orion Press, 1965), p. 17 and Frantz Fanon, *The Wretched of the Earth*, trans. Constance Farrington (New York: Grove Press, 1968), p. 312.

The postcolonial turn in Francophone studies has led to the privileging of notions such as hybridity and vertical contact (France-Maghreb) in Khatibi's work – those we associate, somewhat reductively or selectively, with the early days of postcolonial theory – at the expense of the Third Worldist inspirations and aspirations of his writings.[7] In this essay, I propose to read Khatibi against the grain of postcolonial Francophone studies, supplementing the important work that has been done on the postcolonial dimensions of his writings – most notably the encounter between French and Arabic – through a study of its tricontinental dimensions. Indeed, Khatibi is one of the thinkers who have most faithfully captured the plurality, multipolarity and transversality of the Third World as project. His writings distil the energy of the 'decolonial generation' and reclaim or rearticulate a more dynamic understanding of postcoloniality, one that, drawing on Françoise Lionnet and Shu-mei Shih, I dub *transcolonial*: a condition that is not exclusively shaped by the legacies of colonialism, but is in an active sense structured through horizontal forms of relationality. Thus revised, decolonization represents, in Khatibi's terms, a 'chance of thought', a 'double critique', an 'other-thinking' that moves beyond the Manichean world dissected by Memmi and Fanon.[8]

Even in texts that adopt a Moroccan and Maghrebian frame of reference – *Le Roman maghrébin*, *Maghreb pluriel*, *Amour bilingue* – the Third World looms large. In the introduction to his 1968 study of

7   The spirited debates around the very notion of the postcolonial at the moment of the emergence of the field show that postcolonial studies have always been concerned with horizontal relations across the Third World. See in particular Anne McClintock, 'Pitfalls of the Term "Post-Colonialism"', *Social Text* 31/32 (1992), pp. 84–98 and Ella Shohat, 'Notes on the "Post-Colonial"', *Social Text* 31/32 (1992), pp. 99–113.

8   Khatibi uses the expressions 'decolonial generation' and 'chance of thought' in the seminal essay 'Pensée-autre': 'se décoloniser, c'est cette *chance* de la pensée' ['to decolonize oneself is this *chance* of thought']. Abdelkébir Khatibi, *Maghreb pluriel* (Paris: Denoël, 1983), pp. 15–16; *Plural Maghreb*, pp. 4–5 (original italics). For a succinct definition of transcolonialism, see Françoise Lionnet and Shu-mei Shih, 'Introduction: Thinking through the Minor, Transnationally', in *Minor Transnationalism*, ed. Françoise Lionnet and Shu-mei Shih (Durham, NC: Duke University Press, 2005), pp. 1–23 (p. 11). See also Moura's brief comments on the promising turn towards 'transcolonial studies' and, in his response to Moura, Michel Naumann's call for a 'South–South dialogue'. Moura, 'Le Postcolonial dans les études littéraires en France', in Smouts, *La Situation postcoloniale*, pp. 114–15, pp. 117–18.

the Maghrebian novel – a monograph that in all other respects focuses on Maghrebian literature and the French colonial experience – Khatibi enjoins his compatriots to look beyond France to forge transversal relations with the rest of the Third World:

> Une des conditions de l'édification d'une culture nationale décolonisée est de faire justement éclater les rapports unilatéraux unissant la métropole à ses anciennes colonies, de multiplier les contacts avec le monde extérieur, de faire jouer d'autres circuits et de promouvoir la collaboration effective entre pays du Tiers-Monde.[9]

> [One of the conditions of a decolonized national culture is precisely to break apart the unilateral relations tying the metropole to its former colonies, to multiply contacts with the outside world, to bring into play other circuits and promote real collaboration between the countries of the Third World.]

Over the course of the next 15 years, Khatibi would advance the twin notions of 'double critique' and 'other-thinking' as the condition of possibility for these new forms of circulation and relationality. But it is in the work he began producing in the 1980s – the period that coincides, somewhat paradoxically, with the adoption of Khatibi into the canon of postcolonial Francophone texts – that the decolonial stakes of the Third World project come most fully into view.

I focus in this essay on a flashpoint of transcolonial solidarity, one that radiates throughout Khatibi's writings and illuminates several of his key concepts: Palestine. The Palestinian question has played a seminal if neglected role in Khatibi's *œuvre*, from the central notion of a plural Maghreb to his musings on language, colonialism and 'pensée-autre', an expression he initially coined, as I will elaborate below, in response to the massacre of Palestinian fighters by Jordanian troops in 1970. In what follows, I examine the central importance of the Palestinian question in Khatibi's writings, from his 1974 polemical essay on Zionism, *Vomito blanco*, to his epistolary exchanges with the Egyptian Jewish psychoanalyst Jacques Hassoun in the 1980s.

9 Abdelkébir Khatibi, *Le Roman maghrébin* (Paris: Maspéro, 1968), p. 14.

Palestine as Horizon of Thinking

The subtitle of this section is adapted from an early version of what is probably Khatibi's most influential text, published in its definitive form under the title 'Pensée-autre' in his 1983 collection of essays *Maghreb pluriel*. Written for 'Du Maghreb', a 1977 special issue of *Les Temps Modernes* co-edited by Khatibi, Abdelwahab Meddeb and Noureddine Abdi, 'Le Maghreb comme horizon de pensée' is a condensed version of 'Pensée-autre', with one important excision: Palestine. In both versions of the essay, the final section, entitled 'De la différence intraitable' ['On intractable difference'], culminates in an appeal for a double critique of Western and Arab metaphysics, an intractable thinking of difference that Khatibi names 'pensée-autre' or 'other-thinking'. Let me cite the conclusion of the first version of this essay, which retains the titular notion through the phrase 'le Maroc, en tant qu'horizon de pensée' ['Morocco as horizon of thinking'] and elucidates the image of a plural Maghreb so central to Khatibi's thought:

> — Double critique, dites-vous?
> — Critique des deux métaphysiques, de leur face à face. En fait, un choix, un seul choix est possible: penser le Maroc tel qu'il *est*, comme un site topographique entre l'Orient et l'Occident. Le Maroc, en tant qu'horizon de pensée, est encore innommable. D'une part, il faut l'entendre résonner dans sa propre langue (ses langues); et d'autre part, seul le Dehors repensé, décentré, subverti, détourné de ses déterminations dominantes, peut nous éloigner de l'identité aveugle et de la différence sauvage. Seul le Dehors repensé peut déchirer notre nostalgie du Père et l'arracher à son sol métaphysique – ou du moins l'infléchir vers un tel arrachement. Vers une pensée souveraine, souverainement orpheline. Tel est l'autre versant de la différence intraitable et telle est notre relation à la pensée d'une telle différence.

> [— Double critique, you say?
> — Critique of these two metaphysics, of their confrontation. In fact, only one choice is possible: thinking Morocco as it *is*, as a topographical site between the East and the West. As a horizon of thinking, Morocco remains unnameable. On the one hand, one should listen to it resonate in its own language (its languages); on the other, only the outside rethought, decentred, subverted, diverted from its dominant determinations can allow us to go beyond senseless identity and savage difference. Only the outside thus rethought can tear our nostalgia for the Father away from its metaphysical ground – or at least bend it toward such a tearing. Toward a sovereign thought, a supremely orphaned thought. Such is the other

side of intractable difference, such is our relation to the thought of this difference.][10]

In the paragraph that immediately precedes this call for intractable difference and other-thinking, Khatibi gives a concrete example of what he names here 'savage difference': the Arab repression of Palestinian nationalism. Note that Palestine offers, in this instance, an example of Arab intolerance and identitarian violence, rather than Israeli colonialism. In other words, Palestine appears in Khatibi's text as a critique of Arab, not Western, metaphysics:

> — C'est pourquoi il faut fixer notre attention sur le face à face de ces deux métaphysiques, dont l'une efface l'autre. Nous sommes saisis dans cet écart, en un geste inouï.
> — C'est ce que vous appelez 'la différence intraitable'?
> — Oui. Et il y a d'autres écarts, d'autres ruptures qui déchaînent la violence des uns et des autres. L'identité aveugle et la différence sauvage en sont des démonstrations visibles à coup d'œil, et dirait-on, à coup de mitraillette. Au nom de l'unité communautaire des Arabes, on massacre la Palestine. La mitraillette est au bout de la théologie comme un sinistre déchaînement de la métaphysique. La différence intraitable est un dessaisissement de la métaphysique par une double critique, un double combat, une double mort.[11]

> [— This is why we must focus our attention on the confrontation of these two metaphysics, one of which erases the other. We are caught in this gap, in an as yet inconceivable gesture.
> — So this is what you call 'intractable difference'?
> — Yes. And there are other gaps, other ruptures that are unleashed in the violence of some against the others. Senseless identity and savage difference offer visible and, shall we say, ballistic evidence of it. In the name of the communal unity of the Arabs, Palestine is massacred. The machine gun is at the end of theology like a sinister unleashing of metaphysics. Intractable difference is a relinquishing of metaphysics through a double critique, a double combat, a double death.]

---

10 Abdelkébir Khatibi, 'Le Maghreb comme horizon de pensée', *Les Temps Modernes* 375 bis (1977), pp. 7–20 (p. 20), reprinted in Abdelkébir Khatibi, *Penser le Maghreb* (Rabat: Société Marocaine des Editeurs Réunis, 1993), pp. 123–36 (p. 136). With minor modifications, I have translated citations from 'Le Maghreb comme horizon de pensée' with an eye to P. Burcu Yalim's translation of the final section of 'Pensée-autre' (Khatibi, 'Other-Thought', pp. 22–3).

11 Khatibi, 'Le Maghreb comme horizon de pensée', pp. 19–20.

Palestine is not named in the final version of this essay, which glosses over this exemplary case through the rather vague formulation 'vous avez des exemples [de cette violence], partout dans le monde arabe, iranien' ['You have examples of this [violence] everywhere in the Arab and Iranian world'].[12] 'The Iranian world' constitutes a somewhat surprising interjection in a text that takes aim at 'Arab metaphysics'. One might speculate that in 1981, the year he drafted the final version of this essay, Khatibi felt that it was more fitting to invoke the Islamic revolution than the Palestinian question. Yet restoring Khatibi's mention of Palestine is crucial, I contend, to grasping the significance and import of the notions of other-thinking and double critique he would elaborate in later texts. In what follows I track the articulation of these twin concepts to the question of Palestine, offering a transcolonial genealogy of Khatibi's thought.

Palestine was at the forefront of Khatibi's mind as he was formulating his thoughts on Maghrebian plurality, and the concepts that would come to be most intimately associated with Khatibian thought: other-thinking, double critique and, as I will show in the final section of this essay, *bi-langue* and the notion of the professional stranger or foreigner. In the mid-1960s, Khatibi had been involved with a Marxist–Leninist group of poets and artists that produced what remains one of the most important venues of Third Worldist thought, the journal *Souffles*. It is in the pages of *Souffles* that Khatibi published some of his first poems, as well as a summary of *Le Roman maghrébin*, which would receive a lengthy, if somewhat critical, review by Tahar Ben Jelloun (then known as Tahar Benjelloun), another contributor who made his literary debut in the journal. Khatibi ceased contributing to *Souffles* after its 1968 shift to an explicitly Marxist–Leninist and pan-Arabist editorial line, with the notable exception of the 1969 special issue 'Pour la révolution palestinienne' ['For the Palestinian Revolution'], the planning stages of which began immediately after the June 1967 Arab–Israeli War. Unlike Tahar Ben Jelloun and Mostafa Nissabouri (E. M. Nissaboury), who had also distanced themselves from *Souffles* by the time the Palestine issue went to print, Khatibi did not contribute a poem, artwork or essay to this issue. But his name features prominently in the relatively short list of signatories (nine in total) of the centrepiece editorial on Palestine, 'Appel aux écrivains maghrébins' ['Appeal to Maghrebian Writers']. Tying the Palestinian struggle to the fight against neocolonialism and 'internal

12   Khatibi, 'Pensée-autre', p. 38; 'Other-Thought', p. 22.

colonialism' in Morocco, the appeal calls upon Maghrebian writers to cease imitating derelict French and Arabic literary models to forge new poetic forms, in concert with Mashriqi and Palestinian avant-garde writers, fit to the task of decolonizing Arab literature, 'regardless of its language of expression'.[13] It is notable that the appeal condemns both French and Zionist cultural imperialism and deculturation, and what it calls the 'defeatist jeremiads and morbid prayers' of *adab al-hazima*, the 'literature of defeat' that flourished after *al-naksa* ('the setback' of June 1967) and which the signatories of the appeal dismiss as hopelessly nostalgic, if not reactionary.[14] Here, in succinct, bullet-point form, is an example of what, anticipating Khatibi, we might call a 'double critique' of neocolonialism and nativism:

> Les écrivains maghrébins, regroupés autour de la revue SOUFFLES, signataires du présent appel,
> [...]
> *Affirment*
> — Que l'apport de cette révolution quant à nous écrivains maghrébins est décisif. Cette révolution
> — Impose aujourd'hui une radicalisation de nos options et de nos engagements
> [...]
> — fait sentir l'urgence d'affermir la lutte contre le néo-colonialisme (sous toutes ses formes et notamment culturelle) qui déploie, bien que sous des formes subtiles, les mêmes moyens que la colonisation impérialo-sioniste en Palestine, en vue de la déculturation de nos peuples
> — rend plus évidente la nécessité que nous avions toujours proclamée de la remise en question des contenus et des formes sclérosés de notre culture traditionnelle ainsi que des démarches mystificatrices de la culture occidentale bourgeoise qui ont jusqu'à maintenant constitué au Maghreb les éléments majeurs de blocages intellectuels et psychiques

> [The Maghrebi writers who have gathered around the journal *Souffles* and who have signed this appeal,
> [...]
> Affirm

13 Abdelkébir Khatibi, with Tahar Benjelloun, Bensalem Himmich, Abdellatif Laâbi *et al.*, 'Appeal to Maghrebi Writers', trans. Anne-Marie McManus, in Olivia C. Harrison and Teresa Villa-Ignacio (eds), *Souffles-Anfas: A Critical Anthology from the Moroccan Journal of Culture and Politics* (Stanford, CA: Stanford University Press, 2016), p. 210.

14 Ibid., p. 211.

— that the implications of this revolution for us Maghrebi writers are decisive. This revolution

— forces us, today, to radicalize our choices and our engagements [...]

— reveals the urgent need to redouble the struggle against neocolonialism (in all its forms, notably cultural), which deploys the same methods, albeit in more subtle ways, as imperial-Zionist colonization in Palestine to bring about the deculturation of our peoples

— confirms the need that we have long proclaimed to call into question the ossified contents and forms of our traditional culture and the mystifying reasoning of bourgeois Western culture that have constituted, to the present day, the primary elements of intellectual and psychic obstacles in the Maghreb.][15]

Even more radical in its condemnation of cultural imperialism than Khatibi's *Le Roman maghrébin*, the appeal Khatibi signed in 1969 takes up his call to 'faire jouer d'autres circuits et [...] promouvoir une collaboration effective entre pays du Tiers Monde' ['bring into play other circuits and promote real collaboration between the countries of the Third World'], enshrining Palestine as the figure of Third Worldist solidarity par excellence in the decolonial era.[16]

In 1974, Khatibi published an essay that makes good on the appeal's promise of transcolonial 'radicalization' under the title *Vomito blanco: le sionisme et la conscience malheureuse* (Vomito blanco: Zionism and unhappy consciousness). The first text by Khatibi explicitly to engage with the Palestinian question, *Vomito blanco* is also an early exercise in double critique. Focused almost entirely on Zionist ideology and its support in the French left – the book refutes Jean-Paul Sartre's 'conditional Zionism' and the 'impasse' of Memmi's anticolonial Zionism – *Vomito blanco* also, at key points, articulates a critique of Arab regimes and Arab ethno-nationalism, announcing the movement of 'double critique' that he began working on in the eponymous essay published in 1970, and subsequently developed in 'Le Maghreb comme horizon de pensée' and 'Pensée-autre'.[17] Connecting Khatibi's earlier militancy within the *Souffles* movement to the philosophical and poetic texts that have been the focus of postcolonial readings of Khatibi, *Vomito blanco* represents,

15   Abdelkébir Khatibi, with Tahar Benjelloun, Bensalem Himmich, Abdellatif Laâbi *et al.*, 'Appel aux écrivains maghrébins', *Souffles* 15 (1969), pp. 99–100; 'Appeal to Maghrebi Writers', pp. 209–10.

16   Khatibi, *Le Roman maghrébin*, p. 14.

17   Abdelkébir Khatibi, *Vomito blanco: le sionisme et la conscience malheureuse* (Paris: Union générale d'éditions, 1974), pp. 48, 104.

I argue, an important pivotal point and early staging ground for his signature concepts of double critique and other-thinking.

Vomito blanco was born, Khatibi tells us in his preface, from two separate moments of extreme nausea: 'ce texte a été précédé par deux envies de vomir, la première fois, provoquée par la semaine rouge de Jordanie en septembre 1970, et la deuxième fois, deux ans après, par le déchaînement raciste après le coup de force de *Septembre Noir* à Munich' ['this text was preceded by two occasions when I felt the need to vomit, the first provoked by the red week in Jordan in September 1970, the second, two years later, by the unleashing of racism after the *Black September* attacks in Munich'].[18] This 'pamphlet' was written, Khatibi tells us, in an attempt to 'translate' the 'rage' he felt before Arab anti-Palestinian violence and Western anti-Arab racism.[19] It is of note that Khatibi begins his critique of Zionism by invoking not a Zionist crime but the bloody massacre, by King Hussein's troops, of thousands of Palestinian *feda'in* and civilians in Jordanian refugee camps in September 1970. Double critique, and the condemnation of Arab violence against Palestinians, is foundational to Khatibi's critique of the violence of the Israeli state.

Vomito blanco maintains a tone of moral outrage and political pathos throughout the text. But nowhere does the tone of the essay strike us as more poignant than when Khatibi is speaking of his own relation to Jews. Note the abrupt shift in tone from a caustic denunciation of leftist Zionism – here Khatibi is condemning Robert Misrahi's conflation of anti-Zionism and anti-Semitism – to a lyrical appeal to what we might call, previewing Khatibi's later writings, other-thinking:

> Mais étant sémite et violemment antiraciste moi-même, je me sens notoirement concerné. Devinant la misère effroyable de l'esprit nazi, je me manifeste radicalement chaque fois qu'on exprime des sentiments bizarres vis-à-vis des Juifs. Dans ma société, je combats l'affirmation ethnique. Mais qu'ai-je à me justifier? Ma chance est une morale ouverte, un jeu infini où l'identité irréductible n'a plus de sens. Qu'est-ce donc que la judéité? Qu'est-ce donc que mon arabité? N'ai-je pas dit que le dépassement de soi-même ou de son identité folle exige d'autres valeurs, plus ensoleillées, plus gaies, plus légères, quelque univers insaisissable où la sensation du possible excède toute idéologie.[20]

18   Ibid., p. 1.
19   Ibid., p. 2.
20   Ibid., p. 86.

[Being a Semite and a virulent anti-racist, however, [accusations of anti-Semitism] concern me to the utmost degree. Knowing the terrible wretchedness of the Nazi spirit, I protest vehemently whenever bizarre sentiments towards Jews are expressed. In my society, I combat ethnic claims. But why should I justify myself? My chance is an open morality, an infinite game where irreducible identity no longer has any meaning. What, then, is Jewishness? And what, then, is my Arabness? Haven't I said that going beyond oneself or one's mad identity demands other values, sunnier, happier, lighter values, some ungraspable universe where the sensation of possibility exceeds all ideology.]

An ungenerous reader might interpret this passage as a denial (*une dénégation*) that betrays a suspect attitude towards Jews, particularly in light of other passages, most notably in Khatibi's autobiographical texts, where he admits to his own 'bizarre' behaviour as a child. In *La Mémoire tatouée*, an autobiographical novel published in 1971, the narrator describes his escapades in the Jewish quarters of Essaouira: 'Le mellah n'est pas loin, d'autres odeurs, un autre dialecte légèrement chantant qui me faisait pouffer. Je happais des calottes de vieux bonhommes, et les vendais. Avec l'argent, on recommençait dans l'autre sens' ['The Jewish quarter is not far, other odors, another lightly sing-song dialect that made me burst out laughing. I snatched the skullcaps of old gents, and sold them. With the money, we started over the other way'].[21] But Khatibi has dwelled on this autobiographical vignette elsewhere, clarifying the importance of these 'bizarre' encounters with the Jewish world of his childhood in the formation of his thought of plurality. In *Le Même Livre*, a five-year epistolary exchange with the Egyptian Jewish psychoanalyst Jacques Hassoun published in 1985, he returns to this memory to evoke what he calls his 'Jewishness':

> Je veux raconter, parce que ces petits détails me font remonter le temps de ma 'judaïté', qui est, que je le veuille ou non, un tatouage de ma pure enfance.
>
> D'habitude, c'était nous, les enfants, qui allions attaquer au Mellah. Par exemple, à Essaouira, ville qui était très peuplée alors par les Juifs, nous volions des chéchias au vieux Juifs pour pouvoir les revendre. Mais je ne dois pas exagérer en ce sens parce que ça va réveiller de vieux

---

21 Abdelkébir Khatibi, *La Mémoire tatouée: autobiographie d'un colonisé* (Paris: Denoël, 1971), reprinted in *Œuvres de Abdelkébir Khatibi I: Romans et récits* (Paris: La Différence, 2008), pp. 9–113 (p. 36); *Tattooed Memory*, trans. Peter Thompson (Paris: L'Harmattan, 2016), p. 44. Translation modified.

démons. Je ne dois pas généraliser. Je l'ai fait une fois, une seule, et c'était trop facile pour nous – enfants – sans courage aucun, de chiper ainsi une calotte. Que dire? Plus que cela, nous répétions le geste ailleurs, dans le cimetière juif où nous volions des gri-gri, mais nous faisions de même dans les marabouts musulmans. Je devais avoir cinq/six ans.[22]

[I want to tell this story, because these small details enable me to return to the time of my 'Jewishness', which is, like it or not, a tattoo of my pure childhood.

Usually it was us children who would go on rampages in the Mellah. For example, in Essaouira, a city where there was then a sizeable Jewish population, we would steal old Jews' skullcaps and resell them. But I should be careful not to go too far, because if I do I will awaken old demons. I should not generalize. I did this once, only once, and it was too easy for us kids to filch a skullcap, without any courage whatsoever. What can I say? More than this, we would repeat the gesture elsewhere, in the Jewish cemetery where we would steal amulets, but we would do the same in the tombs of Muslim saints. I must have been five or six.]

Might we read this vignette as a belated response to the speculative chiasmus articulated in *Vomito blanco*: 'Qu'est-ce donc que *la judéité*? Qu'est-ce donc que *mon arabité*?' The 'other direction' evoked in *La Mémoire tatouée* would thus signal an unravelling of the very distinction between Jews and Arabs, Jews and Muslims, evidenced in *Le Même Livre* by the child's parallel escapades in the Jewish cemetery and the tombs of marabouts. This multidirectionality – 'on recommençait dans l'autre sens' – is what enables Khatibi to collapse the parallelism of the first expression to speak of '[his] "Jewishness"'.

Before tackling the question of Jews and Arabs in *Le Même Livre*, let me conclude my remarks on the double critique that makes possible the unravelling of Jewish and Muslim/Arab identities in *Vomito blanco*. An unrelenting and at times polemical critique of leftist Zionism, *Vomito blanco* is also aimed at Arabist essentialism, rejecting a dualistic understanding of 'the Israeli–Arab conflict' – Jews versus Arabs – in favour of a deconstructive approach to the 'madness' of identity ['[l']identité folle'], ideology, metaphysics. It is not surprising that Khatibi ends up advocating in this text for what today we would call the one-state solution, reproducing, in the annex that closes the book, calls by the Palestine Liberation Organization's left wing for a democratic state for

22 Abdelkébir Khatibi and Jacques Hassoun, *Le Même Livre* (Paris: Editions de l'Eclat, 1985), p. 107.

Jewish, Muslim and Christian citizens alike.[23] Khatibi's questioning of
Arabness and Jewishness as stable identities in the musings cited above
are deeply political, and connected to his recuperative interpretation of
Marxism in the second half of the book. For Khatibi, Marxism represents
more than a struggle between the oppressed and their oppressor – what
we might call, transposing the terms of class struggle into the colonial
context and harkening back to my introductory remarks, the colonial
dialectic. More profoundly, Marxism enables the overcoming of the
dialectic itself, in a great reshuffling of the order of things:

> La lutte des classes n'est pas simplement une dialectique entre dominateurs
> et dominés, mais bien cette question illimitée d'introduire un désordre
> permanent dans l'existence des hommes et de leur communication [...] Le
> révolutionnaire est un *passeur*: il brise les idoles mais n'est jamais sûr de
> ses projets, de son avenir.[24]

> [Class struggle is not simply a dialectic between the dominators and the
> dominated, it is rather the limitless question of introducing permanent
> disorder in the existence of men and in their communication [...] The
> revolutionary is one who *passes*: he breaks idols but is never sure of his
> plans, of his future.]

Echoing the positions published in *Souffles*'s Palestine issue, Khatibi
concludes that *'only a generalized class struggle in the Middle East
will liberate the Palestinians and Zionism from the national question'*
– the national question, understood here in the sense of identity-based

---

23   Khatibi includes, in an annex, two unattributed 'Palestinian documents'.
Khatibi, *Vomito blanco*, pp. 155–78. As best I can tell, the first, entitled 'Sionisme
et révolution palestinienne', is excerpted from a 1970 document by the Popular
Democratic Front for the Liberation of Palestine. Parts of this text can be found
on the communist website lesmaterialistes.com. See Front Démocratique Populaire
de Libération de la Palestine (FDLP), 'Des propositions stériles à la solution
démocratique (10 sep 1970)': http://lesmaterialistes.com/fdlp-propositions-steriles-
solution-democratique-1970 (accessed 14 Dec. 2017). Entitled 'Pour un Etat
démocratique', the second text included in Khatibi's annex is excerpted from
Fath's 1970 document, 'Pour un Etat démocratique en Palestine' (General Union
of Palestine Students, 1970). See the third section of the text posted on the Belgian
Marxist–Leninist website, Centre Marxiste-Léniniste-Maoiste [B], 'Fatah: La
révolution palestinienne et les Juifs – 1970' (7 Dec. 2016): https://web.archive.org/
web/20180103193639/www.centremlm.be/Fatah-La-revolution-palestinienne-et-
les-Juifs-%E2%88%92-1970 (La nouvelle Palestine démocratique) (accessed 1 June
2020).
24   Khatibi, *Vomito blanco*, p. 95, original italics.

nationalism or ethno-nationalism.[25] The shape of the nation is not predetermined, it is to be constructed through the revolutionary struggle, no matter the religion, nationality or ethnicity of the revolutionaries. It should not surprise us, then, that *Vomito blanco* quickly went out of print in Israel, where the Israeli Black Panthers – a radical Mizrachi ('Oriental Jewish') organization that styled itself after the Black Panther Party and identified with the Palestinians – disseminated pirated copies of the book, to Khatibi's delight.[26]

All but ignored in France, to this date untranslated into English or any other language, *Vomito blanco* is seldom discussed by Khatibi critics, let alone taught in Francophone postcolonial classes.[27] Yet this text represents a milestone in the development of Khatibi's intellectual itinerary, laying the ground for the central notions of double critique, other-thinking, *bi-langue*, and the professional stranger or foreigner. It is to these latter two notions that I now turn.

The Language of the Other

If other-thinking and double critique are Khatibi's most well-travelled concepts, he is best known in the field of French and Francophone studies for his writings on language in the postcolony. Engaging critically with his literary elders and especially Albert Memmi, who famously predicted that 'colonized literature in European languages appears condemned to die young', Khatibi developed a sophisticated understanding of plurilingualism, diglossia and what he calls *bi-langue* (literally 'bi-language'; more accurately, 'bifurcated tongue') from his early study of the anti- and postcolonial Maghrebian novel, to the essays and novels he published some fifteen years later, most notably *Amour bilingue*, 'Bilinguisme et littérature' ['Bilingualism and Literature'] (both published in 1983) and *Le Même Livre* (1985). Here is how the narrator characterizes *bi-langue* in Khatibi's allegorical tale of postcolonial plurilingualism, *Amour*

25   Ibid., p. 101, original italics.
26   Abdelkébir Khatibi, 'Droit à la raison', in *Paradoxes du sionisme* (Rabat: El Kalam, 1990), pp. 13–25 (p. 21).
27   To my knowledge, Lionnet is the only critic to take seriously the importance of *Vomito blanco* in the trajectory of Khatibi's thought. Françoise Lionnet, 'Counterpoint and Double Critique', in Behdad and Thomas, *A Companion to Comparative Literature*, p. 398.

bilingue: 'Oui, mais de langue en langue, un événement apparaît et disparaît, un événement exceptionnel qui demande une énergie extraordinaire. Evénement que nous appelons bi-langue, différence de toute pensée qui s'affirme et s'abolit dans la traduction' ['Yes, but from language to language, an event appears and disappears, an exceptional event which requires extraordinary energy. An event we call *bi-langue*, different from all thinking which affirms itself and obliterates itself in translation'].[28]

In an essay on Abdelwahab Meddeb's novel *Talismano*, written around the time Khatibi was drafting *Amour bilingue* and published alongside 'Double critique' and 'Pensée-autre' in *Maghreb pluriel*, Khatibi explains *bi-langue* thus:

> J'ai suggéré – et Kateb l'a déclaré très nettement – que l'écrivain arabe de langue française est saisi dans un chiasme, un chiasme entre l'aliénation et l'inaliénation (dans toutes les orientations de ces deux termes): cet auteur n'écrit pas sa langue propre, il transcrit son nom propre transformé, il ne peut rien posséder (si tant soit peu on s'approprie une langue), il ne possède ni son parler maternel qui ne s'écrit pas, ni la langue arabe écrite qui est aliénée et donnée à une substitution, ni cette autre langue apprise et qui lui fait signe de se désapproprier en elle et de s'y effacer. Souffrance insoluble lorsque cet écrivain n'assume pas cette identité entamée, dans *une clarté de pensée qui vit de ce chiasme, de cette schize.*

> [I suggested – and Kateb stated it very clearly – that the Arab writer of French language is caught in a chiasmus, a chiasmus between alienation and inalienation (in all dimensions of the two terms) – this author does not write his proper language, he transcribes his proper name transformed; he cannot possess anything (if ever one appropriates a language), he possesses neither his maternal speech that is not written nor the written Arabic language that is alienated and given to a substitution, nor this other learned language that signals him to disappropriate and erase himself therein. Insoluble suffering when the writer does not assume this instituted identity, in *a clarity of thought that lives on this chiasmus, this split.*][29]

---

28   Albert Memmi, *The Colonizer and the Colonized*, p. 111. Abdelkébir Khatibi, *Amour bilingue* (Montpellier: Fata Morgana, 1983), reprinted in *Œuvres de Abdelkébir Khatibi I: Romans et récits* (Paris: La Différence, 2008), pp. 205–83 (p. 249); *Love in Two Languages*, p. 67. Translation modified.

29   Khatibi, 'Bilinguisme et littérature", in *Maghreb pluriel*, 177–207 (p. 201); Khatibi, 'Bilingualism and Literature', in *Plural Maghreb*, 117–40 (pp. 134–35). Original italics.

The bifurcated thinking evoked here should, of course, immediately evoke Khatibi's twin concepts, double critique and other-thinking. If *bi-langue* is a response to the 'linguistic drama' of the 'colonized writer' so forcefully evoked by Memmi at the height of the anticolonial struggles of the Maghreb, other-thinking and double critique are its conditions of possibility. Neither the language of the colonizer nor the language of the colonized, *bi-langue* is perhaps the only idiom fit to the task outlined by Khatibi in *Le Roman maghrébin*: 'éclater les rapports unilatéraux unissant la métropole à ses anciennes colonies' ['to break apart the unilateral relation tying the metropole to its former colonies']. Put otherwise, plurilingualism, other-thinking and what Khatibi names 'other-literature' represent the writer's way out of the colonial dialectic. As the *récitant* joyfully declares at the close of *Amour bilingue*, summoning 'une littérature-autre selon une pensée non moins autre': 'Apprends-moi à parler dans tes langues' ['an other-literature according to thinking that is no less other': 'teach me to speak in your languages'].[30]

It is important to note that French is not the only 'language of the other' in Khatibi's work. Though it is not named in *Amour bilingue*, one of the languages summoned by Khatibi around this time is Hebrew. I return in closing to *Le Même Livre*, which distils many of the ideas Khatibi was elaborating in the late 1970s and early 1980s – *pensée-autre*, double critique, *bi-langue* – and connects them, explicitly and implicitly, to the question of Palestine-Israel and, even more intimately, Jews and Arabs. Here is how Khatibi presents this 'exercise in alterity' in his first letter, written on 6 September 1980:

> Correspondance ni fausse ni vraie, au-delà de cette opposition [...] à partir de ce qui nous agite tous deux, identité en traverses pour libérer tant soit peu le débat confus qui règne entre ceux qui se considèrent comme arabes ou juifs, pour accueillir le non-dit.[31]

> [A correspondence neither false nor true, beyond this opposition [...] starting from what animates us both, an identity crossed to liberate ever so slightly the confounding debate that prevails between those who consider themselves Arab or Jewish, in order to welcome the unsaid.]

30 Memmi, *The Colonizer and the Colonized*, p. 108; Khatibi, *Le Roman maghrébin*, p. 14; Khatibi, *Amour bilingue*, p. 283; *Love in Two Languages*, p. 118.
31 'La Langue de l'autre' is the title of a collection of texts and interviews on language. Abdelkébir Khatibi, *La Langue de l'autre* (New York: Les Mains secrètes, 1999); Khatibi and Hassoun, *Le Même Livre*, pp. 9, 12–13.

There is a telling ambiguity in Khatibi's formulation of a singular identity (Arab-Jewish?) subject to multiple displacements ('identité en traverses') and the telescoping of Arabs and Jews in the expression 'ceux qui se considèrent comme arabes ou juifs', which can also be read as 'those who consider themselves Arab or (alternatively) Jewish'. The correspondence that follows is, as promised and performed here, an exercise in the deconstruction of the opposition between Jews and Arabs.

I have already discussed Khatibi's evocation of 'ma "judaïté"':[32] his escapades in the mellah and his evocation of the Jewish Arabic dialect of Essaouira ['another lightly sing-song dialect that made me burst out laughing'],[33] which resembles, we learn in a letter written in 1984, the dialect of his Fassi grandfather, that is, a patrilineal and familial tongue: 'entre les Juifs et les Fassis, existait pour moi cette ressemblance linguistique' ['between the Jews and the Fassis, there was for me this linguistic similarity'].[34] Like Khatibi, Hassoun situates his 'identité en traverses' between Jewishness and Arabness in the act of listening (*entendre*, meaning 'to hear' and also 'to comprehend') and in language: 'Quel héritage me permet-il aujourd'hui de considérer que sans "ma judaïté" je ne saurais entendre "mon arabité", et que sans celle-ci, celle-là serait nulle et non advenue [...] Est-ce le dialecte alexandrin qui revient en français me hanter?' ['What heritage allows me to consider that without "my Jewishness" I would not be able to understand "my Arabness", and that without the latter, the former would be null and void [...] Is it the Alexandrine dialect that returns to haunt me in French?'].[35]

Ironically, Khatibi and Hassoun cannot correspond in their Judeo-Arabic languages. 'Je suis condamné pour ma part', writes Hassoun, 'à écrire le français en arabe ou en hébreu' ['For my part, I am condemned to write French in Arabic or Hebrew'].[36] For Khatibi, this double alienation represents an 'incalculable' chance to restore what has been 'lost' between Jews and Muslims:

> Et nous nous exprimons, n'est-ce pas? dans une langue 'intermédiaire' qui est la singularité de ce français, alors que j'ignore l'hébreu, ou plutôt je le méconnais sans l'ignorer totalement. Nous avons deux langues en

---

32   Khatibi and Hassoun, *Le Même Livre*, p. 107.
33   Khatibi, *La Mémoire tatouée*, p. 36; *Tattooed memory*, p. 44.
34   Khatibi and Hassoun, *Le Même Livre*, p. 108.
35   Ibid., p. 76.
36   Ibid., p. 15.

commun, plus ou moins l'hébreu. J'imagine que ce 'plus ou moins' donne
vie à ce début de correspondance. Ce passage de main à main aura été
incalculable.[37]

[We express ourselves, do we not? in an 'intermediary' tongue that is
the singularity of this French language, while I do not know Hebrew,
or rather I misrecognize it without completely ignoring it. We have two
languages in common, plus or minus Hebrew. I imagine that this 'more
or less' gives life to this new correspondence. The passage from one hand
to another will have been incalculable.]

Towards the end of their epistolary exchange, Khatibi speculates that
writing in French has allowed them to speak more freely of the Judeo–
Arab question, 'dans une langue étrangère à l'hébreu, à l'arabe' ['in a
language foreign to Hebrew, to Arabic'].[38] By contrast, Hassoun prefers
to cast doubt on the neutrality of French in the very terms of the question:
'Au fond qu'est-ce que le conflit judéo-arabe? Le formuler en ces termes
n'est-ce pas céder à la langue importée? [...] Je crois que tout ce que j'ai
écrit depuis 1975/77 tourne autour de cette blessure de la langue' ['But
what is the Judeo–Arab conflict? Do we not give in to the imported
tongue by speaking of it in these terms? [...] I think that everything I have
written since 1975/77 concerns this wound of language'].[39] *Bi-langue*, or
more fittingly *pluri-langue*, does not concern only the native tongue and
the colonial tongue, it encompasses all the languages on the map of (post)
colonial diglossia, including the languages of Jews and Arabs, made
unrecognizable to each other (Khatibi's 'méconnaissance de l'hébreu')
through what Derrida, in his book-length response to Khatibi, names
'the double interdict': the suppression of the colonized tongues, and the
foreclosure, in French, of Jewish–Arab relationality.[40]

37 Ibid., p. 24.
38 Ibid., p. 123.
39 Ibid., pp. 101–2.
40 Jacques Derrida, *Monolingualism of the Other, or, The Prosthesis of Origin*,
trans. Patrick Mensah (Stanford, CA: Stanford University Press, 1998), p. 31. For
a comparative study of the relation between the double interdict and the question
of Jews and Arabs in Derrida and Khatibi, see Olivia C. Harrison, 'Abrahamic
Tongues: Abdelkébir Khatibi, Jacques Hassoun, Jacques Derrida', in *Transcolonial
Maghreb: Imagining Palestine in the Era of Decolonisation* (Stanford, CA: Stanford
University Press, 2016), pp. 101–28.

Literary Internationalism

I have argued that Palestine served as a crucial point of articulation for the concepts central to Khatibi's *œuvre* – other-thinking, double critique and *bi-langue* – imagined as ways to exit the colonial dialectic. It is not a contradiction to suggest that Khatibi remains, in this reading, one of the most important writers and theorists of *la Francophonie*, conceived not as a subsidiary of metropolitan literature but as a platform for what Khatibi calls 'literary internationalism'. Let me loop back, in closing, to the question of Francophone literature and what I am calling the transcolonial turn.

Khatibi wrote frequently about the predicament of the postcolonial Francophone writer, beginning in the 1980s and culminating in his exchanges with his fellow 'Franco-Maghrébian' Jacques Derrida in the 1990s.[41] 'Literary internationalism' is the name he gives to the 'littérature-autre' summoned in the closing pages of *Amour bilingue*, in a book he began writing towards the end of his epistolary exchange with Hassoun, *Figures de l'étranger dans la littérature française*. Against the grain of the apparent Orientalism and exoticism of the works he analyses – by Victor Segalen, Roland Barthes and Jean Genet, among others – Khatibi looks for signs of 'literary internationalism': 'ces "affinités électives" qui traversent les frontières' ['these "elective affinities" that cross borders'].[42] The final chapter, on Genet's account of the Palestinian revolution, *Un captif amoureux* (by far the longest chapter, 'Ultime dissidence de Genet' [Genet's ultimate dissidence] takes up almost a third of Khatibi's study) is particularly instructive because this is where, while identifying with Genet's love for Palestine, Khatibi nevertheless distinguishes his own approach to the colonized other:

> Le dernier livre est la dernière étape d'une dissidence d'abord contre la France, contre l'Occident. Dissidence que venait alimenter d'autres insurrections, individuelles ou collectives: *Black Panthers, Les Palestiniens, Baader*. C'est la première fois qu'au cours de son œuvre, Genet propose une identification imaginaire à des groupes de résistance, car ce poète se désirait radicalement seul, d'une solitude irrémédiable et sans réconciliation. Le voici qui s'identifie par l'effet de son art à un peuple, le peuple palestinien. Prenons-en acte tout en maintenant le texte sous son jeu de simulacres. Le peuple palestinien est sans terre et

41   Derrida, *Monolingualism of the Other*, p. 11.
42   Khatibi, *Figures de l'étranger*, p. 14.

sans nation certes, mais il est tout de même le mouvement collectif d'une mémoire et d'une histoire. Comment Genet écrit-il *Souvenirs I* et *II* alors que la question de la Palestine est aussi une destruction de la mémoire, le rapt d'un nom et d'une culture? Comment peut-on signer ce livre, assumer sa signature jusqu'à la mort sans exproprier le Palestinien de son territoire imaginaire? Question éthique, politico-éthique, insoluble dans ce livre; et elle ne pouvait l'être, car c'est la beauté d'un désastre, d'une apocalypse poétique, qui construit l'architecture de cet ouvrage. Architecture un peu en ruine, parfois informe, mais d'une splendeur redoutable. *C'est au lecteur qui s'identifie autrement au Palestinien d'en saisir les paradigmes d'élaboration, les palindromes.*[43]

[This last book is the final stage of a dissidence that articulates itself first against France, against the West. A dissidence nourished by other insurrections, individual and collective: *the Black Panthers, the Palestinians, Baader.* It is the first time in the course of his writing that Genet proposes an imaginary identification with resistance groups, for this poet wished himself radically alone, in an irremediable, irreconcilable solitude. And now he is using his art to identify with a people, the Palestinian people. Let us take note of this while maintaining the text in its play of simulacra. The Palestinian people is without a land and nation, true, but it is nonetheless the collective movement of a memory and a history. How can Genet write *Souvenirs I* and *II* when the question of Palestine is also a destruction of memory, the abduction of a name and culture? How can one sign this book, carry one's signature until death, without expropriating the Palestinian from his imaginary territory? An ethical, political-ethical question that remains insoluble in the book; it cannot be solved, for it is the beauty of a disaster, of a poetic apocalypse, that constitutes the architecture of this book. An architecture somewhat in ruins, sometimes out of shape, but formidably beautiful. *It is up to the reader who identifies otherwise with the Palestinian to grasp the paradigms of its elaboration, its palindromes.*]

Khatibi implicitly gestures to his own identification to Palestine in the passage I have underlined: he is the reader who, by virtue of his own relation to Palestine, is in a position to analyse Genet's status as an 'exote', a position he ventriloquizes thus: 'L'Etranger demeure toujours l'horizon de mon voyage' ['The Stranger always remains the horizon of my voyage'].[44] In the framing chapters of the book, Khatibi introduces a figure that captures his approach to language and his conception of

43   Ibid., pp. 135–6. Final italics are mine.
44   Ibid., p. 33.

relationality, the professional stranger or foreigner: 'Je dirai plus loin ceci: je viens de loin et l'étranger vient de plus loin au cœur de ma mémoire et de sa dispersion soit dans la nostalgie, soit dans la méconnaissance et la dénégation' ['Later I will say this: I come from far away and the stranger comes from farther away still in the heart of my memory and its dispersion, whether in nostalgia or in ignorance and denial'].[45]

If Palestine is one of Khatibi's horizons of thought, as I have suggested, might we also read Khatibi's relation to the stranger/foreigner through the twin figures of the Jew, the Arab in *Vomito blanco* and *Le Même Livre*? Nostalgia, misrecognition, denial are, after all, the objects of double critique in *Vomito blanco* and *Le Même Livre*, which reject Zionism and Arab nationalism, intolerance and 'savage difference' in favour of 'intractable difference' and 'other-thinking'. Recall that *Le Même Livre* is billed as an 'exercice d'altérité [...] un exercice de reconnaissance [...] Et c'est vers l'Etranger – quel qu'il soit et d'où qu'il vienne – que se tourne ce livre' ['an exercise in alterity [...] an exercise in recognition/gratitude [...] And it is toward the Stranger – whoever he may be and wherever he may come from – that this book is turned'].[46] If Hebrew is a language that Khatibi 'misrecognizes', he is able to 'recognize' it by writing a book with an other, or perhaps 'his' other, an Arab Jew. This is why Khatibi is able to say, in the final pages of 'Nationalisme et internationalisme littéraires' ['Literary nationalism and internationalism'], the coda of his book on French representations of otherness: 'Voici: je suis moi-même, presque, un *étranger professionnel*, dans la mesure où l'écriture ne me préoccupe maintenant que comme un *exercice d'altérité cosmopolite*, capable de parcourir les différences' ['Here it is: I am myself almost a professional stranger, to the extent that writing now only preoccupies me as a *cosmopolitan exercise in alterity*, capable of traversing differences'].[47]

In light of the transcolonial genealogy of Khatibian thought I have sketched in this essay, I propose that we take seriously Khatibi's conception of literary internationalism, building on the important vertical work that has been done in postcolonial Francophone studies to develop a horizontal, transcolonial approach to the field. As my reading of the place of Palestine in Khatibi's work shows, such an approach does not imply a naïve understanding of the power relations that continue to

45   Ibid., p. 11.
46   Khatibi and Hassoun, *Le Même Livre*, pp. 9–10.
47   Khatibi, *Figures de l'étranger*, p. 211. Original italics.

govern our purportedly postcolonial world nor, for that matter, 'world literature'. On the contrary, transcoloniality demands constant vigilance to the vestiges and 'recursive qualities' of empire, stressing, or simply reactivating, the anti- and the de- within the postcolonial.[48] For, as a careful reading of Khatibi's *œuvre* reveals, the postcolonial has always been transcolonial.

48 Ann Laura Stoler, *Duress: Imperial Durabilities in Our Times* (Durham, NC: Duke University Press, 2016), p. 26.

CHAPTER SEVEN

Segalen and Khatibi

Bilingualism, Alterity
and the Poetics of Diversity

Charles Forsdick

Tout reste à penser en dialogue avec les pensées et
les insurrections les plus radicales qui ont ébranlé
l'Occident et continuent à le faire, selon des voies
elles-mêmes variables.

[Everything remains to be thought in dialogue with
the most radical thoughts and insurgencies that have
shaken the West and still do, in ways themselves
different.]

Abdelkébir Khatibi[1]

Segalen se soumet à l'exigence du dehors, il en fait
une loi d'écriture. Il ne peut écrire que sur ce dehors,
sur les étrangers. Dehors du territoire et marges du
livre français, dehors des valeurs de l'écrivain, de son
système de référence. Tel est cet exercice d'une altérité
et d'une altération en marche.

[Segalen submits to the demands of what is outside
and makes of these a law of writing. He can write only
about this outside, about strangers. Outside the field
and margins of French literature, outside the values of

---

1   Abdelkébir Khatibi, *Maghreb pluriel* (Paris: Denoël, 1983), p. 12; *Plural
Maghreb: Writings on Postcolonialism*, trans. P. Burcu Yalim (London: Bloomsbury,
2019), p. 2.

the writer, of his own system of reference. Such is this
exercise of alterity and alteration in action.]

Abdelkébir Khatibi[2]

Baton Rouge, 1992: Glissant and Khatibi

The 1992 meeting between Edouard Glissant and Abdelkébir Khatibi
at Louisiana State University (LSU) in Baton Rouge is customarily
understood in the context of the genesis of Jacques Derrida's *Le
Monolinguisme de l'autre*. This is a text that emerged in large part from
the Algerian philosopher's long keynote talk delivered on that occasion
(but drew also on its author's previous interventions on the subject in
Paris and Montreal).[3] The colloquium, presided over by Glissant (then
the distinguished professor in the department of French Studies at LSU),
was dedicated to 'Echos from Elsewhere/Renvois d'ailleurs', and focused
under this title on a range of issues relating to *la Francophonie* outside
France. The dialogues it triggered between the three postcolonial thinkers
are implicitly inscribed in *Le Monolinguisme de l'autre*, where Derrida
quotes from both Glissant's *Discours antillais* and Khatibi's *Amour
bilingue*. It is arguable that Derrida and Glissant found themselves
closely aligned here as a result of their language use (Creole may function
as the dominant language in Martinique, but Glissant's relationship to
French is similarly exclusive and alienating);[4] however, as Dominique
Combe has suggested, Derrida's primary interlocutor in the work – in
terms of the concepts and tropes, such as *tatouage* and *bi-langue*, on
which he draws, and of the other texts, most notably *Maghreb pluriel*,
with which he engages in a tangle of 'citations enchâssées' ['embedded
quotations'] – remains Khatibi, to the extent that 'monolingualism of the
other' can even be seen as 'une co-production de Khatibi et de Derrida'
['a co-production by Khatibi and Derrida'].[5]

---

2   Abdelkébir Khatibi, *Figures de l'étranger dans la littérature française* (Paris:
Denoël, 1987), p. 15. Unless otherwise stated, translations are the author's.

3   On this subject, see Dominique Combe, 'Derrida et Khatibi – autour du
Monolinguisme de l'autre', *Carnets: revue électronique d'études françaises*, 2nd
ser. 7 (2016), pp. 6–11.

4   See Boniface Mongo-Mboussa, 'Edouard Glissant entre Derrida et Khatibi',
Africultures (Jan. 2013): http://africultures.com/edouard-glissant-entre-derrida-
et-khatibi-11272

5   Combe, 'Derrida et Khatibi', p. 2.

Having met for the first time in 1974, the contact between Derrida and Khatibi continued across the three decades until the former's death in 2004. As Tina Dransfeldt Christensen argues, their dialogue constitutes an 'interpenetration of postcolonial and poststructuralist theory',[6] a process underpinned by a common commitment to linguistic deconstruction, but one in which there are nevertheless clear creative tensions as they explore – from their distinctive perspectives – the politics and poetics of monolingualization before and after decolonization. The divergence between the Algerian philosopher and Moroccan sociologist has been explored elsewhere, with an emphasis often put on Khatibi's privileging of the differently diglossic situation in which he operated, contrasting written French with spoken Arabic and generating in the process a reflection on differing patterns of alienation. For Felisa Reynolds, '[t]he titular *Other* in *Monolingualism of the Other* is none other than Khatibi, and Derrida's *monolingualism* is in conversation with Khatibi's *bilingualism*'.[7] Such readings, however important for understanding the genesis of such a key theoretical text, often fail nevertheless to account for the role of Glissant in this trio of postcolonial intellectuals present at Baton Rouge. Although writing from a Martinican and not North African perspective, Glissant had a similar interest in the tensions between the monoglossic and the polyglossic, as well as in the various forms (literary and other) that linguistic plurality might take. Direct links between Glissant and Khatibi may thus not be evident, but it is quite possible to suggest indirect connections in the light of their shared colonial education (albeit in markedly different contexts), their focus (not unusual amongst 'Francophone' writers) on a complex and often troubled relationship with the French language, their commitment to a sociological reflection on the afterlives of empire and their ability to work across a range of genres (most notably fiction, poetry and the essay).

These are specific links evoked by scholars such as Mireille Rosello and Naïma Hachad,[8] with the former teasing out connections between

---

6   Tina Dransfeldt Christensen, 'Towards an Ethics of Bilingualism: An Intertextual Dialogue between Khatibi and Derrida', *Interventions: International Journal of Postcolonial Studies* 19.4 (2017), pp. 447–66 (p. 448).

7   Felisa Reynolds, 'Khatibi as Derrida's Foil: Undermining the Last Defender of the French Language', *Contemporary French and Francophone Studies: Sites* 18.2 (2014), pp. 199–206 (p. 200).

8   Mireille Rosello, 'Linguistic Encounters: Maghrebian "Langualization"

Caribbean creolization and the 'langualization' evident in Khatibi's work, and the latter identifying a shared commitment to rooting their work in 'une subjectivité travaillée par la pluralité' ['subjectivity wrought by plurality'].[9] Like Rosello, Hachad foregrounds the importance of language, seeing evidence in both authors that 'l'appropriation de la langue de domination et sa transformation en langage répond non seulement à une absence d'histoire, mais aussi à une carence langagière' ['the appropriation of the language [*langue*] of domination and its transformation into speech [*langage*] answers not only to an absence of history, but also to a linguistic deficit'].[10] Although we lack any real traces of any dialogue between Glissant and Khatibi on the occasion of the LSU conference, the underlying links between the two – as Boniface Mongo-Mboussa notes – remain subtle but strong:

> Si la filiation [de Khatibi] à Derrida est affichée, la relation à Edouard Glissant est souterraine. Elle est présente à travers cette volonté chez les deux écrivains d'être, chacun à sa manière, ethnologue de soi-même; elle se traduit par leur attachement à Segalen, l'inventeur du Divers; elle se manifeste du point de vue du discours, par le recours au fragment, à ce va-et-vient entre fiction, essais et poésie; il se traduit enfin par la volonté des deux auteurs d'agir chacun dans son lieu tout en pensant avec le monde, selon la formule d'Edouard Glissant.[11]

> [If [Khatibi's] filiation to Derrida is visible, the relationship to Edouard Glissant is subterranean. It is present through this desire of the two writers to be, each in his own way, an ethnologist of himself; it is reflected in their attachment to Segalen, the inventor of Diversity; it is manifested from the point of view of discourse, by the recourse to the fragment, to this coming and going between fiction, essays and poetry; it is finally translated by the desire of the two authors each to act in his own location while at the same time thinking with the world, to quote the formula coined by Edouard Glissant.]

It is striking that the early twentieth-century writer, traveller and theorist of the exotic Victor Segalen (1878–1919) is presented here as one

in Francophone Fiction', in *France and the Maghreb: Performative Encounters* (Gainesville: University Press of Florida, 2005), pp. 74–108 and Naïma Hachad, 'Parole de l'abîme d'Edouard Glissant et d'Abdelkébir Khatibi', *Revue des sciences humaines* 309 (2013), pp. 125–40.

  9 Hachad, 'Parole de l'abîme', p. 125.
 10 Ibid., p. 136.
 11 Mongo-Mboussa, 'Edouard Glissant entre Derrida et Khatibi'.

of several factors associating the two thinkers and writers. It is true that both Glissant and Khatibi provide evidence of a lifelong engagement with his early twentieth-century body of work, but it is also arguable that Segalen's influence in fact actively underpins the other commonalities identified here by Mongo-Mboussa, all of which are also characteristic of the early twentieth-century author's work: auto-ethnography (central to Segalen's works such as *Equipée* and the *Essai sur soi-même*); an interest in the workings of fragmentation (central to a text such as the *Essai sur l'exotisme*), together with a complementary exploration of intergeneric voguing; and a relational dexterity – key to Segalen's 'esthétique du Divers' ['aesthetics of Diversity'] – that is committed to linking the local and the global. As a result, the disruptive role of Segalen in the thinking of key Francophone postcolonial intellectuals merits closer scrutiny. This role is presented by Khatibi himself as double-edged: indicating, on the one hand, 'une voie nouvelle en rupture avec l'exotisme de *Bajazet* ou de *Salammbô* et avec les formes tradition-nelles' ['a new path breaking with the exoticism of *Bajazet* or *Salammbô* and with traditional forms']; yet introducing, on the other, the voice of the colonized into the literary text, notably that of 'l'autre en tant que tel, le colonisé tahitien qui se met à faire une ethnologie des conquérants' ['the other as other, the colonized Tahitian beginning to undertake an ethnology of the conquerors'].[12]

Segalen and his Readers

Glissant and Khatibi were introduced to Segalen's work in the 1950s, and each sustained a dialogue with his writing and thought – a striking example of what Khatibi identified in *Maghreb pluriel* as 'les pensées [...] les plus radicales qui ont ébranlé l'Occident et continuent à le faire' ['the most radical thoughts [...] that have shaken the West and still do'] – over the remaining decades of their lives.[13] To understand the dialogue between Victor Segalen and two of the most important Francophone postcolonial intellectuals of the twentieth and early twenty-first

12   Christine Buci-Glucksmann, Antoine Raybaud, Abdelhaï Diouri, Marc Gontard, Abdesslam Benabdelali, Abdelfattah Kilito, Abdallah Bounfour, Jacques Hassoun and Réda Bensmaïa, *Imaginaires de l'autre: Khatibi et la mémoire littéraire* (Paris: L'Harmattan, 1987), p. 174.
13   Khatibi, *Maghreb pluriel*, p. 12; *Plural Maghreb*, p. 2.

centuries, there is a need initially to explore the wider reception of the author's work. Following his death in 1919, Segalen developed a reputation for being a difficult author, in terms both of the subjects he broached and of the lexical, stylistic and generic experimentation he deployed in order to explore them. Largely ignored during its author's lifetime, when – before his premature death at the age of 41 – only three books from among his otherwise substantial *œuvre* had appeared (*Les Immémoriaux* (1907), *Stèles* (1912) and *Peintures* (1916)), Segalen's work has relied on the advocacy and interpretation of a network of prominent readers to ensure its continued visibility. This process began shortly after his death when, despite the apparent efforts of Paul Claudel and Saint-John Perse to play down the importance of his Chinese writings, an eclectic group of French and Francophone European authors committed themselves to communicating the originality and urgency of Segalen's writings. The Belgian surrealist Norge describes the impact of discovering *Stèles* whilst visiting *bouquinistes* on the banks of the Seine in the 1930s; other readers included the novelist and translator Francis de Miomandre and the poet Pierre Jean Jouve, with further homage paid by a series of writers ranging from Henri Michaux to Roger Caillois, from Michel Leiris to Francis Ponge; Segalen also acted as a key interlocutor for later twentieth-century travel writers, notably Nicolas Bouvier, Michel Le Bris and Kenneth White, providing through his figure of the *exote* the possibility of a distinctive mode of journeying in an age of mass displacement; and in parallel to these dialogues his work has also attracted increasing attention from anthropologists and ethnographers – such as Francis Affergan, James Clifford, Michael Gilsenan and Jean Jamin – who were seeking to negotiate the tensions between cultural difference and more radical understandings of alterity. This ethnographic engagement formed part of a wider theoretical interrogation of Segalen's work as the twentieth century drew to a close, in association primarily with discussions of exoticism and alterity in the work of Jean Baudrillard (*L'Autre par lui-même* and *La Transparence du Mal*) and Tzvetan Todorov (*Nous et les Autres*).[14]

---

14   For a more detailed analysis of Segalen and his readers, see Charles Forsdick, *Victor Segalen and the Aesthetics of Diversity: Journeys between Cultures* (Oxford: Oxford University Press, 2000), pp. 14–22 and Charles Forsdick, 'L'Exote mangé par les hommes: From the French Kipling to *Segalen le partagé*', in Charles Forsdick and Susan Marson (eds), *Reading Diversity* (Glasgow: University of Glasgow French and German Publications, 2000), pp. 1–22.

These networks of readers (and the active dialogues amongst them) become particularly apparent in a volume that emerged from a 1981 conference in Rabat on bilingualism, amongst the contributors to which were four very different writers heavily influenced by Segalen: the Chinese translingual author François Cheng; the author and scholar Eliane Formentelli; and Khatibi and Todorov themselves. In identifying Khatibi as 'un compagnon d'emblée reconnu, un guide' ['a companion recognized from the outset, a guide'],[15] Cheng points here to the elective affinities that often emerge amongst such *segaléniens*. In fact, Segalen surfaces only occasionally in the discussions in *Du bilinguisme*: in a text that would subsequently be integrated into *Maghreb pluriel*, Khatibi associates him with 'la jouissance du plurilinguisme textuel' ['the pleasure of textual plurilingualism'];[16] but the author's influence nevertheless underpins more subtly a number of the exchanges in the volume, revealing the ways in which his work – described by Edouard Glissant in *L'Intention poétique* as '*en avant* du monde' ['*ahead* of the world']*[17] – had a significant impact on literature and thought in the French-speaking world in the later twentieth century. Prominent among these readers were a number of Francophone postcolonial authors, with Khatibi's engagement complemented most notably by that of several French Caribbean authors (including Glissant himself and Patrick Chamoiseau), but also by writers in the French Pacific as well as in Brittany. As such, in the terms of Silke Segler-Messner, Segalen may be seen to have 'balisé le chemin de l'évolution de l'écriture dans l'espace francophone' ['marked out the path of the evolution of writing in the French-speaking world'].[18]

Glissant and Khatibi both discovered Segalen early in their careers, the former when he was a doctoral student and emerging writer in Paris, the latter a *lycéen* in Casablanca.[19] This initial encounter was in the context

---

15   François Cheng, 'Le Cas du chinois', in Jalil Bennani *et al.*, *Du bilinguisme* (Paris: Denoël, 1985), pp. 227–42 (p. 240).

16   Abdelkébir Khatibi, 'Incipits', ibid., pp. 171–95 (p. 180).

17   Edouard Glissant, *L'Intention poétique* (Paris: Seuil, 1969), p. 96.

18   Silke Segler-Messner, 'Victor Segalen et la poétique de l'altérité dans la théorie littéraire postcoloniale (Glissant, Khatibi)', in Silke Segler-Messner (ed.), *Voyages à l'envers: formes et figures de l'exotisme dans les littératures post-coloniales francophones* (Strasbourg: Presses universitaires de Strasbourg, 2009), pp. 69–86 (p. 71).

19   For existing studies of Khatibi and Segalen, see Marc Gontard, 'Théorie de la différence chez Victor Segalen', in Buci-Glucksmann *et al.*, *Imaginaires de*

of a resurgence of interest in the author following publication of a special
issue of *Les Cahiers du Sud* devoted to him in 1947 and the appearance
of a volume of selected works with Le Club du Meilleur Livre in 1955.
The ideological niche in which these initial readings occurred was,
crucially, that of the rapid shift towards decolonization, meaning that
Segalen played a role alongside key thinkers such as Césaire, Fanon and
Memmi in the formation of these major intellectual and literary voices
of the post-war period. The subsequent emergence of a 'postcolonial'
Segalen in the 1960s and 1970s reflects significant divergence in readings
of the writer's work and in interpretations of his thought, with more
conservative critics (often committed to reducing this contribution to
a post-symbolist context) dismissing such analyses as anachronistically
'tiers-mondistes' ['Third Worldists']. Echoing the positions of Glissant
and Khatibi, Martine Astier Loufti discovered, however, in Segalen,
'une réplique proprement littéraire à l'impérialisme' ['a genuinely literary
response to imperialism'].[20] She praises his poetic and ethical challenge
to the voicelessness of the colonized but concludes that this ultimately
led to failure: 'parce qu'il demeura ignoré, ce message reste la tentative la
plus dérisoire et la plus pathétique pour s'opposer à la puissance poussée
de l'impérialisme' ['because he remained ignored, this message remains

---

l'autre, pp. 65–79. See also Nathalie Roelens, 'L'amour bilingue: lire Khatibi et
Segalen', in *Approches interdisciplinaires de la lecture, 10: lire entre les langues*
(Reims, EPURE, 2017), pp. 61–80. In the introduction to his translation of *Le
Lutteur de classe à la manière taoïste* [*Class Warrior – Taoist Style* (Middletown,
CO: Wesleyan University Press, 2017)], Matt Reeck also notes the extent to
which – in the light of Khatibi's engagement with his work – 'Segalen's writings
about world cultures – whether in Tahiti or China – stand as an underdeveloped
narrative thread in Francophone literature' (p. xi). On Glissant and Segalen, see
Jean-Louis Cornille, 'La Mémoire courte des poètes immémoriaux (Glissant
et Segalen)', in *Plagiat et créativité: (treize enquêtes sur l'auteur et son autre)*
(Amsterdam: Rodopi, 2008), pp. 171–82; Charles Forsdick, 'From the "Aesthetics
of Diversity" to the "Poetics of Relating": Segalen, Glissant and the Genealogies
of Francophone Postcolonial Thought', *Paragraph* 37.2 (2014), pp. 160–77;
Jean-Louis Joubert, 'Poétique de l'exotisme: Saint-John Perse, Victor Segalen et
Édouard Glissant', *Cahiers du CRLH* 5 (1988), pp. 281–95; and Jean-Pol Madou,
'Le Germe et le rhizome', in *Le Clézio, Glissant, Segalen: la quête comme
déconstruction de l'aventure* (Chambéry: Editions de l'université de Savoie,
2011), pp. 73–80.

20   Martine Astier Loufti, *Littérature et colonialisme: l'expansion coloniale en
vue dans la littérature romanesque française, 1871–1914* (Paris and The Hague:
Mouton, 1971), p. 132.

the most derisory and pathetic attempt to oppose the driven power of imperialism'].[21]

The afterlives of Segalen's work in the writings of Chamoiseau, Glissant, Khatibi and other major postcolonial writers and thinkers reveal in retrospect the limitations of Astier Loufti's judgement, and the ways in which the early twentieth-century author may now be seen to be central to understandings of what Chris Bongie identified as the 'post/colonial', i.e. an approach to cultural production that eschews the reductive linearity of the historically colonial and postcolonial, and suggests instead more complex exchanges across and around the processes of decolonization.[22] Segalen's reflections on exoticism, otherness, alterity, cultural hegemony, bilingualism and the poetics of cross-cultural production proved from the 1950s onwards to be fertile inspiration for subsequent authors seeking to investigate these topics in the wake of colonial empire. Khatibi himself underlined the importance of this particular elective affinity when he described in an interview with Jean Scemla in the mid-1980s – in the context of his self-positioning in relation to *la Francophonie* – the way in which '[il] [s]e sentai[t] aussi proche de Segalen que de certains francophones et même [...] de certains maghrébins' ['he felt as close to Segalen as he did to certain Francophone writers and even certain North African writers'].[23]

Khatibi as Reader of Segalen

Shortly before his death, Jorge Luis Borges is reported to have commented, to an unidentified 'French poet friend': 'The French talk about Valéry and even the preposterous Péguy with adoration – don't they know that in Victor Segalen they have one of the most intelligent writers of our age'.[24] Focusing on the perceived difficulty of the author's work, already mentioned above, he continued: 'You can read Segalen in less than a

21   Ibid., p. 137.

22   See Chris Bongie, *Islands and Exiles: The Creole Identities of Post/Colonial Literature* (Stanford, CA: Stanford University Press, 1998).

23   Jean Scemla, 'Entretien avec Khatibi', *Bulletin de l'Association Victor Segalen* 2 (1989), pp. 9–10 (p. 9).

24   Cited by Andrew Harvey and Ian Watson, 'Introduction', in Victor Segalen, *Paintings*, trans. Andrew Harvey and Ian Watson (London: Quartet Books, 1991), pp. vii–ix (p. vi).

month, but it might take you the rest of your life to begin to understand him'. Like Glissant, Khatibi falls into the group of readers who, having encountered Segalen in the 1950s, spent much of the rest of his life grappling with his *œuvre*. Although important in this regard, Segalen was far from the only French writer who for Khatibi falls into this category. He makes clear his relationship to French literature: 'J'écris depuis l'enfance sous le signe de la littérature française, de sa langue à laquelle j'ai été donné. [...] Parler dans une langue et écrire dans une autre, est une expérience étrange et peut-être radicale' ['I have written since childhood under the sign of French literature, of its language to which I have been given. [...] Speaking in one language and writing in another is a strange and perhaps radical experience'].[25] In *Le Scribe et son ombre*, an autobiographical reflection published a year before his death, he describes in detail the wide and eclectic reading practices that underpin the progressive *bricolage* central to his own thought:

> Au lieu de me chercher un ou plusieurs maîtres dont je ne saurais comment me libérer, je sentais depuis mon adolescence, confusément et avec une fidélité continue, que je devais pluraliser mon approche de la pensée des autres. Plutôt des textes tutélaires que des maîtres à vénérer, et qui forment une sorte de bibliothèque mobile dans le temps de mes lectures et écritures.[26]

> [Instead of seeking out one or several masters from whom I would not know how to free myself, I felt since my adolescence, confusedly and with a continuous fidelity, that I had to pluralize my approach to the thought of the others. Tutelary texts instead of masters to venerate, and which form a sort of mobile library in the time of my readings and writings.]

La Mémoire tatouée sets out the clear impact a series of authors had already had on the author in his childhood and adolescence. The breadth and depth of these exchanges is illustrated by the contributions to a 1987 collection entitled *Imaginaires de l'autre: Khatibi et la mémoire littéraire*, in which a number of the essays explore dialogues with other writers including poets such as Rimbaud.[27] Baudelaire played a key role too, serving as Khatibi's 'premier maître en mélancolie déliée' ['first

---

25 Abdelkébir Khatibi, *La Langue de l'autre* (New York and Tunis: Les Mains Secrètes, 1999), p. 115.
26 Abdelkébir Khatibi, *Le Scribe et son ombre* (Paris: La Différence, 2008), p. 24.
27 See Buci-Glucksmann *et al.*, *Imaginaires de l'autre*.

mentor in melancholia unbound'].[28] In *La Mémoire tatouée*, the autobiographical narrator goes on to provide a clear insight into his reading
as a solitary adolescent and into the particular 'fraternités littéraires'
['literary brothers'] he cultivated: 'Mes dieux étaient de préférence des
poètes marginaux' ['my preferred gods were marginal poets'], he notes,
'exilés, fous, suicidés, morts jeunes ou tuberculeux, ceux-là mêmes que je
savais perdus à tout jamais dans la souffrance pure' ['the suicides, exiles,
crazy, tubercular or dead young, the very ones I knew to be forever lost
in pure suffering'].[29] With his premature death, almost certainly as a
result of suicide, Segalen is clearly prominent in such a catalogue, but
Khatibi extends his field of reference in the text to other writers, such
as Laforgue and Mallarmé, and also broadens his field of reference to
include later authors such as Sartre.

The specific impact of Segalen emerges in *La Mémoire tatouée*, in the
section relating the narrator's time at the Lycée Lyautey in Casablanca,
where his literature teacher – described as 'ce fakir solitaire, perdu dans
un groupe d'enfants coloniaux et bien gâtés' ['this lonely fakir, lost in
a group of spoiled, colonial kids'][30] – introduces him to the author of
Les Immémoriaux. (It is striking that the word 'immémorial' recurs
as a leitmotiv in the text, as the narrator describes Moroccan culture
subject to French colonial domination.) The immediate context is a
dual one of sexual and political awakening: Khatibi seeks to distinguish
himself from his background as he attempts to attract the attention of
his peers, 'un groupe en majorité féminin et français' ['a group that
was mostly girls and French'], whilst at the same time channelling into
forms of resistance his growing sense of the cultural alienation his
education entails: 'Le professeur de littérature devina le jeu. Il m'aida.
Quand il expliquait Segalen en insistant sur la mort des cultures, je
savais qu'il me donnait des armes' ['The literature professor figured out
my game. He helped me. While he was explaining Segalen and insisting
on the death of cultures, I knew he was arming me'].[31] This initial
encounter is discussed more fully in the interview with Jean Scemla,

28   Khatibi, *La Langue de l'autre*, p. 119.
29   Abdelkébir Khatibi, *La Mémoire tatouée: autobiographie d'un décolonisé*
(Paris: Denoël, 1971), reprinted in *Œuvres de Abdelkébir Khatibi I: Romans et
récits* (Paris: La Différence, 2008), pp. 9–113 (p. 55); Abdelkébir Khatibi, *Tattooed
Memory*, trans. Peter Thompson (Paris: L'Harmattan, 2016), p. 72.
30   Khatibi, *La Mémoire tatouée*, p. 71; *Tattooed Memory*, p. 95.
31   Ibid., p. 71; p. 94.

conducted at a seminar on Segalen that Khatibi had organized in 1984 at the Collège de Philosophie in Vincennes. Here, he notes how the discovery of the Breton author was for him, the only Moroccan pupil in the class, 'quelque chose d'assez beau et d'assez libérateur' ['something quite beautiful and liberating'].[32] The following year, in a discussion at a conference in Morocco, Khatibi summarized the nature of this liberation as he described the core question he had discerned in Segalen's work: 'comment fonder, littéralement parlant, l'étranger en moi?' ['how, literally, to create the stranger in myself?'].[33]

After this initial introduction to Segalen, Khatibi went on to read *Stèles* and then – presumably in the context of writing the relevant chapter in *Figures de l'étranger* – to engage with the author's wider *œuvre* (at that stage, in the 1980s, still scattered across multiple editions, often hard to locate, and some of which he read in manuscript) and also much of his correspondence. From Khatibi's later writing on Segalen emerges a purposeful attention to the materiality of the author's work, an attention to the multiple (and often limited) editions in which it appeared, and an interest in the circuitous routes whereby it has reached its readers. The initial encounter had been more visceral and lacked any overtones of the bibliophilia to which Segalen's work lends itself. In *La Mémoire tatouée*, Khatibi did not in fact specify the text he initially read as a *lycéen* in 1957, although it becomes clear that this was *Les Immémoriaux*, a novel republished in 1956 as one of the inaugural titles in Plon's 'Terre humaine' series. Khatibi describes to Scemla in the 1984 interview the impact of this work on his thinking, both in terms of the bilingual poetics of the ethnographic novel, in which the French is shaped lexically and syntactically by the presence of Tahitian, and in terms of the status of its protagonist Térii, a character seen as 'désaxé, désorbité par rapport à sa planète mythologique' ['misaligned, disoriented in relation to his mythological planet'].[34] *Les Immémoriaux* allowed Khatibi to discover – even before he had read Claude Lévi-Strauss – 'une unification de l'ethnologie et de la littérature' ['a unification of ethnography and literature'], and led him for the first time to detect the method which would become common in many of his earlier works, rooted in '[s]on désir de [se] changer, de transformer [s]on aliénation en une activité intellectuelle, curieuse du

---

32   Scemla, 'Entretien avec Khatibi', p. 9.
33   Buci-Glucksmann *et al.*, *Imaginaires de l'autre*, p. 175.
34   Scemla, 'Entretien avec Khatibi', p. 9.

regard de l'autre dans l'image de soi' ['his desire to change, to transform his alienation into an intellectual activity, curious about the gaze of the other in the image of oneself'].[35] As Nathalie Roelens concludes in one of the few existing studies of the pair, part of the convergence of Segalen and Khatibi is rooted in an 'immersion lectorielle' ['readerly immersion'] experienced by their readers:

> une immersion, voire une communion poétique, qui accepte une perte de sens au profit d'un gain d'atmosphère, 'une extase d'envoûtement', une ouverture vers une autre culture, un amour bilingue mais aussi une entrée en connivence avec un milieu, avec la chair du monde.[36]

> [an immersion, even a poetic communion, which accepts a loss of meaning in return for a gain of atmosphere, 'an ecstasy of bewitchment', an opening towards another culture, a bilingual love but also a connivance with a milieu, with the flesh of the world.]

Segalen's ethnographic novel presents – in a Polynesian context – themes that would be central to Khatibi's own early emerging thought: 'amnésie, rupture dans l'histoire, la mémoire et dans l'identité' ['amnesia, rupture in history, memory and identity'], and it depends also on a central narrative constructed around the dilemma that Derrida himself would later identify in Khatibi, namely 'cette césure entre la littérature orale et la littérature écrite' ['break between oral and written literature'].[37] The discussion of *Les Immémoriaux* in *Figures de l'étranger*, published three decades after this initial encounter, provides a clear account of what initially drew Khatibi to that text: its author acts as 'le témoin d'une culture colonisée et détruite dans sa parole' ['the witness of a culture colonized and destroyed in its voice itself']; yet his aim nevertheless is to discern traces left by this destruction, 'd'écrire cette survie, de l'exprimer dans sa force' ['to write this survival, to express it in its power'], an objective manifested not least in the very language of the text, 'cette accumulation lancinante du lexique maori' ['this haunting accumulation of Maori words'].[38] The parallels between *Les Immémoriaux* and *La Mémoire tatouée* are, as a result, evident, for the impact of European culture – British in Tahiti, French in Morocco – leads to what Khatibi

---

35 Khatibi, *Le Scribe et son ombre*, pp. 41, 42.
36 Roelens, 'L'amour bilingue', p. 78.
37 Scemla, 'Entretien avec Khatibi', p. 10.
38 Abdelkébir Khatibi, 'Célébration de l'Exote', in *Œuvres de Abdelkébir Khatibi III: Essais* (Paris: La Différence, 2008), pp. 137–61 (p. 142).

dubs in his novel 'une déchirure de la mémoire' ['a rip in the memory'].[39]
What interests him, however, is not only the author's capacity to discern
this violent amnesia but also his ability to construct a poetics around it:

> Pas de folklore donc, ni de littérature coloniale, mais une écriture du
> Dehors qui accueille le lieu de l'autre dans mon langage, dans mon
> espace imaginaire. Différence distante: c'est lorsque l'autre est maintenu,
> respecté dans sa singularité que je peux être reçu peut-être par lui.[40]

> [No folklore, then, or colonial literature, but a writing of what is outside
> which welcomes the place of the other into my language, into my
> imaginary space. Distant difference: it is when the other is maintained,
> respected in its singularity that I can perhaps be received by it].

That Khatibi should have engaged with Segalen in this way is not
surprising. *La Mémoire tatouée* makes clear the role played by French
writers, from early in his life, in the elaboration of his thought. As
with other postcolonial writers who have been influenced by Segalen
(especially Glissant), the rapport remains an evolving and iterative one,
dependent on a progressive exploration of the earlier author's *œuvre*
that is sympathetic but far from sycophantic, and in which there is
room for criticism of aspects relating in particular to the assumptions
of the colonial context from which this work emerged. The engagement
of Francophone authors with Segalen often proves dialogic in this
way, implying a clear evolution in the way his work is understood in a
postcolonial frame. In the interview with Scemla, Khatibi describes his
relationship with Segalen along these lines: 'il faut s'éloigner de Segalen
tout en le mangeant, c'est-à-dire en l'absorbant magiquement' ['we must
distance ourselves from Segalen at the same time as we consume him,
i.e. as we absorb him magically'].[41] The figurative use of consumption
recalls the anthropophagic aesthetics of Brazilian modernism, a process
of absorbing hegemonic cultural production on a supposedly marginalized colonial periphery, but it suggests also a remaking of that culture
in a way that provincializes the former centre. Khatibi's engagement with
Segalen is thus parallel in a number of ways to that evident in Edouard
Glissant's work, not least in that any sense of intellectual convergence is
tempered by a firm awareness of the divergence associated with Segalen's
distinctiveness.

39   Khatibi, *La Mémoire tatouée*, p. 34; *Tattooed Memory*, p. 42.
40   Khatibi, *Figures de l'étranger*, p. 28.
41   Jean Scemla, 'Entretien avec Khatibi', p. 10.

For Khatibi, 'son œuvre appartient à une époque déterminée historiquement et est liée à la biographie d'un individu, d'un Breton qui s'appelait Victor Segalen' ['his work belongs to a historically determined period and is linked to the biography of an individual, a Breton, named Victor Segalen'].[42] Building from these specifics, he notes a particular objection to Segalen's anti-modernist political stance, 'ses positions d'aristocrate royaliste, face à la révolution russe ou chinoise' ['his self-positioning, when faced with the Chinese and Russian Revolutions, as a royalist aristocrat'][43] and his reading of the more testing chapters of *Equipée* (on indigenous women and on what Segalen calls the 'hommes de bât' ['packsaddle men']) in *Figures de l'étranger* leads a clear statement of its author's location in a particular ideological niche:

> cet exote est un ethnocentriste, un aristocrate atavique et qui fait retour sur lui-même dans le même cercle des valeurs et des préjugés, la même tradition de la méconnaissance et de la dénégation. Cependant, c'est là un retour qui, d'une manière ou d'une autre, déstabilise cet européocen-trisme et cette image d'autosuffisance.[44]

> [this exote is an ethnocentrist, an atavistic aristocrat who turns back on himself into the same circle of values and prejudices, the same tradition of ignorance and denial. However, this is a return which, in one way or another, destabilizes this Eurocentrism and this image of self-sufficiency.]

In similar terms, Glissant would note, '[c]'est le premier qui a posé la question de la diversité du monde, qui a combattu l'exotisme comme forme complaisante de la colonisation; et il était médecin sur un bâtiment militaire' ['he was the first person to pose the question of the diversity of the world, who fought exoticism as a complacent form of colonization – and he was a doctor on a military vessel'].[45] Both thinkers persist nevertheless in their engagement with Segalen's thinking and poetic practice, acknowledging the elements that jarred in their decolonial and postcolonial present, yet foregrounding those aspects that resonate with their contemporary concerns.

42   Ibid.
43   Buci-Glucksmann *et al.*, *Imaginaires de l'autre*, p. 174.
44   Khatibi, 'Célébration de l'Exote', p. 158.
45   Edouard Glissant, *Introduction à une poétique du Divers* (Paris: Gallimard, 1996), p. 90.

Figures de l'étranger: The 'Exote' as 'Étranger professionnel'

There is a need, therefore, to acknowledge the evolution inherent in Khatibi's engagement, for it reveals a shift from deploying the anti-colonial ammunition with which Segalen provides the young *lycéen* during the first phase of his reflection – 'la phase ou la période dite décoloniale, la souffrance due à la colonisation, au bilinguisme, à une certaine perte de l'identité' ['the phase or period known as decolonial, the suffering caused by colonization, bilingualism, a certain loss of identity'] – to a later stage when, moving away from a specific focus on Moroccan and Maghrebian culture and identity, the author focused instead on 'la notion même d'étranger, d'extranéité' ['the very notion of foreigner, extraneousness'].[46] This later approach, expressed in particular in *Figures de l'étranger*, but also illustrated in other contemporary creative works such as *Un été à Stockholm*, owed much to Segalen, in whose writing Khatibi had discerned a clear slippage of language and culture ('une dissociation systématique entre son territoire, sa terre natale et sa langue qui doit s'exiler' ['a systematic disassociation between his territory, his native land and his language forced into exile']) as well as a consequent migration and decentring of linguistic resources, resulting in a threat to the ethnolinguistic nationalism underpinning much discourse on French identity ('une langue [...] appartient à ceux qui l'exercent et l'aiment suffisamment pour la travailler, la transformer' ['a language belongs to those who use it and love it enough to work on it, to transform']).[47]

Figures de l'étranger – in which the study of Segalen stands alongside chapters on Aragon, Barthes, Duras, Genet and Ollier – represents a shift in his relationship with French literature, based on a particular willingness to engage with 'une littérature capable de parcourir les différences culturelles, de civilisation, de langue' ['a literature capable of navigating cultural differences, in terms of civilization and languages'] – and to ask a key question that reveals the rich dialogue with French literary production evident throughout his thought and literary practice: 'comment, jusqu'à maintenant, la littérature française a-t-elle parcouru ces différences?' ['how, until now, has French literature navigated these differences?'].[48] The emphasis is on a type of literary text described

46   Scemla, 'Entretien avec Khatibi', p. 9.
47   Ibid.
48   Khatibi, *Figures de l'étranger*, p. 9.

as the '*récit des langues*' ['*language narrative*'],[49] a work in which an apparent monolingualism is in constant tension with a more radical multilingual poetics. The corpus on which Khatibi focuses is made up of authors who have received '*l'étranger en tant que l'imaginaire d'une langue*' ['the stranger as the imaginary of a language'],[50] a tendency in which Segalen is seen as foundational:

> Victor Segalen a été parmi les fondateurs de cette internation, de cette modernité littéraire. Son œuvre voulait faire sortir la littérature française de son ethnocentrisme et de ses domaines trop nationalistes. [...] Il s'agit de se *désenclaver* par rapport à la tradition de son pays d'origine. En ce sens, l'Exote ne fait pas d'exotisme: '... C'est l'histoire de la littérature (française) qu'il faudrait composer', écrit-il dans ses notes sur l'exotisme.[51]

> [Victor Segalen was among the founders of this inter-nation, this literary modernity. His work sought to bring French literature out of its ethnocentrism and its excessively nationalistic domains. [...] It is about *opening up* the self in relation to the tradition of one's country of origin. In this sense, the Exote does not indulge in exoticism: '... It is the history of literature (French literature) that needs to be composed', he wrote in his notes on exoticism.]

The impact of the author of *Stèles* becomes apparent: far from being limited to playing a role in Khatibi's postcolonial critique of exoticism, he contributes to his more general understanding of the place of literature as an intervention in history, culture and society. This approach is developed in the opening chapter of *Figures de l'étranger*, 'Célébration de l'exote', devoted to Segalen and underlining his key role in the volume. Segalen's work (and in particular his elaboration of the figure of the *exote*) recurs as a point of reference in subsequent chapters. *Figures de l'étranger* reveals, as a result, the full extent of Khatibi's familiarity with his predecessor's *œuvre*. It also underlines the ways in which his reading of Segalen's work challenged previous critical readings of it, and locates this early twentieth-century aesthetics of diversity in a firmly postcolonial context. The detailed engagement draws on a range of texts, largely from the so-called 'Chinese cycle' of Segalen's work, and shows an interest also in the author's biography. *Stèles* is thus presented as a foundational example of a text articulating, in a colonial

---

49 Ibid., p. 11.
50 Ibid., p. 14.
51 Ibid., p. 15.

and post-symbolist context, the migration of signs between cultures, but Khatibi draws also on *Equipée* (a text whose manuscript he had studied at the Bibliothèque nationale), acknowledging the geographical displacement with which Segalen complemented his experimental poetics, as well as the *Essai sur l'exotisme*.

In *Figures de l'étranger*, Khatibi is also inspired by Segalen's own figure of the *exote* to elaborate his notion of the *étranger professionnel* ['professional stranger']. As Segler-Messner notes, the *exote* accordingly plays the role of 'initiateur d'une forme alternative de description littéraire narrative, qui explore les espaces et les lieux, relevant de l'entre-deux, d'une troisième dimension de l'autre' ['initiator of an alternative form of literary narrative description, which explores spaces and places, relating to the inbetween of a third dimension of the other'].[52] It is such an approach to reading Khatibi via Segalen (and, arguably, Segalen via Khatibi) that reveals the particular richness – both conceptual and creative – of their achronological encounter. Khatibi discerned in Segalen the refusal of any notion of universal unity and detected instead a diversity or plurality underpinning human cultures and societies, observations theorized most notably in the *Essai sur l'exotisme* and illustrated in the poetics underpinning his *œuvre*. This notion of a heterogeneity countering an entropic drift towards homogeneity is described by Khatibi. In his discussion of the tensions between nationalism and literary internationalism in *Figures de l'étranger*, he challenges the conception of the nation itself as homogeneous: 'Toute nation est, en son principe, une pluralité, une mosaïque de cultures, sinon une pluralité de langues et de généalogies fondatrices, soit par le texte, soit par le récit vocal, ou les deux à la fois' ['Every nation is, in principle, a plurality, a mosaic of cultures, if not a plurality of languages and founding genealogies, either by the text or by spoken narrative, or both at once'].[53]

There is resonance in particular between Khatibi's reflection on the semiotics of culture, evident, for instance, in his interest in tattoos, and Segalen's own engagement with the sign systems underpinning the cultures with which he comes into contact, notably in Polynesia (where, in *Les Immémoriaux*, he too focuses on tattoos) and in China (where ideograms form a particular of his focus, in particular in *Stèles*). Khatibi describes Segalen's engagement with Chinese culture in terms of the

52   Segler-Messner, 'Victor Segalen et la poétique de l'altérité', p. 84.
53   Khatibi, *Figures de l'étranger*, p. 209.

French author's response to 'le mouvement cursif de sa calligraphie' ['the cursive movement of calligraphy'],[54] an approach that resonates with his own work in texts such as *L'Art calligraphique de l'Islam*, written with Mohamed Sijelmassi. As Segalen sees ideograms inscribed on funerary monuments as repositories of ancient China, so, for Khatibi, Arabic calligraphy is itself characterized by an 'ensourcement miraculeux' ['miraculous implantation'].[55] He states 'un amour prononcé pour la calligraphie arabe, chinoise et japonaise' ['a pronounced love for Arabic, Chinese and Japanese calligraphy'], detecting in such writing 'une sorte d'écriture au second degré, où, lisible et illisible, la langue voilait les mots derrière leur dessin' ['a sort of second-degree writing in which, legible and illegible, language concealed words behind their drawing'].[56] The parallel is explored by Nathalie Roelens, for whom '[t]out comme *Stèles* est hanté, quant à son style, par l'espacement lapidaire de son objet, le style de Khatibi épouse les courbes de la calligraphie arabe' ['just as *Stèles* is haunted, as far as its style is concerned, by the lapidary spacing of its object, Khatibi's style embraces the curvature of Arabic calligraphy'].[57]

Building on this analysis, Khatibi discerns in *Stèles* evidence of Segalen's precocious 'désir du bilinguisme et des intersignes migrateurs d'une civilisation à l'autre' ['desire for bilingualism and for signs migrating between civilizations'].[58] It is important to note, however, the practical poetic status of this desire. He concludes – in a discussion following Marc Gontard's presentation on his work at a 1985 conference in Morocco, published in *Imaginaires de l'autre* – that Segalen failed to discover 'une langue tournée vers le dehors concret, en dialogue avec l'Asie' ['a language oriented towards a concrete outside, in dialogue with Asia'], but offered nevertheless a radical destabilization of French literature: 'cette déstabilisation de la littérature française dont le territoire s'ouvre à un inconnu réel' ['this destabilization of French literature whose territory is opened to an unknown real'].[59] As such, a text such as *Stèles* contributes to the concept of untranslatability as Khatibi develops

---

54 Khatibi, 'Célébration de l'Exote', p. 147.
55 Khatibi and Sijelmassi, *L'Art calligraphique de l'Islam* (Paris: Gallimard, 1994), p. 25.
56 Khatibi, *La Langue de l'autre*, p. 117.
57 Roelens, 'L'amour bilingue', p. 72.
58 Khatibi, *Figures de l'étranger*, p. 20.
59 Buci-Glucksmann *et al.*, *Imaginaires de l'autre*, p. 173.

it in *Figures de l'étranger*, seen not as the inability of the literary text to capture the world in its cultural and literary complexity but as a quality inherent in all literature, capturing the diglossic tension of the spoken and written, and the multiple languages embedded within what is apparently monolingual. One of the most sustained illustrations of this approach is evident in *Amour bilingue*, a text in which – in Dransfeldt Christensen's terms – 'two languages confront each other and transfer meaning to each other without uniting in synthesis'.[60] The core concept of *bi-langue* is double-edged, stressing the dialogic nature of language to deconstruct both the colonizing hegemony of French and the claims to uniqueness of Arabic. The associated idea that Khatibi dubs 'double-critique' – engaging with both Western ethnocentrism and theocratic hegemony – emerges from the linguistic situation of an increasingly uneven diglossia in which he had found himself since childhood: 'le dialecte est inaugural dans le corps de l'enfant; la langue écrite est apprise ensuite, et en période coloniale, cette langue, cette écriture arabes, ont été combattues, refoulées et remplacées au service de la langue française' ['the dialect is inaugural in the body of the child; the written language is learned afterward, and in the colonial period, this Arabic language and writing were fought against, suppressed and replaced in the service of the French language'].[61]

Conclusion

The focus on bilingualism and the 'double critique' reveals the role played by Segalen in the elaboration of some of the core ideas underpinning Khatibi's work, an influence rooted in particular in the dialogue between diversity (as articulated in the *Essai sur l'exotisme*) and plurality (as explored in *Maghreb pluriel*). The radical and arguably – for many of his contemporaries – unpalatable dimension of Segalen's thought was centred on his 'refus radical d'une unité universelle, à laquelle il substitue l'affirmation d'une pluralité existentielle' ['rejection of universal unity and the substitution of an existential plurality'].[62] Commenting on Henri Bouvelet's 1910 poetry collection *Le Royaume de la Terre*, he notes, for instance, in the *Essai sur l'exotisme*: 'Cette notion de l'homogénéité

---

60   Dransfeldt Christensen, 'Towards an Ethics of Bilingualism', p. 463.
61   Khatibi, *Maghreb pluriel*, p. 187; *Plural Maghreb*, pp. 123–4.
62   Segler-Messner, 'Victor Segalen et la poétique de l'altérité', p. 75.

totale me paraît [...] ou hérésie ou impuissance' ['This muddled idea about a total homogeneity seems to me either heretical or impotent'].[63] These tensions between the homogeneous and the heterogeneous are central to one of the core texts of postcolonial studies, Edward Said's *Orientalism*, a critique of the totalizing and exoticizing Western colonial gaze that both erodes the singularity of colonized cultures and denies their inherent diversity. Said included Segalen amongst those European authors and thinkers complicit in such strategies,[64] and as a result failed to acknowledge the ways in which – including in dialogue with postcolonial intellectuals such as Glissant and Khatibi – his work sought to develop new understandings of exoticism that converged with those developed subsequently by postcolonial critics. The dominance of discussions of Orientalism by Edward Said have also eclipsed the contribution of Khatibi to the field, not least in the collection of essays published as *Maghreb pluriel* in 1983. In a 1974 article subsequently included in that volume, 'Décolonisation de la sociologie', Khatibi had sought ways to 'décentrer en nous le savoir occidental' ['decentre within us Western knowledge'], a manoeuvre that would mature into his elaboration of the *double-critique* mentioned above. Rooted in what Khatibi dubs a *pensée-autre*, this is an approach that eschews any 'naïve déclaration d'un droit à la différence' ['naïve declaration of a right to difference'] and seeks instead 'une pensée plurielle (à plusieurs pôles de civilisation, à plusieurs langues, à plusieurs élaborations techniques et scientifiques)' [plural thought (with several poles of civilization, several languages, several technical and scientific elaborations)'].[65] Developing a distinctively Segalenian reflection on the decline of diversity, he continues: 'Transmutation d'un monde sans retour sur ses fondements entropiques' ['Transmutation of a world without return to its entropic foundations'], and states that 'une pensée qui ne soit pas *minoritaire*, *marginale*, *fragmentaire* et *inachevée*, est toujours une pensée de

63 Segalen, *Essai sur l'exotisme*, in *Oeuvres complètes*, ed. Henry Bouillier, 2 vols (Paris: Laffont, 1995), 1.745–81 (p. 762); *Essay on Exoticism: An Aesthetics of Diversity*, trans. Yaël Schlick (Durham, NC: Duke University Press, 2002), p. 40.
64 On Segalen and Said, see Forsdick, 'Edward Said, Victor Segalen and the Implications of Post-Colonial Theory', *Journal of the Institute of Romance Studies* 5 (1997), pp. 323–39.
65 Abdelkébir Khatibi, 'Pensée-autre', in *Œuvres de Abdelkébir Khatibi III: Essais* (Paris: La Différence, 2008), pp. 9–27 (pp. 10, 11); *Plural Maghreb*, pp. 1–2, 4.

l'ethnocide' ['a thought that is not *minoritarian, marginal, fragmentary and incomplete* is always a thought of ethnocide'].[66]

The thought of Khatibi and Segalen – Moroccan and French, colonized and colonizer, colonial and postcolonial – is in permanent tension, converging and diverging. What unites the two thinkers and authors is an unexpected invisibility in much postcolonial thought, epitomized by the ways in which a key figure such as Edward Said marginalized the relative importance of both of their bodies of work, absorbing Segalen into a homogenized catalogue of Orientalists, and dismissing Khatibi as a 'nice guy but peripheral', 'a kind of Moroccan equivalent of Derrida'.[67] As this chapter has demonstrated, Segalen plays an undeniable role in the emergence and evolution of Khatibi's thought, according to a dialogic process of progressive absorption and distancing; yet, at the same time, following a postcolonial counterflow, Khatibi's engagement with Segalen casts the writings of the twentieth-century *exote* himself in a fresh light, offering new readings of his work. Khatibi comments on the inherent diversity of the Francophone world: 'le monde francophone est métissage, mixité avec des bilinguismes et des multilinguismes divers' ['the French-speaking world is hybridity, diversity, with its varied bilingualisms and multilingualisms'].[68] His analysis not only draws on Segalen's work in reaching this conclusion, but also inscribes Segalen into an analysis of the Francophone world that transcends those previous understandings limited by chronology (i.e. focused exclusively on the second half of the twentieth century) or by geography (i.e. creating a clear distinction between France and the wider Francosphere). Segler-Messner makes it clear that these genealogies are complex ones, and that any linear relationship linking Segalen and Khatibi that suggests reductive patterns of influence and intellectual legacy is disrupted by a clear differentiation of the two authors: Khatibi, she writes, seems to 'personnifier cet autre, que Segalen tentait de devenir lui-même et qui prend désormais lui-même la parole' ['personify that other whom Segalen sought to become himself and who nowadays does the talking'].[69]

66   Khatibi, 'Pensée-autre', pp. 11, 13; *Plural Maghreb*, pp. 4, 6.
67   For Said's comments on Khatibi, see Françoise Lionnet, 'Counterpoint and Double Critique in Edward Said and Abdelkébir Khatibi: A Transcolonial Comparison', in Ali Behdad and Dominic Thomas (eds), *A Companion to Comparative Literature* (Chichester: Wiley Blackwell, 2011), pp. 387–407 (p. 399).
68   Khatibi, *La Langue de l'autre*, p. 132.
69   Segler-Messner, 'Victor Segalen et la poétique de l'altérité', p. 85.

Khatibi evidently draws on Segalen at different points throughout his career, reading him dialogically to elaborate his own thought and to develop the key concepts that serve as its vehicle. This implicit, achronological dialogue between the two authors ranges from the early exploration of decolonization and acculturation in readings of *Les Immémoriaux*, to a reflection in Khatibi's later work on the links between the Segalenian *exote* and the *voyageur professionnel*. The emergence of Khatibi's deconstruction of dichotomies such Occident/ Orient in *Maghreb pluriel* or his elaboration of a distinctive creative practice in a novel such as *Amour bilingue* can be usefully read in the light of his reading of works by Segalen, most notably the *Essai sur l'exotisme* and *Stèles*. Understanding Segalen actively as an interlocutor with Khatibi not only illuminates the Moroccan thinker's own reflection on translation, transnationalism and the aesthetics of diversity but also (and equally importantly) invites a rethinking of Segalen's own early twentieth-century analysis of exoticism in a postcolonial frame. Such an approach not only reverses this vector conventionally associated with intellectual influence but also proposes new readings of Segalen's own work, unimagined and unimaginable by his contemporaries.

CHAPTER EIGHT

Khatibi and Derrida

A 'Franco-Maghrebian' Dialogue

Dominique Combe
Translated from the French by *Jane Hiddleston*

In the three volumes published posthumously by Editions de la Différence, Khatibi's works are classified according to their genre. The first volume, 'Romans et récits', includes *Le Livre du sang* (1979), *Amour bilingue* (1983), *Un été à Stockholm* (1990) and also *La Mémoire tatouée* (1971), with its subtitle 'autobiographie d'un décolonisé'. The second volume brings together Khatibi's poetic works, starting with *Le Lutteur de classe à la manière taoïste* (1976) and the play *Le Prophète voilé* (1979). The third volume comprises a thematic anthology of various critical and theoretical essays on Islam, identity and art, together with extracts from *Maghreb pluriel* (1983) and *Figures de l'étranger* (1987). Although useful to the reader discovering Khatibi in all his diversity, this division by genre is misleading because it artificially separates his theoretical reflection from his literary production. The separation of genres does not account for the constant interaction in Khatibi's novelistic, poetic and critical works between his creative imagination and his theoretical reflection, his work as a social scientist. Beyond the works clearly identified as essays, including *La Blessure du nom propre* and *Maghreb pluriel*, Khatibi's thought is also developed in the 'novel' *Amour bilingue*, in the 'autobiography' *La Mémoire tatouée* and the 'poems' of *Le Lutteur de classe*.

Born in Morocco in 1938, Khatibi studied sociology at the Sorbonne during the 1960s. He also learned structural linguistics, semiology and poetics, which were then on the rise, at the École Pratique des Hautes Études. His work can also be set in the context of the theoretical

avant-garde, of structuralism and *Théorie d'ensemble*.[1] It is during
this period that he met Roland Barthes, who wrote a short article
about him entitled 'Ce que je dois à Khatibi' in 1979, which serves as
a preface to the volume of Khatibi's essays mentioned above. In 1965,
Khatibi defended his first thesis, on the genre of the Maghrebian novel,
which was then published by Editions Maspéro in 1969, before going
back to teach in Morocco, where he became involved in the university
union. In 1966, together with Abdellatif Laâbi, Tahar Ben Jelloun
and Mohammed Khaïr-Eddine, he contributed to the founding of the
review *Souffles*. *Souffles* focused on literature, art and socio-political
reflection, and was deeply marked by the French avant-garde and
by Marxist–Leninist thought, mobilized in opposition to Hassan II
and in support of the 'third-worldist' struggle, which led to its being
suspended in 1972.

Having attended Barthes's seminar, and as a result of his close
relationship with artists, Khatibi maintained a totalizing conception of
'writing', based for him on the graphic sign in all its Eastern and Western
forms – tattoo, drawing, calligraphy, letters, the trace. He defended
Barthes's idea of the 'Text' transcending distinctions between genres.
Barthes also underlines his proximity with Khatibi in what he called
his 'entreprise sociologique' ['sociological enterprise']: 'Khatibi et moi,
nous nous intéressons aux mêmes choses: aux images, aux signes, aux
traces, aux lettres, aux marques' ['Khatibi and I are interested in the
same things: images, signs, traces, letters and marks'].[2] In *Figures de
l'étranger*, published in 1987, Khatibi wrote a long essay on Barthes's
Japan, on the questions raised by *L'Empire des signes*.[3] Japanese culture
and particularly calligraphy are the subject of a profound reflection in
his essays, for example in his reading of *Eloge de l'ombre* by Tanizaki in
French translation.[4]

1   Tel Quel, *Théorie d'ensemble* (Paris: Editions du Seuil, 1968).
2   Roland Barthes, 'Ce que je dois à Khatibi', in Abdelkébir Khatibi, *Œuvres de Abdelkébir Khatibi III: Essais* (Paris: La Différence, 2008), p. 7.
3   Abdelkébir Khatibi, *Figures de l'étranger dans la littérature française* (Paris: Denoël, 1987), pp. 57–85.
4   Abdelkébir Khatibi, *Ombres japonaises* (Montpellier: Fata Morgana, 1988), reprinted in *Œuvres de Abdelkébir Khatibi III*, pp. 208–32.

The Meeting between Khatibi and Derrida

The editors of the first volume of Khatibi's *Œuvres* published by Editions de la Différence in 2008 included a short text by Derrida as a preface, where he writes: 'ce que Khatibi fait de la langue française, ce qu'il lui donne en lui imprimant sa marque, est inséparable de ce qu'il analyse de cette situation dans ses dimensions linguistiques, certes, mais aussi culturelles, religieuses, anthropologiques, politiques' ['what Khatibi does with the French language, what he gives to it by leaving his mark on it, cannot be dissociated from what he analyses in this situation in all its linguistic but also its cultural, religious, anthropological and political dimensions'].[5] Khatibi's relationship with Derrida, as with Barthes, is in all respects essential for the development of his work. It was with the intellectuals of the Latin Quarter in Paris that Khatibi first met the philosopher, in 1974, at the time of the publication of *La Blessure du nom propre* and his anti-Zionist pamphlet *Vomito blanco*. They belonged to the same generation born between the wars (Derrida in 1936 and Khatibi in 1938), and they frequented the same intellectual circles. Above all, they were both born on the other side of the Mediterranean in the colonial context, Khatibi in Morocco and Derrida in Algeria, and were students during the Algerian War of Independence. Their meeting gave rise to an unfailing friendship which lasted until Derrida died in 2004. A reader also of Frantz Fanon and engaged in anticolonial critique, Khatibi explicitly refers to Derrida in his article 'Décolonisation et sociologie' published in 1974 and reprinted in *Maghreb pluriel* in 1983. He makes the necessary connection between decolonization and deconstruction, working against 'logocentrism' and ethnocentrism. Several years before the publication of Edward Said's *Orientalism* in 1978, Khatibi calls us to 'décentrer en nous le savoir oriental' ['decenter in us Western knowledge'] and to 'nous dé-centrer par rapport à ce centre, à cette origine que se donne l'occident' ['to decenter ourselves with respect to this center, this origin that the West gives itself'].[6]

The dialogue between Khatibi and Derrida is pursued from one article and one book to another, from the gathering that formed *Du bilinguisme*

5 Jacques Derrida, 'Exergue', in Abdelkébir Khatibi, *Œuvres de Abdelkébir Khatibi I: Romans et récits* (Paris: Editions de la Différence, 2008), p. 7.

6 Abdelkébir Khatibi, *Maghreb pluriel* (Paris: Denoël, 1983), p. 54; *Plural Maghreb: Writings on Postcolonialism*, trans. P. Burcu Yalim (London: Bloomsbury, 2019), p. 30.

to the Cerisy conference of 1992, up to 'Variations sur l'amitié' published in the *Cahier de l'Herne* in 2004. From 2001 onwards, Derrida regularly visited Khatibi in Morocco. Khatibi enters into dialogue with Derrida in a series of four texts: 'Le point de non-retour', 'Lettre ouverte à Jacques Derrida', 'Le nom et le pseudonyme' and 'Variations sur l'amitié', published together in *Jacques Derrida, en effet* in 2007. Again the two thinkers find themselves concerned with the same questions of language, writing, the 'trace' and 'la différence intraitable' ['intractable difference']. It is through his dialogue with Barthes and Derrida that Khatibi conceptualizes the difference between East and West. *Maghreb pluriel* invents a 'pensée autre' ['other-thought']. At the same time, it is through these dialogues about the Maghreb that Derrida comes to propose the idea of 'le monolinguisme de l'autre' ['the monolingualism of the other']. Algeria was an omnipresent reality in Derrida's thinking from his first texts, though mostly implicitly, as is testified by a long unpublished letter to Pierre Nora in 1961 about Algerian Jews. Here Derrida defends Camus against Nora himself and against Sartre.[7] Having left Algiers in 1949 to study in Paris, he went back to carry out his military service as a teacher in 1957–9, during the war. After that, he did not go back to Algeria until 1971. This did not prevent Algeria from playing a decisive role in the development of his thought, as he recounts with strong feeling in an interview with Mustapha Chérif:

> l'héritage que j'ai reçu de l'Algérie est quelque chose qui a inspiré mon travail philosophique, tout le travail que j'ai poursuivi à l'égard de la pensée occidentale. Les questions que j'ai été amené à lui poser depuis une certaine marge n'auraient pas été possibles si, dans mon histoire personnelle, je n'avais été Algérien.[8]

> [the heritage I received from Algeria inspired my philosophical work, all the work I did on Western thought. The questions I asked about it from a certain marginal position would not have been possible if my personal history had not been Algerian.]

Derrida finds in his dialogue with Khatibi an opportunity to demonstrate the role of the Maghreb, and of his native Algeria, in the deconstruction of Western metaphysics.

---

7   The letter was published with the re-edition of Pierre Nora's *Les Français d'Algérie* (Paris: Christian Bourgois, 1961), pp. 271–99.

8   Mustapha Chérif, Jean-Luc Nancy, Hélène Cixous *et al.*, 'Le vivre-ensemble', in *Derrida à Alger: un regard sur le monde* (Algiers: Barzakh/Arles: Actes Sud, 2008), pp. 15–18 (p. 16).

The Conference at Baton Rouge and the Genesis of
Le Monolinguisme de l'autre

The dialogue between Khatibi and Derrida continued in Baton Rouge in 1992, this time in a transatlantic context. Both of them participated in the bilingual conference *Renvois d'ailleurs/Echos from Elsewhere* organized at the State University of Louisiana by Patrick Mensah and David Wills. Edouard Glissant presided over this conference devoted to literary 'francophonie' outside of France. It brought together both writers and critics of francophone literature, among whom one of the most important was Khatibi. Derrida gave a long presentation subsequently published in 1996 with the title *Le Monolinguisme de l'autre*. The two texts he cites in an epigraph help anchor the question of language in literature, under the aegis of a 'politique de l'amitié' ['politics of friendship']. Alongside a citation from Glissant's *Le Discours antillais* of 1981, Derrida reproduces an extract from Khatibi's *Amour bilingue*, a philosophical fiction where the 'bilangue' is the central figure.

At the conference, Derrida tested some of the hypotheses he had already articulated at the Sorbonne at a meeting of the Collège International de Philosophie and in Montreal. These hypotheses were published in Quebec in 1982 under the title *L'Oreille de l'autre*.[9] *Le Monolinguisme de l'autre* brings together these works fuelled by his exchanges with Glissant and above all Khatibi, to whom the essay is dedicated. Attentive reading of *Le Monolinguisme* reveals in this way the hidden presence of Khatibi's thinking on language. Around French and Arabic, and languages in general, he raises questions of the difference between East and West, and the relationship between Derrida and Khatibi and the Maghreb, Algeria and Morocco. The philosophical question of language is always broached through the singular and historically and geographically situated experience of these two French speakers originating from the Maghreb. This emblematic cultural situation – Khatibi was born in El Jadida to a Muslim, Arabic-speaking family and Derrida was born in Algiers to a Jewish, French-speaking family – is the object of a theoretical reflection that also extends further into 'francophonie' and writing more broadly. Derrida's remarks, like those of Khatibi, in this

9 Claude Lévesque and Christie V. McDonald (eds), *L'Oreille de l'autre: otobiographies, transferts, traductions. Textes et débats avec Jacques Derrida* (Montreal: VLB, 1982).

way take on a general, even universal and paradigmatic significance relating to literature and philosophy as such.

The Search for a Genealogy of an Exemplary Franco-Maghrebian

Albert Memmi argues that 'le colonisé semble condamné à perdre progressivement la mémoire' ['the colonized seems condemned to lose his memory'].[10] In order to understand the stakes of the dialogue between Derrida and Khatibi on language it is necessary to take into account the death of Derrida's mother in Nice, and with that the death of his memory of Algeria. At the end of her life, Georgette was aphasic and amnesiac. The 'autobiographical' project of 'anamnesis' undertaken in 'Circonfession', a text written between January 1989 and April 1990 and published in 1991, continued in *Le Monolinguisme*, attempts to respond to this aphasia-amnesia by means of the 'témoignage' ['testimony'] and 'attestation' of a 'franco-maghrébin exemplaire' ['exemplary franco-Maghrebian'], to his mother 'qui mourait en perdant la mémoire, la parole et le pouvoir de nommer' ['who was dying while losing her memory, her speech and her power of naming'].[11] With the amnesia and the death of his mother, which followed that of his father Aimé, Derrida's personal memory of Algeria seems threatened. This text is then the metaphysical attempt to return by means of voluntary memory to his inaccessible Algerian origins, of which the autobiographical narrative can only ever be a 'prosthesis'. In this way Derrida attributes the 'pulsion généalogique' ['search for a genealogy'] and his 'mouvement compulsif vers l'anamnèse' ['compulsive movement towards anamnesia'] at work in his autobiography to his situation as a 'franco-maghrébin', as an Algerian Jew who speaks French and has no stable model of identification. *Le Monolinguisme* in this way retraces the genealogy of the 'metaphysical' desire for autobiography against the background of cultural amnesia. This problem also affects native Muslims. But, as a

---

10   Albert Memmi, *Portrait du colonisé, précédé du portrait du colonisateur* (Paris: Gallimard, 2008), p. 121; *The Colonizer and the Colonized*, trans. Howard Greenfeld (London: Earthscan, 2003), p. 147.

11   Jacques Derrida, *Le Monolinguisme de l'autre, ou, La Prothèse de l'origine* (Paris: Galilée, 1996), p. 117; *The Monolingualism of the Other, or, The Prosthesis of Origin*, trans. Patrick Mensah (Stanford, CA: Stanford University Press, 1998), p. 60.

result of the interdependence between colonizer and colonized in the system described by Memmi in *Portrait du colonisé, précédé du portrait du colonisateur*, amnesia affects all Algerians.

From the second chapter of *Le Monolinguisme de l'autre*, the paradox 'on ne parle jamais qu'une seule langue' and 'on ne parle jamais une seule langue' ['we only ever speak one language' and 'we never speak only one language'] raises the question of memory.[12] Writing is a form of anamnesia: 'on se rappelle, on s'inquiète, on se met en quête d'histoire et de filiation' ['one recollects, one troubles oneself, one goes in search of history and filiation'].[13] Derrida's approach here also echoes, as if in counterpoint, Khatibi's first great narrative, *La Mémoire tatouée*, with its subtitle 'autobiographie d'un décolonisé'. Khatibi paints a fictional portrait of the relationship between a high school boy and French language and culture – a central issue in the first narratives in French published in the Maghreb in the 1950s: Albert Memmi's *La Statue de sel*, Mouloud Feraoun's *Le Fils du pauvre* and Driss Chraïbi's *Le Passé simple*. This autobiography can be coupled with the theoretical essays brought together by Khatibi in *Maghreb pluriel* in 1983. *Le Monolinguisme de l'autre* and *La Mémoire tatouée* can moreover be associated with the 'autobiographical turn' taken by French literature between 1970 and 1990, along the lines of Roland Barthes in *Roland Barthes par lui-même* (1975) and above all in *La Chambre claire* (1980). Khatibi and Derrida participate in the same philosophical tradition that stretches from Augustine to Descartes and Nietzsche, revisited by Derrida in *Otobiographies: l'enseignement de Nietzsche et la politique du nom propre* in 1984. If it was until then only implicitly present, Algeria returns, in Derrida's pursuit of anamnesia, in the 59 digressive, elliptical fragments of 'Circonfession'.

Anamnesia is not just the effect of a 'nostalgérie' revivified by the death of Derrida's mother and the anguish of forgetting. It also responds urgently to political circumstances. Hélène Cixous affirms that, just as she would not have written *Les Rêveries de la femme sauvage* 'avant de s'être sentie autorisée et sollicitée par [s]es amis algériens' ['before feeling authorized and invited to do so by her Algerian friends'], Derrida would not have undertaken to write *Le Monolinguisme* if he had not opened again the dialogue with is native Algeria and Algerians

12   Derrida, *Le Monolinguisme de l'autre*, p. 21; *The Monolingualism of the Other*, p. 7.
13   Ibid., p. 22; p. 8.

during the civil war of the 1990s.[14] *Le Monolinguisme* is anchored in the tragic moment of the Black Decade which followed the victory of the Front Islamique du Salut in the elections, the military coup d'état of 1991, the deposition of President Chadli Benjedid and the appointment of Mohammed Boudiaf, which triggered the civil war and Islamist terrorism. The singular, personal and familial history of the 'franco-maghrébin exemplaire' meets the history of the Algerian people, who play out again the scene of the armed conflict for independence. This situation, which Derrida followed closely, again opens in him the Algerian wound which will not heal.

The 'Linguistic Drama': Monolingualism, Bilingualism, Diglossia

As in *La Mémoire tatouée*, in *Le Monolinguisme de l'autre*, 'le personnage principal est le Français' ['the main character is the French language'], as Hélène Cixous puts it in her *Portrait de Jacques Derrida en Jeune Saint Juif* published in 1991.[15] The French Algeria in which Derrida was brought up, like Khatibi's Morocco under the Protectorate, was the setting for a colonial drama of domination *of* and *by* language. This was a drama that Memmi analysed in 1957 in *Portrait du colonisé*, on the basis of his own Tunisian experience as an Arabic-speaking Jew educated in the French school. Derrida no doubt read the *Portrait*, with its preface by Sartre. In what was supposed to be 'colonial bilingualism' and turned out in reality to be a 'linguistic duality', the 'indigenous' language, dominated by French in Morocco, Tunisia and a fortiori in Algeria, was systematically devalued even by those who spoke it, fascinated by the prestige of the language of the Other:

> Dans le conflit linguistique qui habite le colonisé, sa langue maternelle est l'humiliée, l'écrasée. Et ce mépris, objectivement fondé, il finit par le faire sien. De lui-même, il se met à écarter cette langue infirme, à la cacher aux yeux des étrangers, à ne paraître à l'aise que dans la langue du colonisateur. En bref, le bilinguisme colonial n'est ni une diglossie, où coexistent un idiome populaire et une langue de puriste, appartenant tous les deux au même univers affectif, ni une simple richesse polyglotte, qui

14   See Hélène Cixous, 'Celle qui ne se ferme pas', in Chérif, Nancy, Cixous *et al.*, *Derrida à Alger: un regard sur le monde*, pp. 45–58 (p. 53).
15   Hélène Cixous, *Portrait de Jacques Derrida en Jeune Saint Juif* (Paris: Galilée, 1991), p. 105.

bénéficie d'un clavier supplémentaire mais relativement neutre; c'est un drame linguistique.

[In the linguistic conflict within the colonized, his mother tongue is that which is crushed. He himself sets about discarding this infirm language, hiding it from the sight of strangers. In short, colonial bilingualism is neither a purely bilingual situation in which an indigenous tongue coexists with a purist's language (both belonging to the same world of feeling), nor a simple polyglot richness benefiting from an extra but relatively neuter alphabet; it is a linguistic drama.][16]

This drama, which makes of the colonized 'un étranger dans son propre pays' ['a stranger in his own land'] is completely different from the virtuosic and fertile plurilingualism of Central European Jewish writers such as Freud, Kafka and Elias Canetti, who have an equal mastery of German, sometimes Yiddish, and often other languages.[17] George Steiner described this polyglot situation:

I have no recollection whatever of a first language. So far as I am aware, I possess equal currency in English, French, and German. [...] My natural situation was polyglot, as is that of children in the Val d'Aosta, in the Basque country, in parts of Flanders, or among speakers of Guarani and Spanish in Paraguay. It was habitual, unnoticed practice for my mother to start a sentence in one language and finish it in another. At home, conversations were interlinguistic not only inside the same sentence or speech segment but as between speakers. Only a sudden wedge of interruption or roused consciousness would make me realize that I was replying in French to a question put in German or English or vice versa. [...] This polyglot matrix was far more than a hazard of private condition. It organized, it imprinted on my grasp of personal identity, the formidably complex, resourceful cast of feeling of Central European and Judaic humanism.[18]

Sent by his family to the franco-Moroccan school, Khatibi was certainly like Steiner educated between languages. But he mastered those languages to unequal levels: 'à l'école, un enseignement laïc, imposé à ma religion; je devins triglotte, lisant le français sans le parler, jouant avec quelques bribes de l'arabe écrit, et parlant le dialecte comme quotidien. Où, dans ce chassé-croisé, la cohérence et la continuité?' ['at school, secular teaching

16 Memmi, *Portrait du colonisé*, p. 125; *The Colonizer and the Colonized*, pp. 151–2.
17 Memmi, *Portrait du colonisé*, p. 124.
18 George Steiner, *After Babel: Aspects of Language and Translation* (Oxford: Oxford University Press, 1975), pp. 115–16.

imposed on my religion; I became trilingual, reading French without speaking it, fooling around with scraps of written Arabic, and speaking my everyday dialect.Where, in all this babble, was there any coherence and continuity?'].[19] 'Linguistic dualism' gave primacy to French as the language of culture and writing, to the detriment of Arabic. Of course, Khatibi speaks Moroccan Arabic, and reads and writes classical Arabic, unlike many Maghrebian intellectuals of his generation, but he thinks, writes and publishes in French.

As a result of this bilingualism, which is really a 'dualism', Khatibi's relationship with French is profoundly different from that of Derrida, who was irremediably monolingual, and this is what was discussed at Baton Rouge. This difference is not only because the history of Algeria as a French 'département', comparable to other 'départements' of metropolitan France, is not the same as that of the Moroccan Protectorate (nor of Tunisia, moreover), where classical Arabic was still taught. It is also because the Jewish community to which Derrida belongs, despite his 'retranchement hors de toute communauté' ['exclusion from every community'], did not have the same status in Morocco or in Tunisia.[20] Algerian Jews who, since the Crémieux decree of 1870, benefited from having French nationality, found themselves separated by the colonial power from local Muslims, Arabs or Berbers alongside whom they lived, often for centuries.[21] They became assimilated as 'French Algerians'. As the language of the colonizer, taught in schools and imposed by the administration, French was to be become their language, and soon their only language. Gradually they lost contact with the Arabic-speaking milieu in which they had previously been fully integrated, to the point of working as interpreters and translators. This assimilation was also accompanied by a secularization leading to a drop in the use of Hebrew, which was reserved for worship, as well as the Judeo-Spanish of their ancestors. The zealous application of anti-Semitic Vichy laws during the war, as a result of which Derrida was excluded from his French school, nevertheless demonstrated the limits of that assimilation. Having lived

19   Abdelkébir Khatibi, *La Mémoire tatouée: autobiographie d'un décolonisé* (Paris: Denoël, 1971), reprinted in *Œuvres de Abdelkébir Khatibi I: Romans et récits* (Paris: La Différence, 2008), pp. 9–113 (p. 40); *Tattooed Memory*, trans. Peter Thompson (Paris: L'Harmattan, 2016), p. 50.

20   Jacques Derrida, *Le Dernier des juifs* (Paris: Galilée, 2014), p. 96.

21   Arabs and Berbers had to be aged 21 before they could apply for naturalisation, which was rarely given.

on the Algerian land for much longer than the colonizers, Jews then became immigrants from within, 'étrangers dans leur propre pays' ['strangers in their own land'], to use Memmi's phrase.[22]

The 'French Algerians' were not a homogeneous community, not even on a linguistic level, despite their assimilation by the colonial schools. Christians of French, Spanish, Italian or Maltese origin, Berber Jews, Sephardis of Spanish origin, Ashkenazis from Central Europe, the 'French Algerians' in their diversity found themselves at the centre of the colonial 'linguistic drama'. Even though French was often not their mother tongue, French Algerians had to make it their reference point. In any case, beyond the Arabic-speaking Jews, those working high up in the colonial administration educated at the Ecole des langues orientales, white priests and several teachers and scholars, few mastered classical Arabic. In Algeria, Arabic and Berber were taught as foreign languages; in Morocco, this was only the case in the French lycées, not in the Franco-Moroccan schools like the one Khatibi attended. Hélène Cixous for this reason regrets that she was forbidden access to Arabic:

> Grandir dans un pays dont on ne parle pas la langue! Vous me direz – ça arrive mais pas ainsi: on grandissait dans un pays insensé. Où la langue natale, celle qu'on disait l'arabe, est déclarée comme morte, reléguée, abaissée, minorisée sur tous les marchés économiques politiques culturels, il y a de quoi rendre différemment fou chacun des peuples qui 'habitent' cet inhabitable. On est à jamais blessé et révolté par cette scène: voir de nos oreilles hommes et femmes non francophones être mutilés diminués, leur langue rendue vaine devant la langue dominante.[23]

> [To grow up in a country whose language you do not speak! You'll tell me that happens, but not in that way: we grew up in a senseless country. Where the native language, Arabic, was declared dead, relegated, denigrated and made into a minor language on an economic, political and cultural level. It is enough to drive those who 'live' in this unliveable

---

22 The situation described by Derrida needs to be further nuanced. In addition to the fact that the Sephardi Jews driven out of Spain (often via Morocco, where they could study) have a different history from the Berber Jews who had lived in Algeria since Antiquity, there was in colonial Algeria, especially in the south and far from the big urban centres, an Arabic-speaking Jewish community, often despised by the Westernized Jews of Oran or Algiers. See Joëlle Allouche-Benyoum and Doris Bensimon, *Juifs d'Algérie hier et aujourd'hui: mémoires et identités* (Paris: Privat, 1989) and Benjamin Stora, *Les Trois Exils, juifs d'Algérie* (Paris: Stock, 2006).

23 Cixous, *Portrait de Jacques Derrida en Jeune Saint Juif*, p. 56.

context mad. We were constantly wounded and revolted by this drama: we would see non-francophone men and women mutilated, diminished, their language made useless by the dominant language.]

Derrida affirms that this situation of linguistic domination resulted in refusing to some access to language. Deprived of the languages of his origins – Arabic, Berber, Judeo-Spanish, even Hebrew – the Algerian Jew[24] is subject to 'l'interdit fondamental, l'interdiction absolue, l'interdiction de la diction et du dire': 'on interdit l'accès au dire, voilà tout, à un certain dire' ['the fundamental interdiction, the absolute interdiction, the interdiction of diction and speech'; 'one forbids access to speech [*au dire*], that is all, a certain kind of speech'].[25] Derrida sees himself in this way as condemned to live in French, his only language, which is nevertheless not his own. 'Il s'est jeté dans la traduction absolue' ['he is thrown into absolute translation'], because, 'il n'y a pour lui que des langues d'arrivée' ['for him, there are only target languages'] in the absence of an original, and originary, language.[26] The 'prosthesis of origin', the subtitle of *Le Monolinguisme*, makes the French language a substitute for this originary language that the Algerian Jew lacks, as he mourns for Berber, Arabic, Hebrew and the Judeo-Spanish of his ancestors.

A Franco-Maghrebian Writer or a Francophone Maghrebian Writer?

Chapter 8 of *Le Monolinguisme* questions the categories of Western thought used to describe the situation of the 'franco-maghrébin': 'tous ces mots: *vérité, aliénation, appropriation, "chez soi", ipséité, place du sujet, loi*, etc., demeurent à mes yeux problématiques. Sans exception. Ils portent le sceau de cette métaphysique qui s'est imposée' ['all these words: *truth, alienation, appropriation, habitation, one's-home* [*chez soi*], *ipseity, place of the subject, law,* and so on remain, in my eyes,

---

24   The use of the capital letter and the singular recalls Sartre's style in *Réflexions sur la question juive*, with which Derrida enters into dialogue in his paper 'Abraham l'autre', in 2000 (reprinted posthumously in *Le Dernier des Juifs* (Paris: Galilée, 2014), p. 98, with a preface by Jean-Luc Nancy).

25   Derrida, *Le Monolinguisme de l'autre*, p. 58; *The Monolinguism of the Other*, p. 32.

26   Ibid., p. 117; p. 61.

problematic. Without exception. They bear the stamp of the metaphysics that imposed itself'].[27] But after listing the metaphysical vocabulary used during his previous chapters, Derrida comes to the heart of his singular situation, with the deictics in italics:

> A travers, justement, *cette* Langue de l'autre, *ce* monolinguisme de l'autre. Si bien que ce débat avec le monolinguisme n'aura pas été autre chose qu'une écriture *déconstructive*. Celle-ci toujours s'en prend au corps de cette langue, ma seule langue, et de ce qu'elle porte le plus ou le mieux, à savoir cette tradition philosophique qui nous fournit la réserve des concepts dont je dois bien me servir.

> [*This* language of the other, *this* monolingualism of the other. So much so that this debate with monolingualism will have been nothing other than a piece of *deconstructive* writing [*écriture*]. Such writing always attacks the body of this language, my only language, and what it bears the most or in the best way, namely, the philosophical tradition that supplies us with the reservoir of concepts I definitely have to use.][28]

The complex process of anamnesia at work in *Le Monolinguisme* makes language the stakes and the principle of deconstruction. The virtuosic usage of a language 'endeuillée du deuil', 'le deuil de ce qu'on n'a jamais eu' ['the bereaved language of bereavement', 'a mourning for what one never had'][29] is mingled with the very experience of deconstruction, which is defined 'à plus d'une langue' ['in more than one language'].[30] In this way the autobiographical narrative – because it is a narrative, however digressive and elliptical it might be – reveals the genesis of Derrida's philosophy, since his introduction to *L'Origine de la géométrie*. The autobiography of the 'franco-Maghrébin exemplaire' or indeed of the 'Juif Algérien', by throwing into question that forbidden language, brings deconstruction into being. It is a question of thinking about language and writing in the general, even universal sense, on the basis of an absolute experience that the exchange with Khatibi sets out to describe.

This contradictory relationship with language defines the condition of the 'franco-maghrébin', itself a new expression and apparently unique to

27 Derrida, *Le Monolinguisme de l'autre*, p. 115; *The Monolinguism of the Other*, p. 59.
28 Ibid., p. 115; p. 59.
29 Ibid., pp. 60–1; p. 33.
30 Jacques Derrida, *Mémoires, pour Paul de Man* (Paris: Galilée, 1988), p. 38.

Derrida. In their dialogue, Derrida and Khatibi's relationship is one of both imitation and rivalry, not to say jealousy (a word often used about language itself), against the background of a friendly complicity. In *Le Monolinguisme*, playing in a virtuoso manner with the use of an address in the second person, Derrida names and reflects on his friend Khatibi, with whom he shares 'un certain destin' ['a certain destiny'], which is to be 'franco-maghrébin', while also distinguishing himself from him in his relationship with language. Derrida presents Khatibi as 'un écrivain maghrébin francophone' ['francophone Maghrebian writer'] rather than 'franco-maghrébin' ['franco-Maghrébian'].[31] Since Khatibi is fundamentally French neither by his nationality nor by his language, Derrida sees himself as more franco-maghrebian than him. Pursuing his reflection he cites the 'franco-Tunisian' writer Abdelwahab Meddeb and his novel *Talismano*, a novel also analysed by Khatibi in 'Incipits' in *Du bilinguisme*, reprinted and developed in *Maghreb pluriel*. Derrida quotes Khatibi, who in turn quotes Meddeb, with a few allusions to Frantz Fanon and Kateb Yacine. At the end of *Le Polygone étoilé*, Kateb describes the 'seconde rupture du cordon ombilical' ['second rupture of the umbilical chord']. His father, literate in Arabic, but anxious that his sons should succeed in life, decides to send him to the French school, cutting him off in this way from his origins:

> Jamais je n'ai cessé, même aux jours de succès près de l'institutrice, de ressentir au fond de moi cette seconde rupture du lien ombilical, cet exil intérieur qui ne rapprochait plus l'écolier de sa mère que pour les arracher, chaque fois un peu plus, au murmure du sang, aux frémissements réprobateurs d'une langue bannie, secrètement, d'un même accord, aussitôt brisé que conclu ... Ainsi avais-je perdu tout à la fois ma mère et son langage, les seuls trésors inaliénables et pourtant aliénés![32]

> [Even on days when the teacher was pleased with me, I never stopped feeling deep inside that second rupture of the umbilical cord, that internal exile which did not bring the schoolboy closer to the mother but tore them apart, each time a little more, against the background of the murmuring of blood, of the disapproving tremblings of a banished language, secretly, broken as soon as concluded ... In this way I lost at once my mother and her language, the only inalienable treasures and yet alienated!]

31   Derrida, *Le Monolinguisme de l'autre*, p. 119; *The Monolinguism of the Other*, p. 62.
32   Kateb Yacine, *Le Polygone étoilé* (Paris: Editions du Seuil, 1997 [1966]), pp. 181–2.

The child is cruelly separated from the Arabophone culture of the mother. Leïla Sebbar, also brought up in Algeria in the French school, also evokes this 'dispossession' in a deeply moving autobiographical narrative. In *Je ne parle pas la langue de mon père* (2003), she in turn stages the tragic rupture of the family. The daughter of an Algerian schoolteacher married to a Frenchwoman, and a *fellagha* [resistance fighter], Sebbar has a complex and ambivalent relationship with the French language – a language that her father, an indigenous Muslim schoolteacher teaches at the Republican school, a language which is no more her own than it is for the Jewish boy Jacques Derrida. The little girl, brought up in the French school where Arabic is prohibited, 'ne parle pas la langue de son père' ['does not speak her father's language'].

However, the situation of the franco-Tunisian writer Abdelwahab Meddeb, culturally Muslim and perfectly bilingual, descended from a family literate in Arabic, is again different. Perhaps Derrida is fundamentally, as he suggests, 'le seul franco-maghrébin' ['the only franco-Maghrebian'], if we can describe in this way a writer devoted to the 'monolinguisme de l'autre' by the circumstances of history – Algeria, Judaism, French nationality, the exclusion from citizenship and from school by Vichy laws, settling in Paris.

Khatibi responds to Derrida's thesis in *Le Monolinguisme* with his beautiful 'Lettre ouverte à Jacques Derrida', printed in the journal *Europe* in 2004. He underlines the difference between the Algerian Jew, who speaks French but has had his citizenship taken away by the Vichy government, and the Moroccan Jew who 'ne perd ni sa citoyenneté, ni sa nationalité et son passeport' ['who has lost neither his citizenship nor his nationality and passport'].[33] Khatibi is no doubt thinking of his friend Edmond Amran El Maleh (who died in 2010), a communist, reader of Jean Genet and author of the magnificent autobiographical narratives *Parcours immobile* (1980) and *Aïlen ou la nuit du récit* (1983), which conjure up memories of Jewish-Arabic Morocco. But, above all, Khatibi deepens Derrida's reflection on the identity of the 'franco-Maghrebian'. Derrida objects to Khatibi that, even without being able to write in Arabic, the Moroccan writer at least possesses a language of his own, one that he can consider as his mother tongue, even if dialectal Arabic to a large extent mixes Arabic

---

33 Abdelkébir Khatibi, 'Lettre ouverte à Jacques Derrida', *Europe* 901 (2004), pp. 201-11, reprinted in *La Langue de l'autre* (New York and Tunis: Les Mains secrètes, 1999), p. 21-33 (p. 26).

and French, making the writer's linguistic identity unstable. Khatibi accepts the contrast between his own personal situation as an 'écrivain maghrébin francophone' ['francophone Maghrebian writer'], of the sort he studied in his thesis on *Le Roman maghrébin*, and that of the 'franco-Maghrebian' Derrida. The francophone Maghrebian writer, who has never been and never will be French, is not monolingual but bilingual, even trilingual, even if his mastery of his languages is not equal. Having adopted the French language as the language of his writing for better or for worse, Khatibi symbolically maintains access to his mother tongue, Arabic, which, even if it was denigrated by colonial history, remains incontestably 'la sienne' ['his']: 'cette langue silencieuse me tenait la main, au-delà de toute aphasie, de toute amnésie' ['that silent language held my hand, beyond all aphasia, all amnesia'].[34] Whilst Derrida is condemned to monolingualism, Khatibi can pride himself on his diglossia – French, the language of his writing, and the Arabic spoken at home: 'en ce sens, ce n'est pas une substitution de la langue maternelle, mais une langue d'écriture en une diglossie incroyable, car il s'agissait de parler dans une langue et d'écrire dans une autre' ['it is in this sense not a substitution of the mother tongue, but a language of writing in an incredible diglossia, because it was a question of speaking one language and writing in another'].[35] It is no doubt true that diglossia puts the francophone Maghrebian writer's mother tongue in an inferior position, but it nevertheless does maintain its usage.

However, the diglossia between French and Arabic at work in *Amour bilingue* is in the end perhaps no less conflictual or paradoxical as the monolingualism of the franco-maghrébian Jew, given the dissymmetry and the unequal power relation between languages in the colonial context. In the essay on Meddeb's *Talismano*, also quoted by Derrida, Khatibi shows that the situation of the francophone Arabic writer is also untenable because it reveals what Memmi called the alienation of colonial bilingualism. Khatibi describes the 'chiasme entre aliénation et inaliénation' ['the chasm between alienation and inalienation'] as a 'schize' ['split'].[36] Transcribing into French his 'nom propre transformé' ['transformed proper name'], which also becomes a pseudonym, the francophone author

34 Khatibi, 'Lettre ouverte à Jacques Derrida', p. 208.
35 Ibid.
36 Khatibi, *Maghreb pluriel*, p. 201; *Plural Maghreb*, pp. 134–5.

ne peut rien posséder (si tant soit peu on s'approprie une langue), il ne possède ni son parler maternel qui ne s'écrit pas, ni la langue écrite aliénée et donnée à une substitution, ni cette autre langue apprise et qui lui fait signe de se désapproprier en elle et de s'y effacer.

[he cannot possess anything (if ever one appropriates a language), he possesses neither his maternal speech that is not written nor the written Arabic language that is alienated and given to a substitution, nor this other learned language that signals him to disappropriate and erase himself therein.][37]

Khatibi, Derrida and Mallarmé

The linguistic alienation created by the separation and hierarchy of languages in the colonial context, experienced in a heightened manner by Derrida and Khatibi, can nevertheless turn out to be creative; it inspires poetry, the invention of a language of one's own. Building on the central thesis of *Le Monolinguisme* as on his own experience of bilingualism in Morocco, emblematic of a sort of ontological bilingualism, Khatibi makes of writing, of all writing, in any language, an experience of 'désappropriation' ['disappropriation']: 'quand j'écris, je le fais dans la Langue de l'autre. Cette langue n'est pas une propriété' ['when I write, it is in the language of the other. This language is not a property'].[38] This is very close to Derrida's remarks on the French language as not 'la sienne' ['his own']. As a writer, Khatibi 'possesses' French no more than any other language:

J'ai toujours senti que la langue en général, et le français en particulier, m'a été prêtée. Je ne suis pas l'héritier direct de cette langue, ni de sa tradition; je n'ai pas l'illusion de parler en son nom, ni avec une autorité qui m'aurait été octroyée de génération en génération, mais elle m'a adopté comme je l'ai adoptée en tant qu'étranger professionnel.[39]

[I have always felt that language in general, and French in particular, was lent to me. I did not directly inherit that language, nor its tradition: I do not feel that I speak in its name, nor with an authority that would have

37 Ibid., p. 201; pp. 134–5.
38 Abdelkébir Khatibi, 'La Langue de l'autre', *Œuvres de Abdelkébir Khatibi III: Essais*, pp. 115–35 (p. 119).
39 Ibid., p. 133.

been bestowed upon me from one generation to another, but rather it adopted me as I have adopted it as a professional stranger.]

In *Portrait du colonisé*, Memmi described the French language as a 'prêt qui, d'ailleurs, ne sera jamais qu'un prêt' ['a loan which can only ever be a loan'].[40] Khatibi conceptualizes bilingualism in a broad sense, not in fact unrelated to monolingualism in that it too makes him a foreigner in language.

This foreignness in language is not unique to the Maghreb, nor to francophone countries outside France. Khatibi also suggests it describes Mallarmé's situation, as he cites the critic Albert Thibaudet: 'il conviendrait de chercher la mesure dans laquelle fut ou non française l'œuvre de Mallarmé' ['we need to discover how far Mallarmé's work was French']. This comparison allows Khatibi to consider himself an 'otage dans la langue française et sa littérature' ['a hostage in the French language and its literature'].[41] The intractable difference between writing in French and speaking in dialectal Arabic is comparable to Mallarmé's separation between the 'brut' ['raw'] and 'essentiel' ['essential'] forms of speech. In 'La Langue de l'autre', with its Derridean subtitle, 'Exercices de témoignage', Khatibi compares speaking in one language and writing in another to Mallarmé's distinction, as it is analysed by Maurice Blanchot, which defines poetry:

> Parler dans une langue et écrire dans une autre est une expérience étrange et peut-être radicale. Je me demande maintenant si Maurice Blanchot n'a pas visé juste: 'Par une division violente, Mallarmé a séparé le langage en deux formes presque sans rapport, l'une la langue brute, l'autre le langage essentiel. Voilà peut-être le véritable bilinguisme'.[42]

> [Speaking in one language and writing in another is a strange and perhaps radical experience. I wonder if Maurice Blanchot got it right: 'in a violent division, Mallarmé separated language into two forms with no connection, one was raw language, the other essential language. Perhaps this is true bilingualism'.]

Derrida in the same way borrows from Mallarmé the term 'idiom'. In 'Crise de vers' (1895), observing 'la diversité, sur terre, d'idiomes' ['the diversity of idioms in the world'], Mallarmé asserts of languages

---

40   Memmi, *Portrait du colonisé*, p. 127.
41   Khatibi, 'La Langue de l'autre: Exercices de témoignage', *Œuvres de Abdelkébir Khatibi III: Essais*, pp. 115–35 (p. 120).
42   Ibid., p. 115.

that: 'imparfaites en cela que plusieurs, manque la suprême' ['many are imperfect, and there is no supreme language'].[43] Derrida's reference to Mallarmé is nevertheless based on a mystical interpretation of the 'défaut des langues' ['lack of languages'] related to the dream of a 'pure langue' or 'reine Sprache' ['pure language'] formulated by Walter Benjamin, who interpreted 'Crise de vers' in 'The Task of the Translator'.[44] This reading owes much to the Jewish mystical tradition of the name. Derrida locates himself not only in Benjamin's genealogy but also that of Franz Rosenzweig and Gershom Scholem. The theory of the 'double état de la parole' ['the dual state of language'] and the 'rémunération du défaut des langues' ['paying the debt of languages'] as it was conceived by Mallarmé remains on the horizon of Derrida and Khatibi's dialogue.

From Algeria to Morocco, which is in some sense the *maghreb* of the Maghreb, from one East to the other, it is always literature in a broad sense, including philosophy, that lies at the heart of the dialogue between Derrida and Khatibi, whether or not they refer directly to Mallarmé, Benjamin, Glissant or Meddeb. Beyond the singular condition of the 'franco-maghrébin exemplaire' and the 'maghrébin francophone', the main stakes of their argument is writing. For Derrida as for Khatibi, it is not just a question of describing the condition of the Maghrebian or franco-Maghrebian, or even the French or francophone writer, the subject of the conference in 1992. Based on the singularity of his own situation and his 'destin', which he considers to be 'exemplaire d'une structure universelle' ['exemplary of a universal structure'], Derrida like Khatibi endeavours to think through the situation of *all* writers, including novelists, poets and philosophers, in relation to language. He argues, 'il en est *toujours ainsi a priori* – et pour quiconque. La langue dite maternelle n'est jamais purement naturelle, ni propre ni habitable' ['it is *always that way a priori* – and for everyone else. The language called maternal is never purely natural, nor proper, nor inhabitable'].[45] At the same time, 'la non identité à soi de toute langue' ['non-identity

---

43 Stéphane Mallarmé, *Igitur – Divagations – Un coup de dés* (Paris: Gallimard, 2003), p. 244.

44 Walter Benjamin's 'The Task of the Translator' is translated by Harry Zohn in Lawrence Venuti (ed.), *The Translation Studies Reader* (London: Routledge, 2000), pp. 15–25.

45 Derrida, *Le Monolinguisme de l'autre*, p. 112; *The Monolinguism of the Other*, p. 58.

of itself of all language'] means that there is not one language, nor the language, nor 'l'idiome ni le dialecte' ['nor the idiom nor the dialect'].[46] The paradox of the franco-Maghrebian's situation, which Khatibi also finds in that of the francophone Maghrebian, defines the condition of the writer towards language. On the basis of the 'aliénation originaire' ['originary alienation'] of all language, it is necessary to write 'à l'intérieur' ['within'] the given language and invent one's own idiom 'en vue de l'idiome absolu' ['with a view to an absolute idiom'].[47] The situation of the franco-Maghrebian in *Le Monolinguisme* allows Derrida in *Parages* to reinterpret Proust's famous statement: 'on n'écrit jamais ni dans sa propre langue ni dans une langue étrangère' ['we write neither in our own language nor in a foreign language'], also quoted by Khatibi. In this way the historical and empirical question – Khatibi as a Muslim writer born in Morocco, and Derrida, a Jewish writer born in Algeria, two French colonies – and its impact on the linguistic dimensions of monolingualism and bilingualism open up the question of the philosophical scope of writing in the most general sense, conceived through the paradox of the franco-Maghrebian. The writer has only one language, and that language is not his own. For Khatibi as for Derrida, the writer can only ever be a professional stranger, 'en deuil de l'origine', as Régine Robin beautifully puts it in her discussion of Yiddish as a language that has irremediably disappeared from but continues to haunt the work of Georges Perec, for example. The loss of Yiddish, like that of Ladino for Elias Canetti, which Régine Robin conceives in Benjaminian terms, is emblematic of the lack which founds the very act of writing, in any language:

> Langue perdue, langue méconnue, langue inconnue, langue en lieu et place d'une autre, troisième langue, langue pure, langue fondamentale, langue de fond, langue maternelle, simplement quelque chose des 'lointains fabuleux' qui s'inscrit dans l'œuvre, dans un travail d'écriture toujours à côté de, pas tout à fait sur le trait, décalé, décentré. Que l'écrivain se trouve au carrefour de plusieurs langues, polyglotte, multilingue, cela ne s'inscrit que dans une langue, langue d'amour ou langue d'emprunt, une langue pour opérer le travail du deuil. C'est LA LANGUE qui fait défaut. Une langue en trop, LA LANGUE EN MOINS. On n'habite jamais sa langue.[48]

46   Ibid., p. 123; p. 65.
47   Ibid., p. 126; p. 67.
48   Régine Robin, *Le Deuil de l'origine: une langue en trop, la langue en moins* (Paris: Editions Kimé, 2003), p. 197.

[A lost language, misrecognized language, unknown language, a language in the place of another, third language, a pure language, a fundamental language, foundational language, mother tongue, simply something from a distant elsewhere inscribed in the work, in the work of writing always alongside, not quite on the line, displaced, decentred. If the writer finds themselves on the crossroads of several languages, polyglot or multilingual, this is recorded in a language, a language of love or borrowed language, to accomplish a work of mourning. It is LANGUAGE which is lacking. A language too much, LANGUAGE ITSELF TOO LITTLE. We do not live in language.]

In this way every writer can say, in their way, that they are a 'franco-maghrébin exemplaire'.

CHAPTER NINE

Maghrebian Shadow

Abdelkébir Khatibi and Japanese Culture

Nao Sawada

> Pour tenir en équilibre une phrase, par exemple la phrase *euphorique* sur le Japon, on doit, par *un vertige artificiel*, donner l'impression d'un plaisir qui vacille sur lui-même. Perte, tremblement, *vacilar*, art de la danse, gestes de l'idée, calligraphie de l'imaginaire.
>
> [In order to keep a sentence in balance – for example, the *euphoric* phrase of Japan – one must, by means of an *artificial vertigo*, give the impression of a pleasure which wobbles on itself. Loss, tremour, *vacilar*, art of dance, gestures of the idea, calligraphy of the imaginary.]
>
> Abdelkébir Khatibi[1]

Introduction

A polymath with a mind open to all experiences, Abdelkébir Khatibi has left us many texts in a variety of genres and covering multiple fields: poems, novels, literary and sociological essays – texts whose main axis is a multifarious reflection on the relationship between the Maghreb and the West: *Maghreb pluriel*, *Le Corps oriental* or *Vomito blanco*.

At first glance, the Far East does not seem to occupy much space in Khatibi's cartography. However, on deeper examination, we do find some

---

1 Abdelkébir Khatibi, 'Le Japon de Barthes', in *Figures de l'étranger dans la littérature française* (Paris: Denoël, 1987), p. 83.

reflections no less stimulating than the ones to which I just alluded on the relationship between the Orients in the plural – namely between the Middle East and the Far East, or, more precisely, between the Orient of the Setting Sun (because the Maghreb means sunset) and the East of the Rising Sun, Japan. Khatibi, a close friend of the author of *L'Empire des signes*, was seduced, in turn, by Japan. He even states that his encounter with Japanese culture dates back to his childhood, to around the age of 13 or 14 years, first through Japanese poetry, in particular the haiku. In the 1970s, he discovered Japanese movies and Japanese calligraphy in Paris. If the haiku and cinema are fairly common points of entry into Japanese civilization, then Khatibi's interest in calligraphy, on the other hand, deserves attention. I will lend it that attention later in this essay. Later, Khatibi tells us that Junichiro Tanizaki (1886–1965) introduced him to Japanese literature. For this reason, Khatibi approaches Japanese culture under the aegis of a Japanese novelist of prime importance. Indeed, guided by the great Japanese master, the Moroccan writer leaves two brief texts on Japanese literature and culture, *Ombres japonaises* and 'Tanizaki revisité', both of which will serve us here as the main corpus for the examination of Khatibi's relationship with Japan. Two short texts, certainly, but ones that are extremely enlightening, and will allow us to understand the socio-cultural vision of the Moroccan writer on Japan.[2] These texts have a dual interest: on the one hand, they allow us to discover some unknown aspects of Abdelkébir Khatibi – his attraction for Japanese culture, for example – and, on the other hand, since he is a fine and brilliant reader of Tanizaki's text – his reading gives us further insight into Japanese culture.

Ombres japonaises is somewhat elliptical, insofar as it supposes a knowledge of *In Praise of Shadows*,[3] Tanizaki's brief essay on Japanese aesthetics, if not exhaustively, at least partially. This Japanese writer's pamphlet is often considered a defence of the Japanese tradition against modern technology. This is certainly not false, because Tanizaki is indeed trying to defend a certain Japanese aesthetic against Western technology using a few recurrent concepts such as *wabi*, *sabi* etc.

---

2   I refer to *Œuvres de Abdelkébir Khatibi III: Essais* (Paris: La Différence, 2008). To these two texts, we can add 'Le Japon de Barthes', a reflection on the relationship of Roland Barthes with Japan, analysed with a fine reading of *The Empire of Signs*. However, to simplify our remarks, we refer to it only incidentally.

3   Junichirô Tanizaki, *In Praise of Shadows*, trans. Thomas J. Harper and Edward G. Seidensticker (Stony Creek, CT: Leete's Island Books, 1977).

However, the stakes of this text do not stop there, and this is what our Moroccan writer highlights; one should not forget that Tanizaki is not a simple traditionalist writer. Far from it: he innovated literary style in the novel as well as in Japanese aesthetics. It is even possible to speak of a modernist dimension in Tanizaki, which I will discuss later.

Fifteen years after the publication of *Ombres japonaises*, Khatibi returns to Tanizaki and Japanese literature in a lecture given, precisely, in Tokyo.[4] There, he more closely addresses the question of eroticism, the body and language, evoking two or three novels by the Japanese writer. In these two texts, we can identify several elements that Khatibi discovers in Japan via Tanizaki: exoticism, eroticism and 'exophony'. I therefore propose to examine the portrait of Khatibi's Japanese culture through the lens of Junichiro Tanizaki, following three problematics: those of exoticism, of the body and languages, and of Eros and Thanatos. But it should immediately be noted that far from being separated, all these elements are intertwined for Tanizaki as well as for Khatibi. In other words, as the Moroccan writer points out, this is a phenomenon of 'intersemiotics'.

Exoticism Beyond the Exotic

It is well known that exoticism is one of Khatibi's central themes, insofar as it is at the same time an object of his criticism and an engine for his thinking. It goes without saying that Khatibi's exploration of

4   On 14 March 2003, at the Maison Franco-Japonaise. The original title was 'La Littérature japonaise vue par un écrivain maghrébin: Tanizaki revisité' ['Japanese literature seen by a Maghrebian writer: Tanizaki revisited']. He gave three more papers: two on 13 March 2003 – 'Figures de l'étranger' ['Figures of the Stranger'] at Chuo University and 'Le roman et l'invention du lecteur' ['The Novel and the Invention of the Reader'] at the Institut franco-japonais de Tokyo, and a third one on 18 March – 'Islam, les Arabes et le désastre annoncé' ['Islam, Arabs, and the Foretold Disaster'] at Hitotsubashi University. He returned to Japan for the last time in March 2007 to participate in the symposium 'Intellectuals in the 21st Century: France, East Asia and the World' at the Franco-Japanese House where he gave a paper entitled 'L'intellectuel et le mondialisme (le cas marocain)' ['The Intellectual and Globalism: The Moroccan Case']. A translation of the latter into Japanese is included in the conference proceedings, Harumi Ishizaki and Hirohide Tachibana (eds), *Nijuiseiki no chisikijin – Furansu, Higashi-Ajia, soshite Sekai* (Tokyo: Ed. Fujiwara, 2009).

Tanizaki is not the result of a naive trip made from an Orientalist standpoint, but an encounter with an *Other*, an Other that is absolutely different, an absolute Other. Following in Victor Segalen's footsteps – Segalen who distinguished three attitudes towards foreigners: that of the tourist, of the folklorist and of the *Exote*[5] – Khatibi tries to opt for this last attitude which consists in refusing any assimilation. But how does one speak of this experience of absolute otherness – which is often ineffable – without reducing it to an established knowledge or falling into a cliché?

> [Ecrire] sur le Japon? et au-delà de tout exotisme? Oui, mais il serait miraculeux que je sois vraiment l'autre, cet autre, pour parler absolument de moi du dehors. Miracle de l'illusion, de la passion et du jeu dangereux, si dangereux du *double*. Peut-être, à propos de ce dernier mot, faut-il faire un *coup double* de chaque pensée, un pour écouter l'exotisme, et l'autre: pour l'amour de la vérité face à chaque étranger.[6]

> [To write] about Japan? and beyond all exoticism? Yes, but it would be miraculous if I really were the other, this other, to speak absolutely of me from outside. Miracle of illusion, of passion, and of that highly dangerous game played with one's *double*. Perhaps each thought needs to be made double [i.e. duplicitous], in order to listen to exoticism and the other, for the love of the truth before each stranger.]

Indeed, writing on Japan without succumbing to exoticism is no easy task. Without mentioning Pierre Loti, even Roland Barthes sometimes seems to fall into some pitfalls. However, Khatibi, very aware of this trap, chose an original way to approach Japan. Following Master Tanizaki's steps like a faithful disciple, blindly, without judging him: 'Tanizaki nous indique une pensée, une seule, celle de l'ombre. Suivons-la' ['Tanizaki conveys to us a thought, only one, that of the shadow. Let's follow it'].[7]

What is intriguing is that we can find in Tanizaki, too, a particular exoticism, one fairly comparable to that of Khatibi.[8] Curious about other

---

5   Cf. Abdelkébir Khatibi, 'Célébration de l'Exote', *Œuvres de Abdelkébir Khatibi III: Essais*, pp. 137–61 (pp. 140–1).

6   Abdelkébir Khatibi, 'Ombres japonaises', *Œuvres de Abdelkébir Khatibi III: Essais*, pp. 207–24 (p. 209); the full version of the text was published as *Ombres japonaises* (Montpellier: Fata Morgana, 1988).

7   Khatibi, 'Ombres japonaises', p. 217.

8   Kan Nozaki, a prominent essayist, scholar and translator of French literature, devotes a particularly remarkable book to this subject: *Tanizaki Junichiro to ikoku*

cultures, about the Occident, China, India, and including a passion for Western culture, the Japanese novelist wrote some stories in his youth whose heroes share his passions. However, this passion does not manifest itself without some reluctance. If the fictional characters are often presented as great admirers – sometimes ridiculously – of the West, the description of scenes, however, remains cold, even ironic. Moreover, we may remember that, as a polyglot, Tanizaki also left excellent translations of Baudelaire, Oscar Wilde and Thomas Hardy.[9]

Khatibi most likely did not know the novels of the young Tanizaki in which foreign characters, including Chinese or Indians, appear. We might also suppose that he was unaware of the Japanese writer's translation work. But that does not matter, because, in spite of everything, it is as if Khatibi had understood in *In Praise of Shadows* all of Tanizaki's fascinations with exotic things. After having quickly evoked the Japanese myth, the cliché of Far Eastern mystery etc., Khatibi places this exoticism in contrast with Tanizaki, admiring the profound simplicity of his response.

> Tanizaki nous propose une pensée de l'ombre. Il en fait un acte d'écriture. C'est une leçon plus ou moins exemplaire: cette pensée ne serait pas, pour les philosophes, une simple contrepartie de celle de 'lumière', c'est-à-dire un platonisme inversé ou un heideggerisme à découvert, mais celle de la technique au cœur de la mémoire japonaise.[10]

> [Tanizaki suggests to us a thought of the shadow. He makes it an act of writing. It is a more or less exemplary lesson: this thought would not be, for the philosophers, a simple counterpart of that of 'light', i.e. an inverted Platonism or an exposed Heideggerianism, but that of the technique at the heart of Japanese memory.]

Tanizaki suggests turning off the light to plunge into darkness. But is it possible to correctly apprehend an object in the shadows? At night,

no gengo [*Tanizaki Junichiro and Foreign Languages*] (Kyoto: Jimbunshoin, 2003; Tokyo: Chukobunko, 2015).

9 *Poems in prose.* Khatibi states that he wrote his first poems aged 12 under the influence of Baudelaire (see 'La Langue de l'autre ['The language of the other'], *Œuvres de Abdelkébir Khatibi III: Essais*, pp. 115–35 (p. 117)). He often speaks of the author of *Les Fleurs du Mal*: 'La mélancolie de la poésie, celle initiée par Baudelaire et qui fut mon bréviaire appris par cœur' ['The melancholy of poetry, the one initiated by Baudelaire and which was my breviary learned by heart']. Ibid., p. 120.

10 Khatibi, 'Ombres japonaises', p. 208.

all the cows are black, as Hegel would say. To look in the dark is to dream, or to watch phantasmatic images in the cinema. Yet Khatibi, endorsing Tanizaki's position and proposal, seeks this impossible gesture in memory of the Japanese tradition. Here is a passage from *In Praise of Shadows* that Khatibi quotes twice in his text:

> A Japanese room might be likened to an inkwash painting, the paper-panelled shoji being the expanse where the ink is thinnest, and the alcove [*Toko no ma*] where it is darkest.[11]

Khatibi added that he isolated this sentence 'en maintenant [son] attention sur le mot "ombre"' ['by keeping [his] attention on the word "shadow"'].[12] However, he does not quote the following passage where the Japanese writer states: 'I marvel at our comprehension of the secrets of shadows, our sensitive use of shadow and light'.[13] Indeed, according to Tanizaki, to really appreciate precious things, one should use not the eyes, but the play of shadow and light, in the manner of Caravaggio's chiaroscuro. Thus, a distinct figure appears in this half-light, that of a female body; *In Praise of Shadows* is also a eulogy of the female body. And as for Khatibi, we know that exoticism often appears in some form or another of attraction to the other sex.

Body and 'Langue(s)'

While one of the main themes of *In Praise of Shadows* is femininity in its corporeality, it is not a corpulent body. Here, again, this is an antithesis of the Greek–Latin vision: a massive nude figure under a midday sunlight. Khatibi tries to follow this path by analysing Tanizaki's other texts: 'The Tattooer' (1910), 'Fumiko's Legs' (1919) and 'A Portrait of Shunkin' (1930). Why does he choose these three texts among Tanizaki's many works? The choice seems extremely suggestive: they are 'intersemiotic' stories. He correctly points out: 'En relisant plusieurs de ses récits, je suis frappé par l'insistance thématique sur l'intelligence artistique du corps féminin' ['In re-reading several of his stories, I am struck by the thematic emphasis on the artistic intelligence of the female body'].[14]

11   Tanizaki, *In Praise of Shadows*, p. 20.
12   Khatibi, 'Ombres japonaises', p. 215.
13   Tanizaki, *In Praise of Shadows*, p. 20.
14   Khatibi, 'Ombres japonaises', p. 227.

What does 'the artistic intelligence of the female body' mean? It means that a body signifies something; and sometimes it is not a 'body proper' nor a naked body, but a dressed body. Dressed, but still, not necessarily in clothes, but sometimes by images, letters or colours. 'Il y a chez Tanizaki, l'idée d'*un corps prothétique* prolongeant l'ombre, et qui, sans son voilement, retomberait vite dans le vide indifférencié' ['in Tanizaki, there is the idea of a *prosthetic body* elongating the shadow, and which, without its veiling, would quickly fall back into the undifferentiated emptiness'], explains Khatibi.[15] In *In Praise of Shadows*, Tanizaki places special emphasis on the aesthetics of the Japanese woman, providing keys to understanding one of the types of women who haunt most of his novels.

Another motif that both writers share is that of tattooing. *The Tattooer* is one of Tanizaki's first stories: a true masterpiece. This is a story of a tattoo artist in old Edo (present-day Tokyo), who tattoos a huge spider on the back of a young geisha. This tattoo will be, contrary to the woman's will, the revelation of her maleficent power over men. As for Khatibi's *Tattooed Memory*, although called a 'novel', it is a hybrid text: somewhere between novel, autobiography and poetry. It is a story of the formation of an identity between the West and the Maghreb. Indeed, it is rather in *Le corps oriental*, that one can find a very interesting analysis of the tattoo,[16] and in particular in *La Blessure du nom propre*.[17] The Moroccan writer reveals the meaning of tattooing in Moroccan society, stating that it is a symbolic representation of the body as a place of language, trace and palimpsest.[18]

If this is the case, the tattoo can also be linked to calligraphy. The tattoo can be considered as a kind of calligraphy engraved on the body, because it is, like calligraphy, an alliance between the sign and the image. Thus, the body becomes meaningful, a surface that speaks. Calligraphy is also a point in common between the Far East and the Maghreb, even if it does not have the same cultural function or form. For the Moroccan writer, who wrote a book about oriental calligraphy, Chinese and Japanese calligraphy was the discovery of a new horizon: 'au départ, l'art de la calligraphie arabe, qui fait partie de la civilisation

15 Ibid., p. 221.

16 Khatibi, *Le Corps oriental* (Paris: Hazan, 2002), p. 67.

17 Khatibi, *La Blessure du nom propre* (Paris: Denoël, 1974).

18 See Abdelkébir Khatibi, 'Tanizaki revisité', *Œuvres de Abdelkébir Khatibi III: Essais*, pp. 225–32 (p. 227).

islamique du signe et de ses puissances décoratives, m'avait sensibilisé à l'originalité de l'art ornemental, du rapport du signe écrit à l'autonomie de la couleur' ['initially, the art of Arabic calligraphy, which is part of the Islamic civilization of the sign and its decorative powers, had made me aware of the originality of ornamental art, of the relationship of the written sign to the autonomy of colour'].[19] We can say that traveling to the Far East for the Maghrebian writer meant meeting the imaginary of the other whose thought is ideographic.

It should be remembered that Tanizaki uses the metaphor of painting in Indian ink to describe the topology of a Japanese house. Japanese calligraphy being both an idea and an image implies a global and polysemic meaning, bringing with it multiple nuances. Henceforth, Tanizaki appears to Khatibi as a smuggler not only for Japanese culture, but also for the question of writing that confronts all contemporary writers: 'depuis un demi-siècle, son texte ne cesse d'être actuel, posant aux écrivains cette question: comment écrire à l'âge de la technique et de son expansion?' ['for half a century, his text continues to be relevant, asking writers this question: how to write in the age of technology and its expansion?'].[20] It is, moreover, for this reason that the shadow haunts literature: 'la littérature: une question d'ombre? Comment aborder cette question entre le silence et la première phrase de lieu, de lieu littéraire sans ses figures' ['literature: a question of shade? How to approach this question between the silence and the first sentence of place, of literary place without its figures'].[21] Following in the steps of Master Tanizaki, Khatibi pushes this investigation to its conclusion:

> Ce témoin ironique de son époque interroge la technique à partir de l'art de vivre, d'écrire. Technique qui altère le corps humain, ses sens, les empreintes du temps sur sa mémoire. Tanizaki remarque avec lucidité que 'le beau n'est pas une substance en soi, mais rien qu'un dessin d'ombres, qu'un jeu de clair-obscur, produit par la juxtaposition de substances diverses'. C'est pourquoi le beau est un paradigme de civilisation et qui change avec la peau.[22]

> [This ironic spectator of his time questions the technique from the art of living, of writing. A technique that alters the human body, its senses, the imprints of time on the human body's memory. Tanizaki remarked

19   Ibid., p. 225.
20   Khatibi, 'Ombres japonaises', p. 218.
21   Ibid., p. 210.
22   Ibid., pp. 217–18.

lucidly that 'beauty is not a substance per se but just a pattern of shadows, a play of light and darkness, created by the juxtaposition of various substances'. That's why beauty is a paradigm of civilization and changes with the skin.]

Thus, another motive appears: that of 'langue'. Everyone knows that the dual meaning of langue (language and tongue) is an almost obsessive subject for Khatibi, both in his novels (*Amour bilingue*) and in his essays (such as *La Langue de l'autre*). In fact, the otherness of a stranger is often revealed in a situation of communication or a realization of the impossibility of communication:

> tout autre est le silence qu'impose, que m'impose une langue étrangère. C'est une différence de corps, non seulement celle que portent cette parole et son silence, mais aussi ce qui les accompagne: gestes, mimiques, regards, postures. Tel geste qui dit 'oui' dans une culture et son code dit 'non' ici ou tout autre chose que j'ignore[23]

> [the silence imposed on me by a foreign language is completely different. It is a bodily difference, not only that of this word and its silence, but also that which accompanies them: gestures, mimicry, looks, postures. A gesture that says 'yes' in a culture and its code says 'no' here or anything else I do not know.]

So, is there nothing that allows us to break this gap, to break that resistance? Why not? Perhaps cooking, for example, as Roland Barthes suggests. Khatibi points out that the cook could be a smuggler, insofar as he is likely to swallow things without us really understanding what it is.

> Tout plat étranger, qui résiste à nos coutumes, libère notre corps de ses conventions premières. Il l'expatrie vers la sphère de son inconnu. C'est pourquoi je jouis de l'étranger, de l'étrangère. Lorsqu'on parle d'une sensation inouïe, indicible, inconnue, inhabituelle (de cette jouissance), ce n'est pas une effusion mystique, mais la touche de l'étranger au creux de mon imaginaire, dans ma langue primitive, organique d'amour. L'étranger – celui que j'aime – donne à l'incroyable le ravissement d'une pure présence, d'une résistance à mes centres de gravité. Il est alors le passeur qui transforme ma solidification doxale, les habitus qui collent à la peau. Je mue.[24]

> [Every foreign dish, which resists our customs, frees our body from our original conventions. It expatriates the body to its unknown sphere.

23 Khatibi, 'Le Japon de Barthes', p. 67.
24 Ibid., p. 78.

That's why I find the stranger delightful. When one speaks of an incredible, unspeakable, unknown, unusual sensation (of this *jouissance*), it is not a mystical bestowal, but the touch of the foreigner in the hollow of my imagination, in my primitive language, my organic tongue of love. The stranger – the one I love – gives to the incredible the rapture of a pure presence, of a resistance to my centres of gravity. He is then the ferryman who transforms my doxical solidification, the habitus that sticks to the skin. I moult.]

If this is so, in the meeting with the stranger, there is sometimes something worse than a process of assimilation; there is a kind of cannibalism. Indeed, exoticism often triggers the appearance of *Eros* and *Thanatos*.

Eros and Thanatos

Tanizaki is a Japanese novelist who revealed a very special masochistic eroticism: *Swastika* (1930) and *Diary of a Mad Old Man* (1961) are good examples. He often writes extremely cruel stories that end badly. We know that Khatibi, too, is fascinated by a violence inherent in love, which could be formulated in the famous expression of the *Thousand and One Nights*: 'Tell me a beautiful story or I will kill you', or, in a slightly modified version, 'Tell me a beautiful story *and* I will kill you'.

Thus, for both, *Eros* and *Thanatos* are two sides of the same coin. It is, moreover, the reason why Khatibi evokes and analyses *The Portrait of Shunkin*, a masterpiece of the Japanese writer, published the same year as *In Praise of Shadows*. This is a tragedy between a young shamisen (traditional Japanese instrument) musician, Shunkin, and her servant and disciple Sasuke. Having become blind, very young, Shunkin, the daughter of a rich family, is forced to become a music teacher. Blindness has given her extraordinary skill in her performance of the instruments but has also made her very withdrawn and extremely nasty. Being materially dependent on her servant, she behaves tyrannically with Sasuke, who secretly becomes her lover. A stranger then attacks Shunkin in the middle of the night and disfigures her. After that, she finally confesses her feelings to Sasuke and makes him promise not to look at her anymore. Sasuke, out of love and devotion, puts out his own eyes, thus descending into absolute darkness. Love makes one blind, it is said, but it is what the disciple did literally, mutilating himself.[25]

25   It should be remembered that blindness is a recurring theme in the Japanese

Let's listen to Khatibi's comment: 'c'est pourquoi le disciple est une ombre de l'ombre. Un double qui subit le châtiment et qui doit sacrifier son corps au corps de l'autre, entre la veille et le sommeil, la nuit et l'autre côté du jour, l'enténèbrement' ['this is why the disciple is a shade of the shadow. A double who undergoes punishment and who must sacrifice his body to the body of the other, between waking and sleeping, at night and on the other side of the day, darkness'].[26] These are very fair remarks. In fact, at the end of the story, we read of a paradox in the vision expressed by Sasuke: asked if blindness is a misfortune, he claims never to have felt so:

> People think it is sad to become blind; but since I lost my sight, that has not been my experience. With me it was quite the reverse; all at once this world became a Paradise, and I seemed to be dwelling in the cup of a lotus flower, together with my teacher [Shunkin]. This was because, when a man becomes blind, he acquires the power of seeing things that were hidden from him when he had his sight. In my case, it was not until I was blind that I fully understood the true beauty of my teacher, or really appreciated the smoothness and glamour of her limbs and the sweetness of her voice. I wonder why it was that I lacked this feeling while I could see.[27]

Thus, Tanizaki shows us an illuminating vision beyond darkness, a little as the mystics do. But let us take another example of the shadow, the shadow of death that Khatibi still finds in Japanese culture, this time, in his article on Jean Genet, 'Ultime dissidence de Jean Genet'. Presenting and analysing *Le Captif amoureux*, the last book by the French writer, Khatibi dwells on one passage where Genet speaks of Japan while he is attending the funeral ceremony in Palestine: 'Obon est le nom que les Japonais donnent à un autre jeu. C'est la fête des morts qui reviennent parmi les vivants pour trois fois vingt-quatre heures' ['Obon is the name the Japanese give to another game. It is the feast of the dead who come back among the living for three times twenty-four hours'].[28] Out of five

---

writer. In fact, he had already published *The Story of the Blind* in 1931, and he later takes up this theme in another story.

26   Khatibi, 'Tanizaki revisité', p. 231.

27   Junichiro Tanizaki, *Ashikari and the Story of Shunkin*, translated from the Japanese by Roy Humpherson and Hajime Okita (Tokyo: The Hokuseido Press, 1936), p. 164.

28   'Ultime Dissidence de Genet', *Œuvres de Abdelkébir Khatibi III: Essais*, pp. 163–205 (p. 183).

hundred pages, why did this short passage on Obon – the only mention of Japan in this novel – draw Khatibi's attention? Well, this time it might be because of the theatrical dimension. Khatibi describes Genet's latest book, with his style of reporting, the stories in his novels and his theatre, as a reinvention of a poetic art.

> C'est une littérature aux limites de ses marges et de ses artifices, mais par là même, elle est innovation, ouverture vers la pensée sur l'Etranger, ouverture et construction d'énigmes qui exigent un mode spécifique de déchiffrement et aussi une cérémonie rituelle aguerrie à des forces de destruction et à leur transformation en une beauté suspendue dans la mémoire.[29]

> [It is a literature at the limits of its margins and artifices, but, by the same token, it is innovation, openness to the thought on the Stranger, openness and construction of puzzles that require a specific mode of deciphering and also a ritual ceremony well hardened by the forces of destruction and their transformation into a beauty suspended in memory.]

And it is precisely in this context that Khatibi evokes the '*Toko no ma*' to which Tanizaki lends such an important place in the Japanese house:[30]

> Lorsque vous regardez une pagode japonaise traditionnelle, elle se découpe dans la nature comme une miniature. Franchissez le seuil, changez la position des murs coulissants selon votre rite du jour et de la nuit, puis allez vers le *Toko no ma*, ce lieu tranquille de méditation et de repos. Si vous fixez le tableau dont le motif change avec chaque saison, vous assisterez à une modification de l'imaginaire. Le tableau *réencadre* la nature (lacs, montagnes et cieux eux-mêmes gradués) à partir d'une pensée idéographique et d'un geste cursif. Et si vous en avez envie, vous prendrez un pinceau pour calligraphier le secret de vos mains, la parure de votre esprit et votre partenaire en sera ravi(e). Mais encadrez toujours: tel serait le mode spectaculaire du lire.[31]

> [When you look at a traditional Japanese pagoda, it cuts itself out into nature like a miniature. Cross the threshold, change the position of the sliding walls according to your rite of day and night, then go to *Toko no ma*, this quiet place of meditation and rest. If you set the table whose

---

29 Ibid.
30 Khatibi quotes his proper passage, with some differences of capitals or in italics, in *Ombres japonaises*.
31 Khatibi, 'Ombres japonaises', p. 192.

pattern changes with each season, you will see a change in the imaginary. The painting *re-frames* nature (lakes, mountains and heavens themselves graduated) starting from an ideographic thought and a cursive gesture. And if you feel like it, you will take a brush to calligraphy the secret of your hands, the adornment of your mind and your partner will be delighted. But always frame: such would be the spectacular mode of reading.]

Conclusion

There are several deep points in common between the Japanese novelist and the Moroccan writer, and it would be possible to point out more. But it is time to conclude by highlighting a few key findings. First of all, let us assert that Tanizaki's essay, despite its misleading title, praises not the shadow itself, but the nuances of shadow that engender luminous figures. According to the Japanese writer, the shadow sharpens not only vision but also the other senses: touch, hearing, smell and even taste. Here is a passage that Khatibi might have quoted.

[When] yôkan is served in a lacquer dish within whose dark recesses its colour is scarcely distinguishable, then it is most certainly an object for meditation. You take its cool smooth substance into your mouth, and it is as if the very darkness of the room were melting on your tongue, even undistinguished yokan can then take on a mysteriously intriguing flavour.[32]

It is therefore a vision diametrically opposed to the Mediterranean vision of Logos. Originating from the monotheistic world, Khatibi's vision of the world remains very close to that of the West. Thus, the Maghreb – this other West – meets Japan – this other East, the Far East. Khatibi states:

ce livre de Tanizaki a été important pour moi doublement: il m'a libéré de l'emprise métaphorique de la lumière, de la clarté, de l'éclat, de l'illumination, de l'extase solaire, qui marquent la pensée grecque et la théologie du monothéisme. D'autre part, en relativisant le mode de refondation du monde des choses dans le langage, Tanizaki nous fit une offrande, à nous, ses lecteurs.[33]

32 Tanizaki, *In Praise of Shadows*, p. 16.
33 Khatibi, 'Tanizaki revisité', p. 226.

[Tanizaki's book was doubly important to me: it freed me from the metaphorical hold of light, clarity, brilliance, enlightenment, solar ecstasy, which mark Greek thought and the theology of monotheism. On the other hand, by relativizing the way of refounding the material world in language, Tanizaki made an offering to us, his readers.]

Secondly, it is worth returning to the question of silence, which is not merely the absence of speech. In *Féerie d'un mutant,* one of his last texts, the hero, Med, visits Japan with his companion, Gabriela. In Nara, more precisely, at the Todaiji temple, which houses a colossal bronze statue of the eighth-century Buddha, in front of the large seated Buddha, they engage in a conversation with a Japanese monk. To the latter who asks them what impressed them the most, the hero answers:

— La puissance de votre silence.
— Intéressant, merveilleux même! Que vous suggère cette puissance?
— Votre sensibilité rentrée, que vous évoquez en surface dans votre sculpture, votre architecture, calligraphie …[34]

[— The power of your silence.
— Interesting, wonderful even! What does this power suggest to you?
— Your withdrawn sensibility, which you evoke on the surface in your sculpture, your architecture, your calligraphy …]

This passage, which could be perceived as a cliché, has a much deeper meaning than it seems, if we refer back to all the remarks we have made in this essay. It is the same for Tanizaki, concerning his apparently traditionalist aspect. It would be better to read Tanizaki as an ultra-modern writer in the guise of a traditionalist. Khatibi has just discovered the true face of the Japanese writer. He is quite right when he writes that, 'il faut surtout reconnaître à Tanizaki un don subtil et rarement acquis par des écrivains professionnels: écrire en pensant, penser en rêvant son expérience de vie et de survie' ['Tanizaki must above all be recognized for his subtle gift, rarely acquired by professional writers: to write while thinking, to think while dreaming of one's experience of life and survival'].[35] In this sense, we can consider the Japanese writer as 'the professional stranger', as defined by Khatibi in *Figures de l'étranger dans la littérature française.* And it is quite possible that the Moroccan writer found a 'Japanese dissident' in

34 Khatibi, *Féerie d'un mutant* (Monaco: La Serpent à plumes, 2005), reprinted in *Œuvres de Abdelkébir Khatibi I: Romans et récits,* pp. 673–711 (p. 699).
35 Khatibi, 'Tanizaki revisité', p. 230.

Tanizaki. Khatibi's declaration of what he owes to the Japanese writer can serve as a conclusion: 'Tanizaki nous fit une offrande, à nous, ses lecteurs. Un don précieux pour moi en tout cas, d'autant plus que je suis toujours intrigué, excité même, par les rapports de résistance et de passage entre les civilisations' ['Tanizaki made an offering to us, his readers. A precious gift for me anyway, especially since I am always intrigued, excited even by the relationships of resistance and transmission between civilizations'].[36]

36   Ibid., p. 226.

13. (August 1990) In Herbeys (France) at Mrs Claudette Oriol-Boyer's home during the summer school, 'Lire, écrire, réécrire' (Chichilianne, University of Grenoble 3/CNRS).

14. (July 1992) With Jacques Derrida in Cerisy-la-Salle during the colloquium 'Le Passage des frontières: Autour du travail de Jacques Derrida'.

15. (July 1992) With French writer Hélène Cixous (right) and French scholar Anne-Emmanuelle Berger (left) in Cerisy-la-Salle during the colloquium 'Le Passage des frontières: Autour du travail de Jacques Derrida'.

16. (1992) In London with Lebanese writer Elias Khoury.

17. (September 1994) In Jerusalem in front of the Dome of the Rock.
Photograph by Mohammed Habib Samrakandi and published with his kind permission.
© Mohammed Habib Samrakandi.

18. (September 1994) With Palestinian leader Yasser Arafat and Moroccan playwright Tayeb Saddiki. Photograph by Mohammed Habib Samrakandi and published with his kind permission. © Mohammed Habib Samrakandi.

19. (November 1995) In Cotonou with Nicéphore Soglo, the then President of Benin, before the Sixth Summit of the Francophonie.

20. (April 1996) In New York during a jazz concert.

21. (July 2000) In Rabat at the Faculty of Law, University Mohammed V.

22. (January 2002) In Rabat with Spanish writer Juan Goytisolo during the colloquium 'Jean Genet: Féerie et dissidence'.

23. (March 2003) In Tokyo.

24. (November 2003) In Paris
with Assia Djebar during the
colloquium 'Assia Djebar: Nomade
entre les murs', organized by
Mireille Calle-Gruber in the period
27–29 November 2003 at La Maison
des Ecrivains. Photograph is property
of Mireille Calle-Gruber and
published with her kind permission.
© Mireille Calle-Gruber – ARCS
(Association 'Archive Claude Simon
et ses Contemporains').

25. (2005) With Moroccan writer
and psychiatrist Rita El Khayat.

26. (2006) In El Harhoura near Rabat with Moroccan journalist and writer
Abdelkrim Ghallab (left) and Iraqi and Morocco-based writer Ali Al-Kasimi (right).

27. (March 2007) During his second visit to Tokyo.

PART THREE

Aesthetics and Art
in the Islamic World
and Beyond

CHAPTER TEN

Reading Signs and Symbols with Abdelkébir Khatibi

From the Body to the Text

Rim Feriani, Jasmina Bolfek-Radovani
and Debra Kelly

Celui qui écrit a à découvrir, à explorer différents lieux
de langage et qui lui sont trop voilés par le secret de
son métier. L'écriture: *initiation* à un secret illisible.

[A person who writes has to discover, to explore
different sites of language, sites which are too well
hidden from him by the secrets of his craft. Writing is
an *initiation* into an unreadable secret.]

Abdelkébir Khatibi[1]

This chapter considers the ways in which Khatibi's practices of
reading contribute to theories of meaning through his thinking on
the deciphering of signs and symbols and of making sense of the
world, and of the worlds of the text, in their multifaceted forms. It
takes as its starting point what Khatibi terms 'l'intersémiotique' in
his introductory essay entitled 'Le cristal du texte' ['The Crystal of
the Text'] in *La Blessure du nom propre*, an important collection of
essays for a better understanding of his work, published in 1974.[2] The
'intersemiotic' concerns migrant signs which move between one sign

---

1 Abdelkébir Khatibi, 'Une psychanalyse personnelle', *Par-dessus l'épaule*
(Paris: Aubier, 1988), pp. 47–71 (p. 69).
2 Abdelkébir Khatibi, *La Blessure du nom propre* (Paris: Denoël, 1974).

system and another, and Khatibi takes as his own project examples from semiotic systems found within Arabic and Islamic cultures, from popular culture, such as the tattoo, to calligraphy and the language of the Qur'an, from the body, including the place of the erotic, to the text and beyond – including storytelling, mosaics, urban space, textiles. His readings reveal the intersemiotic and polysemic meanings created in the movements of these migrant signs between their sign systems. For Khatibi, this 'infinity' of the 'text' is linked also to mobile and migrant identity refracted in the multifaceted surfaces of the crystal (hence the title of the theoretical introductory essay – 'Le cristal du texte') rather than in one reflection as in a mirror. Moving from these concerns through and with which Khatibi develops his radical theory of the sign, of the word and of writing, and from the ways in which these concerns are reflected in the example of his own autobiographical text, *La Mémoire tatouée*, the chapter goes on to investigate how Khatibi's reading strategies may help the reading of other writers with a shared, but varied, relationship to their Islamic heritage.[3] To do this, it takes another precise example in a work by the Algerian writer Assia Djebar whose writing, like that of many other twentieth- and twenty-first-century North African writers, is resonant with Khatibi's intersemiotic theoretical and cultural project, and is concerned also with the individual and the collective, the historical and the contemporary, the political, the social and the linguistic. The chapter ends, then, by considering the implications of Khatibi's reading and writing strategies for writers working with and through an Islamic heritage and significantly, as for Khatibi, the Sufi Islamic heritage.

In the introductory essay to *La Blessure du nom propre*, 'Le cristal du texte', Khatibi presents his theory of the sign in the Arabic language, a theory based on the concept of what he terms an 'intersémiotique transversale' ['transversal intersemiotics']. He defines the calligraphic sign as being at the intersection of two types of discourses, the rationalist discourse of theologians, philosophers and critics on one side, and the mystical discourse on the 'adoration of the divine text and of its infinite meanings' on the other side. Khatibi refers to the Qur'an itself as a 'théorie radicale du signe', a radical theory of the sign, of the Word and of Writing, which he sees as its 'extreme' originality:

---

3   Abdelkébir Khatibi, *La Mémoire tatouée: autobiographie d'un décolonisé* (Paris: Denoël, 1971), reprinted in *Œuvres de Abdelkébir Khatibi I: Romans et récits* (Paris: La Différence, 2008), pp. 9–113.

Car le Coran – et c'est là son extrême originalité – se conçoit comme une théorie radicale du signe, de la Parole et de l'Écriture; *al-qur'ān*: lecture: déchirement et récitation du signe révélé.[4]

[For the Qur'an – and therein lies its extreme originality – is conceived as a radical theory of the sign, of the Spoken Word and of Writing; *al-qur'ān*: reading: the tearing and the reciting of the revealed sign.][5]

The calligraphic sign is not a simple prolongation of the spoken word; instead, its 'sacred' nature results in the production of infinitely refracted meanings:

cette théorie du souffle qui traverse le corps (dans le sens strict: le Coran descend dans le corps), et le sépare, le plie en signes distincts, afin que le croyant éprouve ses fibres comme autant de feuilles cristallines du texte.[6]

[this theory of the breath that traverses the body (in its strictest sense: the verses of the Qur'an descend into the body) and divides it, folds it into distinctive signs so that the believer comes to experience its fibres as a multitude of crystalline leaves of the text.]

However, and this is an important aspect of Khatibi's theory, the calligraphic sign does not only generate infinity of meaning, it also veils or represses other semiotic systems belonging to popular Arab and pre-Islamic culture (such as the practice of tattooing, fairy tales and proverbs, and erotic texts):

La lettre calligraphique – comme trace divine – envahit ainsi tous les arts décoratifs de l'Islam, et complotant sans cesse contre le vide, elle cisèle l'espace en se logeant dans un dedans absolu. Dedans absolu qui permet à la logographie de couvrir, plus ou moins explicitement, d'*autres* systèmes sémiotiques, dont le tatouage. Ces systèmes sémiotiques pour la plupart antérieurs à l'Islam sont donc refoulés, vidés de leur charge symbolique. Mais semblables au langage des rêves, ces hiéroglyphes défigurés déchirent notre imaginaire et regreffent dans le corps et l'inconscient le geste d'une séparation élastique, exigeant – pour être lus – un véritable dessaisissement par rapport à la tyrannie logographique. Ces objets fissurés, comment les lire? Comment percer, crever la clôture logographique?[7]

4 Khatibi, *La Blessure du nom propre*, p. 17.
5 All the translations of quotations from Khatibi's *La Blessure du nom propre* in this chapter are by Jasmina Bolfek-Radovani and Debra Kelly.
6 Khatibi, *La Blessure du nom propre*, p. 17.
7 Ibid., p. 20.

[The calligraphic sign – as a divine trace – invades the realm of the Islamic decorative arts in their entirety and, by repeatedly challenging the space of the void, it reshapes its spaces by lodging itself at the centre of the absolute inside. Absolute inside that allows the logographic system to hide, more or less explicitly, *other* semiotic systems, such as the practice of tattooing. These semiotic systems that for the most part precede Islam are therefore repressed, emptied of their symbolic charge. Similar to the language of dreams, these disfigured hieroglyphs tear apart our imaginary and reintroduce in the body and the unconscious the gesture of a resilient cut that necessitates – in order to be understood – true emancipation from the tyranny of the logographic (the written sign). How is one then to read these fractured objects? How can one make a puncture in the closed system of the written sign?]

The study of an 'intersémiotique transversale' needs to be undertaken at three levels: at the level of a 'sémiotique graphique' ['graphic semiotics'] that brings together the practices of tattooing and calligraphy, at the level of a 'rhétorique du coït' ['rhetoric of coitus'] that relates to the reading of mystical erotic literature, and that of a 'sémiotique orale' ['oral semiotics'] that brings together the proverbial discourse of popular culture transmitted orally through fairy tales and proverbs.[8] The focus here, however, will initially be on Khatibi's extended treatment of the first of these semiotic systems, that of the figure of the tattoo given its place in the title and text of his seminal autobiographical work, *La Mémoire tatouée* (which is further read within its Islamic and Sufi heritage in the second part of this chapter), and also given its significance in *La Blessure du nom propre*, in which Khatibi gives a detailed presentation of the main practices of Moroccan tattooing and of the main characteristics of the semiotic system of the tattoo in a section entitled 'Tatouage: écriture en points' ['Tattooing: Writing in Dots'].[9] Although he defines calligraphy and the art of tattooing under the common name of a 'sémiotique graphique', Khatibi argues that each of these two practices remain fundamentally different, particularly since the practice of tattooing has been relegated to the level of 'popular' art by a monotheistic religious discourse, a discourse that can be said to have assigned an origin or centre to the linguistic sign and system that has repressed any ulterior semiotic systems and practices:

8   Ibid., p. 21.
9   Ibid., pp. 59–129.

[dans le tatouage], il s'agit de l'interdit jeté sur lui par les grandes religions monothéistes, comme si l'écriture divine voulait effacer d'un trait palimpseste toute écriture ultérieure, surtout celle tracée sur le corps.[10]

[[the practice of tattooing] reveals that which has been forbidden by all the main monotheistic religions as if the divine scripture aimed to erase with one single palimpsestic stroke all ulterior writing, especially that which is inscribed on the body.]

The Moroccan practice of tattooing of the (Muslim) body follows specific rules of the spatial arrangement of the tattoos: it is mostly the right side of the front of the body that is tattooed (in contrast, for example, with Polynesian tattoos that are applied to the whole of the body). In addition to this spatial rule, there is a gender sub-distinction: the woman may have tattoos on the front of her body, the man wears tattoos only on the hand, the arm and the forearm. The Moroccan system of corporeal marking is 'semiotically' significant: the rhythmical marking of the body begins with a central tattoo between the eyes known as 'ayyacha' or the 'intersou-cilier' ['between the eyebrows'].[11] In contrast with the linguistic sign whose function is to relay social meaning according to a set of syntactic, semantic and pragmatic rules, for Khatibi, the choice of geometric forms to be imprinted on the 'subverted' Muslim body is random, opening up a space for a pleasurable, polyphonic reading of the tattoos:

Plaisir proféré cependant par une décision de défiguration, à savoir la Subversion sur le corps musulman des interdits qui le nouent [...]. Généraliser, par l'espacement de signes purs, un rythme à lecture polyphonique. C'est en cela que se joue le hasard, par nous suggéré, et que le centre soit un point giratoire qui s'annihile dans la lecture (...).[12]

[Pleasure enacted in the gesture of disfigurement seen as a subversion of the forbidden acts on the Islamic body [...]. To make prevalent, through the spatialization of pure signs, the rhythm of a polyphonic reading. In this way randomness comes into play as we have suggested; the centre becomes a gyratory point that annihilates any reading practice (...)].

Khatibi's own statement about his autobiographical text appears directly linked to the practice and semiotic system of the tattoo: 'J'ai dans *La*

10   Ibid., p. 66.
11   Ibid., p. 87.
12   Ibid., p. 82.

Mémoire tatouée tenté de suivre à la trace les signes et les évènements qui frappent le corps et le marquent définitivement' ['In *La Mémoire tatouée*, I tried to follow the traces of the signs and events that strike a body and mark it permanently'].[13] Khatibi seems to indicate that the clue to the interpretation of this text lies, therefore, in its title and that it deals with the sensory processes of memory and its imprinting or tattooing on the body, both corporal and semiotic. As Lucy Stone McNeece has argued:[14]

> The work's title indicates the way in which Khatibi concretizes the most elusive concepts, affirming the relation of the body and desire to language and writing. The title also establishes the primacy of the sign, or rather of the material signifier, in the formation of personal identity. By the conjunction of 'mémoire' and 'tatouée,' Khatibi articulates the degree to which memory is not cognitive but corporeal, sensuous, and indelible. The emblem of the persistence of sensory impressions is the tattoo, whose markings are a focus of the narrator's early perceptions.[15]

The sign of the tattoo can be read as 'a founding metaphor' in *La Mémoire tatouée* that marks the body of the subject and the body of memory. Yet it is more difficult to explain the polyvalent nature of memory in this text as one that permanently marks the body and at the same time produces a memory that is constantly fleeing, difficult to capture and that distorts the past, as *La Mémoire tatouée* seems to suggest. The cryptic titles of the text's two final parts, 'Série hasardeuse I' and 'Série hasardeuse II', are difficult to understand without drawing once again on Khatibi's theory and notion of the migratory sign that lies at the centre of his definition of 'intersémiotique transversale'. At the very beginning of 'Tatouage: écriture en points' in *La Blessure du nom propre*, the migratory nature of the (Arabic and Berber) sign is considered and explicit reference is made to the idea of 'hazardous' disposition of signs:

> Ce qui suscite notre attention, c'est la migration d'un signe (ou d'un symbole) à un autre, fût-il minime (d'un point, par exemple), et, de

13   Abdallah Bensmaïn, 'Entretien avec A. Khatibi', in *Pro-Culture* 12 – Numéro spécial: 'Khatibi' (Rabat: Imprimerie culturelle et universitaire Mohammed V, 1978), pp. 9–13 (p. 11), quoted in Abdallah Memmes, *Abdelkébir Khatibi, l'écriture de la dualité* (Paris: L'Harmattan, 1994), p. 22.
14   Lucy Stone McNeece, 'Decolonising the Sign: Language and Identity in Abdélkebir Khatibi's *La Mémoire tatouée*', *Yale French Studies* 83 (1993), pp. 12–29.
15   Ibid., p. 13.

proche en proche, le déplacement si ample de graphèmes, ce répertoire inouï d'objets, s'étendant par exemple d'une gravure rupestre à une calligraphie, en passant par un tapis, un tatouage, une vannerie ou un foulard dessiné. Or, ce tremblement de signes n'est rien d'autre que le motif productif (lui-même voyageur) de notre interrogation. Déplacement des signes en une série hasardeuse, et dont la figuration tantôt vibre en décrochant le sens, tantôt fige cette migration en un geste blanc, effaçant en quelque sorte l'espace giratoire qui se réduit ainsi à un point, à une pointe.[16]

[We are particularly interested in the migratory sign (or symbol), whether it is expressed in its minimal form (such as a point, for example) or in its vastest form as a graphic symbol – with its incredible repertoire of objects – spanning from rock art to calligraphic art through carpet design, the practice of tattooing, basketry and scarf design. Yet, this unstable trembling of the sign is nothing else than the productive motif (itself travelling) that lies at the centre of our investigation. Movement of the signs into random series whose arrangement is one moment vibrating to stabilize meaning and the next moment transforming its own movement into a blank gesture, erasing as it were any circular movement thus reduced to one point, one tip.]

And, a little further on:

le tatouage est une écriture en points (c'est le nom utilisé par les Arabes pour le désigner) [...] circulation des signes tantôt inscrits dans le corps, tantôt migrant dans d'autres espaces, signes dont le symbole originaire est souvent perdu pour nous, mais dont l'inscription encore vivante défie nos théories du signe.[17]

[the practice of tattooing is a form of 'writing in points' (name used by the Arabs themselves to designate such a practice) [...] migration of the signs sometimes inscribed on the body, sometimes migrating into other spaces; signs whose original symbol has been lost to us but whose inscription present on the body defies our theories of the sign.]

The 'migratory sign' moves freely between the space of the body and other spaces through the repetition of certain geometric forms travelling freely between different semiotic systems. These semiotic 'borders' are perforated by a constant movement of border-crossing between systems, a type of semiotic wandering. The contradictory character of memory referred to earlier lies in the nature of the sign of the tattoo; it

16   Khatibi, *La Blessure du nom propre*, p. 61.
17   Ibid., p. 64.

possesses not only the capacity to mark permanently the body but it also contains the capacity for random sign arrangement and sign erasure or obliteration. Crucially, for an understanding of Khatibi's notion of an 'intersémiotique transversale', this is a method of reading the text that challenges structuralist semiotic approaches to reading 'texts' in the Barthesian concept of the term, which, of course, extends well beyond literary and other written texts, as for Khatibi, and which may be more familiar to Western readers, especially those familiar with other semiotic theories and methods, such as the Greimassian model and École de Paris semiotics.[18] According to Khatibi, this approach is necessary in order to bypass the 'binarisme métaphysique' ['metaphysical binarism'] contained in the structuralist discourse on language along two poles of meaning, metaphorical and metonymical (syntagmatic and paradigmatic). As he argues in his essay on the tattoo, a multiple, 'oblique' reading is necessary in order to unveil historically repressed semiologic systems:

18   This refers to the work of Algirdas Julien Greimas (1917–92), the Lithuanian specialist in linguistics and semiotics who worked in Paris and wrote in French. He was the author of *Sémantique structurale: recherche de méthode*, the founding text of the École de Paris, a school of semiotic theory, published in French in 1966 but not translated into English until 1983. For a more detailed analysis of how Khatibi's writing resists this 'model' of structural semiotic systems of meaning, see Jasmina Bolfek-Radovani, *Geo/graphies of Loss: Space, Place and Spatial Loss in North African and Canadian Writing in French* (Erlangen: Lambert Academic Publishing, 2015), p. 84, p. 151, pp. 226–7. In the text she discusses Khatibi's approach of 'intersémiotique transversale', in the following way: 'This [oblique] type of reading can be linked to Khatibi's approach and concept of "intersemi-otique transversale". Although Khatibi's analysis of the different semiotic systems in Moroccan culture is extensively discussed by the author in *La Blessure du nom propre*, it becomes less clear how to apply such a reading or approach to the Maghrebian Francophone text. If one assumes that the Maghrebian Francophone text contains a French frame of reference associated with French culture and language, as well as references to traces of other semiotic systems that have been repressed or occulted (both European and Maghrebian), then its status can be viewed as highly ambiguous. The presence of several opposing systems of meaning or frames of references – that of the French (written and oral) language and culture and of the Arabic (written and oral) language and culture – creates a series of oppositions expressed as tensions that uniquely transform the meaning of the Maghrebian Francophone text. Rather than using the concepts of identity and difference in the interpretation of the Maghrebian Francophone text, the notion of the trace becomes instrumental to the way in which one is to interpret the Maghrebian Francophone text' (pp. 226–7).

Déceler une correspondance entre la composition grammaticale et la composition géométrique est utile. Mais il faudrait (comme dans le projet mallarméen) généraliser les nœuds de correspondances, faire éclater chaque fois le paradoxe de leur glissement et exacerber le dénouement intertextuel. Et nécessairement inscrite dans le langage, une lecture multiple, sans cesse oblique, flottante, folle de plaisir, s'attacherait à signifier les systèmes sémiologiques refoulés.[19]

[An identification of the correspondences between the grammatical and the geometrical structures is useful here. However, one would need to describe (as in Mallarmé's project) the knots of correspondences, resolve the paradox of their slippage and untie their intertextual relationship. A multiple, 'oblique', floating, joyful reading necessarily inscribed within the text that would free up the existence of the repressed semiotic systems within that text would then become possible.]

Only this approach, Khatibi argues, offers the potential for a deciphering of the infinite multitude of meanings and signs refracted in the 'crystal' of the text ['le cristal du texte'] that otherwise remain invisible to the reader. Indeed, the argument that Khatibi makes for the method of the 'intersémiotique transversale' and the multiplicity of signs and traces in the language that are reflected in the text and whose meaning is not only explicit but also implicit can be seen to be grounded, on the one hand, in the philosophical tradition of the hermeneutic interpretation of the text as debated in the works of Sufi philosophers and, on the other hand, in Derrida's method of 'deconstruction'. The final part of this chapter explores ways in which this method of reading may be useful to the reading of other Maghrebian texts, but first it returns to Khatibi's own 'mémoire tatouée' and its Islamic and Sufi context.

By using a variety of hypertexts or discourses and semiotic systems in *La Mémoire tatouée*, Khatibi instigates a theory of the sign or an 'intersemiotics' in the movement between the erasure and creation of meaning, meaning that constantly eludes the reader through the polyphony of voices embedded within the text. The reader is invited to decipher the multitude of signs, meanings and codes that are present in the autobiographical discourse and that lead to an intersemiotic encoding–decoding, a process of reading that has the potential to subvert, for example, the Qur'anic discourse through their use of rhetorical figures of the calligraphic sign in the French text. Although, as Abdallah Memmes observes, the process of parodying the Qur'anic

---

19 Khatibi, *La Blessure du nom propre*, p. 117.

text is frequently used in the course of the text, a reader unversed in this Islamic heritage can become aware of this parody only through a process of cultural translation or cultural encoding–decoding and depending on the extent to which she/he is familiar with Qur'anic references, mystical texts or Islamic parables that are inscribed within the text.[20]

While several critical studies have been carried out on the autobiographical dimensions of *La Mémoire tatouée*, fewer critics have fully engaged with the Islamic heritage in Khatibi's work. Of these, Memmes, for example, points to the link between autobiographical writing and textual fragments from the Islamic heritage in *La Mémoire tatouée*. In Memmes's view, while Khatibi's text may give the impression that it follows a conventional Western conception of autobiographical writing in its portrayal of the narrator's development from childhood to adulthood, there are several elements that subvert the chronological order of events. Amongst these elements are the inscription of fragments that belong to the Islamic heritage:

> En effet, partout sont injectés des fragments textuels (hypertextes) qui imitent de façon ludique un ensemble d'hypotextes, appartenant à différents registres sacrés et culturels: le Coran, le hadith, les textes mystiques, les formes du conte, le langage parabolique etc.[21]
>
> [In fact, textual fragments (hypertexts) are injected everywhere and which imitate in a playful way a set of hypertexts belonging to different sacred and cultural registers, such as the Qur'an, the Hadith, mystical texts, storytelling, parabolic language etc.][22]

According to Memmes, the fragments drawn from the sacred and cultural Islamic tradition rupture the temporality of autobiographical writing in Khatibi's text and disrupt the illusion of linearity. As Memmes puts it: 'Ces systèmes d'écriture perturbent ainsi le cours du récit. Au lieu d'être linéaire et progressif, ce dernier avance de rupture en rupture' ['These writing systems thus disrupt the flow of the narrative. Instead of being linear and progressive, the latter moves from one rupture to another'].[23] Khatibi's autobiographical writing in this sense does not

20 Abdallah Memmes, *Abdelkébir Khatibi: l'écriture de la dualité* (Paris: L'Harmattan, 1994).
21 Ibid., p. 29.
22 All the translations of quotations from Abdallah Memmes's *Abdelkébir Khatibi: l'écriture de la dualité* in this chapter are by Debra Kelly and Rim Feriani.
23 Memmes, *Abdelkébir Khatibi: l'écriture de la dualité*, p. 31.

give the illusion of remembering a seamless self.[24] His writing is rather a reflection on the self's different elements, which resonates with the multifaceted idea explored above of 'le cristal du texte'.

For Memmes, *La Mémoire tatouée* pivots around a 'projet théorique du genre [autobiographique]' ['a theoretical project that belongs to [the autobiographical] genre'],[25] which consists in reflecting the dual identity, linguistic as well as cultural, of Khatibi. Hence, the ruptures within the text of Khatibi serve partly to destabilize the linearity of a self-proclaimed memory and to bring to the fore the heterogeneous elements of the cultural and linguistic background from which Khatibi draws. In Memmes's words, autobiographical writing in Khatibi's text 'entend mettre en scène la genèse et l'affirmation de sa dualité culturelle, progressivement assumée et même revendiquée dans le cadre de la dialectique de l'identité et de la différence' ['means setting the scene for the genesis and the affirmation of his cultural duality, which are progressively taken up and even claimed within the dialectic of identity and difference'].[26] *La Mémoire tatouée* is in this sense predicated upon a remembering of the duality of the self and of the dialectic between French and Moroccan cultures, languages and histories.

In a similar vein, Rachida Saïgh Bousta argues that *La Mémoire tatouée* sheds light on the dual cultural heritage that Khatibi draws from as well as on his dual understanding of identity. For Bousta, 'Khatibi revendique son ensourcement culturel double et tentaculaire. L'Occident comme le Maghreb constituent pour lui des composantes identitaires incontournables' ['Khatibi lays claim to his double and sprawling cultural

---

24   It is important to note that Khatibi's experimental forms of exploring the self in writing pre-date those of the better-known French New Novelists. *La Mémoire tatouée* was published in 1971, a whole decade before the writers associated with the New Novel in France turned their attention to the consequences of their writing strategies which subverted the linear, character-driven plots of the traditional novel for new forms of narratives concerned with the self. It is also true of the work of the Tunisian Jewish writer Albert Memmi, in a text such as *Le Scorpion ou La Confession imaginaire*, published two years earlier than Khatibi's, in 1969; and again Memmi explicitly stated the differences between his project and that of his French colleagues. For more details see, for example, Debra Kelly, 'Writing and the Multiple Discourses of Selfhood', in her *Autobiography and Independence: Selfhood and Creativity in North African Postcolonial Writing in French* (Liverpool: Liverpool University Press, 2005), pp. 177–8 and pp. 209–21.

25   Memmes, *Abdelkébir Khatibi: l'écriture de la dualité*, p. 33.

26   Ibid., p. 34.

roots. Both the West and the Maghreb constitute for him essential components of identity'].[27] Khatibi's text revolves around a journey of a self that rides on difference rather than on sameness, indicating that *La Mémoire tatouée* 'est d'emblée errance vers un ailleurs, quête de soi par regards croisés, identité et différence' ['is initially a wandering towards an elsewhere, a quest for a self through diverse perspectives, identity and difference'].[28] While, like Memmes, Bousta stresses the cultural aspect of identity and its centrality in Khatibi's novel, she makes in passing a reference to the close similarity between the writing of *La Mémoire tatouée* and the Sufi works of the medieval scholar Muhyiddin Ibn Arabi: 'Ce type de littérature est particulièrement cultivé par certains soufis tels que Ibn Arabi' ['This type of literature is developed by certain Sufis such as Ibn Arabi'].[29] This remark not only emphasizes the multifarious nature of writing in *La Mémoire tatouée*, which rests on a mixture of genres extending from autobiography, philosophy to essay writing, but also highlights the close connection between Khatibi's writing and the Sufi Islamic heritage.

Taking Bousta's remark on the parallel between Khatibi's text and Ibn Arabi's Sufi writings as a starting point, the nature of this parallel will be further explored through a reading of signs and symbols that have Sufi resonances in *La Mémoire tatouée*. Working with Khatibi's own practice of deciphering of signs and with his own writing – in *La Mémoire tatouée* specifically – a particular example will be taken, namely the ways in which the meaning of visions 'migrates' from the Sufi Islamic heritage. The proposed close textual reading of visions demonstrates that they form a 'tissu' (literally, a 'fabric') of intersemiotic symbols, a key concept applied by Khatibi to his theorizing of the tattoo discussed earlier. In a second stage of the application of this reading method, again echoing that of Khatibi, a further reading of the meaning of visions in Assia Djebar's *Loin de Médine* is proposed, once more with reference to Khatibi's theoretical reading of the practice of the tattoo.

The choice of exploring the relevance of Sufi signs and symbols to Khatibi's own writing practice is motivated by the influence of the

---

27   Rachida Saïgh Bousta, *Lecture des récits de Abdelkébir Khatibi: ecriture, memoire et imaginaire* (Casablanca: Afrique Orient, 1996), p. 11. All the translations of quotations from *Lecture des récits de Abdelkébir Khatibi* in this chapter are by Rim Feriani and Debra Kelly.

28   Bousta, *Lecture des récits de Abdelkébir Khatibi*, p. 13.

29   Ibid., p. 12.

Islamic heritage on Khatibi's works and thought and the many ways in which Khatibi engages with this heritage. Nasrin Qader in her reading of Khatibi's *Le Livre du sang* recognizes that 'Khatibi's engagement with [the mystical tradition of Islam] is no secret, as it traverses the entirety of his *œuvre* [...] This inscription is never a simple repetition but is a rewriting and rethinking of the tradition itself, every time, in a singular way'.[30]

Sufism has many meanings and interpretations and there exist various Sufi schools of thought that are geographically and historically different. Sufism is *tasawwuf* in Arabic and its etymological root stems both from *suf*, which means wool, and from the noun *safa*, which means pure.[31] The eleventh-century Persian Sufi Abd al-Qādir Al-Jīlāni explains that the reason why 'the Sufis are called by this name is [that] their inner world is purified and enlightened with the light of wisdom, unity and oneness'.[32] In *Sufism: The Mystical Side of Islam. Some Developmental Aspects*, Winston E. Waugh also indicates that:

> The term [Sufism] is a very wide one, and it surely conjures up different expressions and so variegated a behaviour pattern that, in its entirety, it defies all human effort to confine it to any one conventional description. Even the Sufis themselves are numerous in the way that they attest to their beliefs. Some describe their movement as a way of life; others describe it as a state of the soul; and yet others talk about it as a relationship to God.[33]

Despite the various and varied forms of Sufism, it is usually broadly understood as the spiritual aspect of Islam. Sufism pivots around the sacred relationship with God and the spiritual seeker's quest for inner realization. It is in this sense that the Sufi Islamic heritage and its resonances in Khatibi's texts, with a particular emphasis on the symbolic dimensions of visions in Sufism, are considered here.

30 Nasrin Qader, *Narratives of Catastrophe: Boris Diop, Ben Jelloun, Khatibi* (New York: Fordham University Press, 2009), p. 153.

31 For a detailed definition of Sufism, see, for example, Titus Burckhardt, *Introduction to Sufi Doctrine* (Bloomington, IN: World Wisdom, 2008); Martin Lings, *What is Sufism?* (Cambridge: Islamic Texts Society, 1999); and Alexander Knysh, *Sufism: A Brief History* (Leiden: E. J. Brill, 2004).

32 Abd al-Qādir Al-Jīlāni, *The Secret of Secrets*, trans. Tosun Bayrak (Cambridge: Islamic Texts Society, 1992), p. 40.

33 Winston E. Waugh, *Sufism: The Mystical Side of Islam. Some Developmental Aspects* (Maitland, FL: Xulon Press, 2005), p. 8.

In this light, visions as symbols in Khatibi's text – and in Djebar's text – are read as forming a 'tissu' (as given above, one way of translating this is as a 'fabric', but perhaps better is 'web'; Khatibi plays with both – and more – of these meanings) of 'points', having 'migrated' from the Sufi heritage and marking the fluctuating memory of the narrators in both *La Mémoire tatouée* and *Loin de Médine*. The following readings reveal how the intersemiotic meaning of visions displays the creativity of a 'tattooed memory' in the same manner that creativity is associated with the Sufi spiritual experience of the sacred. Bearing in mind Khatibi's theoretical concern with the deciphering of signs, the meaning of 'tissu' illustrates the idea of a composition of signs which follows the movement of writing.

According to Khatibi, a 'tissu' is synonymous with 'des dessins décorant le corps: dans le mot *tissu*, il y a l'idée d'une composition microphysique de la matière, l'idée d'un espace rythmé et, *last but not least*, la notion de l'écriture' ['drawings decorating the body: in the word *fabric*, there is the idea of a microphysical and material composition, the idea of a rhythmic space and, last but not least, the notion of writing'].[34] The meaning of 'tissu' needs to be understood in relation to the practice of the tattoo whereby the act of writing or 'tattooing' creates a 'tissu' of interrelated signs and symbols. A 'tissu' is formed, Khatibi writes, through signs that are like tattooed 'points' in a moving 'espace giratoire' ['gyrating space'].[35] In this sense, writing about memory in *La Mémoire tatouée* is similar to a 'tattooed' body of text guided by the rhythm of signs and following the movement of 'migrant symbols'.

In *La Mémoire tatouée*, the narrator's visions resonate with the Sufi spiritual meaning of visions since, as will be demonstrated, they are closely interlinked with meditation, the Qur'an and creativity. At the start of the novel, the narrator describes his mother as an absence who is buried under 'le règne maternel' ['the maternal reign'] and whose memory was erased: 'Mer, mère, mémoire, lapsus échappés à cette frileuse nostalgie' ['Ocean, mother, memory – lapses fleeing from this chill nostalgia'].[36] The narrator's memory of his mother escapes the confines of his nostalgia and the infinitude of oblivion which is alluded to in the infinite nature

34   Khatibi, *La Blessure du nom propre*, p. 80.
35   Ibid., p. 64.
36   Abdelkébir Khatibi, *La Mémoire tatouée* (Paris: Denoël, 1971), reprinted in *Œuvres de Abdelkébir Khatibi I: Romans et récits* (Paris: La Différence, 2008), pp. 9–113 (p. 20); *Tattooed Memory*, trans. Peter Thompson (Paris: L'Harmattan, 2016), p. 25.

of the ocean 'mer'. The lost memory of the mother is thus marked by absence: 'Me revient un lapsus: mère à la place de mémoire, double absence dans un double hasard' ['I just had a slip: mother, instead of memory – double absence in a double fluke'].[37] The silence of the mother, coupled with her lost memory, reinforces her absence from the narrator's childhood memories. As such, the mother is inscribed in 'l'effacement' ['erasure'] and 'l'obscurité' ['darkness'].[38] Yet, despite her absence, the mother's images appear in fractions through visions. It is as though the remembering of the mother is an act of tattooing whereby the narrator's visions symbolize 'points' that mark the body of Khatibi's text.

Through the darkness of a bygone past, images of the absent mother appear to the narrator like visions that manifest themselves to the inner heart of the spiritual seeker. In 'la cuisine obscure et noire de fumée' ['the kitchen, dark and black from smoke'], the narrator sees his mother who 's'asseyait en face de lumière' ['sat facing the light'].[39] When the narrator perceives his mother, he follows the movement of her hands: '[Ma mère] s'occupait de moi et me gâta, on jouait ensemble […] Je suivais, heureux, le mouvement de ses mains' ['She took care of me and spoiled me, we played together […] I was happy following the movement of [her] hands'].[40] As the narrator sees his mother, he speaks of the apparitional form in which she manifests herself: the mother, who, albeit absent, appears in a visionary form as through 'un fragment de vision' ['fragment of vision'].[41]

While the narrator's visions of his mother can be considered as a form of remembering, the meaning of visions in relation to the mother may be interpreted as a symbol of spiritual visions. The word 'méditation' ['meditation'][42] in the final page of the novel and the allusion to the Qur'an cast a different light on the meaning of the narrator's visions. The visions that the narrator receives of his mother are akin to a meditative experience that enables him spiritual access to what is unseen. What the narrator sees does not necessarily belong to a

37 Khatibi, *La Mémoire tatouée*, p. 19; *Tattooed Memory*, p. 20.
38 Ibid., p. 18; p. 20.
39 Ibid., p. 26; p. 32.
40 Ibid., p. 24; p. 29.
41 Ibid., p. 24. In *Tattooed Memory*, p. 28 this phrase is translated as 'everything fades out'. We have instead included our own translation to convey the meaning of visions in relation to the mother.
42 Ibid., p. 113; p. 157.

past history, for he explicitly states that this is an 'œuvre à venir' ['the manuscript to come'],[43] indicating what is yet to come. The symbolic and spiritual aspect of the narrator's visions of his mother is further stressed in the link between 'notre vision actuelle' ['our current vision'], 'signes' ['signs'] and 'le Coran qui suppose mon enfance' ['the Qur'an that supposes my childhood'].[44] Thus, visions of the mother symbolize a spiritual meditation and an uncovering of what is unseen in the same way that a spiritual seeker unravels hidden signs of the Qur'an. Additionally, the mother who belongs to an unseen realm appears to the narrator 'à l'intérieur même' ['in the very interior'][45] of his tattooed memory. This inward aspect of the visions, floating within a 'terrain vague' ['vacant lot'],[46] indicates that the narrator's experience of seeing his mother is an inner experience of an unseen realm.

In the same way that the narrator experiences a visionary encounter with his mother, a Sufi spiritual seeker gains visions of God, who albeit being unseen becomes present to the heart of the seeker. As Firoozeh Papan-Matin writes: 'The unseen is the mystery of God and the hidden realm of realities that are in His vicinity'.[47] However, the seeker's visions form 'windows into the hidden mysteries of both this world and the next'.[48] The visions that a Sufi seeker receives entail an inner perception, in sensible form, of what belongs to the spiritual world. As such, the Sufi seeker 'perceives in sensible imagery some of the things that properly belong to the world of the Unseen'.[49] From this Sufi perspective, the visions of the narrator in Khatibi's text can be read as symbols of spiritual visions. As noted earlier, these visions are closely interlinked with meditation and with the Qur'anic signs that are anchored in the narrator's childhood.

In addition to the connection between the narrator's visions, meditation and the Qur'anic signs, the creative aspect of these visions highlight their

---

43   Ibid., p. 113; p. 157.

44   Ibid., p. 111; p. 152.

45   Ibid., p. 108; p. 146.

46   Ibid., p. 19; p. 21.

47   Firoozeh Papan-Matin, *Beyond Death: The Mystical Teachings of 'Ayn al-Qudat al-Hamadhānī* (Leiden and Boston: Brill, 2010), p. 119.

48   Alexander D. Knysh, 'Dreams and Visions in Islamic Societies: An Introduction', in Alexander Knysh and Özgen Felek (eds), *Dreams and Visions in Islamic Societies* (Albany: SUNY Press, 2012), pp. 1–11 (p. 2).

49   Toshihiko Izutsu, *Sufism and Taoism: A Comparative Study of Key Philosophical Concepts* (London, Los Angeles and Berkeley: University of California Press, 1984), p. 260.

symbolic and spiritual dimensions. The narrator's visions are creative since they engender inner images of an absent yet present mother. Like the mother whose images appear to the narrator through inner visions, the Sufi spiritual wayfarer experiences images of the unseen God. The inner appearance of these images is incumbent upon the love that drives the seeker to the hidden God. In this sense, Henry Corbin explains that spiritual love, in the Sufi sense, is 'situated in the creature who is always in quest of the being whose Image he discovers in himself, or of which he discovers that he himself is the Image'.[50] While God's essence remains hidden from the heart of the spiritual lover, spiritual union with God can be attained through the corporeal apparition of what belongs to the spiritual realm. The spiritual quest, guided by the movement of love, is an apprehension of those forms that manifest themselves to the inner heart of the seeker.

Guided by his love for his mother, whom he refers to as the 'douce mère' ['sweet mother'],[51] the narrator gains inner visions and images of the unseen. Owing to the narrator's passage through the 'chemins' ['pathways'] that 'partent et aboutissent au même noeud' ['part and end up at the same knot'],[52] images of the mother become manifest. The visions of the narrator emblematize a journey within the gyrating space of his 'mémoire nomade' ['nomadic memory'] where 'images légères et mouvantes' ['light and mobile images'][53] reveal themselves to the narrator from within. The narrator's visions of his mother create a space where images flow.

Amongst the vocabulary that the narrator uses to describe his visions is the word 'regard'. The narrator's 'regard' ['glance'] is compared with 'la renaissance d'un espace' ['the renaissance of a space'].[54] Vision as 'seeing' is here a way of recovering 'un puzzle de formes' ['a jigsaw of shapes'] and 'images' ['images'].[55] Thus, the 'regard/look' of the narrator has the spiritual potential of creating an inner space where images of his mother manifest themselves and where the presence of his mother appears in corporeal forms. This importance of the 'look' will be

50   Henry Corbin, *Creative Imagination in the Sufism of Ibn Arabi*, trans. Ralph Manheim (Princeton, NJ: Princeton University Press, 1969), p. 149.
51   Khatibi, *La Mémoire tatouée*, p. 17; *Tattooed Memory*, p. 17.
52   Ibid., p. 29; p. 35.
53   Ibid., p. 29; p. 35.
54   Ibid., p. 29; p. 35.
55   Ibid., p. 29; p. 35.

considered again later in the reading of Djebar's *Loin de Médine* in the final section of this chapter.

The creative aspect of visions in Khatibi's text is further reinforced through the repetitive use of vocabulary pertaining to imagination and dreams. The verb 'to imagine' recurs in its infinitive form 'imaginer' ['imagine'][56] and in the present tense 'j'imagine' ['I imagine'].[57] Furthermore, the narrator asserts that between himself and his mother, 'il y a un rêve entre nous' ['we share a dream'].[58] Gaining access to the mother is mediated through dreams, which is corroborated in the use of the verb 'to dream' in the imperfect tense, 'je rêvais' ['I dreamed'],[59] in the present tense, 'je rêve' ['I [...] now dream of']60 and as well in the noun form in the following statement: 'le seul rêve de mon enfance' ['the only childhood dream'].[61] The tattooed memory in Khatibi's text forms a 'tissu' of intersemiotic visions that follow the rhythm of imagination and dreams as though it were an 'équation de visions qui me font flotter' ['an equation of visions that make me drift'].[62]

It was earlier shown that the narrator's visions form part of Khatibi's intersemiotic project and that these visions are akin to 'points' as explored in Khatibi's own theory on the tattoo. The tattooed memory in Khatibi's text is thus marked by these visions that constitute a creative composition of various images. What also characterizes the act of tattooing is the constant movement of signs. Such a movement, as explained earlier, is displayed in Khatibi's drawing from the Sufi symbolic connotations of visions and inscribing them within his tattooed memory. As such, when the narrator speaks of his 'équation de visions qui me font flotter', he refers to his 'errance' ['roaming'], to his constant 'mouvement' ['movements'][63] and to 'le flux' ['the ebb and flow'][64] of his visionary encounters.

The 'intersemiotic' movement of visions in Khatibi's text are interlinked with desire in the same way the Sufi seeker desires union with the sacred. The narrator's visions of his mother follow the movement of

56   Ibid., p. 24; p. 29.
57   Ibid., p. 18; p. 19.
58   Ibid., p. 16; p. 17.
59   Ibid., p. 25; p. 30.
60   Ibid., p. 20; p. 22.
61   Ibid., p. 20; p. 23.
62   Ibid., p. 102; p. 139.
63   Ibid., p. 102; p. 139.
64   Ibid., p. 80; p. 108.

and 'enchaînement' ['link'][65] to desire, which is a desire to reunite with a hidden 'archet maternel' ['maternal violins'][66] and with the 'douce mère' ['sweet mother'].[67] The narrator thus declares that he is an 'amant de devenir' ['Becoming's lover'],[68] embarking on a 'voyage amoureux' ['love voyage'] seeking 'une tendresse endormante' ['drowsy tenderness'].[69] Seeking the hidden mother is thus akin to a spiritual attainment of an 'oasis' where the narrator can find refuge and reach for safety: 'je suis protégé' ['I am protected'].[70]

The intersemiotic connection between the narrator's visions and his desire to reunite with his mother is further consolidated with the parallel that the narrator establishes between his mother and paradise. At the start of the novel, the narrator expresses his uncertainty about whether he dreamt about paradise: 'Rêvais-je de paradis?' ['Was I dreaming of paradise?'].[71] Two pages later, the parallel between paradise and the mother is clarified when the narrator describes his severance. The narrator indicates how the road to paradise was cut short when he was severed as a child from the maternal breast: 'tout retrouvait le chemin du paradis, bien que la pointe du sein maternel fût alors amère' ['All returned to the path of paradise, though after that my mother's nipple was bitter'].[72] Later in the text, the narrator refers again to paradise, insisting on the necessity of searching for it: 'il faut chercher le paradis' ['you have to find the promised paradise'].[73] Searching for and dreaming about paradise impel the movement of the narrator's visions, which are guided by a desire to attain a lost paradise.

In the same way that the Sufi spiritual connotations of the narrator's visions were explored earlier, paradise may also be interpreted as a symbol that has migrated from the Sufi Islamic heritage and that Khatibi inscribes in his tattooed memory. Sufis use such words as *jannat* and *firdaws* – which translate in English as 'paradise' or 'garden' – to refer symbolically to the hidden realm of God. It is a sacred realm where God manifests Himself to

65   Ibid., p. 110; p. 151.
66   Ibid., p. 13; p. 13.
67   Ibid., p. 17; p. 17.
68   Ibid., p. 105; p. 143.
69   Ibid., pp. 21–2; pp. 24–5.
70   Ibid., p. 104; p. 142.
71   Ibid., p. 15; p. 15.
72   Ibid., p. 16; p. 17.
73   Ibid., p. 33; p. 40.

the heart of the seeker. Sufis interchangeably refer to paradise as 'garden' since these expressions in Arabic are synonymous. In this respect:

> Sufis have drawn from this symbolism and speak of the Garden as designating not only the various levels of paradisal realities but also the Divine Reality beyond Paradise as usually understood. The highest Garden is associated with the absolute Truth, which is one of the Names of the Divine Essence. Hence, we can speak of the Garden of Truth as that reality wherein all the spiritual realities are gathered. The Sufis also speak of the Gardener as God in His absolute and infinite Reality, and of *jannat al-Dhat*, or Garden of the Divine Essence.[74]

Paradise or garden is a symbol that designates the site where the spiritual world appears to the inner heart of the Sufi seeker:

> In the heart, the spiritual man lives in intimacy with God, with the Origin of all those theophanies whose outward manifestations constitute all the beauty that is reflected in the world around us. He lives in that inner garden, that inner paradise, constantly aware of the ubiquitous Gardener.[75]

Within the realm of paradise, the spiritual seeker gains access to the realities of God in the form of inner manifestations. This quest for paradise coincides with visionary encounters with God whereby the seeker can experience 'intimacy' with the spiritual world. It is in this Sufi sense that the mother in Khatibi's text can be read as a symbol of a paradise that the narrator experiences within his inner visions. She manifests herself through images, dreams and imagination, in the same way that the heart of the Sufi seeker experiences manifestations of a hidden paradise.

The intersemiotic relations between visions, desire and paradise in Khatibi's text have therefore been analysed to demonstrate how these visions form a tattooed 'tissu' in his own writing. In this final section, Khatibi's theoretical concern with signs and the tattoo and his practices of reading are taken as a way of reading works by other writers with a shared, although differently experienced, Islamic – and Sufi – heritage. Here, Djebar's *Loin de Médine* is taken as an example. *Loin de Médine* is a text by an Algerian woman writer, published 20 years after *La Mémoire tatouée*, and it is one that does not belong to her own extended practices of autobiographical writing, although it shares

---

74   Seyyed Hossein Nasr, *The Garden of Truth: The Vision and Promise of Sufism, Islam's Mystical Tradition* (New York: HarperOne, 2007), p. xv.
75   Ibid., p. 95.

many of those concerns with excavating a lost past, memory, and female voices and experiences. Taking as a point of departure the symbolic meaning of visions that were associated earlier with Khatibi's theorizing of the intersemiotic composition of 'tissu', the ways in which memory in *Loin de Médine*, in a very similar way to memory in *La Mémoire tatouée*, encapsulates a creative composition of signs is examined. It is also argued that the symbolic meaning of visions in Djebar's novel have 'migrated' from the Sufi Islamic heritage and have been creatively tattooed within the body of the text.

Loin de Médine revolves around a female narrator's remembering of the early years of Islamic history. As the narrator invokes the life of the Prophet Muhammad, she excavates the forgotten lives and voices of women. Through this journey back in history, particular attention is paid in this analysis to the narrator's encounter with the Prophet Muhammad's youngest wife, Aicha. The encounter with Aicha is couched in vocabulary that highlights the spiritual dimensions of the female narrator's as well as Aicha's visions. Whenever Aicha is mentioned in Djebar's text, key semantic words that relate to 'regard' can be detected. One of the possible ways of translating 'regard' in this context is 'eyesight', since Aicha's 'regard' is closely associated with her 'eyes'. For example, there are repeated references to the eyes of Aicha, which are described as 'les yeux ouverts' ['open-eyed'].[76] In addition to the 'eyes', the verb 'to see' is used frequently in connection with Aicha: 'Muette, celle-ci regarde, regarde' ['Silently she looks and looks'] and 'les yeux de Lalla Aïcha, immobilisée, l'ont vu' ['Lalla Aisha's eyes also saw'].[77]

Examining the intersemiotic links between the 'eyes', the action of 'seeing' and the plethora of nouns revolving around these words reveals that the meaning of 'eyesight' is not to be interpreted literally. What can be seen through the 'eyes' of Aicha does not belong to the physical world that she inhabits. Through her encounter with Aicha, the female narrator's visions engender a space where memory is tattooed with images of the unseen. Aicha's vision enables the female narrator to gain access to a hidden realm. As such, Aicha 'voit son destin se dessiner' ['she sees her destiny sketched out'] and her memories catapult her 'dans l'avenir' ['into the future'].[78] Aicha also has the ability to uncover the

76   Assia Djebar, *Loin de Médine* (Paris: Albin Michel, 1991), p. 288; *Far from Madina*, trans. Dorothy S. Blair (Quartet Books: London, 1994), p. 230.

77   Djebar, *Loin de Médine*, p. 292; *Far from Madina*, p. 233.

78   Ibid., pp. 332–3; pp. 267–8.

'secret des adultes' ['the adults' secret'] and to gain access to a veiled 'lumière' ['illumination'].[79] Aicha can even see those who no longer belong to the world of the living. Barira, an ex-slave liberated by Aicha, indicates how the latter's 'eyes' allow her to inhabit a world where her dead father can be found: '[Aicha] yeux ouverts, lèvres serrées, nous contemple, comme si, du côté où vogue l'âme de son père qui, j'en suis sûre, nous écoute, elle s'est installée avec lui' ['open-eyed, lips clenched, gazes on us as if she – as yet the only one not grief stricken – were accompanying her father's soul where it is being borne, from where, I am sure he hears us'].[80] Thus, Aicha's visions of destiny, of the secret of adults, of light and of her father's soul reinforce the inner dimensions of the images that are gained through a spiritual eye.

Owing to Aicha's visions, a spiritual realm opens up to the narrator and which cannot be seen merely through the physical eye. In this sense, through the visionary encounter with Aicha the memory of the female narrator in *Loin de Médine* moves into a reality that lies beyond physical boundaries. This memory, like that of the narrator in *La Mémoire tatouée*, is marked by visionary 'points' that form a 'tissu' of symbols. Gaining access to the female narrator's tattooed memory in *Loin de Médine* therefore demands a deciphering of the inner visions that are spiritually fluctuating, in a constant state of intersemiotic flux.

The 'tissu' of visions in *Loin de Médine* recalls the Sufi experience of unveiling and which consists in the seeker's spiritual access to the unseen. Unveiling for Sufis is:

> the principal mode of access to the supra-sensible world [...] it permits the raising of the veils that the world of the senses (*mulk*) throws over man, thus allowing him to reach the world of the spirit (*malakūt*).[81]

Unveiling is therefore coterminous with a visionary access to a spiritual world and an attainment of spiritual realization. In a similar vein, the female narrator in *Loin de Médine* is constantly encountering veils of silences and veiled female bodies and as she advances in her journey she experiences inner unveiling.

The Sufi spiritual symbolism of visions in *Loin de Médine* also shares the creative aspect of visions that was examined earlier in

---

79   Ibid., p. 297; p. 238.
80   Ibid., p. 288; p. 230.
81   Eric Geoffroy, *Introduction to Sufism: The Inner Path of Islam*, trans. Roger Gaetani (Bloomington, IN: World Wisdom Books), p. 7.

relation to Khatibi's text. It was noted that the narrator's visions in *La Mémoire tatouée* are closely interrelated with dreams and imagination. Similarly, the 'tissu' of visions in *Loin de Médine* is inextricably linked to imagination thus highlighting the creative aspect of the female narrator's visionary encounters. In Djebar's text there is an ensemble of verbs such as 'J'imagine' ['I imagine'],[82] 'Rêver' ['Musing'], 'éclaircir' ['needing clarification'][83] and 'évoquer' ['should be known'].[84] Interpreting these verbs that connote imagination, dreaming and evoking in relation to the female narrator's visions stresses the idea that the latter experiences inner spiritual realization which allows her to see the unseen. Throughout her journey, the female narrator enters a realm where she imagines the 'souvenir' of Aicha that 'trace, dans l'espace de notre foi interrogative, la courbe parfaite d'un météore entrevu dans le noir' ['traces, in the gap of our questioning faith, the perfect curve of a meteor glimpsed in the dark sky'].[85] The tattooed memory in *Loin de Médine* therefore resembles a composition of visions that are intersemiotically related and that creatively engender newly imagined dreams and visions. Like the narrator in Khatibi's text, the female narrator in Djebar's text follows the movement of her visions embarking on a spiritual quest that constantly unfolds a 'tissu' of creative signs and meanings.

The creativity of the female narrator's visions in *Loin de Médine* is reinforced through its close connection with femininity. The narrator gains access to images of female figures in the same way the Sufi spiritual seeker has access to the sacred through the feminine image. Corbin explains that:

> the mystic obtains the highest theophanic vision in contemplating the Image of feminine being, because it is in the Image of the Creative Feminine that contemplation can apprehend the highest manifestation of God, namely, creative divinity.[86]

Spiritual visions, from a Sufi angle, correspond to a manifestation or theophany. Hence the expressions as well as the experience of the sacred are mediated through the very feminine nature of the images that appear to the heart of the seeker. The spiritual experience in this sense brings forth a fusion between creativity, femininity and the sacred. It is thus

82   Ibid., p. 66; p. 52.
83   Ibid., pp. 62–3; pp. 48–9.
84   Ibid., p. 92; p. 73.
85   Ibid., p. 66; p. 52.
86   Henry Corbin, *Creative Imagination in the Sufism of Ibn Arabi*, p. 159.

through the feminine vision that an image is created. Corbin further adds that a 'woman is the being par excellence in whom mystic love (combining the spiritual and the sensible by reciprocal transmutation) attaches to a theophanic Image (*tajallī*) par excellence'.[87] Likewise, the quest for memory in Djebar's text pivots around the symbolic relation between the femininity that Aicha emblematizes and the visionary journey of the female narrator. The visions of the narrator are far from being already formed but are rather created in and through the very process of a journey through a tattooed memory, where theophanic images of unseen women creatively appear to an inner spiritual eye.

To sum up, Khatibi's theorizing of signs foregrounds an intersemiotic deciphering which accounts for the infinity of meanings of a sign and of its crystal refracted dimensions. For Khatibi, calligraphic signs repose on an intersection between rationalist and Sufi mystical discourses. Such an intersection reinforces on the one hand the infinite meanings that a sign can generate and on the other the repression of other semiotic sign systems such as the tattoo. While Khatibi indicates that the tattoo is a popular form of art repressed by the sacred, he reinscribes such a practice within the very same discourse that entailed its exclusion.

As demonstrated in the textual reading of *La Mémoire tatouée*, the tattoo – albeit a popular form of art – is formed of a 'tissu' of visions that draws from and engages with the sacred forms of Sufi symbols. It is as though Khatibi, through his own radical theory of signs, reveals the paradox at the heart of the very practice of the deciphering of signs. Reading the tattooed visions either in *La Mémoire tatouée* or other similar texts such as *Loin de Médine* emblematizes a reading practice that defies a metaphysical binary thinking and celebrates the infinite meanings that are generated by signs and symbols, echoing again Khatibi's theoretical endeavour to 'éclater chaque fois le paradoxe' ['to shatter the paradox every time'].[88]

87   Ibid., p. 162.
88   Khatibi, *La Blessure du nom propre*, p. 117.

CHAPTER ELEVEN

Abdelkébir Khatibi

The Other Side of the Mirror

Lucy Stone McNeece

In spite of the fact that Abdelkébir Khatibi's work has received considerable critical acclaim, especially in the Francophone world, translations
have been slow to appear, and critics are frequently challenged to describe
or classify his writing. His texts are considered 'hybrid' because they
cannot be framed by the categories of conventional genres. Although
several of his theoretical essays, such as those found in *Maghreb pluriel*
(1983) or *Penser le Maghreb* (1993), have been celebrated as prophetic
with respect to postcolonial debates about identity and language, other
texts, which include novels and various kinds of 'récits', continue to
challenge critical discourses, and Khatibi often mixes critical thinking
with imaginative creativity. I have entitled this essay *The Other Side of
the Mirror*, in reference to Lewis Carroll's *Through the Looking Glass*
(1871), as a means of introducing some of the principles that I believe
govern Khatibi's writing. Although we may consider Carroll's work
'child's play' and remote from Khatibi's preoccupations, I believe it may
enhance our reading of several of Khatibi's texts.

In the second of Lewis Carroll's texts about Alice's adventures, Alice
passes through a mirror into an alternative universe that is governed
by the logic of dreams, and where events suggest a radically different
perspective on reality, which, to Alice's confusion, undergoes continuous
transformations. Not only do animals speak and act like humans, the
entire text is structured like a chess game, whose pieces, too, come to life,
suggesting that it is intended as a microcosm of existence. The poem of
the 'Jabberwocky' is written in reverse writing, and it contains invented
and portmanteau words such as those found in Arabic dialects, but
also suggests the hybrid signifying principles of the rebus and those of

Egyptian hieroglyphs or Chinese ideograms. Alice is subject to frequent metamorphoses and is constantly challenged, as are her young readers, to decipher the enigmatic phenomena around her. All the characters and objects in the tale are ciphers. The Red King sleeping under a tree appears to be dreaming, but perhaps it is Alice's dream, or perhaps she exists only within his dream.[1] We are never sure who is directing this serious play. The entire text is a kind of epistemological parable that challenges the complacency of middle-class Victorian society during the apogee of British imperialism, when the English monarchy saw itself as master of much of the world.[2]

I would like to suggest that Khatibi's writing is informed by many of these kinds of subversive epistemological games and reversals, as different as the contexts of Carroll and Khatibi's work may seem. Khatibi's texts may indeed be hybrid, in that they cross generic boundaries, but they are also *hermetic*. I say this not because they often seem obscure or complex, but that the difficulty in classifying or even analysing his writing is due to echoes and traces of certain esoteric traditions that have alternative cosmologies and conceptions of reality and a different relation to signs. Khatibi devoted years of his life to the study of cultures very different from his own, and found that his own national culture, so long overwhelmed by European influences, was in fact a rich tapestry of varied threads, just as he recognized in other cultures the material traces of many buried encounters.

The varied influences present in Khatibi's writing include those of Asian traditions such as the Tao, Buddhism and the Vedas; the Kabbala and Sufism (although its presence is philosophical and poetic rather than religious), but also the hermetic sciences, such as Alchemy, which originated in Egypt and Mesopotamia and then found their way into Greece and its mystery schools, and which were translated and revised by Arabs and Eastern Christians. They entered Europe from Andalusian Spain and also through Italy under the sponsorship of the Medicis and contributed substantially to the revolution in the arts and sciences of the Renaissance.

---

1   In the Chinese Taoist text by Zhuangzi, *Chuang Tzu*, we learn of a similar paradox of a man dreaming of a butterfly but not sure if he is a butterfly dreaming he is a man, or even that he exists only within the butterfly's dream (Kuang-Ming Wu, *The Butterfly as Companion: Meditations on the First Three Chapters of the Chuang Tzu* (New York: SUNY Press, 1990).

2   Lewis Carroll, *Through the Looking-Glass* (London: Macmillan, 1871).

For an understanding of Khatibi's unorthodox style of writing, we may look to the figure of the Egyptian God Thoth, known also to the Greeks as Hermes Trismegistus, the God of writing, art, philosophy, mathematics, music, magic and immortality. He is relevant for several reasons: Thoth-Hermes is above all a messenger, a transmitter of wisdom, and Khatibi speaks often of himself as a 'passeur' ('Je fus donc ce passeur ...' ['I was therefore that ferryman ...']³) and of writing as *transmission*. The term itself is used in Buddhist and Vedic texts as the way in which arcane knowledge may pass from initiates to novices. It is assumed that Thoth-Hermes originated in Mesopotamia under the Sumerians. Much later he became a figure in European alchemy, and Isaac Newton, a pillar of seventeenth-century science and also an avowed alchemist, published a translation of the Emerald tablet, which, although shorter, contains elements found in the *Corpus Hermeticum*. It contains dialogues and the statement, 'as above so below', which has been interpreted to refer to the notion of correspondences and the idea of macrocosm and microcosm.⁴

Thoth-Hermes, or Mercury, in the Roman pantheon, was the moon God, and was associated with the third eye. In Mesopotamian, Indian and Chinese traditions, the moon initially had more significance than the sun; it was associated with the cycles of time, and, by extension, immortality. Thoth-Hermes governs memory, dreams and intuition. He is reflexive and changeable and is master of the rhythms of nature. Water is his element, but as Mercury he is associated with the element of air. He governs language, writing and voyages. He is clever and ambiguous.⁵ We shall find many of these principles in Khatibi's texts. These ancient cultures entertained a relation to signs and images that contrasts with that which has predominated in Europe since the Enlightenment, where, except for certain types of poetry and experiments such as those of the Surrealists and the group Oulipo, signs have lost much of their complex resonance and incantatory force. Khatibi's texts actively explore many

3   Abdelkébir Khatibi, *Amour bilingue* (Montpellier: Fata Morgana, 1983), reprinted in *Œuvres de Abdelkébir Khatibi I: Romans et récits*, pp. 205–83 (p. 247); *Love in Two Languages*, trans. Richard Howard (Minneapolis: University of Minnesota Press, 1990), p. 64.

4   Arthur D. Nock and André-Jean Festugière, *Le Corpus Hermeticum*, vols 1–4 (Paris: Les Belles Lettres, 1946–54).

5   Francis Melville, *Secrets de la haute magie* (Paris: Editions Contre-Dires, 2014), p. 86.

types of signs, reinstating some of their ancient functions as part of his desire to derange entrenched models of thought that have supported dominance and exclusion in several hemispheres.

Proponents of the esoteric or hermetic traditions also had a different conception of the universe and man's place in it. They imagined the cosmos as an integrated sphere that was manifest in multiple phenomena, a space of continuous transformation of diverse elements in an ever-evolving equilibrium, a view quite different from that of the rational individual at the pinnacle of a Great Chain of Being claiming to be master of all he surveys. Within this cosmos in constant transformation, everything is intimately connected as if in dialogue. These ethical principles inform the language of Khatibi's texts which critique the binary (imperial/colonial) vision of north and south, east and west and demonstrate the deep imbrication of apparently opposing cultures and ideologies. He also condemns Islamic dogma and the metaphysics that postulates a mono-logical Oneness. Ideas similar to these esoteric notions are found also in the work of the Argentinian author Jorge Luis Borges, a writer who greatly interested Khatibi. Borges's writing also reflects the degree to which Spanish culture coming to the New World carried with it the hidden imprint of centuries of Andalusian (Arabic) culture.

Khatibi's texts are permeated by his questioning of his own roles as writer, scribe, translator and author. Authors often affirm that their writing is preceded by emotions, images and thoughts that become expressed in words, sentences, paragraphs and texts, but in Khatibi's works we are in the presence of another methodology, one that inverts many of the principles of the former. Khatibi's writing in French is always haunted by the silent presence of the absent Arabic dialect, his mother tongue, which, like the return of the repressed, intrudes and disrupts his written French, which is therefore always a process of translation that tests the limits of intelligibility. But he is also 'subject to' the process of writing for which he often seems to be a *medium*.

We must readjust our notions of the author as 'source', and his relation to the object or subject (in the sense of topic) of writing, for from his earliest texts, such as *La Mémoire tatouée*, Khatibi has thrown this relation into doubt by asserting that in fact writing emerges spontaneously from deep layers of experience which thrust the author into what often seem like acts of improvisation, but which are equally acts of receptivity. They draw upon often forgotten elements of his past, but then, like the erased mother tongue, they resurface in coded ways.

One of the paradoxes of Taoist thought is its celebration of 'forgetting' as a regime that allows for one's natural resources (often referred to generally as 'the body') to become activated. This may help to explain the fertile effects that Khatibi's forgotten dialect has upon his writing in French. And his frequent allusions to wandering ['errances'] or drifting ['dérives'] are a type of *intention-less* movement that in the Tao is associated with discovery and achievement.[6]

Khatibi's 'disponibilité' echoes the notion of 'wu-wei', a type of consciousness that allows things to be as they are instead of interfering in their evolution. To Europeans, schooled to express themselves in external acts of mastery, such an attitude is perceived negatively as either passivity or lack of purpose, whereas in the Chinese traditions, inward stillness ['le vide'] is defined as a source of energy that assures the harmonious development of the world. Khatibi refers often to 'la pensée vide' ['the empty thought'] and all of his texts are essentially paradoxical quests that emerge from a sense of loss. But this emptiness or lack is not what it seems. Although haunted by his past, Khatibi revels in the present moment and places his trust in the future, however uncertain, as we understand from his frequent references to *'divination'* ['divination'], *'promesse'* ['promise'] and a life perpetually *'en devenir'* ['in the making']. The unanswered questions that abound in his texts are not only symptoms of his desire for dialogue, but also attest to the complex relation of memory to imagination, made explicit by his now famous dictum, 'je suis né demain' ['I was born tomorrow'].[7]

The question of authorship for Khatibi is tied to his sense of the writer as a scribe, in the sense that the word had in ninth-century Arabic culture. Paradoxically, many of the scribes in the Abbasid court were Persian, and they brought with them knowledge and refinement from cultures of the East, enriching Arabic culture through their experience and translations. They also participated in the translation of Greek science and philosophy. The function of the scribe, who was required

---

6 'Le bon nageur y parvient tout de suite parce qu'il *oublie* l'eau' ['Good swimmers acquire the ability quickly;– they forget the water'], cited in Jean-François Billeter, *Leçons sur le Tchouang-tseu* (Paris: Editions Allia, 2016, p. 59); *The Sacred Books of China: The Texts of Taoism, Part II*, trans. James Legge (New York: Dover Publications, 1962), p. 16.

7 Khatibi first uttered these words on the occasion of an art exhibit in Rabat. He later repeated it at an exposition at the Arab Institute in Paris. It became one of his favorite dictums.

to master several intellectual disciplines, was to *trans-scribe* realities from language to language and culture to culture, making possible an integrated vision that was superior to its individual parts. It can be said that such activities prepared the way for the revolution of the Renaissance in Europe. The subsequent reversal or 'decline' of the status of Oriental culture tends to obliterate these influences.[8]

Khatibi remembers the moment when, as a young colonized subject, he first discovered his own inner voice capable of (silent) speech in French, his adopted written language. Paradoxically, this moment prefigured his eventual emergence as an autonomous Subject from the long night of indenture to French culture. Indeed, his liberation as an author occurred in and through the language of the Other. This necessary relation, as complex and painful as it often was, is the key not only to understanding Khatibi's experience of his divided nature, but also his notion of hospitality, an ethical and epistemological obligation that he assumed throughout his life.

Khatibi understood early that in order to resist the state of victimization that had been the legacy of French occupation, he had to open his heart and mind to the unknown, and embark upon a perilous but fertile journey to discover other cultures, in order, paradoxically, to know himself. He saw in his own culture's fear and humiliation the danger of self-immolation or compensatory arrogance. Yet he also experienced the lure of becoming an uncritical simulacrum of the Other during his years as a student in Paris, where he became disappointed by the vanity of competing discourses that to him remained abstract and inappropriate to the archaeological and historical work he knew was necessary for Morocco.

Khatibi's interrogation of authorship also denies the role of the author as somehow superior or removed from his narration. In fact, Khatibi writes with the body, with all his senses, immersing himself in his own words and images where he often seems to float (a term he himself uses), transmuting himself into the materiality of signs themselves: 'J'ai rêvé, l'autre nuit, que mon corps était des mots' ['I dreamed, the other night, that my body was made of words'].[9] He surrenders to the powers of

8   This 'decline' continues to be the subject of lively debate in European culture.
9   Abdelkébir Khatibi, *La Mémoire tatouée: autobiographie d'un décolonisé* (Paris: Denoël, 1971), reprinted in *Œuvres de Abdelkébir Khatibi I: Romans et récits* (Paris: La Différence, 2008), pp. 9–113 (p. 53); *Tattooed Memory*, trans. Peter Thompson (Paris: Harmattan, 2016), p. 69.

language more than he 'authors' them: 'La langue nous écrit et nous lit [...]. Le sujet qui écrit n'est pas celui qui écrit, mais il s'entend, il s'écrit, il se lit dans le même acte' ['Language writes us and reads us [...]. The "subject" is not the one who writes, but the one who hears himself, writes himself and reads himself in the same act'].[10] This surrender is at the heart of Khatibi's radical adventure into what he will call 'l'impensé' ['the unthought'] or 'la pensée vide' ['the empty thought'].

Khatibi's writing upsets the scientific principles based on the dualistic vision of Subject and Object, of observer and thing observed, so that they begin to interpenetrate, and this porosity of boundaries and fluidity of identities is endemic to the cosmologies of the Tao and the Vedas as well as to the hermetic sciences. As strange as it may seem, one of the ironies of these neglected traditions is that aspects of very modern science, such as quantum physics and string theory, have reconnected with the ideas of the Greeks, such as Plotinus and Pythagoras, who studied with the Egyptian priests, and with the Arabs who revised their discoveries.

Khatibi's desire to reinscribe the relation of Self and Other within a structure of respect and reciprocity rather than one of dominance and exclusion proceeds from his intuition of analogies between apparently dichotomous entities. This idea is also reflected in the concept of microcosm and macrocosm found in esoteric thought, by which each of the smallest cellular units of life are tied to the very greatest, not only in form, but in function. This is not intended as a metaphor, as most contemporary thinkers would assume. And it is an idea that is consistent with developments in recent science, where correspondences may exist between entities separated by great distances that are able nonetheless to influence each other. Khatibi's writing exhibits an uncanny intuition of these principles. He also sees in literary texts the traces of these concepts. His early appreciation of Baudelaire is not based solely on the poet's aesthetics or his melancholy; it is also epistemological, due to the structure of correspondences in the poet's work that defy conventional logic and cross boundaries of culture, time and space.

Khatibi is haunted by his own deracination and estrangement that issued from being born into a conflicted cultural and linguistic identity. Because of his status as a colonized subject who attended both Qur'anic

---

10   Abdelkébir Khatibi, 'Bilinguisme et littérature', *in Maghreb pluriel* (Paris: Denoël, 1983), pp. 177–207 (p. 181); 'Bilingualism and Literature', in *Plural Maghreb*, trans. P. Burcu Yalim (London: Bloomsbury, 2019), pp. 117–40 (pp. 118–19).

and French schools, he experienced the division of his psyche between the popular imaginary of the world of his Moroccan dialect, never written, and the world discovered through the French language whose writing he mastered rapidly, but delayed speaking. That which Khatibi termed his own 'frailty' and 'instability' (he speaks, too, of an unbalanced gait), his febrile agitation at moments and his passivity at others, are all symptoms of his situation living 'entre-deux', obliged constantly to negotiate his survival in the interstitial spaces between contrary languages, signs and cultural ideals.

Khatibi speaks often of this double self, of the effects of his diglossia, which he traces back to his earliest separation from his mother and his belonging to two cities of origin, Essaouira and El Jadida. His initiation into the world of signs came first from his mother and the women of his family, then the Qur'an, but the mastery of written signs, transmitted through the French language, was an apprenticeship at once painful and ecstatic. The 'exile' that characterized most of Khatibi's life, even after returning to Rabat, is tied to his heightened consciousness of his relation to cultural difference but primarily to the difference endemic to language and his estranged place in it. But, as we know, this 'difference', this gap or chasm, would also become the generative source of Khatibi's unorthodox literary development.

The writing of the Qur'an remained both intimate (threaded into his earliest memories) but to some degree alien, because he felt that it was indentured to a sclerotic patriarchal mentality, providing a certain protection to his people but depriving them of emerging into full autonomy. And the rigid memorization of words he did not understand was an anathema to his adventurous imagination. But the early exposure to the reading of the Qur'an introduced him to the art of calligraphy, that of the painted sign and the spatialization of the word that would preoccupy him throughout his life.

Khatibi's use of written signs reflects an appreciation of their inherent complexity and a far broader conception of the sign than that which has prevailed since the eighteenth century in Europe, the one which was exported to the colonies through French schools. In *Pèlerinage d'un artiste amoureux* (2003), Khatibi recounts the travels across the Mediterranean and within Morocco of his grandfather, an artisan whose perceptions of the world are filtered by his sensitivity to the intricate material forms through which cultures express their values and aspirations. We discover a notion of the sign which includes other signifying modalities in Raïssi's ability to 'read' cultural situations and values inscribed in architecture and design, but also in rhythms and registers of speech and gesture.[11]

Khatibi's exploration of Berber tattoos and carpet design as well as artefacts of other 'civilizations of the sign', led him to revise the history of his own patrimony and which had been distorted in its relations with Europe, which were often seen as one in which Morocco had everything to learn, but also to *un*learn, from France. But he was also inspired to dismantle the shackles of dualistic thinking and the hierarchical categories that Europe believed it inherited from the Greeks. Khatibi revealed that Europe took only what served her interests from that tradition, putting aside all of its *oriental* knowledge.[12]

Khatibi's discovery of Japanese culture revealed to him the beauty of silence, which he learned to appreciate as a positive value rather than a sign of absence, disinterest or ignorance, as it is sometimes understood in Western cultures. Learning about Chinese and Japanese cultures, traditions in which the sign retains its spiritual redolence and polysemic force, Khatibi was dazzled, paradoxically, by their use of shadow in visual representation, which contrasted with the Mediterranean love of sunlight as a paradigm of radiant beauty. The subtle use of stillness, silence and shadow in Asian cultures, allied with the symbolism of the moon, introduced Khatibi to a different aesthetic whose delicacy and discretion resonated with deep affinities of his own.

Writing, which for Khatibi is always at least a bilingual and often a pluri-lingual endeavour (he dreamed of writing 'in languages'), suggests analogies with the texts of both Sufism and the Tao, but also hermetic texts, which are characterized by paradox and oxymoron. We encounter them frequently in Khatibi's texts: 'une violence si douce' ['such a sweet violence'], 'cette joie en détresse' ['this joy in distress'], 'l'os du vide' ['the bone of emptiness'], 'une lenteur ramassée' ['a terse slowness'] and many more, and of course they are also present in the formulation of entire sentences. Khatibi's paradoxes are not signs of a desire to be contrary or obscure; they are for him the only way to 'clarify' language and free it from the accumulated stereotypes embedded in the French language by France's colonial history.

11   The Structuralists, such as Roland Barthes, return to a broader notion of the sign and of writing, as in *Système de la mode* (1967) or *Le Degré zéro de l'écriture* (1953).
12   Many Greeks, like Pythagoras, Plotinus and even Plato, spent long years studying the hermetic sciences with Egyptian priests.

Lao Tzu is said to have declared that the words of truth are always paradoxical. The Tao itself is unnamable (a term used often by Khatibi), but the Tao is often inadequately translated as 'the way', a principle structuring both the cosmos and individual physical experience and consciousness. It is hardly accidental that Khatibi admired Victor Segalen and spent much of his own time travelling. He also describes his own solitary walks, his 'déambulations' ['wanderings'] in his own and foreign cities, which became forms of meditation, allowing Khatibi to observe the unexplored traces of material culture. For Sufis as well as Buddhists, the notion of a 'path' is understood as a progressive divestment of earthly attachments, whereby the individual frees himself from earthly desires and becomes increasingly 'transparent'. Although Khatibi never espouses asceticism, he does try to divest himself of false beliefs and egotistical attitudes.

For Taoists, 'the way' can also be understood as a 'method' by which the individual frees his mind of sterile ratiocination and relaxes in the calm observation of the intuitive actions of the body: 'To a mind that is "still", the whole universe surrenders'.[13] This 'inner quiet' becomes the source of unimagined creative energies. Khatibi and the characters of his texts are creatures of reflection and solitude; they are always 'en retrait' ['withdrawn'], even when actively engaged with others.

Ostracized by the Church and the State, the Hermetic sciences such as Astrology and Alchemy, as well as the science of numbers and letters, but also Gnosticism and varieties of Neoplatonism, were marginalized and frequently condemned as heresies. Certain thinkers, such as Al-Hallāj, Giordano Bruno and many more, were executed by the state and religious authorities. They were considered dangerous because they implied that individuals could have direct contact with the absolute. In modern times, some of these traditions persist in the practices of the Rosicrucians and Freemasons, as well as in various forms of black and white magic, but they are considered by most people to be irrational occult beliefs, without any basis in science. In fact, the esoteric traditions generally disavow the separation of Science and the Arts, because many artistic endeavours, such as architecture, rely on precise geometrical calculations, as do the weaving of carpets and the decorative arts. And navigation as well as the Islamic calendar relied on

---

13   Lao Tzu, *Tao Te Ching*, cited by Arthur Waley, *The Way and its Power: A Study of the* Tao Tê Ching *and its Place in Chinese Thought* (New York: Grove Press, 1958), p. 58.

the exact position of the stars and planets.[14] They were also convinced that all the arts were naturally theoretical, a position Khatibi has often affirmed.[15] Khatibi understood that the arts, like languages, were palimpsests, incorporating buried layers of diverse creations of the past and containing traces of forgotten encounters. Khatibi's keen interest in the plastic arts, as well as in dance and music, especially jazz, issued from his understanding that they were material and spiritual languages that crossed boundaries and expressed universal concepts in a more organic way than could intellectual ideologies and abstractions.

The esoteric sciences also saw history as cyclical rather than linear, although not as a series of static repetitions, but as a spiral evolution.[16] Their vision of time differed from the notion of a chronological sequence of strict cause and effect, and this idea is reflected in many of Khatibi's narratives which leap forward and loop back upon themselves, often confounding his readers who are accustomed to more logical thought processes. The hermetic sciences subscribed to the idea of synchronicity or simultaneity, whereby all events are ever-present, and this is indeed the effect of much of Khatibi's writing, which often includes moments of a trance-like suspension.

Memory constitutes one of Khatibi's persistent obsessions, and in several of his works he explores remote areas of his past, gleaning from them elements that inform his later discoveries. For the Sufis, memory has a dual character: its passive aspect retains impressions (*al-hafz*), but its active nature (*al-dhikr*) is directly related to the spirit that apprehends the timeless presence of eternal essences: 'Si le souvenir peut évoquer le passé dans le présent, c'est que le présent contient virtuellement toute l'extension du temps' ['If memory can evoke the past, it is because the present contains virtually the entire extension of time'].[17]

14　Pythagoras of Samos is credited with perceiving the relation of mathematics to music.

15　Among contemporary scientists whose interests bridge the gap between the hard sciences and the humanities, Nassim Haramein, the director of the Resonance Project in California, is a fine example.

16　In his account of the theories of Ibn Khaldûn in 'Double Critique', Khatibi points out the limitations of Khaldûn's new 'historical' science which fails to analyse sufficiently pertinent historical realities. See Abdelkébir Khatibi, 'Double critique', in *Maghreb pluriel* (Paris: Editions Denoël, 1983), pp. 43–111 (pp. 81–7); *Plural Maghreb*, trans. P. Burcu Yalim, (London: Bloomsbury, 2019), pp. 25–71 (pp. 51–4).

17　Titus Burkhardt, *Introductions aux doctrines ésotériques de l'Islam* (Paris: Editions Dervy, 1996 [1969]), p. 132.

In his essay on Abdelwahab Meddeb's *Talismano*, Khatibi observes that writing in French for an Arab involves incessant reminiscences through the interference of the native dialect which silently displaces and decentres the appropriated language. The memory of Arabic is inscribed indelibly in the senses (the body) of the author:

> Il y a là une force d'amnésie en abîme, la substitution d'une mémoire à une autre, ou plutôt et plus exactement: un enchâssement sans cesse rompu, retrouvé, détaché de son unité, mouvement pris dans un oubli vertigineux, qui travaille à se fragmenter dans fin.

> [Here is a power of amnesia *en abyme*, the substitution of one memory for another, or rather and more precisely – an embedding constantly broken, detached from its unity, movement caught in a vertiginous forgetting, which works to fragment itself endlessly.][18]

And, later in the same text:

> C'est pourquoi cette forme de texte est plus ou moins hermétique: elle se cherche, dans la confusion linguistique, une clarté impossible, *une clarté qui souffre* dans le texte, une clarté frappée par l'impensé.

> [That is why this form of text is more or less hermetic – it seeks, in the linguistic confusion, an impossible clarity, *a clarity that suffers* in the text, a clarity of thought touched by the unthought.][19]

Although dialects are oral forms of Arabic, they share many features with the standard written language. Arabic contains the memory of its archaic forms, bearing traces of earlier Semitic languages such as Aramaic. It cannot be reduced simply to an alphabetical order as European linguists have attempted to do. Khatibi calls their ignorance of the effects of grammar as well as the diacritical marks on the meanings of words 'an ethnocentric reduction'. This language is the vehicle of different structures of thought, and Arabic grammar is often described as an epistemology in itself. As Khatibi affirms, Arabic is structured according to a different logic from that of European languages. And the written language is not a neutral medium of signification, for 'la calligraphie arabe [...] transforme, dans la lecture, l'énoncé même d'un texte; ou bien [...] se réfère à la mystique musulmane des lettres, par exemple' ['Arabic calligraphy [...]

---

18   Khatibi, *Maghreb pluriel*, p. 196; *Plural Maghreb*, pp. 130–1.
19   Ibid., p. 197; p. 131.

transforms, when reading, the very utterance of a text – or [...] refers to the Islamic mysticism of letters'].[20]

Khatibi exploits the polysemy of the language of Arabic, where, like other Semitic languages, words expand into derivations that may seem very distant from one another in meaning, but are connected by common consonantal roots. Reading, therefore, can never be a linear experience, because Arabic moves simultaneously in multiple directions to create meaning, evoking echoes and traces of other encounters as it proceeds. For Khatibi, writing in French is always a mysterious adventure, an activity that resembles a 'combinatoire': 'elle est épreuve, quête, recherche de l'imprévu, sinon de l'inouï' ['it is an ordeal, a quest, a search for the unexpected if not the unheard-of'].[21] It involves a kind of acrobatic dance, giving rise to surprising shifts of register and focus. Khatibi takes risks, playing with French as if it possessed the flexibility and polysemy of Arabic. The effect is to endow familiar words with unexpected connotations, achieved in part by their being displaced from familiar contexts and set against other words that alter their meaning. Khatibi was himself surprised by the discovery of new dimensions of meaning that his writing produced and took pleasure in inventing new words. We only have to think of examples such as 'pensée-autre', 'double critique' and 'aimance', and although the last pre-dates Khatibi's use he endowed it with new resonance.

Khatibi's writing in French itself functions like a palimpsest and engenders mirror-like inversions. The hermetic traditions entertained a conception of truth that is palpable in Khatibi's unorthodox use of language. The European Renaissance and the advent of perspective in painting introduced a notion of truth based upon what the Prince could consume visually in one sitting, an idea that developed into a narrow correlation between reality and visual perception. The oriental traditions, however, conceive of the world as a complex structure of appearances which are most often illusory (*al-Thâhir*) and understand reality as veiled (*al-Bâtin*), hidden, its secrets accessible only by a process that is both a decryption and a type of translation in which meanings often contradict one another. Language may be a privileged vehicle of truth, but its meanings are subject to unexpected metamorphoses. Nonetheless, the apparent and the hidden levels of language are also like

---

20   Ibid., p. 182; p. 119.
21   Abdelkébir Khatibi, *La Langue de l'autre* (New York and Tunis: Les Mains secrètes, 1999), p. 24.

the sides of a coin, and represent, in different ways, the two faces of a larger reality.

Khatibi's texts are permeated by his own shifting perceptions of familiar phenomena and meditations on the paradoxical relation of the visible to the invisible, as of presence to absence and sound to silence. His sensitivity to traces and echoes of all kinds informs his analyses and his creative process, in which he seems to navigate between states of bewilderment and ecstatic vision. He is his own witness, in that he chronicles his desires, dreams, illusions and disillusions, which are revalued and reconfigured by his uncanny play with language.

The dichotomies between the visible and the invisible, between illusion and reality, are in some ways analogous to the relation of dream to waking states, which for the mystical or esoteric traditions was understood very differently from the views prevailing in modern culture. For the ancients, dreams were a mode of consciousness that spoke in riddles, in the language of the rebus, like the Egyptian hieroglyphs, combining iconic, symbolic and phonetic signifying systems in which word-units are broken up and rearranged to form new meanings. For traditional cultures, dreams communicate truths that often cannot be accessed in waking states, and they must be deciphered in order for their wisdom to be effective. Khatibi frequently refers to dreams that mingle with memories and imagination, which for him, too, are alternative means of knowing.

Khatibi describes his early days at school when he lived his life 'à l'envers' ['upside down']: 'Mon rythme, rêver quand travaillaient les autres, lire quand ils dormaient, fuguer, toujours fuguer, regarder par un trou les signes extérieurs' ['My rhythm: dreaming while the others worked, reading when they slept, running away, always running away, watching the signs of the outside world through a hole'].[22] He often refers to himself as a 'dormeur éveillé', or lucid dreamer, by which he may gesture to Marcel Proust and the conundrum of memory and forgetting, but also refers to an expansion of consciousness, in which the paradoxical truths of dreams may become manifest. In fact, his writing resembles the uncanny logic of dreams. He speaks of 'le rêve éveillé de toute écriture' ['the waking dream of all writing'], which he calls 'le rêve fou' ['the mad dream'].[23]

We know that Khatibi was preoccupied with problems of translation, between his native dialect of spoken Arabic and French, between French

22 Khatibi, *La Mémoire tatouée*, p. 54; *Tattooed Memory*, p. 71.
23 Khatibi, *Maghreb pluriel*, p. 197; *Plural Maghreb*, p. 131.

and other languages he learned, such as English and Swedish, but, most importantly, he saw the need for translation *within* French, in order to render it a suppler instrument that could express what had not before been possible for him as a colonized subject: 'langue tierce, le français se substitue à la diglossie en se *traduisant lui-même du français en français*' ['as third language, French substitutes for the diglossia by *translating itself from the French into French*'].[24] Some of the radical epistemological implications of esoteric cultures are transmitted through Khatibi's syntax, which recomposes conventional patterns of Cartesian thought to yield unexpected effects.

Khatibi believed that syntax was an essential feature of his writing: 'Elle initie à l'art de la vie fait rythme' ['It initiates us to the art of life as rhythm'].[25] And also,

> La syntaxe nous apprend à enchâsser et à contrôler le discontinu, à nous éveiller à une fluidité de l'être, à meubler l'ordre par le désordre, le risque par la mesure du silence, de la ponctuation, du vide radieux.[26]

> [Syntax teaches us to embed and control discontinuity, to be stimulated by the fluidity of being, to enrich order with disorder, and risk with the measurement of silence, punctuation and radiant emptiness.]

Khatibi's syntax often reflects that of Arabic in that it diverges from the hierarchical clarity of subordinated clauses typical of French. He makes use of the *masdar*, or verbal noun, which corresponds to the gerund that seems to suspend time. At other moments he simply creates sentences that lack verbs altogether, which is quite common in Arabic. He plays with referents and pronouns, shifting from 'I' to 'he' to 'we' and to 'you', and this slippage of pronouns impedes the reader's ability to discern antecedents and relationships, blurring the writer's tracks, so to speak, and forcing the reader to reconsider the orientation of his statements as well as to whom they refer. This echoes the hermetic notion of plural identities, and it is also evidence of the impact of Khatibi's diglossia on his writing in French. Despite his doubts about

---

24   Khatibi, *Maghreb pluriel*, p. 188; *Plural Maghreb*, p. 124. This is one of the main themes of his article entitled 'Le Nom et le pseudonyme', in Abdelkébir Khatibi, *La Langue de l'autre* (New York and Tunis: Les Mains secrètes, 1998), pp. 36–43.

25   Abdelkébir Khatibi, 'La Langue de l'autre', in *Œuvres de Abdelkébir Khatibi III: Essais* (Paris: La Différence, 2008), pp. 115–35 (p. 126).

26   Ibid.

his own sanity and his obsession with amnesia, Khatibi demonstrates, in his sometimes jazz-like compositions, that nothing is completely lost, everything is always potentially accessible through the act of writing 'in languages'.

It may well be that Khatibi's enthusiastic appreciation of Meddeb's *Talismano* is related to its hermetic character. In his discussion of Meddeb's text, Khatibi seizes upon the title, which in English means 'talisman', but also speaks of Meddeb's transformation of the letters of his own name as signs of a hidden history, referring to the alchemical science of letters in Arabic mysticism. Khatibi speaks of the baroque surface of Meddeb's rhetoric as the author's way of provoking 'un dérangement de la structure monolingue' ['a disruption of the monolingual structure'].[27] Khatibi's writing, too, is elaborate and rife with recondite terms, and seems to want to extend indefinitely the threshold of sense. Pushing the limits of meaning, he often adds a series of phrases that are apposite to the main clause that imbue his thought with contradictory nuances. He also uses words that deviate from the reader's expectations in ways that require 'translation', because their sequence renders their meaning oblique.

Such examples are myriad; here is one from his essay on the Mosaic:

> J'affirme cet enthousiasme de la pensée – dans sa sensualité la plus abstraite qui soit – en tant qu'alternance cadencée entre la gravité d'un jeu somptueux (l'art et ses célébrations) et cette angoisse, parfois terrible et terrifiante, qui nous projette vers l'œuvre aimée, dans l'oubli de toute volonté.

> [I affirm this willingness of thought – in its most abstract sensuality – as cadenced alternation between the gravity of a splendid play (art and its celebrations) and this anguish, at times terrible and terrifying, which projects us toward the beloved work of art, in the forgetting of all will.][28]

His sentences seem to resonate after they end, as if we are witnessing only the minute visible part of a vast process of reflection that moves like a river carrying along images of which we only catch glimpses before they disappear into the current. His writing suggests affinities with hermetic elements of both water and air. In *La Mémoire tatouée* and *Amour bilingue* there are passages where Khatibi swims alone under

---

27   Khatibi, *Maghreb pluriel*, p. 197; *Plural Maghreb*, p. 131.
28   Khatibi, 'Questions d'art', in *Maghreb pluriel*, pp. 209–54 (p. 239); 'Questions of Art', in *Plural Maghreb*, pp. 141–73 (p. 153).

the stars when he feels extremes of either joy or pain. The sea evokes memories of his mother(s), but we recognize that such experiences are more than strong sensory or sensual pleasures: they speak of an ontological sympathy with the elements that conditions Khatibi's entire vision of the world.

We remember the strange exultation he experiences when, caught by waves in a violent storm, he wades back into the water to be buffeted further by the waves; or when he swims at night for hours or floated, gazing up at the stars.

> Ce qu'il aimait dans la mer, c'était cette antique idée de l'errance, qui retenait, dans ses plis, sa folie de la langue. [...] Balancement euphorique: être cet écoulement, n'être que cet écoulement. Il regarda le bleu du ciel. Ce regard lui donna un tel désir de vie.

> [What he loved about the sea was the ancient idea of wandering which kept, in its folds, its madness of language. [...] Euphoric balancing: to be this flow, to be nothing but this flow. He looked up at the blue of the sky. This glance gave him such an appetite for life.][29]

Khatibi's association with the element of air is evident in the countless images of birds such as the swallow and the magic falcon, just as they are in his frequent use of words connoting winged flight to describe his own emotional states. Other aspects that speak of the ethereal dimension of his character are found in his 'oisiveté' ['idleness'], his 'détachement' ['detachment'], his 'volatilité' ['volatility'] and his 'égarement' ['wandering']. As we have observed, such states are valued positively by Asian cultures, and they connote spiritual intelligence in the hermetic sciences. Indeed, Khatibi's writing exhibits aspects of what we might term 'alchemical' processes. Transmuting the complexity of individual sensory and emotional experience into spiritual insight, it moves relentlessly along a horizontal plane, but often seems to collapse into vertigo, or be drawn upward in a kind of vertical trance, as his words ply through veils of perplexity or dejection towards a dream of clarity and coherence. At other times, he acts upon language as might a master craftsman working with wood or stucco, much like Raïssi in *Pèlerinage*, seeing in inarticulate matter and emotional chaos the potentiality of pure forms which he arduously refines out of opacity into illumination.

Despite, or perhaps because of, its complexity, much of Khatibi's writing involves the transmutation of meaning from what we may term

---

29 Khatibi, *Amour bilingue*, p. 235; *Love in Two Languages*, pp. 44–5.

a consolidated, reified state to one of mobility and lightness. To take but one example, in his description of the mosaic, Khatibi offers a metaphor for the process of writing by entering into the movement of the plastic forms of a figure that is both a symbol and the vehicle of the transformation of matter into spirit. Its contemplation induces a sort of trance:

> Je ne décrirai pas la rosace. Elle se décrit elle-même [...] cette mosaïque est un rythme, allant de la matière au signe et du signe au langage. Langage qui, au gré de son expansion, se déploie, s'écoule, jaillit dans ces motifs de décoration encore innomés.

> [I shall not describe the *rosace*. It describes itself [...] this mosaic is a rhythm, going from the matter to the sign and from the sign to language. Language, which, as it expands, unfolds, flows, and springs forth in these as yet unnamed decorative motifs.][30]

We have seen that Khatibi's revolutionary writing bears traces of ancient esoteric traditions that empower him to renew and revise our modern cultural investments. These congealed ideologies have effaced alternative ways of seeing, thinking and writing and have obscured epistemological and ethical principles that are urgently needed in the modern world. As a final paradox, we may think of Khatibi's work as a modern analogy of the work accomplished centuries ago by the Islamic thinkers who translated and revised the traditions of Asia, Mesopotamia, Egypt and Greece, transmitting knowledge that was essential to the flowering of European modernity.

---

30   Khatibi, *Maghreb pluriel*, p. 229; *Plural Maghreb*, pp. 152–3.

CHAPTER TWELVE

The Carpet as a Text, the Writer as a Weaver

Reading the Moroccan Carpet with Abdelkébir Khatibi

Khalid Lyamlahy

Ce n'est pas un hasard si j'ai choisi le tapis.

[It is no coincidence that I chose the carpet.]

Abdelkébir Khatibi[1]

In 1985, Abdelkébir Khatibi opened his contribution to a colloquium dedicated to his works with this original reflection: 'il faudrait regarder un beau tapis comme on lit une page d'Aristote, c'est-à-dire avec la même force d'attention' ['one must look at a beautiful carpet as one reads a page by Aristotle, that is, with the same acute attention'].[2] Khatibi's call to read the carpet as a text, and, even more, one of Greek philosophy, suggests that the carpet is not only a woven fabric whose reading requires a high degree of mental focus but also an intricate web of representations, images and meanings. Khatibi's interest in the carpet, which has surprisingly received little attention, is all the more important

---

1   In Christine Buci-Glucksmann, Antoine Raybaud, Abdelhaï Diouri, Marc Gontard, Abdesslam Benabdelali, Abdelfattah Kilito, Abdallah Bounfour, Jaques Hassoun and Réda Bensmaïa, *Imaginaires de l'autre: Khatibi et la mémoire littéraire* (Paris: L'Harmattan, 1987), p. 183. Unless otherwise stated, all translations are the author's.

2   Abdelkébir Khatibi, 'Intersignes', ibid., pp. 123–31 (p. 123).

in that the carpet can also be read, as I would argue in this essay, as a metaphor for his prolific and multidimensional œuvre. For Khatibi's work skilfully weaves together a wide range of sources and materials borrowed as much from Western philosophy and literature as from Islamic and Moroccan culture.

In her oft-quoted article, Françoise Lionnet has demonstrated that 'Khatibi's method of double critique is the philosophical equivalent of a material practice best described by a sewing or stitching metaphor used in the arts of weaving or quilting'[3] and which consists in a 'constant back-and-forth to link and delink different objects as well as different analytics'.[4] This motion, central to Khatibi's dialectical writing, is 'directed forward and back towards what precedes it so as to overlap with it, envelop it, and then point toward its exterior so as to move beyond it'.[5] While Lionnet's reading has the merit of bringing to light Khatibi's interest in the process of weaving in relation to his philosophical thought, I would argue that this interest needs further investigation in the field of artistic creation. More specifically, Khatibi's reading of the Moroccan carpet weaves together socio-cultural, semiotic and literary meanings, and encourages a more complex understanding of the weaving process itself in relation to religious practice, feminine agency and narrative techniques. My main focus throughout this essay will be on *Du signe à l'image: le tapis marocain*, an art book written by Khatibi in collaboration with Moroccan anthropologist and museologist Ali Amahan, first published in 1995 and translated into English three years later. The historical and technical sections of the book were written by Amahan while Khatibi contributed the introduction, the third section on the aesthetics of the carpet and a series of scattered notes and reflections. The book features an impressive number of photographs of carpets from museums and private collections, accompanied by a selection of poems, tales, literary texts and fragments of thought. This hybrid and multilayered structure reproduces the layout of the carpet as a combination of shapes, units and colours. The journey from the sign to the image suggested by the title is further reflected in the structure

---

3   Françoise Lionnet, 'Counterpoint and Double Critique in Edward Said and Abdelkébir Khatibi: A Transcolonial Comparison', in Dominic Thomas and Ali Behdad (eds), *A Companion to Comparative Literature* (Chichester: Wiley Blackwell, 2011), pp. 387–407 (p. 392).

4   Ibid., pp. 404–5.

5   Ibid., p. 405.

of the book itself: the Moroccan carpet allows for a circulation of signs and significations between texts and illustrations, orality and writing, literature and art.

In the final section of *Du signe à l'image*, Khatibi identifies five possible levels on which the carpet can be approached. The historical and technical approach identifies and describes forms, styles, schemes and materials used in carpet manufacturing. The linguistic or onomastic approach explores the names of these elements and how they relate to the surrounding human and natural environment. The semiotic, ethnologic and anthropologic approaches consider the carpet as respectively a composition of signs, a reflected image of social structures and a laboratory of human imaginaries. While the volume draws on these various analytical techniques, Khatibi contends that the study of the carpet entails an immersion into 'l'image ornementale de la pensée' ['the decorative image of thought'].[6] In the English translation, this immersion is significantly described as 'communion', a word that emphasizes the seductive nature of the carpet as a piece of art that encourages dialogue and harmony with signs, forms and colours.

For Khatibi, I would argue, writing about the Moroccan carpet is first a continuation of his broader project of decolonizing Moroccan culture and promoting its popular forms, which he initiated in his early sociological work and developed throughout his subsequent publications, including *La Blessure du nom propre* (1974) and the three volumes written in collaboration with Mohamed Sijelmassi.[7] Khatibi's interest in the Moroccan carpet is later confirmed by his contribution to the catalogue of a significant exhibition organized between December 2004 and March 2005 at the Institut du Monde Arabe in Paris.[8] As Khatibi explains in his late autobiography, *Le Scribe et son ombre*, all these contributions share the same goal: 'réhabiliter, ou plutôt restituer à la culture populaire, quand elle n'a pas disparu, sa dignité théorique' ['rehabilitate popular culture, or, rather, if it hasn't disappeared, restore

6 Abdelkébir Khatibi and Ali Amahan, *Du signe à l'image: le tapis marocain* (Casablanca: LAK International, 1994), p. 168; *From Sign to Image: the Moroccan Carpet* [trans. anon.] (Casablanca: LAK International: 1997), p. 168.

7 See their *L'Art calligraphique arabe* (Paris: Editions du Chêne, 1976), *L'Art calligraphique de l'Islam* (Paris: Gallimard, 1994) and *Civilisation marocaine: arts et cultures* (Arles: Actes Sud, 1999).

8 See Abdelkébir Khatibi, 'Le Tapis dans l'imaginaire de l'Orient', in *Le Ciel dans un Tapis* (Ghent: Editions Snoeck, 2004), pp. 40–9.

its theoretical dignity'].[9] The carpet, like other forms of popular culture, suffers from a lack of theoretical consideration and is often reduced to a folkloric or banal object of decoration. Thus, Khatibi's and Amahan's volume seeks at once to challenge this commonplace by outlining the complexity of the carpet as a cultural product, and to recover its history from the legacy of colonial scholarship.

In the historical section of *Du signe à l'image*, Amahan notes how the French Department of Indigenous Arts began, soon after the Protectorate, to take an interest in the carpet industry and produced a significant although incomplete catalogue of Moroccan carpets. Khatibi's and Amahan's book – without being exhaustive – still provides an original postcolonial Moroccan response to the early investigations conducted by French scholars. Amahan's contribution, for instance, draws on and offers a critical overview of the work of Prosper Ricard, the honorary director of the 'Service des Métiers et des Arts Marocains' ['Department of Moroccan Arts and Professions'], created at the initiative of Marshal Lyautey. This postcolonial dimension is also visible on a symbolic level as the Moroccan carpet has shown an impressive ability to resist the import of foreign products and techniques, thanks paradoxically to the measures taken by the colonial power itself. In a publication dated 1952, Ricard is pleased to note that,

> pour le maintien de traditions aussi originales et affirmées, au triple point de vue de la technique, du décor ou du coloris [...] le gouvernement du Protectorat a pris dès le début les mesures de protection, d'encouragement et de propagande qui s'imposaient.[10]

> [In order to maintain, from a technical, decorative, and colour-based perspective, such original and well-established traditions [...] the government of the Protectorate has taken from the outset the appropriate measures in terms of protection, encouragement and propaganda.]

As explained by Amahan, these measures included technical studies, quality control and financial aid. Although the aim of the colonial power was to control cultural production and make carpets available for the French market, 'les tapis marocains ont pu résister à l'invasion de nouveaux produits et de nouvelles techniques, introduites d'ailleurs avec la colonisation' ['Moroccan carpets were able to withstand the invasion of new products and techniques introduced from outside along

---

9   Abdelkébir Khatibi, *Le Scribe et son ombre* (Paris: La Différence, 2008), p. 49.
10   Prosper Ricard, *Tapis Marocains* (Paris: Georges Lang, 1952), p. 12.

with colonisation'].[11] Produced in cities (like Rabat, Casablanca and Fez) and mountain regions (the Middle and the High Atlas), moving between Oriental borrowings, local traditional styles and new transgressive models, the history of the Moroccan carpet can be seen as a reflected image of the longevity, the diversity and the complexity of Moroccan identity. Reading the Moroccan carpet is another way of revisiting postcolonial history through the lens of artistic creation.

My second contention, which I will develop in this essay, is that Khatibi uses the Moroccan carpet as a disguised way to reflect on literary creation. By exploring the aesthetics of an art piece that conveys multiple meanings, resists unidirectional readings, favours interplay between form and content and fosters dialogue between reality and the imaginary, Khatibi foregrounds his reading of the Moroccan carpet in an original and productive dialogue with literature. The carpet as a text and the writer as a weaver are the two foundations of a dynamic representation of the act of creation that echoes Khatibi's multilayered intellectual and literary production. This essay will demonstrate that Khatibi conceives of the Moroccan carpet not only as a geometric and chromatic composition, but also as an intersemiotic surface that conveys and challenges a wide range of meanings, grounded in religious, social, spatial, temporal and literary spheres. In this fragmented yet inspiring approach to the Moroccan carpet, Khatibi offers a practical model of interdisciplinary thought while acknowledging the open-ended nature of literary and artistic creation. Furthermore, there is something in the Moroccan carpet that resists commentary and drives the writer to the fascinating if not troubling realm of rituals, mystery and magic. 'On peut enrouler un tapis comme un talisman et le dérouler comme un hiéroglyphe' ['One can roll up a carpet like a talisman and unroll it in the form of a hieroglyph']:[12] the carpet awakens desire and stimulates thought and imagination beyond critical discourse.

An Intersemiotic Surface

Khatibi's reading of the Moroccan carpet is based on the pivotal notion of the intersign. Throughout the volume, Khatibi insists on the way in

---

11   Khatibi and Amahan, *Du signe à l'image*, pp. 39–40; *From Sign to Image*, p. 40.
12   Ibid., p. 150; p. 150.

which the carpet embodies various signs, combines different levels of representation and draws inspiration from other artistic disciplines. As he puts it in the final section, the design of the carpet is characterized by three signs: 'les signes codés et connus par les usagers, les signes d'un langage oublié et fragmentaire, et les signes imaginaires, inventés par les tisseuses et les tisseurs' ['coded signs known to their users, signs from a forgotten and fragmentary language, and imaginary signs invented by the weavers themselves'].[13] As a result, the manufacture of the Moroccan carpet is a multilayered process of codification, recovery and invention. By embedding various categories of signs, the carpet exemplifies the ideas of encounter and fusion in the realm of artistic creation. In his introduction, Khatibi notes that these ideas are not specific to Moroccan carpets: 'dans les tapis-jardins d'Orient', for instance, 'la fête du regard nous prépare à un admirable dialogue entre différents arts' ['Feasting our eyes on the garden-like carpets of the Orient is a prelude to a wonderful dialogue between the different arts'],[14] including calligraphy, mosaics and architecture. This artistic dialogue as a basis for critical discourse finds a resonance in a number of Khatibi's works. In *L'Art calligraphique de l'Islam*, one of the three collective art books written with Sijelmassi, Khatibi reads the work of Iranian painter Charles Hossein Zenderoudi as 'une fête de signe que le tapis persan, immémorialement, a légué à la plus haute tradition de l'art' ['a feast of signs which the Persian carpet has immemorially bequeathed to the highest art tradition'].[15] Each of Zenderoudi's paintings is based on 'l'illusion de la réversibilité: tantôt ce tableau représente l'apparence d'un manuscrit, tantôt celui d'un talisman ou d'un tapis ou d'un arabesque' ['an illusory reversal: the painting has at times the appearance of a manuscript and at other times that of a talisman, a carpet or an arabesque'].[16] The work of Islamic art gains from the reversibility, interlacing and transfer of artistic patterns. An object of artistic dialogue, the carpet is an emblematic symbol of this 'civilisation du signe' ['civilisation of the sign'] that is Islam.[17]

With this in mind, reading the Moroccan carpet amounts to searching for a secret embedded not only in a web of ethnological symbols,

13   Ibid., p. 159; p. 156.
14   Ibid., p. 13; p. 13.
15   Abdelkébir Khatibi, 'Calligraphie et peinture contemporaine', in *Œuvres de Abdelkébir Khatibi III: Essais* (Paris: La Différence, 2008), pp. 249–60 (p. 252).
16   Ibid., p. 252.
17   Khatibi and Amahan, *Du signe à l'image*, p. 13; *From Sign to Image*, p. 13.

geometric forms and vivid colours, but also in its coded language. The carpet demands an approach located 'entre le langage et l'a-langage' ['between language and a-language'], namely in the intersign, that is 'l'intervalle qui migre d'une marque à l'autre, d'une trace à l'autre' ['the space that migrates from one symbol to another, from one sign to another'].[18] According to this approach, the carpet can be conceived of as 'une surface intersémiotique' ['an intersemiotic surface']:[19] it borrows signs from artistic disciplines as diverse as pictography, tattoos, pottery, architecture and ceramics. Besides this first level of interplay, located in the combination of geometric forms and colourful motifs, Khatibi identifies a second level embodied in the surface of the carpet 'qui imite l'espace de jeux réels: l'échiquier; le damier ...' ['[that is] an imitation of a real playing surface, a draught or chess board'].[20] The intersign entails a movement not only from one sign to the other, but also between reality and imagination, model and representation. If the carpet is based on the pure repetition and symmetry of colours, shades, lines and decorative effects, it is the combination of these two principles that creates the enchanting illusion of movement. Illusory effects emerge from the intertwining of shades and colours, longitudinal and transversal motifs, central and bordering patterns.

Deeply influenced by these illusory effects, any visual aspect of the carpet strengthens the notion of the intersign. The eye of the viewer follows the lines of the carpet, flows across its surface, and navigates between its signs. This mobility in perception is reflected in Khatibi's notion of 'intersémiotique comparée entre les arts ornementaux' ['comparative intersemiotics of ornamental arts'],[21] a cross-disciplinary approach that focuses on the dialogue between distinct artistic disciplines of the sign. Khatibi writes, for instance, that 'l'art du tapis est une calligraphie des formes' ['the art of the carpet is a calligraphy of shapes'][22] and provocatively adds that 'on pourrait fixer du regard un tapis comme on admire un tableau, lire la composition de ce tapis ainsi qu'une partition musicale, ou même y prélever le pas de danse qui est esquissé sur tel ou tel motif' ['one could look hard at a carpet, as one admires a painting, read the composition of this carpet like a musical score, or

18   Ibid., p. 62; p. 62.
19   Ibid., p. 62; p. 62.
20   Ibid., p. 82; p. 82.
21   Khatibi, *Le Scribe et son ombre*, p. 51.
22   Khatibi and Amahan, *Du signe à l'image*, p. 90; *From Sign to Image*, p. 90.

even imagine a dancer stepping lightly from one motif to another'].[23] The comparison with painting, music and dance suggests that the vision of the carpet triggers a broad range of sensorial experiences: the intersemiotic gives way to synaesthesia. To borrow Baudelaire's words from one of his poems in which he describes synaesthesia, 'les parfums, les couleurs et les sons se répondent' ['perfumes, colours, sounds may correspond'] on the surface of the carpet.[24] Its rich, intricate and multilayered web of signs creates connections not only within the body but also between body and thought, thought and non-thought, language and silence. In *Penser le Maghreb*, Khatibi explains that pictorial orientalism was born from the confrontation of Western aesthetics and oriental intersemiotics. Painters such as Delacroix and Matisse found inspiration in the possibility of approaching Moroccan nature as a site of colour and autonomy, 'comme un tapis floral qui serait devenu un paradis terrestre' ['as a floral carpet that would have become an earthly paradise']:[25] nature as a space where signs keep circulating between artistic disciplines, foregrounding an intersemiotic understanding of beauty and meaning.

In the context of Moroccan society, the intersemiotic nature of the carpet is also fuelled by the permanent dialogue between signs that belong to oral and popular culture, such as the magic hand or 'khamsa', the eye and certain plants and animal motifs, and signs that remain fundamentally obscure and unfathomable. Khatibi sees in the combination of these two categories a productive paradox: the carpet sends and does not send a message, it figures both memory and loss, representation and mystery. The carpets from the Middle Atlas region, for instance, feature signs of 'tifinagh', an ancient script that has been used recently in Morocco to write Amazigh (or Berber) languages. The carpet becomes an element of junction between past and present, a living memory of old scripts, an invitation to go back in time in search for lost symbols and representations, and to bridge the gap between forgotten signs and new forms of representation. And here again, the carpet fuels the dynamics of artistic creation. In *Maghreb pluriel*, for

23 Ibid., p. 62; p. 62.
24 Charles Baudelaire, *Les Fleurs du Mal* (Paris: Gallimard, 1972), p. 38; *Flowers of Evil*, trans. James McGowan (Oxford: Oxford University Press, 1993), p. 19.
25 Abdelkébir Khatibi, *Penser le Maghreb* (Rabat: Société Marocaine des Editeurs Réunis, 1993), p. 100.

instance, Khatibi describes the work of Moroccan abstract painter Ahmed Cherkaoui as a 'calligraphie des racines' ['calligraphy of roots'][26] in reference to the inspiration he draws from Moroccan popular culture. Like a craftsman, Cherkaoui invents his own motifs and forms within the broader intersemiotic space of tattoos, carpets, and other decorative work, turning his painting into a rewriting of signs deeply rooted in the Moroccan cultural and social environment.

In and Beyond Religious Practice

One aspect that explains the recurrence of the carpet in Khatibi's *œuvre* is its multifunctional role. Not only is the carpet a piece of Moroccan art but it also serves religious, social, literary and symbolic purposes. Throughout his fictional, theoretical and poetic works, Khatibi refers to the carpet as a shifting product, subject to description, reformulation and transgression.

The religious signification of the carpet is of particular interest. Khatibi's and Amahan's volume opens with a Surah from the Qur'an that describes the paradise promised to the faithful as a carpet-decorated space. In his introduction, Khatibi reveals that the same image has obsessed him throughout the preparation of the book: 'la correspondance du jardin, du tapis et du paradis, comme [...] l'une des plus métaphoriques que l'art ait produites en terre d'Islam' ['metaphorical garden or paradise, surely one of the richest images produced by Islamic art'].[27] If this evocation draws a link between the carpet as a material object and the garden as a model of perfection, it also echoes the opening image of the carpets laid before the faithful in the promised paradise. The carpet is a piece of art that bridges the material and religious orders: it is at once an earthly and heavenly object.

Needless to say, the carpet has a significant role in religious practice. Muslim worshippers use for their daily prayers small rugs decorated with a niche that represents the mihrab of the mosque and featuring reproductions of holy places such as the Kaaba. Larger carpets are laid in and often out of mosques to allow for collective prayers. Khatibi is

26 Abdelkébir Khatibi, *Maghreb pluriel* (Paris: Denoël, 1983), p. 218; *Plural Maghreb: Writings on Postcolonialism*, trans. P. Burcu Yalim (London: Bloomsbury, 2019), p. 143.

27 Khatibi and Amahan, *Du signe à l'image*, p. 13; *From Sign to Image*, p. 13.

attentive to this aspect and, in *Le Corps oriental*, he reads the carpet as a fundamental piece of the space of meditation, hospitality and protection offered by the mosque and its refined architecture:

> Cette miniaturisation de l'espace, qui est une forme de désir et de quiétude (*sakina*), le croyant la vit à ces instants avec un certain plaisir quand il plie et replie le petit tapis de prière (*sajjada*) qui évoque – pour ceux qui sont initiés à l'imaginaire du monothéisme islamique – la correspondance entre le jardin, le tapis et le Paradis: métaphore inépuisable en effets décoratifs.

> [This spatial miniaturization, which is a form of desire and quietude (*sakina*), is experienced by the worshipper in these moments with a certain pleasure as he folds and refolds the small prayer rug (*sajjada*). For those initiated into the imaginary of Islamic monotheism, the prayer rug evokes the correspondence between garden, carpet and Paradise: a metaphor with endless decorative effects.][28]

The repeated act of unfolding and folding the prayer rug not only marks the renewable immersion of the Muslim worshipper in religious peace but also triggers a unique form of desire and pleasure. In Islamic practice, the carpet is at once functional and metaphorical: it allows for the condition of cleanliness during prayers and reproduces the correspondence between earthly decoration and heavenly harmony. In his analysis of the Rabat carpet, Khatibi observes that the perfection of floral patterns idealizes the sign by creating 'une nostalgie du paradis' ['a sort of nostalgic return to Eden'].[29] In the Islamic tradition, this nostalgic return is precisely the metaphorical counterpart of the act of praying: surrendering to the divine power and seeking the initial locus of serenity and pleasure. Khatibi's insistence on desire enriches the religious dimension of the carpet and redefines worship as a sensorial experience located beyond theology and dogmatism.

This effort to enrich and extend the religious significance of the carpet is developed throughout Khatibi's works. In *Pèlerinage d'un artiste amoureux*, a novel that recounts the journey of a Moroccan artisan, Hadj Raïssi, the carpet takes on various meanings. Following his departure from Fez, Raïssi stops at the tomb of a Moroccan saint where he meets a strange man 'à l'allure insolite, assis, immobile, couvert

28   Abdelkébir Khatibi, 'Le Corps Oriental', in *Œuvres de Abdelkébir Khatibi III: Essais* (Paris: La Différence, 2008), pp. 89–111 (p. 99).
29   Khatibi and Amahan, *Du signe à l'image*, p. 139; *From Sign to Image*, p. 139.

d'une robe rapiécée et multicolore' ['bizarre-looking, sitting unmoving, covered with a patched and multi-coloured robe'] and whose secret is yet to be revealed.[30] The man's multi-coloured robe and mysterious identity are conflated with the image of the carpet as an ambiguous and cryptic object: 'Se prenait-il pour un motif de tapis ou pour le tapis lui-même?' ['Did he take himself for a carpet motif or for the carpet itself?'].[31] The carpet operates beyond religion as an esoteric and holy secret grounded in the cult of Moroccan saints and open to investigation and transmission. Later in the narrative, Raïssi's wife Dawiya tells him about a snake that was hidden in a prayer rug at the sanctuary of the Ancestor. Like carpets, beasts are inhabited by spirits and meanings: a sign from the snake saves Dawiya and invites her to reconsider the significance of the sanctuary as a space for peace and quietude. In the sanctuary, the carpet is endowed with a magical power: it operates beyond the realm of religious practice and belief as a supernatural element that sheds meaning on its surrounding.

The most appealing and provocative diversion of the religious function of the carpet operates through an association with the register of sexuality. In *Le Livre du sang*, a novel woven around the figure of the androgynous, sexual intercourse between Muthna and 'Le Maître' takes place on 'le petit tapis de prière' ['the small prayer rug'].[32] Khatibi's description of the carpet, partly reproduced in *Du signe à l'image*, is worth quoting in length:

> On peut toucher du regard les magnifiques formes de ce tapis – soigneusement usé – avant de s'incliner vers lui avec un fléchissement de détente et de désir [...] Le tapis suspend cette courbure mobile qui module chaque partie du corps pour ensuite l'abandonner à un délicat chavirement. Oui, le Tapis s'ouvre à une paix étrange, si étrange que le lieu qui l'abrite se perd en fable silencieuse, parfois si étincelante de fantaisie. Il appelle à maintenir dans le royaume de la terre l'espace d'un monde enchanté de désir et tissé par des esprits et des mains invisibles.
>
> [One can grasp by sight the magnificent forms of this neatly worn out carpet before leaning towards it in a bending of relaxation and desire [...]

---

30 Abdelkébir Khatibi, *Pèlerinage d'un artiste amoureux* (Monaco: Editions du Rocher, 2003), reprinted in *Œuvres de Abdelkébir Khatibi I: Romans et récits* (Paris: La Différence, 2008), pp. 471–672 (p. 579).

31 Ibid., p. 579.

32 Abdelkébir Khatibi, *Le Livre du Sang* (Paris: Gallimard, 1979), reprinted in *Œuvres de Abdelkébir Khatibi I: Romans et récits*, pp. 115–204 (p. 187).

The carpet suspends this moving curve that modulates each part of the body and then abandons it to a delicate capsizing. Yes, the carpet opens to a strange peace, so strange that the place that shelters it is lost in a silent fable, sometimes glaringly fanciful. It calls to maintain, within the kingdom of earth, a world space enchanted with desire and woven by invisible spirits and hands.][33]

In a transgressive movement, Khatibi turns the prayer carpet into an active and powerful element of sexual desire, as emphasized by the shift from lower case ('tapis') to capital letter ('Tapis'). Sexual intercourse on the carpet becomes a form of subverted prayer driven not only by the quest for pleasure but also by the experience of strangeness, fantasy and enchantment. The parallel with religion is made more visible when the text refers to the geometric signs of the carpet as elusive and evanescent, including, at its centre, 'la trace tremblante d'une rosace, tremblante pour autant qu'elle s'efface au fur et à mesure que s'annule le regard. Rosace entourée par un entrelacs serré et qui, en allant vers le centre, éclate en polygone étoilé – astre de l'Islam' ['the shivering trace of a rosette, shivering to the extent that it fades away as the gaze turns blank. A rosette that is surrounded by a tight interlacing and, while moving to the centre, breaks into a starred polygon – the star of Islam'].[34] This formal and sensorial subversion works to challenge the dogmatic reading of one of the most popular geometric forms in Islam: the evanescence of the trace of the Islamic rosette gives way to the emergence of desire and freedom. The whole process is depicted as this 'superbe pensée du Signe qui fait tomber les ceintures les moins débridées et les cœurs les plus pudiques!' ['superb thought of the sign that unbuckles the least unbridled belts and seduces the most prudish hearts!']:[35] the carpet liberates discourse and representation from prudery and conservatism, giving shape to what Khatibi describes elsewhere as 'l'arabesque érotique' ['the erotic arabesque'].[36] Both the androgynous and the carpet embody a sense of transgressive variation by appropriating and diverting religious symbols towards the realm of sexual desire. Driven by Khatibi's subversive vision, a peculiar tension arises from the confrontation of both realms.

33   Ibid., p. 187.
34   Ibid., p. 188.
35   Ibid.
36   Khatibi, *Pèlerinage d'un artiste amoureux*, p. 640.

A Spatial and Social Object

Besides its religious function, the carpet is a key element of spatial arrangement. Its image and perception are tied up with the space in which it is disposed. This is all the more true in a country like Morocco where homes are traditionally decorated with a large variety of carpets and rugs. In this context, the carpet as a spatial object is in constant dialogue with its surrounding.

Khatibi is particularly attentive to this aspect. He notes, for instance, that the Rabat carpet 'fait partie du lieu qui l'abrite' ['is an integral part of the space that accommodates it'] and serves as 'un "chemin bas" [qui] oriente votre regard et votre pas dans la salle, il brode en quelque sorte votre orientation dans l'espace' ['a "pathway" [that] guides your eyes and your footsteps into the room; in a manner of speaking, it embroiders one's spatial orientation'].[37] In the traditional Moroccan town house, the carpet serves as the transition from one space to another and embodies the distribution of light and colour. The spatial function of the carpet is based on a peculiar contradiction as ornamentation '[est] un art d'agencer les différentes parties entrant dans la composition de l'espace' ['harmonizes the different elements of spatial composition'], and, in this sense, 'elle produit l'espace en le voilant, elle l'agrandit en l'adoucissant' ['creates space in the very act of concealing it, enlarges it by softening it'].[38] The Rabat carpet at once encloses and frees space: the eye's attention is simultaneously attracted by the central medallion and left free to wander over the bordering shades and beyond. In terms of spatial organization, the carpet is at once a fixed fragment and an element of transition from one space to another. The effect of a decorative motif as important as the rosette is described as 'un vertige de symétrie' ['a dizzying symmetry'][39] for it keeps disrupting and reorganizing space within the carpet and, by extension, in its surroundings. As a result, looking at a carpet entails a spatial movement on two levels: on the surface of the carpet, from one motif or one colour to another, and around the carpet, from the space it accommodates to the one it introduces.

Similarly, in Khatibi's novels, the carpet often serves to introduce and differentiate space. In a passage from *La Mémoire tatouée*, Khatibi opens his account of a visit to India with the image of the carpet:

37 Khatibi and Amahan, *Du signe à l'image*, p. 125; *From Sign to Image*, p. 125.
38 Ibid., p. 125; p. 125.
39 Ibid., p. 130; p. 130.

'Hantise ce tapis kilométrique de l'hôtel et qui m'accompagnait jusqu'à la chambre' ['Haunted by the kilometres of that carpet, which kept with me till I got to my room'].[40] The carpet is recovered by the author's selective memory and described as a haunting object, at once dispropor-tionate and central to the experience of spatial orientation in a foreign country. A similar link between spatiality and the carpet is staged in *Un été à Stockholm*, when the narrator, Gérard Namir, visits the apartment of air hostess Lena in the Swedish city, and notes that 'les tapis, les tentures et le fauteuil' ['the carpets, the hangings and the armchair'] constitute 'un à-peu-près ornemental qui convenait à ce lieu de séjour et de passage, adaptable […] à un décalage horaire vécu régulièrement par elle' ['an approximate ornamentation that suited this place of residence and transit, and adaptable […] to the jet lag she regularly experienced'].[41] Here, the carpets are not only an element of interior design but also a reflected image of Lena's occupation as they evoke endless mobility as well as spatial and temporal instability.

Khatibi's approach to the relationship between space and carpet is inscribed within a broad perspective. The spatial function of the Moroccan carpet extends to the way in which it embodies geographic and social modes of distribution. The carpet is not only an intersemiotic surface and a spatial object but also an element of social representation and connection. In his description of the floral-inspired decorations of the city carpet, Amahan notes that 'on en dénombre plus de cinq inspirés de l'environnement de la tisseuse, ce dont témoignent les représen-tations zoomorphes (cigogne), les thèmes floraux (vigne), ou empruntés au mobilier (théières)' ['more than five are inspired by the weaver's environment, including zoomorphic representations (the stork), floral themes (the vine), or borrowings from the household (the tea-pots)'].[42] As in Khatibi's texts, the carpet serves as a mirror reflecting a social reality with its network of patterns and differences. In the Middle Atlas region, for instance, which provides the greatest number of styles, 'chaque formation sociale (tribu, voire fraction), a sa spécificité' ['each social

40   Abdelkébir Khatibi, *La Mémoire tatouée: autobiographie d'un décolonisé* (Paris: Denoël, 1971), reprinted in *Œuvres de Abdelkébir Khatibi I: Romans et récits* (Paris: La Différence, 2008), pp. 9–113 (p. 101); *Tattooed Memory*, trans. Peter Thompson (Paris: L'Harmattan, 2016), p. 138.

41   Abdelkébir Khatibi, *Un été à Stockholm* (Paris: Flammarion, 1990), reprinted in *Œuvres de Abdelkébir Khatibi I: Romans et récits*, pp. 285–379 (p. 331).

42   Khatibi and Amahan, *Du signe à l'image*, p. 52; *From Sign to Image*, p. 52.

group (tribe or even family group) has its particular characteristics'].[43] In some tribes, the manufacture of the carpet 'constitue un prélude aux préparatifs du mariage puisque le tapis fait partie du trousseau de la mariée' ['constitutes a prelude to marriage preparations, the carpet forming part of the bride's trousseau'].[44] Thus, the carpet is as much a distinguishing social feature as a symbolic element of union: it operates at once to define and connect, to offer and combine.

The duality of this social role is reflected in *Pèlerinage d'un artiste amoureux*, when Raïssi reaches Marrakesh and is hired to finalize the decoration of a house. The carpet then reappears with a social signification:

> J'étais le seul habitant de cette grande demeure. J'y avais une chambre, un lit et un tapis de l'Atlas: laine teinte au henné, géométrie de carrés et de rectangles mobiles, entre le noir, le blanc, le violet et l'orange. Couleurs qui symbolisent, me dit-on, la division d'un pâturage collectif, chaque famille ayant sa part, irriguée par la source du voisin. La vallée toute proche s'élève ainsi vers l'Atlas, de tapis vert en tapis blanc, là où la neige s'illumine.[45]

> [I was the only inhabitant of this huge house. I had a room, a bed and an Atlas carpet: a henna-dyed wool with geometric squares and rectangles moving between black, white, purple and orange. Colours that symbolize, I am told, the division of a collective pasture, with each family having its share irrigated by the source of the neighbour. The nearby valley thus rises towards the Atlas, from green to white carpet, where the snow lights up.]

The colourful carpet serves here as an artistic reproduction of geographic and social identity. Its religious function is clearly overshadowed by the geometric symbolism of territorial allocation. Mobility is inscribed in the circulation of both geometric forms and natural landscapes: the Moroccan land becomes a carpet of signs and meanings laid before the reader. Furthermore, the unfinished house and Raïssi's excitement about his work suggests that the various meanings surrounding the carpet – including the religious one – resist fixity and are radically open to variation and reconstruction.

---

43 Ibid., p. 57; p. 57.
44 Ibid., p. 60; p. 60.
45 Khatibi, *Pèlerinage d'un artiste amoureux*, p. 590.

Artistic Creation and Feminine Agency

A fundamental aspect of the carpet's social signification is its implication of feminine agency. In his contribution to *Du signe à l'image*, Khatibi is particularly attentive to the way in which the carpet rehabilitates women's agency and constitutes a form of feminine expression and creativity:

> Le tapis est, au Maroc, cet espace plastique où la femme, surtout la femme, a dessiné sa capacité d'inventer ou d'improviser des formes. Rêverie active qui s'appuie sur une technique millénaire contraignante, et sur une esthétique très codée, avec laquelle la femme lie et délie la technique des mains.

> [In Morocco, the carpet is a blank page on which women, in particular, have demonstrated their ability to invent or improvise shapes. Their hands weave the fluent text of their imagination across a frame of precise and ancient techniques with their own highly formalised aesthetic code; tying and untying, these hands release their secret message.][46]

As suggested by the references to plasticity, aesthetics and technicity, Khatibi acknowledges the craftsmanship of Moroccan women as a process of creation that combines imagination and precision, creativity and mastery. The carpet embodies what Khatibi defines elsewhere as 'un art au féminin' ['a feminine art'],[47] namely a unique feminine ability to operate across disciplines by creating original forms that spark desire and celebrate the ritual of creation. This sense of commitment is reflected in one of the popular chants reproduced in the introduction and in which women symbolically address wool:

> Nos peines, nous te les offrons avec joie,
> Que sont-elles à côté de tes inestimables bienfaits
> O laine, sur nous ta baraka pleine de vertus!

> [We offer you our sufferings with joy,
> What are they beside your priceless favours,
> O wool, may your blessing full of virtue be on us!][48]

Carpet-making involves not only effort but also patience and engagement. As suggested by the word 'baraka', which refers in Moroccan dialect to

---

46   Khatibi and Amahan, *Du signe à l'image*, p. 15; *From Sign to Image*, p. 15.

47   Khatibi, *Penser le Maghreb* (Rabat: Société Marocaine des Editeurs Réunis, 1993), p. 110.

48   Khatibi and Amahan, *Du signe à l'image*, p. 16; *From Sign to Image*, p. 16.

abundance and wealth, the manufacturing process is experienced as a virtuous circle that celebrates women's agency and gives sense and dignity to their subjectivities.

Feminine dedication is also at the core of the significant ritual that accompanies the various phases of manufacturing. It is the Moroccan woman who leads and controls the process of creation, as exemplified by the preparation of the warp:

> Pendant l'opération d'ourdissage elles prennent soin de déposer dans un tamis (*boussiyar*) du henné, du sucre et des grain de blés. Tout homme qui passe à proximité d'elles est frappé par un rondin de fil. Il doit nécessairement, pour éviter qu'un malheur ne s'abatte sur lui, offrir quelques pièces d'argent aux femmes.

> [During the preparation of the warp, they are careful to place some henna, sugar and grains of wheat in a sieve (*bousiyar*). Any man passing close to them is struck by a stick of yarn. To avoid misfortune falling on him, he is obliged to offer a few pieces of silver to the women.][49]

Feminine agency hinges on a powerful fusion with natural elements that fuels the women's ability to invent new motifs, whilst men are kept away and forced to abide by the rules of manufacturing. Dyeing, for instance, is accompanied with a specific ritual:

> Avant d'exécuter cette opération, la femme prend un bain purificateur après avoir distribué figues et dates, elle s'enferme ensuite pour que personne ne vienne perturber son espace devenu sacré. Elle ne sera visible et visitable qu'à la fin de l'opération.

> [Before the dyeing begins, the woman first distributes figs and dates, then takes a cleansing bath. Afterwards, she shuts herself away and no one is allowed to disturb her. Only when her work is complete will she emerge from her sacred isolation.][50]

Khatibi's rendering of the manufacturing process insists on both feminine agency and the sanctity that surrounds the creative process. Manufacturing a carpet is a long, subtle and demanding process that requires a form of absolute and almost religious devotion.

The leading role of women is brilliantly illustrated in a Moroccan story included in Khatibi's and Amahan's volume. After the death of his father and the loss of his fortune, the son of a merchant is inspired by

---

49 Ibid., p. 92; p. 92.
50 Ibid., p. 92; p. 92.

the talent and intelligence of his wife, as she fabricates splendid carpets and asks him first to offer them to three power representatives in town before making them pay the higher cost of three merchant ships. The woman's genius is reflected in her ability to weave not only eye-catching carpets but also an astute plan to help her husband to recover his lost wealth. The narrative itself is driven by her ideas, queries and decisions. Unsurprisingly, Khatibi writes elsewhere in the volume that 'le tapis est, au Maroc, un talisman plastique de la femme' ['in Morocco, the carpet is a plastic talisman of womankind']:[51] there is something magical in the way in which women weave together the common threads of carpets and of narration. Like the writer himself, the Moroccan woman is the weaver who creates desire out of innovation, the gifted creator who gives sense to the act of creation.

This magical power of feminine creativity is reflected in a passage from *Triptyque de Rabat*, when the protagonist Idris observes the transfiguration of his house into an erotic site around the geometric motifs of a carpet. From the sensual arrangement of these motifs emerge, 'par quelque miracle visuel du tapis, le corps esquissé d'une danseuse berbère' ['by some visual miracle of the carpet, the sketched body of a Berber dancer'] and 'un langage oublié, mémoire paradisiaque des femmes' ['a forgotten language, the heavenly memory of women'].[52] Khatibi's reference to the Berber dancer and memory is a tribute to the creative performance of Moroccan women. Their skill consists in a dream-like ability to carve desire and sensuality on the surface of the carpet, and miraculously resists the passage of time through creation. Later in the novel, the death of Idris's friend and mentor, the politician A.L., is caused by his fall on 'un tapis natal, lui rappelant les femmes de son village, l'une après l'autre, assises devant le métier à tisser, muettes, figées en une image d'hiver' ['a native carpet reminding him of the women of his village, one next to another, sitting in front of the loom, silent and frozen in a winter picture'].[53] This contrast between physical death and memory revival draws once again on the powerful evocation of women weaving the threads of the carpet. Their silence and immobility emphasize their dedication to the task and turn the carpet into a living memory of their individual and collective agency.

51   Khatibi and Amahan, *Du signe à l'image*, p. 144; *From Sign to Image*, p. 144.
52   Abdelkébir Khatibi, *Triptyque de Rabat* (Paris: Noël Blandin, 1993), reprinted in *Œuvres de Abdelkébir Khatibi I: Romans et récits*, pp. 381–469 (p. 388).
53   Ibid., p. 467.

Khatibi's reading of the carpet in dialogue with feminine subjectivity is further developed in his poetic work around the concept of 'aimance', a form and a language of love that liberate pleasure and bring together the affinities and contradictions of loving relationships. In his 'Notes pour les femmes' ['Notes for women'], a series of fragmented thoughts about women and 'aimance', Khatibi compares 'le repos de l'aimante' ['the repose of the lover'] to 'le paradigme d'une tapisserie ou l'idée d'une pensée sertie de simples gestes' ['the paradigm of a tapestry or the idea of a thought inlaid with simple gestures'].[54] Like courtly love, the dynamic ability of 'aimance' to spark off desire through a combination of solicitude, hospitality and gentleness is reminiscent of the very structure of the carpet as a feminine composition of varying and seductive motifs. Khartibi's book of 'aimance' has therefore 'la rigueur d'une tapisserie ductile, enrichie par ses couleurs et ses signes entrecroisés: mémoire et devenir, Amour et Aimance' ['the rigour of a ductile tapestry, enriched with its interlaced colours and signs: memory and becoming, Love and "Aimance"'].[55] The carpet is at once a feminine masterpiece of rigour and precision, and a reflected image of the dynamics of variation and exchange that defines the concept of 'aimance'. In *Dédicace à l'année qui vient*, the dialogue between the poet and his 'aimante' is significantly developed around the motifs of the carpet:

> Quadruple signe
> Sur le tapis qui te porte:
> Quel hiéroglyphe
> De ta forme imaginale
> Lie et délie
> Ma pudeur latente?[56]

> [A quadruple sign
> On the carpet that carries you:
> Which hieroglyph
> Of your imaginal form
> Ties and unties
> My latent modesty?]

---

54   Abdelkébir Khatibi, 'Les Deux Livres de chevet', in *Œuvres de Abdelkébir Khatibi II: Poésie de l'aimance* (Paris: La Différence, 2008), pp. 83–121 (p. 87).
55   Ibid., p. 100.
56   Abdelkébir Khatibi, *Dédicace à l'année qui vient* (Montpellier: Fata Morgana, 1986), p. 28.

The lover's portrait is confused with the surface of the carpet. Geometric signs disrupt the poet's reserve and reproduce the desired image of his lover. Thus, the carpet becomes a transitional object in the experience of seduction, a metaphorical element in the loving relationship.

Beyond its dialogue with feminine subjectivity, the concept of 'aimance' holds a creative potential that mirrors the aesthetics of the carpet. In his correspondence with Moroccan psychoanalyst Rita El Khayat, Khatibi argues that the word itself is 'comme le premier fil d'un tapis, de sa trame. On peut rêver, penser, déraisonner à partir de ses résonances qui sont nombreuses' ['like the first thread of a rug, of its fabric. We can dream, think, unreason, starting from its numerous resonances'].[57] Writing about the notion of 'aimance' amounts to weaving a carpet of dream and thought around loving and friendly relationships. Its dynamic and multilayered meaning is a permanent call for literary, poetic and intellectual creation. Like the carpet, it is a living piece that bridges art, thought and society.

Writing the Carpet, Weaving the Text

Khatibi's interest in the carpet also serves the broader project of reflecting on the aesthetics of artistic and literary creation. Writing about the carpet is yet another way to probe the process of writing itself. If the Moroccan women's hands have passed on to the carpet 'le tracé d'une énergie vitale, les paradigmes d'un récit' ['a living text, the outline of a narrative'],[58] Khatibi's aim is to perpetuate this gesture of transmission by rehabilitating Moroccan popular culture and finding a new model to think through the intricate and multilayered process of writing. The concept of variation, at the core of Khatibi's literary and intellectual production, is central to his textual interest in the Moroccan carpet. The carpet is a text in that it weaves together various levels of representation, decoration and referencing. The writer is a weaver in that he works to perform an act of creation and to preserve

---

57   Abdelkébir Khatibi and Rita El Khayat, *Correspondance ouverte* (Rabat: Marsam, 2005), p. 9; *Open Correspondance: An Epistolary Dialogue*, trans. Safoi Babana-Hampton, Valérie K. Orlando and Mary Vogl (New Orleans: UNO Press, 2011), p. 29.
58   Khatibi and Amahan, *Du signe à l'image*, p. 14; *From Sign to Image*, p. 14.

an ancestral tradition in permanent dialogue with his social identity, as well as with local history and geography.

The parallel between texts and carpets is first visible at the level of production. Interestingly, Moroccan carpets have been produced through both the mimicry of old articles and the manufacturing of new pieces. This combination of reproduction and innovation, borrowing and renewal, is one of the distinguishing features of literary texts, and more specifically of Khatibi's novels which build on ancient and contemporary works while introducing new topics to Moroccan literature, such as bilingualism in *Amour bilingue*, queer identity in *Le Livre du sang* and transhumanism in *Féérie d'un mutant*.

Like texts, carpets are also made to travel and circulate. This is not only the case with the flying carpet, a recurring trope in Persian and Arab mythology, but also in the exchange and commercialization of carpets. In the historical section of *Du signe à l'image*, Amahan explains that, throughout Moroccan history, carpets have been offered by sultans as presents to foreign ambassadors and rulers, or included among the products exported to sub-Saharan Africa and Europe. A piece of local craftsmanship and artistic creation, the Moroccan carpet has gained a universal dimension through economic and symbolic exchange, as evidenced by its documented presence at the second Universal Exhibition to be held in Paris in 1867.

This notion of mobility is central to Khatibi's aesthetics. Not only do his works keep moving from one discipline to the other, but each text also embodies the idea of travel and displacement. Reading *La Mémoire tatouée*, *Pèlerinage d'un artiste amoureux* or *Féérie d'un mutant* amounts to looking at a series of multicoloured carpets whose motifs and patterns are in constant motion. If 'le trait essentiel d'un tapis est de varier les mêmes motifs en les transposant' ['the essential feature of a carpet is its variation of familiar motifs by shuffling them around'],[59] Khatibi's texts turn this variation into a multifaceted process that operates on linguistic, geographic and temporal levels. For Khatibi, the act of 'reading' the carpet involves a process of appropriation and translation. He argues, for instance, that when we see a carpet from the Atlas region, we must 'traduire cette construction de formes imaginaires, de lui donner un lieu pensé et pensant dans la topographie de l'imaginaire' ['translate this structure of imaginary shapes, and

---

59 Ibid., p. 152; p. 152.

consciously place it in the landscape of our imagination'].⁶⁰ The same process can be used to approach the intricate and shifting structures of Khatibi's novels. The dizzying variation of spatial settings is an invitation to extend the reader's landscape of imagination. As with the carpet, variation needs to be read and reproduced in the act of reading itself.

As a result, the carpet, I would argue, serves also as source for literary inspiration. In one of the fragments included in the volume, Khatibi compares the carpet to 'la surface d'une pure illusion' ['this surface of pure illusion'] on which impressions float.⁶¹ The combination and variation of colours, shapes and decorative motifs create an almost fictional space in which the writer can find models of representation and creation. When speaking of a carpet, we say that 'il est disposé, en désir, à toute position érotique, à toute prière, à toute supplique' ['it is laid before us, an invitation to desire, to pray, to plead'].⁶² The carpet holds layers of hidden and coded messages, a fictional potentiality embedded in the many stories it can tell. The global symmetry of the carpet stems from the way in which its many variations decorate, influence and counterbalance one another: as in a narrative, the composition is based on contrast, dialogue and harmony.

The correspondence of carpets and texts also hinges on the key element of language. In a volume written in dialogue with Derrida's thought, Khatibi invokes the image of the carpet in his discussion of the interference between native and adopted languages in colonized Algeria:

Comment les particularités d'un idiome dit natal sont-elles effacées et retraduites dans la langue d'arrivée? Dans quel enjeu de palimpseste? Quelque chose s'est-il dissimulé, caché à tout jamais dans un tapis de hiéroglyphes et de codes, désormais muets, sinon frappés d'aphasie, par surimposition sur l'idiome métropolitain de la littérature française?⁶³

[How are the peculiarities of a native idiom erased and retranslated in the target language? What is at stake in this palimpsest? Is anything concealed, forever hidden in a carpet of hieroglyphs and codes that are now silent, if not stunned into aphasia, being superimposed on the metropolitan idiom of French literature?]

60   Ibid., p. 14; p. 14.
61   Ibid., p. 44; p. 44.
62   Ibid., p. 54; p. 54.
63   Abdelkébir Khatibi, *Jacques Derrida, en effet* (Neuilly-sur-Seine: Al Manar, 2007), p. 26.

The dynamics of linguistic contact between Algerian and French entails a juxtaposition of signs and a transposition of features. This process inevitably causes a loss or at least a shift of meanings. As in some obscure motifs in the carpet, a gap is created between the signifier and the signified as a whole layer of indistinct signs is left unexplained. Interestingly, Khatibi's and Amahan's volume includes in its final pages a table of the Tifinagh alphabet and a glossary providing the transcribed version of technical words borrowed from Tamazight, Moroccan dialect and occasionally classical Arabic. Some of these words are mentioned and explained throughout the volume. In so doing, *Du signe à l'image* reproduces in its very composition the multilingual act of creation exemplified by the Moroccan carpet. The latter is approached as a multilingual construct, a multilayered object of knowledge, as suggested by the extensive bibliography and the closing section that introduces the preliminary processes in the manufacture of the carpet. Reading the volume inevitably triggers a desire to look at the carpet not only as a piece of Moroccan art but also as a broader metaphor for artistic creation and multilingual creativity, pushed to the point of disrupting the order of signification. When commenting on the corpora of the Rabat carpet's signs, Khatibi observes that 'entre le motif et son nom, il n'y a pas nécessairement une correspondance à résonance figurative' ['there is not necessarily any figurative relationship between a motif and its name'].[64] The relationship between the signified and the signifier is disrupted in favour of a non-figurative approach that encourages freedom and circulation. Similarly, and like the multicoloured surface of a Moroccan carpet, the hybrid nature of the volume invites the reader to wander between images of carpets, fragments of thought, excerpts of narratives and translated chants. Like writing, reading becomes a weaving process that operates between reality and fiction, between textuality and iconography.

It is my contention that between the lines and illustrations of *Du signe à l'image* there is hidden a portrait of the Moroccan writer as a weaver of artistic craftsmanship, popular culture and literary creation. The Moroccan woman is haunted by her creation: 'Pour tisser, disait-elle, il faut être habitée (*maskouna*). C'est ce que pense et sent tout artiste' ['to weave, she used to say, one must be possessed (*maskouna*). This is what every artist feels and thinks'].[65] Similarly, Khatibi is haunted as much by

64 Khatibi and Amahan, *Du signe à l'image*, p. 132; *From Sign to Image*, p. 132.
65 Ibid., p. 92; p. 92.

the carpet as he is by the act of writing itself. The carpet symbolizes the extreme experience of immersion and dedication that allows the creation of intricate structures and navigation between motifs and colours to experience the magical pleasure of creation. Variation is a skill that is required in both literary writing and carpet manufacturing. Khatibi aptly notes that 'le style d'une tisseuse ou d'un tisseur réside dans la manière de varier les motifs, et souvent les mêmes motifs. D'où cet amour pour le détail, cette miniaturisation qui provoque notre rêverie devant un tapis' ['the style of a weaver lies in the way he or she varies the motifs, often the same ones. Hence the love of detail, this miniaturisation which causes us to daydream when looking at a carpet'].[66] The same can be said about Khatibi as a writer: his style lies in the way in which he has continuously varied the same motifs throughout his work: alterity, bilingualism, travel, but also the fundamental encounter of Western and Oriental cultures.

In *Du signe à l'image*, this last motif is visible in Khatibi's reference to both Henry James and Scheherazade. In the former's famous novella 'The Figure in the Carpet', Hugh Vereker, a fashionable writer, confides in the narrator that a magic formula, 'something like a complex figure in a Persian carpet', is hidden in his works. In his search for the missing figure, the narrator rereads Vereker's work, consults his friends, but comes to understand that the riddle has no answer. For James's magic formula is precisely to have captured the attention of the reader throughout the story, using a series of incidents and surprises to revive the quest. The effect produced by Vereker's works is similar to that of the carpet as described by Khatibi: 'toucher du regard sans s'attarder [...] caresser le regard [...] le flatter, grâce à une participation magique au monde des apparences' ['to catch your eye without ever holding your gaze, to soothe, to flatter the spectator through a magical participation in the world of appearances'].[67] The surface of the carpet, like that of the text, is the object of an open-ended quest for meaning that can only lead to the pleasure of searching itself. As Khatibi writes elsewhere in the volume, 'l'art du tapis nous apprend à sa manière l'art de la trace et de la "filature"' ['the carpet teaches you the art of tracking, of following the thread'].[68] The variations of motifs and the transition from one motif to another require a constant movement that mirrors the construction

66   Ibid., p. 132; p. 132.
67   Ibid., p. 132; p. 132.
68   Ibid., p. 160; p. 160.

of narratives. This skill is fully mastered by Scheherazade who weaves stories together to delay her execution. Khatibi argues that 'ce n'est point un hasard si Shéhérazade invente l'image du tapis volant: elle doit vivre coûte que coûte entre le récit et la mort' ['it is not by chance that Scheherazade invented the image of the flying carpet – she had to live, regardless of the consequences, between the story and death'].[69] It is in this intermediary space that Scheherazade embodies not only a feminine agency which mirrors that of Moroccan women weaving carpets in the mountains but also the skill of evading death in the act of creation. More specifically, the flying carpet is a narrative trope that emphasizes both the power of the imagination and the ideas of variation and mobility associated with the carpet.

Scheherazade's stories are unfolded like endless carpets of signs and surprises. Similarly, Moroccan carpets are laid before the viewer as fascinating stories waiting to be read and recounted. The writer as a weaver is one who draws on the narrative and fictional potential of the carpet to give substance to an aesthetics of dialogue, desire and variation. Khatibi's transdisciplinary work is an invitation to read and recount the story of the carpet in order to restore the dignity of popular culture and evade the death of imagination and creativity.

69 Ibid., p. 62; p. 62.

CHAPTER THIRTEEN

The Artist's Journey, or, the Journey as Art

Aesthetics and Ethics in *Pèlerinage d'un artiste amoureux* and Beyond

Jane Hiddleston

> L'artiste serait-il en tous temps un étranger profes-
> sionnel? Celui qui vient pour annoncer aux hommes
> qu'ils ne sont ni perdus, ni chassés du paradis.
>
> [Might the artist always be a professional stranger?
> The one who announces to men that they are neither
> lost nor expelled from paradise.]
>
> Abdelkébir Khatibi[1]

Khatibi's notion of the 'étranger professionnel' (professional stranger),
as it is conceived in *Figures de l'étranger dans la littérature française*
and dramatized in *Un été à Stockholm*, is well known as a figure for
his commitment to transnational thinking. The professional stranger
is a traveller of the mind, adopting a dynamic and non-proprietary
mode of interaction with the world, and refusing rooted or identitarian thinking in favour of the continual embrace of the unfamiliar.
Jean Genet, Khatibi suggests, offers an apt example, as someone who
travels across countries, cultures and borders, to the extent that, 'sa
langue "maternelle" est sa patrie nomade, le lieu de sa généalogie

---

1   Abdelkébir Khatibi, *Pèlerinage d'un artiste amoureux* (Monaco: Editions du
Rocher, 2003), reprinted in *Œuvres de Abdelkébir Khatibi I: Romans et Récits*
(Paris: La Différence, 2008), pp. 471–672 (p. 517).

textuelle' ['his mother tongue is his nomadic native land, the place of his textual genealogy'].[2] And Genet's writing, moreover, is the trace of this transcultural movement, the product of an imaginary that pays no heed to origins and borders, inscribed in an idiom that gestures towards the multiple other languages with which it comes into contact. Like Genet, the central character of Khatibi's *Un été à Stockholm*, a simultaneous interpreter spending the summer at a conference on neutrality in the Swedish capital, is also a professional traveller, not so much this time as a result of his writing but as a result of the attentiveness to linguistic dialogue and difference that drives his work as a translator. Khatibi's protagonist here too is a perpetual wanderer, whose linguistic border-crossings are mirrored in his nomadism, in his transient relationships, in his appreciation of Sweden's political neutrality, and in his enjoyment of the sense of elusiveness created by the city's architecture. More recently, however, it is the character of Raïssi in *Pèlerinage d'un artiste amoureux* who personifies the professional stranger most fully, not only through his journeying but also through the artistic vision with which he apprehends the world and which encapsulates at the same time Khatibi's own unique and liberatory aesthetics.

Published towards the end of Khatibi's career in 2003, *Pèlerinage* is loosely based on the life story of the author's grandfather, and narrates the travels of its protagonist, a 'stucateur' (an artist who works in stucco), against the backdrop of Morocco's history before and after the French Protectorate. Suffering from asthma caused by the dust produced by his work, Raïssi nevertheless exhibits his artistic vision throughout the narrative, and sets out on the pilgrimage referred to in the book's title in search of refreshment and renewal. Two events conspire to trigger his departure from Fez. First, after a storm loosens the stones of a wall, he discovers inside it a letter, written by a certain Rachid Madroub, beseeching the finder of the missive to make the journey to Mecca as a penance for the death of a woman after a terrible accident, whose body he buried in the wall. Secondly, Raïssi is moved to travel after a passionate affair with 'la Sicilienne', the wife of the sterile master of a house he is working on, who goes on to bear his child. In the first case, the journey represents spiritual renewal, but it is also significant that it is the story of another man's pain that is capable of catalysing Raïssi's wandering. In the second case, the departure represents acceptance

---

2   Abdelkébir Khatibi, *Figures de l'étranger dans la littérature française* (Paris: Denoël, 1987), p. 137.

of the fleeting nature of love relationships, the embrace of movement as opposed to any claim for ownership of the lover. The rest of the narrative of *Pèlerinage* links art, the journey, spirituality and love in a rich interweaving that traces the rest of Raïssi's life story while also uniting and developing many of Khatibi's major aesthetic, ethical and political concerns through his own intellectual career. An 'étranger professionnel' par excellence, Raïssi also reflects in intricate and subtle form the many conceptual dimensions of Khatibi's theory of art and its resonance in all his thinking, as it ranges from anti-colonialism to transnationalism, and to the profound but all too often ignored shared history of Judaism, Christianity and Islam.

Raïssi's work as a sculptor and moulder shapes his vision of the world in ways that serve to enact some of the core principles of Khatibi's philosophy of art. Raïssi's life has indeed from the outset been steeped in art:

> Il était né en quelque sorte dans l'art ornemental. D'une manière ou d'une autre, sa vie allait se développer avec cette force malléable que permet le plâtre qu'il fallait sculpter, découper, mouler, peindre selon la composition de l'ensemble. Raïssi s'attardait sur les jeux des claustras à entrelacs de mailles du plâtre ou bien sur les arabesques où la calligraphie venait libérer la danse des signes.[3]

> [He was somehow born in ornamental art. One way or another, his life would develop with that malleable force that plaster allows, and that it can sculpt, cut out, mould and paint according to the shape of the whole. Raïssi lingered over the play of the panels interlaced with the mesh of plaster or on the arabesques where calligraphy came to free the dance of signs.]

The malleability of plaster, here, and the ability of the sculptor to shape and mould it, also figure the changing fortunes of Raïssi's life, as if both are formed creatively. The interlacing of the mouldings with calligraphy, moreover, displays the dynamism of artistic forms reflecting back on one another, inviting a conception of art as this 'danse des signes', eschewing more simplistic models of signification. As Khatibi muses elsewhere, it is the open-ended and allusive effects of the interaction between different kinds of signs, ('signe écrit, coloré, cryptographique' ['the written, coloured, or cryptographic sign']) that liberates the process of signification, so that they become 'signes qui disent autre chose que

3 Khatibi, *Pèlerinage d'un artiste amoureux*, p. 474.

la langue' ['signs which say something other than language'], and here too Raïssi's immersion in art forms since his childhood seems to promise this aesthetic suggestiveness.[4] Indeed, he describes his art as a 'harmonie stable, entre la matière, la forme et le signe décoratif' ['stable harmony, between substance, form, and decorative sign'], as if these precisely work together and respond to one another on multiple levels.[5] In addition, the narrative stresses repeatedly that the sculptor's vision is one that is alert to change, to the nuances of light and shade. Raïssi's work at the Sebtis' house (where he meets 'la Sicilienne') can be seen from multiple angles, as 'son modelé se nuance selon la lumière et les jeux de transparence' ['its modelling nuanced by the light and the play of transparency'], again reflecting a form that shifts as it is perceived from different perspectives.[6] Again, as in Khatibi's more theoretical studies on Islamic art, what is privileged here is not so much art as denotation, as the conveyor of a transcendental signified, but rather art as a play on forms transforming themselves and reflecting back on themselves. Khatibi indeed describes his study of various art forms in *La Blessure du nom propre* as the effort to 'prendre en écharpe toute cette agitation du signe et du sens' ['to touch indirectly this agitation of sign and meaning'], and Raïssi's aesthetic reflections similarly convey an alertness to this 'agitation'.[7]

The pilgrimage of the work's title is filtered, then, through this artistic vision, at the same time as the journey itself reflects Raïssi's and Khatibi's experience of art as ongoing reflection and discovery. If, as we saw in the quotation reproduced at the beginning, the artist is an apt example of the 'étranger professionnel', Raïssi's travelling is infused with his experience as an artist and vice versa. He sees the world itself as an aesthetic form: the clouds he gazes at as the ship departs are like a tapestry, and, later, a chessboard is like a mosaic. The environment is repeatedly perceived as an interplay of shapes and patterns. The principles of decorative composition, as he learned them from his uncle, also serve to inform the artist's view of the landscape, as the uncle insists on 'l'harmonie des couleurs, la pureté des formes et une géométrie totale' ['the harmony of colours, the purity of forms and a total geometry'].[8] This language of

---

4   See Khatibi in Hassan Wahbi (ed.), *La Beauté de l'absent: entretiens avec Abdelkébir Khatibi* (Paris: L'Harmattan, 2010), p. 31.

5   Khatibi, *Pèlerinage d'un artiste amoureux*, p. 516.

6   Ibid., p. 487.

7   Abdelkébir Khatibi, *La Blessure du nom propre* (Paris: Denoël, 1986), p. 13.

8   Khatibi, *Pèlerinage d'un artiste amoureux*, p. 499.

decoration and ornamentation once again allows form to express itself in suggestive and affective ways, a dance of shapes and signs as opposed to a denotative system. What fascinates Raissi is precisely 'la liberté indéterminée du geste, d'où pouvait jaillir l'image d'une mosaïque "en soleil", ou celle d'un tapis de signes improvisés, où viendrait s'asseoir, par une substitution enchantée, l'Amante qui l'attendait' ['the indeterminate freedom of gesture, from which the image of a mosaic in the sun could spring, or that of a carpet of improvised signs, where the lover who awaited him would come and sit, in an enchanted substitution'].[9] Art is in this way produced out of gesture and movement, out of the fleeting play of sunlight, for example, just as the lover's passing presence might capture the artist's passion in a moment. Aesthetic form can be detected everywhere and is constantly changing, offering up endless suggestive possibilities that transcend any reductive equivalence between sign and meaning. The pilgrimage, then, turns out to be this journey through artistic perception, it is the expansion and exploration of a mode of seeing. Raïssi is in no way looking for religious truth, nor is he travelling to Mecca in order to fulfil scriptural doctrine; rather, it is in order to open up his vision of the world.

Both art and the journey are the catalysts for renewal. The text opens with Raïssi's asthma attack, connoting restriction and suffocation, but a heavy rainstorm cleans the air and loosens the stones to allow him to discover the letter that will change the course of his life. The cadi encourages him to make the pilgrimage by reminding him of the story of the seven sleepers, referred to in the Qur'an, according to which seven youths hide in a cave in Ephesus to escape religious persecution only to reawaken three hundred years later, 'annonçant le Jugement dernier!' ['announcing the Last Judgment!'].[10] The emergence from the cave, reflective also of Raissi's discovery of Rachid Madroub's letter in the stones of the wall, generates a new realization, an increased depth and clarity of insight. In *La Blessure du nom propre*, moreover, Khatibi explains how the story of the seven sleepers inaugurates the Islamic theory of signification in its dramatization of the opposition between the flawed sign, 'muet et errant' ['silently wandering'] and divine illumination. It is from here that Khatibi traces the juxtaposition between the obscurity of, 'd'une part la Parole-Raison (Nut'q) enfermée dans l'imitation (théologiens, philosophes, juristes et commentateurs), de

---

9   Ibid., p. 500.
10   Ibid., p. 485.

l'autre l'adoration du texte et de son sens infini (prophètes, mystiques, poètes)' ['on the one hand, the Rational Word (Nut'q) replicated without deviation by theologians, philosophers, jurists and commentators; on the other hand, the text's infinite meaning adored by prophets, mystics and poets'].[11] This distinction demonstrates Khatibi's fascination in particular with Sufi mysticism, with this spiritual suggestiveness as opposed to theological doctrine, which will also inform Raïssi's vision. In referring to the seven sleepers, then, the narrative announces a moment of opening out, an apprehension of the infinite possibilities of signification and a transcendence of everyday human meaning. The journey undertaken as a result of this opening out, moreover, triggers a renewed understanding of the potentiality of signification that brings at the same time the continual rebirth of the self: 'dès qu'il quitte son pays, le pèlerin se déstabilise, orphelin en état de réincarnation' ['when he leaves his country, the pilgrim is unsettled, an orphan being reincarnated'].[12] The pilgrim apprehending this aesthetic depth also becomes aware of his own depths; his spiritual journey uncovers his own infinite capacity for renewal.

As in many of Khatibi's other works, this kind of aesthetic reflection is resonant in the conception of love relationships. Love stories are woven into and in turn become shaped by Raïssi's artistic vision and itinerant living. As I have mentioned, it is the passionate affair with 'la Sicilienne' that inaugurates Raïssi's departure, and Khatibi is stressing here, as he does elsewhere, the contingency of even the most intense experiences of love. The description of the lovers' intimacy conveys devotion but also movement and change. The affair itself will not be able to last, and in the lovers' complicity what they appreciate is the restlessness of the body and its endless recreation: 'la Sicilienne savait inventer l'amour, le faire avec volupté, en soutenant l'énergie plastique du partenaire. Il était illuminé par cette extraordinaire souplesse du corps et de l'esprit, si bien que, d'une union à l'autre, s'affirmait un désir continu' ['the Sicilian woman knew how to invent love, to make love with delight, supporting the flexible energy of her partner. He was lit up by the extraordinary suppleness of her body and mind, so much so that between each of their meetings was formed a continuous feeling of desire'].[13] This suppleness and flexibility, integral to Raïssi and Khatibi's artistic vision, is at the same time here associated with that aesthetic openness, as if the body

---

11   Khatibi, *La Blessure du nom propre*, pp. 19–20.
12   Khatibi, *Pèlerinage d'un artiste amoureux*, p. 501.
13   Ibid., p. 489.

too resists determinate signification to be appreciated as an endlessly dynamic and suggestive form. The spiritual, the sensual and the artistic coalesce in the evocation of the woman's 'sexe paré de mille noms, chiffres et symboles occultés' ['sex decorated with a thousand names, figures and hidden symbols'].[14] In becoming more intimate, moreover, it is as if the lovers become more unknown to one another, as proximity generates the perception of hidden depths. This association between love and transformation is crystallized also by the pregnancy of 'la Sicilienne', which of course on the one hand represents new life, though also on the other hand augurs the end of her relationship with Raïssi. She must bring the child up as if he were the son of her husband, but when he resembles Raïssi so closely he realizes he has to leave. The arrival of new life generates the continuation of the journey.

Later in the text, after completing the pilgrimage and returning to Morocco, Raïssi meets and marries Dawiya, and nearly forgets 'la Sicilienne'. Tellingly, however, he notes that this very distancing in a sense brings her closer to him: 'j'avais la vive impression d'être lié à elle, à eux, par cet oubli et cet éloignement mêmes' ['I had the vivid impression of being connected to her, to them, by this forgetting and distancing themselves'].[15] Forgetting and moving on are paradoxically signs of fidelity to their original embrace of human suppleness and flexibility. Even more, some years after his marriage to Dawiya, Raïssi takes another wife, Mademoiselle Matisse, an action that Dawiya accepts (with some resignation) and which again represents an acceptance of change and evolution in love relationships. And Mademoiselle through her music also opens Raïssi up once again to the reinvention of himself and his vision as an artist:

> En sa compagnie, mon œuvre de stucateur s'ouvrit à de nouvelles formes. Cette œuvre, qui est un ensemble de traces de mon propre itinéraire, reste dispersée dans des lieux différents, demeures, mosquées, places publiques. Ce sont des traces périssables, remplaçables. J'ambitionnais d'enrichir les figures de l'imagination artistique, de trouver un secret initiatique transmissible de maître à disciple. Je serais alors réincarné dans la main du stucateur, comme le compositeur l'est dans le doigté de l'instrumentaliste. Voilà que la musique, qui se dessinait sur mes sensations et mes émotions, réveillait en moi ce désir inassouvi d'invention.[16]

14 Ibid.
15 Ibid., p. 605.
16 Ibid., p. 642.

[In her company, my work as an artist in stucco was opened up to new forms. This work, which is the ensemble of traces of my own itinerary, is dispersed in different places, homes, mosques and public places. They are perishable, replaceable traces. I had the ambition to enrich the figures of artistic imagination, to find an initiatory secret that could be transmitted from master to disciple. I would be reincarnated in the hand of the stucco artist, as the composer is by the dexterity of the instrumentalist. The music, which resonated on my sensations and emotions, awakened in me this unsatisfied desire for invention.]

Here again, intimacy, art and rebirth are intertwined. Mademoiselle's music casts Raïssi's own work in a new light, and allows him to perceive how, just as harmonies move through time, his sculptures and mouldings evolve. His relationship with Dawiya changes, though does not end, as a result of Mademoiselle's intervention, and at the same time his artistic vision is altered through the analogy with music. Furthermore, he sculpts while Mademoiselle plays the piano, but the changing image he has of her as she moves through the music, and also around the room, influences his art. And, just as Khatibi celebrated the criss-crossing of art forms in *La Blessure du nom propre* (the 'signe écrit, coloré, cryptographique', cited earlier), so here too does Raïssi add to his moulding 'une touche musicale' ['a musical touch'].[17] As love changes, then, so too does the form of art produced, as that original perception of formal potentiality is here further expanded and accomplished on another level.

Raïssi's contingent and dynamic love relationships perform Khatibi's conception of 'aimance' as a form of friendship open to contingency and recreation. 'Aimance' is at the same time an ethical interaction; it eschews domination and mastery and remains sensitive to the unfamiliarity of the other, just as Khatibi's artist remains open to multiple formal potentialities. Originating in a notion of courtly love, and developed in depth by Jacques Derrida in *Politiques de l'amitié*, 'aimance' names the love in friendship as well as respect for the other's difference. In Khatibi's words:

Le devoir d'Aimance – une volupté qui libère la mémoire du Plaisir, son jeu imprévisible. Il lui faut une hospitalité souple, avenante, singulièrement accordée sur les plages de l'imagination: vent et tempête délicate, cheval solaire retournant à ses caresses, cercle ouvert vers les yeux de l'Initiée, par-dessus l'épaule qui voit ce qu'elle touche.[18]

17   Ibid.
18   Abdelkébir Khatibi, *Aimance* (Neuilly-sur-Seine: Al Manar, 2003), p. 14.

[The work of Aimance – a delight which liberates the memory of Pleasure, its unpredictable play. It needs a supple, appealing hospitality, singularly fitted to the range of the imagination: a delicate wind and storm, a horse of the sun returning to its caresses, a circle open to the eyes of the Initiated, over the shoulder of the one who sees what she touches.]

This insistence on the imagination emphasizes how this concept of love at the same time borrows from Khatibi's aesthetic vision in its embrace of different modes of perceiving and seeing. Exemplified by the love affairs of the 'étranger professionnel' of *Un été à Stockholm*, moreover, 'aimance' refers to love in movement, the love of the traveller, perhaps, and although the disregard for marital fidelity (and for the woman's suffering) at times seems troubling in Khatibi's characters, this insistence on contingency in love can also be construed not so much to necessitate separation but to invite an awareness of human change. If it can also be understood to characterize the turbulent interlingual relationship between an Arabic-speaking man and a French woman in *Amour bilingue*, it perhaps represents both dialogue and complicity, and untranslatability or opacity between lovers. And if it demands a peaceful living-together in an awareness of the limits of the self and of our knowledge of the other, this then informs not only the life of the couple but also a broader world vision: 'c'est un acte, une affinité active, entre les hommes, les hommes et les femmes, les animaux et leurs semblables, les plantes et toute chose initiatique de l'existence. Une relation de tolérance réalisée, un savoir-vivre ensemble, entre genres, sensibilités, pensées, religions, cultures diverses' ['it is an act, an active affinity, between men, men and women, animals and those like them, plants and all things that exist. A fully realized relation of tolerance, an ability to live together, between genders, sensibilities, modes of thought, religions and diverse cultures'].[19]

This insistence on tolerance is another central feature of the artist's journey in *Pèlerinage* and occupies an important role not only in Khatibi's ethical philosophy but also in his religious and political thought. If Raïssi's journey is redolent with a form of Islamic spiritual thinking, it is, as I have suggested, in no way an affirmation of doctrinal law, and his spiritual development occurs not only through aesthetic discovery but also through the discovery of other religions. References are made throughout the text to the comparability and shared history

19 Abdelkébir Khatibi, *Jacques Derrida, en effet* (Paris: Al Manar, 2007), p. 69.

in particular of the three monotheisms, and Raïssi's spiritual journey is informed as much by his contacts with people of other religions as by his knowledge of Islamic scripture. Raïssi's dialogues with representatives of other religions are crucial performances, then, of Khatibi's own commitment to resisting atavistic theocracy and to conceiving spiritual learning as the result of both ongoing effort and exchange.

From the beginning, the pilgrimage is associated with religious diversity, in that the captain of Raïssi's ship carrying Muslim pilgrims is a Christian. When the ship docks at Algiers, however, Raïssi is shocked by the divisiveness of the French secular regime, according to which the state claims to replace God. Secularism paradoxically here erects boundaries between religions rather than allowing itself to enter into dialogue with them in ways that might better accommodate local communities. While the storyteller Anasse tells the Algerian man that, in Morocco, 'quand une mère musulmane se dépêche pour aller faire ses courses, il lui arrive de confier le bébé à sa voisine juive pour le garder ou l'allaiter. L'inverse aussi' ['when a Muslim mother hurries to do the shopping, she sometimes gives her baby to her Jewish neighbour to look after and feed. The other way round too'], Algeria is conjured as a country of conflict, tension and division.[20] In his conversation with the artist–priest in Malta, moreover, Raïssi seeks to articulate the differences between Islamic and Christian belief systems, yet the priest–artist encourages reconciliation. Raïssi insists that Jesus cannot be the son of God, and describes him as 'un orphelin, un éternel orphelin, l'imam des errants' ['an orphan, an eternal orphan, the imam of wanderers'], but the priest–artist reminds him that, as a pilgrim himself, Raïssi too is 'un errant, à la trace de notre Christ' ['a wanderer, like our Christ'], and, he goes on, 'peut-être êtes-vous aussi chrétien que moi, et moi, aussi musulman que vous' ['perhaps you are as Christian as I am, and I am as Muslim as you are'].[21] Khatibi at the same time underlines in this encounter the fraternity in the exchange between artists, as if it is indeed their aesthetic vision that allows them to trace their complicity: 'quand deux artistes fraternisent provisoirement, ils refondent le monde en beauté et se donnent une religion universelle qui justifie leur métier' ['when two artists temporarily become friends, they recreate the world in beauty and give themselves a universal religion that justifies their profession'].[22] If Raïssi evidently travels in a world where

20   Khatibi, *Pèlerinage d'un artiste amoureux*, p. 508.
21   Ibid., p. 522.
22   Ibid.

people find it difficult to understand one another's religions, Khatibi seems to be suggesting here that aesthetic sensibility – that openness to multiple forms – might help to envision spiritual sharing.

These traces of a dialogue between religions are given fuller expression by Khatibi in his earlier correspondence with the Egyptian Jewish psycho-analyst Jacques Hassoun in *Le Même Livre* (*The Same Book*). The title of this work itself refers to the parallels between the two holy books, the Torah and the Qur'an, as well as the wider history of dialogue between the two religions that has come to be so disastrously forgotten in the sequence of conflicts since the Second World War, the formation of the state of Israel, and the demise of colonialism. Khatibi and Hassoun's own correspondence then develops that dialogue in its exploration of comparable rituals, customs and practices, and in its own open and dynamic form as correspondence. Importantly, for example, Khatibi notes in both religions the interdiction of the image and commitment to the word, and this privileging of non-iconic forms of representation again relates to the aesthetic vision of endless suggestibility as opposed to a straightforward referentiality. On the one hand, then, the volume stresses the recent destructive history of conflicts between Judaism and Islam, as theocracy has become hardened, and 'nous sommes empoisonnés par notre archaïsme exclusif' ['we are poisoned by our exclusive archaism'].[23] This ideological hardening is what has caused the entrenchment of the division between Israel and Palestine, notes Khatibi, as he vilifies the exorbitance of the demand for recognition by the state of Israel, at the same time as he criticizes the inability of Arab states to accord both Palestinians and Jews with equal recognition. On the other hand, however, *Le Même Livre* also envisions a new, alternative dialogue, performed in the correspondents' own letter writing, and which indicates something of the power of art, or here literature, in keeping a dynamic form of relationality alive. At the same time, in a deft interweaving, this dialogue is also conceived as another form of 'aimance', as the ethics of openness, might, according to Khatibi, also offer a way forward from the present conflict between Judaism and Islam:

> Et bien, j'aimerais dire quelques mots, non pas de l'amitié en général (il n'y a que des amitiés), mais sur ce qui, du judaïque à l'islamique, transforme le mépris et la haine en contrat blanc, où rien n'est effacé, mais où le mépris se suspend dans sa trace archaïque, dans son fond

23 Abdelkébir Khatibi and Jacques Hassoun, *Le Même Livre* (Paris: Editions de l'éclat, 1985), p. 87.

abîmé. Rien n'est effacé, mais la connaissance de l'autre, du Juif, de mes pères et frères, permet de me dégager d'une certaine représentation mythique, de la haine ancestrale. Il n'y a pas d'amour entre les gens du Livre partagé. Il n'y a que ce rapport au Livre et au sacré.[24]

[So I would like to say a few words, not on friendship in general (there are only friendships), but on what, from the Jewish to the Islamic, transforms hatred and scorn into a white contract, where nothing is effaced, but where scorn is suspended in its archaic trace, in its ruined foundation. Nothing is effaced, but the knowledge of the other, of the Jew, my father and brothers, allows me to free myself from a mythical form of representation, from ancestral hatred. There is no love between the people of the shared Book. There is only this relationship with the Book and with the sacred.]

The relinquishment of that mythical hatred and the acceptance of difference and evolution in people and in thought would, for Khatibi, perhaps trigger the start of a dialogue built out of an intercultural ethical and aesthetic vision.

In *Pèlerinage d'un artiste amoureux*, religious dialogue is also part of a wider vision of the rich dynamism of communities that have maintained their historical cultural plurality. Malta and Alexandria are both stopping points on the pilgrimage where Raïssi is struck by the energetic jostling of religions and cultures, and these places serve to crystallize at the same time Khatibi's wider vision of transnationalism and intercultural creativity. The small island of Malta, for example, is a meeting point for people and communities from across the world: 'ils se promenaient au milieu de cette foule mélangée où les Maltais côtoyaient des Arabes, des Africains, des Asiates, des Anglais, des Australiens de passage' ['they walked in the mixed crowd where Maltans crossed paths with Arabs, Africans, Asiatics, English and Australians passing through'].[25] It is also multilingual, though importantly this is not in the sense that various communities speak particular languages but in the sense that Italian, Maghrebian and English words can crop up at any time, as 'il y a toujours de la place pour une autre langue, pour d'autres langues' ['there is always a place for another language, for other languages'].[26] As in *Maghreb pluriel*, Khatibi perceives here not just the use of more than one language, but an open-ended 'pensée en langues' ['thought in

24 Ibid., p. 139.
25 Khatibi, *Pèlerinage d'un artiste amoureux*, p. 511.
26 Ibid., p. 512.

tongues'], where languages can accommodate and inflect one another within single sentences rather than living side by side without contact. Moreover, perhaps more antagonistically, Alexandria is also a site of cultural plurality, as, arriving there after the shipwreck, Raïssi is told, 'dans cette ville c'est un jeu d'échecs: musulmans, juifs, grecs orthodoxes et catholiques, d'autres catholiques – arméniens, syriaques, chaldéens – coptes orthodoxes, maronites, protestants, que sais-je, moi!' ['in this city it's like a game of chess: Muslims, Jews, Orthodox and Catholic Greeks, other Catholics – Armenian, Syrian, Chaldean – Orthodox Copts, Maronites and Protestants, all sorts!']27 Relationships between the communities here are figured as rather more tense than in Malta, but the kindness that Raïssi receives from his hosts hints at Khatibi's vision of a more open form of multiculturalism. The shipwreck is no doubt a signifier for the devastating disorientation that might occur through the process of unmooring, but the relationships that Raïssi forms through his journey across cultures nevertheless foreground the enrichment created by encounters with different peoples and modes of life.

Khatibi's vision of transnationalism, multilingualism and religious dialogue as it is conjured both in *Pèlerinage* and across his work is crucially, however, rooted in his critique of colonial thinking. Raïssi's story begins with his departure on pilgrimage in March 1897 and ends after Moroccan independence, so that the history of the French Protectorate provides the tense backdrop for his life. To a certain extent, it is striking that despite this chronology colonialism is not a dominant preoccupation for Raïssi, as if the subtlety of his artistic, spiritual and affective journey transcends the crude political tensions of the French colonial project. During the period of the occupation, Raïssi acknowledges the French presence but insists on continuing to focus on his own survival and enrichment. And later, while his son Mohammed is moved to participate in the resistance in the lead-up to decolonization, Raïssi remains more concerned with aesthetic and affective liberation. War, observes Mademoiselle Matisse, is the very enemy of art, which as we have seen rests on openness, on receptiveness to creative possibility, and Raïssi is keen to protect his artist's vision. Nevertheless, Raïssi's slight disengagement from colonial history serves at the same time to emphasize the contingency of such political projects, the fragility even of ambitious political regimes, and their transgression of what emerge as core human ethical principles.

27 Ibid., p. 546.

The destructiveness of the colonial vision is first evoked through Raïssi's discovery of Algeria during the pilgrimage. As I have mentioned, Algiers is portrayed as a city where secularism has divided and fractured religious communities, where state control has immobilized people: 'le pays était déchiré, lézardé, par des passions adverses, des conquêtes, par une mainmise soutenue sur la ville, la montagne, la plaine, le désert si proche. Il fallait donc vivre dans la nuit blanche, ne pas douter de soi, éternellement se replier sur sa force, sinon on mourrait de syncope, de paralysie, de déraison' ['the country was torn apart, cracked, by opposing passions, by conquests, by the sustained control of the cities, the mountains, the plains and the desert close by. You had to live staying awake at night, not doubt yourself, constantly drawing on your strength, otherwise you would die by blacking out, becoming paralysed or mad'].[28] This divisiveness is a shock to the Moroccan traveller, accustomed to a more peaceful cohabitation of cultural diversity, and yet Khatibi goes on in the latter part of the narrative to track the destructive stages of France's interference in Morocco. Noting the irony of the participation of Moroccan soldiers in both world wars despite their mistreatment by the French, for example, Raïssi records the horrific imbalance between respective forces in the subjugation of the rebellion led by Abd El Krim. A fierce anticolonialist who set out to create the independent Republic of the Rif, Abd El Krim was defeated in a fierce battle by French and Spanish forces in 1926 – about which Raïssi observes: 'pour le battre, on mobilisa 320,000 soldats français et 100,000 espagnols et leurs mercenaires, contre 75,000 résistants marocains dont 20,000 seulement étaient armés!' ['to overthrow him, they mobilized 320,000 French soldiers and 100,000 Spanish soldiers with their mercenaries, against 75,000 resisting Moroccans of which only 20,000 were armed!'].[29] Colonial violence may have been more intense and long-lasting in Algeria than in Morocco, then, but Khatibi nevertheless draws attention to the brutality of the French in Morocco, as the quest for dominance is backed up here too by real atrocities. While Raïssi seeks peace, however, his son Mohammed's activities in the resistance are on some level justified by the violence of the French repression. And if by the 1950s Raïssi is ageing, and observes the rebellion with a sort of stunned detachment, Khatibi again contrasts his spiritual openness and contemplativeness with references to the horror

28   Ibid., p. 508.
29   Ibid., p. 621.

of the anticolonial conflict: 'deux années de lutte continue: attentats, bombes, incendies, sabotage de voies ferrées' ['two years of continued struggle: attacks, bombs, fires, the sabotage of railways'].[30]

This contrast between Raïssi's spiritual and artistic world vision and the antagonism of colonial conflict is also evidently a performance of the opposition between colonial thinking and the 'pensée autre' ['other-thought'] in *Maghreb pluriel* (*Plural Maghreb*). At the opening of this most famous of Khatibi's works, he cites Fanon's assertion that in the wake of European colonialism, 'il faut trouver autre chose' ['we must find something different'], and this shift in Fanon from the acerbic critique of colonial brutality to a call for the invention of an alternative mode of thought forms the starting point for Khatibi's 'pensée autre' ['other-thought'].[31] While Fanon's work is above all devoted to the mining of colonial Manicheanism, moreover, Khatibi picks up where the former left off in his insistence on transcending that very binary structure to accommodate an alternative political, ethical and aesthetic world view. The early pages of *Maghreb pluriel* capture, like *Pèlerinage*, both the destructiveness of the 'jeu européen' and the suggestive possibilities of this 'other thought', as Khatibi argues:

> Quoi qu'il en soit, cet intime de notre être, frappé et tourmenté par la volonté de puissance dite occidentale, cet intime qui est halluciné par l'humiliation, la domination brutale et abrutissante, ne peut être résorbé par une naïve déclaration d'un droit à la différence, comme si ce 'droit' n'était pas déjà inhérent à la loi de la vie, c'est-à-dire à la violence insoluble, c'est-à-dire à l'insurrection contre sa propre aliénation.

> [In any event, the core of our being, touched and tormented by the so-called Western will to power, this innermost element that suffers from humiliation and violent and stupefying domination, cannot be resolved by a naïve declaration of a right to difference, as if this 'right' were not already inherent to the law of life, which is to say, the insolvable violence, or yet in other words, the insurgency against its own alienation.][32]

European colonialism leaves behind a history of brutality, but this cannot be properly countered by a form of self-affirmation that follows the same

---

30 Ibid., p. 667.

31 Abdelkébir Khatibi, *Maghreb pluriel* (Paris: Denoël, 1983), p. 12; *Plural Maghreb: Writings on Postcolonialism*, trans. P. Burcu Yalim (London: Bloomsbury, 2019), p. 1.

32 Khatibi, *Maghreb pluriel*, pp. 11–12; *Plural Maghreb*, pp. 1–2.

binary logic. The assertion of a distinct and particularized Islamic, Arab identity, suggests Khatibi, would comply with the same metaphysics as colonialism, bringing confrontation and division. Religious atavism operates according to the same logic as colonial domination in its insistence on origins and on a totalizing identity, and both are conceived as manifestations of ideological violence.

Having testified, like Raïssi, to the brutality caused by this kind of dominative ideology, Khatibi again like the artist-pilgrim offers not so much a strategy for practical decolonization as a world view of a completely different order. The resistant activities of figures such as Mohammed may have their place, and yet Khatibi like Raïssi is more interested in a philosophy that can accommodate cultural plurality, multilingualism and movement. The 'pensée autre', moreover, is not only one that celebrates the transcultural contacts Raïssi saw in Malta, for example, but it also knows its own limits and is able to embrace change in the way in which Raïssi's artistic vision also allows, since, 'une pensée qui ne s'inspire pas de sa pauvreté est toujours élaborée pour dominer et humilier; une pensée qui ne soit pas *minoritaire, marginale, fragmentaire et inachevée*, est toujours une pensée de l'ethnocide' ['a thought that is not inspired by its own poverty is always elaborated in order to dominate and humiliate; a thought that is not *minoritarian, marginal, fragmentary, and incomplete* is always a thought of ethnocide'].[33] Furthermore, steeped in Derrida's critique of Western metaphysics, Khatibi's 'double critique' of both colonialism and theocracy heralds a new conception of language, and although multilingualism is only referenced in passing in *Pèlerinage*, the broader unhinging of the sign from the transcendental signified is clearly at the basis both of Raïssi's aesthetic vision and of Khatibi's anticolonial critique. The 'pensée autre' is also, then, a 'pensée en langues' reminiscent of the movement and criss-crossing of forms evoked earlier, as Khatibi champions 'une mondialisation des codes, des systèmes et des constellations de signes qui circulent dans le monde et au-dessus de lui (dans un sens non-théologique)' ['a globalizing translation of the codes, systems, and constellations of signs that circulate in the world and above (in a nontheological sense)'].[34] Raïssi's artistic vision and Khatibi's anticolonial critique are both different ways of rejecting logocentrism, or the capture and containment of a transcendental meaning within the

33 Ibid., p. 18; p. 6.
34 Ibid., p. 60; p. 35.

sign. Both rather celebrate the continual movement and reshaping of forms as they mutually respond to one another.

In these ways, *Pèlerinage* draws together multiple and various threads in Khatibi's thought into the narrative of its protagonist's life span. What is perhaps so apt and so revealing about this late novel, moreover, is precisely its reformulation of philosophical reflection into the story of a journey, where the protagonist's development prevents the sort of reductive abstraction that Khatibi's thought sets out to reject. Khatibi's theoretical style is itself often difficult and abstruse, partly because he constantly resists facile argument and proceeds, like Derrida, through readings rather than through assertion.[35] The exposition of theoretical reflection through the narrative of a journey for this reason works appropriately to highlight Khatibi's attachment to thought itself as a continual process. *Pèlerinage* is, importantly, moreover, the story not only of a pilgrimage to Mecca, but of a pilgrimage through life; it is the narrative of the evolution of an 'étranger professionnel' rather than a history with a single purpose or end. Indeed, the cadi on the ship transporting the pilgrims to Mecca reminds them that 'le pèlerin deviendra peu à peu le voyage lui-même' ['the pilgrim will gradually become the journey itself'], as if the real journey is that of the inner life of the traveller.[36] And certainly Raïssi himself constantly undergoes rebirth, as the narrative frequently refers to his reincarnation at different stages on his journey through life. This emphasis on evolution is perhaps why the narrative perspective shifts halfway through the novel from the third person to the subjectivity of the first. After the death of his mother, Raïssi undergoes a transformation, 'réincarnation en narrateur qui, désormais, racontera sa propre histoire' ['reincarnation as a narrator, who, from then on, will tell his own story'].[37] The emergence of a narrating 'je' here dramatizes the process of self-creation through story-telling, through reflecting on experiences and creating links oneself. Accompanied by the 'l'Ange qui me parle, l'Esprit qui me visite' ['the Angel who speaks to me,

---

35   Khatibi argues in this regard that 'Celui qui se plaint de la difficulté d'un texte avoue indirectement que c'est la relation entre lui et ce texte qui est difficile. Il faut que le lecteur se mette en jeu' ['The one who complains about the difficulty of a text admits that it is his relationship to that text that is difficult. The reader must bring himself into play']. See *L'Œuvre de … Abdelkébir Khatibi* (Rabat: Marsam, 1997), pp. 25–6.

36   Khatibi, *Pèlerinage d'un artiste amoureux*, p. 498.

37   Ibid., p. 575.

the Spirit who visits me'], Raïssi goes on to note that he travels through life in search of his own secret, as these figures guide him, probe him and usher him through his periods of self-questioning.[38] And if, as Raïssi later owns, 'la vie est un rêve à interpréter' ['life is a dream to interpret'], then it is clear that this imaginative questioning will never produce an accomplished meaning or end.[39]

It is through art, ultimately, that Khatibi, with Raïssi, suggests we might accept and reflect upon this movement. Art, of which literature is just one example, performs movement, and is presented as a continual process of reshaping or remoulding in infinite new forms, and this is why the artist is perhaps a pre-eminent example of the 'étranger professionnel'. Crucially, moreover, whilst Khatibi is in no way committed to Islamic scripture, this deconstructive view of aesthetic creation is associated with a form of Islamic thought, just as Raïssi's artistic vision is expanded and developed through his spiritual pilgrimage. Khatibi's affirmation of aesthetic experimentation is perhaps summarized most succinctly in *Pèlerinage* when Raïssi reflects on his son Abdellah learning the secret of decorative art through his reading and rewriting of the Qur'an. Raïssi recalls how, 'enfant, n'avait-il pas appris, comme moi, à l'école coranique, le dessin et le palimpseste sur la planche, avec une encre brune et délébile!' ['as a child, did he not learn at the Qur'anic school, as I did, drawing and layering on a board, with brown erasable ink!'], and he goes on, 'écrire, effacer, recommencer, jusqu'à la fin des temps ...' ['writing, effacing, starting again until the end of time ...'].[40] Just as the child learns by writing and rewriting, here too Raïssi suggests that art is brought into being by this continual reworking, as each creation engenders recreation. Decorative art, like writing, Khatibi suggests, is this process of sculpting and resculpting, in a provisional overlaying of forms.

The concluding chapter of *Maghreb pluriel* also captures this interpenetration of artistic creation with growth and reinvention, and indeed the inclusion of this section on 'Questions d'art' in a volume on decolonization and bilingualism invites further reflection on the connections between these aspects of Khatibi's thought. The striking opening image of the chapter also anticipates Raïssi's view of art and is worth quoting at length:

38   Ibid., p. 580.
39   Ibid., p. 647.
40   Ibid., p. 626.

J'évoque ainsi l'image d'un arbre gigantesque, et dont les branches, en dehors du tronc, reviennent amplement vers la terre et s'y enfoncent avec fougue. La solidité du tronc persiste, mais aperçue en filigrane. Aperception voilée par les branches qui participent ainsi à l'être de la racine et à l'être de la branche.

Dans ce geste, la racine revient, écartée, à son propre élément. Sans doute, le destin de l'arbre est de prendre racine et de marcher vers le ciel, mais ici l'arbre s'enracine et s'élance selon un élan double et circulatoire, comme si le deuxième mouvement de son élan (les branches voilant le tronc) libérait l'arbre de la terre, et la terre de sa profondeur. De ce fait, la liane déborde les éléments qui la soutiennent et l'irriguent. Le sang de la pensée est une fiction de l'arbre.

[I thus evoke the image of a gigantic tree whose branches, apart from the trunk, abundantly come down to the ground, and with passion sink into it. The strength of the trunk persists but is noticed implicitly – apperception veiled by the branches that thus contribute to the being of the root and to the being of the branch.

In this movement, the root returns, deviated, to its own element. No doubt, the tree's destiny is to take root and stretch out to the sky, but here the tree takes hold and soars up in accordance with a double and circulatory impetus, as if the second movement of its impetus (branches veiling the trunk) freed the tree from the earth, and the earth from its depth. Thereby, the liana overflows the elements that sustain and nourish it. The blood of thought is a fiction of the tree.][41]

Here, the work of art is compared with the growth of a tree, whose branches stretch down and re-join the soil, to refuel and recreate itself in an endless circular but life-giving structure. This re-energizing of the roots (of the tree and of the art work) both sustains the creative impulse and allows the roots themselves to transcend their own anchorage in the soil, as if the life source can be both maintained and liberated at once. Just as Abdellah writes, effaces, and rewrites, the art work, in this analogy with the tree, regenerates itself in its continual return to its own beginning.

The creative and regenerative work of the artist turns out to be a crucial element in Khatibi's thought, and at moments such as this he aptly uses aspects of Islamic aesthetic thought to give form to the broader 'pensée autre' that underpins his philosophy of anticolonialism as well as of religious and cultural interaction. As I have suggested,

41 Khatibi, *Maghreb pluriel*, pp. 213–14; *Plural Maghreb*, pp. 141–2.

his late novel *Pèlerinage d'un artiste amoureux* succeeds in using the story of the artist's pilgrimage to bring together these various strands of thought. One of the most significant achievements of Khatibi's work is his ability to bring Islamic or often Sufi aesthetics and thought into dialogue also with significant aspects of French and francophone critical thought, as the references to Derrida alongside calligraphy in *Maghreb pluriel*, for example, demonstrate. Raïssi's artistic vision, the 'étranger professionnel' and the 'pensée autre' more broadly all combine a vision of aesthetic creation and contingency with a commitment to cultural dialogue and plurality indebted both to deconstruction and to Islamic art. Khatibi's aesthetics here might also be conceived to resonate with that of major postcolonial thinkers and writers such as the Martinican Edouard Glissant, in that Glissant too revolts against colonialism as a form of representation founded on 'le Même' by sketching a poetics of multilingualism, movement and contingency. Glissant's 'poétique de la Relation' is not only, like Khatibi's aesthetics, an affirmation of transnational creativity but it is also a celebration of art as process, as Glissant argues:

> C'est aussi que la poétique de la Relation est à jamais conjecturale et ne suppose aucune fixité d'idéologie. Elle contredit aux confortables assurances liées à l'excellence supposée d'une langue. Poétique latente, ouverte, multilingue d'intention, en prise avec tout le possible. La pensée théoricienne, qui vise le fondamental et l'assise, qu'elle apparente au vrai, se dérobe devant les sentiers incertains.

> [In addition, the poetics of Relation remains forever conjectural and presupposes no ideological stability. It is against the comfortable assurances linked to the supposed excellence of a language. A poetics that is latent, open, multilingual in intention, directly in contact with everything possible. Theoretician thought, focused on the basic and fundamental, and allying these with what is true, shies away from these uncertain paths.][42]

Like Khatibi, Glissant too combines creative theoretical writing with novels and poetry to demonstrate how abstract argument can be superseded by the more nuanced embrace of contingency enacted by literature and art. Khatibi's achievement throughout his work, and, I have

42 Edouard Glissant, *Poétique de la Relation* (Paris: Gallimard, 1990), p. 44; *Poetics of Relation*, trans. Betsy Wing (Ann Arbor: University of Michigan Press, 1997), p. 32.

suggested, perhaps particularly synthetically in *Pèlerinage*, is precisely to have elucidated both the place of this aesthetics in Maghrebian history and its far-reaching resonance for our understanding of colonialism, religion and culture in the twentieth and twenty-first centuries.

PART FOUR

Translations

CHAPTER FOURTEEN

Excerpts from Abdelkébir Khatibi, *La Blessure du nom propre* (Paris: Editions Denoël, 1974)

Translated from the French by *Matt Reeck*

Translator's Note

La Blessure du nom propre (1974) is Abdelkébir Khatibi's second major work, published three years after *La Mémoire tatouée*. It is a fascinating, enigmatic text of five chapters: 'Le discours parémiologique' ['Paremiological Discourse'], 'Tatouage: écriture en points' ['Tattooing: Writing in Dots'], 'La rhétorique du coït' ['The Rhetoric of Sex'], 'Le tracé calligraphique' ['The Calligraphic Trace'] and 'La voix du récit' ['The Voice of the Narrative']. In choosing these objects of study, Khatibi means to bring attention to forms of Moroccan popular culture. His method aims to excavate through the evidence of a material trace the latent excess and intersemiotic potential within these forms of culture.

Both intersemiotics and Khatibi's idea of double critique define the scope of this work. The latter, summarized in an essay in *Maghreb pluriel*, is by now recognized as an essential part of Khatibi's legacy concerning the decolonization of sociology in the Maghreb. Yet the first time that Khatibi outlined his double critique took place contemporaneous to completing *La Blessure du nom propre*. The month after writing this book's introduction, Khatibi gave an interview to Zakya Daoud, the editor of *Lamalif*, in which he outlines his ideas.[1] Khatibi's double critique takes aim both at the European social sciences and their

---

1 Abdelkébir Khatibi, 'Il faut s'essayer à une double critique permanente: Interview with Zakya Daoud', *Lamalif* (1 Feb. 1973), pp. 32–4.

concepts, linked historically to imperial hegemony; and at the forms of knowledge of 'dominated', or colonized, societies. The nature of his double critique explains in part this work's difficulty. The reader must be not only cognizant of both the history of concepts of European social sciences and the history of Moroccan forms of cultural interpretation, but also understand that Khatibi means to revise the rubrics of both.

Khatibi aims to combat the history of concepts of European sociology by focusing on popular culture, peasant culture, mystical religious culture and oral culture, and by denying the utilitarianism of colonial anthropology and sociology, bent on helping the colonial power rule its subjugated people. The semiotic focus of the work is by itself a challenge to conventional sociology, reliant upon analyses of data. In fact, in *Le Scribe et son ombre*, Khatibi notes that by the late 1960s semiology had replaced sociology as the focus of his critical interest. From that standpoint, then, the overtly literary quality of the work, perhaps mistakenly seen as a de rigueur set of references to the chief theoreticians of the 1960s, is rather an unconventional, indiscriminate borrowing. Khatibi's weaving together of these threads of thinking with ones from Islamic and Arabic sources points to how Khatibi's intersemiotic method locates meaning in relation, or in the 'intersign'.[2] (See David Fieni's work in the bibliography below.)

That is to say, Khatibi's intersemiotics is not that of Roman Jakobson. For Jakobson, intersemiotic 'transmutation' – a form of translation – designates 'an interpretation of verbal signs by means of signs of nonverbal sign systems'.[3] This might characterize Khatibi's views on proverbs, whose meaning, he believes, is cemented through the social milieu of their iteration, and 'ritual time'. But it does not help explain his interest in calligraphy or tattoos. Instead, Khatibi teases out the material traces within sign systems. These resilient signs leap energetically across sign systems. Volatile and alive, these signs suggest through their migration how relations of difference constitute the fiber of semantic and semiotic meaning.

Khatibi writes as well against the prevailing social forces that constrain Moroccan intellectual culture in the era of decolonization. First, independence brought a non-dialectic form of political thinking,

---

2   David Fieni, 'Introduction: désappropriation de soi et poétique de l'intersigne chez Khatibi', *Expressions maghrébines* 12.1 (2013), pp. 1–17.

3   Roman Jakobson, 'On Linguistic Aspects of Translation', in Lawrence Venuti (ed.), *Translation Studies Reader* (London: Routledge, 2012, pp. 126–31).

largely theological and theocratic. National culture was prized above all else, but this culture was merely that of the middle class. Lastly, independence signified the triumph of the orthodox, puritanical, Islam of the cities over the fundamentally mystical form of Islam practised by the peasant masses. Instead of advocating a polarized and inherently repressive form of post-independence national culture, Khatibi attempts a dialectic form of political thinking that traces a national culture only insofar as popular culture allows.

Excerpt 1 The Text's Crystal

The dreamed-of book will hover in its most intense moments around several insistent themes: gyratory movement, the wound of the name, a volatile carving, an oblique slap, the point of an argument and the point of a nib. And in this agitation, migratory signs – from one semiotic system (tattooing or calligraphy) to another (writing) – will retain an interrogative movement, ceaselessly provocative.

Does something like an intersemiotics exist from one semiotic system to another? And, more precisely for us, there is this question: at what moment is knowledge seized by a text, by writing? There is a transference of knowledge to writing in which a hushed emotion and meditative jouissance harmonize in an art of living. There is such an outlay of happy laughter and the scriptural dispersion of the body that the dryness of knowledge capsizes into fiction, without their antagonism ceasing to be virulent. How could one live like this? Or, in other terms, how does one establish the power of jouissance? I borrow the phrase 'the power of jouissance' from Roland Barthes, to whom our generation owes a more exact – and especially more jubilant – understanding of the text.

Yet this implies a given context where the subject of the énoncé toggles – by a vibratory and almost evanescent asceticism – in a voluptuous consciousness of the self, or, as Georges Bataille says, a consciousness that 'no longer has any object'. And because sensitive to a critical effacement that pierces and overwhelms it, the subject begins an ascetic practice: to renounce again and again, and so to the other torn desire suggests its vital space – its capacity to breathe, to laugh, and to make love. It is thus violence without hysteria; the subject opens itself to its wound, just as it gives in to every oscillation between nonsense and the pure sign. The orphaned teasing apart of meaning resides there. My joy, my asceticism, resides there. And in this double bind, the concept of the book is strategically brought into question, both in its closure and its institution.

This movement does not contradict an Orphic slap, such as this Chinese image – absent from the texts that follow – that returns repeatedly to me, bringing with it the decorative motifs that flavour the text. It is said that after having attended a party of 'floating cups', Wang Xizhi (301–361) invented his famous calligraphic writing, the most beautiful, reputedly, in all of Chinese art. Let us imagine a rather small, lively river that allows the guests of the Emperor to place floating cups full of wine upon the river's current. Each would drink, refill the cup, and set it on its way to the next guest along the river – and so on until nightfall. The poem also tells us that returning home completely drunk, Wang Xizhi completed a work of calligraphy so beautiful it would become inimitable. What of this image? In what could such an imperial fury of heavenly bureaucracies justify a power of jouissance? Does such a suspect nostalgia silence history? But it is not an archaic image: the fragmented body – of which we speak freely these days – can be decisive in a work so violent and jubilant that it is able to animate Mallarmé's 'pure rhythmic motifs of being'. To catch unawares all of this agitation of the sign and meaning, this is the project hereby sketched out, laid out baldly in its two faces: the ascetic and the Orphic. The project is also positioned in the following way: the texts and the semiotic systems under investigation here all belong to Arab culture, and particularly to the popular culture of Morocco; they are united by a concern of intersemiotic organization. Migratory signs are the gyratory themes of these texts, signs themselves suspended in this mnemonic incandescence that constitutes the Name. Thus the title of this text pivots around the question of its reinscription: what justifies it (what is a title but 'the held mail of no one?')[4] is not so much its empirical use in our analysis of Arab calligraphy (Figure 13), referring to a royal signature – tyrannical symbol of power and of its appropriation; but rather its polysemic capacity that opens the pages of the text to a combinatory play and the fiery veiling of chance.

So the book – a strategic reply to textual memory – and the concept of the book will both be defined as an infinite wound of the Name: in the old French word 'blecier' there is the notion of murder; and, without

---

4   See the postface on the sign in Pierre Klossowski's *Les Lois de l'hospitalité* (Paris: Gallimard, 1965).

a doubt, the text is the secretly gyratory place of the mortal activation of our destiny. In the wound, between the wound and the Name, what is at play is essentially the inscription of the Orphic body, shredded, but evaporated in its musical being, delivered over to excess, but excess veiling itself in a cruel reconciliation with nature. Never will any alibi be able to delimit the search for identity (here, the Name)[5] within a simple mirroring of the self and its intimate theatre; never will knowledge be able to pretend to end in theory the infinity of the text. If the title of a text has any reason for its selection, it is as the punctual effect of the propagation of meaning and its disorder, which writing scans and consumes. And the 'author' never knows whether their text has realized a stroke of genius or its opposite.

It is time, then, to leave behind the Hindu proverb 'your Name is your destiny' and no longer consider identity as a divine fatality fixed at a centre and origin, but put the Name in play according to the crystal of the text: this mirroring of the self transforming, recombining in the riffling of meaning. Your Name is your destiny, like the crystalline index of an infinite wound to the Orphic text because no text can easily dismiss the mythic work that animates and traverses it. And in this sense, the science of the text is hardly capable of residing (at the price of what blindness!) in the depths of this mythic work of writing, and when it has to change paths, the science of the text is forced into blind formalism. No doubt, to reconstruct the text in the manner of a Russian doll – by unpacking and packing of structural unities – incites a certain epistemological pleasure. Reduced to this show of legerdemain, the enigmas of the text disappear in the illusion of a logical, classificatory infinity.

One can always attempt a science of language more subtle and likely to unknot the formalist activity of our era, and which can put a finger on a scientific and critical semiotics of the text and its own laws.[6] I will retain several themes of this form of questioning, in particular the notion of intertextuality. Meanwhile, the attention given to Arab culture and its theories of the sign returns us with yet more appreciation to the work of Jacques Derrida, although in no way do I pretend to treat the entire breadth of his work here. One crucial argument in

---

5   Remember what Jean Starobinski said about the Saussurian anagram: 'Poetic discourse is only, thus, the second *way of being* of a name'. See his *Les mots sous les mots* (Paris: Gallimard, 1971), p. 37.

6   I am thinking particularly of Julia Kristeva's *Sèméiotikè: recherches pour une sémanalyse* (Paris: Seuil, 1969).

his work motivates me. And that is how the metaphysics of the sign, in returning to a Western logocentric tyranny, is hidden from itself while hiding the intelligibility of other cultures: all critical writing can thus only be a heliotropic tearing of the historical being, erasing, though its interrogation, the limits of that tyranny: centre, origin, the opposition of the signifier and signified, of the intelligible and sensible. It will be a monumental critique through which the concepts of being and non-being will be exceeded. At the threshold of this renunciation of the self a theoretic pause intervenes, and, following the example of Derrida, we can ask ourselves, 'Are we Greek? Are we Oriental?' Unifying this vacillating double identity makes the text an orphaned being, a being of exile. It is in the interval, itself nomadic, of such an identity that destiny finds and wounds itself. 'Are we Greek? Are we Oriental?' This is what that means: in the knowledge of the text, its gem of many facets, particularly here in relation to the divine body as intersign, there is a place where the power of jouissance changes in color like in approaching a poison. An intersign is a mark, an index, or, as the dictionary tells us, a 'mysterious relation between two things'. For us, it is a blood crystal with many facets and a regular tip whose glassy, fragile iridescence wounds the body and the Name, while reinscribing in a different fashion the crystalline symmetry of identity and difference. From the first definition to the second, it is the question of the sign in its full extent that is at stake; from a positivist semiotics to a transversal intersemiotics, it is again the concept of writing that must be invested in the body while placing it as a challenge against the Qur'an and the Arabic language.

In fact, the semiotic systems presented here exist chiefly in relation to Islam and its fundamental semiotics, either as a system that constitutes a veiled, masked propagation of the divine intersign (calligraphy); or that develops in the interstice of the trace suppressed by Islam (tattooing as the arche-writing of the empty sign); or that is based upon an oral semiotics, no doubt determined by the text of the Qur'an, but whose formal structure goes back to the primitive Story (proverbs and fairy tales); or, finally, that bears directly upon the erotic semiotics of a written text, *The Perfumed Garden*. Each and every one arising in what we call popular culture, all of these semiotic systems reverberate in the Islamic context like a cross-holding, a fiery mirroring of the sign instituted by the Qur'an – 'a clear word' revealed to Muhammad as a supreme sign of life, death and the Very Great Violence.

The Qur'an owes its extreme originality to how it defines itself as a radical theory of the sign, of the Word and of Writing; *al-qur'ân* – the reading, parsing and recitation of the revealed sign. What we mean by Gabriel's command to Muhammad to read and to repeat the Name of Allah in 'opening his chest' is exactly the theory of the breath that passes through the body (in the exact sense that the Qur'an descends into the body) and that splits it, that folds it into distinct signs, so the believer experiences these fibres as so many crystalline leaves of the text. The prophetic intersign is a breath, an ecstatic discourse, whose plasticity is governed by, accounted for, and veiled and unveiled in the body: 'Do not follow blindly what you do not understand: ears, eyes, and heart, you will have to speak for them all.'[7] Allah holds in his breast the interpretation of signs and, at the same time, he affirms the clarity of his message. Thus, the Qur'an marks the sign in its double face of veiling and unveiling. A hidden god, Allah directs the order of the 'Unknowable', but he lavishes visible, audible and tactile – in short, readable – signs upon humankind and the universe. In this relation between God and humankind, the Prophet is not considered the governor of interpretation; he is a simple transmitter, there to give people a 'clear warning'.

How could humankind – this sign created out of a 'drop of sperm' – seize this gesture of presence and absence, if not in the midst of the greatest solitude? Allah is not a god that loves, like in Christianity: he demands from the believer a complete submission to the Qur'an. This violent submission to the text will condition the entire status of writing as a body, as a divine intersign. And we know, moreover, what Allah promises to the non-believer: he will be turned into an animal, a mineral, left forever in Hell, this 'Hated Future'; he promises a 'rupture of the ears', an 'uncircumcised heart'. It is Allah who holds men up, and because the non-believer turns his back on the 'clear word', Allah will turn his face to the eternal fire.

This divine envelopment of the body is admirably recounted in the allegory of the Men of the Cave, plunged into silence for three hundred years: 'We sealed their ears with silence in the cave for years'.[8] There is a state between sleeping and wakefulness, during which, projected to the centre of the cave, the body is reflected to the right and the left of the cave through the rotation of the sun. It is thus a place of suspension, sheltering within the limits of the day and the night. In

7   The Qur'an, 17:36. All translations are from The Qur'an, trans. M. A. S. Abdel Haleem (Oxford: Oxford University Press, 2004).

8   The Qur'an, 18:10.

waking, the Sleepers find again the pulsation of time and recover their senses. What does this waking mean? This allegorical setting defines the Qur'anic theory of the sign, divided between a nocturnal identity marking humankind without God as a blind, dumb and lost sign, and an illuminated sign, coming from the tree of the 'good word'. It is said that 'Allah made the night and the day as two signs, and he darkened the sign of the night and brightened the sign of the day'.[9]

This opposition of diurnal and nocturnal determines the status of Arabic, which Allah chose over all 'barbarian' languages to make clear the signs of his Word: 'We have made the signs clear for those who have knowledge'.[10] A strategic intelligibility enters into conflict with the symbolic and parabolic discourse of the Qur'an. From this, the two principal movements that excavate the logocentric closure of Islam become evident: on the one hand, the Rational Word (Nut'q) replicated without deviation by theologians, philosophers, jurists and commentators; on the other hand, the text's infinite meaning adored by prophets, mystics and poets. Yet it is in an interstitial space where the calligraphic trace opens as a sacred celebration of the sign. Far from being a simple graphic supplement to the word, the calligraphic trace is a composition inside the text, a crystalline production of the linguistic body itself.

The calligraphic letter as divine trace invades all of the decorative arts of Islam; ceaselessly vying against the void, it carves out space while inhabiting an absolute interior, an absolute interior that allows logography to cover, more or less explicitly, other semiotic systems, like tattooing.

These semiotic systems that arose for the most part before Islam are thus suppressed and emptied of their symbolic charge. But like in the language of dreams these deformed hieroglyphs rip through our imagination and imprint in the body and in the unconscious the gesture of an elastic separation, requiring, in order to be read, a true divestment of logocentric tyranny. How are we to read these torn objects? How are we to pierce and collapse logocentric closure?

To offer such a glimpse of the Arab semiotics of popular culture will require us to attempt the timely analyses of many different semiotic systems: fairy tales and proverbs, calligraphy and tattooing, and, finally,

9   The Qur'an, 17:12.
10 The Qur'an, 6:97.

the erotic text of Nafzawi. Why exactly have I chosen these systems whose allure seems so fragmentary?

My analyses are organized according to two themes. The first is that all of these semiotic systems are a translation of the body and its jouissance: from the trace of the tattoo to incestuous passion (shown here by the story of 'The Talking Bird') there is the deployment of euphoric writing. The economy of the text and of pleasure is found here.

The second theme deals with a transversal intersemiotics where knowledge is torn again and again, folded and caught unawares by textual necessity. It is an intersemiotics along three axes:

1. A graphic semiotics (tattooing, calligraphy), understood in its symbolic density; in the case of tattooing, the empty sign (anaphora) reproduces a suppressed arche-writing; in the case of calligraphy, it deals with an over-determined mirroring of the linguistic code.

2. A rhetoric of love-making, called by the ancient Chinese 'the art of the bed chamber'. I have chosen *The Perfumed Garden* because this text remains principally oral, in the manner of *One Thousand and One Arabian Nights*. Thus, it is situated between learned and popular culture.

3. An oral semiotics (fairy tale, proverb) that will helps us determine the relation of the voice to myth.

The interest in these semiotic systems would be futile if it did not bring up, at the level of writing, the originality of cultures and, more importantly, the relation of the text and the historical being; without this, it would remain akin to this nostalgic pleasure that certain disillusioned diplomats experience in arranging flower bouquets or Zen gardens or learning how to shoot arrows while timing the breath. The retranslation of popular semiotics forces us to relinquish such nostalgia. To listen to popular culture is a strong ideological intervention that suffuses and contaminates every decision of speech. To write is thus to open in the body that speaks the process of historical meaning, by which a class war takes places also within the text.

The subject draws to itself the exteriority that creates it. And that will dissolve it.

January 1973

Excerpt 2 The Calligraphic Trace

1 The Fissure of the Sign
A sovereign form of writing, calligraphy denounces, subverts and reverses the very substance of language while transporting it to an other-space, one whose arrangements subject language to an overdetermined variation. It is this movement vacillating between sound and the written mark that we investigate here. Like Chinese calligraphy, Arabic calligraphy is an unheard form of the sign and a rhetoric of over-signification. A rhetoric? Usually this word is reserved for literary acts. But in this habit there is a strange deviation. For Western knowledge originates and fixes meaning within the confines of the spoken word, credited with the double virtue of being the reservoir of meaning and of coming before the written mark. The written mark, by consequence, is obscured, made distant in a secondary function, a function of transvestism.[11] We wish to investigate here this largely forgotten, repressed premise: calligraphic writing is a system of rhetorical figures that doubles and redoubles spoken language by a process of ordered over-signification. It is a system that puts language into intersemiotic dialogue.

First, we must distinguish between two facets of Arabic rhetoric: *al-bayân* is not simply the set of figures ('beauty marks', says Ibn Khaldun) that organizes discourse. It is, more generally, the art of precise and elegant exposition, that is, a general rhetoric that applies equally to speaking and writing. 'Writing and speaking share the virtue of Bayân', al-Qalqashandi writes.[12] Just as the spoken word must be eloquent in order to convince, the calligraphic trace has the ability to insert itself into the semantic process and to open this process to over-signification.

Without the refined rigour of the calligraphic trace, the text is disfigured, as is the process of reading. 'The qalam [pen] is one of two tongues', as Arabic linguists have said. The expression must be understood in both senses of the word 'tongue'. But the image itself troubles and betrays: it can either point to a material knowledge of the sign or serve as the basis for a theological and bureaucratic order, as

11   See Jacques Derrida, *De la grammatologie* (Paris: Editions de Minuit, 1967).
12   Ahmad Al-Qalqashandi, *Subh al-a'sha* [1412], vol. 3 (Cairo, 1914). [Translator's note: see also Tarek Galal Abdelhamid and Heba El-Toudy (eds), *Selections from* Subh al-a'sha *by al-Qalqashandi, Clerk of the Mamluk Court. Egypt: 'Seats of Government' and 'Regulations of the Kingdom', from Early Islam to the Mamluks* (London: Routledge, 2017).]

in the example of celestial bureaucracies. As the double of the tongue and as 'the tongue of the hand', the qalam records and fixes the word of God. By the qalam, history is transmitted, that is to say, justified by the reproduction of the metaphysical trace. Al-Qalqashandi, a celestial scribe, maintains the ambivalence of the question. 'What is the spoken word?' he asks in a dialogue. 'It's the wind passing'. 'And who can tame it?' 'Writing'.[13] Thus, the dialectic of the speech and writing, especially for Islamic metaphysics, plays with a mode and a theory of the sign that is very specific: Allah is the Creator, who transmits to the prophets the messages carried through – and woven upon – their breath. And their bodies are made to dance in a parabolic movement to the rhythm of rhymed prose.

The originating sign is revealed to Muhammad in a strange vanishing: the divine word is whispered into the transfigured body. This evanescent body, made radiant in a flash, in the blink of an eye, is transported outside of time. Divine rhetoric and eloquence are this sealed presence, tattooed – in writing – onto an evanescent body. Tradition tells us that this experience is known to ordinary people only in dreams: only a dream has the quality of being suffused, produced, by angelic writing, justifying Freud's contention. Muhammad said, 'I received (from God) words brimming with meaning in the most concise utterance possible'. This is, of course, the goal of all rhetoric, but here it is tied to a writing system subject to dissolution. In fact, God treats the universe like a palimpsest. The Qur'an states this very clearly, 'God erases or confirms whatever He will, and the source of Scripture is with Him'.[14] The human body is a movement of four phases: God kills,[15] gives life, kills, and finally gives life in the beyond, deep in the double book of judgment – paradise and hell.

All of Islamic tradition insists on the Qur'an's revelation as being one of the greatest miracles (i'jâz): in the verb 'ajaza, there is the idea of shattering powerlessness. Rhetoric is thus the product of a miracle whose deciphering imposes on humankind the process of over-signification. Such are, for example, the mysterious isolated letters (fawâtih) that begin certain of the Qur'an's surahs – arbitrary letters outstripping the norms of linguistic economy. What utterance do these signs that decorate the Qur'an hide in their scattered, glittering appearance? Theologians can

13 Al-Qalqashandi, *Subh al-a'sha* [1412], vol. 3.
14 The Qur'an, 13:39.
15 The state before birth: no relation at all to metempsychosis.

conclude without contradicting themselves that 'the letters in question were revealed so as to carry the challenge to its paroxysm in order to show all Arabs the incapacity of men to produce a comparable book'.[16] One of the secrets of the Qur'an is that it transformed letters understood as pure signs into an over-signifying rhetorical argument and that it split the sign from its message, from its utterance, so that in the ear of the believer meaning remains eternally suspended, distant and shifting. 'I will have my sign raised up from the horizon', Muhammad said. The message of the Qur'an is linked to this metamorphosis of language into an enigmatic distraction, a divine game by which the prophets reinvent language. As Massignon says about these isolated letters, 'Visions of the Prophet, first in luminous, sonorous touches, isolated consonants at the head of certain surahs, before he makes clear how to coordinate them in words, then in sentences'.[17] Countering this mystical experience, the disguising of the linguistic sign and its transport bring into being a double writing: a divine writing, the inimitable model of rhetoric; and a worldly writing, which is secondary, derived from the first (in the sense of 'drifting away'), whose function is to make the model into an idol, to fetishize it, and to attempt to depict its miraculous movement. This movement is accomplished by calligraphy with its extreme rigour – which extends to the pure sign, in a process that requires a mystical, fetishizing asceticism.[18] The qalam is like the soul of the spoken word, a geometric soul, Plato would have said; it must decipher, transcribe the inimitable spoken word, and it will be repeated in the calligram up to the blind spot of gyratory movement: death, the veil put back in place, the void wiped out by the hand of God.

To capture this mystical dimension of the sign, let us turn for a moment to the foundational myth of the origin of Arabic writing. All

16   S. M. Sadr, 'Les fawâtih ou lettres isolées', in *Les cahiers de l'Oronte* (Beirut, 1966). [Translator's note: the complete reference is: Seyyed Moussa Sadr, 'Les Fawatih ou lettres séparées', in *Les Cahiers de l'Oronte* 5 (Beirut, 1966), pp. 30–31.]

17   *Opera minora*, vol. 2, p. 554. [Translator's note: Khatibi here refers to Louis Massignon's *Opera minora*, vol. 2 (Paris: Presses universitaires de France, 1969).]

18   In the Buddhist scribes and monks, we find the same mystical asceticism with respect to the calligraphic trace: 'Thus a certain Buddhist monk, isolated for thirty years at the top of pavilion, made this his sole occupation.' See 'L'écriture chinoise', in *L'écriture et la psychologie des peuples* (Paris: Armand Colin, 1963). [Translator's note: Khatibi probably refers here to Jacques Gernet's 'La Chine: Aspects et fonctions de l'écriture', in *L'écriture et la psychologie des peuples: XXIIe Semaine de Synthèse* (Paris: Armand Colin, 1963), pp. 29–49.]

Revelation, the Qur'an teaches, is signed and recorded in an explicit writing. The divine power of such a Revelation is graduated and centred on the miracle of the Qur'an. The Qur'an transcends all previous texts; it establishes and governs their hierarchy. What is the source of this power? The mythic system responds by returning to the origin of writing. Here are four versions of this response:

1. Adam wrote words and books three centuries before his death, and after the flood every people discovered his book.

2. Allah reveals writing to Adam in 21 tablets.

3. According to Muhammad, every people of belief has a book and the book of Adam is corresponds exactly to the Arabic alphabet.

4. The 28 Arabic letters are the divine incarnation in the human body.

If God is the inventor of the Arabic alphabet, then, how are we to distinguish between sacred alphabets and worldly ones? What is the status of difference between languages? Arabic linguists use two distinctions: a mythic distinction – only the alphabets of revealed texts have the mark of the divine hand; and a logical distinction – based upon the arbitrary relation between the phoneme and the written mark. Arabic scholars clearly grasped the principle underlying this relation: 'In general', says al-Qalqashandi, 'there is no established relation between meaning and the sounds of speech, or between phonemes and written marks. From this source the diversity of languages springs'.[19] Jacques Derrida was able to analyse rigorously how the theory of the sign, founded upon the principle of arbitrariness, is linked to the metaphysics of absence and presence. It goes without saying that this hypothesis must be verified and examined in different cultural contexts. The Platonic tradition reduces the written mark to a function of transvestism, because the truth of that sign, the spoken word, is the origin of meaning. In Arabic learning, the sign is split, rent, in a different way. 'Writing', al-Qalqashandi says, 'is more useful than speech because the latter conveys only the present, while the former conveys both presence and absence'. The Platonic sign is reversed, though the argument still remains within the closure of metaphysics. Writing and the speech thus share the force of Bayân; the process of signification is the very same as that of the sign in its entirety. It is a process of unveiling that Arabic authors explain well: 'Bayân is

19   al-Qalqashandi.

everything that lifts the veil of a meaning (ma'nâ) to the point where it can be understood by the spirit'.[20] 'Bayân', says al-Jahiz, 'is the general name of everything that helps you unveil meaning'.[21] For al-Jahiz, the theory of Bayân, centred on the concept of unveiling, puts signs into five categories:[22]

speech

writing

gestures 'with the hand, the head, the eyes, the eyebrows and the shoulders; with clothing and the sword when the interlocutors are at a distance'

al-uqud: the act of counting without speaking or writing, that is to say with the fingers and their joints

an-nisbâ: the spoken word of the earth, of the heavens, and of the wind, for example. The mystical notion that inspires the astrological theories of Arabic writing and that makes this alphabet correspond to the lunar cycle.

In the same way, the act of writing from the right to left or from left to right: in the first case, the hand follows the movement of the stars that move from West to East; and in the second case, the hand follows the movement of the seven stars that move backwards.

Where can this logical-mystical hierarchy lead us, if not to the splitting of the sign? Without writing, Ibn Khaldun says, the spoken word is dead. At the same time the universal semiotics that makes the stars speak imposes on humans the process of a terrorizing spoken word – this exterior and vertiginous voice that holds the secret of meaning suspended twice over, in the voice of God and in the arbitrariness of the sign. Ceaselessly, the divine voice suffuses the body and the visions of humans: what I communicate to my interlocutor is not so much the trace of this voice as the system of the articulation of phonemes. God is the

---

20   In *al-'iqd al-farîd*. [Translator's note: Khatibi refers here to Ibn 'Abd Rabbih's *al-'Iqd al-Farīd*. For the English translation, see *The Unique Necklace*, trans. Issa J. Boullata (Reading: Garnet, 2006).]

21   *Al-bayân wat-tabyyîn*. [Translator's note: Khatibi refers here to Al-Jāḥiz's *al-Bayān wa al-tabyin* (*The Book of Eloquence and Oratory*). See the version edited by 'Abd-al-Salām Moḥammad Hārun, 4 vols. (Cairo, 1949).]

22   *Al-bayân wat-tabyyîn*.

creator of alphabets and compound words, and humans are the artisans of their combinations, situated only on the level of the second articulation. Now it is necessary to cite Ibn Khaldun at length:

> Discourse is formed from compound words that God created in the organ of the tongue, with phonetic combinations produced by the uvula and the tongue, so that humans can communicate their thoughts through language. That is the first step of written communication (kitâba). Writing transforms letters as written marks into the verbal expressions of the imagination, and the latter into the ideas found in the soul. The person who writes thus proceeds without stop from one symbol (dalîl) to another [...] Their spirit, led along in this work, passes from the container to that which it contains: this is the intellectual speculation that allows the expansion of knowledge. The ceaseless repetition of going from the signifier to the signified finishes by producing the habit of discernment (ta'qîl).[23]

One possible reading of this quotation is that the articulation of signs is regulated in the last instance by writing, which is the centre inscribed in the God's word; from there to signification ('the thinking of the soul'), writing assures an economy of rupture and continuity or, if you prefer, of over-determined articulation. Similarly, the process of the sign vacillates between writing as the productive truth of meaning and as oblique writing given breath by a voice external to language, an oblique writing impregnated by an already accredited meaning. Between essence and appearance, writing traces the sign's fissure and the memory of such a movement. It is in the interstices of two forms of writing that Arabic calligraphy compounds the boundless gesture of repetition.

The fissure of the sign, a double writing, a disguising of the divine voice: the setting of calligraphy supplies a transitory, limited fiction that idolizes repetition to the point of exploding the order of language and of giving life to the artifice of the gesture and of vision.

2 Polygraphy
Placed within a general semiotics, calligraphy is, without a doubt, an exalted and mobile rhetoric whose abundance of figures transforms language into a meditative posture. It links and exceeds language in

---

23   Ibn Khaldun, *al-muqaddimah*, translated by Vincent Monteil. [Translator's note: see Ibn Khaldun, *Al-Muqaddimah*, trans. Vincent Monteil (Paris: Sindbad, 1967).]

a tripartite register. Phonetics: the phoneme is of course the basis of its laws and its readability, but the calligraphic trace tears and repairs it in a more musical manner. The phoneme is thus the sign of the birth of polyphony. The calligraphic trace makes possible a reading of multiple dimensions, located each time in the interstice of a circular movement, and it introduces into the linguistic system the sound of a suspended music. Semantics, no less exciting: the over-signification developed in this process annuls the usual meaning that the énoncé produces. In this, there is a sensual pleasure that calligraphic knowledge dramatizes and that is the source of its extreme ambivalence: pleasure, in working against the conventional origin of meaning, creates as an externalized object the substance from which it emerges. And precisely the rhetoric of calligraphy, organized principally by geometry, creates a game of postures. The variety of figures and their delicate bravado correct in some way the restrictions binding language. Through its infinite formulas, calligraphy points to the confinement of meaning and disseminates it through a power replete with jouissance, as if in the movement back and forth across these three levels, the mark, the gesture and musicality composed, by an expansion of language, a moving arrangement.

What is the semiotic status of such a movement? With his habitual rigour (a rigour of jouissance), Lévi-Strauss shows us an approach related to music and Chinese calligraphy:

> Like the latter – but because it is a sort of secondary form of painting – music refers back to a primary level of articulation created by culture: in the one instance, there is a system of ideograms; in the other, a system of musical sounds. But by the mere fact of its creation, the pattern makes explicit certain natural properties: for instance, graphic symbols, particularly those of Chinese writing, display aesthetic properties independent of the intellectual meanings they are intended to convey; and it is these properties that calligraphic art exploits.[24]

If we consider the double articulation no longer as a dogma but as a simple postulate of an overt strategy, we are led, it seems to me, to an even more radical perspective. It is a radicalization suggested by Igor Stravinsky, who enigmatically stated, 'Music is first calligraphy'. This

24 *Le cru et le cuit*, p. 29. Translation from *The Raw and the Cooked: Introduction to a Science of Mythology: I*, translated from the French by John Weightman and Doreen Weightman (New York: Harper Row, 1969), p. 21.

is a semiotic reversal whose full significance (which is conceivably immense) we are incapable of measuring, but that provides for our text the necessary jouissance: the subtle emotion that sings out from the pleasure of writing, and that dissolves delicately through the back-and-forth motion into the pure sign: the effacement of rhetorical abundance, the taking flight, in return, of the intense dazzling or the violent perfume of a look that is itself calligraphic. The point of an argument, the point of a nib. Then begin again.

Articulated twice, music plays on the artifice of its own unique arrangement; music is capable of implementing (by an internal form of critique) and subverting the codes upon which it is based, whereas calligraphy inscribes its originality and its difference in the existence of a third code, which is this dazzling rhetoric that makes language an externalized object while at the same time inserting it into its own arrangements. It goes without saying that semantically the third code signifies only from within language, and through relation to the two other levels. There is thus an interruption and a displacement of the process; this is sensible work of visual rhetoric.

The gesture of Arabic calligraphy respects this order. It composes letters separately, ties them together, gives voice to them, and finally embellishes the entire énoncé – three moments whose vibratory transposition will have to be discussed later and in relation to the three aforementioned levels, namely the phonetic, the semantic and the geometric. But first, the Jakobsonian problematic – remarkable in itself – must be dealt with, 'the analogy between the role of grammar in poetry and the role of composition in painting',[25] as Massignon's love for analogies must be dealt with as well. While discussing Arab arts, Massignon writes, 'the triple vocalization is thus the basis of Arabic grammar: the I'râb. And it is the basis of Semitic musical semantics'. A little further on, he writes, 'the triple vocalization is the basis of Semitic musical semantics. The relation of rhythm (that weakens its units) to melody (that attains the soul) is the same as the relation of the

---

25   Roman Jakobson, 'Sur l'art verbal de W. Blake et d'autres peintres-poètes', in *Change* (Paris: Seghers/Laffont, 1972). [Translator's note: the complete reference is Roman Jakobson, 'Sur l'art verbal de William Blake et d'autres peintres-poètes', in N. Chomsky, R. Jakobson and M. Halle, *Hypothèses: trois entretiens et trois études sur la linguistique et la poétique,* '*Change*' (Paris: Seghers/Laffont, 1972), pp. 75–102.]

consonant-based theme (that provides the formula of for the idea) to the vocalization of final sounds (that makes the phrase comprehensible)'.[26]

Calligraphic writing is no longer confined to a strictly linguistic order; it is the resonance of its phonetic-semantic geometry. Language precedes it, but the calligraphic trace peels back the veil of its order. The analogy between the Arab language and the arts is no longer valid. Arab music is principally homophonic, melodic, and vocal; it is based on the interval of the fourth; the temporality of the calligraphic trace is polyphonic, intertextual, and intersemiotic. It is through the help of new musical languages that one day it will become possible to analyse the relation between calligraphy and music. Polyphony? It is more accurate to speak of polygraphy. What sings out here, what makes the calligram exceed language, is this subtle and powerful non-linguistic combination that suffuses language, disfigures it, and announces a flamboyant celebration of the sign. The visible surface is of course language, but the voyage and the reading necessary for such a migration of vision sets in play a fiction (of meaning) in nothing less than a rhetoric-saturated narrative, a logical and spatial-temporal rhetoric, tamed meanwhile by an integral graphic dimension. In Arabic calligraphy, the triple vocalization maintains explicitly the circular signification in the consonant-based body, the horizontal line on which the text is stationed tends to dissolve and to join the oblique and the vertical, or to dissolve into a labyrinthine space of suggestion and drunken analogy. There are so many figures unknitting language in some way, liberating the confounding enigma of desire, the truth beyond the present: the wink.

26   Louis Massignon, *Voyelles sémitiques et sémantique musicale*, in *Parole donnée* (Paris: Union générale d'éditions, Collection 10/18, 1970). [Translator's note: Khatibi refers to Louis Massignon's article 'Voyelles sémitiques et sémantique musicale', in *Parole donnée* (Paris: Julliard, 1962), pp. 379–85. See also *Encyclopédie de la Musique I* (Paris: Fasquelle, 1958), pp. 77–83.]

CHAPTER FIFTEEN

Excerpts from Abdelkébir Khatibi and Jacques Hassoun, *Le Même Livre* (Paris: Editions de l'Eclat, 1985)

Translated from the French by *Olivia C. Harrison*

Translator's Note

In 1985, Abdelkébir Khatibi and the Egyptian Jewish psychoanalyst Jacques Hassoun published an epistolary book comprising some 40 letters exchanged over a nearly five-year period, from July 1980 to March 1985. Entitled *Le Même Livre* [*The Same Book*], the book was conceived as an attempt to think through 'the Judeo–Arab question' from the plural sites of Khatibi's and Hassoun's past and present trajectories: pre-1956 Egypt and contemporary Cairo, French-ruled Essaouira and postcolonial Morocco, France and the Francophone Mediterranean, and Spain, among other sites.[1] Playing on the Arabic notion *ahl al-kitab*, the people of the Book common to Jews, Christians and Muslims, *Le Même Livre* centres round the twin figures of the Semite – the Jew and the Arab – as they have been articulated in theological, political and poetic discourses in order to question, and move beyond, the opposition naturalized in the expression 'Judeo–Arab conflict'. As Hassoun puts it in one of the letters translated below, 'What is the Judeo–Arab conflict in the end? Do we not give in to the imported language by speaking of it in these terms?'.[2]

Figuratively speaking, 'the imported language' is the language of political rhetoric and state media, be it Arab, Israeli or Western. And yet,

---

1 Abdelkébir Khatibi and Jacques Hassoun, *Le Même Livre* (Paris: Editions de l'Eclat, 1985), p. 7.

2 Ibid., p. 101.

as Khatibi's and Hassoun's letters make clear, this imported language is also French, the language of the colonizer for Khatibi, the language of exile for Hassoun, and for both, the language that helped widen the schism between Arabness – impervious to assimilation, according to French colonial doctrine – and Jewishness. No surprise, then, that Hassoun asks Khatibi, immediately after evoking the French language, if he was 'touched' by the departure of Moroccan Jews, in both senses of that term (the French word, 'atteint', also evokes the notion of being 'afflicted' by an illness, as well as the image of reaching a distant shore). The letters translated below are some of the most moving in the book, capturing the exquisite pain of exile (from Egypt) and of separation (between Jews and Arabs) while attempting to restore what Khatibi playfully calls 'a Semitic archaism!'[3] 'Without "my Jewishness"', avows Hassoun, 'I would not be able to comprehend "my Arabness", and without the latter the former would be null and void'.[4] To which Khatibi responds: 'my "Jewishness" [...] is [...] a tattoo of my purest childhood'.[5] Within and between the Judeo–Arab schism, Khatibi and Hassoun are able to carve out a chiasmic Judeo–Arab identity.

Khatibi published *Amour bilingue*, his allegory of *bi-langue* – 'bifurcated tongue', Khatibi's signal contribution to theories of postcolonial multilingualism – as well as his seminal collection of essays, *Maghreb pluriel*, in 1983. *Figures de l'étranger dans la littérature française*, his plea for 'literary internationalism', came out in 1987. As the reader will discover when reading the excerpts below, Khatibi's epistolary exchanges with Hassoun are a laboratory and sounding board for the notions he was developing at this time: other-thinking, double critique, *bi-langue* and the professional stranger or foreigner. More profoundly still, they evidence the intricate connection between these key Khatibian notions and 'the Judeo–Arab question'. In a 1982 letter, Khatibi explains *bi-langue* thus: 'to write, to attempt to write not only the unsaid, but to make visible, beyond any notion of origins, an antecedence of simulacra and appearances'.[6] Previewing the dialogue Khatibi would have with another Francophone Jewish exile, Jacques Derrida, in the 1990s, *Le Même Livre* is a deconstruction of identity, be it religious, ethnic, cultural or linguistic. In place of the identity of

3   Ibid., p. 24.
4   Ibid., p. 76.
5   Ibid., p. 107.
6   Ibid., p. 53.

the self, Khatibi and Hassoun offer 'an identity of crossings, so that we may free ourselves from the confounding debate opposing those who consider themselves Arab or Jewish in order to welcome the unsaid'.[7] Against sameness, then, an 'exercise in alterity' written in the pages of *The Same Book*.[8]

The Same Book (excerpts)

El Harhoura, 27 June 1984

My dear Jacques, this will not be my last letter. This correspondence is a game of letters, where each player places his pawn, you might say. Do you remember our initial agreement? Let me cite my letter from 6 September, 1980, which says: '… a correspondence that is neither false nor true, beyond this opposition, a correspondence that is destined to be written and printed'. On the basis of the Judeo–Arab conflict, of course.

Very well. I will continue with the enigma of the election (an enigma that remains to be analysed) which is also the exclusion of the Jews, given that being elected by one's own god also means being excluded from the rest of the world. This is a myth, of course, but it has taken root in the body of the Jew, as an illusion historically founded on this situation, the relation of election/exclusion. It seems to me that this ancestral and tribal atavism is what entertains belief in Judaic monotheism, and not the reverse. Take, for example, this absurd if not incomprehensible phrase by Marina Tsvetaieva, cited by the remarkable poet Paul Celan: 'All poets are Jews'. In a noble sense, we can say, can we not, that what defines the Jew is a certain relation to the Book, to the sacred text. Being Jewish would be inherent to this relation to the sacred: it is no longer a question of particularism, nor the singularity of a specific people, but an essential relation to being: we are Jewish insofar as we have become *readers* of a book, and of a prophetic book. When Allah tells Muhammad: 'إقرأ' ['read'] he recalls through this *fiat* the command to read that is given to us. In this way, the question of my bilingualism between Allah and the letter, or rather the message the prophet sends himself, also comes to graft itself between the command to *read* in a language and to write in another. In this way, the Jewish diaspora lives in a foiled double command. See how Celan uses Hebrew, a dead language in the small Tower of Babel of this excellent poet.

7   Ibid., p. 13.
8   Ibid., p. 9.

But Tsvetaieva's phrase is also imbued with indignity, in the sense that it carries poetry towards the privilege that the Jews bestow upon themselves even as they suffer from and pay a heavy price for it. It reinforces tribal prejudice. In any case, however we read the ambiguity of this sentence, it still poses a great risk, the vehicle for a war of signatures. What of the *trauma* between the voice and the written word in the Jewish experience? What is irremediable in the illusion of election? I am orienting you towards this question again, even though you have spoken about it in your letters.

Last month there was a double 'political' event in Morocco: the Congress of Jews of Moroccan descent, which was closely followed by a day dedicated to al-Quds, as if by linking these two events and neutralizing them, one could recognize not the State of Israel, but the Sephardim and thus also the people of Israel. A conjuring trick no doubt. On the official Moroccan side, there was an appeal to Abrahamic solidarity. Public opinion was somewhat dubious: how do you explain the presence, in Morocco, of Israeli senators who live, where else, in Israel? According to the official casuistry, a Moroccan, Jewish or not, never loses his nationality, even if he rejects or changes it. (Born a Moroccan, a Moroccan remains Moroccan, in death.) Hence the old anecdote about Moroccan Jews: when they leave they take the keys of the house with them. Their house cannot be expropriated, it is – in its own way – sacred. In lieu of a set of keys, there is, it seems, always a guardian who stays after the departure of the Jewish community. A witness, often old, abandoned, one who remains, remains that persist in this myth. But the drama of these witnesses is pitiful, theirs is more a decomposition than an act of witnessing, they are those who guard the dead rather than hopeful survivors. I saw the guardian of El Jadida, my native city, and felt sorry for him. El Maleh tells this story rather well in his book *Parcours immobile*. It begins with the epigraph of the last Jew who died in Assila, in the north of Morocco.

I told you that I attended a small conference of Arab and Spanish writers in Ronda, a gorgeous eagle-city perched over impressive valleys, and one of the last cities conquered by the Catholic Kings. This is the city the poet Rilke adopted as his destinal city.

It is only now that the 'return of the repressed' is appearing in Spain, albeit in a marginal way. The novelist Goytisolo proposes the notion of '*mudejar*' to speak of the cultural *métissage* between what is Hispanic and what is Arab. He wishes to turn *métissage* into a form of writing that is traversed by this plural identity, by the sensibility formed throughout the history of such a long struggle. In his books, he tries to practise this form, far from any notion of folklore. To make the other intervene in your writing like something that is inherent to your own body. It seems to me that this experience can go much further than any form of exoticism in French literature, which remains attached to a mythology of fantasies and irresponsible leisure. In the best of cases, it is a 'romantic' nostalgia in the vein of Chateaubriand. Segalen was the one who opened the gates to an aesthetics of the stranger or foreigner that respects this figure in its irreducible difference.

Spain is moving and marching forth. At the same time this forward movement makes apparent the force of memory. Strange impression of *returning* to Spain. As a Moroccan, I return to it at the intersection of two chiasma, two traumatic chiasma. The first is the Arab defeat over there, in the melancholy of speaking and writing poems about it; the second is the colonial one, which continues to work through us. For example, my French language – which was first imposed upon me – is an *irremediable* language, a traumatic event, a violent uprooting. The day I understood that one has to *transform* the irremediable, my 'style' became the cutting edge of a sentence that must welcome decomposition and humiliation in order to bear witness beyond trauma. We write only the irremediable, but we die from it if we do not return it to the suffering that belies it. This is how I write, I think. Have faith in my friendship. I send you my greetings.

A. Khatibi

On this 2nd of July, 1984

My dear Adbelkebir,

I don't know if at this time of the day – 6 o'clock in the morning – in this month of July of the year of grace I don't know what, since after all grace is what is the most contested and the least shared, I can write anything of value about the typographical sign called the hyphen which links the *two* terms Judeo and Arab. Grammatically speaking, I should have written 'the terms'… but my writing betrayed me; as if each term were marked by a third term hidden behind I know not what curtain, which I imagine dyed in all the colours of a rainbow as ancient as the mantle that covered that old drunk Noah, whose nudity distressed at least one of his sons: Sem, our common eponymous ancestor.

It seems to me that this third term demarcates a field: I was dumbfounded that during the Lebanon war the Israelis declared

– amongst other justifications – that they were intervening to protect the poor persecuted Christian communities. I am surprised to read Israeli propandists-*hystorians* write that 'the Arabs have always banned the Jews from the city of Jerusalem'... when the Arabs were the ones to let them live there when they conquered the city, unlike the Byzantines who expelled them from the city and the Crusaders who slaughtered them.

But also ... of late Arab polemicists (I am thinking in particular of that heap of counter-truths and ramblings that is Ibrahim Amin Ghali's *Egypt and the Jews in Antiquity*) have been writing that the 'torturers of Jesus' – the Jews, *of course* – 'are, have been, and forever will be ... traitors to be banished'. And so, the time has come when Jews and Arabs parade around heaping praise upon the imaginary Christians who were, in the West, let's not forget it, persecutors of the worst kind (the predatory kind). See the Jew and the Arab pointing fingers at each other and chanting 'he's the bad guy!! he's the bad guy!!!'

A strange paradox indeed. A pirouette of history, as if the tired but not yet exhausted actors were thumbing their noses in the direction of the audience, an audience wildly amused by these absurd contortions and overly theatrical displays of flattery.

Can you imagine Ishaq and Ishmael singing in a broken chorus: 'Save! Save *Yerushalayim/El Quds* in the Name of the Sacred Heart!'? It would be hilarious. The burlesque is the order of the day. It prevails. Will it prevail for much longer? Or will it disappear amidst the boos of spectators who are said to be 'clear-eyed and outraged'? Suspense ...

I don't know if I'm making any sense this morning. But I have the strange feeling that the third term that intrudes into a confrontation that has lasted fifteen hundred years is the one a friend of mine dubbed 'the acrobat'.

With this irreverence I end these lines, which appeared unannounced in place of the erudite and solemn letter I had resolved to send you.

Yours truly
Jacques Hassoun

El Harhoura, 8 July 1984

Our letters *crossed paths*, my dear Hassoun. And indeed they were, they are destined to cross paths continually. The one you call 'the acrobat' is for me the *postman*: he distributes and disperses letters while leaving some of them blank. What can we do but write on the trace of this blankness, sealed here (in the Jewish and Arab debate) with something irremediable.

I am convinced that one can write only from the irremediable and from a traumatic trace, whether it is occasioned by an event or a complete fiction. The letter is always based on something traumatic, to be returned, turned over if we are to read its trace.

How might we read the advent of monotheism from this point of view? From the point of view of the biographic 'tradition' ['السيرة'] of Muhammad, Allah sends Muhammad a letter or rather an illegible message. The prophet must transmit this message without altering it, he listens to it and repeats it and it is the scribe – the third party between Allah and the prophet – who records it. From the very beginning, there is a dissymmetry of destination, a dissymmetry of reading and writing. He does not read or write, he repeats what he hears. It seems to me that this dissymmetry is also what defines the traumatic event as it is produced in imagination. There is a dissociated gesture in the inscription of this archaism, such that there is an identity between God and the Book.

If I remind you of this story it is to return to the 'incurable' relation between monotheism and writing. For example, I live this relation in my experience of bilingualism, an experience I have recounted elsewhere. Yesterday I remembered that I dedicated the second edition of my book *La Mémoire tatouée* to my mother, who is illiterate. In a way, I took the place of God while my mother took the place of the prophet. This inversion is already at play in the dissymmetry of the prophetic message. A very curious operation, and yet I *signed* it, for better and worse. Of course, this is not a perfect analogy, since God dedicates (himself) to himself, he sings his own praise.

What about the Jewish Mother in her sacrifice to the Book? It seems to me that in this respect the Jews and the Arabs have repressed the maternal figure with the same violence, and that Christianity wanted to salvage an undesirable relation between the Book and the Mother. Thanks to the trinity, Christianity reintroduced the image of the *flesh* in the letter, between creation and pro-creation, as if it wanted to radicalize a new hierarchy in the notion of the Book made flesh. To an extent it feminized writing: Nietzsche says this very clearly in many passages. The passion of the One (amongst Jews and Arabs) eliminates the feminine One for the Other, which is a masculine figure. It seems to me that this Hegelian mediation (remember Hegel and Derrida's reading in his unforgettable *Glas*, which defends the impregnable position of the Mother) is lacking in the Semitic passion of the One.

The One: a number, the first, and at the same time, a *name*, the other name of God.

This passion extends to the social structure (that of the Semitic peoples) following the ethnological law of the highly codified exchange of women, mothers, wives, concubines, slaves.

Christianity introduced the *three* in order give woman a place, and also to fix her in the tender cruelty of dogma. Between Christian love and Semitic passion, God has changed scenes.

But what about the Jewish Mother?

The summer continues, with the pleasures of water and voyagers. I have real dizzy spells, but a poem awaits me, a poem that I hope will be close to the Ocean.

I hope your summer will be a beautiful one.

Faithfully yours,
A. Khatibi

Paris, on this 14 July 1984

My dear Abdelkébir,

Here we are again, taking up the pilgrim's pen one after the other to try to say, again and again, of what loss we are – most of us – the witnesses. My last letter stunned me after the fact. What is the Judeo–Arab conflict in the end? Do we not give in to the imported language by speaking of it in these terms? For those who have been brought up in an Arabic culture (language, customs, table and bed manners) saying Judeo–Arab conflict would imply an existential tear, a schism, more than a split, that could be cured only through the work of writing about and theorizing this apparently inextricable situation. In this way 'أكتب' ['write'], rather that 'إقرأ' ['read'], would come to index our existence. Hence the tendency to drift towards chronicles or tales of nostalgia, which have flooded us all these past years. Perhaps this is a way to account for what, in the trace, grates at us, makes us start, like an old wound that reminds he who suffers from it, whenever the season changes, that *it* is still alive. Lovecraft gave us a repulsive image of this process; Juda Halévi (Aboul Hassan El-Lawi), a heroic poetics. I think that everything I have written since 1975/77 revolves around this wound of language, which encroaches upon the ultimate border represented by the letter. A wound of language, that is to say a wound of the symbolic that muddles the cards to the point that at every turn an image appears that refers back only to itself, that insists, appears, disappears and throws the player onto the playing deck.

I would like to think that the exchange we have established allows us to identify this wound in the place where it seems to be active.

This is why I say that the Judeo–Arab conflict is a displaced state conflict. A conflict that has, perhaps, animated ancient grievances, ancient misunderstandings … At this point I would like to ask you: And you, do you feel touched by the departure of the Moroccan Jews you lived with? How did this absented part of the Moroccan people move you? I hope that one day you will be able to give me an answer.

But let me come back to one of your questions: the question concerning the relation of the Jewish mother to the Book. The figure of the mother is omnipresent in Judaism. But in a very specific way: the more Judaism was detached from its environment, the more it was subjected to economic and social hardships, the more women were cloistered and confined to the four corners of their house. During periods of good fortune (the Fatimid era in Egypt until the beginning of the Mamluk era, in Kurdish or Yemenite communities living in remote valleys) women were teachers, predicators, and could even have their 'Kenisseth el moualamath' (Synagogue of Female Teachers), as they did in Cairo in the eleventh century. So there was a time when their freedom could be imagined. This possibility disappeared when the Jews were forced into a position of defence. Through their bodies, women represent the destiny of their clan. This is why they are closest to the real. Guardians of *the sanctity of the home*, they are responsible for baking the bread and removing the *hala*, the portion of the dough that is burned to represent the sacrifice; they are responsible for purity and impurity on their days of menstruation, they are responsible for lighting the oil lamp that marks the border between the days of feast and the days of toil and vanity. They mark the limit, they represent it. They are the ones who make space around the place that will be occupied by the one and only Book (*el-Mousshaf*). But my generation discovered Europeanized women. School teachers in Cairo, in the Schools of Saint-Joseph-of-the-Apparition (!) or the Schools of the Jewish Community 'Moses of Cattaoui Pacha'. Like many women of their generation, they tolerated the ubiquitous presence of the Hebrew Book as long as it did not stop their children from entering the only culture they deemed worthy of the name, French culture. And, while they knew the Arabic language well, they generally knew nothing of Hebrew (except for the benediction over the Friday night lamp). Though this may seem somewhat anecdotal, it shows that we are still dealing with the *three*, as long as (for the Semite) the three does not enter into manifest discourse. This is why I consider your remarks on the opposition between Semitic passion and Christian love to be on the mark. Love expatiates. Passion howls. The Semite, the Jew wishes to ignore love and the pangs of the heart. Remember this anecdote – a persistent one, it seems – of the Alexandrine rabbi Mordekhay 'Anzarouth, who would exhort us not to say that we loved the divinity in our hearts, but to venerate it in even the most futile actions of our daily life, for in speaking of the heart ['قلب'] the human only ever expresses the vile behaviour of a dog ['كلب']. And this rabbi would rail against the West and its lures by recalling the prophetic phrase: '*from the North evil will come …*'

I would have liked to ask you more about Arab monotheism (and to what extent it relies, or not, on the notion of the *Umma* – the Arab Nation) but I will come back to this question in another letter.

For now, let me say that the Jewish mother, eternally grieving for her mother and her daughters, is the woman who announces (too loudly?) her passion for her father and her sons and the respect she claims to have for her husband. How is she woman? How does she introduce femininity into monotheistic discourse? Through her very abstraction …

Summer is approaching … As of 6 July, I am the grandfather of a little girl named Helen Rosa. I am delighted.

I will write soon … An article by Lyotard and the reactions it provoked will be my pretext. For he speaks of the foreclosure of the mother amongst the Jews … a bizarre expression, opposed to everything Lacan says about foreclosure.

In the meantime, I wish you an excellent week (amongst the Jews of Egypt we would say ['جمعتك خضرا']: may your week be green).

Yours truly
Jacques Hassoun

Tangier, 24 July 1984

And so it is from this city, Jacques, that I congratulate you on your grandfatherhood. I don't know if I will ever experience this feeling, but I imagine one must feel like an ancestor, somewhere between the fashioning of the name (repeated three times) and the fashioning of the body, which is more fraught. In any case, I wish you, or rather I would wish to bless you, yes, to bless you (strange, isn't it) but in the name of no god. And isn't that what we wanted, what we desired; to poke fun – without too much blasphemy – at the end of all monotheism. But monotheism has yet to destroy itself in the violence and apocalypse it contains before we can find the time to poke fun at it. After 'our' death, it will continue to give birth to the survivors that torment us, those of which we are speaking here.

I would rather not wait to answer your question about how I felt after the departure of Moroccan Jews. First, because I feel like it, and also because movements of departure, voyage and exodus excite my imagination. As we know, the movement of writing recalls the voyage. Writing is separation, nostalgia, the to-and-fro of traces and their effacement, even, in a sense, when 'not sitting'. Well, let us begin!

When I recall the Jews of my childhood today, words like ['زيم']⁹ or ['ماء الحياة']¹⁰ come to my lips, so to speak. That 'crispy', unsalted bread always intrigued me. It is only later that, thanks to a Jewish (and communist) friend, I was able to discover, to really savour the sweets, wines and 'heavenly' delicacies of Jewish Moroccan cuisine, a cuisine that we are steadily losing and that has exiled itself to other mouths, other 'ventriloquists'. This would usually happen after the feast of Mimouna. I want to tell this story, because these small details enable me to return to the time of my 'Jewishness', which is, like it or not, a tattoo of my purest childhood.

Usually it was us children who would go on rampages in the Mellah. For example, in Essaouira, a city where there was then a sizeable Jewish population, we would steal old Jews' skullcaps and resell them. But I should be careful not to go too far, because if I do I will awaken old demons. I should not generalize. I did this once, only once, and it was too easy for us kids to filch a skullcap, without any courage whatsoever. What can I say? More than this, we would repeat the gesture elsewhere, in the Jewish cemetery where we would steal amulets, but we would do the same in the tombs of Muslim saints. I must have been five or six.

At the time, I could also make out a phonetic and tonal difference that made us laugh. The ['ا'] (*a*) in place of the ['ق'] (*q*), for example. This phonetic transformation also exists among the Muslims of Fez, and my grandfather was Fassi. I never knew him, and around me a very guttural dialect was spoken, the dialect of my region, the Doukkala. There was, for me, a linguistic similarity between the Jews and the Fassis. Later, I

---

9 *Zim*: unleavened bread. [Author's note.]
10 *Ma' el haya*: fig alcohol. [Author's note.]

learned that it came from the culture of the Moors. My phonetic schema was slightly disturbed.

All this does not amount to much; and yet these slight traces of cultural difference intrigued us and fed our imaginary 'superiority' over the Jews. Superiority or disdain for a people that, relegated to a lower caste, burrows itself in difference.

But today I think that my affective make-up as a child was more complicated than this. In biographical terms, from a very young age I experienced (through a series of circumstances that would no doubt be too long and tedious to recount) a whole network of cultural elements: at once Arab, Muslim, Berber, French, Jewish and – in my city – an entire Portuguese mythology. Wasn't the marabout of our city a Portuguese convert who betrayed his people during the siege of Mazagan (*Mazagao*) by the Moroccans of that era? This marabout is the patron saint of the city. A Portuguese *canonized* by the people: an ordinary story, rather than a miraculous one, of what was required in Morocco to become a saint. More than this, one had to be a *foreigner* (to the tribe, the clan, the nation and even one's religion in this case).

I remember than on the occasion of Independence, after the speech of King Mohammed V (so beloved by the Jews), we felt, I felt quite satisfied. I had welcomed the news of the appointment of a Jewish minister in the national government. Amongst the youth of Independence, we had discussed and debated this appointment. But I heard no trace of anger, no indignation. It was simply part of the new (and always so ancient) political chessboard.

But I have forgotten what is perhaps the most important thing, the essential element of my affective life in relation to the Jews. I already told you this story in one of my letters, the terribly symptomatic and tragic story of a relative married to a Jewish woman. I knew him well and loved him. I got to know his converted Jewish wife (who later returned to her faith) at the crossroads between faith and abdication. I loved her as one loves a foreign mother, a mother who is nevertheless secondary.

And so I can respond in the affirmative to your question: yes, I was moved by the departure of the Jews. I still am, in a different way of course, but how? A society that does not tolerate its minorities is itself intolerable. One has only to see the silence surrounding Berber culture in Morocco: there isn't even a university professorship on the subject. And yet this problem – a very specific one to be sure – is enormous. As for the Judeo–Arab question, my point is not to raise the question of the mutual responsibility attributed either to Zionist propaganda (which made every effort to frighten and turn the Jewish minority away from its natural homeland to its mythical homeland) or to the Muslims themselves or the propaganda of inter-Arab nationalism, but also to underscore the limits inherent in theocratic societies, which always contain within them forces of rejection and exclusion. And this is true of Judaism also. Today Muslims tear one another apart, they exclude one another and destroy themselves in the lost figure of the One. We can laugh about the carcass of the symbolic father on either side, we can also survive it, like in the Egyptian cycle of the dead, where each caste, each sect dreams of traversing the itinerary of its own immortality. Immortality, that is to say, the death of others, their effacement.

What we need is a strategy that better understands these intimations of apocalypse, a strategy that would be able to reorient us towards more modern realities and mythologies, those that are already underway: the globalization of techniques that are in the hands of a few world powers, the marginalization of the 'Third-World', a process of impoverishment seemingly without end, and the neutralization of the old world of our dreams, its myths and its spectres. And lots of other questions. But, speaking of Israel, or rather the State of Israel, what is clear is that it is the laboratory, a singular laboratory between the death of the gods and the supremacy of strategists. I send you my greetings.

A. Khatibi

Notes on Contributors

Assia Belhabib is Professor of French, Francophone and Comparative Literature at the University Mohammed V in Rabat (Morocco) and a literary critic. Her publications explore the universal dimension of literature and include *La langue de l'hôte: Lecture de Abdelkébir Khatibi* (Editions Okad, 2009). She has also edited several collective volumes *Littérature et Altérité* (Editions Okad, 2009), *Le jour d'après* (Editions Afrique-Orient, 2010), *Quand le printemps est arabe* (Editions La Croisée des Chemins, 2014) and *Abdelkébir Khatibi, Quels héritages?* (Edition de l'Académie du Royaume du Maroc, 2020).

Jasmina Bolfek-Radovani is a Visiting Research Fellow at the University of Westminster. A graduate of the same institution, she holds a PhD in Francophone literary and cultural studies and a monograph based on her thesis, *Geo/graphies of Loss: Space, Place and Spatial Loss in North African and Canadian Writing in French*, was published in 2015. Her research interests include the study of literary and cultural productions of space in the areas of the Francophone Maghreb and Canada. She has published several articles in peer-reviewed journals and has given a number of conference presentations, both nationally and internationally. Jasmina is a multilingual poet and the creator of the multilingual poetry project 'Unbound'; her multilingual poetry performances 'Reveries about Language' (in London and Zagreb) received funding from the Arts and Humanities Research Council-funded *Language Acts and Worldmaking* small grants programme in 2018 and 2019.

Dominique Combe is Professor of French literature and literary theory at the École Normale Supérieure (Paris) and Dean of International Relations. He is also in charge of the joint Master's 'Littératures' (ENS/PSL). He has taught in various universities in France (Avignon,

Sorbonne-Nouvelle) and abroad as a permanent or visiting professor (University of Cairo, University of Fribourg, University of Oxford, Middlebury College, University of Montreal, University of Tokyo). His main research fields are literary theory, poetics, and francophone and French modern poetry. He has published eight books about nineteenth and twentieth century French poets (Rimbaud, Césaire, Bonnefoy), literary genres, and francophone and postcolonial literature (French Antilles, Maghreb, Middle East, Quebec, Europe), including recently the revised edition of *Littératures francophones – questions, débats, polémiques* (Presses Universitaires de France, 2019). He is a member of the 'République des Savoirs', a research team in humanities, sciences and philosophy.

Rim Feriani is Educational Director at The Muhyiddin Ibn Arabi Society (MIAS), UK. She had previously lectured in Arabic language at King's College, London and taught Arabic language and cultural studies in the Department of Modern Languages and Cultures at the University of Westminster, London. Her doctoral thesis (2016) demonstrates how the works of three internationally acclaimed writers of the twentieth and twenty-first centuries, the Algerian Assia Djebar, the Moroccan Tahar Ben Jelloun and the British Indian Salman Rushdie creatively engage with the Islamic heritage. Combining Ibn Arabi's Sufi thought with Paul Ricoeur's hermeneutic approach, it explores the symbolic and ontological underpinnings of the Sacred, providing a broader understanding of their literary works. She has published on her research and presented papers at King's College, Birkbeck College University of London, University of Cambridge, Warwick University and Bristol University.

Charles Forsdick is James Barrow Professor of French at the University of Liverpool. His books include *Victor Segalen and the Aesthetics of Diversity* (Oxford University Press, 2000) and *Toussaint Louverture: A Black Jacobin in the Age of Revolution* (Pluto, 2017). He has also edited or co-edited several volumes, including: *Francophone Postcolonial Studies: A Critical Introduction* (Arnold, 2003), *Postcolonial Thought in the French-Speaking World* (Liverpool University Press, 2009) and *The Black Jacobins Reader* (Duke University Press, 2016). He is co-editor of the Glissant Translation Project and was, until 2020, AHRC Theme Leadership Fellow for Translating Cultures.

Olivia C. Harrison is Associate Professor of French and Comparative Literature at the University of Southern California. Her publications include *Transcolonial Maghreb: Imagining Palestine in the Era of Decolonization*, an anthology-in-translation of the Moroccan journal *Souffles*, and essays on Maghrebi literature, Beur and banlieue cultural production, and postcolonial theory. She is currently working on a monograph about the intersection of antiracism and Palestine solidarity movements in France, and researching the recuperation of minority discourses by the French far- and alt-right for a book tentatively titled *The White Minority*.

Jane Hiddleston is Professor of Literatures in French at the University of Oxford, and Official Fellow in French at Exeter College, Oxford. She has published widely on francophone literature and postcolonial theory, including most recently *Decolonising the Intellectual: Politics, Culture, and Humanism at the End of the French Empire* (Liverpool University Press, 2014) and *Writing After Postcolonialism: Francophone North African Literature in Transition* (Bloomsbury, 2017). She is currently working on a study of Fanon and literature, entitled *Frantz Fanon: Literature and Invention*.

Debra Kelly is Professor Emerita in Modern Languages, School of Humanities, University of Westminster, London. She has published widely in French and Francophone literary and cultural studies, including *Autobiography and Independence. Selfhood and Creativity in North African Postcolonial Writing in French* (Liverpool University Press, 2003). Her current research focuses on the historical and contemporary French and Francophone communities in London, and she is co-editor of *A History of the French in London. Liberty, Equality, Opportunity* (Institute of Historical Research Publications, 2013). She is also a Senior Associate Research Fellow at King's College London working on the flagship Arts and Humanities Research Council-funded project *Language Acts and Worldmaking*, a research centre within King's Art and Humanities Research Institute.

Khalid Lyamlahy is Assistant Professor of French and Francophone Studies at the University of Chicago. He holds a PhD from the University of Oxford (St Anne's College) and his work focuses on North African Francophone literature in relation to political, social and cultural debates in the region and beyond. His research interests include contemporary fiction and poetry in French, literary theory and translation, and his articles have appeared in *Research in African Literature, The Journal of North African Studies*, the *Irish Journal of French Studies* and *Revue Roland Barthes*. His current research explores questions of identity and alterity in post-2011 Maghrebi fiction. Besides his academic work, he has published a novel, *Un Roman Etranger* (Présence Africaine Editions, 2017) and is a regular contributor to several literary magazines in France and the US.

Lucy McNeece has a PhD from Harvard University and is Emeritus professor of Comparative Literature and Francophone Studies. She served as chair of the Comparative Literary and Cultural Studies program at the University of Connecticut, as well as director of the Middle East Studies Center. During her tenure she directed several plays from the Francophone Arab world. She has lived and taught in Morocco and Tunisia. Since her retirement, she has done research at The French Institute of the Middle East (IFPO) and The American University (AUB) in Beirut. She lives in Paris, where she has obtained a master's degree in modern Arabic literature at the National Institute of Oriental Cultures and Languages (INALCO). She has published primarily on writers of the Maghreb, but also on writers from Turkey and Lebanon. Her research focuses on the contemporary novel, theatre and cinema of the Islamic world.

Matt Reeck has published translations from French, Hindi, Urdu and Korean. He has won awards from the Fulbright Foundation, the PEN/ Heim Fund and the National Endowment for the Arts. His translation of Khatibi's *Class Warrior—Taoist Style* was published by Wesleyan University Press in 2017. In Spring 2021, he will be the Translator in Residence at Princeton University. *The Ethics of Description*, his monograph on a minor tradition within French modern travel writing, will be published in the Routledge Research in Travel Writing series in 2021.

Alison Rice is Dr William M. Scholl Associate Professor of French and Francophone Studies and Chair of the Department of Romance Languages and Literatures at the University of Notre Dame. Her first book, *Time Signatures: Contextualizing Contemporary Francophone Autobiographical Writing from the Maghreb* (Lexington Books, 2006), focuses on Hélène Cixous, Assia Djebar and Abdelkébir Khatibi.

Polygraphies: Francophone Women Writing Algeria (University of Virginia Press, 2012), examines the work of seven prominent women writers from Algeria. Her current book project, 'Francophone Metronomes: Worldwide Women Writers in Paris', is complemented by a series of filmed interviews available at the following website: https://www.francophonemetronomes.com/.

Nao Sawada is Professor of French Literature at Rikkyo University in Tokyo. He took his doctorate in philosophy at University of Paris 1. He is author of a number of books, notably on Sartre: *Yobikake no keiken, Sarutoru no moraruron* (The Call to Adventure: An Ethical Reading of Sartre, 2002), and on contemporary French philosophy (*Jean-Luc Nancy*, 2013). He has translated into Japanese many of Sartre's books, including *Les Mots* (*The Words*). He has also translated a number of novels and essays by contemporary francophone authors, such as Philippe Forest (*Sarinagara*), Tahar Ben Jelloun (*Moha le fou Moha le sage*) and Abdelkébir Khatibi (*Maghreb pluriel*).

Andy Stafford is a specialist of the work of Roland Barthes. He has published widely on African and Caribbean literature in French and on the photo-text (Liverpool University Press 2010). His chapter on Abdellatif Laâbi's prison poetry is due to appear in a volume on confinement (Classiques Garnier 2021, Michaël Abecassis and Maribel Peñalver Vicea eds). He is senior lecturer at the University of Leeds and in 2019 was visiting professor at the University of Paris-Sorbonne-Nord.

Edwige Tamalet Talbayev is Associate Professor of French at Tulane University. A scholar of Maghrebi literature and Mediterranean Studies, she is the author of *The Transcontinental Maghreb: Francophone Literature across the Mediterranean* (2017) and the co-editor of *The Mediterranean Maghreb: Literature and Plurilingualism* (2012) and *Critically Mediterranean: Temporalities, Aesthetics, and Deployments of a Sea in Crisis* (2018). She is currently at work on several projects that examine borders and migration from the standpoint of water as an epistemological site. She is editor of *Expressions maghrébines*, the peer-reviewed journal of the *Coordination Internationale des Chercheurs sur les Littératures Maghrébines*.

Alfonso de Toro is Professor Emeritus for Romance Philology at the University of Leipzig and Director of the Transdisciplinary

Ibero-American and Francophone Research Centre at the same university. He is also the director of the series *Theory and Critique of Culture and Literature, Theory and Praxis of the Theatre, Passagen* (OLMS) and *Transversalité* (L'Harmattan). His long list of publications include *Borges infinito. Borgesvirtual* (OLMS, 2008) and *Epistémologies. 'Le Maghreb'* (L'Harmattan, 2009/2011). He edited an issue of *Expressions maghrébines* on Dispositifs autobiographiques et historiques: Epistémologies transversales (2011) and co-edited the collective volume *The World in Movement: Performative Identities and Diasporas* (Brill, 2019). He is also the Corresponding Member of the Chilean Language Academy Abroad and received several distinctions including the 'Gabriela Mistral Medal with the rank of Great Officer' and the distinction of 'Officier dans l'ordre des Palmes académiques'. https://home.uni-leipzig.de/detoro/.

Bibliography

Books by Abdelkébir Khatibi
(including Co-authored and Co-edited Volumes)

Anthologie des écrivains maghrébins d'expression française. Co-edited with Albert Memmi, Jean Déjeux, Jacqueline Arnaud and Arlette Roth. Paris: Présence Africaine, 1964.

Bibliographie de la littérature nord-africaine d'expression française. Co-edited with Albert Memmi, Jean Déjeux, Jacqueline Arnaud and Arlette Roth. Paris: Editions Mouton, 1965.

Bilan de la sociologie au Maroc. Rabat: Publications de l'Association pour la Recherche en Sciences Humaines, 1967.

Le Roman maghrébin. Paris: Maspero, 1968.

Etudes sociologiques sur le Maroc. Ed. Abdelkébir Khatibi. Rabat: Société d'études économiques, sociales et statistiques, 1971; 2nd edn, Bulletin *économique et social* du Maroc, 1978.

La Mémoire tatouée: autobiographie d'un décolonisé. Paris: Denoël, 1971. Reprinted in *Œuvres de Abdelkébir Khatibi I: Romans et récits.* Paris: La Différence, 2008, pp. 9–113.

La Blessure du nom propre. Paris: Denoël, 1974.

Ecrivains marocains: du Protectorat à 1965. Co-edited with Mohammed Benjelloun Touimi and Mohammed Kably. Paris: Sindbad, 1974.

Vomito blanco: le sionisme et la conscience malheureuse. Paris: Union générale d'éditions, 1974.

L'Art calligraphique arabe. Co-authored with Mohamed Sijelmassi. Paris: Editions du Chêne, 1976. Republished as *L'Art calligraphique de l'Islam.* Paris: Gallimard, 1994.

Le Lutteur de classe à la manière taoïste. Paris: Sindbad, 1976. Reprinted in *Œuvres de Abdelkébir Khatibi II: Poésie de l'aimance.* Paris: La Différence, 2008, pp. 9–35.

La Peinture de Ahmed Cherkaoui. Co-authored with Edmond Amran El Maleh, Toni Maraini and Mohammed Melehi. Casablanca: Shoof, 1976. Reprinted as *Ahmed Cherkaoui: la passion du signe.* Paris: Editions Revue noire, 1996.

Le Livre du sang. Paris: Gallimard, 1979. Reprinted in *Œuvres de Abdelkébir Khatibi I: Romans et récits*. Paris: La Différence, 2008, pp. 115–204.

Le Prophète voilé. Paris: L'Harmattan, 1979.

De la mille et troisième nuit. Tangier: Presses des Editions marocaines et internationales, 1980. Reprinted as 'Nuits blanches', in *Ombres japonaises*. Montpellier: Fata Morgana, 1988, pp. 9–32.

Amour bilingue. Montpellier: Fata Morgana, 1983. Reprinted in *Œuvres de Abdelkébir Khatibi I: Romans et récits*. Paris: La Différence, 2008, pp. 205–83.

Maghreb pluriel. Paris: Denoël, 1983.

Du bilinguisme. Co-authored with Jalil Bennani, Ahmed Boukous, Abdallah Bounfour, François Cheng, Eliane Formentelli, Jacques Hassoun, Abdelfettah Kilito, Abdelwahab Meddeb and Tzvetan Todorov. Paris: Denoël, 1985.

Le Même Livre. Co-authored with Jacques Hassoun. Paris: Editions de l'éclat, 1985.

Dédicace à l'année qui vient. Montpellier: Fata Morgana, 1986.

Figures de l'étranger dans la littérature française. Paris: Denoël, 1987.

Ombres japonaises. Montpellier: Fata Morgana, 1988. Reprinted in *Œuvres de Abdelkébir Khatibi III: Essais*. Paris: La Différence, 2008, pp. 208–32.

Par-dessus l'épaule. Paris: Aubier, 1988.

Un été à Stockholm. Paris: Flammarion, 1990. Reprinted in *Œuvres de Abdelkébir Khatibi I: Romans et récits*. Paris: La Différence, 2008, pp. 285–379.

Paradoxes du sionisme. Rabat: Al Kalam, 1990.

Penser le Maghreb. Rabat: Société Marocaine des Editeurs Réunis, 1993.

Triptyque de Rabat. Paris: Noël Blandin, 1993. Reprinted in *Œuvres de Abdelkébir Khatibi I: Romans et récits*. Paris: La Différence, 2008, pp. 381–469.

Du signe à l'image: le tapis marocain. Co-authored with Ali Amahan. Casablanca: LAK International, 1994.

Peintres de Doukkala. Co-authored with Moulim El Aroussi. Casablanca: Association des Doukkala, 1994.

Poésie 94, n° 53 (June 1994). 'L'Aimance'. Ed. Abdelkébir Khatibi. Paris: Seghers/Maison de la Poésie.

'Civilisation de l'intersigne'. Conference presented at the Université de Rennes, 6 Apr. 1995 and at Berkeley, University of California, 14 Apr. 1995. Rabat: Dossiers Ouverts, 1996.

Le Livre de l'aimance. Casablanca: Marsam, 1995.

L'Alternance et les partis politiques. Casablanca: Eddif, 1998.

Civilisation marocaine: arts et cultures. Co-edited with Mohamed Sijelmassi. Arles: Actes Sud, 1999.

La Langue de l'autre. New York and Tunis: Les Mains secrètes, 1999.

Vœu de silence. Neuilly-sur-Seine: Al Manar, 2000. Reprinted in *Œuvres de Abdelkébir Khatibi II: Poésie de l'aimance.* Paris: La Différence, 2008, pp. 161–77.

L'Art contemporain arabe: prolégomènes. Neuilly-sur-Seine: Al Manar, 2001.

Chemins de traverse: essais de sociologie. Rabat: Editions Okad, 2002.

Le Corps oriental. Paris: Hazan, 2002.

Aimance. Neuilly-sur-Seine: Al Manar, 2003.

Féerie et dissidence: colloque Jean Genet. Co-edited with Marie Redonnet. Rabat: Okad, 2003.

Pèlerinage d'un artiste amoureux. Monaco: Editions du Rocher, 2003. Reprinted in *Œuvres de Abdelkébir Khatibi I: Romans et récits.* Paris: La Différence, 2008, pp. 471–672.

Correspondance ouverte. Co-authored with Rita El Khayat. Rabat: Marsam, 2005.

Féerie d'un mutant. Monaco: Editions du Rocher, 2005. Reprinted in *Œuvres de Abdelkébir Khatibi I: Romans et récits.* Paris: La Différence, 2008, pp. 673–711.

Quatuor poétique: Rilke, Goethe Ekelof, Lundkvist. Neuilly-sur-Seine: Al Manar, 2006. Reprinted in Abdelkébir Khatibi, *Œuvres de Abdelkébir Khatibi II: Poésie de l'aimance.* Paris: La Différence, 2008, pp. 179–91.

Jacques Derrida, en effet. Neuilly-sur-Seine: Al Manar, 2007.

Œuvres de Abdelkébir Khatibi I: Romans et récits. Paris: La Différence, 2008.

Œuvres de Abdelkébir Khatibi II: Poésie de l'aimance. Paris: La Différence, 2008.

Œuvres de Abdelkébir Khatibi III: Essais. Paris: La Différence, 2008.

Le Scribe et son ombre. Paris: La Différence, 2008.

Le Chemin vers l'autre: entretiens (27–31 Octobre 2008). Co-authored with Samuel Weber. Rabat: Faculté des Lettres et des Sciences Humaines de Rabat, 2012.

Texts, Articles and Chapters by Abdelkébir Khatibi

'Histoire et sociologie au Maroc, note sur le problème de l'idéologie', *Hespéris-Tamuda* 7 (1966), pp. 101–5.

'Justice pour Driss Chraïbi', *Souffles* 3 (1966), p. 48.

'Le Maroc à l'heure du scoubidou', *Lamalif* 2 (15 Apr. 1966), pp. 19–23.

'Perception et fonction de l'enquête de l'opinion', *Bulletin ESM* 101–2 (Apr.–Sept. 1966), pp. 169–72.

'Poèmes', *Souffles* 2 (1966), p. 16.

'Roman maghrébin et culture nationale', *Souffles* 3 (1966), pp. 10–11.

'Stratification sociale et développement', *Bulletin ESM* 106–7 (July–Dec. 1967), pp. 171–3.

'Avant-propos', *Bulletin ESM* 109 (Apr.–June 1968), p. 1.

'Avant-propos', *Souffles* 10–11 (1968), pp. 4–5.

'Deux propositions sur le changement social et l'acculturation', *Annales marocaines de sociologie* 1 (1968).

'Abdellatif Laâbi, *Race* and E. M. Nissabouri, *Plus haute mémoire*', *Souffles* 13–14 (1969), p. 35.

'Appel aux écrivains maghrébins'. Co-authored with Tahar Benjelloun, Bensalem Himmich, Abdellatif Laâbi, Azeddine Madani, Ahmed Madini, Abdelaziz Mansouri, Ahmed Mejjati and E. M. Nissabouri, *Souffles* 15 (1969), pp. 99–102.

'La jeunesse est un espoir conditionné' (interview with Abdelkébir Khatibi), *Lamalif* 31 (July–Aug. 1969), pp. 46–50.

'Avant-propos', *Bulletin ESM* 118–19 (1970), p. 3.

'Avant-propos', *Etudes sociologiques sur le Maroc*. Rabat: Publications de la Société d'Etudes économiques, sociales et statistiques, 1971.

'Bagatelles', *Les Lettres Nouvelles* (Nov. 1971), pp. 29–37.

'Hiérarchies pré-coloniales – les théories', *Bulletin ESM* 120–1 (Jan. 1971), pp. 27–62. Republished as 'Etat et classes sociales', in Abdelkébir Khatibi (ed.), *Etudes sociologiques sur le Maroc*. Rabat: Société d'études économiques, sociales et statistiques, 1971; 2nd edn, Bulletin *économique et social* du Maroc, 1978, pp. 3–15.

'Vingt bagatelles sur la dépossession', *Les Lettres Nouvelles* (Mar. 1971), pp. 125–8.

'Culture nationale et culture de classe au Maroc', *Intégral* 5–6 (Sept. 1973), p. 20.

'Il faut s'essayer à une double critique permanente: Interview with Zakya Daoud', *Lamalif* 57 (1 Feb. 1973), pp. 32–4.

'Le Maghreb comme horizon de pensée', *Les Temps Modernes* 375 bis (1977), pp. 7–20 (p. 20). Reprinted in *Penser le Maghreb*. Rabat: Société Marocaine des Editeurs Réunis, 1993, pp. 123–36.

'Repères', in *Pro-Culture* 12 – Numéro spécial: 'Khatibi'. Rabat: Imprimerie culturelle et universitaire Mohammed V, 1978, pp. 48–52.

'Pour un compromis saharien', *Le Monde*, 2–3 Sept. 1979. Reprinted in *Penser le Maghreb*. Rabat: Société Marocaine des Editeurs Réunis, 1993, pp. 117–19.

'Présentation', in *La Mémoire tatouée: autobiographie d'un colonisé*. Paris: Union générale d'éditions, Collection 10/18, 1979, pp. 9–13.

'Préface', in Paul Pascon, *Etudes rurales: idées et enquêtes sur la campagne marocaine*. Rabat: Société Marocaine des Editeurs Réunis, 1980, pp. i–viii.

'Incipits', in Jalil Bennani *et al.*, *Du bilinguisme*. Paris: Denoël, 1985, pp. 171–95.

'Avant-propos', co-authored with N. Bouderbala, A. Diouri, M. Fay, A. Herzenni and L. Zagdouni, in 'Paul Pascon: 30 ans de sociologie au Maroc', *Bulletin ESM* 155–6 (Jan. 1986), pp. 5–6.

'Exergue', in Fatima Mernissi, *Le Maroc raconté par ses femmes*. Rabat: Société Marocaine des Editeurs Réunis, 1986, pp. 7–10.

'En guise de conclusion', in 'En hommage à Paul Pascon: colloque international sur le devenir de la société rurale au Maroc', *Bulletin ESM*, 159–61 (1987), p. 293.

'Intersignes', in Christine Buci-Glucksmann, Antoine Raybaud, Abdelhaï Diouri, Marc Gontard, Abdesslam Benabdelali, Abdelfattah Kilito, Abdallah Bounfour, Jaques Hassoun and Réda Bensmaïa, *Imaginaires de l'autre: Khatibi et la mémoire littéraire*. Paris: L'Harmattan, 1987, pp. 123–31.

'Mémoire d'une quête', in 'En hommage à Paul Pascon: colloque international sur le devenir de la société rurale au Maroc', *Bulletin ESM* 159–61 (1987), pp. 9–12.

'La Passion du livre vivant', *Regards* 1 (1988), pp. 46–9.

'Un chasseur d'empreintes', in Daoud Aoulad-Syad, *Marocains*. Paris: Contrejour/Agadir: Belvisi, 1989.

'Lettre – Préface', in Marc Gontard, *La Violence du texte: étude sur la littérature marocaine*. Paris: L'Harmattan, 1993, pp. 7–9.

'Amitié truquée (Lettre ouverte à Tahar Ben Jelloun en réponse à son livre *La soudure fraternelle*)', *République Internationale des Lettres* 5 (8 July 1994), pp. 56–7.

'Le Point de non-retour', in *Le Passage des frontières: autour du travail de Jacques Derrida*. Colloque de Cerisy. Paris: Galilée, 1994, pp. 445–9.

'L'Envol des racines', *Ahmed Cherkaoui: la passion du signe*. Paris: IMA, 1996.

'Un étranger professionnel', *Etudes françaises* 33.1 (1997), pp. 123–6.

'Paradigmes de civilisation', in *L'Œuvre de… Abdelkébir Khatibi*. Rabat: Marsam, 1997, pp. 69–87.

'Lettre ouverte à Jacques Derrida', in *La Langue de l'autre*. New York and Tunis: Les Mains secrètes, 1999, pp. 21–33. Reprinted in *Europe* 901 (2004), pp. 201–11.

'Paradigmes de civilisation', *Civilisation marocaine: arts et cultures*. Ed. Abdelkébir Khatibi and Mohamed Sijelmassi. Arles: Actes Sud, 1999, pp. 10–15.

'Préface', in Kacem Zhiri, *Panorama Islamique*. Casablanca: Najah el Jadida, 1999, p. 7.

'Préface', in Abdellatif El Bayati, *La Symphonie des nuits diaprées: récit autobiographique*. Rabat: Marsam, 2001, pp. 9–10.

'Tanizaki revisité: Méditation sur la littérature japonaise' (2003), in *Œuvres de Abdelkébir Khatibi III: Essais*. Paris: La Différence, 2008, pp. 225–32.

'Le Tapis dans l'imaginaire de l'Orient', in *Le Ciel dans un tapis*. Ghent: Editions Snoeck, 2004, pp. 40–9.

'Cervantès et la modernité' (2005), in *Œuvres de Abdelkébir Khatibi III: Essais*. Paris: La Différence, 2008, pp. 233–41.

'Préface', in Siham Issami, *Les Amants de l'ailleurs*. Neuilly-sur-Seine: Al Manar, 2005, pp. 7–8.

'Témoigner en images', *Regards des photographes arabes contemporains*. Paris: IMA, 2005.

'La Vestale et la guérillère: à propos de *L'Amour, la fantasia*', in *Assia Djebar, nomade entre les murs: pour une poétique transfrontalière*. Ed. Mireille Calle-Gruber. Paris: Maisonneuve & Larose, 2005, pp. 107–13.

'Préface', in Mohammed Cherkaoui, *Exposition des tableaux des merveilles cosmiques*. Rabat: Imprimerie Al Maarif Al Jadida, 2006, pp. 5–6.

'Témoigner à distance', in *Genèses, généalogies, genres: autour de l'œuvre d'Hélène Cixous*. Ed. Mireille Calle-Gruber and Marie-Odile Germain. Paris: Galilée and Bibliothèque Nationale de France, 2006, pp. 153–61.

'L'Intellectuel et le mondialisme', in Centre Marocain de Pen International, *L'Intellectuel, la société, le pouvoir*. El Jadida: Editions Okad, 2007, pp. 9–20.

'Comment fonder poétiquement une nation en exil?', in Mahmoud Darwich and Rachid Koraïchi, *Une nation en exil: hymnes gravés* suivi de *La Qasida de Beyrouth*. Algiers: Barzakh/Arles: Actes Sud, 2009, pp. 15–21.

'Postface', in Abdallah Bensmain, *Le Retour du muezzin*. Paris: Publisud, 2011, pp. 195–8.

Translations

Al-Riwaya Al-Magharibia. Trans. Mohammed Berrada. Rabat: Publications du Centre Universitaire de la Recherche Scientifique, 1971.

Al-Issmo Al-Arabiyo Al-Jarih. Trans. Mohammed Bennis. Beirut: Dar Al-Aouda, 1980.

Al-Mounadil Al-Tabaki Ala Al-Tarika Al-Taouia. Trans. Kadhim Jihad. Casablanca: Toubkal, 1980.

Annakd Al-Mouzdawaj. Trans. Adonis, Abdesslam Benabdelali and Zoubida Bourhil. Beirut: Dar Al-Aouda, 1980/Rabat: Okad, 1990.

Fi Al-Kittaba wa Ttajriba. Trans. Mohammed Berrada. Beirut: Dar Al-Aouda, 1980/Rabat: Okad, 1989.

Diwan Al-Khatte Al-Arabi. Trans. Mohammed Berrada. Beirut: Dar Al-Aouda, 1981.

Addakira Al-Mawchouma. Trans. Boutros Hallaq. Rabat: Institut Arabe pour la Recherche et la Publication & Société Marocaine des Editeurs Réunis, 1984.

'Double Criticism: The Decolonization of Arab Sociology'. In *Contemporary North Africa: Issues of Development and Integration*. Ed. Halim Barakat. Washington, DC: Center for Contemporary Arab Studies, 1985, pp. 9–19.

'Traces of a Trauma: On *Marrakch médine*'. Trans. Cecile Lindsay. In *The Review of Contemporary Fiction* 8.2 (1988), pp. 107–13.

'Space, Time, Culture: Reflections on Urban Life in Morocco'. In *Urbanism in Islam: The Proceedings of the International Conference on Urbanism in Islam (ICUIT)*. Ed. Yukawa Takeshi. Tokyo: The Middle Eastern Culture Center, vol. 2 (1989), pp. 273–81.

Love in Two Languages. Trans. Richard Howard. Minneapolis: University of Minnesota Press, 1990.

'Literary Nationalism and Internationalism'. In *Crisscrossing Boundaries in African Literatures*. Ed. Kenneth W. Harrow, Jonathan Ngaté and Clarisse Zimra. Annual Selected Papers of the ALA 12/1986. Washington, DC: Three Continents Press/African Literature Association, 1991, pp. 3–10.

Sayf fi Stockholm. Trans. Farid Zahi. Casablanca: Toubkal, 1992.

Annabiy Al-Moukanaa. Trans. Mohammed Kaghat. Kuwait City: Ministère de la Communication, 1993.

'A Colonial Labyrinth'. Trans. Catherine Dana. In *Yale French Studies* 83.2 (1993), pp. 5–11.

'How I Dream the Coming Century'. In *Civilisation de l'intersigne*. Trans. Faiza Shereen. Rabat: Dossiers Ouverts, 1996, pp. 29–54.

The Splendor of Islamic Calligraphy. Trans. James Hughes. London: Thames & Hudson, 1996.

From Sign to Image: The Moroccan Carpet. Trans. anon. Casablanca: LAK International, 1997.

Thoulathiat Al-Ribat. Trans. Farid Zahi. Casablanca: Arrabita, 1998.

'Diglossia'. Trans. Whitney Sanford. In *Algeria in Others' Languages*. Ed. Anne-Emmanuelle Berger. Ithaca, NY: Cornell University Press, 2002, pp. 157–60.

'L'intellectuel et le mondialisme (le cas marocain)' (2007). Trans. into Japanese in *Nijuiseiki no chisikijin – Furansu, Higashi-Ajia, soshite Sekai*. Ed. Harumi Ishizaki and Hirohide Tachibana. Tokyo: Ed. Fujiwara, 2009.

'Frontiers: Between Psychoanalysis and Islam'. Trans. P. Burcu Yalim. *Third Text* 23.6 (2009), pp. 689–96.

'The Language of the Other: Testimonial Exercises'. Trans. Catherine Porter. *PMLA* 125.4 (2010), pp. 1002–19.

Open Correspondance: An Epistolary Dialogue. Trans. Safoi Babana-Hampton, Valérie K. Orlando and Mary Vogl. New Orleans: UNO Press, 2011.

Nahwa Fikr Moughayir. Trans. Abdesslam Benabdelali. Doha: Ministry of Culture, Arts, and Heritage, 2013.

'Appeal to Maghrebi Writers'. Co-authored with Tahar Benjelloun, Bensalem Himmich, Abdellatif Laâbi, Azeddine Madani, Ahmed Madini, Abdelaziz Mansouri, Ahmed Mejjati and E. M. Nissabouri. Trans. Anne-Marie McManus. In *Souffles-Anfas: A Critical Anthology from the Moroccan Journal of Culture and Politics*. Ed. Olivia C. Harrison and Teresa Villa-Ignacio. Stanford, CA: Stanford University Press, 2016, pp. 209–13.

'The Maghrebi Novel and National Culture'. Trans. Claudia Esposito. In *Souffles-Anfas: A Critical Anthology from the Moroccan Journal of Culture and Politics*. Ed. Olivia Harrison and Teresa Villa-Ignacio. Stanford, CA: Stanford University Press, 2016, pp. 56–8.

'Poems'. Trans. Lucy R. McNair. In *Souffes-Anfas: A Critical Anthology from the Moroccan Journal of Culture and Politics*. Ed. Olivia Harrison and Teresa Villa-Ignacio. Stanford, CA: Stanford University Press, 2016, pp. 37–8.

Tattooed Memory. Trans. Peter Thompson. Paris: L'Harmattan, 2016.

Class Warrior – Taoist Style. Trans. Matt Reeck. Middletown, CT: Wesleyan University Press, 2017.

Plural Maghreb. Trans. P. Burcu Yalim. London: Bloomsbury, 2019.

Secondary Works

Ahnouch, Fatima. *Abdelkébir Khatibi: la langue, la mémoire et le corps*. Paris: L'Harmattan, 2004.

Al-Jāḥiẓ. *al-Bayān wa al-tabyin (The Book of Eloquence and Oratory)*. Ed. ʿAbd-al-Salām Moḥammad Hārun, 4 vols. Cairo, 1949.

Al-Jīlāni, Abd al-Qādir. *The Secret of Secrets*. Trans. Tosun Bayrak. Cambridge: Islamic Texts Society, 1992.

Al-Qalqashandi, Abū al-ʿAbbās Ahmad. *Ṣubḥ al-Aʿshá fī Ṣināʿat al-Inshāʾ* [1412], 14 vols. Cairo: al-Matbaʿa al-Amiriya, 1903–19.

——. *Selections from* Ṣubḥ al-Aʿshā *by al-Qalqashandī, Clerk of the Mamluk Court. Egypt: 'Seats of Government' and 'Regulations of the Kingdom', from Early Islam to the Mamluks*. Ed. Tarek Galal Abdelhamid and Heba El-Toudy. London: Routledge, 2017.

Allouche-Benyoum, Joëlle and Doris Bensimon. *Juifs d'Algérie hier et aujourd'hui: mémoires et identités*. Paris: Privat, 1989.

Apter, Emily. *The Translation Zone: A New Comparative Literature*. Princeton, NJ: Princeton University Press, 2006.

Astier Loufti, Martine. *Littérature et colonialisme: l'expansion coloniale en vue dans la littérature romanesque française, 1871–1914*. Paris and The Hague: Mouton, 1971.

Bacri, Roland. *Trésors des racines pataouètes*. Paris: Belin, 1983.

Barbery, Muriel, Tahar Ben Jelloun, Alain Borer *et al.* 'Manifeste pour une littérature-monde en français', *Le Monde des Livres*. Online. 15 Mar. 2007: www.lemonde.fr/livres/article/2007/03/15/des-ecrivains-plaident-pour-un-roman-en-francais-ouvert-sur-le-monde_883572_3260.html.

Barthes, Roland. *Le Degré zéro de l'écriture*. Paris: Le Seuil, 1953.

——. *Système de la mode*. Paris: Le Seuil, 1967.

——. *L'Empire des signes*. Geneva: Skira, 1970/Paris: Flammarion, 1980.

———. 'Historical Discourse'. Trans. Peter Wexler. In *Structuralism: A Reader*. Ed. Michael Lane. London: Jonathan Cape, 1970, pp. 145–55.

———. 'Ce que je dois à Khatibi'. In *Pro-Culture* 12 – Numéro spécial: 'Khatibi'. Rabat: Imprimerie culturelle et universitaire Mohammed V, 1978, pp. 7–8. Reprinted in *L'Œuvre de … Abdelkébir Khatibi*. Rabat: Marsam, 1997, pp. 121–3, and as 'Exergue', in *Œuvres de … Abdelkébir Khatibi III: Essais*. Paris: La Différence, 2008, pp. 7–8.

———. 'The Three Points of Entry', *S/Z* [1970]. Trans. Richard Miller. New York: Hill & Wang, 1974, pp. 214–16.

———. *The Empire of Signs*. Trans. Richard Howard. New York: Hill & Wang, 1982.

Baudelaire, Charles. *Les Fleurs du mal*. Paris: Gallimard, 1972 [1857].

———. *Flowers of Evil*. Trans. James McGowan. Oxford: Oxford University Press, 1993.

Baudrillard, Jean. *La Transparence du mal: essai sur les phénomènes extrêmes*. Paris: Galilée, 1990.

———. *The Transparency of Evil: Essays on Extreme Phenomena*. Trans. James Benedict. London and New York: Verso, 1993.

Belhabib, Assia. *La Langue de l'hôte: lecture de Abdelkébir Khatibi*. El Jadida: Okad, 2009.

—— (ed.). *Le Jour d'après: dédicaces à Abdelkébir Khatibi*. Casablanca: Afrique Orient, 2010.

Ben Jelloun, Tahar. 'Bibliographie critique maghrébine: Abdelkébir Khatibi', *Le Roman maghrébin*', *Souffles* 13–14 (1969), pp. 32–4.

———. *Eloge de l'amitié*. Paris: Arléa, 1994.

Benabdelali, Abdesslam. *Abdelkebir Khatibi: l'étranger professionnel*. Casablanca: Centre Culturel du Livre, 2019.

Benjamin, Walter. 'The Task of the Translator'. Trans. Harry Zohn. In *The Translation Studies Reader*. Ed. Lawrence Venuti. London: Routledge, 2000, pp. 15–25.

Bensmaïa, Réda. 'Multilingualism and National "Character": *On Abdelkébir Khatibi's "Bilanguage"*'. In *Algeria in Others' Languages*. Ed. Anne-Emmanuelle Berger. Ithaca, NY: Cornell University Press, 2002, pp. 161–83.

———. *Experimental Nations: Or, the Invention of the Maghreb*. Trans. Alyson Waters. Princeton, NJ: Princeton University Press, 2003.

———. 'Media-Terranean, or Between Borders: Nabile Farès's *Un passager de l'Occident*'. In *The Mediterranean Reconsidered: Representations, Emergences, Recompositions*. Ed. Mauro Peressini and Ratiba Hadj-Moussa. Ottawa: University of Ottawa Press, 2005, pp. 109–23.

Bensmaïn, Abdallah. 'Entretien avec A. Khatibi'. In *Pro-Culture* 12 – Numéro spécial: 'Khatibi'. Rabat: Imprimerie culturelle et universitaire Mohammed V, 1978, pp. 9–13.

Berdouzi, Mohamed. *Structures du Maroc précolonial*. Casablanca: Editions La Croisée des Chemins, 2012.

Berger, Brigitte and Peter L. Berger. *Sociology: A Biographical Approach*. Harmondsworth: Penguin, 1976 [1972].

Bernabé, Jean, Raphaël Confiant and Patrick Chamoiseau. *Eloge de la créolité*. Paris: Gallimard, 1989.

——. *In Praise of Creolness*. Trans. M. B. Taleb-Khyar. Paris: Gallimard, 1993.

Bhabha, Homi. *The Location of the Culture*. London and New York: Routledge, 1994.

Billeter, Jean-François. *Leçons sur le Tchouang-tseu*. Paris: Editions Allia, 2016.

Bolfek-Radovani, Jasmina. *Geo/graphies of Loss: Space, Place and Spatial Loss in North African and Canadian Writing in French*. Erlangen: Lambert Academic Publishing, 2015.

Bongie, Chris. *Islands and Exiles: The Creole Identities of Post/Colonial Literature*. Stanford, CA: Stanford University Press, 1998.

The Book of Chuang Tzu. Trans. Martin Palmer with Elizabeth Breuilly, Chang Wai Ming and Jay Ramsay. London: Penguin Books, 2006.

Bourneuf, Roland and Réal Ouellet. *L'Univers du roman*. Paris: Presses universitaires de France, 1981.

Bourqia, Rahma. *La stratification sociale. Note de synthèse* (2006) – available at www.ires.ma/wp-content/uploads/2017/02/GT2-1.pdf.

Bousta, Rachida Saïgh. *Lecture des récits de Abdelkébir Khatibi: ecriture, memoire et imaginaire*. Casablanca: Afrique Orient, 1996.

Braidotti, Rosi. 'Thinking with an Accent: Françoise Collin, *Les cahiers du Grif*, and French Feminism', *Signs* 39.3 (2014), pp. 597–626.

Buci-Glucksmann, Christine and Antoine Raybaud, Abdelhaï Diouri, Marc Gontard, Abdesslam Benabdelali, Abdelfattah Kilito, Abdallah Bounfour, Jacques Hassoun and Réda Bensmaïa. *Imaginaires de l'autre: Khatibi et la mémoire littéraire*. Paris: L'Harmattan, 1987.

Burckhardt, Titus. *Introductions aux doctrines ésotériques de l'Islam*. Paris: Editions Dervy, 1996 [1969].

——. *Introduction to Sufi Doctrine*. Bloomington, IN: World Wisdom, 2008.

Cagne, Jacques. '"Bilan de la sociologie au Maroc" de Abdelkébir Khatibi', *Bulletin ESM* 106–7 (1967), pp. 174–9.

Carroll, Lewis. *Through the Looking Glass*. London: Macmillan, 1871.

Centre international de synthèse. *L'écriture et la psychologie des peuples*. Paris: Armand Colin, 1963.

Cervantès Saavedra, Miguel. *Don Quichotte de la Manche*. 2nd edn. Paris: Gallimard, 1973 [1605; 1615; 1961].

Chamoiseau, Patrick. 'Pour Abdelkébir Khatibi'. In *Ecarts d'identité* 114 (2009), p. 4.

Charoub, Akim. '*La Mémoire tatouée* de Abdelkébir Khatibi', *Jeune Afrique* 558 (1971), p. 50.

Cheng, François. 'Le cas du chinois'. In Jalil Bennani *et al.*, *Du bilinguisme*. Paris: Denoël, 1985, pp. 227–42.

Chérif, Mustapha, Jean-Luc Nancy, Hélène Cixous *et al.* 'Le vivre-ensemble'. In *Derrida à Alger: un regard sur le monde*. Algiers: Barzakh/Arles: Actes Sud, 2008, pp. 15–18.

Cherribi, Sam and Matthew Pesce. 'Khatibi: A Sociologist in Literature'. In Kirsten Ruth Bratt *et al.* (eds), *Vitality and Dynamism: Interstitial Dialogues of Languages, Politics and Religion in Morocco's Literary Tradition*. Leiden: Leiden University Press, 2014, pp. 177–84.

Cixous, Hélène. *Portrait de Jacques Derrida en Jeune Saint Juif*. Paris: Galilée, 1991.

———. 'Celle qui ne se ferme pas'. In *Derrida à Alger: un regard sur le monde*. Algiers: Barzakh/Arles: Actes Sud, 2008, pp. 45–58.

Combe, Dominique. 'Derrida et Khatibi – autour du *Monolinguisme de l'autre*', *Carnets: revue électronique d'études françaises*, 2nd ser. 7 (2016), pp. 6–11.

Corbin, Henry. *Creative Imagination in the Sufism of Ibn Arabi*. Trans. Ralph Manheim. Princeton, NJ: Princeton University Press, 1969.

———. *Histoire de la philosophie islamique*. Paris: Gallimard, 1986.

Cornille, Jean-Louis. 'La Mémoire courte des poètes immémoriaux (Glissant et Segalen)'. In *Plagiat et créativité: (treize enquêtes sur l'auteur et son autre)*. Amsterdam: Rodopi, 2008, pp. 171–82.

Dakhlia, Jocelyne. '"No man's langue": une rétraction coloniale'. In *Trames de langues: usages et métissages linguistiques dans l'histoire du Maghreb*. Ed. Jocelyne Dakhlia. Paris: Maisonneuve et Larose, 2004, pp. 259–71.

———. *Lingua Franca: histoire d'une langue métisse en Méditerranée*. Arles: Actes Sud, 2008.

De Toro, Alfonso. 'Jorge Luis Borges. The Periphery at the Center/The Periphery as Center/The Center of the Periphery: Postcoloniality and Postmodernity'. In *Borders and Margins: Post-Colonialism and Post-Modernism*. Ed. Fernando de Toro and Alfonso de Toro. Frankfurt am Main: Vervuert, 1995, pp. 11–45.

———. 'La postcolonialidad en Latinoamérica en la era de la globalización. ¿Cambio de paradigma en el pensamiento teórico-cultural latinoamericano?'. In *El debate de la postcolonialidad en Latinoamérica: una postmodernidad periférica o Cambio de paradigma en el pensamiento latinoamericano*. Ed. Alfonso de Toro and Fernando de Toro. Frankfurt am Main: Vervuert, 1999, pp. 31–77.

——. 'Jenseits von Postmoderne und Postkolonialität. Materialien zu einem Modell der Hybridität und des Körpers als transrelationalem, transversalem und transmedialem Wissenschaftskonzept'. In *Räume der Hybridität. Postkoloniale Konzepte in Theorie und Literatur.* Ed. Christof Hamann and Cornelia Sieber. Hildesheim, Zurich and New York: Olms, 2003, pp. 15–52.

——. *Estrategias de la 'postmodernidad' y la 'postcolonialidad' en Latinoamérica. 'Hibridez' y 'Globalización'.* Frankfurt am Main: Vervuert, 2006, pp. 9–36.

——. 'Globalization – New Hybridities – Transidentities – Transnations: Recognition – Difference'. In *New Hybridities.* Ed. Frank Heidemann and Alfonso de Toro. Hildesheim, Zurich and New York: Olms, 2006, pp. 19–37.

——. 'Jorge Luis Borges: Translatio e Historia'. In *In memoriam Jorge Luis Borges.* Ed. Rafael Olea Franco. Colóquio Internacional, Centro de Estudios Lingüísticos y Literarios, Cátedra Jaume Torres Bodet. Mexico City: Colegio de México, 2008, pp. 191–236.

——. *Epistémologies: Le Maghreb.* Paris: L'Harmattan, 2010 [2008].

——. 'Le "plurilinguisme de l'autre": performativité et transversalité de la langue', *Expressions maghrébines* 12.1 (2013), pp. 85–101.

De Toro, Fernando. 'From Where to Speak'. In *Borders and Margins: Post-Colonialism and Post-Modernism.* Ed. Fernando de Toro. Frankfurt am Main: Vervuert, 1995, pp. 131–48.

——. *New Intersections: Essays on Culture and Literature in the Post-Modern and Post-Colonial Condition.* Madrid: Iberoamericana/Frankfurt am Main: Vervuert, 2003.

Deleuze, Gilles. *Différence et répétition.* Paris: Presses universitaires de France, 1968.

Derrida, Jacques. *De la grammatologie.* Paris: Editions de Minuit, 1967.

——. *Mémoires, pour Paul de Man.* Paris: Galilée, 1988.

——. *Le Monolinguisme de l'autre, ou, La Prothèse d'origine.* Paris: Galilée, 1996.

——. 'Fidélité à plus d'un: mériter d'hériter où la généalogie fait défaut'. In *Idiomes, nationalités, déconstructions: rencontre de Rabat avec Jacques Derrida.* Paris: Intersignes/Casablanca: Editions Toubkal, 1998, pp. 221–65.

——. *The Monolingualism of the Other, or, The Prosthesis of Origin.* Trans. Patrick Mensah. Stanford, CA: Stanford University Press, 1998.

——. 'Exergue'. In *Œuvres de Abdelkébir Khatibi I: Romans et récits.* Paris: La Différence, 2008, p. 7.

——. *Le Dernier des juifs.* Paris: Galilée, 2014.

Dhaouadi, Muhammad. 'The Concept of Change in the Thought of Ibn Khaldun and Western Classical Sociologists', *Islam Arastirmalari Dergisi Sayi* 16 (2006), pp. 43–87.

Djebar, Assia. *Loin de Médine*. Paris: Albin Michel, 1991.

——. *Far from Madina*. Trans. Dorothy S. Blair. London: Quartet Books, 1994.

——. *Ces voix qui m'assiègent … en marge de ma francophonie*. Paris: Albin Michel, 1999.

Dransfeldt Christensen, Tina. 'Towards an Ethics of Bilingualism: An Intertextual Dialogue between Khatibi and Derrida', *Interventions: International Journal of Postcolonial Studies* 19.4 (2017), pp. 447–66.

Duvignaud, Jean. 'La Sociologie et le tiers monde'. In *Introduction à la sociologie*. Paris: Gallimard, 1966, pp. 133–48.

El Fassi, Nacer. 'Avant-propos', *Bulletin ESM* 100 (1966), p. 5.

El Jabbar, Nabil. *L'Œuvre romanesque d'Abdelkébir Khatibi: enjeux poétiques et identitaires*. Paris: L'Harmattan, 2014.

El Khatibi, Mourad (ed.). *Né demain: hommage à Abdelkébir Khatibi (11 février 1938–16 mars 2009)*. Tangier: Slaiki Akhawayne, 2014.

El Merabet, Lahoucine. *Abdelkébir Khatibi: la sensibilité pensante à l'œuvre dans* Le Livre du sang. Paris: L'Harmattan, 2018.

Fanon, Frantz. *The Wretched of the Earth*. Trans. Constance Farrington. New York: Grove Press, 1968.

Farès, Nabile. *Le Miroir de Cordoue*. Paris: L'Harmattan, 1994.

Fennane, Abdelghani (ed.). *Celui qui vient de l'avenir: Abdelkébir Khatibi*. Casablanca, Editions Toubkal, 2020.

Fieni, David. 'Introduction: Khatibi's "Place of Hostage"', *PMLA* 125.4 (2010), pp. 1002–19.

——. 'Introduction: désappropriation de soi et poétique de l'intersigne chez Khatibi', *Expressions maghrébines* 12.1 (2013), pp. 1–17.

Forsdick, Charles. 'Edward Said, Victor Segalen and the Implications of Post-Colonial Theory', *Journal of the Institute of Romance Studies* 5 (1997), pp. 323–39.

——. 'L'exote mangé par les hommes: from the French Kipling to *Segalen le partagé*'. In *Reading Diversity*. Ed. Charles Forsdick and Susan Marson. Glasgow: University of Glasgow French and German Publications, 2000, pp. 1–22.

——. *Victor Segalen and the Aesthetics of Diversity: Journeys between Cultures*. Oxford: Oxford University Press, 2000.

——. 'From the "Aesthetics of Diversity" to the "Poetics of Relating": Segalen, Glissant and the Genealogies of Francophone Postcolonial Thought', *Paragraph* 37.2 (2014), pp. 160–77.

Foucault, Michel. *Les mots et les choses*. Paris: Gallimard, 1979 [1966].

——. *The Order of Things: An Archaeology of the Human Sciences*. Trans. anon. London: Routledge, 2011.

Gallissot, René (ed.). *Sur le féodalisme*. Paris: Editions sociales, 1971.

Geoffroy, Eric. *Introduction to Sufism: The Inner Path of Islam*. Trans. Roger Gaetani. Bloomington, IN: World Wisdom Books, 2010.

Glissant, Edouard. *L'Intention poétique*. Paris: Seuil, 1969.

———. *Poétique de la relation*. Paris: Gallimard, 1990.

———. *Introduction à une poétique du divers*. Paris: Gallimard, 1996.

———. *Poetics of Relation*. Trans. Betsy Wing. Ann Arbor: University of Michigan Press, 1997.

———. *Traité du tout-monde*. Paris: Gallimard, 1997.

Gómez Peña, Guillermo. *The New World Border: Prophecies, Poems and Loqueras for the End of the Century*. San Francisco: City Lights, 1996.

Gontard, Marc. *Le moi étrange: littérature marocaine de langue française*. Paris: L'Harmattan, 1981.

———. 'Théorie de la différence chez Victor Segalen'. In Christine Buci-Glucksmann, Antoine Raybaud, Abdelhaï Diouri, Marc Gontard, Abdesslam Benabdelali, Abdelfattah Kilito, Abdallah Bounfour, Jaques Hassoun and Réda Bensmaïa, *Imaginaires de l'autre: Khatibi et la mémoire littéraire*. Paris: L'Harmattan, 1987, pp. 65–79.

———. *La Violence du texte: étude sur la littérature marocaine*. Paris: L'Harmattan, 1993.

Guillebaud, Jean-Claude. *La Refondation du monde*. Paris: Seuil, 1999.

———. *Re-Founding the World: A Western Testament*. Trans. W. Donald Wilson. New York: Algora Publishing, 2001.

Hachad, Naïma. 'Parole de l'abîme d'Edouard Glissant et d'Abdelkébir Khatibi', *Revue des sciences humaines* 309 (2013), pp. 125–40.

Hammoudi, Abdellah. 'Segmentarity, Social Stratification, Political Power and Sainthood: Reflections on Gellner's Theses', *Hespéris-Tamuda* 15 (1974). Reprinted in *Economy and Society* 9.3 (1980), pp. 279–303.

Hargreaves, Alec G., Charles Forsdick and David Murphy (eds). *Transnational French Studies: Postcolonialism and Littérature-Monde*. Liverpool: Liverpool University Press, 2010.

Harrison, Olivia C. 'Abrahamic Tongues: Abdelkébir Khatibi, Jacques Hassoun, Jacques Derrida'. In *Transcolonial Maghreb: Imagining Palestine in the Era of Decolonisation*. Stanford, CA: Stanford University Press, 2016, pp. 101–28.

Harrison, Olivia C. and Villa-Ignacio, Teresa (eds). *Souffles-Anfas: A Critical Anthology from the Moroccan Journal of Culture and Politics*. Stanford, CA: Stanford University Press, 2016.

Hart, D. 'Making Sense of Moroccan Tribal Sociology and History', *Journal of North African Studies* 6.2 (2001), pp. 11–28.

Harvey, Andrew and Ian Watson. 'Introduction'. In Victor Segalen, *Paintings*. Trans. Andrew Harvey and Ian Watson. London: Quartet Books, 1991, pp. vii–ix.

Hél-Bongo, Olga. 'Polymorphisme et dissimulation du narratif dans *La Mémoire tatouée* d'Abdelkébir Khatibi', *Études littéraires* 43.1 (2012), pp. 45–61.

———. *Roman francophone et essai: Mudimbe, Chamoiseau, Khatibi*. Paris: Honoré Champion, 2019.

Hiddleston, Jane. *Understanding Postcolonialism*. Abingdon: Routledge, 2014 [2009].

'Hommage à Abdelkébir Khatibi (1938–2009)', *Celaan Revue/Revue Celaan*, 9.9 (2011).

Horden, Peregrine and Nicholas Purcell. *The Corrupting Sea: A Study of Mediterranean History*. Oxford: Wiley Blackwell, 2000.

Ibn ʿAbd Rabbih. *The Unique Necklace (al-ʿIqd al-Farīd)*. Trans. Issa J. Boullata. Reading: Garnet, 2006.

Ibn Khaldun. *Al-Muqaddimah*. Trans. Vincent Monteil. Paris: Sindbad, 1967.

Izutsu, Toshihiko. *Sufism and Taoism: A Comparative Study of Key Philosophical Concepts*. London, Los Angeles and Berkeley: University of California Press, 1984.

Jakobson, Roman. 'Sur l'art verbal de William Blake et d'autres peintres-poètes'. In N. Chomsky, R. Jakobson and M. Halle, *Hypothèses: trois entretiens et trois études sur la linguistique et la poétique, 'Change'*. Paris: Seghers/Laffont, 1972, pp. 75–102.

———. 'On Linguistic Aspects of Translation', *Translation Studies Reader*. Ed. Lawrence Venuti. London: Routledge, 2012, pp. 126–31.

Joubert, Jean-Louis. 'Poétique de l'exotisme: Saint-John Perse, Victor Segalen et Édouard Glissant', *Cahiers du CRLH* 5 (1988), pp. 281–95.

Kant, Emmanuel. *Perpetual Peace: A Philosophical Sketch*. Philadelphia: Slought Foundation *et al.*, 2010 [1795]: https://slought.org/media/files/perpetual_peace.pdf.

Kelly, Debra. *Autobiography and Independence: Selfhood and Creativity in North African Writing in French*. Liverpool: Liverpool University Press, 2005.

'Khatibi in English', *Celaan* 16.2–3, Spring & Summer 2020 (New York: Skidmore College, 2020).

Klossowski, Pierre. *Les Lois de l'hospitalité*. Paris: Gallimard, 1965.

Knysh, Alexander D. *Sufism: A Brief History*. Leiden: E. J. Brill, 2004.

———. 'Dreams and Visions in Islamic Societies: An Introduction'. In: *Dreams and Visions in Islamic Societies*. Ed. Alexander Knysh and Özgen Felek. Albany: SUNY Press, 2012, pp. 1–11.

Kristeva, Julia. *Sèméiotikè: recherches pour une sémanalyse*. Paris: Seuil, 1969.

Lacoste, Yves. *Ibn Khaldoun: naissance de l'histoire, passé du Tiers-Monde*. Paris: Maspero, 1966.

Lamrhili, Ahmed Kohen (ed.). *Abdelkébir Khatibi*. Rabat: Okad, 1990.

Laroui, Abdellah. *L'histoire du Maghreb: un essai de synthèse*. Paris: Maspero, 1970.

Lévesque, Claude and Christie V. McDonald (eds). *L'Oreille de l'autre: otobiographies, transferts, traductions. Textes et débats avec Jacques Derrida.* Montreal: VLB, 1982.

Lévi-Strauss, Claude. *The Raw and the Cooked: Introduction to a Science of Mythology: I.* Trans. John Weightman and Doreen Weightman. New York: Harper Row, 1969.

Lings, Martin. *What is Sufism?* Cambridge: Islamic Texts Society, 1999.

Lionnet, Françoise. *Postcolonial Representations: Women, Literature, Identity.* Ithaca, NY: Cornell University Press, 1995.

——. 'Counterpoint and Double Critique in Edward Said and Abdelkébir Khatibi: A Transcolonial Comparison'. In Dominic Thomas and Ali Behdad (eds), *A Companion to Comparative Literature.* Chichester: Wiley Blackwell, 2011, pp. 387–407.

Lionnet, Françoise and Shu-mei Shih. 'Introduction: Thinking through the Minor, Transnationally'. In *Minor Transnationalism.* Ed. Françoise Lionnet and Shu-mei Shih. Durham, NC: Duke University Press, 2005, pp. 1–23.

Lukács, Georg. 'On the Nature and Form of the Essay: Letter to Leo Popper' [1911]. In *Soul and Form.* Trans. Anna Bostock. New York: Columbia University Press, 2010, pp. 16–34.

——. 'The Ideology of Modernism' [1957]. Reprinted in *Marxist Literary Theory.* Ed. Terry Eagleton and Drew Milne. Oxford: Blackwell, 1996, pp. 141–62.

Mabrour Abdelouahad (ed.). *Hommage à Abdelkébir Khatibi: Actes du Colloque international du 26 et 27 mars 2008.* El Jadida: Publications de la Faculté des Lettres et des Sciences Humaines d'El Jadida, 2009.

McClintock, Anne. 'Pitfalls of the Term "Post-Colonialism"', *Social Text* 31/32 (1992), pp. 84–98.

McNeece, Lucy Stone. 'Decolonising the Sign: Language and Identity in Abdélkebir Khatibi's *La Mémoire tatouée*', *Yale French Studies* 83 (1993), pp. 12–29.

——. 'Rescripting Modernity: Abdelkébir Khatibi and the Archeology of Signs'. In *Maghrebian Mosaic: A Literature in Transition.* Ed. Mildred Mortimer. Boulder, CO: Lynne Rienner Publishers, 2011, pp. 81–98.

Madelain, Jacques. *L'Errance et l'itinéraire: lecture du roman maghrébin de langue française.* Paris: Sindbad, 1983.

Madou, Jean-Pol. 'Le Germe et le rhizome'. In *Le Clézio, Glissant, Segalen: la quête comme déconstruction de l'aventure.* Chambéry: Editions de l'université de Savoie, 2011, pp. 73–80.

Mallarmé, Stéphane. *Igitur – Divagations – Un coup de dés.* Paris: Gallimard, 2003.

Massignon, Louis. 'Voyelles sémitiques et sémantique musicale'. In *Parole donnée.* Paris: Julliard, 1962, pp. 379–85.

——. *Opera minora*, vol. 2. Paris: Presses universitaires de France, 1969.

Melville, Francis. *Secrets de la haute magie*. Paris: Editions Contre-Dires, 2014.

Memmes, Abdallah. *Abdekébir Khatibi: l'écriture de la dualité*. Paris: L'Harmattan, 1994.

Memmi, Albert. *La Statue de sel*. Paris: Corréa, 1953.

——. *Agar*. Paris: Corréa, 1955.

——. *Portrait du colonisé, précédé du portrait du colonisateur*. Paris: Gallimard, 2008 [1957].

——. *The Colonizer and the Colonized*. Trans. Howard Greenfeld. New York: Orion Press, 1965; London: Earthscan, 2003.

——. *Anthologie des écrivains français du Maghreb*. Paris: Présence africaine, 1969.

——. *Le Scorpion ou La Confession imaginaire*. Paris: Gallimard, 1969.

Mignolo, Walter. *The Darker Side of Western Modernity: Global Futures, Decolonial Options*. Durham, NC: Duke University Press, 2011.

——. *Local Histories/Global Designs: Coloniality, Subaltern Knowledges, and Border Thinking*. Princeton, NJ: Princeton University Press, 2012.

Mongo-Mboussa, Boniface. 'Edouard Glissant entre Derrida et Khatibi', *Africultures* (Jan. 2013). Available at http://africultures.com/edouard-glissant-entre-derrida-et-khatibi-11272.

Moura, Jean-Marc. *Littératures francophones et théorie postcoloniale*. Paris: Presses universitaires de France, 1999.

——. 'Le Postcolonial dans les études littéraires en France'. In *La Situation postcoloniale: les* postcolonial studies *dans le débat français*. Ed. Marie-Claude Smouts. Paris: Presses de la Fondation Nationale des Science Politiques, 2007, pp. 98–119.

Musette [Auguste Robinet]. *Cagayous, ses meilleures histoires: introduction, notes et lexique par Gabriel Audisio*. Paris: Gallimard, 1931.

Nadel, Siegfried F. *La Théorie de la structure sociale*. Trans. Jeanne Favret. Paris: Editions de Minuit, 1970.

Nasr, Seyyed Hossein. *The Garden of Truth: The Vision and Promise of Sufism, Islam's Mystical Tradition*. New York: HarperOne, 2007.

Naville, Pierre. 'Classes sociales et classes logiques: note sur le réalisme des classes', *Année sociologique*, 1960, pp. 3–77. Reprinted in *Classes sociales et classes logiques*. Paris: Presses universitaires de France, 1961.

Nejjar, Saïd. *Bibliographie de l'œuvre de Abdelkébir Khatibi*. Rabat, Institut Universitaire de la Recherche Scientifique, 2001.

Nock, Arthur D. and André-Jean Festugière. *Le Corpus Hermeticum*, vols 1–4. Paris: Les Belles Lettres, 1946–54.

Nora, Pierre. *Les Français d'Algérie*. Paris: Christian Bourgois, 1961.

Nozaki, Kan. *Tanizaki Junichiro to ikoku no gengo* [*Tanizaki Junichiro and Foreign Languages*]. Kyoto: Jimbunshoin, 2003; Tokyo: Chukobunko, 2015.

L'Œuvre de ... Abdelkébir Khatibi. Rabat: Marsam, 1997.

Ortiz, Fernando. *Contrapunteo cubano del tabaco y el azúcar*. Havana: Editorial de Ciencias Sociales, 1983 [1940].

Papan-Matin, Firoozeh. *Beyond Death: The Mystical Teachings of 'Ayn al-Qudat al-Hamadhānī*. Leiden and Boston: Brill, 2010.

Piser, Celine. 'Silent Multilingualism: Language Politics in the Mediterranean', *Critical Multilingualism* 5.2 (2017), pp. 64–86.

Planas, Natividad. 'L'Usage des langues en Méditerranée occidentale à l'époque moderne'. In *Trames de langues: usages et métissages linguistiques dans l'histoire du Maghreb*. Ed. Jocelyne Dakhlia. Paris: Maisonneuve et Larose, 2004, pp. 241–57.

Pro-Culture 12 – Numéro spécial: 'Khatibi'. Rabat: Imprimerie culturelle et universitaire Mohammed V, 1978.

Qader, Nasrin. *Narratives of Catastrophe: Boris Diop, Ben Jelloun, Khatibi*. New York: Fordham University Press, 2009.

The Qur'an. Trans. M. A. S. Abdel Haleem. Oxford: Oxford University Press, 2004.

Rachik, Hassan and Rahma Bourqia. 'La Sociologie au Maroc: grandes étapes et jalons thématiques', *SociologieS: théories et recherches*. Online. 18 Oct. 2011: http://journals.openedition.org/sociologies/3719.

Reeck, Matt. 'Introduction'. In *Class Warrior – Taoist Style*. Middletown, CT: Wesleyan University Press, 2017, pp. vii–xv.

——. 'The Poetics of the Orphan in Khatibi's Early Work', *Journal of French and Francophone Philosophy* 35.1 (2017), pp. 132–49.

Revue Celfan/Celfan Review 8.1–2, 'Abdelkébir Khatibi' (Nov. 1988–Feb. 1989). Philadelphia: Temple University, 1990.

Reynolds, Felisa. 'Khatibi as Derrida's Foil: Undermining the Last Defender of the French Language', *Contemporary French and Francophone Studies: Sites* 18.2 (2014), pp. 199–206.

Ricard, Prosper. *Tapis marocains*. Paris: Georges Lang, 1952.

Rice, Alison. *Time Signatures: Contextualizing Contemporary Francophone Writing from the Maghreb*. Oxford: Lexington Books, 2006.

Robin, Régine. *Le Deuil de l'origine: une langue en trop, la langue en moins*. Paris: Editions Kimé, 2003.

Roelens, Nathalie. 'L'Amour bilingue: lire Khatibi et Segalen'. In *Approches interdisciplinaires de la lecture, 10: lire entre les langues*. Reims, EPURE, 2017, pp. 61–80.

Rosello, Mireille. *France and the Maghreb: Performative Encounters*. Gainesville: University Press of Florida, 2005.

The Sacred Books of China: The Texts of Taoism, Part II. Trans. James Legge. New York: Dover Publications, 1962.

Sadr, Seyyed Moussa. 'Les Fawatih ou lettres séparées'. In *Les Cahiers de l'Oronte* 5 (Beirut, 1966), pp. 30–1.

Said, Edward. *Orientalism*. New York: Vintage Books, 1994 [1978].

Sartre, Jean-Paul. *Réflexions sur la question juive*. Paris: Gallimard, 1946.

Scemla, Jean. 'Entretien avec Khatibi', *Bulletin de l'Association Victor Segalen* 2 (1989), pp. 9–10.

Sefrioui, Ahmed. *La Boîte à merveilles*. Paris: Editions du Seuil, 1954.

Segalen, Victor. *Essai sur l'exotisme*. In *Œuvres complètes*. Ed. Henry Bouillier, 2 vols. Paris: Laffont, 1995.

——. *Essay on Exoticism: An Aesthetics of Diversity*. Trans. Yaël Schlick. Durham, NC: Duke University Press, 2002.

Segler-Messner, Silke. 'Victor Segalen et la poétique de l'altérité dans la théorie littéraire postcoloniale (Glissant, Khatibi)'. In *Voyages à l'envers: formes et figures de l'exotisme dans les littératures post-coloniales francophones*. Ed. Silke Segler-Messner. Strasbourg: Presses universitaires de Strasbourg, 2009, pp. 69–86.

Serfaty, Abraham. 'Progrès technique et développement', in *Bulletin ESM* 109 (Apr.–June 1968), pp. 3–17.

——. 'Cultures et progrès scientifique', *Souffles* 13/14 (1969), pp. 7–15.

——. 'La francophonie contre le développement', *Souffles* 18 (Mar.–Apr. 1970), pp. 26–34.

Shohat, Ella. 'Notes on the "Post-Colonial"', *Social Text* 31/32 (1992), pp. 99–113.

Smouts, Marie-Claude. 'Introduction: le postcolonial pour quoi faire?'. In *La Situation postcoloniale: les* postcolonial studies *dans le débat français*. Ed. Marie-Claude Smouts. Paris: Presses de la Fondation Nationale des Science Politiques, 2007, pp. 25–66.

Starobinski, Jean. *Les mots sous les mots*. Paris: Gallimard, 1971.

Steiner, George. *After Babel: Aspects of Language and Translation*. Oxford: Oxford University Press, 1975.

Steinmetz, George. 'Sociology and Colonialism in the British and French Empires, 1945–1965', *Journal of Modern History* 89 (2017), pp. 601–48.

Stétié, Salah. 'Questions sur un très vieux rivage'. Online. 8 Dec. 2011: http://salahstetie.net/?p=130.

——. 'A Question upon a Very Old Shore'. Online. 10 Apr. 2014: http://salahstetie.net/?p=1007.

Stoler, Ann Laura. *Duress: Imperial Durabilities in Our Times*. Durham, NC: Duke University Press, 2016.

Stora, Benjamin. *Les Trois Exils, juifs d'Algérie*. Paris: Stock, 2006.

Tanizaki, Junichirô. *Ashikari and the Story of Shunkin*. Trans. Roy Humpherson and Hajime Okita. Tokyo, The Hokuseido Press, 1936.

——. *In Praise of Shadows*. Trans. Thomas J. Harper and Edward G. Seidensticker. Stony Creek, CT: Leete's Island Books, 1977.

Todorov, Tzvetan. *L'Homme dépaysé*. Paris: Editions du Seuil, 1996.

Touraine, Alain. 'Faux et vrais problèmes'. In *Une société fragmentée? Le multiculturalisme en débat*. Ed. Michel Wieviorka. Paris: Editions de la Découverte, 1997.

Tzu, Lao. *Tao Te Ching*. Trans. D. C. Lau. New York: Penguin Books, 1963.

Wahbi, Hassan. *Les Mots du monde: Khatibi et le récit*. Agadir: Publications de la Faculté des Lettres et Sciences Humaines, 1995.

——. *La Beauté de l'absent: entretiens avec Abdelkébir Khatibi*. Paris: L'Harmattan, 2010.

——. *Abdelkébir Khatibi: l'Esprit de la lettre*. Rabat: Marsam, 2014.

Waley, Arthur. *The Way and its Power: A Study of the* Tao Tê Ching *and its Place in Chinese Thought*. New York: Grove Press, 1958.

Waterbury, John. *The Commander of the Faithful: The Moroccan Political Elite. A Study in Segmented Politics*. New York: Columbia University Press, 1970.

Waugh, Winston E. *Sufism: The Mystical Side of Islam. Some Developmental Aspects*. Maitland, FL: Xulon Press, 2005.

Woodhull, Winifred. *Transfigurations of the Maghreb: Feminism, Decolonisation, and Literatures*. Minneapolis: University of Minnesota Press, 1993.

Wu, Kuang-Ming. *The Butterfly as Companion: Meditations on the First Three Chapters of the Chuang Tzu*. New York: SUNY Press, 1990.

Yacine, Kateb. *Le Polygone étoilé*. Paris: Editions du Seuil, 1997 [1966].

Zouggari, Ahmed. 'Abdelkébir Khatibi, une carrière dédiée aux Sciences humaines et sociales', *Bulletin ESM* (July 2009), pp. 7–9.

Index

Abd El Krim 318
Abdelmalek, Anouar 44
Abdelmoumen, Mélikah 126n3
Abdi, Nourredine 154
Abraham 2, 208n24
    Abrahamic monotheism 91, 143
    Abrahamic solidarity 350
Académie du Royaume du Maroc 18
Académie française 23
acculturation 10, 37, 44, 149, 195
Adam 341
Adonis (Syrian poet) 17n46, 18
Affergan, Francis 178
Africa 12, 91, 94
    North Africa 15, 56, 90
    Sub-Saharan Africa 299
aimance 4, 17, 23, 29, 35, 273, 297–8,
    312–13, 315
Al-Alam (Moroccan newspaper) 20
Al-Andalus 104, 106, 262
    Andalusian *Convivencia* 104
    Andalusian culture 264
    Andalusian *Reconquista* 104
Al-Asas (Moroccan journal) 18
Al-Hallāj 270
Al-Ittihad Al-Ichtiraki (Moroccan
    newspaper) 20
Al-Jahiz 342
Al-Jīlāni, Abd al-Qādir 249
Al Ma'arri 26
Al-Nahda (Arab renaissance) 20
Al-Naksa 157

Al-Qalqashandi 338–9, 341
Al-Yawm Assabi 20
alchemy 262–3, 270
Alexandria 316–17
Algeria 13, 29, 59, 98, 100, 140,
    199–204, 206–7, 211, 215–16,
    300, 314, 318
    Algerian dialect 301
    Algerian Jews 200, 202, 206, 208,
        211
    Algerian War of Independence 199
    Algerian writers and artists 10, 15
    Algerians 203–4
    French Algerian dialect 100
    French Algerians 206–7
Algiers 99–100, 200–1, 207n22, 314,
    318
alienation 29, 129, 164, 166, 175, 183–5,
    208, 212–13, 216, 319
alterity 28, 94–5, 99, 105, 117, 119–20,
    139, 165, 170, 173–4, 178, 181,
    302, 349
Amahan, Ali 8, 35, 280, 282, 287, 292,
    295, 299, 301
Amazigh (or Berber)
    culture 46, 358
    dancer 296
    Jews 207
    language(s) 21, 75, 98–9, 207–8,
        242, 286
    people 91, 206
    proverbs 59n61

roots 7
tattoos and carpet 269
tribalism 47, 59
amnesia 97–8, 129, 185–6, 202–3, 212,
    272, 276
anamnesia (or anamnesis) 95, 104,
    202–3, 209
androgynous 146, 289–90
Annales marocaines de sociologie
    (Moroccan publication) 20,
    45n13
années de plomb (or Years of Lead)
    14, 48
anthropology 62, 330
    anthropological approaches 281
    anthropological 'other' 53
    anthropological process 133
    anthropologists 178
    colonial anthropology 281, 330
    Western anthropology 62
anticolonial
    conflict 319
    critique 33, 199, 320
    protests 4
    struggles 165
    theory 151
    thinking 37
anticolonialism 323
Aoulad-Syad, Daoud 9n20
Apter, Emily 149
Arab
    arts 345
    identity 13, 101, 320
    music 346
    nationalism 170, 359
    writer 164
Arab-Israeli War 156
the Arab Spring 14
the Arab world 9, 19, 21, 45, 59, 91,
    107, 132
arabesques 8, 284, 290, 307
Arabic
    alphabet 341
    culture 265, 354
    grammar 272, 345

language 2, 4, 19–21, 24, 75, 83, 85,
    91, 98–101, 103, 117, 136, 140,
    142–3, 146, 152, 164, 166–7,
    175, 192, 201, 206–8, 210–13,
    238, 244, 249, 256, 272–5, 301,
    334, 336, 341, 355
    philosophy 34, 143
    writing 340, 342
Arabness 34, 160, 162, 166, 348
Arabs 38, 104–5, 143, 155, 161, 165–7,
    206, 243, 262, 267, 316, 340,
    348, 352–3
Aragon, Louis 188
architecture 169, 232, 269, 270, 284–5,
    288, 306
Aristotle 58, 91, 143, 279
Arnaud, Jacqueline 9, 49
Aron, Raymond 6, 49
art
    books 9, 280, 284
    decorative art 240, 270, 322, 336
    forms 37, 308, 312
    work 323
    world 112
Artaud, Antonin 15
artisan 8, 268, 288, 343
artistic
    concepts 113
    craftsmanship 301
    creation and (re)production 9, 15,
        280, 283–4, 286, 293–4, 298–9,
        301, 322
    dialogue 284
    disciplines 8, 284–6
    endeavours 270
    expression 116
    forms, objects and patterns 7, 284,
        307
    friendships 14
    imagination 312
    intelligence 224–5
    perception 309
    prose 76
    vision 306, 308, 310, 312, 319–20,
        322, 324

Ashcroft, Bill 131
Asia 191, 278
    Asian sources 37
    Asian traditions/cultures 262, 269, 277
Assila 350
Astier Loufti, Martine 180–1
astrology 270, 342
the Atlantic Ocean 2–3, 7, 97
the Atlas 293, 299
    the High Atlas 283
    the Middle Atlas 283, 286, 292
authorship 265–6
autobiography 16, 33, 131, 197, 202–3, 209, 225, 248, 281
    autobiographical work or writing 1, 16, 22–3, 240, 246–7, 256

Baader 168–9
Babana-Hampton, Safoi 35, 298n57
Bachelard, Gaston 26
Balandier, Georges 49
Balzac, Honoré de 64
baraka 294
Barthes, Roland 19, 26, 29–30, 50, 57, 59n60, 64, 92, 112, 117, 135, 168, 188, 198–200, 203, 219n1, 222, 227, 269n11, 331
    Barthesian 42, 52, 64, 244
Bastide, Roger 61
Bataille, Georges 60, 331
Baton Rouge 174–5, 201, 206
Baudelaire, Charles 27, 182, 223, 267, 286
Baudrillard, Jean 112, 178
Beckett, Samuel 15, 25
Bel Hachmy, Abdelkader 49n29
Belhabib, Assia 18–19, 36, 111–23
Belhachmi, Ahmed 49n29
Ben Jelloun, Tahar 10, 15, 30n84, 45n13, 91n5, 142, 150n2, 151n5, 156, 157n13, 158n15, 198, 249n30
Benabdelali, Abdesslam 17, 19–20
Benjamin, Walter 215

Benjelloun, Abdelmajid 17n46
Benjelloun Touimi, Mohammed 9n21, 50n29
Bennis, Mohammed 20
Bensmaïa, Réda 33, 92
Bensmain, Abdallah 16, 242n13
Berber *see* Amazigh
Berdouzi, Mohamed 43
Bernabé, Jean 84
Berque, Jacques 28, 54
Berrada, Mohammed 19–20
Bhabha, Homi 32, 126–8, 130
bi-langue 25, 32, 92–3, 95, 102–3, 117, 137, 149, 156, 163–5, 167–8, 174, 192, 348
Bibliothèque Nationale du Royaume du Maroc 10n23, 43n5
bilingualism 12, 24–5, 74, 79, 92–3, 103–4, 117, 125, 132, 149, 163, 173, 175, 179, 181, 184–5, 188, 191–2, 194, 201, 204–6, 211–14, 216, 269, 299, 302, 322, 349, 353
Black Decade 204
Black Panthers 163, 168–9
Black September 159
blackness 34
Blanchot, Maurice 26, 214
body 2–3, 9, 11, 24, 37, 65, 70–3, 76, 78, 94, 107, 126–8, 136, 146, 192, 209, 221, 224–7, 229, 237–44, 250–1, 265–6, 270, 272, 286, 290, 296, 306, 310, 331–7, 339, 341–2, 346, 349, 351, 356
Bolfek-Radovani, Jasmina 37, 237–60
Bongie, Chris 181
border thinking 32, 149n2
Borges, Jorge Luis 26–27, 135, 142, 181, 264
Bounfour, Abdallah 17, 24
Bourqia, Rahma 57n54, 61n66
Bouvelet, Henri 192
Bouvier, Nicolas 178
Braidotti, Rosi 126

Brazilian modernism 186
Bruno, Giordano 270
Buci-Glucksmann, Christine
    17n48
Buddha 232
Buddhism 262–3, 270, 340n18

Cagne, Jacques 47, 56
Caillois, Roger 178
Cairo 347, 355
Calle-Gruber, Mireille 14
calligraphy 3, 7–8, 37, 115, 191, 198,
    219–20, 225, 231–2, 238, 240,
    268, 284–5, 287, 307, 324, 330,
    331–2, 334, 336–7, 338, 340,
    343–6
    Arabic 191, 226, 272, 338, 343,
        345–6
    Chinese 191, 225, 338, 344
    Islamic 7, 35
    Japanese 191, 220, 225–6
Camus, Albert 123, 200
Canetti, Elias 205, 216
capitalism 33, 60
Caracas 94
Caravaggio 224
the Caribbean 84, 176, 179
carpet *see* Moroccan carpet
    the flying carpet 299, 303
Carroll, Lewis 261
Casablanca 2, 4–5, 179, 183, 283
    riots (1965) 50, 52, 55
Catholics 104, 317, 350
Celaan revue 18
Celan, Paul 349
Cervantes 27, 126, 137–40, 142,
    146
Césaire, Aimé 180
Chamoiseau, Patrick 27, 33n91, 84,
    179, 181
Chateaubriand, René de 351
Cheng, François 24, 179
Cherkaoui, Ahmed 9n20, 287
Cherkaoui, Mohammed 16
Chikhi, Beïda 15

childhood 2, 4–5, 9, 73, 160–1, 182,
    192, 220, 246, 251–2, 254, 308,
    348, 357
China 190–1, 223, 265n6
    Chinese art 332
    Chinese culture 190, 269
    Chinese ideograms 262
    Chinese traditions 263, 265
Choukri, Mohammed 52
Chraïbi, Driss 2, 10–11, 50, 203
Christianity 126, 134, 138, 144, 307,
    335, 353–4
    Christians 99, 101, 121, 162, 207,
        262, 314, 347, 352
cinema 112, 114, 220, 224
Cixous, Hélène 29, 150, 203–4, 207
class struggle 6, 59, 162
Claudel, Paul 178
Clifford, James 178
colonial
    anthropology 330
    domination 183, 320
    history 212, 269, 317
    violence 318
colonialism 27, 34, 38, 45–6, 90, 94,
    103–4, 131, 152–3, 155, 157, 315,
    317, 319–20, 324–5
coloniality 32–3
colonization 31, 59, 70, 79, 129, 132,
    158, 187–8
Combe, Dominique 28, 37, 174,
    197–217
Commonwealth 150–1
communism 58, 61
Confiant, Raphaël 84
Convivencia see Al-Andalus
Corbin, Henry 57n54, 253, 259–60
Cordoba 23
Corneille, Pierre 4
cosmopolitanism 68, 94, 113, 123,
    131–2, 135, 170
Creole 174
créolité (creoleness) 84
creolization 99, 176
cultural diversity 140, 144, 318

Dakhlia, Jocelyne 98–9, 101–2
Dana, Catherine 35
dance 219, 271, 273, 286, 307, 309, 339
Daoud, Zakya 329
decolonial 32, 53, 85, 152–3, 158, 187–8
decolonization 6, 10, 28, 31, 36–7, 39, 41, 44, 53, 90, 132, 151–3, 175, 180–1, 195, 199, 317, 320, 322, 329–30
deconstruction 28, 32, 37, 57, 131–2, 134, 166, 175, 195, 199–200, 209, 245, 324, 348
deculturation 46, 157–8
Déjeux, Jean 9, 49
Delacroix, Eugène 286
Deleuze, Gilles 127, 133n22
Delhi 23
Derrida, Jacques 26, 28–30, 37, 74, 79–80, 97–101, 105, 112, 119, 125–6, 138, 145, 150, 167–8, 174–6, 185, 194, 197–217, 245, 300, 312, 320–1, 324, 333–4, 341, 348, 353
    Le Monolinguisme de l'autre 29, 74, 174, 200–4, 208–11, 213, 216
    Politiques de l'amitié 29, 312
Descartes, René 203
Dhaouadi, Muhammad 60n64
difference 12, 17, 23–4, 30, 32, 64, 81, 90, 94, 107–9, 120–2, 127, 133, 141, 145, 154–5, 164, 170, 178, 186, 188, 193, 248, 268, 306, 312, 316, 319, 330, 351, 358
    intractable difference 12, 118, 154–5, 170, 200, 214
diglossia 37, 92–3, 132, 149, 163, 167, 192, 204, 212, 268, 275
Diop, Papa Samba 27
Djebar, Assia 10, 14, 84, 142, 150–1, 238, 248, 250, 254, 256–60
Djemeri, Taieb 49n29
Dostoevsky, Fyodor 27

double critique 12, 27, 32, 35–6, 90–1, 127, 132–6, 143–4, 149, 152–9, 161, 163–5, 168, 170, 192–3, 273, 280, 320, 329, 348
Doukkala (Moroccan region) 9n20, 357
Dransfeldt Christensen, Tina 175, 192
dream 72, 111, 115, 119, 146, 215, 224, 232, 240, 254–6, 259, 261–3, 266, 269, 274, 277, 296, 298, 302, 322, 331, 336, 339, 359
Duras, Marguerite 188
Durkheim, Emile 57, 61–3
Duvignaud, Jean 45, 50

the East 12, 20–1, 91, 97, 154, 200–1, 215, 219–20, 223, 225–6, 231, 342, 264
École Pratique des Hautes Études (EPHE) 49–50, 197
Edwards, Bryan T. 35n99
Egypt 262, 278, 347–8, 352, 355–6
Eid El Kebir 2
El Aroussi, Moulim 9n20
El Bayati, Abdellatif 16
El Fassi, Nacer 44
El Jadida 2, 17–18, 21, 52, 201, 268, 350
El Khatibi, Mourad 19
El Khayat, Rita 35, 112, 122, 298
El Maleh, Edmond Amran 9n20, 211, 350
Elhariry, Yasser 35
eroticism 9, 221, 228, 238–40, 290, 296, 334, 337
errantry 2, 4, 23, 25
esotericism 262, 264, 267, 270–1, 274–5, 278, 289
Essaouira 3, 160–1, 166, 268, 347, 357
estrangement 105, 267
ethnocentrism 131–2, 187, 189, 192, 199, 272
ethnography 50, 53, 61, 177–8, 184–5
ethnology 6, 176–7, 184, 281, 284, 354

étranger professionnel (*professional stranger*) 25–6, 36, 65, 67–71, 74, 76–9, 87, 123, 139, 149, 156, 163, 170, 188, 190, 213–14, 216, 232, 305–8, 313, 321–2, 324, 348
Eurocentrism 187
Evans-Pritchard, Edward Evan 61
exile 65–6, 74, 85, 105, 183, 188, 210, 268, 334, 348, 357
exote 169, 178, 187–90, 194–5
exoticism 30, 37, 107, 111, 145, 168, 176–8, 181, 187, 189–93, 195, 221–4, 228, 351

fairy tales 239–40, 334–5, 337
Fanon, Frantz 28, 150–2, 180, 199, 210, 319
Farès, Nabile 15, 91n8, 96
Favret, Jeanne 61–2
feminine agency 8, 280, 294–6, 303
femininity 34, 224, 259–60, 356
Fennane, Abdelghani 19
Feraoun, Mouloud 203
Feriani, Rim 37, 237–60
feudalism 47, 57, 60, 63
Fez 283, 288, 306, 357
Fieni, David 85, 330
folklore 7, 106, 186, 222, 282, 351
Formentelli, Eliane 24, 179
Forsdick, Charles 13, 37, 151n5, 173–95
Foucault, Michel 26, 141–2
Francophone
    literature 9, 168, 201
    studies 149, 151–2, 163, 170
    world 74, 194, 261
    writers 118, 168, 175, 177, 179, 181, 186, 212, 215
Francophonie 45n14, 168, 174, 181, 201
French
    culture 22, 244n18, 266, 355
    identity 188
    language 4–5, 21, 24–5, 49, 73–7, 81, 83, 85, 87, 97, 100–1, 103–4, 117, 119–20, 125, 129–30, 136, 142, 146, 149–52, 164–7, 174–5,
184–6, 192, 199, 202–8, 211–14, 247, 264–6, 268–9, 272–5, 301, 332, 348, 351
    left 14, 158
    literature 151, 173, 182, 186, 188–9, 191, 203, 300, 351
    orientalists 7, 28
    Protectorate 4, 6, 38, 46, 204, 266, 282, 306, 317
    school 3, 204, 206, 210–11, 268
Freud, Sigmund 26, 205, 339

Gallissot, René 60
Gellner, Ernest 61–2
Genet, Jean 25, 168–9, 188, 211, 229–30, 305–6
Ghali, Ibrahim Amin 352
Gilsenan, Michael 178
Glissant, Edouard 31, 150–1, 174–7, 179–82, 186–7, 193, 201, 215, 324
globality 31, 63, 118
globalization 31, 114–15, 118, 122, 359
Goethe 27, 126, 130n15
Goldmann, Lucien 50
Gómez-Peña, Guillermo 128, 145
Gontard, Marc 17n48, 33, 179n19, 191
Goytisolo, Juan 107, 350
Greece 56, 262, 278
Greek
    mythology 4
    philosophy 91, 265, 279
Greimas, Algirdas Julien 244
Griffiths, Gareth 131
Guillebaud, Jean-Claude 122
Gurvitch, Georges 6, 47, 49, 53, 60

Hachad, Naïma 175–6
the Hadith 246
haiku 220
Halévi, Juda 354
Hallaq, Boutros 20
Hammoudi, Abdellah 61n66
Hardy, Georges 46
Hardy, Thomas 223

Harrison, Olivia C. 27, 35–6, 38, 149–71, 347–59

Hart, David 61

Hassan, Kadhim Jihad 20

Hassan II (King) 198

Hassoun, Jacques 20, 24, 28, 107, 112, 122, 153, 160, 166–8, 315, 347–59

Havana 23

Hebrew 100, 165–7, 206, 208, 349, 355

Heidegger 143, 223

Hél-Bongo, Olga 33n91, 47n22

Heraclitus 26

hermeticism 37, 262–4, 267, 269–77

Hespéris-Tamuda (Moroccan journal) 45, 54, 61n66

Hiddleston, Jane 1–38, 106, 108, 111, 149n2, 197, 305–25

hieroglyphs 239–40, 262, 274, 283, 297, 300, 336

the High Atlas *see* Atlas

Himmich, Bensalem 157n13, 158n15

hospitality 93, 101, 114, 135–9, 142, 266, 288, 297, 313

Howard, Richard 34

Hughes, James 35

Hussein (King) 159

hybridity 32, 36, 92, 99–100, 107, 123, 127–31, 136–8, 140, 143–6, 152, 194, 225, 261–2, 280, 301

hybridization 22, 29–30, 145

Ibn Arabi 248, 253n50

Ibn Khaldun 26, 57–9, 61, 63, 271n16, 338, 342–3

identity 1, 7–13, 15, 31–2, 66, 70–1, 73, 84, 86, 90, 94–5, 98, 101, 103–5, 107–8, 118, 121–2, 126, 128–9, 134–5, 137–9, 144, 146, 150, 154–5, 160–2, 164–6, 185, 188, 197, 205, 211–12, 216, 225, 238, 242, 247–8, 261, 267, 283, 289, 293, 299, 320, 333–4, 336, 348–50, 353

and difference 8, 65, 247–8, 334

idiom 2, 4, 71, 76–7, 84–7, 89, 92, 94–5, 98–102, 106, 109, 129–30, 134, 165, 204, 214, 216, 300, 306

the Idrisids 58

Ikken, Aïssa 15

illumination 231, 258, 277, 309

imperialism 33–4, 132, 157–8, 180–1, 262

India 223, 291

Institut de Sociologie 6, 44, 47

Institut du Monde Arabe 19, 281

Intégral (Moroccan journal) 64n74

inter-lingual 93

interculturality 2, 90, 95, 104, 106–7, 316

interlangue 82, 84–6, 93, 104, 108

internationalism 25, 93, 168, 170, 190, 348

intersemiotic(s) 7–8, 37, 221, 224, 237–8, 240, 242, 244–5, 248, 250, 254–60, 283, 285–7, 292, 329–34, 337–8, 346

intersign 113–14, 191, 283, 285, 330, 334–5

intertextuality 7, 245, 333, 346

intractability 24, 36

Islam 9, 28, 46, 90–1, 101, 126, 143, 197, 239–40, 249, 284, 288, 290, 307, 314–16, 331, 334, 336

Islamic

aesthetics 323–4

art 2, 240, 284, 287, 308, 324

body 241

calendar 270

civilization 105, 226

cultures 238–9, 280

dogma 264

heritage 238, 240, 246, 248–9, 255–7

history 2, 257

identity 320

idioms 85

influence 8

metaphysics 229

mysticism 273

parables 246
scripture 2, 314, 322
sources 330
theology 90–1
theory 309
thinkers 278
thought 91, 313, 322
tradition 246, 288, 339
world 9, 33, 36, 235
Israel 155, 159, 163, 165, 315, 347,
    350–1, 352, 359
Israeli-Arab conflict 161
Issami, Siham 16
Italian language 98, 100, 129, 316

Jakobson, Roman 330, 345
James, Henry 302
Jamin, Jean 178
Japan 198, 219–33
Japanese
    calligraphy *see* calligraphy
    culture 37, 219–33, 269
    poetry 220
jazz 271, 276
Jerusalem or al-Quds 350, 352
Jesus 314, 352
Jewishness 34, 160–2, 166, 348, 357
Jews 38, 98–9, 159–61, 165–7, 200,
    206–7, 315, 317, 347–50, 352–3,
    355, 355–8
Jordan 153, 159
jouissance 78, 179, 228, 331, 334, 337,
    344–5
Jouve, Pierre Jean 178
Judaism 28, 52, 211, 307, 315, 355, 359
Judeo-Arab conflict 167, 347, 349,
    354–5
Judeo-Arabic 100, 166
Judeo-Spanish 206, 208

Kabbala 262
Kably, Mohammed 9n21
Kafka, Franz 29, 142, 205
Kateb, Yacine 10, 92, 164, 210
Kelly, Debra 33, 37, 237–60

Kenitra 18
Khaïr-Eddine, Mohammed 198
Khalil Gibran, Gibran 4, 26
khamsa 286
Khatibi, Abdelkébir
    Aimance 29, 312
    L'Alternance et les partis politiques
        14, 16
    Amour bilingue 24, 29, 34, 36, 77,
        80, 102–4, 107, 117, 126, 152,
        163–5, 168, 174, 185, 192, 195,
        197, 201, 212, 227, 276, 299, 313,
        348
    Anthologie des écrivains
        maghrébins d'expression
        française 49
    L'Art calligraphique arabe 19
    L'Art calligraphique de l'Islam 191,
        284
    La Beauté de l'absent 26, 31
    Bilan de la sociologie au Maroc 6,
        47, 57
    La Blessure du nom propre 7, 19,
        35, 38, 197, 199, 225, 237–8, 240,
        242, 281, 308–9, 312, 329–46
    Bulletin économique et social du
        Maroc (Bulletin ESM) 6, 43–4,
        54, 56
    Chemins de traverse 112
    Civilisation de l'intersigne 113
    Civilisation marocaine: arts et
        culture 7n15, 281n7
    Le Corps oriental 9, 219, 225, 288
    Correspondance ouverte 35, 298
    Dédicace à l'année qui vient 297
    Du bilinguisme 24, 112, 179, 199,
        210
    Du signe à l'image: le tapis
        marocain 8, 35, 37, 279–303
    Féerie d'un mutant 69, 114, 232,
        299
    Figures de l'étranger dans la
        littérature française 25, 27, 35,
        126, 168, 184–5, 187–90, 192,
        197–8, 232, 305, 348

Imaginaires de l'autre: Khatibi et la mémoire littéraire 17, 126, 182, 191

Jacques Derrida, en effet 29, 200

La Langue de l'autre 18, 29, 35, 74, 126, 227

Le Livre de l'aimance 29

Le Livre du sang 53, 116, 197, 249, 289, 299

Le Lutteur de classe à la manière taoïste 19, 31, 35, 42, 197

La Mémoire tatouée 3, 5, 15, 19, 21–3, 31, 34, 41–2, 50–4, 56, 64, 126, 131, 135, 143, 160–1, 182–6, 197, 203–4, 225, 238, 240, 242, 245–8, 250, 256–60, 264, 276, 291, 299, 329, 353

La Mille et deuxième nuit 19

La Mort des artistes 5

Le Même livre 20, 28, 35, 38, 160–1, 163, 165, 170, 315, 347–59

Le Prophète voilé 5, 19, 197

Le Roman maghrébin 9–10, 19, 22, 42, 47, 51, 152, 156, 158, 165, 212

Le Scribe et son ombre 1, 7, 16, 22, 26, 30, 36, 65, 71, 182, 281, 330

Maghreb pluriel 12–13, 19, 24, 27–8, 34, 73, 76, 102, 105, 112, 126, 152, 154, 164, 174, 177, 179, 192–3, 195, 197, 199–200, 203, 210, 219, 261, 286, 316, 319, 322, 324, 329, 348

Œuvres Complètes 29, 30, 42, 199

Ombres japonaises 27, 220–1

Paradoxes du sionisme 35

Pèlerinage d'un artiste amoureux 37, 68, 121, 268, 277, 288, 293, 299, 305–25

Penser le Maghreb 13, 126, 261, 286

Triptyque de Rabat 19–20, 296

Un été à Stockholm 19, 23, 25, 29, 36, 69, 77, 81, 84, 114, 188, 197, 292, 305–6, 313

Vomito blanco 14, 19–20, 27, 36, 52, 153, 158–63, 170, 199, 219

Kierkegaard 26

Kilito, Abdelfattah 16–17, 24, 142

Klossowski, Pierre 332n4

Kolin-Kobayashi, Minol 27

the Koran *see* the Qur'an

Kourouma, Ahmadou 25

Kristeva, Julia 57–8

Laâbi, Abdellatif 10–11, 43, 51, 53, 198

Laâbi, Jocelyne 44n10

Lacoste, Yves 57, 59

Laforgue, Jules 183

Lamalif (Moroccan journal) 43, 44n11, 48n23, 56n49, 63n72, 329

language 2–3, 5, 15, 24, 25–30, 32–7, 67–8, 70–1, 73–87, 92–5, 98–104, 106–9, 111–12, 116–23, 125–39, 141–6, 153–4, 157, 163–7, 169, 174–6, 182, 185–6, 188–93, 200–17, 221, 225, 227–8, 232, 237–8, 242, 244–7, 261, 263, 264, 266–9, 271–8, 284–6, 297, 300, 306, 308, 316–17, 320, 324, 333, 336, 338, 340–1, 343–9, 351, 354–5

European languages 163, 272

foreign language(s) 77, 93, 117, 137, 216, 227

language politics 85

lingua franca 98–101

Semitic languages 272–3

Lanly, André 100–101

Lao Tzu 26–7, 270

Laroui, Abdallah 12, 28, 59

Laroui, Fouad 142

Latin Quarter 199

Lazarev, Grigori 57n52

Le Bris, Michel 178

Le Chatelier, Alfred F. 46

Le Cœur, Charles 49

Lebanon war 351

Lefebvre, Henri 6

Leiris, Michel 178

Leopardi, Giacomo 26
Leroi-Gourhan, André 6, 26
Lévi-Strauss, Claude 184, 344
Lindsay, Cecile 35
Lionnet, Françoise 32–3, 76, 152, 280
logocentrism 131–2, 199, 320, 334, 336
London 23
Loti, Pierre 222
Lukaćs, Georg 50–2
Lyamlahy, Khalid 1–38, 279–303
Lyautey
    Lycée 5, 183
    Marshal 46, 282
Lyotard, Jean-François 356

Maeterlinck, Maurice 27
Maghreb 2, 9–16, 20–1, 24, 29, 31,
    36, 89–92, 94–6, 98–107, 126,
    133–4, 152–4, 158, 165, 200–1,
    203, 215, 219–20, 225, 231,
    247–8, 329
    Arab Maghreb Union 13
    Maghreb studies 13
    Maghrebian history 325
    Maghrebian identity 15, 90, 98, 104
    Maghrebian literature 102, 140, 153
    Maghrebian novel 10, 118, 153, 163,
      198
    Maghrebian writer(s) 10–11, 104,
      156–7, 208, 210, 212, 226
Makhzen 46, 59, 63
Mallarmé, Stéphane 25, 27, 183,
    213–15, 245, 332
Malta 314, 316–17, 320
Mammeri, Mouloud 10
Maoism 52
Maraini, Toni 9n20
Marcus Aurelius 26
Marrakesh 4–5, 293
Martinique 174
Marx, Karl 26, 47, 48, 52–3, 57–64
Marxism 42, 48, 53, 64, 162
Maspéro (French publisher) 198
Massignon, Louis 340, 345
Matisse, Henri 286

Mauss, Marcel 60–1
Mawakif (Moroccan journal) 20
Mazagan 2, 358
McNeece, Lucy S. 37, 242, 261–78
Meddeb, Abdelwahab 15, 24, 28, 142,
    154, 164, 210–12, 215, 272, 276
medina 2, 9
the Mediterranean 7, 27, 36, 56,
    89–109, 199, 231, 268–9, 347
    Mediterranean diversity 107
    Mediterranean identity 103
    Mediterranean idiom 98–9, 109
    Mediterranean poetics 102
    Mediterranean relations 99, 101
    Mediterranean space 36, 91
    Mediterranean thought 97
    trans-Mediterranean 91, 95, 103
melancholia 95, 105, 183
the Mellah (Jewish quarter) 160–1,
    166, 357
Memmes, Abdallah 245–8
Memmi, Albert 9, 44, 49–50, 52, 97–8,
    102, 108, 142, 150–2, 158, 163,
    165, 180, 202–4, 207, 212, 214
memory 3, 11, 18, 73, 76, 86, 89, 92,
    95, 98, 104, 107–8, 136, 160,
    169–70, 185–6, 202–3, 223–4,
    226, 230, 242–3, 247, 250–5,
    257–60, 263, 265, 271–2, 274,
    286, 292, 296–7, 313, 332, 343,
    351
the Men of the Cave 335
Mensah, Patrick 201
Mesopotamia 262–3, 278
métissage 74, 107–8, 194, 350
Michaux, Henri 25, 52, 178
Michaux-Bellaire, Edouard 46, 59
the Middle Atlas *see* Atlas
Mignolo, Walter 32, 149
Miomandre (de), Francis 178
Misrahi, Robert 159
mobility 4, 99, 278, 285, 292–3, 299,
    303
modernity 32–3, 90, 105, 114, 139, 142,
    189, 278

Mohammed V (King) 46, 358
Le Monde (French newspaper) 13
mondialité 31
Mongo-Mboussa, Mongo 176–7
monolingualism 24, 37, 79, 98–9, 103,
    119, 139, 174, 189, 200, 204,
    209, 211–12, 214, 216, 276
monotheism 91, 104, 143, 231–2,
    240–1, 288, 314, 349, 353,
    356–7
Montagne, Robert 43, 46–7
Montaigne, Michel de 26
Morin, Edgar 53
Moroccan
    Arabic (or dialect) 4, 100, 192, 206,
        211, 214, 264, 268, 294, 301
    art 2, 5, 8, 282, 287, 301
    carpet 8, 37, 243, 270, 279–303, 309
    civilization 7
    culture 1, 2, 5, 8, 43, 45, 183, 247,
        280–1, 287
    independence 4–5, 10, 44, 46–7,
        317, 330–1, 358
    Jews 211, 348, 350, 355, 357
    nationalism 46
    political parties 14
    popular culture 287, 298, 329–32,
        336
    popular proverbs 9, 329–30, 336
    saints 288–9, 357
    tattoos 9, 37, 174, 190, 198, 225,
        238, 240, 242–3, 248, 254, 269,
        285
mosaics 190, 238, 276, 278, 284, 308–9
mother tongue 24, 75–7, 79, 83, 93,
    136–7, 205, 207, 211–12, 217,
    264, 306
Moura, Jean-Marc 150n4, 151n5,
    152n8
mourning 31, 101–2, 105, 208–9,
    217
Muhammad (Prophet) *see* Prophet
    Muhammad
multiculturalism 121, 317
multilingualism (or plurilingualism) 3,

24, 74, 76–7, 81, 85, 92, 101–3,
    137, 143, 163, 165, 179, 189, 194,
    205, 216–17, 269, 301, 316–17,
    320, 324, 348
music 33, 228, 263, 271, 285–6, 311–12,
    333, 344–6
Muslims 99, 101, 161, 166, 202, 206,
    317, 347, 357, 359
mysticism 15, 72, 215, 229, 238, 240,
    246, 249, 259, 260, 273–4, 276,
    310, 330–1, 336, 340, 342
mythology 4, 7, 106, 184, 299, 351,
    358–9

Nadel, Siegfried F. 61n66
Nafzawi 337
Nancy, Jean-Luc 30–1
Naville, Pierre 49, 56
neo-imperialism 33–4
Neoplatonism 270
Newton, Isaac 263
Nietzsche 26, 116, 203, 353
Nissabouri, Mostafa 11, 156
Noah 351
nomadism 58, 127–9, 135, 143, 145,
    253, 305–6, 334
Nora, Pierre 200
Norge (pseudonym of Georges Mogin)
    178

the Occident 12, 22, 91, 109, 126, 129,
    131–2, 134, 137, 140, 143–4, 154,
    168, 173, 177, 195–9, 223, 247
    see also the West
Ollier, Claude 29, 35, 74–5, 188
One Thousand and One Nights 228,
    337
opacity 36, 102, 277, 313
Orient 12, 22, 70, 91, 126, 129, 132,
    134, 137, 140, 143–4, 154, 195,
    220, 284
Orientalism 30, 168, 193, 286
Orlando, Valérie K. 35
Orphelin (orphan) 31, 41–2, 53–4, 154,
    310, 314, 331, 334

Orphic
    body 333
    myth 53, 332
    text 333
Ortiz, Fernando 135
Oulhaci, Abdelkader 49n29
Oulipo 263

painting 114, 224, 226, 231, 273, 284–7,
    344–5
Palestine 27, 36, 52, 153–8, 162, 165,
    168–70, 229, 315
    Palestine Liberation Organization
        161
    Palestinian writers 157
    Palestinians 36, 159, 162–3, 169,
        315
pan-Arabism 13, 156
Papan-Matin Firoozeh 252
Paris 14–15, 19–20, 22–3, 26, 44,
    48–50, 53, 61, 67–8, 174,
    199–200, 211, 220, 244, 266,
    281, 299, 354
Pascon, Paul 6, 43–4, 47, 61
pataouète 100
Péguy, Charles 181
PEN International 17
pensée autre (*other tought* or *other
    thinking*) 12, 25, 28, 30, 32–4,
    90–1, 127, 132–4, 143–4, 149,
    153–4, 158, 164–5, 193, 200, 273,
    319–20, 323–4
pensée en langues 144, 316, 320
pensée plurielle 118, 193
pensée vide 265, 267
performativity 36, 125–46
The Perfumed Garden 334, 337
Perse, Saint-John 178
philosophy 5–6, 22, 26, 30, 34, 91, 123,
    134, 143, 202, 209, 215, 248, 263,
    265, 279–80, 307, 313, 320, 323
phonetics 129, 274, 343–6, 357–8
photography 9n20, 14, 114, 280
pilgrimage 306, 308–11, 314, 316–18,
    320–2, 324, 354

Piser, Celine 103
Plato 26, 223, 269n12, 270, 340–1
Plotinus 267, 269n12
pluri-langue (or *pluri-language*) 95,
    129–30, 140, 167
plurilingualism *see* multilingualism
Poésie 94 (French journal) 17
poetry 4, 11, 17, 27, 29, 42, 50, 52–3,
    76, 116, 126, 175–6, 213–14,
    220, 225, 263, 324, 345,
    350
polygraphy 343, 346
Polynesia 185, 190, 241
polyphony 95, 123, 134, 241, 245, 344,
    346
Ponge, Francis 178
Porter, Catherine 35, 150n3
Portuguese 2, 85, 98, 129, 358
postcolonial
    history 283
    nations 45
    studies 150–1, 193
    theory 31, 150–2
    thought 10, 30–2, 174, 194, 324
    turn 152
post-colonialism 143
post-coloniality 130–1, 143
post-structuralism 48, 57, 63–4
pottery 285
Présence Africaine Editions 9n21, 49,
    97n35
Prévert, Jacques 64
Pro-Culture (Moroccan journal)
    18
Prophet Muhammad 257, 334–5,
    339–41, 353
Propp, Vladimir 58n55
Proust, Marcel 216, 274
Pythagoras 267, 269n12

Qader, Nasrin 30, 33, 91, 249
qalam 338–40
the Qur'an 28, 238–9, 245–6, 250–2,
    268, 287, 309, 315, 322, 334–6,
    339–41

Qur'anic
    discourse 245–6
    school 3, 267–8, 322
    signs 252, 336

Rabat 6, 18–20, 24, 43–4, 47, 131, 179,
    268, 283, 288, 291, 301
Rachik, Hassan 57n54
Racine, Jean 4
rationalism 12, 90, 121, 238, 260
Raybaud, Antoine 17n48, 177n12,
    279n1
realism 11, 56
Reconquista see Al-Andalus
Reeck, Matt 31, 33, 35, 38, 84, 329–46
relationality 106, 152–3, 167, 170, 315
religious dialogue 316–17
Renaissance 262, 266, 273
Reynolds, Felisa 175
rhetoric 32, 240, 245, 276, 329, 337–40,
    343–7
Ricard, Prosper 282
Rice, Alison 26, 33, 36, 38, 65–87
the Rif (Moroccan region) 46, 318
Rilke, Rainer Maria 27, 350
Rimbaud, Arthur 25, 27, 182
Robin, Régine 216
Roelens, Nathalie 185, 191
Ronda (Spanish town) 104, 350
rosace 278, 290
Rosello, Mireille 86, 175–6
Rosenzweig, Franz 215
Roth, Arlette 9, 49

the Saharan 7, 13
    the Saharan conflict 13
Said, Edward 32, 127, 193–4, 199
Saïgh Bousta, Rachida 18, 247–8
Salafism 12
Sansal, Boualem 142
Sartre, Jean-Paul 158, 183, 200, 204,
    208n24
Sawada, Nao 37, 219–33
Sayad, Abdelmalek 44
Scemla, Jean 181, 183–4, 186

Scheherazade 302–3
Scholem, Gershom 215
sculpture 232, 307–8, 312, 322
Sebbar, Leïla 211
Second World War 52, 67, 315
secularism 8, 205–6, 314, 318
seduction 2, 22, 117, 220, 281, 290,
    297–8
Sefrioui, Ahmed 49n29
Segalen, Victor 13n32, 37, 107, 168,
    173–95, 222, 270, 351
Segler-Messner, Silke 179, 190, 194
segmentarity 61–4
Sem 351
semantics 92, 95, 106, 133–4, 241, 257,
    330, 338, 344–6
semiology 1, 3, 66, 113, 197, 244–5,
    330
semiotic systems (or sign systems) 7, 23,
    37–8, 190, 238–41, 243–5, 260,
    330–2, 334, 336–7
semiotics 38, 190, 221, 240, 244, 333–4,
    336–7, 342–3
Semitic
    languages 272–3
    passion 354, 356
    peoples 354
Serfaty, Abraham 43, 45n14, 53
sexuality 12, 78, 122, 138, 289–90
Sijelmassi, Mohamed 7, 19, 191, 281,
    284
Smouts, Marie-Claude 150n4, 151n5,
    152n8
social
    stratification 47, 56, 60n63, 61n66,
    63
    structures 11, 60, 281, 354
    struggle 48
sociology 6–7, 20, 22, 26, 36, 41–64,
    197, 329–30
    sociological fieldwork 54
    sociological research 42
    sociological writing 42–3
Sorbonne 5, 10, 22, 44, 68, 197,
    201

Souffles/Anfas (Moroccan journal)
　10–12, 41, 43, 45, 49–50, 52–3,
　156–8, 162, 198
Spain 56, 104–7, 262, 347, 350–1
Spanish
　culture 264
　forces 318
　identity 107, 140, 207
　language 81, 85, 94–5, 98, 100, 106,
　　142, 205
　writers 350
spatiality 292
spatialization 241, 268
Stafford, Andy 32, 36, 41–64
Starobinski, Jean 333n5
Steiner, George 205
Steinmetz, George 43–4, 49
Stendhal 4, 27
Stétié, Salah 97
Stockholm 23
Stravinsky, Igor 344
structuralism 59n60, 198, 244, 269n11
the Suez Canal 96–7
Sufism 248–9, 250, 252–6, 258–60, 262,
　269–71
　Sufi aesthetics 324
　Sufi heritage 37, 238, 240, 248, 250,
　　257
　Sufi mysticism 260, 310
　Sufi philosophers 245
　Sufi writings 248
Surrealism 56, 178, 263
Sweden 23, 69, 306
Swedish (language) 81, 275
synaesthesia 286
synchronicity 271
syntax 24, 76, 83, 119, 275

Tahiti 177, 184–5
Talbayev, Edwige Tamalet 36, 89–109
Talisman 276, 283–4, 296
Tamazight 21, 100, 301
Tanizaki 27, 37, 198, 219–33
Tao 262, 265, 267, 269–70
　Taoism 265, 270

tattooing 225, 239–43, 250–1, 254, 329,
　331, 334, 336–7
Les Temps Modernes 12, 20, 154
theatre 5, 50, 77–8, 116, 141, 230,
　333
theology 30, 90–1, 143, 155, 232, 288
the 'third space' 32, 126, 128, 137
the Third world 54, 151–3, 158, 359
　Third Worldism 152, 156, 158, 180,
　　198
Thompson, Peter 34
Tiffin, Helen 131
Tifinagh 286, 301
Todorov, Tzvetan 24, 111, 178–9
Tokyo 221, 225
tolédance 132, 137, 143, 146
Toledo 142
the Torah 28, 315
de Toro, Alfonso 32, 36, 125–46
de Toro, Fernando 127–9
traditionalism 11–12, 221, 232
trance 271, 277–8
trans-Mediterranean *see*
　Mediterranean
transcolonial 27, 36, 149, 152–3, 156,
　158, 168, 170–1
transculturalism 96, 127, 129, 131, 133,
　137, 306, 320
transdisciplinarity 6–7, 79, 131, 303
translation 4, 7, 19–21, 23–4, 34–5,
　37–8, 65–87, 91, 93, 102, 114,
　136, 143–4, 149, 164, 195, 198,
　208, 223, 246, 261, 263–5,
　273–6, 281, 299, 320, 327–59
transnationalism 2, 26, 34, 36–7, 39,
　87, 92–3, 101, 103, 195, 305, 307,
　316–17, 324
transparency 36, 81–2, 93, 111–13, 116,
　123, 270, 308
trauma 95–6, 101–2, 104–8, 350–1, 353
travel 2, 6, 23, 25, 36, 38, 43, 65–6,
　68–72, 74, 77–9, 86–7, 131, 135,
　149, 176, 178, 226, 243, 268,
　270, 299, 302, 305–6, 308–9,
　313–14, 318, 321–2

tribal system 59–63, 349–50
Tripoli 99
Tsvetaieva, Marina 349–50
Tunis 99
Tunisia 45, 50, 56, 204, 206
Turkish (language) 98–100

UNESCO 47
unhomeliness 32, 128
Union Nationale des Etudiants Marocains (UNEM) 13
Union Socialiste des Forces Populaires (USFP) 14
universalism 31, 119, 123, 134
universality 120, 122, 134
University Chouaïb Doukkali (El Jadida) 17
University Mohammed V (Rabat) 6, 19, 49
untranslatability 24, 79, 93, 102, 191, 313
urbanism 44

Valéry, Paul 26–7, 108, 181
the Vedas 262–3, 267
Verhaeren, Emile 27
Villa-Ignacio, Teresa 10n23, 50n31, 51n36, 157n13
vocabulary 22, 119, 209, 253–4, 257
Vogl, Mary 35

Wahbi, Hassan 18, 26, 31
wandering 21, 23, 137, 146, 243, 248, 265, 277, 291, 301, 306, 309, 314

Waterbury, John 61n65
Weber, Samuel 19
the West 12, 21–2, 33, 91, 104–6, 112, 118, 122, 132, 144, 154, 169, 173, 177, 199–201, 219, 223, 225, 231, 248, 264, 342, 352, 356
  see also the Occident
Western culture(s) 8, 22–3, 134, 158, 223, 269
Western ego 30, 109
Western knowledge 144, 193, 199, 338
Western thought 123, 200, 208
White, Kenneth 178
Wilde, Oscar 223
Wills, David 201
Woodhull, Winifred 34
world literature 151, 171

Xizhi, Wang 332

Yalim, P. Burcu 34
the 'Years of Lead' *see* années de plomb
Yiddish 205, 216

Zahi, Farid 20
Zaki, Maria 16
Zebdi, Kamel 49n29
Zen 337
Zenderoudi, Charles Hossein 284
Zhiri, Kacem 16
Zionism 14, 27–8, 52, 153, 157–9, 161–2, 170, 199, 358